Police Station Adviser's Index

AUSTRALIA
Law Book Co. Sydney

CANADA AND USA
Carswell Toronto

NEW ZEALAND
Brooker's Auckland

SINGAPORE and MALAYSIA
Sweet & Maxwell Asia
Singapore and Kuala Lumpar

POLICE STATION ADVISER'S INDEX

BRIAN SPIRO, LLB
Partner, BCL Burton Copeland

and

STEVEN BIRD, LLM
Partner, Birds Solicitors

LONDON
SWEET & MAXWELL
2005

Published in 2005 by Sweet & Maxwell Limited
100 Avenue Road
London NW3 3PF
Typeset by Servis Filmsetting Ltd.
Printed and bound in Great Britain by William Clowes Ltd, Beccles, Suffolk

First edition 1995
Second edition 1999
Third edition 2005

No natural forests were destroyed to make this product;
only farmed timber was used and replanted

A CIP catalogue record for this book is available from the
British Library

ISBN 0421 88510 6

Contents

Preface

The first edition of this book was written shortly after the implementation of the provisions of the Criminal Justice and Public Order Act 1994 that so profoundly altered the suspect's right of silence. The second edition incorporated the many changes introduced by the subsequent case law and significant new legislation including the Proceeds of Crime Act 1995, the Police Acts of 1996 and 1997, and the Crime and Disorder Act 1998.

If it was ever thought that the courts and legislature would then allow the police and legal adviser time to adjust to the new rules and regulations, such notions were soon proven to be naive. In writing this new edition we have had to deal not only with the ever growing body of domestic and European case law but also incorporate the many changes introduced by an unprecedented flurry of legislation impacting either directly or indirectly upon the work of the police station adviser. This includes: the Human Rights Act 1998, the Access to Justice Act 1999, the Criminal Justice and Court Services Act 2000, the Regulation of Investigatory Powers Act 2000, the Powers of the Criminal Courts (Sentencing) Act 2000, the Terrorism Acts of 2000 and 2001, the Criminal Justice and Police Act 2001, the Police Reform Act 2002, the Proceeds of Crime Act 2002, the Extradition Act 2003, the Sexual Offences Act 2003, the Asylum and Immigration Act 2004, and, perhaps most significantly, the Criminal Justice Act 2003. In addition, there have been many significant changes to secondary legislation, necessitating major changes to sections of the book on topics as diverse as legal aid (now referred to as "public funding"), duty solicitors and police misconduct.

The apparently insatiable desire of lawmakers to interfere in the relationship between the law enforcer and alleged law breaker highlights, if such emphasis was needed, that the time a suspect spends in police detention remains the most critical of the entire criminal justice process. This book is designed to provide authoritative answers quickly in a situation where time is short and the pressure is high. It also seeks to give the adviser some practical guidance on dealing with the various areas of law which one confronts daily in advising suspects in police detention.

This third edition deals with the many recent changes to the law on and other issues arising in connection with police station work, and incorporates the newly revised PACE Codes of Practice introduced on August 1, 2004 as well as reproducing them in full together with the relevant legislation in the appendices.

Once again thanks are due to others and we would particularly like to acknowledge the invaluable assistance of Diane Calnan, Stephen Davies, Helen Harper, Nahid Khaliq, Tom McNeill, Paul Morris, Johann Oosthuizen, Somaya Ramadhan, Hannah Raphael, Durran Seddon, John Vorster, Nicky Meech and the team at Thomson Sweet and Maxwell, and all of our colleagues at BCL Burton Copeland and Birds Solicitors. Finally, much love and thanks are due to our long suffering families who have had to endure too many evenings and weekends in our absence as we have grappled with the writing of this book.

We have sought to state the law as at March 1, 2005.

Brian Spiro and Steven Bird

Preface to Second Edition

The first edition of this book was written shortly after the implementation of the Criminal Justice and Public Order Act 1994 and published in September 1995. We did not then know how the courts would interpret the fundamental changes introduced by the Act and hence some of our commentary was perforce speculative.

Over the last four years there have been a number of important decisions interpreting the 1994 Act. As a result, we have reorganised and re-written the "Advising the Suspect" and "Right of Silence" Chapters so that they now adjoin each other in the book and are more easily accessed. We have dealt with all of the leading cases on section 34 so that those becoming lost in the legal fog can see their way through more clearly.

The time a suspect spends in the police station remains the most critical of the entire criminal justice process and this edition is intended to provide authoritative answers quickly in a situation where time is short and the pressure is on. It also seeks to give the adviser some practical guidance on dealing with the various areas of law which one confronts daily in advising suspects in police detention.

This second edition not only deals with the recent case law on section 34 of the CJPOA 1994 and other issues arising in police station work but also incorporates the new revised PACE Code A (Stop and Search) and changes introduced by the Crime and Disorder Act 1998, Proceeds of Crime Act 1995, Police Acts 1996 and 1997, the Duty Solicitors Arrangements 1997 and the Police (Conduct) Regulations 1999. Once again the Codes are reproduced in full together with all of the relevant sections of the CJPOA 1994 and PACE 1984.

Once again thanks are due to others and we would particularly like to thank Nicola Fleming and all our colleagues at Simons Muirhead & Burton; Wing Commander G. J. Harding; Peter Dovey and David Benson as PSDS; Martin Carroll at the Legal Aid Board; and all those at Sweet & Maxwell.

We have sought to state the law as at August 1, 1999.

Brian Spiro & Steven Bird

Preface to First Edition

This index has been designed as a comprehensive reference guide for all lawyers, be they qualified or not, who represent clients in police detention.

It is often said that the most critical juncture in the criminal process is the period spent by a suspect in the police station. During such time he may be subject to interview, search, identification and other procedures, and thereafter vital decisions will be made as to whether charges should be brought and bail be granted. Each of these processes is likely to have a profound effect upon any subsequent criminal proceedings. For these reasons, the police station adviser must not only be experienced and well informed but also have ready access to authoritative explanations of each area of the relevant law. It is intended that this work will provide such guidance and be of particular benefit in situations where information is needed literally at one's fingertips.

The index covers fully the significant changes introduced by the Criminal Justice and Public Order Act 1994; most notably the severe limitations imposed upon the common law right of silence. It incorporates the newly revised PACE 1984 Codes of Practice and reproduces these, together with relevant sections of the Police and Criminal Evidence Act 1984 and the Criminal Justice and Public Order Act 1994, in the appendices.

Most of the index topics are divided into three sections. First, there is an account of the law. Secondly, we explain the practice and procedure in how the law operates. Lastly, under the heading of "Practical Guidance", we discuss the most common problems that arise, suggest methods of dealing with them, and give other professional "tips".

We can only apologise for the constant use of the male pronoun throughout the index—clarity having won the battle against political correctness—we certainly intend no disrespect to any female colleagues, clients, or police officers.

As is inevitably the case when writing such a work there are many other persons to whom we are deeply indebted. Particular thanks are due to Anthony Burton, David Walsh, Judy Morgan, Richard Locke, Caroline Flambard and the rest of Simons, Muirhead and Burton; Cecily Engle; Charlotte Friedman and

Cathryn Bird; and Leanne Hicks and Mary Kenny of FT Law and Tax.

We have sought to state the law as at June 1, 1995.

Brian Spiro and Steven Bird

Guide to Using the Index as a Textbook

This book is primarily intended to be used by practitioners whilst in the police station and is organised into chapters in alphabetical order for ease of reference.

It can also be used as a textbook by those new to police station work (such as those studying to become accredited representatives).

To use the Guide as a textbook, the index headings should be read in the following order.

GENERAL PROCEDURE

Accepting Instructions and Preparation
Arrestable and Serious Arrestable Offences
Suspect's Rights
Custody Records
Detention Periods and Reviews
Warrants of Further Detention
Information Gathering
Health of Suspect
Advising the Suspect—Right of Silence
Advising the Suspect—Preparation for Interview
Interviews under Caution
Financial Interviews
Statements under Caution
Identification Procedures
Search of Premises
Search of Person
Samples—Intimate, Non-intimate and Handwriting
Charging and Alternatives
Bail
Fingerprints and Photographs
Complaints

SPECIAL CATEGORIES OF SUSPECT

Armed Services
Immigration Aspects
Juvenile Suspects
Mentally Disordered Suspects
Terrorist Suspects
Volunteers

MISCELLANEOUS

Duty Solicitors
Solicitors' Representatives
Interpreters
Public Funding

List of Abbreviations

AA 1955	Army Act 1955
ACSA 2001	Anti-Terrorism, Crime and Security Act 2001
AFA 1955	Air Force Act 1955
AIA 1996	Asylum and Immigration Act 1996
AIAA 1993	Asylum and Immigration Appeals Act 1993
AI(TC)A 2004	Asylum and Immigration (Treatment of Claimants, etc) Act 2004
AJA 1999	Access to Justice Act 1999
BA 1976	Bail Act 1976
CA 1989	Children Act 1989
CDA 1998	Crime and Disorder Act 1998
CDS(G)R 2001	Criminal Defence Service (General) No.2 Regulations 2001
CJA 1987	Criminal Justice Act 1987
CJA 1988	Criminal Justice Act 1988
CJA 1991	Criminal Justice Act 1991
CJA 1993	Criminal Justice Act 1993
CJA 2003	Criminal Justice Act 2003
CJCSA 2000(A)(O) 2004	Criminal Justice and Court Services Act 2000 (Amendment) (order) 2004
CJPA 2001	Criminal Justice and Police Act 2001
CJPOA 1994	Criminal Justice and Public Order Act 1994
CLA 1967	Criminal Law Act 1967
CJACCCP 2004	CJA 2003, Conditional Cautions: Code of Practice 2004
CJCSA 2000	Criminal Justice and Court Services Act 2000
C(SA)R 1991	Children (Secure Accommodation) Regulations 1991
CYPA 1933	Children and Young Persons Act 1933

DSA 2001	Duty Solicitor Arrangements 2001
DVCVA 2004	Domestic Violence, Crime and Victims Act 2004
EA 2003	Extradition Act 2003
ECHR	European Convention on Human Rights
FCA 1981	Forgery and Counterfeiting Act 1981
GCC 2004	General Criminal Contract 2004
HOC 66/1990	Home Office Circular 66/1990 (Provision for Mentally Disordered Offenders)
HOC 78/1992	Home Office Circular 78/1992 (Detention of Juveniles)
HOC 18/1994	Home Office Circular 18/1994 (Cautioning of Offenders)
HOC 12/1995	Home Office Circular 12/1995 (Mentally Disordered Offenders: Inter-agency Working) and accompanying booklet
HOC 34/1998	Home Office Circular 34/1998 (New Bail Measures in The Crime and Disorder Act 1998)
HOC 9/1999	Home Office Circular 9/1999 (Guides to the key Provisions in The Crime and Disorder Act 1998)
HOC 60/2003	Home Office Circular 60/2003 (Criminal Justice Act 2003: Changes Affecting PACE)
HOC 61/2003	Home Office Circular 61/2003 (Bail Elsewhere Than At a Police Station)
HRA 1998	Human Rights Act 1998
IA 1971	Immigration Act 1971
IAA 1999	Immigration and Asylum Act 1999
LA 2003	Licensing Act 2003
MCA 1980	Magistrates' Courts Act 1980
MCA 1988	Malicious Communications Act 1988

MDA 1987	Ministry of Defence Act 1987
MHA 1983	Mental Health Act 1983
NCIS(C)R 1998	NCIS (Complaints) Regulations 1998
NCS(C)R 1998	National Crime Squad (Complaints) Regulations 1998
NDA 1957	Naval Discipline Act 1957
NPR(PO)(A)R 2003	National Police records (recordable Offences) (Amendment) Regulations 2003
NPR(RO)(A)R 1997	National Police Records (Recordable Offences) (Amendment) Regulations 1997
NPR(RO)R 1985	National Police Records (Recordable Offences) Regulations 1985
OAPA 1861	Offences Against the Person Act 1861
OPA 1959	Obscene Publications Act 1959
PA 1996	Police Act 1996
PA 1996(CTP)O 1999	Police Act 1996 (Commencement and Transitional Provisions) Order 1999
PA 1997	Police Act 1997
PACE 1984	Police and Criminal Evidence Act 1984
PACE(AAF)O 1997	PACE 1984 (Application to the Armed Forces) Order 1997
PACE(CP)(AF)O 2003	PACE 1984 (Codes of Practice) (Armed Forces) Order 2003
PACE(TI)(No 1)O 1991	Police and Criminal Evidence Act 1984 (Tape Recording of Interviews) (No. 1) Order 1991
PCA 1978	Protection of Children Act 1978
PCC(S)A 2000	Powers of the Criminal Courts (Sentencing) Act 2000

P(C)R 2004	Police (Conduct) Regulations 2004
P(C & M)R 2004	Police (Complaints and Misconduct) Regulations 2001
POCA 2002	Proceeds of Crime Act 2002
PRA 2002	Police Reform Act 2002
RIPA 2000	Regulation of Investigatory Powers Act 2000
RR(A)A 2000	Race Relations (Amendment) Act 2000
RRD(SPS)R 2003	PACE 1984 (Remote Reviews of Detention) (Specified Police Stations) Regulations 2003
RTA 1988	Road Traffic Act 1988
SOA 1956	Sexual Offences Act 1956
SOA 2003	Sexual Offences Act 2003
SOA 1959	Street Offences Act 1959
TA 1968	Theft Act 1968
TA 1984	Telecommunications Act 1984
TA 2000	Terrorism Act 2000
VATA 1983	Value Added Tax Act 1983
YJCEA 1999	Youth Justice and Criminal Evidence Act 1999

Table of Cases

Table of Statutes

Table of Statutory Instruments

Table of European Legislation

Accepting Instructions and Preparation

THE LEGAL ADVISER'S RESPONSIBILITIES

Suspects under criminal investigation will look to their legal advisers not only for advice on the law but also for a protective shield between them and the police. Rightly or wrongly, suspects will often fear that they are in danger of being abused, tricked or otherwise mistreated by the police and they will expect their advisers to shelter them from any such behaviour.

It is usually the case that the adviser's presence will in itself ensure that the suspect is treated properly by those in authority. However, this is not a guarantee and the adviser must always be alert and prepared to intervene where necessary to ensure that the police are not in breach of any of the relevant rules or obligations, as detailed under the other index headings in this book.

The primary responsibility of the adviser is to act in the best interests, and upon the instructions of the suspect, subject to legality and the professional rules of conduct. Indeed, the PACE 1984 Codes of Practice recognise this, by stating that the solicitor's role in the police station is "to protect and advance the legal rights of their client".

PACE 1984, Code C, Note for Guidance 6D
R. v McFarlane, The Times, March 24, 1999

For further details of the implications of these responsibilities, refer to the **Advising the Suspect—Preparation for Interview** index heading.

PREPARATION BEFORE ATTENDING POLICE STATIONS

Office systems

The need for solicitors to provide an efficient and professional service to their clients is complicated by the facts that suspects are often arrested out of normal office hours and that such arrests are intrinsically unpredictable in terms of both when and how often they occur. This means that it is imperative to have in place clear office systems which are understood by all members of staff likely to be involved in criminal work in any way.

Different practices will approach this need in different ways and the types of systems introduced will often depend upon the size and location of the firm. However, a basic model will include:

(a) properly trained reception staff who are aware of how to react to and deal with telephone calls requiring immediate attention;

(b) clear procedures whereby the appropriately qualified police station advisers are easily contactable in the event that they are out of the office (usually done by the provision of mobile phones and/or pagers);

(c) an emergency telephone number for the use of suspects and police out of office hours; and

(d) rotas for advisers to attend police stations, both in and out of office hours.

As a result of public funding requirements for Criminal Defence Service suppliers and improved practice management standards generally, most firms generate a number of standardised forms including a "police station attendance report form" for use by their staff whilst in attendance at a police station. Use of such a form should ensure that all significant details, events and times are properly recorded; a properly completed form proving a valuable aid, both at the police station and thereafter.

Individual adviser's systems

The well-organised office must be matched by the well-organised police station adviser.

As well as having a thorough understanding of and experience in the nature of the work, advisers should consider maintaining a pre-packed briefcase which is always to hand, ready for an attendance at a police station at short notice. This should contain:

(a) supplies of stationery, including headed notepaper and carbon paper, in the event of written representations having to be made whilst at the police station;

(b) proof of identity;

(c) a stock of the requisite Criminal Defence Service application and report forms;

(d) a stock of the firm's standardised police station attendance report forms;

(e) cigarettes (nothing will enamour a non-smoking adviser to a smoking client as much as his foresight in bringing tobacco!);

(f) a copy of PACE 1984 as amended and the latest versions of the Codes of Practice;

(g) copies of Home Office Circulars HOC 66/1990, 78/1992, 18/1994, 12/1995, 34/1998, 9/1999, 60/2003, 61/2003; and the "Conditional Cautions: Code of Practice 2004"

(h) a copy of the local police force policy statement on cautioning;

(i) a copy of the Code for Crown Prosecutors;

(j) a local street map; and

(k) a copy of this book!

The legal adviser should also ensure that he acquires the habit of maintaining and preserving accurate contemporaneous notes of all work done. Such notes may be required to enable another lawyer to take over conduct of the matter if necessary and may also be vital in support of any future argument as to what did or did not occur during the suspect's detention. The notes may also be important in the event of a suspect later disputing either the advice received or the instructions given, and may be required to justify billing.

ACCEPTING INSTRUCTIONS FROM THE SUSPECT

Introduction

When instructions to act are received direct from the suspect, whether he is in custody or not, there are no difficulties in accepting and acting upon them.

It is important to check with the suspect that he has not already instructed another lawyer. If he is telephoning from custody then the adviser should also check this point with the custody officer and, in particular, ensure that a duty solicitor has not been called out by the police on behalf of the suspect.

Suspects in custody

When the suspect is in police custody, any telephone conversation might be overheard by police officers. If a phone call

PACE 1984, s.58 and

Code C, para. 6.1, Notes for Guidance 1E, 6J and Annex B

involves the taking of instructions or the giving of advice then the adviser should request that the suspect be allowed to talk in private, which is his right other than in exceptional circumstances.

If for any reason it is not possible for the suspect to talk in private, the adviser should tell the suspect only to answer questions with a "yes" or "no" and structure the conversation accordingly.

PACE 1984, Code C, Note for Guidance 6A

If the conversation results in an agreement that the adviser attend the suspect in person, the adviser should ensure that he advises the custody officer of this, as well as giving an estimated time of arrival. The suspect should be advised not to speak to the police about the allegations under investigation before the adviser's arrival and, the custody officer should be told that this advice had been tendered.

Suspects not in custody

There will be occasions when advisers are contacted by suspects who are not in custody but are aware that they are under investigation and that the police are endeavouring to locate them.

The adviser should carefully explain what is likely to happen if the suspect surrenders to the police on a voluntary basis, as well as the consequences of failing to do so, whilst ensuring that the suspect is aware that the decision as to which course to follow rests with him alone. Nothing should be said that could be interpreted as an active encouragement to the suspect to evade police detection. Indeed, the suspect should be advised that it may be in his interests to surrender voluntarily, as this has the advantages of:

(a) allowing an arrangement to be made by the adviser for surrender at a time convenient to both the police and the suspect when, if appropriate, the adviser can also be in attendance; and

(b) assisting in later representations for bail.

ACCEPTING INSTRUCTIONS FROM THE POLICE

It is sometimes the case that initial contact with the adviser is made by the police telephoning on behalf of a suspect in custody.

In such circumstances, the adviser should insist that the suspect be brought to the phone, in order that instructions can be taken from him in person. Once this has been arranged, the adviser should proceed upon the basis that he is receiving instructions direct from the suspect, as described in the previous section.

ACCEPTING INSTRUCTIONS FROM THE DUTY SOLICITOR TELEPHONE SERVICE

Police station duty solicitors normally receive their initial call from the duty solicitor call centre phone service. If on rota, the solicitor is obliged to accept and act upon the call, unless already engaged in acting for another suspect or has a conflict that prevents him from acting for this suspect. If not on rota, the solicitor may accept Panel and Back-up cases and "must use all reasonable endeavours to do so".

DSA 2001, para. 5.4 GCC 2004, Contract Spec. Pt B, paras 8.2.2–8.2.4

Refer to the **Duty Solicitors** index heading for further details.

ACCEPTING INSTRUCTIONS FROM A THIRD PARTY

Acting on the instructions

There will be occasions when the adviser is first contacted by a concerned third party, such as a relative, friend or associate of the suspect.

The adviser is entitled to act upon such contact and accept instructions to act for the suspect, as long as he is satisfied that the instructions are genuine. Confirmation from the suspect must also be obtained as soon as contact is made with him.

R. v Sally Jones (1984) Crim. L.R. 357; *Al-Sabah v Ali and others, Independent*, January 27, 1999

When speaking to a third party, efforts must be made to obtain as much detail as possible as to the suspect's full name, address and date of birth, as well as the circumstances of the arrest, including the identity of the arresting officers. If the suspect uses aliases then the third party should be asked whether he knows which name was given on arrest.

Locating the suspect

The first difficulty after receiving instructions from a third party may be in locating the suspect.

If the third party is unable to assist in identifying the police station to which the suspect was taken, the adviser should first contact the police station local either to the suspect's address or to the place of arrest. Even in cases where the suspect has been arrested by or on behalf of another police force, he will often have been taken to the local police station first. If the local station is not a "designated" station then the nearest such station should be the next point of inquiry.

PACE 1984, ss 56, 58; and Code C, para. 5.5, Note for Guidance 5D and Annex B

When telephoning a police station, the adviser should speak to the custody officer, who is normally obliged to confirm whether or not a suspect is in detention. The custody officer may refuse to provide such confirmation, perhaps because the suspect is being held incommunicado and/or access to a legal representative is being denied.

Such a refusal to give out information may itself suggest that the suspect is in detention. In such circumstances, the adviser should ask that his interest be noted on the custody record and that he be telephoned as soon as the custody officer is in a position to respond to the inquiry. Thereafter, the adviser should not rely upon the custody officer's co-operation but continue to telephone at regular intervals of between 15 and 30 minutes and repeat the initial inquiry.

The suspect has not asked for representation

A common difficulty arises when the custody officer confirms that the suspect is being detained but insists that he has not asked for legal representation.

PACE 1984, Code C, Annex B, para. 4

In such circumstances, the officer should be reminded that access to legal advice cannot be delayed on the ground that an adviser has been asked to attend a police station by a third party and that PACE 1984, Code C specifies that:

PACE 1984, Code C, para. 6.5

> "Whenever legal advice is requested, and unless Annex B applies, the custody officer must act without delay to secure the provision of such advice. If, on being informed or reminded of this right, the detainee declines to speak to a solicitor in person, the officer should point out that the right includes the right to speak with a solicitor on the telephone . . ."

It is notable that this provision does not specify that the request for legal advice has to come from the suspect rather than from a third party.

Therefore, it should be made clear by the adviser that he insists on speaking to the suspect on the telephone.

PACE 1984, Code C, para. 6.15 and Annex B, para. 4

If, despite these representations, the custody officer refuses to allow the suspect to come to the telephone, the adviser should state that this leaves no option but for him to attend the police station in person, thereby invoking those provisions of PACE 1984 which require that the suspect be advised of the adviser's presence upon his arrival.

The suspect does not wish to be advised

On occasion the custody officer will state that the suspect has made the positive assertion that he does not wish to receive legal advice or representation. If this has occurred, the custody officer is obliged to ask the suspect for his reasons for declining legal advice and to note these in the custody record or interview record as appropriate. However, the suspect is not obliged to give reasons for declining legal advice and should not be pressed to do so.

PACE 1984, Code C, para. 6.5 and Note for Guidance 6K

In such circumstances, the adviser should still attempt to speak to the suspect directly, so as to have this information confirmed. Such a request may be declined, because the police may fear that the adviser will attempt to persuade the suspect to alter his decision; however, the police are specifically embargoed from doing or saying anything with the intention of dissuading a suspect from obtaining legal advice and therefore it is arguable that the police are not permitted to refuse the adviser's request simply because of this fear of "interference".

PACE 1984, Code C, para. 6.4

If the request is refused then the adviser should ask that the call be noted on the custody record, together with the requirement that he be contacted if and as soon as the suspect changes his mind. Alternatively, if there are grounds for disbelieving a claim by the police that the suspect has refused legal representation, the adviser should consider attending the police station in person, thereby invoking those PACE 1984 provisions which require that the suspect be advised of his presence upon arrival.

PACE 1984, Code C, para. 6.15 and Annex B, para. 4

INFORMATION TO BE OBTAINED FROM THE POLICE

At various stages during the accepting of instructions, it is likely that the adviser will have reason to speak to the custody officer. The adviser should also ensure that he speaks to an investigating officer involved in the enquiry for further information about the allegation(s).

During any such conversations, it is important to obtain from the police as much information as possible that will assist in advising the suspect. This should include:

(a) whether the suspect is a volunteer or under arrest;

(b) the grounds for detention;

(c) whether the suspect is a juvenile and/or suffering from a mental disorder or any particular medical complaint;

(d) whether the suspect is a fluent English speaker or requires the services of an interpreter;

(e) the names and ranks of the investigating officers;

(f) whether the suspect was arrested under warrant and, if so, details of this;

(g) the time and place of arrest and the time of arrival at the police station;

(h) the time that the detention was authorised;

(i) the reasons for arrest and details of the offence(s) for which the suspect is in detention;

(j) whether there has been any search of the suspect's person or premises and, if so, details of these;

(k) whether there have been any interview(s) and, if so, details of these;

(l) whether other suspects are also in custody; and

(m) the next steps the police propose to take as part of their investigation.

INITIAL ADVICE TO THE SUSPECT

Introduction

The index heading **Advising the Suspect—Preparation for Interview** deals with this issue in detail. This section therefore only provides an introduction to the main issues which most commonly arise in advising a suspect over the telephone prior to or instead of an attendance at a police station.

Once the adviser has obtained as much information as possible from the police, he is then in a position to commence discussions with the suspect.

The two primary concerns at this stage are to give initial advice and to decide whether an attendance upon the suspect in person is required.

As explained earlier, the adviser should initially endeavour to ensure that the suspect can speak in private, failing which he must tailor his questions so that the suspect need only answer "yes" or "no".

Obtaining information

Before offering advice, the adviser should obtain as much information as possible from the suspect, including:

(a) confirmation of the name he gave to the police on arrest and whether this is an alias;

(b) confirmation that he requires the adviser to act;

(c) the brief circumstances surrounding the arrest;

(d) whether any admissions have been made or incriminating evidence found;

(e) whether the suspect has any complaints about police behaviour; and

(f) whether the suspect wishes the adviser to attend the police station.

The adviser should also outline any information gained from the police to the suspect and seek confirmation that it accords with the suspect's understanding of events to date.

The adviser is now in a position to offer initial advice. The nature and extent of this advice will depend upon whether the police propose to interview the suspect and/or whether it is agreed that the adviser will be attending the police station.

Adviser to attend the police station

If the adviser is to attend the police station, the suspect should be informed of the expected time of arrival and advised that he should not agree to be interviewed or answer any questions about the allegation(s) until the adviser's arrival.

Adviser not to attend the police station

If the adviser is not to attend the police station, the suspect should be advised as to the likely future events, as well as being reminded that the right to legal advice continues and that he can ask to speak to a lawyer again at any future stage whilst in detention.

PACE 1984, s.58 and Code C, para. 6.1

Situations where an attendance is not required will be uncommon. They will usually arise when:

(a) the allegation(s) are relatively trivial;

(b) the suspect is familiar with police station procedures and happy to be advised simply over the telephone;

(c) there is no issue as to police bail; and/or

(d) the police have confirmed that they do not wish to interview the suspect.

Duty solicitor's obligations

GCC 2004, Contract Spec. Pt B, paras 8.2.6

Duty solicitors must remember that they are obliged to attend a suspect at a police station where:

(a) the suspect has been arrested for an arrestable offence and is to be interviewed;

(b) the suspect is to be subject to an identity parade, group or video identification, or confrontation;

(c) the suspect complains of serious maltreatment by the police; or

(d) the suspect is a youth or person at risk.

INFORMING THE POLICE OF INTENTIONS

Once a suspect has received advice, the adviser should speak again to the custody officer.

PACE 1984, Code C, para. 6.6

The custody officer should be told of the adviser's intentions. If these are that the adviser will be attending the police station then the expected time of arrival should be given and confirmation sought that no interview will commence or, if already commenced, will be stopped and not continue until his arrival.

PACE 1984, Code C, para. 6.6 and Annex B

There are certain circumstances under which the police may commence or continue an interview without waiting for the arrival of the adviser: these are detailed under the **Suspect's Rights** index heading. However, it should be noted that if the reason given by the police for starting or continuing an interview is that the adviser's expected time of arrival is too far ahead and awaiting his arrival will "cause unreasonable delay to the process of investigation", the adviser should consider declining to accept the suspect's instructions and advising the suspect and custody officer of this, in order that alternative arrangements can be made for a more conveniently located solicitor to attend in his place.

PRACTICAL GUIDANCE

(1) Faxed letters

It may be appropriate to send letters by fax to the police station confirming initial conversations or agreements. For example, if the adviser has been told that the suspect has stated that he does not require legal advice then, as well as asking the custody officer to note the adviser's interest in the matter, this interest should be confirmed in a letter sent by fax to the police station marked for the custody officer's attention. The letter should state, *inter alia*, that the adviser should be contacted immediately if and when the suspect has a change of mind.

Such letters and the accompanying fax time log may be of great relevance in any future proceedings where such events are in dispute.

(2) Passing information to third parties

The adviser may be asked by the suspect to contact a third party and advise him of the suspect's arrest and surrounding circumstances. Such a request should be acted upon only with the upmost caution, as it may be the case that the third party is also a suspect and will seek to evade arrest once receiving the information or is otherwise an associate of the suspect and will attempt to interfere with the course of justice.

It is suggested that the safest course for the adviser is to inform the suspect that the request will only be acted upon if the suspect consents to the adviser first informing the custody officer of the proposed contact and ascertaining that the police do not have any sustainable objection to the contact being made.

(3) Acting for more than one suspect

PACE 1984, Code C, Note for Guidance 6G

It is perfectly proper for an adviser to act for more than one suspect who is under investigation. However, if upon taking instructions it becomes clear that there is a conflict of interest between the suspects, the adviser can only act for those suspects who are not in conflict with each other. The custody officer should then be advised of the situation, so that alternative arrangements can be put in hand for separate legal representation.

(4) Police information given in confidence

The adviser must never agree to accept information from the police in confidence, as this will conflict with his overriding obligations to the suspect.

The Guide to the Professional Conduct of Solicitors (Law Society)

There are exceptions to this rule where the information could cause harm to the suspect because of his physical or mental condition or if the information relates to certain orders or warrants under DTA 1994 or TA 2000, whereby it is an offence to make disclosures that are likely to prejudice the investigation of the offence.

If information is tendered in confidence but not accepted as such then it is for the adviser to decide whether to relay the information to the suspect. Clearly, it must be so relayed if it is of any relevance to the suspect's current situation and does not fall within one of the defined exceptions.

Advising the Suspect—Preparation for Interview

This chapter deals with advising the suspect at the police station prior to interview with the police and preparing the suspect for that interview. Advice in relation to the right of silence is contained in the **Advising the Suspect—The Right of Silence** index heading. Prior to meeting the suspect to provide this advice, the adviser will have obtained as much information from the police as possible (refer to the **Accepting Instructions** and **Information Gathering** index headings).

RECORDS

The adviser must keep detailed and contemporaneous notes of events which take place at the police station, as it is always possible that he will have to give evidence of any untoward occurrences and possibly even reasons for certain advice, notwithstanding the existence of legal privilege.

It is extremely useful for the adviser to carry a *pro forma* attendance note for completion as the case progresses at the police station. Such attendance notes should include details of the following (note that this list is by way of guidance rather than exhaustive):

(a) time of and reason for arrest;

(b) time of arrival of suspect at police station;

(c) relevant times for detention periods and reviews;

(d) custody number;

(e) identity of the officer in the case and arresting officer;

(f) time and content of telephone calls;

(g) time of arrival of adviser at the police station;

(h) time and details of information given to the adviser by the police and the identity of the officer providing the information;

(i) time and details of interview(s) between the adviser and the suspect (and appropriate adult if relevant), including careful notes of the suspect's instructions and the advice given;

(j) time and a detailed note of formal police interview(s), as it is not good enough to rely on obtaining a copy of the tape(s) at a later date;

(k) time and content of any representations made by the adviser, for example at the review of detention or bail stage;

(l) time and details of any identification procedure;

(m) time and details of any requests for and provision of, or refusal to provide samples and details of the advice given;

(n) time and details of any injuries to or complaints by the suspect, including diagrams if appropriate;

(o) details of any other feature of the case such as intimate searches; and

(p) time of departure from the police station and any follow-up action taken, such as informing relatives or arranging sureties.

MESSAGES

It is not uncommon for suspects to ask the adviser to pass on a message to a friend or relative outside the police station. The adviser must take the utmost care not to be party to passing on a message, however innocent it may appear, which is likely to further crime or lead to the destruction of evidence. If the adviser has any doubt about passing on the message then he should not do so unless, with the consent of the suspect, he has raised the matter with the police.

INITIAL INTERVIEW BETWEEN ADVISER AND SUSPECT

The importance of the initial interview between the adviser and the suspect cannot be overemphasised. It provides the adviser with the opportunity to reassure the suspect that he has someone "on his side" who will support the suspect and protect his rights in the often hostile atmosphere of the police station. It is a chance to build a rapport with the suspect and to instil confidence that the adviser will be able to deal with the police and the case in an effective manner.

PACE 1984, s.58

This interview must be held in private, which means out of the hearing and view of others. If no private facilities are available, the interview should not take place and the reason explained to the suspect, who should also be advised to say nothing to the police until after such a private consultation has taken place.

The adviser should not be forced to go into a cell with the suspect, although this may be the private facility offered by the police: an interview in such circumstances could be potentially dangerous for the adviser and the police are known not to respond to cell buzzers with great alacrity. An interview room or other detention room can usually be provided and the adviser should request the use of such a room. However, the adviser should be aware that the police may have the ability to listen to conversations in some interview rooms.

Introduction to the suspect

The adviser should explain to the suspect that the role of the adviser is to protect and advance the legal rights of the suspect while in the police station.

PACE 1984, Code C, NfG 6D

He should make sure that the suspect understands that all information passed between suspect and adviser is confidential and will not be disclosed to the police or to any other party without the consent of the suspect.

If the adviser is not a solicitor, his exact status should be explained to the suspect, as required under Law Society guidelines. This explanation will have the effect of nullifying any sharp police practice at a later stage of referring to the status of the adviser in such a way as to attempt to undermine the confidence of the suspect in his adviser.

If the adviser has been called to the police station as duty solicitor (or a representative of the duty solicitor), he should explain to the suspect that he is completely independent of the police and is a solicitor (or an accredited representative) in private practice or a member of the Public Defender Service who happens to be on duty at that time for that area. Many suspects may still harbour concerns that the duty solicitor is "the police solicitor" and early reassurance that this is not the case is often helpful.

The suspect ought to have been told that he is entitled to legal advice whilst in police custody free of charge. However, some suspects may not have fully understood this and the adviser should ensure that he explains to the suspect that no charge will be made for advice received while in the police station (unless an agreement has been reached with an "own client" for the attendance to be privately funded notwithstanding the suspect's right to free legal advice).

Many suspects are anxious to know what is going to happen to them while in police custody. Although it is rarely clear what will be the exact course of events, the adviser can let the suspect know what is likely to happen in general terms. It may be that such general information at this early stage will help to limit the natural anxiety of a suspect in police detention.

ASSESSING FITNESS TO BE INTERVIEWED

PACE 1984, Code C, paras 3.5–3.10

Before taking any initial instructions from a suspect, the adviser should make some assessment of whether the suspect is fit to be interviewed. It is helpful to start with the risk assessment which will have been carried out by the custody officer.

The suspect must be considered fit for interview by the custody officer before each interview. Annex G to Code C provides some guidance on fitness for interview.

PACE 1984, Code C, Annex G, para. 2

A suspect may be at risk in an interview if it is considered that:

(a) conducting the interview could significantly harm the detainee's physical or mental state;

(b) anything the detainee says in the interview about their involvement or suspected involvement in the offence about which they are being interviewed **might** be considered unreliable in subsequent court proceedings because of their physical or mental state.

PACE 1984, Code C, Annex G, para. 3

In assessing whether the suspect should be interviewed, the following must be considered:

(a) how the suspect's physical or mental state might affect their ability to understand the nature and purpose of the interview, to comprehend what is being asked and to appreciate the significance of any answers given and make rational decisions about whether they want to say anything;

(b) the extent to which the suspect's replies may be affected by their physical or mental condition rather than representing a rational and accurate explanation of their involvement in the offence;

(c) how the nature of the interview, which could include particularly probing questions, might affect the suspect.

Any health care professional consulted about a suspect's fitness for interview must consider the suspect's functional ability rather than simply relying on a medical diagnosis. It is possible for a person with severe mental illness to be fit for interview.

PACE 1984, Code C, Annex G, para. 4

A health care professional should advise on the need for an appropriate adult to be present at any interview, whether reassessment of the person's fitness for interview may be necessary if the interview lasts beyond a specified time, and whether a further specialist opinion may be required.

PACE 1984, Code C, Annex G, para. 5

When the health care professional identifies any risks they should be asked to quantify the risks and they should inform the custody officer whether the suspect's condition is likely to improve, will require or be amenable to treatment, and indicate how long it may take for such improvement to take effect.

PACE 1984, Code C, Annex G, para. 6

The health care professional's determination and any advice or recommendations should be made in writing and form part of the custody record.

PACE 1984, Code C, Annex G, para. 7

Once the health care professional has provided that information, it is a matter for the custody officer to decide whether or not to allow the interview to go ahead and if the interview is to proceed, to determine what safeguards are needed.

PACE 1984, Code C, Annex G, para. 8

Notwithstanding that it is for the police to decide if the suspect is fit to be interviewed and the advice of a health care professional may have been sought, if the adviser forms the opinion that the suspect is unfit to be interviewed by police, he should object to any proposed interview and request that the objection be noted on the custody record. A separate record should be made in the adviser's own notes of the objection, the reasons for it and the police response to it.

It may also be appropriate to seek an independent medical opinion as the suspect has the right to be examined by a doctor of his choice and the cost of such an opinion can be claimed under the General Criminal Contract if it is reasonably incurred in the suspect's best interests.

PACE 1984, Code C, para. 9.8

GCC 2004, Pt C, para. 1.18

If the police insist on going ahead with an interview, the adviser should consider advising the suspect not to answer questions and a note of the reasons for the advice made. However, there is a great risk of an adverse inference as the court is likely to prefer the view of the qualified health care professional to that of the medically unqualified legal adviser.

R. v Condron (1997) 1 Cr. App.R. 185

If the suspect appears to be mentally disordered or mentally vulnerable, the adviser should, subject to the suspect's instructions, so inform the custody officer. Having been told in good faith that the suspect appears to be mentally disordered, the

PACE 1984, Code C, para. 1.4

suspect must then be treated as if he were mentally disordered and all the safeguards for such suspects must be applied. For more detail, refer to the **Mentally Disordered Suspects** index heading.

PACE 1984, Code C, para. 12.2

PACE 1984, Code C, para. 9.8

A suspect may be unfit for a variety of other reasons, such as stress, anxiety for the safety of his children or tiredness. The suspect will be entitled to a period of eight hours' continuous rest in any 24-hour period and, if he is tired, he may prefer to take advantage of this provision by taking his rest at that time, leaving him more refreshed for interview at a later stage. If stress is an issue, the suspect should be advised to request a clinical examination, which will mean that a health care professional will have to be called as soon as practicable.

R. v Bowden [1999] 4 All E.R. 43

Any objection to the fitness of a suspect to be interviewed must be noted by the adviser and a request made that the objection be noted on the custody record. If the interview takes place despite these objections, the adviser should repeat the objection at the start of the interview on tape. He should be careful not to refer to any privileged conversation or reasons for any advice already given to the suspect as such comments may waive the privilege attached to those consultations.

TAKING INITIAL INSTRUCTIONS

The adviser should have obtained as much information from the police as possible about the alleged offence before speaking to the suspect (see the **Information Gathering** index heading).

It is often a helpful way to start taking the suspect's initial instructions by telling the suspect what the police are alleging. The suspect should be told that the police will not necessarily have given the adviser the full details and that what they have said will usually reflect only part of the story.

As a safeguard against any subsequent ethical difficulties, the adviser could inform the suspect at this early stage that if he tells the adviser that he is guilty of the offence but that he wishes positively to deny the offence (rather than remaining silent), the adviser will not be able to continue to act for him.

The suspect should then be allowed to tell his version of events, if possible without interruption, after which the adviser should take him through it again in more detail, asking the sort of questions that the police may ask in the interview.

The adviser will need to have a knowledge of the elements of the offence(s) alleged and the defences available. It is obviously not for the adviser to help the suspect construct his defence but it is helpful to know what the suspect believes his defence to be and to consider whether such a defence is valid. The suspect should be asked about potential alibi or other witnesses.

The suspect should be asked about the circumstances of the arrest, whether anything has already been said to the police and/or whether any police questions have been met with silence. Information about items found at arrest or on a subsequent search should also be obtained. It is only after obtaining as much information as possible from the suspect that proper and informed advice can be given about whether the suspect ought to answer questions in interview.

Finally, it is important to obtain information about the suspect's background and, in particular, whether they have previously been arrested or convicted. This may be helpful for considerations in relation to bail or whether a matter could potentially be dealt with by way of caution, reprimand or final warning. Equally, it will of assistance in considering whether evidence of the suspect's character could become admissible in due course under the provisions of the Criminal Justice Act 2003.

CJA 2003, s.98–110 and s.112

ETHICAL DIFFICULTIES WITH INSTRUCTIONS

It is sometimes the case that the suspect has given the police details of a false identity by giving a false name, date of birth or address or a combination of all three.

If this fact comes to the attention of the adviser, he is put in a difficult position: if the suspect has given details of a false identity to avoid the police finding out about previous convictions or outstanding warrants, or to prevent a search of his premises, the adviser cannot be party to the suspect persisting in the deception and should withdraw from acting for the suspect, without informing the police of the reasons for that withdrawal. If, on the other hand, the suspect intends not to persist with the fake details, then the adviser can continue to act for him.

A suspect who has provided false details to the police should be advised of the consequences of so doing, which may include prosecution for wasting police time or attempting to pervert the course of justice, although the latter charge has been discouraged by the Court of Appeal except in serious cases. The suspect should also be advised of the likelihood of his true identity subsequently being established, for example following the taking of fingerprints or use of Livescan.

R. v Sookoo [2002] EWCA Crim. 800

If a suspect decides not to provide the police with any details of his identity at all (or only partial details such as name but not address), no such ethical problems arise, as no deception is being practised on the police. The suspect should, however, be advised as to the other difficulties that such a refusal may present, the most obvious being that bail after charge will be refused on the grounds that no address has been provided. Again his identity is likely to be discovered by the use of fingerprints, if he has previously had his fingerprints taken.

A suspect may intend to mislead the police in other ways. A suspect may tell the adviser that he is guilty but that he wishes to put forward a false account in interview. The adviser could not be party to such a deception and would have to withdraw but must not reveal the reason for that withdrawal. If the suspect admits guilt to the adviser but intends not to answer questions in interview, the adviser can continue to act without any problem. If subsequently, during the interview, the suspect does put forward a version of events which the adviser knows to be false, he should withdraw from the case but only once the interview has finished and not during the course of the interview, as that would effectively indicate that the suspect is not telling the truth and would be a breach of confidence.

If the suspect tells the adviser he is innocent but will accept guilt in the interview, the adviser is not obliged to withdraw but ought to consider it and should advise the suspect strongly against taking such a course of action. The suspect will find it very difficult to convince a court that he confessed falsely, particularly in the presence of a legal adviser. He could also be placing himself at risk of prosecution for attempting to pervert the course of justice and/or wasting police time if the deception is later revealed.

ARGUMENT THAT NO INTERVIEW SHOULD TAKE PLACE

PACE 1984, s.34(1), 37

This argument is considerably more difficult than it once was and is likely to be available only in very limited circumstances. The authority to detain a suspect is vested in the custody officer and derives from s.34(1) of PACE 1984, read in conjunction with s.37 of the same Act (refer to the **Detention Periods and Reviews** index heading).

Under s.34(1), a "person arrested for an offence shall not be kept in police detention except in accordance with the provisions of this Part of this Act".

Prior to charge, the relevant provision of the Act is s.37, which states that:

> where a person is arrested for an offence . . . or returns to a police station to answer bail, the custody officer . . . shall determine whether he has before him sufficient evidence to charge that person with the offence for which he has been arrested and may detain him [for the purpose of charging].

Section 37(7) goes on to state that if, at any time during a suspect's detention, the custody officer determines that there is sufficient evidence on which to charge the suspect, he must either be so charged or released.

PACE 1984, s.37

These provisions of the Act should be read in conjunction with the Codes of Practice with which there would appear to be some conflict—see below.

Section 34(1)(a) of the Criminal Justice and Public Order Act 1994 states:

> where, in any proceedings against a person for an offence, evidence is given that the accused at any time before he was charged with the offence, on being questioned under caution by a constable trying to discover whether or by whom the offence had been committed, failed to mention any fact relied on in his defence in those proceedings . . . being a fact which, in the circumstances existing at the time, the accused could reasonably have been expected to mention . . . then the court or jury, in determining whether the accused is guilty of the offence charged, may draw such inferences from the failure as appear proper.

CJPOA 1994, s.34(1)(a)

Therefore if the police have (or believe that they have) sufficient evidence to charge the suspect before any interview then any questions they put to the suspect will not be for the purpose of "trying to discover whether or by whom the offence had been committed". These questions would therefore fall outside of the ambit of s.34. If the questions do not fall within the section then no adverse inference can be drawn from a failure to answer them.

The only question which should be permissible at this point is "Do you have anything you wish to say?" Once again, this is not a question seeking to discover whether the suspect had committed the offence or whether the offence had been committed and falls outside of the scope of s.34.

R. v Pointer [1997] Crim. L.R. 676; *R. v Gayle* [1999] Crim. L.R. 502

However, the adviser should be aware that this argument is considerably more difficult since the initial cases of *Pointer* and *Gayle* as a result of recent case law and the most recent PACE 1984 Codes of Practice.

Under Code C the interview of a person about an offence with which that person has not been charged or for which they have not been informed they may be prosecuted, must cease when:

PACE 1984, Code C, para. 11.6

(a) the officer in charge of the investigation is satisfied all the questions they consider relevant to obtaining accurate and reliable information about the offence have been put to the suspect, this includes allowing the suspect an opportunity to give an innocent explanation and asking questions to test if the explanation is accurate and reliable, *e.g.* to clear up ambiguities or clarify what the suspect said;

(b) the officer in charge of the investigation has taken account of any other available evidence; and

(c) the officer in charge of the investigation, or in the case of a detained suspect, the custody officer, reasonably believes there is sufficient evidence to provide a realistic prospect of conviction for that offence.

PACE 1984, Code C, para. 16.1

Furthermore, when the officer in charge of the investigation reasonably believes there is sufficient evidence to provide a realistic prospect of conviction for the offence, they shall without delay inform the custody officer who will be responsible for considering whether the detainee should be charged.

R. v Van Bokkum and others [2000] 6 *Archbold News* 2, CA

R. v Elliott [2002] EWCA Crim. 931

Even prior to the change in the Code specifically to allow the suspect to be given an opportunity to give an innocent explanation and asking questions to test if the explanation is accurate and reliable, the Court was beginning to take a more robust view, *i.e.* that "sufficient evidence to prosecute" (the expression used in the old Code) must involve some consideration of any explanation or lack of it from the suspect. In *Elliott* the court reviewed the previous authorities and held that:

(a) even if the interviewing officer believed that there was sufficient evidence to justify charging the suspect, he was not prohibited from offering the defendant the opportunity to explain his account of the incident;

(b) moreover, whether "an offence had been committed" for the purposes of s.34 of the CJPOA 1994 depended as

> much on the availability of defences as it did on the proof of actus reus and mens rea. For example, if the defendant had been acting in self defence, his actions would not have been unlawful and he would have committed no offence.

None of the previous authorities appear to have considered the duty of the custody officer under s.37 of PACE 1984 but have, instead, concentrated on the provisions of the Codes of Practice and the term "sufficient evidence to prosecute" rather than "sufficient evidence to charge". If these terms can be distinguished, this argument will still be available. For instance, "sufficient evidence to charge" may equate to sufficient evidence to establish a prime facie case (without consideration of any explanation from the suspect) whereas "sufficient evidence to prosecute" has been judicially interpreted to involve some consideration of any explanation or lack of it from the suspect.

R. v Elliott [2002] EWCA Crim. 931

Notwithstanding the current state of the case law and the current wording of the Codes, where the adviser is representing a suspect who does not wish to be interviewed but against whom there appears to be sufficient evidence to charge him, he should consider making representations to the investigating and custody officer that the suspect should either be so charged or released. The adviser may wish to highlight the duty of the custody officer under s.37 of PACE 1984 and point out the mandatory nature of that duty notwithstanding any apparent conflict with the Codes. It may be helpful to ask the custody officer whether he believes that at that stage there is sufficient evidence to charge the suspect. If he agrees that there is, the suspect should be charged. If he does not, what further evidence can be obtained from an interview in which the suspect remains silent which would subsequently justify a charge?

If such representations are made, they must be noted by the legal representative and a request made that they be recorded on the custody record.

If the custody officer does not accede to the representations and an interview takes place, the adviser should consider stating at the start of the interview and on the tape that in his opinion the detention of the suspect is now unlawful under s.37(1) and (7) of PACE 1984 because the police have sufficient evidence to charge the suspect.

He should also consider advising the suspect on the tape, in the present tense and in the presence of the police officers not to answer the questions which will be put to him. This should not waive the privilege attached to the earlier private consultation between legal representative and suspect and will prepare the ground for submissions at trial that no adverse inference be drawn as a result of the silence of the suspect in interview.

If an interview either does not take place or does proceed but is met with silence, this will still leave open the question as to whether the suspect should reply orally or in writing to the caution on charge.

ADVICE ON WHETHER TO ANSWER QUESTIONS

Advice to the suspect on whether or not to answer questions is dealt with in the **Advising The Suspect—Right of Silence** index heading.

OTHER AREAS FOR ADVICE

During the initial interview, the adviser should also be in a position to advise on any other matters which may be relevant to the individual case, such as whether or not to provide fingerprints, samples of handwriting or intimate or non-intimate samples before charge, or whether to agree to any identification procedure. These matters are all dealt with in detail under their relevant index headings.

Notes of significant statements or silences

PACE 1984, Code C, para. 11.4

It is often the case that the suspect will be offered the arresting officer's notes and asked to read them and sign them to confirm their accuracy. The note of what was said or not said on arrest or subsequently will be put to the suspect in interview if it is considered to be a "significant statement or silence".

If the suspect disagrees with the note, it may well be prudent to make this clear by endorsing the officer's notebook to this effect. Whether the suspect should positively assert his version of events rather than just his disagreement with the officer's version is a matter which must be decided on a case-by-case basis. However, Code C provides that, where there is a disagreement, the details of that disagreement shall be recorded by the officer and the suspect invited to sign the further notes to confirm that they accurately reflect his disagreement with the original notes. Any refusal to so sign shall also be recorded.

PACE 1984, Code C, NfG 11E

There are often advantages to putting disagreements on record at an early stage, particularly if the officer has recorded the suspect as making admissions on arrest (or making no comment when he did in fact say something).

Where there is no disagreement with the notes, the question of whether to sign them will depend on what was said (or not said) and the individual circumstances of the case. Obviously, if the suspect made an immediate denial which is consistent with his version of events in interview, it will be useful to confirm the notes as accurate. However, there would be no advantage in signing notes which are effectively a confession unless the suspect is clear in his instructions that he is admitting guilt.

SUSPECT'S DECISION

The suspect should always be told that whether he answers questions or provides samples, etc. is entirely his choice: the adviser is there only to advise and not to make the decisions for the suspect. Some suspects will look to the adviser and rely on him more heavily than others but in all cases the suspect must make the decisions.

PREPARATION FOR INTERVIEW

The adviser should explain to the suspect in general terms what is likely to happen in the interview. This will include basic information, such as where everyone will sit and how the interview will be recorded, as well as more specific information such as how to deal with a "no comment" interview or a reminder that nothing is "off the record" in the police station, so that it is not just what is said on tape that matters.

The suspect should be reminded that he has the right to ask for and obtain legal advice in private at any time and that this means that he can interrupt the interview to request such advice. Although some police officers will not like this, the suspect is entitled to have the interview suspended to receive further legal advice and it will be for the adviser to insist that such advice be allowed.

PACE 1984, s.58

PACE 1984, Code C, NfG 6D

The suspect should be told that he will not get help in answering questions by way of prompts from the adviser or by the adviser answering the question on the suspect's behalf.

If, in a "no comment" interview, the suspect is asked if he will agree to an identification procedure or to give certain samples, the adviser should suggest that the matter be dealt with outside of the interview. Even where instructions have been taken and the suspect indicated his agreement to such a course to the adviser before the interview, the adviser will not know whether he has changed his mind during the course of the interview or requires further advice before consenting.

A suspect who is going to answer questions should be told not to be aggressive, sarcastic or facetious in his answers. The demeanour of the suspect in interview will be very important if the audio or videotape of the interview is subsequently played at trial.

The suspect should be made aware of certain tactics that the police may employ either to trick him into saying something he does not want to say or to get him to answer questions if the interview is one in which comment is declined. Obviously, tactics vary from officer to officer, but some general guidance will be helpful (refer to the **Interviews under Caution** index heading).

If the suspect elects not to answer questions, he should be told of the best method of doing this in interview: this is normally to confirm his identity and, if appropriate, that he understands the caution and thereafter to reply to every question by saying "no comment", which is generally easier than silence.

The suspect must be given the opportunity to ask the adviser any questions he may have before the commencement of any interview. The suspect should be told not to speak to any police officers outside of the interview room and/or in the absence of the adviser and reminded again of the right to interrupt the interview for further advice.

Advising the Suspect—Right of Silence

RIGHT OF SILENCE—THE LAW

THE COMMON LAW

The general principle

The old common law rule was that a suspect had the right to remain silent and hence refuse to answer questions or otherwise comment at any stage during a criminal investigation or subsequent trial. The exercise of this right could not amount to evidence against the suspect, nor could it corroborate any other evidence.

R. v Forbes [1992] Crim. L.R. 593

In any trial, the prosecution could not comment upon the fact that the defendant had remained silent. A judge could make some limited comment to a jury but not so as to imply that silence was any indication of guilt.

R. v Gilbert (1977) 66 Cr. App.R. 237

During Crown Court trials, advocates and the trial judge would remind the jury of the defendant's right of silence when appropriate, although there was no embargo as such upon a jury drawing their own inferences in instances where a defendant had refused to answer questions.

The common law position still applies where the questioning is not under caution or falls within PACE 1984, Code C, Annex C (see below).

CJPOA 1994, ss 34(2A), 36 (4A), 37(3A) as amended by YJCEA 1999, s.58
PACE 1984, Code C, Annex C

Exceptions to the general principle

Prior to CJPOA 1994 there were a number of exceptions to the common law right of silence. There is an obligation on a person to co-operate or provide information in the following situations:

(a) Silence in the face of the victim's accusation

When a defendant remained silent in the face of a direct accusation by the alleged victim when it would be reasonable to expect the defendant to have protested or have made some form of denial, the prosecution could comment on, and the court or jury draw adverse inferences from, this silence.

R. v Christie [1914] A.C. 545;
R. v Horne [1990] Crim. L.R. 188

(b) Criminal Justice Act 1987, s.2

It is an offence to fail to answer questions, furnish information or produce documents to Serious Fraud Office investigators during a "section 2" interview.

It should be noted that any answers given by a suspect under this provision cannot be used as evidence against him in any future criminal trial, other than to rebut a different version of events if such is expounded by the suspect during the trial.

(c) Company legislation

When Department of Trade and Industry inspectors are appointed to investigate the affairs of a company, ss 431–441 of the Companies Act 1985 require officers and agents of the company to assist the inspectors when asked to so do. This assistance may include the answering of relevant questions.

The Insolvency Act 1986 and Financial Services Act 1986 include similar provisions for investigations into insolvent companies and insider dealing allegations, respectively.

Saunders v UK (1997) 23 E.H.R.R. 313; *R. v Staines and Morrisey* [1997] Crim. L.R. 825

The European Court of Human Rights has held that it would infringe Art.6 of the European Convention on Human Rights (the right to a fair trial) if answers given during questioning under this legislation were to be used as evidence against the suspect in any future criminal trial. However, the Court of Appeal held subsequent to the ECHR decision that such evidence was not required to be excluded.

However, guidance from the Attorney-General issued after both decisions advises that answers obtained as a result of compulsory questioning under the various Acts which allow it should not be used as evidence or in cross-examination unless the defendant introduces them himself or the prosecution is based on a failure or omission to mention facts when required by statute to do so. This guidance was followed by legislation which now prohibits the use of evidence obtained from compulsory disclosure under a number of Acts relating to financial investigations.

YJCEA 1999, s.59, Sch. 3

THE CRIMINAL JUSTICE AND PUBLIC ORDER ACT 1994

The CJPOA 1994 materially affects the common law rules on the right of silence but it has not removed that right. A suspect can still choose to remain silent when questioned about an offence, although, in certain circumstances, adverse inferences can be drawn from that silence.

Silence when questioned or charged

The prosecution may call evidence during criminal proceedings of a defendant's failure to mention any fact relied upon in his defence, either:

(a) at any time before charge on being questioned under caution by a constable (or other investigating officer) trying to discover whether or by whom the offence(s) had been committed; or

CJPOA 1994, s.34(1), (4)

(b) on being charged or being officially informed that he might be prosecuted.

This provision can only operate if the circumstances at the time were such that the suspect could reasonably have been expected to mention the fact.

Once evidence of the silence has been called by the prosecution, the court or jury may draw such inferences "as appear proper" from the defendant's silence.

CJPOA 1994, s.34(2)

Silence when asked about objects, substances or marks

The prosecution can call evidence and the court or jury can draw such inferences "as appear proper" during criminal proceedings when a suspect under arrest fails to account for any object, substance, mark or mark on an object found on his person, on his clothing or otherwise in his possession, or in any place in which he was at the time of arrest.

CJPOA 1994, s.36 (1)–(2)

Silence in these circumstances is only relevant when the police have a reasonable belief that the object, substance or mark may be attributable to the suspect's participation in a crime specified by the police and the suspect is so informed, asked to comment and warned as to the possible effect of his silence in "ordinary language".

CJPOA 1994, s.36 (1)(b)–(d),(4)

A substance or mark on clothing is defined as including the "condition" of the clothing.

CJPOA 1994, s.36 (3)

There is no reasonableness requirement so that a simple failure to account for the object, substance or mark will allow the court to draw inferences. However, in deciding what inference is "proper" the court will have to consider the reason for the refusal.

The section also applies regardless of whether the matter not mentioned is a fact relied upon as part of the defence at trial.

Silence when asked to account for presence at a place

The prosecution can call evidence and the court or jury can draw such inferences "as appear proper" during criminal proceedings when a suspect arrested at a place at or about the time the offence is alleged to have been committed fails to account for his presence at that place.

CJPOA 1994, s.37 (1)–(2)

CJPOA 1994, s.37 (1)(b)–(c),(3)

Silence in these circumstances is only relevant when the police have a reasonable belief that the suspect's presence at that place and at that time may be attributable to his participation in the commission of the offence and the suspect is so informed, asked to account for his presence and warned as to the possible effect of his silence in "ordinary language".

CJPOA 1994, s.38 (1)

"Place" is defined as including any building, part of building, vehicle, vessel, aircraft, hovercraft or "any other place whatsoever".

There is no reasonableness requirement so that a simple failure to account for presence at the place will allow the court to draw inferences. However, in deciding what inference is "proper" the court will have to consider the reason for the refusal.

The section also applies regardless of whether the matter not mentioned is a fact relied upon as part of the defence at trial.

Silence at trial

CJPOA 1994, s.35 (2)

Where a defendant of any age chooses either not to give evidence or not to answer certain questions without good cause during his trial, it will be permissible for the court or jury to draw such inferences "as appear proper" from this silence.

CJPOA 1994, s.35 (5)

It will be presumed that the defendant has no "good cause" to remain silent unless he is entitled to refuse to answer questions by virtue of any Act of Parliament or on the grounds of privilege, or as a result of the court excusing him from answering in the exercise of its "general discretion".

CJPOA 1994, s.35 (3)

Inferences in these circumstances specifically include inferences as to guilt.

CJPOA 1994, s.35 (1)

This rule is subject to the court determining that the suspect's physical or mental condition is not such that it is undesirable for him to give evidence.

General matters

The CJPOA 1994 does not remove the right of silence. Rather, it permits the prosecution to comment upon and for the court or jury to draw inferences from a suspect's exercise of this right in the defined circumstances.

CJPOA 1994, s.38 (3)–(4); *R. v Abdullah* [1999] 3 *Archbold News* 3, CA

It is specifically legislated that a suspect/defendant's silence cannot by itself raise a sufficient inference for his case to be committed to the Crown Court, for him to be found to have a case to answer or for him to be convicted.

CJPOA 1994, ss 34(5), 36(6),

CJPOA 1994 provides that none of its provisions prejudices the admissibility in evidence of a suspect's silence which would have been permissible under the previous common law rules and earlier statutory exceptions.

37(5), 38(5)

CJPOA 1994 also specifies that none of its provisions prejudices any of a court's pre-existing powers to exclude evidence at its discretion, including exclusion by the prevention of the putting of questions.

CJPOA 1994, s.38 (6)

Restriction on drawing adverse inferences from silence and terms of the caution when the restriction applies

(a) The restriction on drawing adverse inferences from silence

The conditions under which adverse inferences may be drawn from a suspect's failure or refusal to say anything about their involvement in the offence when interviewed, after being charged or informed they may be prosecuted are subject to an overriding restriction on the drawing of adverse inferences from that silence which applies:

PACE 1984, Code C, Annex C; CJPOA 1994, ss 34, 36, 37 as amended by YJCEA 1999, s.58

(i) to any detainee at a police station who, before being interviewed or being charged or informed they may be prosecuted has:

- asked for legal advice;
- not been allowed an opportunity to consult a solicitor, including the duty solicitor; and
- not changed their mind about wanting legal advice.

This condition will apply when a suspect who has asked for legal advice is interviewed before speaking to a solicitor either because his right to consult a solicitor is being delayed or the interview is urgent.

However, it does not apply if the suspect has nominated or selected a solicitor from a list but that solicitor cannot be contacted, has previously indicated they do not wish to be contacted, or having been contacted, has declined to attend, and the suspect has been advised of the Duty Solicitor Scheme but has declined to ask for the duty solicitor.

(ii) to any person charged with, or informed they may be prosecuted for, an offence who:

- has had brought to their notice a written statement made by another person or the content of an interview with another person which relates to that offence;

- is interviewed about that offence; or
- makes a written statement about that offence.

(b) Terms of the caution when the restriction applies

When a requirement to caution arises at a time when the restriction on drawing adverse inferences from silence applies, the caution shall be:

> "You do not have to say anything, but anything you do say may be given in evidence."

Whenever the restriction either begins to apply or ceases to apply after a caution has already been given, the person shall be re-cautioned in the appropriate terms. The changed position on drawing inferences and that the previous caution no longer applies shall also be explained to the detainee in ordinary language.

The restriction on drawing inferences from silence does not apply to a person who has not been detained and who therefore cannot be prevented from seeking legal advice if they want to.

RIGHT OF SILENCE—THE CASE LAW

Since the CJPOA 1994 came into force there have been a number of decisions which have sought to interpret the law as it now stands in relation to silence at interview (s.34) and at trial (s.35). This section will only consider the case law in relation to s.34.

Legal and professional privilege

Privilege attaches to most communications between the suspect and legal adviser in the police station. The privilege belongs to the suspect and not the adviser and should rarely be waived. In certain circumstances there is no choice but to do so and it is a matter of some concern that defendants in criminal trials are now often placed in the position where they have seriously to consider waiving privilege in order properly to defend themselves.

What is clear is that the adviser must be extremely cautious in what is said in the police station and in particular on the interview tape. An opening statement that the suspect has been advised to remain silent for specific reasons is likely to waive the suspect's privilege for the whole of the pre-interview consultation.

If any such statement is to be made, reference to advice should be given in the present tense so that in effect the advice is being given at the time of the interview and in the presence of the police. This advice will not be subject to privilege but the previous consultation should remain privileged.

A simple statement that the suspect has been advised not to make any comment will not waive any privilege but neither is it likely to assist in persuading a jury or magistrate not to draw an inference adverse to the suspect in the absence of further elaboration.

R. v Condron (1997) 1 Cr. App.R. 185; *R. v Bowden* [1999] 4 All E.R. 43

In addition any statement made by the adviser may be used against the suspect at trial should his position change. The comments by the adviser will be admissible and deemed to have been made with the consent of the suspect.

R. v Fitzgerald [1998] 4 *Archbold News* 2, CA

1. When can an inference be drawn?

It will only be possible for an adverse inference to be drawn under s.34 when all of the conditions of that section are satisfied.

CJPOA 1994, s.34(1)

The conditions are:

R. v Argent (1997) 2 Cr. App.R. 27

(a) There must be proceedings for an offence;

(b) The failure to mention facts must occur before charge;

(c) The failure must occur during questioning under caution;

(d) The questioning must be directed to trying to discover whether or by whom the alleged offence was committed;

(e) The fact not mentioned is relied on by the defence at trial; and

(f) The suspect/defendant could reasonably have been expected to mention the fact.

Proceedings for an offence

It is therefore clear that s.34 applies only in criminal proceedings.

Failure to mention facts must occur before charge

If following charge, a fact emerges which will be relevant and relied upon at trial, no inference can be drawn from the failure to mention it. Thus no inference can be drawn if at the time of the interview the fact is not known to the suspect. For example, if the suspect does not provide an explanation for his semen being present on the garment of a complainant in a sexual

R. v N [1999] Crim. L.R. 61

offence allegation which he subsequently provides at trial, no inference can be drawn if the presence of the stain was unknown to all parties at the time of the interview as the forensic tests had not been completed.

R. v B (MT) [2000] Crim. L.R. 181

In some situations, it may not be obvious whether the suspect knew of the fact at the time of interview or charge. In order for an adverse inference to be drawn, the Crown would have to prove that he did know of the fact at the relevant time.

Failure must occur during questioning under caution

Should no caution have been administered before questioning then no inference can be drawn from failure to mention a fact during the course of that questioning. This would apply both where the suspect was at the time an uncautioned volunteer or being spoken to in another capacity and had not been cautioned and where he was a suspect and the police had omitted to caution him when they clearly should have done so.

CJPOA 1994, s.34(1)(b)

An inference may also be drawn if the suspect fails to mention a fact when he is charged which he later relies on at trial.

R. v Dervish [2002] 2 Cr. App.R. 6

Although inferences are usually invited from silence in interview rather than on charge, there are circumstances where an inference from silence on charge may be drawn. If the suspect has used a prepared statement in earlier interviews and information is then disclosed to him which was not known when the statement was prepared, if no supplementary statement is used and no comment made on charge, an adverse inference may subsequently be drawn about any failure to mention facts relating to the newly disclosed information.

Questioning must be directed to trying to discover whether or by whom the alleged offence was committed

PACE 1984, s.34(1), s.37

If the custody officer considers that there is sufficient evidence to charge a suspect, then he must either be charged or released and any further detention of that suspect for any purpose other than charge may be unlawful.

R. v Pointer [1997] Crim. L.R. 676; *R. v Gayle* [1999] Crim. L.R. 502

If the police have (or believe that they have) sufficient evidence to charge the suspect before any interview, then any questions they put to the suspect will arguably not be for the purpose of "trying to discover whether or by whom the offence had been committed". These questions would therefore fall outside of the ambit of s.34. If the questions do not fall within the section then no adverse inference can be drawn from a failure to answer them.

Arguably the only question which would may permissible at this point is "Do you have anything you wish to say?" Once again this is not a question seeking to discover whether the suspect had committed the offence or whether the offence had been committed and falls outside of the scope of s.34.

However, it will not be in every case that the police have a *prima facie* case that they need to charge without interview and each case will be considered on its facts.

R. v Ioannou [1999] Crim. L.R. 586; *R. v McGuinness* [1999] Crim. L.R. 318

This argument is particularly difficult in the light of the Codes of Practice and recent case law which confirms that "sufficient evidence to prosecute" (the expression in the old Codes) involves some consideration of any explanation or lack of it from the suspect. Under the Codes, the officer in charge of the investigation may be able to question the suspect until he is satisfied that all the questions he considers relevant to obtaining accurate and reliable information about the offence have been put to the suspect which includes allowing the suspect an opportunity to give an innocent explanation and asking questions to test if the explanation is accurate and reliable, *e.g.* to clear up ambiguities or clarify what the suspect said. Once he or the custody officer reasonably believes there is sufficient evidence to provide a realistic prospect of conviction for that offence, he should be charged. There remains a conflict between the provisions of the Codes and those of PACE 1984.

R. v Elliott [2002] EWCA Crim. 931

PACE 1984, Code C, para. 11.6

Fact not mentioned is relied on by the defence at trial

This condition appears to involve two considerations:

(i) Did the suspect fail to mention the fact

If the suspect mentions matters briefly either in a short oral or written statement or by answering some questions and not others but in giving evidence gives more details, then he may be deemed to have mentioned the fact previously and no inference should be drawn. Therefore, the submission of a written statement claiming self defence has been considered sufficient to mention the facts relied upon when further detail or "flesh on the bones" was given at trial.

R. v McGarry [1999] Crim. L.R. 316

The purpose of s.34 is to encourage early disclosure of the defence and does not extend to allowing the police to cross-examine a suspect upon his account. It is the disclosure of the facts relied upon which is important.

R. v Knight [2003] EWCA Crim 1977

However, in a case where the bare bones of an alibi were given to the solicitor at the police station but not revealed to the police, and a full and detailed account emerged in a later alibi notice (now defence statement), the Court of Appeal did not consider that the judge was obliged to say that the defendant had sufficiently

R. v Taylor [1999] Crim. L.R. 77

explained his whereabouts, and that his failure to do so to the police was through reluctance to admit other criminality.

R. v Turner [2003] EWCA Crim. 3108

The Court of Appeal has also stated that the "growing practice" of submitting a pre-prepared statement and declining to answer questions in interview may prove a dangerous course for an innocent person who subsequently discovers at trial that something significant has been omitted but that no such problem would arise following an interview where the suspect gives appropriate answers to the questions.

(ii) Did he rely upon the fact at trial.

A fact can be relied upon by the defendant or other defence witness giving evidence of it.

R. v Hart and McLean [1998] 6 *Archbold News* 1, CA

R. v Webber [2004] UKHL 1

A defendant may also be treated as having relied upon a fact if it is put in cross-examination to a witness. A positive suggestion put to a witness by or on behalf of a defendant might amount to a fact relied upon in his defence even if that suggestion was not adopted by the witness. The word "fact" covers any alleged fact which was in issue and was put forward as part of the defence case.

R. v Moshaid [1999] Crim. L.R. 1

A defendant who merely puts the Crown to proof would not be relying on any facts in his defence and the section would not bite.

Suspect could reasonably have been expected to mention the fact

R. v Argent (1997) 2 Cr. App.R. 27

There is no easy answer as to whether the suspect could reasonably have been expected to mention a fact at the time of the interview or on charge. It is a question of fact with a subjective test as the court must have regard to "the actual accused with such qualities, apprehensions, knowledge and advice as he is shown to have had at the time".

The Court of Appeal gave a non-exhaustive list of matters which ought to be considered as potentially relevant, namely:

- time of day;
- age;
- experience;
- mental capacity;
- state of health;
- sobriety;

- tiredness;
- knowledge;
- personality; and
- legal advice.

As stated above this list is not exhaustive and to it one may wish to add:

R. v Roble [1997] Crim. L.R. 449

- lack of disclosure of the police case;
- lack of admissible evidence against the suspect;
- complexity of the evidence;
- age of the allegation; and
- behaviour of the police.

(a) Legal advice

The effect of legal advice on whether an adverse inference can be drawn has developed in recent years, not always in a coherent or uniform way. However, it is clear that the suspect cannot rely solely on the fact that he was advised to say nothing in interview by his legal adviser in order to avoid an adverse inference being drawn.

R. v Condron and Condron (1997) 1 Cr. App.R. 185; *R. v Van Bokkum and others* (2000) 6 *Archbold News* 2, CA

What is important is not the quality of the advice but the effect of the advice on the suspect and whether in the circumstances it was reasonable for him to take the advice and not answer questions. This is most likely to mean that the reasons for the advice will have to be explained and privilege waived. The waiver will extend to the whole of the consultation and not merely the discreet piece of advice.

The fact that the suspect has been advised by his legal representative to remain silent must be given "appropriate weight" by the court. It is important whether the decision to remain silent was genuinely made as a result of legal advice rather than because there was no innocent explanation or none that would stand up to scrutiny.

Condron v UK [2000] Crim. L.R. 679; *R. v Betts and Hall* (2001) 2 Cr.App.R. 257

However, once it is shown that the advice (of whatever quality) has genuinely been relied on as the reason for the suspect's remaining silent, adverse comment may still be allowed. It is not necessarily unreasonable to expect the suspect to mention the facts in question notwithstanding the advice received. What is reasonable depends on all the circumstances.

R. v Howell [2003] Crim. L.R. 405

In the case of *Howell* the court did not consider the following to be good reasons not to mention facts later relied upon:

- absence of a written statement from the complainant (if adequate oral disclosure of the complaint has been given),
- the possibility that the complainant may not pursue his complaint, nor
- a belief by the solicitor that the suspect would be charged in any event whatever he says.

The court held that "there must always be soundly based objective reasons for silence, sufficiently cogent and telling to weigh in the balance against the clear public interest in an account being given by the suspect to the police. Solicitors bearing the important responsibility of giving advice to suspects at police stations must always have that in mind".

R. v Robinson [2003] EWCA Crim. 2219

It is for the jury to consider whether a defendant could reasonably have been expected to mention in interview the facts on which he later sought to rely.

R. v Hoare (2004) 148 S.J. 473, CA

The fact that advice has been given to remain silent remains an important consideration but not one that automatically excludes an adverse inference because the defendant has a choice to accept or reject the advice and is warned in the caution that a failure to mention any facts that he relied on at trial might harm his defence.

R. v Beckles [2004] EWCA Crim. 2766

Therefore, where a defendant relies on a solicitor's advice as an explanation for not mentioning in interview any fact relied on at trial, the crucial question for the jury is whether the facts relied on at trial were facts which the defendant might reasonably have been expected to mention at interview. If the jury considers that the defendant has genuinely relied on the advice, it is not necessarily the end of the matter. For instance, the jury might not consider it reasonable to rely on a solicitor's advice as a convenient way of disguising a true motivation for not mentioning facts. If the jury concludes that the suspect had been acting unreasonably in remaining silent despite having genuinely relied upon the advice of their legal representative, they might draw an adverse inference from his failure to mention the relevant facts.

R. v Imran and Hussein [1997] Crim. L.R. 754

(b) Disclosure

The police are not obliged to make full disclosure of their case at the police station. Indeed they are not obliged to make any disclosure. Police officers will rarely disclose all that they know of the case before interview as they may wish to get the suspect to commit himself to an account before presenting him with contradictory evidence. This is a tactic which has caused the Court of Appeal no concerns at all but if the police have misled the suspect or his adviser then any evidence subsequently obtained from the interview would be susceptible to an argument that it be excluded.

Should the adviser feel that inadequate disclosure has been made to the extent that he cannot properly advise the suspect, it is likely that the court may feel that it was reasonable for the suspect not to answer questions. However, one can never be certain at such an early stage in proceedings what decisions will be taken further down the line.

R. v Roble [1997] Crim. L.R. 449

(c) Physical or mental state of the suspect

The physical or mental state of the suspect may well be a factor in deciding whether he should answer questions in interview. The court must look at the particular circumstances facing the particular suspect including all of his particular concerns, illnesses and fears. If the adviser considers that the suspect is not fit enough to deal properly with the interview but the health care professional certifies that he is fit to be interviewed, it is likely that the latter's view will be preferred.

R. v Condron and Condron (1997) 1 Cr.App.R. 185; *R. v Kavanagh* unreported, February 7, 1997

In *Howell* the court briefly set out the kind of circumstances relating to the suspect's condition which may justify silence, namely ill-health, in particular mental disability, confusion, intoxication and shock.

R. v Howell [2003] Crim. L.R. 405

(d) Complexity and/or age of the case

If the allegation is complex or extremely old, it is arguable that it would be reasonable for the suspect to remain silent as no immediate response is appropriate. An inability genuinely to recollect events without reference to documents which are not to hand or communication with other persons who may be able to assist the suspect's recollection, may be considered to justify silence.

R. v Roble [1997] Crim. L.R. 449

R. v Howell [2003] Crim. L.R. 405

Obviously if the police provide detailed disclosure and allow the suspect sufficient time to consider matters (by disclosing matters well in advance of the interview), it will be less likely that silence would be considered reasonable.

2. What inferences can be drawn?

The court can draw such inferences "as appear proper" from the failure to mention the fact at interview or charge which is

CJPOA 1994, s.34(2)

R. v Beckles and Montague [1999] Crim. L.R. 148
R. v Betts and Hall (2001) 2 Cr.App.R. 257

subsequently relied upon at trial. The inference must be relevant to the determination of guilt but there is otherwise no restriction on what inference may be drawn.

The jury should be directed that they must only draw an inference where they are satisfied that the suspect had no innocent explanation or none that would stand up to scrutiny. The Court of Appeal has considered a number of different possible inferences which it would be open to the court to draw.

(a) Recent fabrication

R. v Condron (1997) 1 Cr. App.R. 185

The most likely inference to be drawn when a suspect gives an explanation at trial but has refused to answer questions at the police station is that the account given at trial has been fabricated since arrest and is therefore false. The defendant will have had the benefit of full disclosure of the case against him with access to all of the statements relied upon and will have had ample time to consider his position.

(b) Not thought through all of the facts

R. v Daniel [1998] Crim. L.R. 818

In a similar vein to recent fabrication, the court may consider that the suspect had not had the opportunity at the police station to think through his account fully whereas at trial he would have done so.

(c) Not willing to be subjected to questioning

R. v Daniel [1998] Crim. L.R. 818

R. v Randall [1998] 6 *Archbold News* 1, CA

The court may consider that the suspect had made up his account prior to interview but did not want to give his account to police at the time of interview because he knew he would be subjected to further probing questions about it which he did not want to or could not answer. For example, if the suspect had put forward an alibi and named witnesses, he may have feared that the police would contact them before he had an opportunity to do so. In many cases this may not in fact be an unreasonable fear!

R. v Howell [2003] Crim. L.R. 405

Indeed in *Howell* one of the circumstances most likely to justify the suspect's silence was his inability genuinely to recollect events without communication with other persons who may be able to assist his recollection. This may in certain circumstances include alibi or other potentially important witnesses.

PRACTICAL GUIDANCE

Each case has to be judged on its own individual circumstances and there is no easy answer as to whether a suspect should or should not be advised to answer questions.

The information available to the adviser at the stage that advice on this crucial aspect of the suspect's case is required is usually limited to what has been gleaned from the police and the suspect. The information is not always reliable from either source and, as a result, the safest course is often to advise the suspect to remain silent.

Equally, it is impossible for the adviser at the police station to know what view will be taken by others at a later stage in proceedings of the advice given at this early stage. The adviser can never know with any degree of certainty whether the suspect's reliance on his advice will ultimately be considered reasonable.

Even following the changes introduced by CJPOA 1994, the starting point for advice to a suspect should still be that he remain silent. It is accepted, however, that silence is not always in the best interests of the suspect.

The adviser will have to take a number of issues into consideration before advising a suspect whether or not to answer questions.

Disclosure of the police case

Determining whether the police have made sufficient disclosure to the adviser of the evidence existing against the suspect is extremely important when advising a suspect whether or not to answer questions.

A careful note should be made by the adviser of the information provided by the police and of whether the adviser considers that information to be sufficient disclosure of the case against the suspect. If insufficient information is made available to the adviser, the suspect should be advised not to answer police questions and the reasons for such advice should be noted. Although not certain, remaining silent may be considered reasonable in these circumstances.

If, at a subsequent trial, the prosecution invite an adverse inference to be drawn by the court from the suspect's silence in interview, reasons for that silence may need to be given. Assuming the waiver of legal privilege, it may be that the adviser will be called upon to explain the advice given to the suspect not to answer questions in an attempt to demonstrate that the suspect could not have reasonably been expected to have mentioned at that time facts upon which he subsequently sought to rely. The court will then be able to consider whether in the circumstances it was as a matter of fact reasonable of the defendant to rely on the advice of his legal adviser. It is not the correctness of the advice that matters, rather the reliance of the suspect upon it and whether it was reasonable for him to do so in the circumstances.

Strength and/or admissibility of the police evidence

Having elicited as much information as possible from the police, the adviser should consider whether the evidence against the suspect is likely to be admissible in court and, if so, the apparent strength of that evidence.

This is not an easy task, in view of the fact that the police may not have disclosed the entirety of the evidence against the suspect to the adviser or may have put a slant on it so as either to underplay or to overplay the strength of their case.

Where the evidence appears weak or potentially inadmissible, the best advice may be to remain silent. An adverse inference as a result of silence cannot be the only evidence against a suspect and the suspect should be careful not to create a case for the police against himself by answering questions and thereby providing evidence that the police would otherwise not have obtained.

Strength of the suspect's case

If a suspect can answer the police case in its entirety, it will normally be in his interests to answer police questions.

This should lead to the police taking no further action if the suspect's version of events is accepted. If the police do not accept what is said, the suspect has put his version on record at the earliest opportunity, which will be of assistance at trial.

If the suspect is clear in his instructions that he will be answering questions and that he will be relying in his defence on particular points he will wish to raise at trial, he should be reminded to mention these points in interview. Failure to do so may have the effect of weakening the credibility of his case at any subsequent trial and attracting an adverse inference even though other matters have been raised and questions answered.

Caution should always be exercised, as the adviser will not know if the police have any other evidence which will tend to contradict the suspect's version and which has not been disclosure prior to interview. This is especially the case if staged discloure is being used.

If the suspect has an alibi or wishes to rely on a specific defence, such as self-defence, there may be advantages to disclosing this to the police in interview, particularly as failure to do so could weaken the credibility of that defence at any subsequent trial. Again, caution is required, particularly as alibi witnesses may be reluctant to speak to police officers, who may be more interested in destroying than confirming the suspect's alibi. It may be more prudent to set out the bones of the defence in a written statement without the detail, although this is not guaranteed to prevent an adverse inference at a later stage especially if detailed questions are asked about the alibi by police in interview.

R. v Lewis [2003] EWCA Crim. 223

Advantages of admitting guilt

In cases where the prosecution evidence appears strong and the suspect has admitted guilt to the adviser, it may be in his interests to admit that guilt to the police in interview.

Some consideration will usually be given by the sentencing court to the suspect's early admission of guilt and co-operation with police.

An admission of guilt may also lead to the offence being dealt with by way of a caution, warning or reprimand rather than prosecution. It may be prudent for the adviser to raise the matter with the police before any interview takes place (refer to the **Charging and Alternatives** index heading).

Bad Character

In certain circumstances the fact that the suspect has previous convictions or has previously been in trouble with the police may become admissible at his trial. Where possible, the adviser should ensure that nothing said or done at the police station makes this eventuality more likely.

CJA 2003, ss 98 –106

Evidence of the "bad character" of the defendant is admissible at a trial if:

CJA 2003, s.101(1)(a)–(g)

- all parties agree;
- the evidence is adduced by the defendant himself or is given in answer to a question asked of him in cross-examination and intended to elicit it;
- it is important explanatory evidence;
- it is relevant to an important matter in issue between the defendant and the prosecution;
- it has substantial probative value in relation to an important matter in issue between the defendant and a co-defendant;
- it is evidence to correct a false impression given by the defendant; or
- the defendant has made an attack on another person's character.

CJA 2003, s.102

Evidence is important explanatory evidence if without it the court would find it impossible or difficult properly to understand other evidence in the case and its value for understanding the case as a whole is substantial.

CJA 2003, s.103

Matters in issue between the defendant and the prosecution include the question of whether the defendant has a propensity to commit offences of the kind with which he is charged (unless it makes it no more likely that he committed the offence charged), and whether the defendant has a propensity to be untruthful (except where it is not suggested his case is untruthful in any respect).

CJA 2003, s.105

The defendant will be considered to give a false impression, which can be corrected by evidence of his bad character, if he is responsible for making an express or implied assertion which is apt to give the court a false or misleading impression of him. The defendant is to be treated as being responsible for such an assertion if it is made in the proceedings or if he makes the assertion on being questioned under caution, before charge, about the offence with which he is charged or on being charged with the offence or officially informed he may be prosecuted for it.

CJA 2003, s.106(1)

The defendant makes an attack on another person's character if he adduces evidence attacking that person, asks any questions in cross-examination intended to elicit such evidence or evidence is given about the other person on being questioned under caution before charge about the offence with which he is charged or on being charged with the offence or officially informed he may be prosecuted for it.

CJA 2003, s.106(2)

Evidence attacking the other person's character means evidence to the effect that the other person has committed an offence (whether a different offence from the one with which the defendant is charged or the same one) or has behaved or is disposed to behave in a reprehensible way.

It therefore follows that the adviser will have to seek as much information from the suspect (and the police) about the suspect's previous convictions and dealings with police. If the suspect with a previous history is likely to be putting forward an account, he should be warned that in the above circumstances he may be opening the door for the Crown to inform the court about his previous convictions at any subsequent trial.

It may be more prudent in certain cases not to make accusations about other persons involved in the investigation including police officers. Equally, positive assertions about the character of the suspect should be avoided if it might be said to create a false impression.

These provisions apply to all trials starting after December 15, 2004 regardless of whether the police station appearance (and the assertion) took place before that date.

R. v Bradley [2005] EWCA Crim. 20

Ability of the suspect

Some suspects are incapable of remaining silent in the face of police questions, whereas others may find silence almost second nature.

Some suspects may be likely to do themselves an injustice by answering questions in interview for a variety of reasons: they may have specific fears about police officers, the welfare of their children or being locked up, or they may have a propensity to tell lies to get out of stressful situations. Poor memory, anxiety, physical discomfort, depression, confusion or an inability to distinguish between what the person has observed and what they have been subsequently told may all be factors which need to be taken into account when advising the suspect whether or not he ought to answer questions in interview.

The factors for consideration mentioned above do not comprise an exhaustive list, and it will be for the adviser to make a judgment on the individual circumstances of each case and the individual characteristics of each suspect as to whether silence is advisable.

Notwithstanding that an adverse inference may be drawn at a later stage, if the adviser believes that the suspect would not do himself justice in interview, the suspect should be advised not to answer questions. The adviser should make a careful note of the reasons for the advice.

Making an oral or written statement

Whilst it was previously accepted good practice for a suspect to be advised either not to answer any questions or to answer all questions, it may now be necessary to consider advising a third course.

Given that a "no comment" interview may subsequently attract adverse inferences, the adviser may consider advising the suspect to make a short statement at the start of the interview briefly outlining the facts on which he may seek to rely in any trial but thereafter decline to answer any further questions.

For this course of action to be effective, the suspect will have to be sufficiently articulate to make the statement and sufficiently intelligent to understand the reasons for it.

The adviser may also consider the possibility of preparing a written statement under caution with the suspect in the initial interview dealing with the points on which he is likely to rely at any trial and submitting this to the police in the interview, after which the suspect shall decline to comment further (refer to the **Statements under Caution** index heading). It has been accepted by the Court of Appeal that this course of action constitutes the mentioning a fact when questioned or at charge, although recently the Court has warned that such a course is not without risks if something important which is later relied upon is omitted from the statement.

R. v McGarry [1999] Crim. L.R. 316.

R. v Turner [2003] EWCA Crim. 3108

Submitting a written statement may prove to be a preferable course of action, as it may be less likely to cause any of the problems associated with an interview in which only some questions are answered and would not depend on the ability of the suspect to make the statement orally and refrain from commenting once he had finished.

This strategy means that the suspect will have committed himself to the account. It will not avoid an inference if an important fact relied upon is omitted. In addition, in certain cases it may provide evidence which the police do not otherwise have, for example, evidence of identification if the suspect claims to have acted in self-defence thus putting himself at the scene of the offence and as responsible for striking the complainant.

Statement taken from suspect but not served on police

The most likely or common adverse inference to be drawn is one of recent fabrication. In order to combat this particular inference, the adviser can take a statement from the suspect before the interview, which is signed by the suspect and the legal adviser, dated and timed.

This statement should then be kept by the legal adviser and not served on the police. It is helpful if it is taken on a separate piece of paper from the bulk of the notes forming the advice to the client.

R. v Condron (1997) 1 Cr. App.R. 185; *R. v Wilmot* (1989) 89 Cr.App.R. 341, CA

If the client seeks to put forward the same defence at court and the prosecution seek to have an adverse inference drawn, *i.e.* that it has recently been fabricated, it is open to the defence to produce the statement in rebuttal. This will not waive privilege.

If the account has changed the statement is never used but the defendant may have to live with the adverse inference. This tactic will not avoid inferences other than recent fabrication.

Statement on charge

Another tactic designed to combat the limitations on silence imposed by CJPOA 1994 is to follow a "no comment" interview with a statement when the suspect is cautioned after charge by the custody officer.

In the past, it was rare for a suspect to say anything at this stage but CJPOA 1994 specifies that the failure of a suspect to mention facts on being charged or officially informed that he might be prosecuted may lead to an adverse inference. Therefore, the suspect has an opportunity on charge to make a statement which may be either oral (and then recorded in writing by the custody officer) or written in advance, by or on behalf of the suspect, as a statement under caution.

CJPOA 1994, s.34(1)(b)

In any such statement, the suspect can present the issues on which he may seek to rely at trial: if the suspect does so at charge shortly after any interview, a court may have greater difficulty in seeking to draw adverse inferences from his silence in interview particularly an inference of recent fabrication.

If a statement after charge is made, the police may seek to re-interview the suspect. However, as he has now been charged, the police would only be able to ask questions about the offence if it is:

PACE 1984, Code C, para. 16.5

(a) necessary for the purpose of preventing or minimising harm or loss to some other person or to the public;

(b) necessary for clearing up an ambiguity in a previous answer or statement; or

(c) in the interests of justice that the person should have put to him, and have an opportunity to comment on, information concerning the offence which has come to light since he was charged or informed he would be prosecuted.

If the police did seek to ask further questions relying on one of the above conditions, the suspect should be advised again and may decide either to repeat the statement made on charge or, more likely, to decline to comment.

No adverse inference can be drawn from silence in such an interview and the appropriate caution is:

PACE 1984, Code C, para. 16.5

> You do not have to say anything, but anything you do say may be given in evidence.

Custody officers are not always happy to have to take a verbatim note of the suspect's statement, particularly given that they by and large still expect and, to an extent, encourage silence on charge.

If this course is to be followed, the adviser will have to be sure of the ability of the suspect to deal with the situation in this way and will have to remain in the police station whilst the suspect is being charged to ensure he is allowed to make the statement, that it is properly recorded in writing and that no further interview after charge takes place without satisfaction of one of the conditions in Code C, para. 16.5.

Accounting for marks, items or presence at a particular place

It is clear that, once arrested and cautioned, the suspect must not be interviewed about the alleged offence other than in a police station (or equivalent place of detention), except under the limited emergency provisions provided for under Code C to avoid harm to evidence or persons, alerting others yet to be arrested or hindering the recovery of property.

This means that the police are not entitled to ask questions relating to marks or items found on an arrested suspect or to his presence at a particular place until he is taken to the police station and interviewed in the normal manner under caution. Should such an "interview" have taken place (and have been recorded in an officer's notebook), it would arguably be inadmissible in any subsequent trial and the suspect should be advised not to endorse the accuracy of the notes of this "interview".

Obviously, the suspect will be questioned about the marks, items or his presence at the place in question in interview and will need to be advised whether or not to answer questions about such issues.

PACE 1984, Code C, para. 10.10

When a suspect interviewed at a police station or authorised place of detention after arrest fails or refuses to answer certain questions, or to answer satisfactorily, after due warning, a court or jury may draw such inferences as appear proper. However, such inferences may only be drawn when:

(a) the restriction on drawing adverse inferences from silence does not apply; and

(b) the suspect is arrested by a constable and fails or refuses to account for any objects, marks or substances, or marks on such objects found:

- on their person;
- in or on their clothing or footwear;

- otherwise in their possession; or
- in the place they were arrested;

(c) the arrested suspect was found by a constable at a place at or about the time the offence for which that officer has arrested them is alleged to have been committed, and the suspect fails or refuses to account for their presence there.

When the restriction on drawing adverse inferences from silence applies, the suspect may still be asked to account for any of the matters in (b) or (c) but the special warning described below will not apply and must not be given.

For an inference to be drawn when a suspect fails or refuses to answer a question about one of these matters or to answer it satisfactorily, the suspect must first be told in ordinary language:

PACE 1984, Code C, para. 10.11

(a) what offence is being investigated;

(b) what fact they are being asked to account for;

(c) this fact may be due to them taking part in the commission of the offence;

(d) a court may draw a proper inference if they fail or refuse to account for this fact;

(e) a record is being made of the interview and it may be given in evidence if they are brought to trial.

Unlike s.34, an adverse inference may be drawn even if there was a reasonable explanation for the silence at the time. However, one would expect that should such an explanation be available, the court would be reluctant to draw any inference adverse to the suspect.

SUSPECT'S DECISION

The suspect should always be told that whether he answers questions or provides samples, etc. is entirely his choice: the adviser is there only to advise and not to make the decisions for the suspect. Some suspects will look to the adviser and rely on him more heavily than others but in all cases the suspect must make the decisions.

Armed Services

INTRODUCTION

Members of the armed services are subject not only to the normal criminal law but also to a number of specific prohibitions, as laid down in AA 1955, AFA 1955 and NDA 1957.

The majority of PACE 1984 provisions apply to the investigation of offences and to individuals arrested under the provisions of these regulating Acts in the normal way, and it is important to note that, when a member of the armed services is being investigated or detained by the civil police, he is treated no differently than if he was a civilian: all of the PACE 1984 provisions and Codes of Practice will operate.

PACE 1984, s.113(1); PACE(AAF)O 1997

Therefore, this section will only deal with those special procedures that apply when members of the armed services are being investigated or detained by services police.

ARMED SERVICES OFFENCES—THE LAW

All armed services personnel are subject to English criminal law, wherever they are serving in the world. They are also subject to an additional set of offences, as laid down in their relevant regulating Act. Civilians accompanying the armed forces overseas may also be subject to the Service Disciplinary system.

AA 1955, ss 24–69, 70; AFA 1955, ss 24–69, 70; NDA 1957, ss 2–42, 48

ARMED SERVICES OFFENCES—PRACTICE AND PROCEDURE

Personnel subject to the Army Act 1955 or the Air Force Act 1955

For those of the rank of non-commissioned officer or below, trivial cases are invariably dealt with summarily by a commanding officer, with more serious offences being referred to a court-martial.

AA 1955, s.76; AFA 1955, s.76

Such offences alleged against those below the rank of lieutenant-colonel or wing-commander can be dealt with summarily by an "appropriate superior authority", but are otherwise dealt with by way of a district or general court-martial.

For officers of or above the rank of lieutenant-colonel or wing-commander, any offence, however trivial, may only be dealt with by way of a general court-martial.

Personnel subject to the Naval Discipline Act 1957

NDA 1957, s.52D

Any person below the rank of officer may be tried summarily, other than for an offence of murder: they are invariably so tried unless either the case involves a legally complex matter or it is considered that the commanding officer's powers of summary punishment (dismissal and 90 days' imprisonment) are insufficient. In such instances, the matter will be put before a court-martial.

NDA 1957, s.48

Any officer subject to an allegation must be tried by way of a court-martial other than in times of war, when a special disciplinary court may be established.

MINISTRY OF DEFENCE AND SERVICES POLICE—CODES OF PRACTICE

MDA 1987, s.2(1), (3)

Ministry of Defence police officers are "constables" as defined by PACE 1984 and, as such, are subject to the normal PACE 1984 Codes of Practice when investigating an offence alleged against a member of the armed services.

PACE 1984, s.113(2)–(3); PACE(AAF)O 1997; PACE(CP)(AF) O 2003

Services police are treated as "constables" for the majority of PACE 1984 purposes. However, the standard PACE Codes of Practice do not apply, rather they are subject to the special services police Code of Practice for the Questioning and Treatment of Persons; Code of Practice for the Identification of Persons Suspected of Offences; and Code of Practice for the Tape Recording of Service Police Interviews with Suspects, as issued by the Secretary of State pursuant to his obligations under PACE 1984.

KEY DIFFERENCES IN THE SERVICES POLICE CODES

There are a number of differences between the PACE Codes of Practice and the services police Codes.

The right to legal advice

When a suspect is interviewed by service police, he is entitled to legal advice in the usual way and this can only be denied in exceptional circumstances (for example for "security reasons") and after the interviewing officers have consulted with a senior officer and a service lawyer.

Such advice must be given by a qualified lawyer, who can either be a lawyer of the suspect's own choice, a duty solicitor or a lawyer chosen from a list of lawyers who have previously indicated their willingness to provide assistance. Advisers who are not qualified lawyers are not entitled to act, but solicitor's clerks will be allowed to do so unless it is held that their visit would hinder the investigation of the offence.

The right to an impartial observer

An accused member of the armed services has the right to ask for an impartial observer to be present at any interview. Such an observer may be in addition to a lawyer.

Disciplinary proceedings

All service police are required to observe all provisions of the services police special codes of practice. A failure to do so may render him liable to disciplinary action. In particular, the codes provide that any discriminatory behaviour on the grounds of a person's gender, colour, race, ethnic or national origin may render a service policeman, like any member of the armed services, liable to disciplinary action.

DETENTION RIGHTS

Services police can only detain a suspect for the period of any interview or interviews. Thereafter, the suspect may be held in custody by other service authorities under powers conferred by the relevant services Act and regulations.

This means that the suspect's rights whilst in detention are not governed by PACE 1984 but rather by the relevant services Act and the special services police Code of Practice for the Questioning and Treatment of Persons. These are similar to the rights enjoyed by those detained by civil police and, in particular, include the right not to be held incommunicado and any continued detention must be authorised by, and regularly reviewed by, the suspect's commanding officer.

REMUNERATION

Advice and representation of a member of the armed services who is being interviewed in connection with a "serious services offence" can be remunerated under the General Criminal Contract.

GCC 2004, Pt A, para. 2.2.1(c)

PRACTICAL GUIDANCE

(1) The prosecution process

The services police rarely have the same degree of control over the prosecution process as their civil counterparts: they are usually used by the suspect's commanding officer to gather evidence and then report back. The commanding officer will then normally consult with his legal staff before deciding whether or not to instigate formal disciplinary action and, if so, in what form.

(2) Provision of the Codes of Practice

The Services Police Codes of Practice should be provided to a suspect's adviser by the interviewing officer upon request.

(3) Security

When visiting military establishments, the adviser should always ensure that he carries proper proof of identity. Failure to do so may result in a refusal of admission.

(4) Further information

Those who either represent or intend to represent armed services personnel on a regular basis should obtain from HMSO the relevant publications: *The Manual of Military Law*, *The Manual of Air Force Law* and *The Manual of Naval Law*.

Arrestable and Serious Arrestable Offences

INTRODUCTION

All offences can be categorised as non-arrestable, arrestable or serious arrestable offences. A suspect can still be arrested for a non-arrestable offence if the general arrest provisions apply or if the enabling legislation for that offence provides a power of arrest (*e.g.* affray).

However, only an arrestable offence (as defined) can ever fall within the definition of a serious arrestable offence. When an offence is classified as an arrestable or serious arrestable offence, the legislation allows the police to use certain powers which they cannot use in relation to any other offences.

ARRESTABLE OFFENCES—THE LAW

Definition

Arrestable offences are those offences which are arrestable by virtue of PACE 1984 s.24 and are defined by that section as:

PACE 1984, s.24(1)

(a) offences for which the sentence is fixed by law;

(b) offences which are punishable by imprisonment of five years on a first conviction of someone of 21 years of age or over, including criminal damage and aggravated vehicle taking (where the aggravation relates to damage) even where the value is such that only summary trial is possible;

(c) offences listed in Sch.1A (as amended), namely an offence under the:

PACE 1984, s.24(1)(c), (2) and Sch. 1A (as variously amended)

(i) customs and excise Acts as defined by the Customs and Excise Management Act 1979 for which a person may be arrested;
(ii) Misuse of Drugs Act s.5(2) possession of controlled drug in respect of cannabis or cannabis resin;
(iii) Official Secrets Act 1920 which is not otherwise arrestable;
(iv) Official Secrets Act 1989 except those under s.8(1),(4) or (5);

(v) Prevention of Crime Act 1953 s 1(1), *i.e.* prohibition of carrying offensive weapons without lawful authority or excuse;

(vi) section 139(1) of the Criminal Justice Act 1988, *i.e.* having article with blade or point in public place;

(vii) section 139A(1) or (2) of the Criminal Justice Act 1988, *i.e.* having article with blade or point (or offensive weapon) on school premises;

(viii) Theft Act 1968, s.12(1) or 25(1), *i.e.* taking a motor vehicle without authority or going equipped for stealing;

(ix) Theft Act 1978, s.3, *i.e.* making off without payment;

(x) Sexual Offences Act 1956, s.22 or 23, *i.e.* causing prostitution of women or procuration of a girl under 21 years of age;

(xi) Sexual Offences Act 1985, s.1, *i.e.* kerb-crawling;

(xii) Obscene Publications Act 1959, s.2, *i.e.* publication of obscene matter;

(xiii) Protection of Children Act 1978, s.1, *i.e.* indecent photographs and pseudo–photographs of children;

(xiv) Criminal Justice and Police Act 2001, s.46, *i.e.* placing advertisements in relation to prostitution;

(xv) Wildlife and Countryside Act 1981 s.9(1) and (2) or 6, *i.e.* taking, possessing, selling *etc.* of wild birds in respect of a bird included in Sch. 1 of the Act or any part of or anything derived from such a bird;

(xvi) Wildlife and Countryside Act 1981, s.1(5), *i.e.* disturbance of wild birds, s.9, 13(1)(a) or (2) *i.e.* taking, possessing, selling *etc.* of wild animals or plants or s.14, *i.e.* introduction of new species;

(xvii) Civil Aviation Act 1982, s.39(1), *i.e.* trespass on aerodrome;

(xviii) Aviation Security Act 1982, s.21C(1) or s.21D(1), *i.e.* unauthorised presence in a restricted zone or on an aircraft;

(xix) Road Traffic Act 1988, s.103(1)(b), *i.e.* driving while disqualified;

(xx) Road Traffic Act 1988, s.170, *i.e.* failure to stop and report an accident causing personal injury;
(xxi) Road Traffic Act, s.174, *i.e.* false statements and withholding material information;
(xxii) Criminal Justice and Public Order Act 1994, s.166, *i.e.* sale of tickets by unauthorised persons;
(xxiii) Criminal Justice and Public Order Act 1994, s.167, *i.e.* touting for car hire services;
(xxiv) Police Act 1996, s.89(1), *i.e.* assaulting a police officer in the execution of his duty or a person assisting such an officer;
(xxv) Protection from Harassment Act 1997, s.2, *i.e.* harassment;
(xxvi) Criminal Justice and Public Order Act 1994, s.60AA(7), *i.e.* failing to comply with requirement to remove disguise;
(xxvii) Crime and Disorder Act 1998, s.32(1)(a) *i.e.* racially or religiously aggravated harassment;
(xxviii) Football Spectators Act 1989, s.14J or 21C, *i.e.* failure to comply with requirements imposed by or under a banning order or a notice under s.21B);
(xxix) any offence under the Football (Offences) Act 1991;
(xxx) Criminal Justice and Police Act 2001, s.12(4), *i.e.* failure to comply with requirements imposed by constable in relation to consumption of alcohol in public place;
(xxxi) Criminal Justice Act 1925, s.36, *i.e.* untrue statement for procuring a passport;
(xxxii) Wireless Telegraphy Act 1949, s.14(1)—offences triable either way;
(xxxiii) Firearms Act 1968, s.19—carrying a firearm or imitation firearm in a public place in respect of an air weapon or imitation firearm;
(xxxiv) Civil Aviation Act 1982, s.60 contravening an air navigation order where the offence relates to a provision which prohibits specified behaviour by a person in an aircraft towards or in relation to a member of the crew or a provision which prohibits a passenger being drunk in an aircraft;
(xxxv) Public Order Act 1986, s.19, *i.e.* publishing, etc. material likely to stir up racial on religious hatred;

(xxxvi) Criminal Justice and Police Act 2001, s.46—placing of advertisements in relation to prostitution;

(xxxviii) Sexual Offences Act 2003, ss 66, 67, 69, 70 and 71—exposure, voyeurism, intercourse with an animal, sexual penetration of a corpse and sexual activity in a public lavatory;

(d) conspiracy, attempt (except for a summary only offence) or incitement, aiding, abetting, counselling or procuring any of the above offences.

DVCVA 2004, s.10(1)
LA 2003, s.143(1)
PACE 1984, s.24(4)

Common assault will become an arrestable offence when the Domestic Violence, Crime and Victims Act 2004 comes into force. Failure to leave licensed premises will be an arrestable offence when the Licensing Act 2003 comes into force.

Statutes enacted after PACE 1984 came into force which create new offences may include a power of arrest although they would not be "arrestable offences" unless they fell within s.24 as defined above.

Consequences

(a) When can an arrest be made

Any person (including but not limited to a police officer) may arrest without a warrant:

PACE 1984, s.24(3)

(a) anyone who is in the act of committing an arrestable offence;

(b) anyone whom he has reasonable grounds for suspecting to be committing such an offence;

PACE 1984, s.24(5)

(c) anyone who is guilty of having committed an arrestable offence where such an offence has been committed; or

(d) anyone whom he has reasonable grounds for suspecting of being guilty of having committed an arrestable offence where such an offence has been committed.

A police officer may arrest without warrant not only in the above circumstances but also if:

PACE 1984, s.24(6)

(a) he has reasonable grounds for suspecting that an arrestable offence has been committed and reasonable grounds for suspecting the person arrested to be guilty of the offence;

(b) someone is about to commit an arrestable offence; or

(c) he has reasonable grounds for suspecting that the person arrested is about to commit such an offence.

PACE 1984, s.24(7)

(b) Time in Custody

Time in custody can only be extended beyond 24 hours if the offence under investigation is an arrestable offence by authorization of a superintendent. The maximum period of detention that can be authorised for an arrestable offence is 36 hours. Beyond that a warrant of further detention is required and the offence must be a serious arrestable offence (see **Detention Periods and Reviews** Index heading).

PACE 1984, s.42 as amended by CJA 2003, s.7

(c) Search of premises

If an officer of the rank of inspector or above has so authorised, the police may enter and search any premises occupied or controlled by a person who is under arrest for an arrestable offence, if there are reasonable grounds for suspecting that there is evidence on the premises, other than items subject to legal privilege, that relates to that offence, or to some other arrestable offence which is connected with or similar to that offence.

PACE 1984, s.18

(d) Delay in access to writing material and telephone call

Allowing the suspect to be given writing materials on request and to telephone one person for a reasonable time may be denied or delayed if the suspect is detained in connection with an arrestable and an officer of inspector rank or above considers sending a letter or making a telephone call may lead to interference with, or harm to, evidence connected with an arrestable offence, or interference with, or physical harm to, other people, or lead to alerting other people suspected of having committed an arrestable offence but not yet arrested for it, or hinder the recovery of property obtained in consequence of the commission of such an offence.

PACE 1984, Code C, para. 5.6
PACE 1984, Code C, Annex B, para. 1

These privileges may also be delayed if the offence is a drug trafficking offence and the officer has reasonable grounds for believing the suspect has benefited from drug trafficking, and the recovery of the value of his proceeds from drug trafficking will be hindered by the exercise of either right, or if the offence

PACE 1984, Code C, Annex B, para. 1

is one to which the Criminal Justice Act 1988, Pt VI (confiscation orders) applies and the officer has reasonable grounds for believing the suspect has benefited from the offence, and the exercise of either right will hinder the recovery of the value of the property obtained by the suspect from or in connection with the offence, or the value of the pecuniary advantage derived by the suspect from or in connection with it.

PACE 1984, s.56; PACE 1984, Code C, para. 5.1

This is separate from the suspect's right to have someone informed of their whereabouts as soon as practicable which cannot be delayed for an arrestable offence.

SERIOUS ARRESTABLE OFFENCES—THE LAW

Definition

Certain arrestable offences are always serious:

PACE 1984, s.116(2), Sch. 5, Pt I as amended by CJPA 2001, s.72 and SOA 2003 s.140, Sch. 7

(a) offences specified in PACE 1984, Sch. 5, Pt I:

- (i) treason;
- (ii) murder;
- (iii) manslaughter;
- (iv) kidnapping;
- (v) An offence under s.170 of the Customs and Excise Management Act 1979 prohibiting the importation of indecent or obscene articles.

(b) an offence under an enactment specified in PACE 1984, Sch. 5, Pt II:

PACE 1984, s.116(2), Sch. 5 Pt II as variously amended latterly by SOA 2003 s.140, Sch. 7

- (i) Explosive Substances Act 1883, s.2, *i.e.* causing an explosion likely to endanger life or property;
- (ii) Firearms Act 1968, ss 16, 17(1) and 18, *i.e.* possession of firearms with intent to injure, use of firearms and imitation firearms to resist arrest and carrying firearms with criminal intent;
- (iii) Taking of Hostages Act 1982, s.1, *i.e.* hostage taking;
- (iv) Aviation Security Act 1982, s.1, *i.e.* hijacking;
- (v) Criminal Justice Act 1988, s.134, *i.e.* torture;
- (vi) Road Traffic Act 1988, s.1, *i.e.* causing death by dangerous driving;
- (vii) Road Traffic Act 1988 s.3A, *i.e.* causing death by careless driving when under the influence of drink;
- (viii) Aviation and Maritime Security Act 1990, ss 1, 9 and 10, *i.e.* endangering safety at aerodromes,

hijacking of ships and seizing or exercising control of fixed platforms;

(ix) Channel Tunnel (Security) Order 1994 (SI 1994/570) arts 4 and 5, *i.e.* hijacking of Channel Tunnel trains and seizing or exercising control of the tunnel system;

(x) Protection of Children Act 1978, s.1, *i.e.* indecent photographs and pseudo-photographs of children;

(xi) Obscene Publications Act 1959, s.2, *i.e.* publication of obscene matter;

(xii) Sexual Offences Act 2003 s.1 and 5, *i.e.* rape and rape of a child under 13 years of age;

(xiii) Sexual Offences Act 2003 s.2 and 6, *i.e.* assault by penetration and assault by penetration of a child under 13 years of age;

(xiv) Sexual Offences Act 2003 s.4 and 8, *i.e.* causing a person to engage in sexual activity without consent where the activity involved penetration and the same offence with a child under 13 years of age;

(xv) Sexual Offences Act 2003 s.30, *i.e.* sexual activity with a person with a mental disorder impeding choice where the touching involved penetration;

(xvi) Sexual Offences Act 2003 s.31, *i.e.* causing or inciting a person with a mental disorder impeding choice to engage in sexual activity involving penetration.

Causing or allowing the death of a child or vulnerable adult will be a serious arrestable offence when the Domestic Violence, Crime and Victims Act 2004 comes into force.

DVCVA 2004, s.58(1), Sch. 10, para. 24

(c) offences specified in para. 1 of the Proceeds of Crime Act 2002, *i.e.* drug trafficking offences, namely:

(i) unlawful production or supply of controlled drugs;

(ii) possession of controlled drug with intent to supply;

(iii) permitting certain activities relating to controlled drugs under Misuse of Drugs Act 1971 s.8;

(iv) assisting in or inducing the commission outside the UK of an offence punishable under a corresponding law;

(v) Fraudulent evasion, importation and exportation of drugs;
(vi) manufacture or supply of a substance for the time being specified in Sch. 2 to Criminal Justice (International Co-operation) Act 1990 as a substance useful for the manufacture of controlled drugs;
(vii) using a ship for illicit traffic in controlled drugs.

(d) any offence under ss 327–329 of the Proceeds of Crime Act 2002, namely:

(i) concealing, converting, disguising or transferring criminal property;
(ii) entering into or becoming concerned in an arrangement knowing or suspecting it to facilitate the acquisition, retention, use or control of criminal property by or on behalf of another person;
(iii) acquiring, using or possessing criminal property.

PACE 1984, s.116(3) and (6)

Any other arrestable offence can be serious if the actual, intended or likely consequences of its commission are:

(a) serious harm to the security of the state or to public order;

(b) serious interference with the administration of justice or the investigation of offences or of a particular offence;

(c) the death of any person;

(d) serious injury to any person;

(e) substantial financial gain to any person; or

(f) serious financial loss to any person.

PACE 1984, s.116(7) and (8)

Loss is "serious" if it is serious for the person suffering that loss, having regard to all the circumstances and "injury" includes any disease and any impairment of a person's physical and mental condition.

PACE 1984, s.116(4)

An arrestable offence which entails the making of a threat is serious if carrying out the threat would be likely to lead to any of the above consequences.

TA 2000 s.41, Sch. 8

A suspect detained on suspicion of being a terrorist is no longer governed by PACE 1984—see **Terrorist Suspects** index heading.

Consequences

(a) Extension of time in custody beyond 36 hours

It is only possible to apply to the Magistrates' Court for a Warrant of Further Detention to extend the time in custody beyond 36 hours where the offence under investigation is a serious arrestable offence (refer to the **Detention Periods and Reviews** and **Warrants of Further Detention** index headings).

PACE 1984, s.43

(b) Access to a telephone

The right of the suspect to make a telephone call to a friend or member of his family can only be denied or delayed if the suspect is detained in connection with a serious arrestable offence and an officer of inspector rank or above considers the telephone call may lead to interference with, or harm to, evidence connected with a serious arrestable offence, or interference with, or physical harm to, other people, or lead to alerting other people suspected of having committed a serious arrestable offence but not yet arrested for it, or hinder the recovery of property obtained in consequence of the commission of such an offence.

PACE 1984, s.56

PACE 1984, Code C, Annex B, para. 1

This right may also be denied or delayed if the serious arrestable offence is a drug trafficking offence and the officer has reasonable grounds for believing the suspect has benefited from drug trafficking, and the recovery of the value of his proceeds from drug trafficking will be hindered by the exercise of either right, or if the offence is one to which the Criminal Justice Act 1988, Pt VI (confiscation orders) applies and the officer has reasonable grounds for believing the suspect has benefited from the offence, and the exercise of either right will hinder the recovery of the value of the property obtained by the suspect from or in connection with the offence, or the value of the pecuniary advantage derived by the suspect from or in connection with it.

PACE 1984, Code C, Annex B, para. 2

(c) Access to legal advice

As with the suspect's right to have someone informed of their whereabouts as soon as practicable (above), their right of access to legal advice can only be denied or delayed when a serious arrestable offence is under investigation and an officer of inspector rank or above has reasonable grounds to believe that the solicitor requested will, inadvertently or otherwise, pass on a message from the suspect or act in some other way which will lead to any of the consequences outlined above (refer to the **Suspect's Rights** index heading).

PACE 1984, s.58

PACE 1984, Code C, Annex B, paras 1–3

PACE 1984, Code C, para. 5.6; PACE 1984, Code C, Annex B, paras 1 and 2

(d) Delay in access to writing material and telephone call

Allowing the suspect to be given writing materials on request and to telephone one person for a reasonable time may be denied or delayed when a serious arrestable offence is under investigation and an officer of inspector rank or above considers the exercise of the right may lead to any of the consequences outlined above.

PACE 1984, Code C, para. 5.6

In this case reference to a serious arrestable offence may also apply to an arrestable offence.

(e) Search warrants

PACE 1984, s.8

A search warrant under s.8 of PACE 1984 can only be issued by magistrates if the offence under investigation is a serious arrestable offence.

PACE 1984, s.18

The right of police to enter and search any premises occupied or controlled by a person who is under arrest for an arrestable offence in the appropriate circumstances, also applies if the offence is a serious arrestable offence.

NON-ARRESTABLE OFFENCES—THE LAW

PACE 1984, s.25(1)

If a police officer has reasonable grounds for suspecting that an offence which is non-arrestable has been committed or attempted, or is being committed or attempted, he may arrest the suspect only if the general arrest conditions (see below) are satisfied, as a result of which it appears to the officer that the service of a summons is impractical or inappropriate.

The general arrest provisions are:

PACE 1984, s.25(3)

(a) the name of the suspect is unknown or cannot be readily ascertained;

(b) the officer has reasonable grounds for believing that the name given by the suspect is false;

(c) the suspect has failed to give a satisfactory address or the officer has reasonable grounds for believing that the address is not satisfactory for service of a summons;

(d) the officer has reasonable grounds for believing that arrest is necessary to prevent the suspect from:

    (i) causing physical injury to himself or any other person;
    (ii) suffering physical injury;
    (iii) causing loss or damage to property;

(iv) committing an offence against public decency; or
(v) causing an unlawful obstruction of the highway; or

(e) the officer has reasonable grounds for believing that arrest is necessary to protect a child or other vulnerable person from the suspect.

None of the consequences which flow from an offence being categorised as an arrestable or serious arrestable offence apply to non-arrestable offence even if the enabling legislation has provided a power of arrest (*e.g.* affray). Therefore a suspect arrested for a non-arrestable offence cannot be kept in custody for more than 24 hours, cannot have their right to inform someone of their arrest, access to legal advice or writing materials or a personal telephone call denied or delayed and cannot have their premises searched under s.18 of PACE 1984.

The adviser should also be aware that the police have other powers of arrest, *e.g.* for breach of the peace, for breach of bail, to take fingerprints or samples.

PRACTICAL GUIDANCE

(1) Classification of offence

When first receiving a call from the police station, the adviser should always identify whether the offence for which the suspect has been arrested is arrestable or not. If the offence is arrestable, the adviser will need to consider whether there is a likelihood that the offence could come within the definition of a serious arrestable offence.

(2) Enhanced powers

The adviser should have in mind the enhanced powers of the police which are triggered by the classification of an offence as an arrestable or serious arrestable offence.

(3) Representations

If the police are attempting to use the extra powers conferred on them by PACE 1984, the adviser should consider making representations to the relevant authorising officer as to whether the offence under investigation is indeed an arrestable or serious arrestable offence.

Often, no such representations can be made as the offence clearly comes within the definition. However, it may be necessary to request more details from the police as to the individual circumstances of the case, in order to come to any determination as to whether it could fall within the definition.

R. v Smith [1987] Crim. L.R. 579

This would be particularly true where the police were relying on the loss or injury caused or financial gain made in the case to justify the classification of the offence as a serious arrestable offence. For instance, an offence of robbery or theft may become a serious arrestable offence if the amount of the loss is considered to be substantial to the person who has suffered the loss. What is considered substantial will not be the same in each case. There is scope to argue that in the individual case the loss should not be considered as substantial to the loser especially if it is a financial institution or large organisation.

(4) Records

Any such representations ought to be recorded on the custody record and the adviser should make his own detailed note of both the representations and the response of the police officer.

ANNEX—LIST OF ARRESTABLE OFFENCES

This list contains some of the more common arrestable offences and is not meant to be exhaustive:

abduction;
abstracting electricity;
acquiring, using or possessing criminal property;
aggravated vehicle taking (if the aggravation relates to damage);
arson;
assault:
- — ABH (OAPA 1861, s.47);
- — unlawful wounding (OAPA 1861, s.20);
- — GBH (OAPA 1861, s.18);

assaulting a police officer in the execution of his duty;
blackmail;
bladed article—possession in public place and on school premises
bomb hoaxing;
buggery:
burglary;
causing death by careless driving when under the influence of drink;

causing death by dangerous driving;
concealing, converting, disguising or transferring criminal property;
conspiracy;
corruption;
counterfeiting currency;
criminal damage (regardless of value);
cruelty to children;
deception;
driving while disqualified drugs:

- — possession of Class A or B drugs;
- — possession of cannabis or cannabis resin;
- — production;
- — possession with intent to supply;
- — supply;
- — importation;

explosions:

- — attempting to cause explosions;
- — causing an explosion likely to endanger life or property
- — conspiracy to cause explosions;

explosives—using or making;
failure to comply with requirements imposed by constable in relation to consumption of alcohol in public place;
failure to comply with requirements imposed by or under a banning order;
failure to comply with requirement to remove disguise;
failure to stop and report an accident causing personal injury;
false accounting;
firearms—possession without a certificate upwards;
forgery
fraudulent trading;
going equipped for theft;
handling stolen goods;
harassment (including aggravated and racially aggravated harassment);
immigration—assisting illegal entry;
importation of drugs;
incest;
indecency between males over 21 and those under 18;
indecent assault on a man, woman or girl under 13;

indecent photographs of children (except possession);
intercourse (and attempt) with a girl under 13;
intimidation of witnesses, jurors and others;
kerb-crawling;
kidnapping and false imprisonment;
making off without payment;
manslaughter;
murder;
offensive weapons—possession;
official secrets offences;
perjury;
perverting (or attempt to pervert) the course of justice;
prostitution:

- — causing prostitution of women;
- — procuration of a girl under 21;
- — living off immoral earnings;

public nuisance;
publication of obscene matter (OPA 1959, s.2);
publication of racially inflammatory material;
rape;
riot;
robbery;
sexual offences (other):

- — causing or inciting a person with a mental disorder impeding choice to engage in sexual activity involving penetration;
- — sexual activity with a person with a mental disorder impeding choice where the touching involved penetration
- — causing a person to engage in sexual activity without consent where the activity involved penetration and the same offence with a child under 13 years of age living off immoral earnings;
- — assault by penetration and assault by penetration of a child under 13 years of age causing prostitution of women;

taking a vehicle without consent;
theft;
threats to damage property;
threats to kill;
ticket touting;
touting for car hire services;
untrue statement for procuring a passport;

VAT—conduct involving an offence under VATA 1983, s.39(1),(2); and
violent disorder.

NB: attempting, aiding, abetting, counselling or procuring an arrestable offence is also an arrestable offence (unless an attempt relates to a summary only offence). Common assault will become an arrestable offence when the Domestic Violence, Crime and Victims Act 2004 comes into force.

Bail

INTRODUCTION

The Criminal Justice and Public Order Act 1994 and Crime and Disorder Act 1998 introduced major changes to the law governing a defendant's right to bail in advance of any court appearance, as well as giving the police the power to arrest without warrant a suspect who fails to answer to police bail.

The Criminal Justice Act 2003 has further reformed the area with the introduction of "street bail", and a new procedure for seeking advice from the Director of Public Prosecutions (through a suitably authorised Crown Prosecutor) as to whether to charge a suspect once bail has been granted.

The Extradition Act 2003 applies the provisions of the Bail Act 1976 to those involved in **extradition** proceedings.

There are a number of special bail provisions which apply to **juvenile suspects, mentally disordered suspects** and **terrorist suspects**: the reader should refer to these respective index headings for further details of these.

BAIL BEFORE CHARGE—THE LAW

Introduction

The police are at liberty to release a suspect before charge at any time and for any reason. However, there are certain statutory obligations which must be read in conjunction with this general power.

Street bail (as introduced by CJA 2003, s.4)

CJA 2003 amends PACE 1984 by permitting a suspect who has been arrested in a place other than a police station to be released on bail at any time before he arrives at a police station. In such circumstances no bail conditions are imposed save for the obligation that the suspect attend a police station at some later date.

PACE 1984, s.30A (1)–(5)

The powers contained within the Bail Act 1976 are specifically excluded from street bail

PACE, s.30C(3)

The constable must give the person a notice in writing before he is released; detailing the offence for which he was arrested and the grounds for the arrest. The notice must also inform him that he is to subsequently attend a police station. The notice may specify the police station he is required to attend and the time of

PACE 1984, s.30B (1)–(7)

the attendance; if it does not, then the person must be given a subsequent notice with this information. If the suspect is later required to attend a different police station or at a different time to that in the original notice, then he must be given notice in writing of any such change(s).

PACE 1984, s.30C (1)–(2)

Should it be determined that a person who has been required to attend a police station is not now required to do so, then he is to be given a notice in writing confirming this.

PACE 1984, s.30C (4)

A person released on street bail may still be re-arrested without a warrant if new evidence justifying a further arrest has come to light since his release.

Decision on arrival at police station

PACE 1984, s.37 (1)–(2); CJPOA 1994, s.29(4)(a); CJA 2003, s.87(6)

Once a suspect has been arrested and brought to a police station, the custody officer must determine whether there is sufficient evidence with which to charge him with the offence for which he has been arrested. However, once s.87 of Criminal Justice Act 2003 comes into force, the custody officer will have to request that an officer of the rank of superintendent or above who has not been directly involved in the investigation make this decision.

PACE 1984, s.37(9)

If there is insufficient evidence, the suspect must be released unless the custody officer determines that his detention is necessary to secure or preserve evidence or to obtain evidence by questioning, or that the suspect is not in a fit state to be released.

Release without bail or on bail

PACE 1984, s.37(2)

If the suspect is released upon arrival at a police station, this may either be "without bail" or "on bail". A release without bail is an unrestricted or unconditional release, whereas a release on bail means a release subject to condition(s).

PACE 1984, s.37(8)

If the suspect is released pending a decision as to whether or not he should be prosecuted, the custody officer is obliged to inform him of this situation.

The continuing obligation to release

PACE 1984, s.37(7)

If at any time during a suspect's period in detention the custody officer determines that there is sufficient evidence with which to charge him with the offence for which he was arrested then the suspect must either be so charged or released without charge. Such a release will be either without bail or on bail.

Bail pending the DPP's advice

PACE 1984, s.37 (7);

The suspect may be released without charge and on bail for the purpose of sending to the DPP (or an appropriately authorised

Crown Prosecutor as his agent) such information as to allow him to decide whether there is sufficient evidence for the suspect to be charged with an offence; if so, which offence he should be charged with; and whether or not the suspect should be cautioned. If it is decided that the suspect should not be charged or cautioned, then he is to be informed in writing of this decision by the custody officer; otherwise the suspect should be charged or cautioned accordingly. If it is not possible to caution the suspect in such circumstances then he is to be charged instead.

CJA 2003, Sch. 2 para. 2; PACE 1984, s.37B; CJA 2003, Sch. 2, para. 3

If the suspect is released on bail pending a decision of the DPP, the custody officer may appoint a different time or an additional time at which the suspect is to attend at the police station to answer to his bail. The exercise of this power must be communicated to the suspect in writing. In addition, if the suspect returns to a police station to answer bail after being granted bail under the DPP provisions, or is otherwise in police detention, then he may be kept in police detention to enable him to be dealt with in accordance with the process of cautioning/charging as outlined in the DPP provisions, or for him to be dealt with for any breaches of bail under the provisions. If the suspect is deemed to be not "in a fit state" to be dealt with, then he may be kept in police detention until such time as he is so fit.

PACE 1984, s.37D; CJA 2003, Sch. 2, para. 3

Bail on expiry of the detention period

If a suspect's detention period expires without having been properly extended by either the police or the magistrates' court and he has not been charged with an offence, then he must be released either without bail or on bail.

PACE 1984, ss 42 (10), 43(15), (18), 44(7), 47(7); CJPOA 1994, s.29(4) (e); *R. v Taylor (Leroy)* [1991] Crim. L.R. 541

Bail conditions

Whenever a suspect is released "on bail" before charge it is for the custody officer to appoint the venue of the police station and the date and time for the suspect's return.

PACE 1984, s.47(3)

The obligation to return to the appointed venue at the appointed time is a condition that will always attach to such bail. However, the custody officer may give subsequent written notice to the suspect cancelling the obligation

PACE 1984, s.47(4)

Powers enabling the police to impose post-release bail conditions, as *per* BA 1976, in general only apply when a defendant is being bailed after charge. Hence, the police cannot normally seek any of the normal post-release bail conditions (such as a condition of residence or curfew restriction) when a suspect is being bailed before charge. They can seek pre-release conditions by demanding a surety and/or a security. The exception to

PACE 1984, ss 37(7) (a)–(d), 37B, 47(1), 47(1A)–(1F), 47(8); CJPOA 1994, ss 27(1), 28; MCA 1980, s.43; BA 1976, s.3(1)–(5)

this is situations when a suspect is released for the purpose of enabling the DPP to make a decision as to whether there is sufficient evidence to charge him. In these cases, post-release bail conditions may be set.

CDA 1998, s.54(1), HOC 34/1998

Although securities are normally sought when it is feared that the suspect may abscond from the jurisdiction, they can be required even in cases where it appears that the accused is likely to remain in Great Britain. So, for example a security may be required as an alternative to a surety where the accused cannot provide a suitable surety.

Liability to rearrest and the detention clock

PACE 1984, s.47(2)

A suspect released on police bail prior to charge can be rearrested without warrant in respect of the same offence if new evidence justifying a further arrest comes to light subsequent to his initial release.

PACE 1984, s.47(7); CJPOA 1994, s.29(4)(e)
PACE 1984, s.47(6); CJPOA 1994, s.29(4)(d)
R. v Taylor (Leroy) [1991] Crim. L.R. 541

If a suspect is rearrested under this provision, the detention clock starts again. This contrasts with the situation when a suspect returns to the police station in answer to bail or is arrested for non-attendance. In these circumstances, the detention clock does not restart and the time he spent in detention prior to the earlier release still counts for the purposes of calculating his period in detention upon return to the police station.

BAIL BEFORE CHARGE—PRACTICE AND PROCEDURE

Street bail (as introduced by CJA 2003, s.4)

It is expected that "street bail" will be primarily used when a suspect's identity and address are clearly established, the offence is minor, there is no need to impose specific bail conditions, and there is no need, or no immediate need, to interview the suspect. Home Office guidelines identify four key considerations as to how constables should use their discretion in deciding whether to grant "street bail":

HOC 61/2003

- the nature of the offence;
- the ability to progress the investigation at the police station;
- the level of confidence in the suspect answering bail; and
- the level of awareness and understanding of the procedure by the suspect.

It is suggested that the period of street bail should be for a period of no longer than six weeks, and that the norm should be two weeks.

HOC 61/2003

The police may delay either taking a suspect to a police station or releasing him on street bail if necessary to carry out reasonable investigations. Any such delay must be for a period of no longer than 6 hours.

PACE 1984, ss 30(2), (10), (10A)

If a suspect fails to answer to street bail then the police have a power of arrest and, once arrested, the suspect must be taken to a police station as soon as practicable.

PACE 1984, s.30(D)

Police use of bail before charge

The police invariably use bail before charge as a device to provide themselves with further time to investigate the suspect and the circumstances of the allegation(s) against him.

It stops the detention clock from running whilst allowing the police the opportunity to interview witnesses, conduct forensic examinations, arrange identification parades, seek legal advice and follow any other line of inquiry.

PACE 1984, s.47(1); CJPOA 1994, s.27(1)

Consequences of failure to surrender

Whilst such inquiries are undertaken, the suspect is at liberty but under a legal obligation to return to the designated police station for further questioning, a further extension of bail or a release without charge, or for charging.

A failure to surrender to bail is an offence unless the suspect has "reasonable cause" and the suspect may be arrested without warrant if he fails to surrender at the appointed police station at the appointed time.

BA 1976, s.6; PACE 1984, s.46; CJPOA 1994, s.29(2)

If so arrested, the detention clock does not restart and the time spent in detention prior to the release on bail will count for the purpose of calculating his period in detention after arrest.

PACE 1984, s.47(6); CJPOA 1994, s.29(4)(d)

If a suspect has been released on bail for the purpose of obtaining the DPP's advice, then a constable may arrest him without warrant if he fails to surrender to bail or the constable has reasonable grounds for believing that he has broken any other of his conditions of bail. If at the time of this arrest the DPP has not yet given his decision, then it is for the custody officer to decide whether to charge the suspect and whether to release him on bail or without bail. If he is released without charge but on bail, then he can only be released under the same bail conditions as applied before his arrest.

PACE 1984, s.46A; CJA 2003, Sch. 2 para. 5; PACE 1984, s.37C; CJA 2003, Sch. 2 para. 3

PACE 1984, s.37D; CJA 2003, Sch. 2 para. 3

In such circumstances, the custody officer may invoke the same power to appoint a different time or an additional time for the suspect to attend the police station as under the normal provisions for bail pending the DPP's advice (see **Bail pending the DPP's advice** above).

Sureties and securities

In practice, the police seldom require either a surety or a security as a pre-release condition of bail before charge. It is only likely to occur when the allegation is of a relatively serious nature and/or the bail return date is some considerable time in the future. Other factors, such as a lack of community ties, may also affect this decision.

A "surety" is a person prepared to act as a financial guarantor for the suspect's return to the appointed location at the appointed time, while a "security" is money or other valuable item(s) surrendered by or on behalf of the suspect, normally but not necessarily, in order to answer any fear that he will not remain within Great Britain until the date of his surrender.

BA 1976, s.3(4); BA 1976 s.3(5)

Return of property

Any of the suspect's property seized from him on arrival at the police station on the grounds that it might be used to:

(a) cause physical injury to any person;

(b) damage property;

(c) interfere with evidence; or

(d) assist in an escape,

must be returned to the suspect when he is released, whether without bail or on bail.

PACE 1984, s.22(3)

BAIL AFTER CHARGE—THE LAW

Introduction

PACE 1984, s.38(1); CJPOA 1994, s.28(2)

Once a suspect has been charged, the normal rule is that he should be released either without bail or on bail pending a first court appearance.

There are a number of exceptions to this rule, as well as provisions for the imposition of both pre-release and post-release bail conditions.

Suspects normally prohibited from the grant of bail

Under Art.5(3) ECHR, all accused must be considered for bail and any blanket embargo on bail is a violation of the accused's fundamental rights. However, a certain category of suspect will normally be prohibited from the grant of bail in anything other than "exceptional circumstances".

CC v United Kingdom (1999) Crim. L.R. 228

Such suspects are those charged with (or convicted of):

CJPOA 1994, s.25; CDA 1998, s.56; SOA 2003, Sch. 6 para. 32(2)

(A) murder;

(B) attempted murder;

(C) manslaughter; and

(D) the following sexual offences:

(i) rape under the law of Scotland or Northern Ireland;
(ii) rape as defined in s.1 SOA 1956;
(iii) rape as defined in s.1 SOA 2003;
(iv) assault by penetration;
(v) causing a person to engage in sexual activity without consent where the activity involved penetration;
(vi) rape of a child under 13;
(vii) assault of a child under 13 by penetration;
(viii) causing or inciting a child under 13 to engaged in sexual activity, where the activity involved penetration;
(ix) sexual activity with a person with a mental disorder impeding choice, where the activity involved penetration;
(x) causing or inciting a person with a mental disorder impeding choice to engage in sexual activity where the activity involved penetration was caused; and
(xi) an attempt to commit any of the sexual offences listed above;

when the suspect has been previously convicted within the UK of:

(a) any of the above offences; or
(b) culpable homicide; and

if the previous conviction was for manslaughter or culpable homicide, he received a sentence of imprisonment (or long-term detention if then a child or young person).

CJPOA 1994, s.25(4)

A suspect will falls into this category above even if he has an outstanding appeal against either conviction or sentence.

CJPOA 1994, s.25(5)

A "conviction" is defined as including a finding of not guilty by reason of insanity, a finding that the defendant did the act or made an omission although unfit to plead, and a conviction for which the suspect was placed on probation or discharged (absolutely or conditionally).

CJPOA 1994, s.25(1)

The "exceptional circumstances" that will justify a police officer in granting bail to such a suspect after charge are not defined and it is difficult to envisage a scenario in which the adviser could persuade the police to grant bail prior to a first court appearance. However, custody officers have been advised to consult a more senior officer and/or the CPS before authorising such a release and have been reminded of the need to make a full written note on the custody record of the reasons for granting bail if it is granted.

HOC 34/1998

Other exceptions to the right to bail

Other than those normally prohibited from the grant of bail, a suspect must be released unless he falls into one of these categories:

PACE 1984, s.38(1), 63B; CJPOA 1994, s.28(1)–(2); CJA 2003, s.5(2)(b)

(a) the suspect's name and address cannot be ascertained or the custody officer has reasonable grounds for doubting whether such details as supplied by him are *bona fide*;

(b) the custody officer has reasonable grounds for believing that the suspect will fail to appear in court to answer to bail;

(c) in the case of a suspect arrested for an imprisonable offence, the custody officer has reasonable grounds for believing that the detention is necessary to prevent him from committing an offence;

(d) in the case of a suspect aged above 18, the custody officer has reasonable grounds for believing that the detention is necessary to enable a sample to be taken from him;

(e) in the case of a suspect arrested for a non-imprisonable offence, the custody officer has reasonable grounds for believing that the detention is necessary to prevent him from causing physical injury to any other person or from causing loss of or damage to property;

(f) the custody officer has reasonable grounds for believing that the detention of the suspect is necessary to prevent him from interfering with the administration of justice or with the investigation of an offence or offences;

(g) the custody officer has reasonable grounds for believing that the detention of the suspect is necessary for his own protection; or

(h) in the case of a suspect who is a juvenile, the custody officer has reasonable grounds for believing that he ought to be detained in his own interests.

If the suspect is detained for purposes of drug testing, detention is limited to six hours from the time when he was charged.

PACE 1984, s.38(2)

If one of these exceptions is deemed to apply then the custody officer may authorise that the defendant be detained prior to his appearance before a magistrates' court.

PACE 1984, s.38(2)

Bail conditions

When a defendant is bailed after charge, it is for the custody officer to appoint the venue of the magistrates' court and the date and the time for his first appearance.

PACE 1984, s.47(3)

The obligation to attend the appointed court at the appointed time is a condition that will always attach to such bail, although these details may be varied or cancelled in advance of the due date by the court.

MCA 1980, s.43(1); PACE 1984, s.47(8)(a)

The police can impose not only pre-release bail conditions (requiring a surety and/or a security) but also post-release bail conditions once a defendant has been charged.

PACE 1984, s.47(1); CJPOA 1994, s.27 (1)

Bail conditions can only be imposed if such appear necessary to the custody officer in order to secure that the defendant:

PACE 1984, s.47(1); CJPOA 1994, s.27(1), (2)(b), (3); BA 1976, s.3(6), PCC(S)A 2000, s.165(1), Sch. 9 para. 51; CJPA 2001, s.131(1), (3)

(a) surrenders to custody;

(b) does not commit any offence whilst on bail;

(c) does not interfere with witnesses or otherwise obstruct the course of justice;

(d) makes himself available for the purpose of enabling inquiries or a report to be made to assist the court in dealing with him for the offence; or

(e) attends an interview with an authorised advocate or litigator before the time appointed for him to surrender to custody.

PACE 1984, s.47(1); BA 1976, s.3(6), 3(A)

The custody officer may impose any of the post-release bail conditions that a court could impose (such as a curfew restriction, a condition of residence or a requirement not to contact others), apart from a condition to reside in a bail hostel, a condition to attend a medical examination or a condition to attend a person compiling a court report.

PACE 1984, s.38(1); CJPOA 1994, s.27(3); BA 1976, s.3A(5)

Bail conditions may only be imposed to the extent that they appear necessary to the custody officer to prevent a failure to surrender, the commission of an offence or an interference with witnesses or the course of justice.

PACE 1984, s.38; CJA 2003, s.88(1)

It should be noted that when CJA 2003 Pt X comes into force (governing retrial for serious offences) the custody officer can only release on bail a person charged under these provisions if bail is subject to a duty to appear before the Crown Court within 24 hours.

BAIL AFTER CHARGE—PRACTICE AND PROCEDURE

Police use of bail after charge

Prior to CJPOA 1994, it was not possible for the police to grant bail to a suspect after charge with any post-release conditions other than the obligation to attend court.

As a result, many suspects were held in police custody prior to their production before the court in order to allow the Crown Prosecution Service to request that bail conditions be imposed.

The rationale behind the new law was that this would no longer occur, and the fact that the police can now impose virtually the same conditions as a court has led to a greater number of suspects being released on police bail after charge than happened prior to CJPOA 1994.

However, the adviser should always be alert to the risk that the police will attempt to impose conditions upon bail in circumstances where they would have not been sought in the past. The adviser must be prepared to argue that the suspect should be released on unconditional bail in appropriate cases even if the police are suggesting that conditions be imposed that the suspect can meet.

Custody officer's obligations in considering bail

PACE 1984, s.38(2A);

When considering whether there are substantial grounds for believing that if the suspect was bailed he would fall into one of the categories giving grounds for the refusal of bail, the custody officer must have regard to the same considerations as those regarded by a court in relation to the bail position of a defendant accused or convicted of an imprisonable offence.

CJPOA 1994, s.28(3)

These considerations are:

(a) the nature and seriousness of the offence (and the probable method of dealing with the suspect if found guilty);

(b) the character, antecedents, associations and community ties of the suspect;

BA 1976, Sch.1, Pt 1, para. 9

(c) the suspect's record as respects the fulfilment of his obligations under previous grants of bail;

(d) the strength of the evidence against the suspect.

There are three exceptions to this obligation. The custody officer need not have regard to these considerations in assessing the grounds relating to:

(a) the suspect's name and address;

(b) the suspect's own protection; and

(c) (for juveniles only) the suspect's own interests.

Need for advisers to make bail applications

It is part of the adviser's duties to make extensive representations to the custody officer on behalf of a suspect after charge if bail is in issue. Such representations will be analogous to a fully argued application for bail before the magistrates' court.

Issues to be addressed may include:

(a) whether any of the "exceptions to the right to bail" can be properly deemed to apply;

(b) if so, whether the police concerns can be met by the imposition of bail conditions; and

(c) what will or will not be appropriate bail conditions in all the circumstances of the case.

Power to vary bail conditions

Once a custody officer has imposed bail conditions, the suspect has the right to apply to vary these. An application to vary may be made to the original custody officer, or another custody

CJPOA 1994, s.27(3)–(4); BA 1976, s.3A(4);

MCA 1980, s.43B

officer serving at the same police station or to a magistrates' court. Any officer (or court) hearing the application may remove the conditions or vary them.

Advisers must, however, be aware of the fact that a "variation" may involve the imposition of more stringent conditions: therefore, an application should not be made lightly. However, the right does provide the suspect with an instant appeal process that may be of use if it is felt that unnecessary and onerous bail conditions have been imposed. An application to vary should certainly be considered if unrealisable conditions have been imposed, such as an excessive and unobtainable surety requirement.

Written notice of bail decisions

CJPOA 1994, s.27(4) and Sch. 3; BA 1976, s.5

When a custody officer grants bail or imposes or varies bail conditions, he must make a written record of the decision and if the custody officer is so asked by the suspect, he must supply him with a copy of the record as soon as practicable after it is made.

CJPOA 1994, s.27(4) and Sch. 3, para. 2; BA 1976, s.5A; CJPA 2001, s.129(2)

There is an additional requirement that, when the decision relates to bail conditions (either their imposition or their variation), the custody officer must give his reasons: this is to enable the suspect to consider applying for a variation of the conditions. The reasons must be noted in the custody record and the suspect must be given a copy of the note.

Magistrates' courts powers to reconsider bail decisions

CJPOA 1994, s.27(4) and Sch. 3, para. 3; MCA 1980, s.43B

Where a custody officer grants bail to a suspect and imposes or varies bail conditions, a magistrates' court has the power either to remove or to vary such conditions upon the **suspect's application**.

This power enables an application to be made for a removal or variation of bail conditions prior to what would otherwise be the suspect's first court appearance. However, it is important to be aware that the court's powers on hearing the application include the imposition of more onerous conditions and even the withholding of bail.

CJPOA 1994, s.30; BA 1976, s.5B; CJPA 2001, s.129(3); EA 2003, ss 198(1),(6)

The **prosecution** also has the **right to apply** to the magistrates' court either for the withholding of bail granted or for a variation of bail conditions imposed by either the police or the magistrates' court. However, such an application can only be made if new information has become available since the original decision was taken and if the offence charged is not a summary-only matter. These provisions apply whether the suspect has been granted bail by either a magistrates' court or a constable in either criminal or extradition proceedings.

Consequences of failure to comply with bail conditions

Once on bail, a suspect is legally obliged to return to the designated court at the appointed time: a failure to surrender to bail is an offence unless the suspect has "reasonable cause".

BA 1976, s.6(1); BA 1976, s.7(1)–(3)

Where a suspect who has been released on bail in connection with extradition proceedings is under a duty to surrender into the custody of a constable, a magistrates' court may issue a warrant for his arrest should he fail to surrender to custody at the appointed time.

BA 1976 s.7 (1A), (1B); EA 2003, s.198 (1), (7)

A suspect released on bail regarding criminal or extradition proceedings may be arrested without warrant if a police officer has reasonable grounds for believing he is unlikely to surrender and the court can issue a warrant for arrest if he does fail to so surrender.

BA 1976, s.7(4A); EA 2003, s.198(1), (9)

In addition, he may be arrested without warrant by a constable if the officer has reasonable grounds for believing that he is likely to break any of his bail conditions or has reasonable grounds for suspecting that he has broken any such conditions.

A suspect arrested as a result of failing to surrender to the custody of the court is to be brought as soon as is practicable and in any case within 24 hours of arrest before a justice of the peace; unless he has been arrested within 24 hours of the time appointed for him to surrender to custody, in which case he is to be brought before the court to which he was to have surrendered to custody.

BA 1976, s.7 (3), (4), (4B); EA 2003, s.198(11)

Return of property

As for a suspect bailed before charge, certain property seized upon arrival at a police station must be returned once a suspect is released after charge.

For further details refer, to the "**Return of property**" heading under the "**Bail before charge—practice and procedure**" section above.

PRACTICAL GUIDANCE

(1) Improper offer/denial of bail by police

In considering bail issues, the adviser must be aware that either the offer of bail or the threat of refusal of bail prior to or during a police interview is likely to be interpreted as oppressive behaviour or something likely to make a confession unreliable, rendering the interview inadmissible.

PACE 1984, s.76(2)

(2) Representations for bail before charge

PACE 1984, s.34(2)

In making such representations, the adviser must remember that the custody officer is under an overriding duty to release a suspect immediately upon becoming aware that the grounds for his detention have ceased to apply and when there are no other grounds to justify detention.

PACE 1984, Code C, para. 1.1

This is supported by the PACE 1984 Codes of Practice, which state that all suspects must be "released as soon as the need for [their] detention no longer applies".

(3) The detention clock and representations

The fact that the detention clock stops upon the granting of bail before charge can be used in support of representations that a suspect be given bail pending further inquiries.

Circumstances may arise whereby the police investigation has reached a temporary impasse and the adviser can remind the custody officer that the detention clock is running and that all parties would be better served by releasing the suspect on bail pending the police's resolution of their difficulties.

(4) Confirmation of bail return date

Once a suspect/defendant has been released on bail, the adviser should always make a diary note to check with either the police or the magistrates' court (as appropriate) in advance of the due return date and obtain confirmation that the date stands.

If the suspect is on bail before charge then the adviser should also inquire of the officer in the case as to his intentions upon the suspect's surrender.

(5) Representations for bail after charge

In making representations that a suspect should be released after charge, the adviser should include, as appropriate, argument that:

(a) none of the exceptions to bail as of right apply. All of the exceptions require an element of "reasonableness" in the custody officer's decision process, enabling an argument to be put that a proposed decision to refuse release is not reasonable; or

(b) the release may be subject to conditions, for example a security of money or some other item of value such as jewellery, a passport or a motor vehicle. Thus, if a custody officer argues that bail cannot be given because of a professed fear that the suspect is likely to leave the country, this can be countered with the argument that the surrender of the suspect's passport by way of security reduces any such risk to the point where it is no longer a reasonably held fear.

(6) The decision to grant bail after charge

The decision whether or not to grant bail after charge is one of profound significance.

There can be little doubt that, if the police grant bail, the suspect is likely to remain on bail thereafter unless he commits a further offence or breaks any bail conditions, or new adverse information comes to the attention of the prosecution.

Conversely, if the police refuse bail and the Crown Prosecution Service maintain objections to bail at the magistrates' court, the suspect will be at very real risk of remaining on remand in custody throughout the proceedings.

In these circumstances, the adviser must make the most forceful representations possible when the question of whether or not to grant bail after charge is being made.

(7) Unlawful detentions

In making representations to a custody officer, it may assist to emphasise that an unlawful detention, which will include a detention where there are no proper grounds to justify it, may give rise to the civil torts of false imprisonment and trespass to the person.

(8) Convenient date

When a suspect is to be released under an obligation either to return to a police station or to appear before the magistrates' court, the adviser should ensure that the date of return is convenient for the suspect before it is fixed.

Charging and Alternatives

CHARGING—THE LAW

Timing and types of decision

As soon as a suspect who has been arrested arrives at a police station, the custody officer must decide whether there is sufficient evidence to charge the suspect with the offence for which he has been arrested.

PACE 1984, ss 37(1), (10)

Thereafter, there is a continuing obligation upon the custody officer to determine whether such evidence exists and once the custody officer is of the view that such evidence does exist then he must either charge (if appropriate, after seeking direction from the CPS) or release the suspect.

PACE 1984, s.37(7)

If the suspect is released without charge this can be either:

PACE 1984, s.37(7)(a)–(c); CJA 2003, Sch. 2, para. 2(4)

(a) on bail in order that the CPS (as agent of the DPP) can make a decision on charge;

(b) without charge and on bail for a purpose other than above (*e.g.* to consult the victim); or

(c) without charge and without bail.

(For further details refer to the **Bail** index heading.)

The latest time at which the decision to charge or release must be made is at the expiry of the detention time limit.

R. v Taylor [1991] Crim. L.R.541

Who makes the decision?

All decisions whether to charge, whether to seek direction from the CPS, whether to release on bail to seek direction from the CPS, or whether to release on bail for another reason lie with the custody officer. In practice, the custody officer will invariably look to the officer investigating the case for guidance, if not for a recommendation, before reaching this decision.

PACE 1984, s.37(7A)

However, an officer of the rank of superintendent or above, who is independent of the investigaion, will make the decision once s.87 of Criminal Justice Act 2003 come into force.

CJA 2003, s.87(6)

How charges are put

Charges are usually put to the suspect by the custody officer in the police station's custody room.

When a suspect is charged, he must be cautioned.

PACE 1984, Code C,

para.16.2

The suspect must be given a written charge notice which, *inter alia*, has noted on it:

PACE 1984, Code C, para. 16.3

(a) the name of the officer in the case;
(b) a case reference number;
(c) the precise charge(s) in law;
(d) so far as possible, the particulars of the charge(s) in simple terms; and
(e) the caution.

If the suspect is to be granted bail then the charge notice should also contain details of the court, date and time at which the suspect is to first appear.

Charging for retrial under CJA 2003

CJA 2003, ss 87–91

It should be noted that when CJA 2003, Pt 10 (Retrial for Serious Offences) comes into force a number of special procedures will operate for the charging of those suspects arrested for the purpose of retrial.

CHARGING—PRACTICE AND PROCEDURE

The decision whether or not to charge

The custody officer's decision will depend upon a number of factors. These include:

(a) the seriousness of the allegation(s);
(b) the strength of the evidence;
(c) the suspect's attitude to the allegation(s);
(d) whether the circumstances are such that the CPS should be consulted for direction; and
(e) whether a preferable alternative means of disposal exists (see below).

The role of the CPS in statutory charging

CJA 2003, Sch. 2; PACE 1984, s.37

Under provisions introduced by CJA 2003, amending s.37 of PACE 1984, responsibility for key charging decisions will shift from the police to the CPS (as agents of the DPP).

The scheme will be governed by special guidance issued by the DPP. Under the guidance the police will continue to be responsible for charging those cases which the custody officer considers suitable for early disposal in the magistrates' court as straightforward guilty pleas and minor matters (such as most road traffic offences and certain street offences). All other cases will be referred to the CPS for decisions on charging.

PACE 1984, ss 37A, 37B

Duty CPS prosecutors will be available in police stations for face-to-face consultations with custody officers during office hours. At other times, officers will be able to speak to duty prosecutors by telephone under the "CPS Direct" facility.

At the date of publication, 'shadow' schemes are operating in over 300 police stations whereby the CPS are being *consulted* for *guidance* on charging as a "dry run" for the statutory scheme. However, the full scheme, under which *legally-binding decisions* are taken by the CPS, is only fully operational in six areas: Cleveland, Kent, Lancashire, Northumbria, South and West Yorkshire. The current plans are for the full scheme to be extended to all other areas in a phased programme to be completed by late 2005.

Interviews and the obligation either to charge or to release

The custody officer has an obligation either to charge or to release a suspect once he is of the view that there is "sufficient evidence to charge . . .". This obligation must be read together with the PACE 1984 Codes of Practice, which provide different criteria for the point in time at which any interview of the suspect must be stopped.

PACE 1984, s.37(7)

An interviewing officer must conclude an interview without delay and bring the suspect before the custody officer to consider whether or not the suspect will be charged, or bailed for the CPS to advise on charge, when the officer in charge of the investigation considers that:

(a) all relevant questions have been put;

(b) the suspect has been allowed an opportunity to give an innocent explanation;

(c) he has taken account of any other available evidence; and

(d) he (or, if the suspect has been detained, the custody officer) reasonably believes there is sufficient evidence to provide a realistic prospect of conviction.

PACE 1984, Code C, paras 11.6, 16.1–16.1B

In light of points (a)—(c) above, it is arguable that the police can continue interviewing a suspect after the point has been reached whereby the custody officer, if aware of all of the facts, would have to decide either to charge or to release the suspect.

PACE 1984, s.34(2); *R. v Canale* (1989) 91 Cr.App.R. 1

It is important that the adviser be aware of this discrepancy. The adviser should be prepared to argue during an interview that because:

(i) the officer in charge has "sufficient evidence to provide a realistic prospect of conviction . . .", and

(ii) all of the other criteria have been satisfied, and

(iii) because of the custody officer's obligation either to charge or to release a suspect once aware that the grounds for his continuing detention have ceased to apply,

then the interview must be brought to an end and a decision be made even if the officer in charge would like to continue the interview.

The suspect's answer to charges

PACE 1984, Code C, paras 16.2–16.3

When a suspect is charged he is given the caution which, *inter alia*, warns of the risk that harm may be done to the defence by a failure to mention something which is later relied on in court (unless the restriction on drawing adverse inferences from silence applies). This caution is also included on the charge notice.

PACE 1984, Code C, para. 16.8

The police are obliged to keep a written record of anything the suspect says when charged.

If a suspect who was legally advised did not answer questions in any previous interview, he should normally reply "no comment" when cautioned after charge unless a tactical decision has been taken to use this opportunity to give some explanation(s) in an attempt to avoid adverse inferences that might otherwise flow as a result of ss 34 to 39 of the CJPOA 1994 (refer to the **Advising the Suspect—Right of Silence** index heading).

However, if the suspect did answer questions in interview it is advisable that he reply "I have nothing to add to my earlier statements". This will prevent any suggestion arising that he has elected to remain silent upon charge, whilst ensuring that a new quasi-interview process does not commence.

A situation may arise whereby the adviser has been instructed by a suspect subsequent to his being interviewed, in which interview the suspect had refused to answer questions.

In such situations, it should be remembered that the suspect will have a further opportunity to explain himself in reply to the caution given after charge. Advice must be given upon this point as if the suspect is about to be interviewed for the first time.

Special provisions for suspects detained for more than one offence

The PACE 1984 Codes of Practice make it clear that when a suspect is detained in respect of more than one offence, it is permissible for the officer in charge of the investigation to delay bringing him before the custody officer until **all** of the earlier defined conditions have been satisfied in respect of **all** of the offences.

PACE 1984, Code C, para.16.1

This does not derogate from the custody officer's mandatory obligations to charge or release a suspect once there is sufficient evidence to charge. This means that it is technically possible for a suspect to be released on one allegation and then rearrested on any remaining allegation(s) if the officer in charge can satisfy the custody officer that there is still insufficient to provide a realistic prospect of conviction and there is a need to interview the suspect further in relation to such remaining allegation(s).

PACE 1984, s.37 (1), (2), (7)

In these circumstances, the adviser must take care when representing a suspect who is being investigated for more than one offence. When, during the course of making representations to the police, the adviser wishes to refer to the s.37(7) provision, this should be with a view to speeding up the interviewing process, rather than by way of argument for an immediate charge or release, which may simply lead to the suspect being rearrested.

ALTERNATIVES TO CHARGE—THE LAW, PRACTICE AND PROCEDURE

Release on bail

It is often the case that the police will release a suspect on bail pending further investigations and/or further consideration of the decision whether or not to bring charges.

Under provisions introduced by CJA 2003, the suspect may also be bailed for the purpose of sending to the CPS (as agent of the DPP) relevant information so as to allow them to determine whether to charge, caution or take no action against the suspect.

PACE 1984, ss 37 (7), 37B; CJA 2003, Sch. 2 paras 2–3

For full details, refer to the separate **Bail** index heading.

No further action

If the police are of the view that, having completed their investigation, there is insufficient evidence to charge the suspect then they will release him unconditionally.

The suspect will normally be advised by the police that "no further action" is to be taken and that the matter is at a conclusion unless fresh evidence comes to light.

The police are empowered to take such a course even when sufficient evidence to charge is in existence. However, this is a rare occurrence and will only normally arise when there are extraordinary features to the case, which may include:

HOC 18/1994

(a) the suspect is mentally disordered or suffering from a severe physical illness, or is a juvenile; and

(b) the allegation is of a relatively trivial nature.

The attitude of the complainant may also be considered as a relevant factor.

Young offender reprimands and final warnings

The system of police "reprimands" and "final warnings" was introduced in order to reduce the likelihood of young offenders re-offending and ensuring a consistent approach by the police when dealing with young offenders. Extensive guidance on the system is contained in the Home Office publications *Final Warning Scheme: Guidance for the Police and Youth Offending Teams* (The Guidance) and *Further Guidance for the Police and Youth Offending Teams* (The Further Guidance).

CDA 1998, ss 65–66

Reprimands are to be available for first-time minor offences. Any re-offending will result in either a final warning or charge. A final warning may also be given for more serious offences without there having been a prior reprimand. Only in exceptional cases will further offending after a final warning result in any police action other than a charge.

Under the system, if a constable is satisfied that:

(a) there is sufficient evidence that the offence has been committed; and

CDA 1998, s.65(2)–(4)

(b) he has sufficient evidence for there to be a reasonable prospect of the child or young person being convicted of an offence; and

(c) the child or young person has admitted the offence; and

(d) the child or young person has not previously been convicted of an offence; and

(e) it would not be in the public interest for the child or young person to be prosecuted

the constable may reprimand the child or young person if he has not previously been reprimanded or warned. Alternatively, he may warn the child or young person if he has not previously been warned—or was previously warned over two years ago and this offence is not so serious as to require a charge being brought. A child or young person offending for the fourth time cannot receive a reprimand or warning in any circumstances and must be charged.

The Home Office has produced guidelines as to when it is and is not in the public interest to prosecute a child or young offender. They are analogous to the public interest principles described in the Code for Crown Prosecutors.

HOC 9/1999, Annex C

Reprimands and warnings must be administered at a police station or any other venue that is 'suitable, easily accessible and secure', and should be administered by a police officer; who can be the police member of a youth offending team (The Further Guidance, paras 8 and 9). If the offender is aged 16 or under, they must be administered in the presence of an "appropriate adult". The officer administering the reprimand or caution should, in normal circumstances, be in uniform. This oral reprimand or warning must be followed by written information to the offender clearly explaining the implications of the reprimand or caution.

CDA 1998, s.65; CJCSA 2000, s.56

Once a child or young person has received a warning he will be referred to the local youth offending team for induction into a rehabilitation programme, unless there are reasons to make this inappropriate.

CDA 1998, s.66(1)

A reprimand, warning or failure to participate in a rehabilitation programme may be cited in future criminal proceedings in the same manner as a conviction.

CDA 1998, s.66(5)

It should be noted that special rules apply under the scheme for child prostitutes, who are recognised as having special needs. In such cases, the initial response will be the "prostitute's caution". This does not require an admission of guilt but is coupled with a specific warning that she will be treated as an offender if her behaviour continues. This special caution does not count towards the final warning system and each case is to be decided upon its own facts as to whether to bring a

HOC 9/1999

young person with a previous "prostitute's caution" into the final warning scheme (including the number of previous such cautions, whether they have been forced into prostitution by coercion, *etc.*).

It should also be noted that The Guidance and The Further Guidance do not prohibit the police from taking informal action by way of 'firm advice' to a child or young offender (or his parents) for minor offending, if it is considered that this is likely to prevent repetition of the offending. However, such "informal cautions" should be limited to exceptional circumstances.

Adult police cautions (the non-statutory scheme)

The police may choose to formally caution an adult offender when:

HOC 18/1994; *Metropolitan Police Commissioner, Ex p. P* (1995) T.L.R. 305 CJACCCP 004, para. 2.2

(a) there is sufficient evidence of the offender's guilt to give a realistic prospect of conviction;

(b) the offender admits the offence;

(c) the offender will give informed consent to the caution;

(d) where possible, the victim has been consulted (although the victim's consent to a caution being administered is not a prerequisite); and

(e) a statutory conditional caution (see below) is not appropriate because either there appear to be no suitable conditions or the offender has already forestalled these (*e.g.* by paying compensation to the victim).

A caution will be recorded by the police. It is not a conviction but can be cited in any future criminal proceedings.

HOC 18/1994

The Home Office Circular 18/1994 (*The Cautioning of Offenders*) provides national guidance on the administration of the caution system. In addition, it makes it clear that each police force is obliged to have its own "force policy statement" on cautioning. Such statements must detail the circumstances in which a caution is likely to be considered.

HOC 18/1994

Certain criteria are common to all police forces in considering the circumstances when a caution may be appropriate:

(a) The nature of the offence

The more serious the offence, the less likely it will be that a caution will be considered appropriate. In particular, cautions should never be given for serious indictable-only offences and only for less serious indictable-only offences when there are exceptional circumstances (such as a young person taking another's pocket money by force, which in law is robbery).

(b) The offender's record

Cautions will not be considered if the offender has a previous caution unless the current allegation is of a trivial nature and there has been a sufficient lapse of time since the first caution.

(c) Likely effectiveness

The police must be satisfied that a caution is "likely to prove an effective means of dealing with the offender".

(d) The suspect's age and health

An elderly offender, or one suffering from some form of mental illness or severe physical illness, is more likely to be dealt with by way of a caution.

(e) The offender's attitude

An offender who is deemed not to have committed the offence wilfully and/or has subsequently demonstrated regret is more likely to be dealt with by way of a caution.

In addition, consideration must always be given to the guidance as to when it is and is not appropriate to charge an offender found within the Code for Crown Prosecutors.

On occasion, an offender will be released only after he has been given an oral warning about his future conduct. This practice is sometimes referred to as the giving of an "informal caution". Such a warning is not a formal police caution and cannot be recorded as such: it is, in effect, a variation upon the taking of "no further action".

Adult conditional cautions (the statutory scheme)

In June 2004 the new statutory system of 'conditional cautions' introduced by Pt 3 of CJA 2003 came into force. Conditional cautions do not replace the non-statutory scheme (see above) but are an alternative option to be used when the police consider that the imposition of conditions attaching to the caution are desirable to address the offender's behaviour (rehabilitative conditions) and/or assist him in making reparation for his offending (reparative conditions).

CJACCCP 2004, paras 1.2, 2.2

Conditional cautions enable offenders to be dealt with other than by charge "where rehabilitative or reparative conditions (or both) are considered preferable to prosecution" by providing

CJACCCP 2004, paras 1.2, 3.2

"a statutory means of enforcing them through prosecution for the original offence in the event of non-compliance."

Five conditions have to be satisfied for a conditional caution to be administered to an adult offender:

(1) The authorised person (police officer, etc.) has evidence that the offender committed an offence;

(2) The relevant prosecutor (CPS, etc.) has decided that there is sufficient evidence to charge and that a conditional caution should be given;

CJA 2003, ss 22(1), 23 CJACCCP 2004, para. 4.1

(3) The offender has admitted to the authorised person that he committed the offence;

(4) The authorised person has explained the effect of a conditional caution to the offender and warned him that failure to comply with any of the attached conditions may result in him being prosecuted for the offence;

(5) The offender has signed a document containing details of the offence, an admission that he committed the offence, his consent to being given a conditional caution and his consent to the attached conditions.

CJA 2003, s.25; CJACCCP 2004, para.2.4

The decision whether to impose a conditional caution will be for the prosecutor (usually the CPS as agent for the DPP) rather than the police and, in reaching their decision, they will follow the Home Office's "Conditional Cautions: Code of Practice".

CJACCCP 2004, para. 3.1

In considering whether to administer a conditional caution, the prosecutor should consider the Code for Crown Prosecutors together with Home Office Circular 18/1994 and other considerations as for the non-statutory scheme (see above).

CJACCCP 2004, para. 3.3

If the offender has recently received a non-statutory caution for the same or similar offence, this will normally preclude him from receiving a conditional caution. However, previous cautions, and even convictions, can be ignored in a decision whether to issue a conditional caution if they were for quite dissimilar offences or over 5 years old.

CJACCCP 2004, para. 2.5 PACE 1984, s.37(7)(a)

The authorised person (*e.g.* police officer) should consult with the relevant prosecutor (*e.g.* CPS) as soon as is practicable, either face-to-face or by telephone, for the decision as to whether to issue a caution. In exceptional circumstances the suspect can be bailed for a sufficient period to enable such consultation to take place.

The prosecutor can advise that the offender be bailed to attend a mediation meeting with the victim if this will assist in the fixing of suitable conditions.

CJACCCP 2004, para. 2.6

Conditions attached to a caution must be:

(a) proportionate;

(b) achievable;

(c) appropriate; and

(d) set within a realistic timetable for completion.

CJACCCP 2004, paras 5.1, 6.1

Proportionate conditions are ones that are neither more onerous nor significantly less than the punishment a court would be likely to give on conviction. Appropriate conditions are those that are relevant to the offence or the offender. The timetable should be realistic so, for example, for summary only offences it must leave enough time for a prosecution to proceed in the event of non compliance.

Examples of rehabilitative conditions include: taking part in a treatment programme for drug or alcohol dependency and attending an anger management course. The conditions may specify that the offender bear the costs of the course. Examples of reparative conditions include: repairing or making good damaged property, paying modest financial compensation and a simple apology. There should always be a condition not to re-offend during the specified timetable.

CJACCCP 2004, paras 5.2, 5.3

When possible with a case where a conditional caution is being considered and there is a personal victim, "restorative justice" trained personnel should contact the victim and seek their views on reparation as a condition of the caution or enquire whether they would like to be involved in a direct or indirect "restorative justice" process. However, the victim's views will not be conclusive as to the decisions whether to offer a caution and what conditions will attach thereto.

CJACCCP 2004, paras 7.1, 8.1

A condition that the offender has contact with the victim, be it direct or indirect, can be imposed as part of the "restorative justice" process, as long as both the offender and the victim agree to such a course.

CJACCCP 2004, para. 8.2

A failure to comply with any of the conditions attached to the caution without reasonable excuse may result in the cancelling of the caution and the commencement of criminal proceedings for the original offence(s). The caution will be admissible in any such proceedings.

CJA 2003, s.24; CJACCCP 2004, paras 10.2, 10.5

CJACCCP 2004, para. 2.8; CJACCCP 2004, para. 11.1

A conditional caution will be recorded by the police. It is not a conviction but can be cited in any future criminal proceedings.

Reporting for summons (written charges and requisitions)

The power to report a suspect for summons is usually operated either when the suspect is a young person or when the alleged offence is of a trivial nature.

It operates by the suspect being released unconditionally pending a future decision by the police as to whether to lay an information before a magistrates' court requesting that a summons be issued.

Summonses may be served upon the suspect personally or by post. In exceptional circumstances, the police may agree to effect service upon the suspect's solicitors, for example when the suspect is illiterate.

When a suspect is released pending a report for summons, he is under no bail obligation. However, if he fails to attend court on the date specified on the summons then the court is empowered to issue a warrant for arrest.

It should be noted that when ss 29 to 31 of CJA 2003 come into force, the summons will be replaced by a scheme of "written charges" and "requisitions". Under this system the custody officer will have the power to release the suspect without charge but on bail and the decision whether to subsequently issue a written charge will then lie with the CPS after considering a written report from the police. If a "written charge" is issued this will be accompanied by a "requisition" requiring the person to appear before a magistrates' court to answer the charge.

CJA 2003, ss 29–31

PRACTICAL GUIDANCE

(1) Representations

Representations by the adviser may play a significant part in determining the police's decision as to how to deal with a suspect once their investigations are either completed or have come to an impasse.

Although the police are under no obligation to hear such representations, they will invariably be considered and should be directed to the officer in the case and/or the custody officer.

It is vital that the adviser be aware of all the options available to the police and attempt to persuade them to follow the course that appears most appropriate in the circumstances and accords with the suspect's instructions.

(2) Disputes

If there is a dispute between the custody officer and an officer in the case of higher rank as to how to deal with the suspect, the matter must be referred to an officer of the rank of superintendent or above who is in charge of the police station.

PACE 1984, s.39(6)

(3) The Code for Crown Prosecutors

The Code for Crown Prosecutors is issued pursuant to s.10 of the Prosecution of Offences Act 1985. It provides guidelines for the Crown Prosecution Service to consider in deciding whether or not to proceed with a prosecution.

It is recommended that advisers have a copy of the current Code to hand, as reference to it in making representations may be of assistance: the police may be dissuaded from bringing charges even where sufficient evidence exists, or persuaded that a reprimand, warning or caution is a more appropriate course of action.

(4) Interviews after charge

The adviser must remember that once a suspect has been charged, the general rule is that he should not be subjected to any further questioning in relation to the offence(s) charged. The exceptions to this rule are:

PACE 1984, Code C, para. 16.5

(a) the questions are necessary for the purposes of preventing or minimising harm or loss to another;

(b) the questions are necessary for clearing up an ambiguity in a previous answer or statement; or

(c) it is in the interests of justice that the suspect has put to him, and has the opportunity to comment upon, information in relation to the offence(s) which has come to light subsequent to charges being put.

(5) Reporting for summons

When a suspect is reported for summons, this has the advantage of enabling further representations to be made after the suspect's release from custody but prior to the decision to commence proceedings by way of summons being taken.

(6) Police cautions—documentation

The adviser should always ensure that he carries copies of HOC 18/1994, the local police force policy statement on cautioning, and the Home Office's "Conditional Cautions: Code of Practice".

Surprisingly often, the adviser will discover that the police are unaware of the precise details contained within these documents and that it is necessary to have their attention drawn to them.

(7) Consequences of a caution

When the police indicate that they are prepared to consider dealing with the suspect by way of a caution, the adviser needs to consider this carefully with the suspect and advise accordingly.

This is particularly the case when the suspect has denied guilt but indicates to the adviser that he is willing to accept a caution because of his fear that a failure to do so will result in charges being brought.

Although the adviser can endeavour to ascertain from the police what course of action they propose to take if the offered caution is refused, it is often the case that the police will either refuse to answer such a question or will indicate that charges will indeed be brought.

In either event, all that the adviser can do is to remind the suspect that:

(a) fingerprints are taken after a caution has been administered;

(b) a caution can only be administered when there is an admission of guilt;

(c) the caution will be formally recorded by the police;

(d) the caution may be cited by the police in future criminal proceedings;

(e) the acceptance of a caution significantly reduces the chance of a caution ever being administered in the future; and

Omar v Chief Constable of Bedfordshire (2002) EWHC 3060

(f) the administering of a caution does not in itself prevent the suspect from being prosecuted unless the suspect has been induced into accepting the caution or has been specifically told that accepting the caution will mean that they will not be prosecuted.

As far as (f) is concerned, before advising a suspect to accept a caution, the adviser should seek the police's unequivocal confirmation that this will mean that there will be no subsequent prosecution unless, for conditional cautions, there has been a breach of the conditions without reasonable excuse.

(8) The Reprimand and Final Warning Scheme

It is recommended that advisers have a copy of the Home Office Guidance which will assist in making representations to the police that a child or young offender suspect should be properly dealt with by way of a reprimand or warning rather than a charge.

HOC 9/1999

Complaints

INTRODUCTION

While attending a suspect detained in a police station, the adviser may hear about from the suspect, or personally witness, matters which give rise to a complaint. Such matters can range from rudeness by police officers, through behaviour which is in breach of PACE 1984 or its Codes of Practice, to serious allegations of assault or the planting of evidence.

Complaint can also be made that an officer is in breach of his general obligations under the Police Code of Conduct. The code includes requirements that officers behave honestly, fairly, politely, impartially and soberly.

P(C)R 2004, Sch. 1

COMPLAINTS UNDER THE POLICE REFORM ACT 2002—THE LAW

Complaints against police and their employees

Part II of the Police Reform Act 2002, which came into force on April 1, 2004, introduced new measures for dealing with police complaints and misconduct. Under the new regime, the Police Complaints Authority (PCA) has been replaced by the Independent Police Complaints Commission (IPCC).

PRA 2002, Pt II and Sch. 3

PRA 2002, s.9

The new procedures apply to complaints made against any person serving with the police. This includes police officers, civilian employees who are under the direction and control of a chief officer and special constables.

PRA 2002, s.12 (7)

A complaint can be made about the conduct of a person serving with the police by:

PRA 2002, s.12 (1)

- members of the public who claim to be the person in relation to whom the conduct took place;
- a member of the public who claims to have been adversely affected by the conduct;
- a member of the public who claims to have witnessed the conduct; and
- a person acting on behalf of any of the above, with their written consent.

PRA 2002, Sch. 3, para. 2

A complaint may be made to the IPCC, the relevant police authority or a chief officer of a police area.

PRA 2002, Sch. 3, para. 2

Where the complaint is submitted to a chief officer of a police area he should take proper steps to obtain or preserve evidence relating to the complaint before determining the "appropriate authority" to investigate the complaint.

PRA 2002, s.29

The "appropriate authority" will be either the chief officer himself or the police authority for the force's area.

PRA 2002, Sch. 3, para. 2

Where a chief officer or police authority determines that it is not the "appropriate authority" the complainant must be notified of the person who is.

PRA 2002, Sch. 3, para. 3

If the police decide to take no action, the complainant must be notified of the grounds on which the decision was made. The complainant then has a right of appeal to the IPCC.

PRA 2002, Sch. 3, para. 4(1), P(C&M)R 2004, reg. 2

Any complaint of misconduct causing death, serious injury, or of a type specified in the regulations laid down by the Secretary of State must be referred to the IPCC. The IPCC can also notify the appropriate authority that it requires the complaint in question to be referred for its consideration.

PRA 2002, Sch. 3, para. 4(2)

Other complaints may also be referred to the IPCC if considered the proper course by the appropriate authority by reason of gravity of the subject matter of the complaint or any other exceptional circumstance.

PRA 2002, Sch. 3, para. 6(2),(3)

Unless a complaint has been referred to the IPCC, it can be resolved by way of local resolution if it would not justify criminal or disciplinary proceedings (even if proved), or the IPCC approves the use of local resolution. This is subject to the complainant agreeing to the complaint being dealt with by way of local resolution.

PRA 2002, Sch. 3, para. 8(2); P(C&M)R 2004

The Secretary of State has issued regulations which specify procedures to be followed when a complaint is dealt with by way of local resolution.

PRA 2002, Sch. 3, para. 9

There is a right of appeal by the complainant to the IPCC in respect of the conduct of the local resolution.

PRA 2002, Sch. 3, para. 16

If a complaint is not dealt with by way of local resolution, an investigating officer is appointed.

PA 1996, s.84(1); PRA 2002, s.36; P(C)R 2004

The ensuing investigation and any resulting disciplinary proceedings are governed by regulations laid down by the Secretary of State pursuant to PA 1996 and PRA 2002 and can result in dismissal, resignation, demotion in rank, fine, reprimand or caution. A special constable can be suspended for up to three months.

PRA 2002, Sch. 3, Pt 3, para. 15

Where an investigation is to be supervised by the IPCC, they have discretionary power to determine the nature of the investigation and whether it is conducted by the police, the IPCC or by the police under the supervision or management of the IPCC.

Complaints against members of NCIS and NCS

PA 1997 placed the National Criminal Intelligence Service (NCIS) on a statutory footing and created a new organisation; the National Crime Squad (NCS).

PA 1997 (as amended by PRA 2002) empowers the Secretary of State to make regulations for the handling of complaints about the conduct of members of both NCIS and NCS, the recording of matters of misconduct, and the investigation of such complaints and matters.

PA 1997, ss 39(1), 83(1) as amended by PRA 2002, s.25

The Police (Complaints and Misconduct) Regulations 2004 came into force on April 1, 2004 and provide that Pt II of the PRA 2002 shall apply equally to members of NCIS and NCS as to other police officers.

P(C&M)R 2004, reg. 29

Under the regulations: any reference to a "police authority" shall apply to the Service Authorities of NCIS and NCS; any reference to a "chief officer" shall apply to the Director Generals of NCIS and NCS; and any reference to a "person serving with the police" shall apply to members of NCIS and NCS.

P(C&M)R 2004, reg. 29

INFORMAL COMPLAINTS—PRACTICE AND PROCEDURE

Occasions will arise when the adviser must consider whether an informal complaint should be made whilst the suspect is still in the police station. There may only be a need to "complain" in the general sense of the word rather than registering a formal complaint. On such occasions the options open to him are as follows:

(1) Making representations

It may be appropriate to make oral representations when the matter being complained of is of a relatively minor nature: it may often be due to a genuine oversight or misunderstanding by the police. Such matters may include the withholding of refreshments for the suspect or questioning in interview which is in danger of becoming overly aggressive.

Representations about such behaviour may be made to any officer involved in the investigation or the custody officer, as appropriate.

If the activity complained of involves the breach of any PACE 1984 provision then the representations should refer to this and the possible consequences (refer to the section **'PACE 1984 provisions for the exclusion of evidence'** below).

(2) Requesting the custody officer to make a note

As an alternative to or in addition to making oral representations, the adviser may ask the custody officer to note the complaint in the custody record.

This can only be a request: neither the suspect nor his adviser has any right to dictate such matters to the custody officer.

(3) Requesting the presence of an officer of higher rank

If a complaint has been made but remains unresolved then the adviser should consider making a request for a meeting with the officer in charge of the station or another senior officer and, if granted, making representations to him. If the officer refuses to take remedial action, he should be asked at least to make a full record of the complaint.

Again, there is no legal right and thus one can only request such a meeting.

(4) Making a full contemporaneous note

Whether or not any other action is taken, the adviser should always take a full contemporaneous note of any instructions from a suspect involving a complaint about his treatment or of any such matters witnessed by the adviser at first hand. Similarly, any remedial action taken or attempted should be noted contemporaneously.

FORMAL COMPLAINTS—PRACTICE AND PROCEDURE

A formal complaint under PRA 2002 can be lodged either before or after departing from the police station. Careful consideration must be given before embarking on this course.

When to complain

A formal complaint against the police or their employees may be lodged whilst the suspect is still in police custody, immediately after the granting of bail but before departing from the police station or at any time thereafter.

What to complain about

Any actions of an individual police officer (or police employee) may be made subject of a complaint. This is the case whether or not the activity complained about is a criminal act or a civil tort, and whether or not it is in breach of PACE 1984 or its Codes of Practice.

Who can complain?

Any person can lodge a complaint, whether or not they are the victim: thus, an adviser can lodge the complaint on behalf of the suspect if he has the suspect's written consent. The adviser is also able to lodge a complaint in his personal capacity if he considers that he has been the victim of police misconduct.

PRA 2002, s.12(1)

How to lodge a complaint

The complaint may be lodged orally or in writing, although the latter is preferable. It may be made to the IPCC, the relevant police authority or the Chief of Police. If made at the police station, it should be addressed to the "Chief Officer of Police' but may be lodged with any officer. It is usually advisable to lodge it with the custody officer or the officer in charge of the police station

How a complaint is dealt with

If the complainant is still in police custody then a record must be made of the complaint, together with any relevant remarks by the custody officer. In addition, a report must be made as soon as practicable to an officer of the rank of inspector or above who is independent of the investigation.

PACE 1984, Code C, para. 9.2, 9.15(a)

The procedures as explained in the previous sections on the law will then come into operation.

Results of an investigation

The process of "local resolution" established by the PRA 2002 has replaced the earlier informal resolution process as under the PA 1996. Complaints that are not of serious misconduct or any other serious matter will be dealt with by way of local investigation and local resolution. The vast majority of complaints will be subject to local handling, or will be subsequently withdrawn by the complainant or will be found to be unsubstantiated. However, when a complaint is upheld, those found to be culpable will be dealt with either by way of internal disciplinary measures or by way of prosecution.

Ex gratia payments can be made to the complainant but these are rare.

Whether to complain

The decision whether or not to lodge a formal complaint is always a difficult one. This is particularly the case when advising a suspect whilst he is still in police custody.

Unless the adviser is lodging a complaint on his own behalf, it should be remembered that the decision remains that of the suspect, although he will invariably look to his adviser for guidance.

In so advising, one should have in mind the following considerations:

(a) Other remedies

Other remedies may exist; if so, it should be decided whether a formal complaint is likely to assist or interfere with these. So, for example, if a civil action against the police is contemplated then some would argue that an omission to lodge a formal complaint at the earliest opportunity has an adverse effect upon such proceedings. On the other hand, others would argue that the greater risk lies in lodging a complaint which is likely to be found to be unsubstantiated.

(b) Support for a future defence

The immediate lodging of a formal complaint may assist future court proceedings. So, for example, if a suspect's defence involves an allegation that evidence was planted upon him by police then this may gain added credence if a complaint in these terms is immediately lodged whilst the suspect is still in police custody.

(c) Police obligations under the Police Reform Act 2002

PRA 2002, Sch. 3, para. 2

Upon the lodging of a complaint, the police are under an obligation to obtain or preserve evidence relating to the conduct complained of.

This may be important, for example, if it is suspected that the fingerprints of an officer are present upon "planted" evidence.

(d) Fear of repercussions

The suspect may fear that if he is to remain detained after the lodging of a complaint then he will fall victim to a police campaign of harassment or even violence whilst in detention. Alternatively, he may be concerned that the complaint will adversely affect the police decision on bail.

(e) Risk of being charged

The lodging of a complaint may increase the risk that the suspect will be charged. This may be a concern about simple vindictiveness on the part of the police or a concern that the police will feel a need to charge the suspect as a defensive measure once the complaint has been lodged. For example, it is often feared that if a complaint involves an allegation of assault, the police will themselves charge the suspect with assault in order that they can subsequently argue that they were acting in self-defence.

NB: The risks inherent in (d) and (e) above may be allayed by the lodging of a complaint immediately after the suspect has been released from custody but prior to his departure from the police station.

(f) Putting the police on prior notice

The making of a complaint may put the police on prior notice of issues to be raised during future criminal proceedings.

If in any doubt the suspect should be advised to consider delaying lodging a formal complaint at this stage. This will give time for more considered thought, as the suspect can always lodge a complaint at a later time.

Request by police to interview complainant

If a complaint is lodged whilst the complainant is still in the police station then he may be asked to be interviewed about it.

It is generally thought inadvisable to agree to such an interview at this time, unless there are clear and positive reasons to do so. One should simply ask the officer to put his request in writing and send this to the adviser in order that the matter can be properly considered.

It should be recalled that there is no obligation on the police to investigate a complaint as soon as it has been made.

Medical examinations

If the complaint involves allegations of assault, the police are under an obligation to call an appropriate health-care professional as soon as is practicable.

PACE 1984, Code C, para. 9.2

However, the complainant is under no obligation to agree to any medical examination. There may be a concern that a police health-care professional lacks the necessary objectivity.

An alternative course is for the adviser to call out an independent doctor. Any fees thereby incurred may be reclaimed

GCC 2004, Pt C, para. 1.18

under the General Criminal Contract as a disbursement if considered in the best interests of the client and reasonably incurred.

A further option is for the complainant to be advised to visit either his own GP or a hospital casualty department immediately after release.

OTHER COMPLAINT PROCEDURES

Breach of the Police and Criminal Evidence Act 1984 Codes of Practice

PACE 1984, s.67(10)–(11)

PACE 1984 specifies that, whilst any breach of the PACE 1984 Codes of Practice does not in itself render an officer liable either to criminal or civil proceedings, the Codes of Practice themselves and hence any breach of them are admissible as evidence in either criminal or civil proceedings

Criminal prosecutions

The police are of course subject to the criminal law themselves. However, no public funding is available for a private prosecution and police prosecutions against their own are not only rare but have a significantly low success rate.

Civil proceedings

Civil proceedings against the police are not common but have the advantage over a criminal prosecution, to the extent that:

(a) public funding is potentially available to the complainant;

(b) the complainant will only have to prove his case "on the balance of probabilities"; and

(c) the complainant, if successful, will be awarded damages.

Police and Criminal Evidence Act 1984 provisions for the exclusion of evidence

In many ways the main deterrent against police impropriety is the awareness that such behaviour will become the subject of complaint in any future trial, such complaint most commonly falling under the mantle of an application for the exclusion of improperly obtained evidence.

The adviser may choose to refer to such a possibility either explicitly or implicitly whilst registering a complaint in the police station. For this reason, it is important for the adviser to be aware of the relevant PACE 1984 provisions and the methods whereby evidence obtained by the police may subsequently be excluded during criminal proceedings. In summary form, the key points are:

(a) **A breach of PACE 1984 or its Codes of Practice** does not automatically render evidence thereby obtained inadmissible. Conversely, evidence may be held to be inadmissible even in instances where there was no breach of PACE 1984 or its Codes of Practice.

R. v Beycan [1990] Crim. L.R.185

(b) **The adviser should intervene** and either attempt to remedy any impropriety or at least put on record his objection to it whilst in the police station. Thus, for example, if the adviser is of the view that a police officer is behaving oppressively during the questioning of a suspect, he should record his objection to this during the interview itself and ask the officer to desist from any further such behaviour. This will of course support any subsequent legal argument *vis-à-vis* the admissibility of evidence.

(c) **Taking contemporaneous notes** of any behaviour, which may later give rise to complaint, is of the utmost importance. There is always the possibility that the adviser may be called as a material witness during an application for the exclusion of evidence in forthcoming proceedings.

(d) **PACE 1984, s.76(2)** provides for the exclusion of confession evidence in certain circumstances. For further details, refer to the **Interviews under Caution** index heading.

R. v Wahab and Cromer (2003) 1 Cr.App.R.15

(e) **PACE 1984, s.78(1)** provides for the exclusion of any evidence if the court considers that its inclusion will adversely affect the fairness of the proceedings. As this section covers any type of evidence, an application for the exclusion of confession evidence may be made under either PACE 1984 s.76(2) or s.78(1) or under both sections.

Thompson v R [1998] 2 W.L.R. 927

(f) **The common law** power of the courts to exclude evidence at their discretion is specifically preserved by PACE 1984. This provision of course covers not only evidence obtained by the police but also other rules of evidence on matters such as hearsay.

PACE 1984, s.82(3); *R. v Smurthwaite and Gill* (1994) 98 Cr.App.R.437

Custody Records

THE LAW

The custody officer is responsible for ensuring that all detainees at a police station are dealt with in accordance with PACE 1984 and the Codes of Practice issued thereunder. The custody officer must open a custody record for each person detained at the police station as soon as practicable and it is his sole responsibility to make sure that all relevant matters are recorded accurately.

PACE 1984, s.39(1)
PACE 1984, Code C, paras 2.1, 2.3

What must be recorded?

Under PACE 1984, a number of different matters, should they occur, must be recorded on the custody record:

(a) When **authorising the detention** of a suspect who has been arrested but not yet charged, the reason for that detention must be recorded. — PACE 1984, s.37(4)

(b) If a suspect is to be **detained for longer than 24 hours**, the reason for the extension of the detention period must be recorded. — PACE 1984, s.42(5)(b)

(c) When a suspect is authorised for **detention after charge**, the reason for the detention must be recorded in his presence unless he is incapable of understanding what is said, violent, likely to become violent or in urgent need of medical attention. — PACE 1984, s.38(3)–(5)

(d) If a **review of detention is postponed**, a record must be made of the reason for that postponement. — PACE 1984, s.40(7)

(e) If a suspect **requests legal advice**, the time of that request must be recorded. — PACE 1984, s.58(2)

(f) If there is to be a **delay in access to legal advice**, the reason for that delay must be recorded. — PACE 1984, s.58(9)

(g) If there is a **delay** in allowing the suspect to **contact friends or family**, the reason must be noted. — PACE 1984, s.56(6)

(h) If any **samples**, whether intimate or non-intimate, are taken, the appropriate information must be recorded on the custody record. — PACE 1984, ss 62(7)–(8), 63(8)–(9)

(i) Details of the **items in the possession of the suspect** on arrival at the police station **may** be recorded on the — PACE 1984, s.54(1)–(2);

CJA 2003, s.8

custody record. It is for the custody officer to decide whether or not to make any such record.

PRACTICE AND PROCEDURE

Record keeping and the role of the custody officer

The manner in which custody records are maintained and the role of the custody officer is set out in some detail in para. 2 of PACE, Code C.

PACE 1984, Code C, para. 2.1

(a) A **separate custody record** must be opened for each person brought to the police station under arrest or who is arrested at the police station having attended voluntarily. No record need be opened for a person who remains a volunteer throughout his time at the police station.

PACE 1984, Code C, paras 1.1A, 2.1, Note for Guidance 1H

(b) Any information to be recorded in the custody record must be so **recorded as soon as practicable**. If there is any justifiable delay in the custody officer carrying out any of the functions specified in the PACE 1984 Codes of Practice, he must indicate on the custody record when the delay has occurred and the reason for it.

PACE 1984, Code C, para. 2.6–2.6A, Note for Guidance 2A

(c) All entries in the custody record must be **timed and signed** by the maker. If the custody record is made on a computer, the entries should contain the identification of the maker. However, the identity of the maker (or any other member of police staff) need not be recorded or disclosed in terrorism enquiries or when there are other reasonable grounds for fearing disclosure will put the person at risk. In such cases the individual shall merely record their warrant or other ID number and name of their police station.

PACE 1984, Code C, para. 2.2

(d) Where any action requires the authority of an officer of a **specified rank**, his name and rank must be noted on the custody record unless the suspect is held in a terrorism enquiry, in which case a warrant or other identification number and the officer's station will suffice.

PACE 1984, Code C, para. 2.3

(e) Although the custody officer is not necessarily the maker of every entry on the custody record, it is his sole responsibility to ensure that the custody record is **accurate and complete**.

(f) If the suspect is **transferred** to another police station, a copy of the custody record must accompany the suspect showing the reason for and time of the transfer.

PACE 1984, Code C, para. 2.3

(g) The **legal representative or appropriate adult must be allowed to consult the custody record** of the detained suspect as soon as practicable after having arrived at the police station.

PACE 1984, Code C, para. 2.4

(h) When a suspect leaves police detention or is taken before a court from police custody, a **copy** of his custody record must be **supplied** to him or his legal representative or appropriate adult on request as soon as practicable; such entitlement lasts for 12 months.

PACE 1984, Code C, para. 2.4A

(i) If a request on reasonable notice is made by the suspect, his legal representative or appropriate adult to **view the original** custody record after release from police detention, that request should be complied with and a note made of the inspection in the custody record.

PACE 1984, Code C, para. 2.5

(j) Should anyone **refuse to sign** the custody record when asked to do so in accordance with the provisions of the PACE 1984 Codes of Practice, the time and fact of that refusal must be noted on the custody record.

PACE 1984, Code C, para. 2.7

OTHER MATTERS TO BE RECORDED

PACE Codes C and D detail a number of matters which must be recorded in addition to those specified in the Act itself. Even when the Code does not specify that a particular record should be on the custody record, it is invariably the case that the custody record is used for such purposes:

(a) Any **comment** made by the suspect in relation to the account given by the **arresting officer** should be noted, although he shall not invite comment on it. The custody officer shall also inform the suspect of the **grounds on which detention has been authorised** as soon as practicable and shall note the grounds and any **comment** the suspect may make, without inviting any such comment.

PACE 1984, Code C, paras 3.4, 3.17

(b) The signature of the suspect confirming **receipt of notice of his rights** whilst in police detention must be obtained.

PACE 1984, Code C, para. 3.2

(c) The signature of the suspect on initial detention indicating whether **legal advice is requested** or whether he wishes to have **someone informed of his detention** at this stage needs to be obtained. If legal advice is refused, the suspect will be asked for his reasons for so doing and, if given, those reasons must be recorded on the custody record.

(d) It is for the custody officer to determine whether a record should be made of **property** the suspect had with him or was taken from him on arrest. If such a record is made, its existence and whereabouts should be noted on the custody record. Any refusal of the suspect to sign the property record should also be recorded and, if the suspect is not allowed to keep any item of clothing or personal effects, the reasons for this must be recorded.

(e) Details must be noted of any **complaint** made by or on behalf of a suspect regarding his treatment since arrest or request for **medical attention**. If it otherwise comes to the officer's notice that a detainee may have been treated improperly or requires medical attention, this must also be noted. Details made for any medical examination, any resulting clinical directions and advice and/or any relevant remarks by the custody officer must also be recorded. Any information about the cause of any injury, ailment or condition is not required to be recorded on the custody record if it appears capable of providing evidence of an offence.

(f) Details shall be recorded of any **medication** that the suspect has in their possession on arrival at the police station together with a note of any such medication they claim to need but do not have with them. Responses received when **attempting to rouse** a person following the Code C, Annex H procedure must also be recorded to ascertain whether clinical treatment is required.

(g) On a **review** of the detention of a suspect, a note must be made of the reminder of the right to legal advice given by the reviewing officer, any grounds for and the extent of any delay in the review, full details of any telephone reviews and the outcome of each review and any application for a **warrant of further detention**.

(h) Whenever the suspect is **not in the custody of the custody officer**, the time and reasons must be recorded. Similarly, if an interview has taken place in a **location other than an interview room** then the details and reasons for this must be recorded.

PACE 1984, Code C, paras 3.5, 6.5

(i) As far as **access to legal advice** is concerned, any request for such advice and the action taken following such a request should be noted. If a legal adviser attends at the police station (either as a result of a request from a third party or otherwise), the arrival of the adviser and whether the suspect wishes to see him should be recorded and the suspect invited to sign the entry.

PACE 1984, Code C, paras 4.4–4.5

(j) If an **interview is started without the legal representative** despite the suspect's request for legal advice then this should be recorded in the **interview record**.

(k) If an **urgent interview of a vulnerable suspect** is conducted under the provisions of para. 11.18 of Code C, the grounds for so doing must be recorded.

(l) If an inspector **refuses access to or excludes from any interview an accredited or probationary representative**, this fact must be noted on the custody record.

PACE 1984, Code C, paras 9.2, 9.5, 9.8, 9.15, 9.16 and Note for Guidance 9G

(m) If a suspect requests that **someone be notified** of his arrest, that request should be noted, together with details of any communications made or received.

(n) In relation to **juvenile and other vulnerable suspects**, details of any special action taken must be recorded, including any action in relation to calling an interpreter. If a juvenile is kept in a cell, the reasons must be noted.

(o) The decision of a **juvenile** suspect not to have an appropriate adult present at an **intimate search** should be recorded.

PACE 1984, Code C, paras 9.15(f), 9.17 and Note for Guidance 9H

(p) If an **intimate search** is undertaken, a record should be made of the parts of the body searched, the person carrying out the search (if this was a police officer, the reason why it was impracticable for a medically qualified person to carry out the search), who was present, the reasons for the search and the results of it.

PACE 1984, Code C, paras 15.12–15.16

(q) The reasons for, persons present and result of a **strip search** should be noted on the custody record.

PACE 1984, Code C, paras 12.10–12.11

(r) Records must be kept of **meals** and any **replacement clothing** offered to the suspect; the reasons why **a juvenile suspect** has been put in a cell; and any use of **restraints** on a suspect whilst in a cell, the reasons for it and, if appropriate, the arrangements for the enhanced supervision of the detainee whilst restrained.

PACE 1984, Code C, paras 6.15–6.16 and Annex B, para. 4

(s) In relation to **identification procedures**, if it is considered **impracticable** to hold an identification parade or video identification despite a request from the suspect, the reasons for this must be noted.

(t) The **refusal** of a suspect to **consent** to any of the various forms of **identification procedures** should be recorded.

PACE 1984, Code C, para. 6.17

PACE 1984, Code C, para. 11.20

(u) As regards the taking of **fingerprints**; a record must be made with reasons if they were taken without consent; if it was the case, that force was used and those present; and confirmation that the suspect has been informed that their fingerprints may be subject of a "speculative search".

PACE 1984, Code C, para. 6.14

PACE 1984, Code C, para. 5.8

(v) A record must be made when a suspect is **searched, examined or photographed**. The record must include details of those carrying out the search, etc. the purpose and outcome, whether the suspect consented and if he did not the reasons why he was searched, etc. without consent, and the circumstances of any force used and details of those who were present.

PACE 1984, Code C, paras 3.24, 8.10

PACE 1984, Code C, Annex A, para. 5

(w) In relation to any **non-intimate samples**, a note must be made of the reasons for taking it and that the suspect consented. In those cases where force can be used if consent is not forthcoming, the circumstances and those persons present must be recorded. A record must also be made of the giving of the warning that any samples taken may be subject of a "speculative search".

PACE 1984, Code C, Annex A, paras 7, 8

PACE 1984, Code C, Annex A, para. 12

(x) In relation to any **intimate samples**, the fact that the suspect has been reminded of his right to legal advice before the taking of a sample must be recorded. A record must also be made of the reasons for the taking of the sample, and that the suspect was given the warning that refusal of consent to the taking of an intimate sample may harm his case at any trial and that any samples taken may be subject of a "speculative search".

PRACTICAL GUIDANCE

(1) Suspect's property

PACE 1984, Code C, paras 8.9–8.11

Section 8 of CJA 2003 amended s.54 of PACE 1984 by removing the previous requirement that the custody officer "record or cause to be recorded" the suspect's property.

The new obligation is for the custody officer merely to "ascertain" what property the suspect has without necessarily recording it and, if he chooses to record it, the record only "may" be part of the custody record (although, if it is not, its existence and whereabouts should be noted on the custody record—see (d) above).

PACE 1984, Code D, para. 3.26

PACE 1984, Code D, para. 3.27

PACE 1984, Code D, paras 4.8–4.9

The adviser must be alert to the possibility that the police have seized property from the suspect that is either of significant monetary/emotional value, or is of potential evidential value. In any of these circumstances the adviser should either ensure that the items are recorded accurately by the police or, if this is not possible, that he has made his own comprehensive record.

(2) Examination of the custody record

PACE 1984, Code D, paras 5.17, 5.18

The PACE 1984 Codes of Practice afford the legal adviser the right to see the custody record on his arrival at the police station. This right should be taken advantage of in every case, because the custody record provides the most important documentary history of the suspect's detention in the police station. It contains information vital to the proper representation of the suspect during his time in police detention.

PACE 1984, Code D, paras 6.10–6.12

The adviser should try to get as much information from the police prior to advising the suspect as possible. Therefore, if the officer in the case is less than forthcoming, sight of the custody record can provide the adviser with great assistance in understanding the police view of the case.

(3) Requests for entries to be made on the custody record

PACE 1984, Code D, paras 6.3, 6.11, 6.12

Although there is no right to have an entry made in the custody record, many custody officers will record representations made by the adviser. This can be a very useful tool in the armoury of the adviser, as it may have a significant effect at any later trial. The mere request for representations to be recorded on the custody record can and sometimes does result in the custody officer reconsidering certain decisions.

It is important for the adviser to keep his own note of all requests for entries to be made on the custody record, in particular if that request is refused.

(4) Copies of the custody record

A copy of the custody record should always be requested if the suspect is subsequently charged or a summons issued against him, as it can assist greatly in the preparation of the suspect's case.

(5) Do the doctor's notes form part of the custody record?

The Code states that if a health care professional has not recorded their clinical findings on the custody record it must be stated on the record where they are recorded.

Often a health care professional will record their findings on a separate document (the "Book 83" in London) and it is unlikely that these notes will form part of the custody record in their entirety and may not be disclosable as of right to the adviser. Generally, however, these notes are disclosed to the adviser with the custody record.

Clearly the health care professional's notes ought to be seen by the adviser as they may contain information about the suspect's state of physical or mental health which could be of great assistance in dealing with and advising him.

PACE 1984, Code C, para. 2.4

If the custody officer shows the adviser the custody record but refuses to show the notes made by the health care professional following any medical examination, the adviser should enquire as to the reasons for the reluctance to disclose the notes. If the custody officer says that they are confidential to the suspect, the adviser should obtain written authority from the suspect to allow disclosure of the health care professional's notes to the adviser.

Detention Periods and Reviews

INTRODUCTION

PACE 1984 provides a statutory mechanism to control the periods of time suspects can be detained in a police station (detention periods) and a system whereby their detention is regularly monitored (detention reviews).

CJA 2003 (by amending the relevant sections of PACE 1984) has modified the procedures by providing for the use of telephones in conducting reviews of police detention and, most significantly, allowed for the extension of the maximum period of detention from 24 hours to 36 hours for *all arrestable offences* (as opposed to the previous law that was limited to *serious* arrestable offences).

CJA 2003, ss 6–7

DETENTION PERIODS BEFORE CHARGE—THE "RELEVANT TIME"

Definition

The period during which a suspect can be detained by the police prior either to a charge being brought or to his release is calculated from the commencement of the "relevant time". This is defined as the earlier of either the time the suspect arrived at the relevant police station or 24 hours after his arrest.

PACE 1984, s.41(2)(a)

In calculating a suspect's period of detention before charge, time will generally run continuously from the commencement of the "relevant time".

Provisos

These rules are subject to a number of provisos:

(a) If a suspect has been **arrested outside of either England or Wales** then the "relevant time" is the earlier of either:

PACE 1984, s.41(2)(b)

(i) his time of arrival at the first police station within the area of England or Wales in which the offence for which he has been arrested is being investigated; or
(ii) 24 hours after the time of his entry into England or Wales.

PACE 1984, s.4l(2)(c)

(b) If a suspect initially attended at the police station as **a volunteer** and he was later arrested, the "relevant time" is the time of his arrest.

PACE 1984, s.4l(2)(ca)

(c) If a suspect attends a police station in answer to "**street bail**" granted under PACE 1984, s.30A, the "relevant time" is the time of his arrival at the police station.

PACE 1984, s.4l(3)

(d) If a suspect has been **arrested in police area 1 for an offence for which his arrest is sought in police area 2** then the "relevant time" is the earlier of either his time of arrival at the first police station in police area 2 or 24 hours after his arrest. This applies provided that the suspect has not been questioned in police area 1 in order to obtain evidence in relation to the offence: if he has been so questioned then this proviso does not apply and the normal rules remain operative.

PACE 1984, s.4l(5)

(e) If a suspect has been **detained in police area 1 and his arrest in relation to another offence is sought in police area 2** and he is then taken to police area 2, the "relevant time" is the earlier of either the time of his arrival at the first police station in police area 2 or 24 hours after leaving the police station in police area 1. This applies provided that no questions have been asked of the suspect in police area 1 to obtain evidence in relation to the offence: if he has been so questioned then this proviso does not apply and the normal rules remain operative.

PACE 1984, s.41(4)

(f) If a suspect has been detained in respect of one offence and is then subsequently **rearrested in respect of another offence** under PACE 1984, s.3l then the "relevant time" remains the same as for the original offence. This means that a subsequent arrest cannot be used as a device to prolong the maximum period of detention prior to charge.

PACE 1984, s.4l(6)

(g) If a suspect, subsequent to his detention, is then **removed to a hospital** for medical treatment then the time spent travelling to and from the hospital and in the hospital does not count in calculating the period of his detention—except for any time spent during these periods questioning the suspect in order to obtain evidence.

PACE1984, s.47(6)–(7)

(h) If a suspect has been **released on bail** with a duty to return to the police station under PACE 1984, s.47(3)(b) and is detained upon his return then, for the purposes of calculating the suspect's time in detention, the "relevant time" is that relating to his initial detention upon his first arrest, unless he is rearrested upon his return, in which case the "relevant time" is calculated from this subsequent arrest.

DETENTION PERIODS BEFORE CHARGE—THE LAW

Removal to a police station

If a suspect is arrested at a place other than a police station then he must be taken to a police station "as soon as practicable after the arrest" or be granted "street bail". However, this can be delayed if necessary to carry out reasonable investigations, such as a PACE 1984, s.32 search of premises. Where there is any such delay, the reasons for the delay must be recorded as soon as the suspect arrives at the police station.

PACE 1984, s.30(1), (10), (11)
R. v Khan [1993] Crim. L.R. 54
R. v Raphaie (1996) Crim. L.R. 812

If the police station to which the suspect has been taken is not a "designated" police station, he must be transferred to such a police station within six hours of his arrival.

PACE 1984, s.30(6)

Release or detention upon arrival at a police station

Once a suspect arrives at a police station the custody officer must determine whether there is sufficient evidence to charge the suspect with the offence for which he was arrested and may detain him for such a period as is necessary to enable him to so determine.

PACE 1984, s.37(1)

If such evidence exists then the custody officer must either charge the suspect or release the suspect without charge, either on or without bail.

PACE 1984, s.37(7)

If no such evidence exists then the custody officer must release the suspect, unless there are reasonable grounds to believe that his detention is necessary either to:

PACE 1984, s.37(2)

(a) secure or preserve evidence; or

(b) obtain such evidence by questioning.

In considering these obligations, the custody officer should be aware of three additional provisions:

(a) There is an overriding requirement that the custody officer release a suspect immediately he becomes aware that the grounds for detention have ceased to apply and that there are no other grounds to justify the suspect's detention.

PACE 1984, s.34(2)

PACE 1984, s.37(9)

(b) If a suspect is not in a fit state to be dealt with either by charge or by release then he may be detained until so fit. This provision may apply, for example, when a suspect is too intoxicated to understand the nature of the charge or release bail conditions.

PACE 1984, s.37(1)

(c) These requirements only apply in the instances when a suspect has been arrested in relation to "an offence". Thus, for example, they do not apply to individuals arrested under BA 1976, s.7, or those in breach of an injunction with a power of arrest attached, or escaped prisoners.

Detention for the first 24 hours

PACE 1984, ss 37(3), 41(1)

Once the custody officer has determined that the suspect's detention is necessary then he can be so detained upon the custody officer's authority for up to 24 hours from the "relevant time" without charge.

PACE 1984, s.37(4)–(6) and Code C, para. 1.8

The grounds for the detention must be advised to the suspect and a written record made of them as soon as is practicable in his presence. This requirement may be obviated if the suspect is incapable of understanding, violent or likely to become violent, or in urgent need of medical attention. In such circumstances, the appropriate explanation must be given as soon as practicable thereafter.

Extension of the first 24-hour detention

PACE 1984, s.42(1), CJA 2003, s.7

An officer of the rank of superintendent or above can extend the first 24-hour period of detention for a period or a sequence of periods totalling a further 12 hours if he has reasonable grounds for believing that:

R. v Chief Constable of Hertfordshire Ex p. Wiles (2002) EWHC 387

(a) it is necessary to secure or preserve evidence relating to an offence for which the suspect is under arrest or to obtain such evidence by questioning;

(b) it is an "arrestable offence"; and

(c) the investigation is being conducted diligently and expeditiously.

PACE 1984, s.42(4)

The first of any such extensions may be granted at any time after the second review of detention (see below) and before the expiry of 24 hours from the "relevant time".

If the officer grants such an extension then he must inform the suspect of the following:

(a) the grounds for the continued detention; and

PACE 1984, s.42(5)

(b) the suspect's right to have a friend or relative or other person known to him with an interest in his welfare advised as to his arrest, if he has not already exercised this right; and

PACE 1984, ss 42(9), 56(1)

(c) the suspect's right to legal advice, if he has not already exercised this right.

PACE 1984, ss 42(9), 58

The officer must record that he has performed these obligations in the custody record.

PACE 1984, s.42(5)(b)–(9)

Before the officer can authorise a further 12-hour extension, he must provide the suspect, or his solicitor if available, with the opportunity to make representations.

PACE 1984, s.42(6)–(8)

Warrants of further detention

Upon the application on oath by a constable supported by an information, a magistrates' court may issue a "warrant of further detention" authorising the suspect's detention in police custody beyond 36 hours from the "relevant time". Such a warrant can authorise a further period of detention of no longer than 36 hours (refer to the **Warrants of Further Detention** index heading).

PACE 1984, s.43

Expiry of authorised detention

Once the maximum time of properly authorised detention has expired, the suspect must either be charged or released, either on or without bail.

PACE 1984, ss 41(7), 42(10), 43(18)

DETENTION PERIODS BEFORE CHARGE—PRACTICE AND PROCEDURE

Representations against detention within the first 24 hours

The statutory obligation upon the custody officer to release a suspect once aware that the initial grounds for detention no longer apply and that no other grounds for detention exist should be read in conjunction with Code of Practice C. The code states that "all persons in custody must be dealt with expeditiously and released as soon as the need for detention has ceased to apply".

PACE 1984, Code C, para. 1.1

By referring to these provisions, the adviser can make representations at any time either to the investigating officer or the custody officer that the suspect should be released, if it can be argued that no proper grounds for detention exist.

It may be argued, for example that even if the police are behaving reasonably in their belief that they are seeking to secure or preserve evidence or are endeavouring to obtain it by questioning, the detention is not "necessary" for them to do so, as required by PACE 1984, s.37(2). Alternatively, it may be argued that, as the suspect will not be answering police questions in interview, there is no prospect of the police obtaining evidence by questioning and to continue a detention for this purpose alone is improper and may amount to oppressive treatment rendering as inadmissible evidence subsequently obtained.

The PACE 1984, s.37(7) obligation upon the custody officer either to charge a suspect or to release him once there is "sufficient evidence to charge" may also be used in such representations. It may be possible to argue that sufficient evidence exists for the suspect to be charged and that nothing can be gained in this respect by further questioning or by further detention for any other reason.

However, it should be noted that the officers are under no statutory obligation to consider any such representations unless they are made either at the point when an extension of the time for detention beyond 24 hours is being considered or at the time of a detention review (see below).

PACE 1984, s.42(6)–(8); *Re An Application for a Warrant of Further Detention* [1988] Crim L.R. 296

Representations against detention beyond 24 hours

The suspect, or his legal adviser if available, has the right to make representations at the time when an extension of the period of detention beyond the first 24 hours is being considered.

PACE 1984, Code C, Note for Guidance 15C

If the suspect is likely to be asleep when such a decision would otherwise be taken then the process should be brought forward to enable such representations to be made.

PACE 1984, s.42(7)

Such representations can either be made orally or in writing. They should include, as appropriate, argument that:

(a) the detention is not "necessary" as required by PACE 1984, s.37(2) to secure, preserve or obtain evidence;

HOC 60/2003, para. 4.4

(b) Home Office Guidelines make it clear that the power should only be used *"sparingly and only where there is full justification"*;

(c) the offence(s) being investigated are not "arrestable offences";

(d) the investigation is not being conducted expeditiously, as required by Code C, para. 1.1;

(e) sufficient evidence now exists with which a decision can be made either to charge or to release the suspect either on or without bail, under PACE 1984, s.37(7);

(f) a detention otherwise than in accordance with PACE Pt IV is unlawful and amounts to false imprisonment; or

(g) if the time of detention is to be extended then this must not be for a period longer than that necessary for the purpose for which the extension is being sought.

Robets v C. C. of Cheshire Constabulary, The Times, January 27, 1999

DETENTION PERIODS AFTER CHARGE—THE LAW

Release or detention

Once a suspect has been charged, the custody officer must order his release, either on or without bail, unless one of the specifically defined exceptions applies.

PACE 1984, s.38(1)

For non-juveniles, these exceptions are:

(a) the suspect's name and address cannot be ascertained or the custody officer has reasonable grounds for doubting whether such details as supplied by the suspect are *bona fide*;

(b) the custody officer has reasonable grounds for believing that the suspect will fail to appear in court to answer to bail;

(c) when the suspect has been arrested for an imprisonable offence, the custody officer has reasonable grounds for believing that the suspect's detention is necessary to prevent him from committing an offence;

(d) when the suspect has been arrested for a non-imprisonable offence, the custody officer has reasonable grounds for believing that the suspect's detention is necessary to prevent him from causing physical injury to any other person or from causing loss of or damage to property;

PACE 1984, s.38(1)(a)–(iiia); CJPOA 1994, s.28(1)–(2)

(e) the custody officer has reasonable grounds for believing that the suspect's detention is necessary to prevent him from interfering with the administration of justice or with the investigation of offences or of a particular offence;

(f) the custody officer has reasonable grounds for believing that the suspect's detention is necessary for his own protection; or

(g) the custody officer has reasonable grounds for believing that the suspect's detention is necessary to enable a sample to be taken from him under PACE 1984, s.63B. In this particular case, the detention may not extend beyond 6 hours after the suspect has been charged.

For juveniles, these exceptions are:

PACE 1984, s.38(1)(b)

(a) any of the above; and

(b) the custody officer has reasonable grounds for believing that the suspect ought to be detained in his own interests.

CJPOA 1994, s.25

Suspects charged with murder, attempted murder, manslaughter, rape or attempted rape cannot be released on bail other than in exceptional circumstances if they have a previous conviction for any such offence.
For further discussion of issues relating to the grant of police bail, refer to the **Bail** index heading.

The authorising of detention

PACE 1984, s.38(2)

Once the custody officer has decided that one of the above exceptions applies, he is entitled to authorise that the suspect be kept in police detention prior to his being produced before a magistrates' court.

Time limits for detention

PACE 1984, s.46(2); *R. v Avon Magistrates' Courts' Committee, Ex p. Broome* [1988] 1 W.L.R. 1246

If the suspect is to be produced before a magistrates' court in the local justice area in which the police station at which he was charged is situated then the suspect must be brought before such a court as soon as is practicable after charge and no later than the first sitting after charge.

PACE 1984, s.46(4)

If, however, the suspect is to be brought before a magistrates' court in any other local justice area, then he must be removed to that area as soon as is practicable and brought before such a court as soon as practicable after his arrival in the area and no later than the first sitting after his arrival.

PACE 1984, s.46(5)–(8)

If no magistrates' court for the relevant area is due to sit within the following 24 hours then special procedures are laid down under which the clerk to the justices must arrange for an extraordinary court to so sit within 24 hours (excluding Sundays, Christmas Day and Good Friday).

None of the normal time limits within which a detained suspect must be brought before a magistrates' court applies if he is in hospital and is not well enough to appear before the court.

PACE 1984, s.46(9)

DETENTION PERIODS AFTER CHARGE—PRACTICE AND PROCEDURE

The right to make representations

When deciding whether to release a suspect on bail after charge, the custody officer is obliged to "have regard to the same considerations as those which a court is required to have regard to in taking the corresponding decisions" when deciding whether any of the exceptions to the normal BA 1976 "right to bail" apply.

PACE 1984, s.38(2); CJPOA 1994, s.28(3)

The court's "considerations" will include defence representations; this means that the suspect or his legal adviser has the right to make full representations to the custody officer before it is decided whether to grant police bail after charge.

Representations

In making representations that a suspect should be released after charge, the adviser should include, as appropriate, argument that:

(a) none of the PACE 1984, s.38 exceptions apply;

(b) whilst the officer in the case may be arguing that one or more of the exceptions do apply, his belief in such is not a "reasonable" one as is required; or

(c) any residual concerns can be allayed by the imposition of suitable bail conditions.

In contentious cases, the adviser must be prepared to put forward as strong and as comprehensive an argument as would be put forward in a full magistrates' court application for bail.

For further guidance on this topic, refer to the **Bail** index heading.

DETENTION PERIODS—PRACTICAL GUIDANCE

When representing a suspect in police detention, it is of vital importance that the legal adviser be fully conversant with the rules governing detention periods and the manner in which representations can be made. The following suggestions may assist.

(1) The detention timetable

As soon as is practicable after arrival at the police station, the "relevant time" should be ascertained and noted: if possible, one should ensure that this time agrees with that in the custody officer's record. Thereafter, a checklist of the future key/trigger times should be prepared and kept under constant review during the suspect's period in police detention. This will assist in ensuring that the suspect is released if a detention period time limit expires prior to it being properly extended.

(2) The meaning of "periods of time"

PACE 1984, s.45(2)

PACE 1984 specifies that any reference to a "period of time" is to be treated as "approximate only".

This is generally interpreted to mean that one should not argue over seconds or minutes in calculating the passage of time, such as during a period of detention. However, any such problems should be avoided if one has agreed the start of the "relevant time" with the custody officer at the outset.

(3) Unlawful detention

Roberts v C.C. of Cheshire Constabulary, The Times, January 27, 1999; *R. v Davison* [1988] Crim L.R. 44

In making any representations to a custody officer in respect of the period for which it is proposed to detain the suspect, it may be helpful to emphasise that an unlawful detention, which will include a detention when there are no proper grounds to justify it, may give rise to the civil torts of false imprisonment and trespass to the person.

An extended detention may also give rise to challenge under the HRA 1998 on the basis that the detention period is disproportionate to the seriousness of the offence and in breach of the suspect's rights under Art. 5 either to be brought promptly before a judge following arrest and detention, or to challenge detention after charge speedily.

In such representations it may assist to emphasise the point that evidence obtained during an unlawful detention may be held to be inadmissible in any resulting court proceedings.

(4) Absence from the police station

If the adviser is concerned that the initial 24-hour period of detention is to be extended under PACE 1984, s.42 during his absence from the police station, then he should ask that the custody record be endorsed with his request that he be contacted prior to the necessary authorisation being considered, allowing sufficient time for him either to return to make representations in person or to make representations by telephone, such representations being proper under PACE 1984, s.42(6)–(8).

The alternative means of dealing with this situation is by the leaving of written representations prior to one's departure from the police station; however, this is a less satisfactory option and should only be used as a last resort.

(5) Keeping the suspect informed

It is important to keep the suspect fully appraised of his situation: this should include a general explanation as to the maximum periods he can be detained prior to charge and after charge, his right to make representations and when, *etc.*

This, of course, is no more than proper solicitor/client conduct but one cannot emphasise too highly that the fear of unlimited detention in police custody is often the most worrying aspect of detention for a suspect—particularly one unacquainted with police powers and procedures.

(6) When time runs

Remember that, when calculating a suspect's period of detention, time "runs" from the relevant time but, when a detention period is to be formally reviewed, time "runs" from the time the detention was authorised.

PACE 1984, ss 40(3), 41(2)

DETENTION REVIEWS—INTRODUCTION

PACE 1984 provides a system of mandatory "reviews" of a suspect's detention in police custody, whether or not he has been charged with an offence.

The only persons to whom such reviews do not apply are:

(a) volunteers;

(b) those removed to a police station as a "place of safety" under MHA 1983; and

(c) those arrested for something other than an offence, for example a person arrested under a fine default warrant or an escaped prisoner.

REVIEWS PRIOR TO CHARGE—THE LAW

The timing of reviews

PACE 1984, s.37(1)–(3)

In calculating when detention reviews fall due, the starting point is the time that the suspect's detention was first "authorised" by the custody officer. This may be different to the "relevant time", often being slightly later.

PACE 1984, s.40(3)(a)

The first review must be no later than six hours from this time and second and subsequent reviews must be carried out no later than nine hours from the time of the immediately preceding review.

PACE 1984, s.40(3)(b)–(c)

These reviews must continue during any period of the suspect's detention prior to charge.

The reviewing officer

PACE 1984, s.40(l)

The reviews must be carried out by an officer of the rank of inspector or above who is independent of the investigation.

Reviewing officer's duties

The purpose of a review is for the reviewing officer to satisfy himself that the original PACE 1984, s.37 grounds for detention continue to apply. In particular, he must consider:

PACE 1984, s.40(8)

(a) whether there is sufficient evidence with which to charge the suspect; and, if there is not, then

PACE 1984, s.40(8)

(b) whether the suspect's detention is necessary to secure or preserve evidence or to obtain evidence by questioning; or

PACE 1984, s.40(9)

(c) if the suspect is being detained as being unfit to be either charged or released—under PACE 1984, ss 37(9) or 37D(5)—whether he is now so fit.

Postponement of reviews

PACE 1984, s.40(4)(a)

A review may be postponed if, in all the circumstances, it is not practicable to carry out the review at the due time.

PACE 1984, s.40(4)(b)

This may arise, for example either because the suspect is being questioned and the review officer is satisfied that an interruption would prejudice the investigation or because no review officer is readily available.

PACE 1984, s.40(5)

However, if a review has been postponed then it must be carried out as soon as is practicable thereafter.

Written notes must be made in the custody record of the grounds for and the extent of any such postponement as well as any comments made by the detainee.

PACE 1984, s.40(7) and Code C, para. 15.5

If a review is postponed then subsequent reviews must not be affected by the earlier postponement. This means that the timing of the subsequent reviews will remain governed by the time when the detention was first authorised and the maximum periods of time permissible between reviews thereafter.

PACE 1984, s.40(6)

Reviews whilst suspect is asleep

If the suspect is likely to be asleep at the time of a review then the review process should be brought forward in order for the suspect, or his representative, to be able to make representations. It is important to note that, unlike the situation when a review is postponed, when a review is brought forward for this or any other reason then subsequent reviews must also be brought forward.

PACE 1984, Code C, Note for Guidance 15C

PACE 1984, s.40(3)

REVIEWS PRIOR TO CHARGE—PRACTICE AND PROCEDURE

Documentation

The time that the suspect's detention is first authorised and the grounds for it must be noted on the custody record.

PACE 1984, s.37(4) and Code C, para. 2.1

The outcome of all reviews must be noted on the custody record.

PACE 1984, Code C, para. 15.16

Disputes

If there is any disagreement between the review officer and a more senior officer on the question of whether a suspect should remain detained, the review officer is obliged to refer the matter immediately to an officer of the rank of superintendent or above who is responsible for the police station.

PACE 1984, s.40(11)

The right to legal advice

Before a review is conducted, the review officer must remind the suspect of his right to legal advice and note that this has been done in the custody record.

PACE 1984, Code C, para. 15.12

Reviews by telephone

Unless reviews by video have been authorised and are practicable (see below), a review during the suspect's first 24 hours of detention may be conducted over the telephone. All other PACE 1984, s.40 requirements must be observed. However, any

PACE 1984, s.40A and Code C, Note for Guidance 15F; CJA 2003, s.6;

HOC 60/2003, para. 4.9

reviews beyond the first 24-hour period of detention must be done by the review officer in person.

HOC 60/2003, para. 3

It is for the review officer to decide on each case individually as to whether to conduct the review in person or by telephone. He must take full account of the needs of the suspect and there will be specific additional considerations if the suspect is a juvenile, mentally vulnerable, suffering from anything other than a routine minor ailment, or there are "presentational or community issues" around the suspect's detention.

Reviews by video

PACE 1984, s.45A RRD(SPS)R 2003

The Secretary of State can introduce regulations allowing for reviews of detention to be performed using video-conferencing facilities. At the time of publication this is only operating as an experiment in two police stations: Alton and Winchester (North Walls), Hampshire.

Representations

PACE 1984, s.40(12)–(13)

The review officer must allow the suspect, or his adviser if available at the time of the review, the opportunity to make oral or written representations. Such representations should deal with the following points:

(a) whether the suspect's detention is necessary to secure, preserve or obtain evidence as required by PACE 1984, s.37(2);

(b) whether there is sufficient evidence to charge the suspect: if there is, PACE 1984, s.37(7) demands that the custody officer either charge the suspect or release him, either on or without bail;

(c) whether the investigation could not properly continue with the suspect on police bail; and

(d) whether the investigation is being conducted "expeditiously", as required by Code C, para. 1.1.

DETENTION REVIEWS AFTER CHARGE

PACE 1984, s.40(1)

Once the suspect has been charged, all of the above review rules and requirements continue to apply. However, the review officer will now be the custody officer.

PACE 1984, s.40(10)

The object of reviews after charge is for the review officer to decide whether the decision to detain the suspect rather than release him is still justified under the provisions of PACE 1984, s.38 (refer to the **Bail** index heading).

DETENTION REVIEWS—PRACTICAL GUIDANCE

In addition to the points already made under the "Detention periods—practical guidance" heading above, a suspect's legal adviser should consider the following points.

(1) Informing police of wish to make representations

The adviser should make it clear to the custody officer whether or not he wishes to make representations at the next review and, if he does, ask that this be noted on the custody record, together with the request that he be contacted prior to the review time. This will prevent any argument arising that he was not "available" (under the provisions of PACE 1984, s.40(12)–(13)) at the appropriate time.

(2) Written or telephone representations

If the adviser is unlikely to be present in the police station at the time of the next review, he may leave written representations with the custody officer with the instruction that these be shown to the review officer at the relevant time.

As an alternative, he may leave a telephone number with the custody officer and instructions that he be telephoned by the review officer at the time of the review in order for him to make appropriate representations.

(3) Adviser's written representations

If written representations are presented to the review officer, he is obliged to retain these.

PACE 1984, Code C, para. 15.5

Therefore, even if making oral representations, it may assist to prepare a written note of these and hand this to the review officer. This is particularly advisable on occasions when the review officer is not making his own notes of the representations.

(4) Retain written records

It is advisable always to retain a full written record of representations made at each review and a record of the review officer's response to them. Wherever practicable, this should be made as a contemporaneous note.

Duty Solicitors

THE DUTY SOLICITOR SCHEME

The Duty Solicitor scheme is governed by the Criminal Defence Service Duty Solicitor Arrangements 2001 (last updated in July 2003). The Criminal Defence Service also publish lengthy guidance in the form of the Duty Solicitor manual (last updated in June 2004). The obligations of the duty solicitor are set out in the General Criminal Contract Specifications Pt B s.8.

Aspects of the scheme seem to be constantly changing as the Legal Services Commission seek to introduce new rules. In order to become a duty solicitor, the solicitor must pass both parts of the Criminal Litigation Accreditation scheme and must now be both a court duty solicitor and a police station duty solicitor unless granted a waiver for either type of scheme. Those solicitors who were duty solicitors prior to April 1, 2001 were passported onto the schemes after that date and did not have to undertake the accreditation schemes.

Any solicitor who was a police station duty solicitor prior to April 2001 but not a court duty solicitor can only remain as a police station duty solicitor if they pass the Magistrates Court Qualification or obtain a waiver (generally only granted on grounds of child care difficulties or disability). A solicitor who was a police station duty solicitor prior to April 2001 but is no longer acting as a duty solicitor can attend duty cases effectively as an accredited representative.

ACCEPTING THE INITIAL CALL

The duty solicitor may be either on rota duty or on the panel. In either case, the initial request for advice will be referred by the Duty Solicitor Call Centre unless the duty solicitor is on rota and already at the same police station as the suspect at the time of the request (as quite often happens), in which case he must notify the Duty Solicitor Call Centre that a request for advice has been accepted directly from the suspect.

GCC 2004, Pt B, para. 8.2.2

If the firm has a duty solicitor on rota duty, the firm is obliged to accept the case unless the rota duty solicitor is already engaged in acting for another suspect at a police station or at court in relation to a hearing of an application for a warrant of further detention or an extension of such a warrant or at

GCC 2004, Pt B, para. 8.2.2

an armed forces custody hearing or if a conflict of interest arises.

GCC 2004, Pt B, para. 8.2.3

The firm may still accept the case if the rota duty solicitor is unavailable as above but another duty solicitor is available to accept the case without delay and is able to arrange attendance at the police station, if necessary, within 45 minutes.

If the rota duty solicitor is unable to accept the case and no other duty solicitor from that firm is available to accept the case, it will be referred to the next duty solicitor on rota duty or, where there is only one duty solicitor on rota duty, it will go to the panel—all duty solicitors on that scheme will be called in turn until one accepts the case.

GCC 2004, Pt B, para. 8.2.4

A duty solicitor who is called because he is on the panel is not obliged to accept the case but the firm must use "all reasonable endeavours" to accept such cases.

GCC 2004, Pt B, para. 8.2.5

With written prior approval from the Legal Services Commission, a firm may use non-duty solicitor staff to receive calls from the Call Centre Service, and such staff may accept a referral from the Service provided that:

(a) the LSC is satisfied that the staff concerned have been effectively trained to undertake such a role; and

(b) there are clear procedures in place for such staff to follow which ensure that referrals are not accepted unless there is a duty solicitor available to make first contact with the client immediately and which ensure that referrals are passed to such solicitors immediately; and

(c) a duty solicitor is available to make first contact with the client immediately and is able to arrange attendance at the Police Station, if necessary, within 45 minutes.

INITIAL ADVICE

GCC 2004, Pt B, para. 8.2.6

Once a case has been accepted, the duty solicitor (whether rota or panel) must provide initial advice personally by speaking directly to the suspect on the telephone unless he is at or near the police station and can immediately advise the suspect in person.

If the police refuse to permit the suspect to speak to the duty solicitor on the telephone, he may attend the Police Station.

If the case is one on which the duty solicitor is obliged to attend the police station, he should tell the suspect that he will be attending himself or by his authorised representative unless there are exceptional reasons for not attending which should be explained to the suspect.

Where a suspect is to be charged with an arrestable offence, the duty solicitor must advise on the implications of the caution which will be given on charge. The solicitor must also consider whether or not he should attend the police station at the time of charge taking into account whether it is possible to give confidential telephone advice and the possible consequences of not making a statement when charged.

GCC 2004, Pt B, para. 8.2.6

POSTPONEMENT OF INITIAL ADVICE ON THE TELEPHONE

The initial advice may only be postponed in the following circumstances:

(a) if the suspect is incapable of speaking to the duty solicitor by reason of drunkenness (and presumably the influence of drugs) or violent behaviour;

(b) if the suspect is in a sleep period;

(c) where an interpreter is required.

GCC 2004, Pt B, para. 8.2.6

The duty solicitor shall make arrangements to provide initial advice as soon as the suspect is capable of speaking to him.

GCC 2004, Pt B, para. 8.2.6

A problem may arise when the duty solicitor is told by the custody officer that the suspect is incapable and may refuse to bring the suspect to the telephone for the duty solicitor to make the assessment personally. If the duty solicitor has any reason to consider the police are not acting properly, he should attend the police station to speak to the suspect directly. Otherwise arrangements should be made to speak to the suspect as soon as he is capable of doing so. This may mean relying on the custody officer to telephone the duty solicitor once the suspect is capable of speaking to him or, more reliably perhaps, telephoning the police station at regular intervals to monitor the progress of the suspect.

USE OF ACCREDITED REPRESENTATIVES IN DUTY CASES

Only once initial advice by telephone has been given by the duty solicitor in person can he arrange for an accredited representative to give advice to the suspect where he considers it appropriate to do so.

GCC 2004, Pt B, para. 8.2.11

If the representative is not an employee of the firm, the travel time claimed must not exceed 45 minutes.

GCC 2004, Pt B, para. 8.2.12

The suspect must be informed of the status of the person giving the advice in these circumstances before such advice is given.

GCC 2004, Pt B, para. 8.2.11

In the circumstances outlined below, Services personnel can only be advised by an accredited representative if that representative is a solicitor.

An accredited representative can only represent a suspect on a warrant of further detention if they are a solicitor.

OBLIGATION TO ATTEND THE POLICE STATION

The duty solicitor should be aware of whether he has an obligation to attend the police station. If so, he should inform the suspect that he or his representative will be attending the police station to provide advice and to attend any interview or identification procedure unless there are exceptional circumstances for not so doing.

GCC 2004, Pt B, para. 8.2.7

A duty solicitor has an obligation to attend the police station either in person or by his representative after having given initial advice at the telephone in the following circumstances:

(a) where the suspect has been arrested in connection with an arrestable offence as defined and the police intend to interview the suspect within the duty period; or

(b) where the police intend to resolve an issue of identification by holding an identification parade, a group or video identification or a confrontation; or

(c) where the suspect is complaining of serious maltreatment by the police; or

(d) where the suspect is a youth or person at risk; or

(e) where representation is required in connection with an application for a warrant of further detention.

GCC 2004, Pt B, para. 8.2.8

If any of these criteria are met, an attendance at the police station will be required unless there are exceptional circumstances which justify non-attendance (which must be explained to the suspect and noted on the file). Exceptional circumstances would include the situation where the suspect expressly instructs the duty solicitor not to attend the police station.

Exceptional circumstances are less likely to arise where serious police maltreatment is alleged or the client is a youth or otherwise at risk.

If the interview or identification procedure is postponed until a time after which the rota duty solicitor is no longer on duty or the panel duty solicitor can no longer conveniently attend, he must make arrangements to ensure that the suspect continues to receive advice either from the rota duty solicitor continuing to act as duty solicitor or from another duty solicitor.

GCC 2004, Pt B, para. 8.6

SERVICES PERSONNEL

Where the suspect is a Services person at a Services establishment or assisting with an investigation by Services police and suspected of offences contrary to the Services Discipline Acts, the duty solicitor must attend personally where he considers attendance necessary for the protection of the suspect's interests and where:

(a) the investigation involves any offences which cannot be dealt with summarily; or

(b) the offences appear to the interviewing Services police to be serious.

GCC 2004, Pt B, para. 8.2.9

If the suspect is a Services person requiring representation at a custody hearing before a judicial officer under the Armed Forces Discipline Act 2000, the duty solicitor shall attend personally upon the suspect to provide advice and assistance (including advocacy assistance).

GCC 2004, Pt B, para. 8.2.10

The duty solicitor cannot delegate to an accredited representative in the case of a Services person in the above circumstances or where representation is required at an application for a warrant of further detention unless that representative is a solicitor. This is also the case where the interview or identification procedure is delayed to a time when the solicitor is no longer on duty.

GCC 2004, Pt B, para. 8.2.11

DISCRETION TO ATTEND THE POLICE STATION

In cases where the duty solicitor is not obliged to attend the police station, he has a discretion to attend, depending on whether he considers attendance in the interests of the suspect.

In exercising such discretion, regard shall be given to whether advice can be given on the telephone with sufficient confidentiality and if he can communicate effectively with the suspect by telephone.

SUFFICIENT BENEFIT TEST

GCC 2004, Pt B, para. 8.2.14

The duty solicitor shall only attend the Police Station when the Sufficient Benefit Test set out in the General Criminal Contract Pt B, Rule 2.5 is satisfied. The Contract states the test to be:

GCC 2004, Pt B, para. 2.5

> "Advice and Assistance may only be provided on legal issues concerning English law and where there is sufficient benefit to the Client, having regard to the circumstances of the matter, including the personal circumstances of the client, to justify work or further work being carried out."

GCC 2004, Pt B, para. 2.5.9

The Sufficient Benefit Test will be satisfied automatically where a client has a right to legal advice or is a Volunteer under the Police and Criminal Evidence Act 1984 or the equivalent legislation applying to armed forces in the case of military investigations. However, the Sufficient Benefit Test is only met automatically for the purposes of initial advice. It must still be applied by the solicitor in determining the extent of the advice which is required (including whether an attendance is necessary and the length of time which should be spent).

GCC 2004, Pt B, para. 8.2.14

The circumstances when this test will automatically be satisfied include:

(a) to provide advice prior to and during interview;

(b) to advise at an identification procedure (including a video identification procedure when the client is not present);

(c) when appropriate, to advise a client who is a youth or person at risk;

(d) when appropriate, to advise on the implications of the caution when the client is charged with an arrestable offence;

(e) to advise when the advice may materially affect the outcome of the investigation and goes significantly beyond initial advice;

(f) to advise a client who complains of serious maltreatment by the police.

TELEPHONE ADVICE ONLY?

In the following cases, the duty solicitor may provide Police Station Telephone Advice only and shall not claim from public funds for any Police Station Attendance unless one of the exceptions below applies:

GCC 2004, Pt B, para. 8.2.17

(a) The suspect is detained in relation to a non-imprisonable offence;

(b) The suspect is arrested on a bench warrant for failing to appear and being held for production before the court, except where the solicitor has clear documentary evidence available that would result in the client being released from custody in which case attendance may be allowed provided that the reason is justified on file;

(c) The suspect is arrested on suspicion of:

  (i) driving with excess alcohol who is taken to the police station to give a specimen (s.5 Road Traffic Act 1988);
  (ii) failure to provide a specimen (ss 6, 7 and 7A Road Traffic Act 1988);
  (iii) driving whilst unfit/drunk in charge of a motor vehicle (s.4 Road Traffic Act 1988).

(d) The suspect is detained in breach of police or court bail conditions

Exceptions

The duty solicitor may attend the police station to advise on any of the above "telephone advice only" matters if one of the following exceptions applies and the Sufficient Benefit Test is satisfied:

GCC 2004, Pt B, para. 8.2.18

(a) an interview or an identification procedure is going to take place;

(b) the suspect is eligible for assistance from an appropriate adult under the PACE Codes of Practice;

(c) the suspect requires an interpreter or is otherwise unable to communicate over the telephone;

(d) the suspect complains of serious maltreatment by the police;

(e) the investigation includes another alleged offence which does not fall within the above criteria;

(f) the duty solicitor is already at the same Police Station, in which case he may attend the suspect but may not claim more than the Police Station Telephone Advice fixed fee.

If any of the above exceptions apply then the duty solicitor must endorse the reasons for attendance on his file, otherwise his claim will be limited to the Police Station Telephone Advice fixed fee.

CONTINUING TO ACT FOR THE SUSPECT

GCC 2004, Pt B, para. 8.5.1

A duty solicitor must inform every suspect that they represent as duty solicitor that he or she is not obliged to instruct the duty solicitor.

GCC 2004, Pt B, para. 8.5.2

If a suspect wishes another solicitor to act, the duty solicitor shall not act unless the named solicitor is not available and the suspect asks the duty solicitor to act on that occasion only.

GCC 2004, Pt B, para. 8.5.3

If the duty solicitor does not continue to act for the suspect, he or she must make available to any solicitor subsequently instructed any relevant information or papers.

NON-DISCRIMINATION

GCC 2004, Pt B, para. 8.6

A duty solicitor must be prepared to carry out his duties so as not to discriminate on grounds of race, gender, sexual orientation, religion, age or disability and regardless of the nature of any offence for which the suspect is under investigation or with which the suspect has been charged or previously convicted.

CDS DIRECT PILOT

From May 2, 2005 a six month pilot is being run by the LSC concerning police station advice in apparently straight forward matters by a new body called CDS Direct.

In summary the CDS Direct pilot will now provide advice in the following circumstances:

(a) When people are detained at police stations in Liverpool or Boston (Lincolnshire), regarding a non-indictable only crime, such as petty theft or drunk and disorderly, where the time of interview is not known when the request for a duty solicitor is made.

(b) When people are detained at any police station in England and Wales where the matter is restricted to telephone advice only, such as driving with excess alcohol or a warrant and a request for a duty solicitor is made.

Should any of the exceptions to the restriction of advice to telephone advice apply, the call will be passed on to the duty solicitor to attend the police station. Equally in the Liverpool and Boston cases, once the time for interview is known the matter will be passed to the duty solicitor.

PRACTICAL GUIDANCE

(1) Telephone service

Make sure that the telephone service is aware that you have taken a call.

Do not contact the police station directly without having first informed the telephone service that you are able to assist as they may be trying to locate another solicitor.

Keep the telephone service informed as to your whereabouts and on which number you can be contacted.

(2) Tools of the trade

Certain publications are extremely useful if not essential, such as:

(a) PACE 1984;

(b) PACE 1984 Codes of Practice;

(c) a copy of this book;

(d) Pt B, para. 8 of the General Criminal Contract; and

(e) duty solicitor identity card

Other items are also invaluable to have at hand and may be seen as essential:

(a) pager;

(b) mobile telephone;

(c) standard police station attendance report forms and notebooks;

(d) application form for legal aid (Form A);

(e) advice and assistance forms (CDS1 and 2);

(f) your firm's headed notepaper, plain paper and sheets of carbon paper—in case written representations or a letter to the suspect need to be written;

(g) business cards;

(h) cigarettes, a box of matches and some sweets; and

(i) a local street map (A–Z).

(3) Initial advice

If you are not able to speak to the suspect as a result of his drunkenness or violent behaviour, do not necessarily rely on the custody officer to call you back. Telephone the police station at regular intervals to check on the state of the suspect.

(4) Obligation to attend

Decide whether the case is one which will require attendance and have the criteria well in mind. Inform the suspect that you or your representative will be attending prior to any interview or identification procedure and give yourself time to speak to the suspect before the interview without the need to make two trips to the police station.

(5) Discretion to attend

If you are not obliged to attend, should you be exercising your discretion in favour of attendance? It is often difficult to communicate with a suspect on the telephone when he is in a busy custody suite surrounded by police officers.

Do not ask questions that may elicit admissions within earshot of police officers. If the suspect is vulnerable for whatever reason, attendance should be the norm.

(6) Introduction to the suspect

At the start of the initial interview with the suspect, inform him that you are an independent legal adviser who happens to be on duty for that area at that time. Some suspects may still believe that the duty solicitor is the "police solicitor" and will need to be reassured that you will be acting in the best interests of the suspect and not the police.

(7) Continuation of instructions

Make sure that the suspect is aware of his right to instruct any firm of solicitors he wishes to instruct and do not force your services onto the suspect.

If the suspect wishes to instruct someone else then tell him to give your details to the new solicitor so that you can forward your notes on request.

Financial Interviews

THE LAW

Introduction

Confiscation of the proceeds of crime, along with the authority to enquire into and restrain a person's assets and income when they are suspected to be the proceeds of crime, is governed by the Proceeds of Crime Act 2002. This is a complex and detailed area of law and, accordingly, this chapter will focus on only those issues that are of most relevance to the adviser when the suspect is in police custody and is to be questioned about his financial affairs either prior to or immediately after charge.

POCA 2002

POCA 2002 created the Assets Recovery Agency with whom the police, the CPS and Customs and Excise have a statutory duty to co-operate. The Agency's primary role is to co-ordinate activity across the UK in recovering "unlawfully obtained assets" from those with "no right to hold them".

Powers under POCA 2002 are in addition to and distinct from other court powers to impose fines, order costs and award compensation.

Confiscation orders under POCA 2002

Upon conviction in the Crown Court the suspect is liable to be made subject to a confiscation order. The Court is obliged to make such an order if:

(a) it determines that a defendant has a "criminal lifestyle" and he has benefited from his "general criminal conduct"; or

POCA 2002, s.6(2)–(3)

(b) it determines that he does not have a "criminal lifestyle" but he has benefited from his "particular criminal conduct".

The court will then decide on the recoverable amount and make an order requiring him to pay that amount.

POCA 2002, s.6(4)–(5)

Financial affairs interviews under POCA 2002

In anticipation of a possible confiscation order, the suspect may be asked to complete a financial affairs interview either before or after charge whilst in police custody.

PACE 1984, Code C, para. 11.6

The PACE Codes of Practice specifically allow for the questioning of a suspect as to his financial affairs under POCA 2002, by way of a formal question and answer record, even if all other conditions for the termination of an interview have been met

There is some protection afforded to a suspect that answers he gives to enquiries as to his financial affairs after conviction cannot be evidence in criminal proceedings against him. However, this protection does not extend to answers given to financial questions put under caution prior to or post charge but before conviction. Thus, any information supplied by the suspect relating to the proceeds of crime whilst in police custody may be used as evidence in respect of the offence itself, if relevant.

POCA 2002, s.18 and Sch. 6, para. 2

There is no offence of refusing to answer such financial affairs interviews, nor can any inferences be drawn from any such refusal in any subsequent trial of the substantive offence(s).

PRACTICE AND PROCEDURE

The interview

In appropriate cases, the police will wish to investigate a suspect's income and assets in order to determine their value and whether they are or appear to be the proceeds of crime. In due course, the police will present their findings to the court if and when the suspect is convicted and a confiscation order is under consideration. Police forces have specially assigned officers or "confiscation units" to perform this task.

As a first step, the police will invariably wish to subject the suspect to a financial affairs interview. This can be done either before or after charge although, other than in the more straightforward instances, it is usually conducted after charge.

Advising the suspect

The suspect is under no obligation to answer questions put during an investigation into his financial affairs pre-conviction, nor can any specific adverse comment be made upon such a refusal, as opposed to the situation during an investigation into the substantive offence(s). The adviser must therefore be clear as to whether questioning of a suspect about his finances is a "financial interview" or part of a normal interview, gathering evidence relating to the possible charge(s).

This is not to say that there is no potential detriment in not answering questions put during a financial interview. If the suspect is to be charged and subsequently convicted, a failure to provide financial information to the court will mean that the police conclusions as presented during confiscation proceedings will be deemed to be accurate. In addition, there are certain instances when the burden of proof in such proceedings will rest with the defendant (see below). For these reasons, a suspect must be advised carefully before deciding to refuse to answer questions put during a financial interview.

If the suspect's financial affairs are both uncomplicated and non-incriminating, he may be happy to answer questions about them instantaneously. In any other circumstances, he may be best advised to indicate that, whilst he is not prepared to answer such questions whilst in police custody following an initial arrest, he will consider answering questions at a later stage.

Although the suspect's unwillingness to assist when first asked will be noted and may, if considered relevant, be reported to the court during confiscation proceedings, it cannot be deemed to be a refusal to co-operate in itself. Obviously, a point will arise in the future when a final decision will have to be taken as to whether or not to consent to a financial interview but it is usually preferable that this be done in a more considered manner and not during a period of detention in a police station.

Delay of suspect's rights and bail

When a suspect is detained at a police station in relation to an offence for which a confiscation order may be made, the police are entitled to delay his rights to have a third party notified of his arrest and access to legal advice if the police consider that the operation of these rights will hinder their recovery of property.

PACE 1984, ss 56, 58

However, a suspect's refusal to submit to financial interview and/or a request for time to consider the matter further cannot legitimately adversely effect the police decision as to whether bail should be granted either before or after charge.

The burden of proof

It should be noted that when a suspect is convicted and the court is considering the making of a confiscation order, POCA 2002 provides for certain presumptions to be made by the court as to his "criminal lifestyle" and the provenance of his income and assets. These presumptions are invariably adverse to the suspect and the burden of proof rests with him to rebut them.

POCA 2002, s.6(7)

The burden of proof being the civil test of "on the balance of probabilities".

This means that it is often the case that the suspect will be best advised to provide answers and information during a financial interview, because a failure to do so will be to his detriment. However, this in itself is not a reason against postponing the financial interview until a later date, when more considered instructions can be taken and advice upon them be given.

PRACTICAL GUIDANCE

(1) Answers leading to fresh inquiries

Answers to financial questions may not only be admissible in the trial of the substantive offence(s) for which the suspect is in detention, if relevant, but may also lead to the police pursuing fresh lines of inquiry. In advising the suspect, it is important for the adviser to remember that such inquiries may result in evidence being obtained which will be admissible in other/new proceedings.

(2) Questionnaires

It is common for the police to use a prepared *pro forma* questionnaire whilst conducting financial interviews.

In such instances, the adviser should insist upon having sufficient time to consider the questionnaire with the suspect before the suspect decides whether or not to agree to its completion.

Such questionnaires are comprehensive and detailed. It will normally require a delay of several days, if not weeks, to take full instructions from the suspect and to tender advice. Only when a suspect has an extremely simple financial profile will it be advisable to consider completing this exercise whilst still in police detention following an initial arrest.

(3) Court's ability to compel answers

In advising a suspect the adviser must appreciate that if the suspect is ultimately convicted and confiscation proceedings are commenced, the Crown court is empowered to require him to give financial information. If the suspect fails without reasonable excuse to comply with any such order then the court is entitled to draw such inference from the failure as it considers appropriate.

Similar rights do not exist enabling the police effectively to compel answers to their financial inquiries.

(4) Restraint orders

In advising a suspect who appears, or is suspected, to have significant financial resources, it will be important to advise him as to the possibility that a restraint order will be obtained by the police. Such orders prohibit the suspect and any other named persons from dealing with any realisable property held by them and can enable the authorities to seize or freeze the property pending any future confiscation order.

Fingerprints and Photographs

FINGERPRINTS—THE LAW

Definition

Any references to "fingerprints" means any record, produced by any method, of the skin pattern and other physical characteristics or features of a person's fingers or palms. The record can be taken electronically on approved devices or in the more traditional manner using ink and paper.

PACE 1984, Code D, para. 4.1, 4.5; PACE 1984, s.61(8A)

Taking fingerprints with consent

The police may take the fingerprints of any person if the appropiate consent is given. The consent can be oral if the person is not at the police station but must be in writing if the person is at the police station.

PACE 1984, s.61(1), (2)

PACE 1984, s.61(7A), (8)

If fingerprints are taken with a suspect's consent, the police must tell the suspect the reasons for taking the fingerprints and that they be subject to a speculative search. This information is to be recorded on the custody record. This information should be given in the presence of an appropriate adult where one is required.

PACE 1984, Code D, para. 4.7

PACE 1984, Code D, para. 2.14

Appropriate consent

If the suspect is under 14 years of age, the appropriate consent is the consent of a parent or guardian. If the juvenile suspect is 14 or over, consent of both juvenile and parent or guardian is required. If the juvenile suspect is in care of the local authority or voluntary organisation, the consent of that authority or organisation is sufficient. If the parent, guardian or representative from the local authority or voluntary organisation is not acting as appropriate adult, their consent can be obtained by telephone but they must be given all the necessary information about the request and be allowed to speak to the juvenile and the appropriate adult if they wish to do so.

PACE 1984, s.65(1)
PACE 1984, Code D, NfG 2A

PACE 1984, Code D, para. 2.12

If the suspect is mentally disordered or otherwise mentally vulnerable the consent is only vaild if given in the presence of an appropriate adult.

PACE 1984, Code D, para. 2.15

The fingerprints of a suspect who requires an appropriate adult must take place in the presence of the appropriate adult.

If fingerprints are taken from a suspect without consent in circumstances where consent is necessary, there may be an action against the police for trespass to the person or assault and the fingerprints may be inadmissible as evidence at any subsequent trial.

Taking fingerprints without consent

Fingerprints can be taken without consent in the following situations:

PACE 1984, s.61(3) as amended by CJA 2003, s.9(2)

(a) If the suspect is detained at the police station in consequence of his arrest for a recordable offence and he has not had his fingerprints taken in the course of the investigation of the offence by police.

PACE 1984, s.61(4) as amended by CJA 2003, s.9(2)

(b) If the suspect is detained at the police station and has been charged with or informed that he will be reported for a recordable offence and he has not had his fingerprints taken in the course of the investigation of the offence by police.

PACE 1984, s.61(3A) as amended by CJA 2003, s.9(3)

(c) In either of the above situations where the suspect has previously had his fingerprints taken but they do not constitute a complete set of his fingerprints or some or all of them are not of sufficient quality to allow satisfactory analysis, comparison or matching.

PACE 1984, s.61(4A); PACE 1984, Code D, para. 4.3

(d) If a suspect answers bail at a police station or court where fingerprints have previously been taken and there are reasonable grounds for believing that they are not the same person and either the court or an officer of at least the rank of inspector authorises the fingerprints to be taken.

PACE 1984, s.61(4A); PACE 1984, Code D, para. 4.3

(e) If a suspect answers bail at a police station or court and claims to be a different person from a person whose fingerprints were previously taken and either the court or an officer of at least the rank of inspector authorises the fingerprints to be taken.

PACE 1984, s.61(6); PACE 1984, Code D, para. 4.3

(f) If a person has been convicted of or cautioned, reprimanded or warned for a recordable offence. If cautioned they must have admitted the offence at the time of the caution.

Recordable offences

PACE 1984, Code D, NfG 4A

A recordable offence is an offence for which a conviction, caution, reprimand or warning is recordable on the police national computer. These offences, *inter alia*, are:

NPR(RO)(A)R 2003

(a) all offences punishable by imprisonment;

(b) offences under SOA 1959, s.1 (loitering or soliciting for the purposes of prostitution);

(c) offences under TA 1984, s.43 (improper use of a public telecommunications system);

(d) offences under RTA 1988, s.25 (tampering with motor vehicles);

(e) offences under MCA 1988, s.1 (sending letters, *etc.* with intent to cause anxiety or distress);

(f) other offences as set out in the National Police Records (Recordable Offences) Regulations 2000 as amended by the National Police Records (Recordable Offences) (Amendment) Regulations 2003.

Speculative searches

Where a person has been arrested on suspicion of being involved in a recordable offence, has been charged or informed that he will be reported for summons for such an offence, any fingerprints taken from him may be checked against other fingerprints held by a law enforcement agency (which includes international agencies) or held in connection with or as a result of an investigation of an offence.

PACE 1984, s.63A(1), (1A), (1B)

Any fingerprints taken from a person who does not fall into the above categories can only be the subject of a speculative search if that person consents in writing, but once given the consent cannot be revoked or withdrawn.

PACE 1984, s.63A(1C), (1D)

Information to be given to the suspect

When fingerprints are taken from a suspect, he must be informed of the reason for the taking of the fingerprints and that they may be the subject of a speculative search. Both the reasons and the warning as to the use of the fingerprints in a speculative search must be recorded as soon as is practicable. If the suspect is in police detention, the record shall be made on the custody record.

PACE 1984, s.61(7), (7A), (8)

PACE 1984, Code D, para. 4.7

Late taking of fingerprints and power of arrest

If a person has been convicted of, cautioned, reprimanded or warned for a recordable offence but has not been in police custody and has not had his fingerprints taken during the course of the investigation or since conviction, he may be required to attend the police station in order that his fingerprints be taken.

PACE 1984, s.27(1)

PACE 1984, s.27(1A)

If a person who has been convicted of, cautioned, reprimanded or warned for a recordable offence and has had his fingerprints taken during the course of the investigation or since conviction, he may still be required to attend the police station in order that his fingerprints be taken, if the original fingerprints do not constitute a complete set or some or all of them are not of sufficient quality to allow satisfactory analysis, comparison or matching.

PACE 1984, s.27(1), (2), (3)

This requirement only lasts for one month from the date of conviction, caution, warning or reprimand. The person shall be given at least seven days in which to attend and the time of day may be specified. Should he fail to comply with such a requirement, he may be arrested without warrant so that his fingerprints can be taken.

Destruction of fingerprints

PACE 1984, s.64(1A)

Where fingerprints are taken in connection with the investigation of an offence they may be retained after they have fulfilled the purposes for which they were taken but shall not be used except for purposes related to the prevention or detection of crime, the investigation of an offence or the conduct of a prosecution.

PACE 1984, s.64(3), (3AA), 3(AC)
R. (on the application of Marper and Another) v Chief Constable of South Yorkshire [2002] 1 W.L.R. 3223; [2003] 1 All E. R. 148;
R. v Jones 21/07/04, unreported
PACE 1984, Code D, Annex F para. 3

Samples must be destroyed if taken from someone other than a suspect once the purpose has been fulfilled unless they were taken for the purposes of an investigation of an offence for which someone has been convicted and a sample was also taken from the convicted person. Consent can be given for the retention of samples taken from non-suspects, such consent once given is irrevocable.

This means that samples from a suspect whether arrested or attending voluntarily do not have to be destroyed even if that person is never charged or, if charged, is subsequently acquitted. These provisions have survived a challenge under the Human Rights Act 1998.

Where fingerprints taken from a non-suspect are to be destroyed, that person can witness their destruction if notice is given to the police within five days of the relevant decision which will lead to their destruction. A certificate of destruction can be requested from the relevant chief officer and should be provided within three months of the request and no copies should be kept.

Terrorist Offences

PACE 1984, s.61(9)

The provisions of PACE 1984 do not apply to a suspect detained under the terrorist legislation. See **Terrorist Offences** index heading.

Immigration provisions

The provisions of PACE 1984 do not apply to a person detained for immigration enquiries. PACE 1984, s.61(9)

A person's fingerprints may be taken for the purposes of Immigration Service enquiries. In these circumstances, fingerprints can only be taken with consent in writing or without consent if the following conditions apply: PACE 1984, Code D, para. 4.10 PACE 1984, Code D, para. 4.11

(a) when it is reasonably necessary for the purposes of identifying a person detained as a liable to examination or removal; IA 1971, Sch. 2, para. 16, 18(2) IAA 1999, s.141(7)(a)

(b) from a person who fails to produce, on arrival, a valid passport with a photograph or some other document satisfactorily establishing their identity and nationality if an immigration officer does not consider the person has a reasonable excuse for the failure; IAA 1999, s.141(7)(b)

(c) from a person who has been refused entry to the UK but has been temporarily admitted if an immigration officer reasonably suspects the person might break a condition imposed on them relating to residence or reporting to a police or immigration officer, and their decision is confirmed by a chief immigration officer; IAA 1999, s.141(7)(c) IAA 1999, s.141(7)(d)

(d) when directions are given to remove a person as an illegal entrant, liable to removal under the Immigration and Asylum Act 1999, s.10, or who is the subject of a deportation order from the UK;

(e) from a person arrested under UK immigration laws under the Immigration Act 1971, Sch. 2, para. 17;

(f) from a person who has made a claim for asylum or under Art. 3 of the European Convention on Human Rights; or IAA 1999, s.141(7)(e)

(g) from a person who is a dependant of someone who falls into (b) to (f) above. IAA 1999, s.141(7)(f)

Police and immigration officers have the power to arrest, without warrant, a person who fails to comply with a requirement imposed by the Secretary of State to attend a specified place for fingerprinting. IAA 1999, s.142(3); PACE 1984 Code D, para. 4.12

Before any fingerprints are taken, with or without consent, the person must be informed: PACE 1984, Code D, para. 4.13

(a) of the reason their fingerprints are to be taken;

PACE 1984, Code D, Annex F, Pt B

(b) the fingerprints, and all copies of them, will be destroyed as soon as practicable if the person from whom they were taken proves they are a British or Commonwealth citizen who has the right of abode in the UK or is a dependent of such a person, or in any event within ten years of being taken or within such period specified by the Secretary of State.

PACE 1984, Code D, para. 4.14

Reasonable force may be used, if necessary, to take a person's fingerprints without their consent.

FINGERPRINTS—PRACTICE AND PROCEDURE

The provisions of PACE 1984, Code D, para. 4 echo the provisions of PACE 1984.

Taking fingerprints with consent

PACE 1984, Code D, para. 4.7
PACE 1984, Code D, Annex F, Pt A

If fingerprints are taken with consent, that consent must be in writing. The suspect must be informed of the reason for taking the fingerprints and informed that they may be used for a speculative search. Fingerprints taken from a suspect do not have to be destroyed.

Taking fingerprints without consent

PACE 1984, Code D, para. 4.3

If the suspect is over the age of ten years, fingerprints may be taken without consent if the conditions outlined above are satisfied. In practice, fingerprints can now be taken routinely whether or not they will assist in the investigation of the offence. The only proviso is whether the offence for which the person is under arrest or with which he has been charged, cautioned, reprimanded or warned is a recordable offence.

Reasonable Force and Records

PACE 1984, Code D, para. 4.6, 4.8

If fingerprints are to be taken without consent reasonable force may be used to take them. If reasonable force is used, a record shall be made of the circumstances and those present.

PACE 1984, Code D, para. 4.8, 4.9

A record shall also be made of the reason for taking the fingerprints without consent and of the fact that the suspect has been told they may be used for a speculative search.

Destruction

Fingerprints need only be destroyed if taken from someone who has not been a suspect in the offence and where there has been no conviction of someone from whom fingerprints were also taken.

PACE 1984, Code D, Annex F, Pt A

When fingerprints are taken from a person in connection with an investigation and the person is not suspected of having committed the offence, they must be destroyed as soon as they have fulfilled the purpose for which they were taken unless:

PACE 1984 Code D, Annex F, para. 1

(a) they were taken for the purposes of an investigation of an offence for which a person has been convicted; and

(b) fingerprints were also taken from the convicted person for the purposes of that investigation.

However the fingerprints may not be used in the investigation of any offence or in evidence against the person who is, or would be, entitled to the destruction of the fingerprints.

It follows, therefore, that fingerprints taken from a suspect for an offence whether arrested or attending voluntarily, do not have to be destroyed even if that person is never charged or, if charged, is acquitted.

The above requirement to destroy fingerprints and restrictions on their retention and use do not apply if the person gives their written consent for their fingerprints to be retained and used after they have fulfilled the purpose for which they were taken.

PACE 1984, Code D, Annex F, para. 2

When a person's fingerprints are to be destroyed any copies of the fingerprints must also be destroyed and the person may witness the destruction of their fingerprints or copies if they ask to do so within five days of being informed destruction is required. Access to relevant computer fingerprint data shall be made impossible as soon as it is practicable to do so and the person shall be given a certificate to this effect within three months of asking. The fingerprints may not be used in the investigation of any offence or in evidence against the person who is, or would be, entitled to their destruction.

PACE 1984, Code D, Annex F, para. 3

Fingerprints taken in connection with the investigation of an offence which are not required to be destroyed, may be retained after they have fulfilled the purposes for which they were taken but may be used only for purposes related to the prevention or detection of crime, the investigation of an offence or the conduct

PACE 1984, Code D, Annex F, para. 4

of a prosecution in, as well as outside, the UK and may also be subject to a speculative search. This includes checking them against other fingerprint records held by, or on behalf of, the police and other law enforcement authorities in, as well as outside, the UK.

PACE 1984, Code D, Annex F, NfG F1

As far as volunteers are concerned, the Code makes it clear that it is important to make sure "innocent volunteers" are not deterred from participating and their consent to their fingerprints being used for the purposes of a specific investigation is fully informed and voluntary. If the police or volunteer seek to have the fingerprints retained for use after the specific investigation ends, it is important the volunteer's consent to this is also fully informed and voluntary. Examples of consent for the various consents are given in the Code.

FINGERPRINTS—PRACTICAL GUIDANCE

The police now have extremely wide ranging powers to take fingerprints without consent. They no longer require authorisation and can request fingerprints from anyone arrested for a recordable offence regardless of whether the fingerprints will tend to prove or disprove their involvement in the offence. In addition, fingerprints taken from a suspect need not be destroyed even if the suspect is not charged, or if charged, is acquitted. Furthermore, fingerprints can be taken by reasonable force if necessary.

If a request is made of the suspect to provide fingerprints (and this may become routine in every case), the adviser should ensure that the offence is, in fact, a recordable offence as, if it is not, no power to take fingerprints without consent exists.

The suspect should also be advised of the power of the police to use reasonable force and the fact that active resistance could lead to charges of obstruction or assaulting a police officer.

PHOTOGRAPHS—THE LAW

PACE 1984, s.64A(1)
PACE 1984, s.64A(6)
PACE 1984, s.65(1)
PACE 1984, Code D, fG 2A

A person detained at a police station may be photographed either with the appropriate consent or, where the appropriate consent is withheld or it is not practicable to obtain it, without such consent. A photograph includes any process by means of which a visual image may be produced, such as a video image.

Appropriate Consent

PACE 1984, Code D, para. 2.12

If the suspect is under 14 years of age, the appropriate consent is the consent of a parent or guardian. If the juvenile suspect is

14 or over, consent of both juvenile and parent or guardian is required. If the juvenile suspect is in care of the local authority or voluntary organisation, the consent of that authority or organisation is sufficient. If the parent, guardian or representative from the local authority or voluntary organisation is not acting as appropriate adult, their consent can be obtained by telephone but they must be given all the necessary information about the request and be allowed to speak to the juvenile and the appropriate adult if they wish to do so.

If the suspect is mentally disordered or otherwise mentally vulnerable the consent is only valid if given in the presence of an appropriate adult.

The photograph of a suspect who requires an appropriate adult must be taken in the presence of the appropriate adult.

PACE 1984, Code D, para. 2.15

Removal of items

The police are entitled to require the removal of any item or substance worn on or over the whole or any part of the head or face of the person to be photographed. If the suspect refuses to remove the item the police can do so. One would assume that this would mean items such as make up, plasters or headgear.

PACE 1984, s.64A(2)

Use of the photograph

The photograph may be used by or disclosed to any person for any purpose related to the prevention or detection of crime, the investigation of an offence or the conduct of a prosecution. This includes criminal activity abroad.

PACE 1984, s.64A(4), (5)

Destruction of a suspect's photograph

A photograph taken under PACE 1984 s.64A does not have to be destroyed but may only be used for the purposes set out in that section, namely for any purpose related to the prevention or detection of crime, the investigation of an offence or the conduct of a prosecution.

PACE 1984, s.64A(4), (b)

PHOTOGRAPHS—PRACTICE AND PROCEDURE

Reasonable Force

If it is established that the suspect is unwilling to co-operate sufficiently to enable a suitable photograph to be taken and it is not reasonably practicable to take the photograph covertly, an officer may use reasonable force both to take the photograph

PACE 1984, Code D, para. 5.14

without the suspect's consent and, for the purpose of taking the photograph, to remove any item or substance worn on or over all or any part of the suspect's head or face which they have failed to remove when asked.

PACE 1984, Code D, para. 5.15

A photograph may be obtained without the suspect's consent by making a copy of an image of them taken at any time on a camera system installed anywhere in the police station.

Information to be given to the suspect

PACE 1984, Code D, para. 5.16

When a suspect is photographed under these provisions or their photograph is obtained from another image as above, the suspect must be informed of the purpose of the photograph and the purposes for which the photograph may be used, disclosed or retained. This information must be given before the photograph is taken, except if the photograph is to be taken covertly or obtained by copying another image from a camera installed elsewhere in the police station. In such a case the person must be informed as soon as practicable after the photograph is taken or obtained.

Documentation

PACE 1984, Code D, para. 5.17

A record must be made when a photograph of the suspect is taken. The record must include the identity of the officer taking the photograph, the purpose of the photograph, the suspect's consent to the photograph or the reason the suspect was photographed without consent

PACE 1984, Code D, para. 5.18

If force is used when taking a photograph, a record shall be made of the circumstances and those present.

Volunteers

PACE 1984, Code D, para. 5.19

PACE 1984, Code D, para. 5.21

When there are reasonable grounds for suspecting the involvement of a person in a criminal offence, but that person is at a police station voluntarily and not detained, the same provisions should apply, except that force may not be used to take a photograph of the person.

PACE 1984, Code D, para. 5.22

PACE 1984, Code D, para. 5.24

In addition, the photographs of persons not detained must be destroyed (together with any negatives and copies) unless the person is charged with, or informed they may be prosecuted for, a recordable offence, is prosecuted for a recordable offence, is cautioned for a recordable offence or given a warning or reprimand for a recordable offence, or gives informed consent in writing for the photograph or image to be retained. This is subject to the need to retain any images under any separate requirement of the Criminal Procedure and

Investigations Act 1996 to retain material in connection with criminal investigations.

The person must be given an opportunity to witness the destruction or to have a certificate confirming the destruction provided they so request the certificate within five days of being informed the destruction is required.

PACE 1984, Code D, para. 5.23

Examples of the purposes for which a photograph can be used

A photograph can be used or disclosed for any purposes related to the prevention or detection of crime, the investigation of offences or the conduct of prosecutions which include:

PACE 1984, Code D, NfG 5B

(a) checking the photograph against other photographs held in records or in connection with, or as a result of, an investigation of an offence to establish whether the suspect is liable to arrest for other offences;

(b) when the suspect is arrested at the same time as other people, or at a time when it is likely that other people will be arrested, using the photograph to help establish who was arrested, at what time and where;

(c) when the real identity of the suspect is not known and cannot be readily ascertained or there are reasonable grounds for doubting the name and other personal details given by the suspect;

(d) when it appears any identification procedure may need to be arranged for which the suspect's photograph would assist;

(e) when the suspect's release without charge may be required, and if the release is on bail to appear at a police station, using the photograph to help verify the person's identity when they answer their bail and if the person does not answer their bail, to assist in arresting them;

(f) when the suspect's release without charge may be required, and if the release is without bail, using the photograph to help verify their identity or assist in locating them for the purposes of serving them with a summons to appear at court in criminal proceedings;

(g) when the person has answered to bail at a police station and there are reasonable grounds for doubting they are the person who was previously granted bail, using the photograph to help establish or verify their identity;

(h) when the person arrested on a warrant claims to be a different person from the person named on the warrant and a photograph would help to confirm or disprove their claim;

(i) when the person has been charged with, reported for, or convicted of, a recordable offence and their photograph is not already on record or their photograph is on record but their appearance has changed since it was taken and the person has not yet been released or brought before a court.

No power of arrest

PACE 1984, Code D, NfG 5C

There is no power to arrest a person convicted of a recordable offence solely to take their photograph. The power to take photographs applies only where the person is in custody as a result of the exercise of another power, *e.g.* arrest for fingerprinting.

When it would not be practicable to obtain the appropriate consent

PACE 1984, Code D, NfG 5D

The circumstances in which it would not be practicable to obtain the appropriate consent for the taking of a photograph include:

(a) when the person is drunk or otherwise unfit to give consent;

(b) when there are reasonable grounds to suspect that if the person became aware a suitable photograph was to be taken, they would take steps to prevent it being taken, *e.g.* by violently resisting, covering or distorting their face etc, and it would not otherwise be possible to take a suitable photograph;

(c) when, in order to obtain a suitable photograph, it is necessary to take it covertly; and

(d) in the case of a juvenile, if the parent or guardian cannot be contacted in sufficient time to allow the photograph to be taken.

PHOTOGRAPHS—PRACTICAL GUIDANCE

The police now have extensive powers to take photographs of suspects with or without their consent. There is little the adviser can do to prevent a photograph being taken except to ensure that the police have the power to do so under PACE 1984, s.64A and under the Code of Practice.

The suspect should be advised that, in a situation where the police are entitled to take a photograph, they can do so using reasonable force if necessary both to take the photograph and to remove any item or substance to enable a suitable photograph to be taken. Active resistance to such a course may lead to a prosecution for obstruction or assaulting a police officer.

If the suspect is a volunteer rather than detained, force cannot be used to obtain the photograph and the suspect would be entitled to resist any attempts to do so. The suspect may decline to sit in front of a camera but the police would be able to obtain an image from other images on cameras throughout the police station. It is, of course, usual for custody suites to have CCTV and images from these systems can easily be used to produce images of suspects.

If a volunteer has his photograph taken, they should be advised as to the destruction requirements. If the volunteer gives consent for a photograph to be retained, it is not clear whether that consent can subsequently be withdrawn. There are no specific provisions in statute or the Codes of Practice concerning photographs unlike those for fingerprints.

SEARCHES AND EXAMINATION TO ASCERTAIN IDENTITY—THE LAW

If an officer of at least the rank of inspector authorises it, a suspect detained in a police station may be searched or examined (or both) for the purpose of ascertaining whether he has any mark that would tend to identify him as a person involved in the commission of an offence, or for the purpose of ascertaining his identity which includes showing that he is not who he claims to be.

PACE 1984, s.54A(1)

PACE 1984, s.54A(11)

Authorisation

Authorisation may only be given if the appropriate consent to a search or examination that would reveal whether the mark in question exists has been withheld or it is not practicable to obtain such consent. Authorisation may also be given if the person in question has refused to identify himself or the officer has reasonable grounds for suspecting that the person is not who he claims to be. Such authorisation may be given orally or in writing, but if given orally must be confirmed in writing as soon as practicable.

PACE 1984, s.54A(2), (3)

PACE 1984, s.54A(4)

Photographing any mark

PACE 1984, s.54A(5)

PACE 1984,s.54A(11)

Any identifying mark found on a search or examination may be photographed with the appropriate consent (defined as above) or without such consent if it is withheld or it is not practicable to obtain it. A photograph includes any visual image such as a video.

Use of photograph

PACE 1984, s.54A(9), (10)

A photograph taken of such a mark may be used by or disclosed to any person for any purpose related to the prevention or detection of crime, the investigation of an offence or the conduct of a prosecution. This includes criminal activity abroad.

Destruction of the photograph

PACE 1984, s.54A(9)

A photograph taken of the mark does not have to be destroyed but may only be used for the purposes set out in that section, namely for any purpose related to the prevention or detection of crime, the investigation of an offence or the conduct of a prosecution.

Who can carry out the search/take the photograph

PACE 1984, s.54A(6), (7)

The search or examination may only be carried out and a photograph of any mark revealed may only be taken by a constable or designated civilian officer of the same sex to the suspect.

SEARCHES AND EXAMINATION TO ASCERTAIN IDENTITY—PRACTICE AND PROCEDURE

PACE 1984, Code D, para. 5.1

The provisions of the Code largely mirror those of the statute.

A person detained at a police station to be searched under a stop and search power is not a detainee for the purposes of these powers.

Authorisation

PACE 1984, Code D, para. 5.2

A search and/or examination to find marks may be carried out without the suspect's consent only if authorised by an officer of at least inspector rank when consent has been withheld or it is not practicable to obtain consent.

PACE 1984, Code D, para. 5.3

A search or examination to establish a suspect's identity may be carried out without his consent only if authorised by an officer of at least inspector rank when the detainee has refused to identify themselves or the authorising officer has reasonable grounds for suspecting the person is not who they claim to be.

Authority for the search and/or examination may be given orally or in writing. If given orally, the authorising officer must confirm it in writing as soon as practicable. A separate authority is required for each purpose which applies.

PACE 1984, Code D, para. 5.8

Any marks that assist in establishing the suspect's identity, or their identification as a person involved in the commission of an offence, are identifying marks. Such marks may be photographed with the suspect's consent or without such consent if it is withheld or it is not practicable to obtain it. Such marks can include scars, injuries and birthmarks.

PACE 1984, Code D, para. 5.4

Who carries out the search

A detainee may only be searched, examined and photographed by a police officer of the same sex.

PACE 1984, Code D, para. 5.5

The thoroughness and extent of any search or examination must be no more than the officer considers necessary to achieve the required purpose. Any search or examination which involves the removal of more than the person's outer clothing shall be conducted in accordance with Code C, Annex A, para. 11. An intimate search may not be carried out under these powers.

PACE 1984, Code D, para. 5.10

PACE 1984, Code D, para. 5.11

Use of photographs

Any photographs of identifying marks taken may be used or disclosed only for purposes related to the prevention or detection of crime, the investigation of offences or the conduct of prosecutions by, or on behalf of, police or other law enforcement and prosecuting authorities inside, and outside, the UK. After being so used or disclosed, the photograph may be retained but must not be used or disclosed except for these purposes. There may be a separate requirement under the Criminal Procedure and Investigations Act 1996 to retain material in connection with criminal investigations.

PACE 1984, Code D, para. 5.6

PACE 1984, Code D, para. 5.7

Reasonable force

If it is established that a person is unwilling to co-operate sufficiently to enable a search and/or examination to take place or a suitable photograph to be taken, an officer may use reasonable force to search and/or examine a detainee without their consent, and photograph any identifying marks without their consent.

PACE 1984, Code D, para. 5.9

Information to be given

When a person is searched, examined or photographed, they must be informed of the purpose of the search, examination or photograph and the grounds on which the relevant authority, if

PACE 1984, Code D, para. 5.16

applicable, has been given, and the purposes for which the photograph may be used, disclosed or retained. This information must be given before the search or examination commences or the photograph is taken.

Documentation

PACE 1984, Code D, para. 5.17

A record must be made when a suspect is searched, examined, or a photograph of the person, or any identifying marks found on them, are taken. The record must include the identity of the officer carrying out the search, examination or taking the photograph, the purpose of the search, examination or photograph and the outcome, the suspect's consent to the search, examination or photograph, or the reason the person was searched, examined or photographed without consent, and the giving of any authority, the grounds for giving it and the authorising officer.

PACE 1984, Code D, para. 5.18

If force is used when searching, examining or taking a photograph a record shall be made of the circumstances and those present.

Volunteers

PACE 1984, Code D, para. 5.19

PACE 1984, Code D, para. 5.20

When there are reasonable grounds for suspecting the involvement of a person in a criminal offence, but that person is at a police station voluntarilyand not detained, a search, examination or photograph of a mark can only be taken if the person consents.

PACE 1984, Code D, para. 5.21

Force may not be used to search and/or examine the person to discover whether they have any marks that would tend to identify them as a person involved in the commission of an offence or to establish their identity, or take photographs of any identifying marks.

PACE 1984, Code D, para. 5.22

The photographs or images of the identifying marks of persons not detained must be destroyed (together with any negatives and copies) unless the person is charged with, or informed they may be prosecuted for, a recordable offence, is prosecuted for a recordable offence, is cautioned for a recordable offence or given a warning or reprimand for a recordable offence, or gives informed consent, in writing, for the photograph or image to be retained.

PACE 1984, Code D, para. 5.23

When the destruction of any photograph or image is to take place, the person must be given an opportunity to witness the destruction or to have a certificate confirming the destruction provided they so request the certificate within five days of being informed the destruction is required.

Examples of the purposes for which a photograph can be used

The examples of purposes related to the prevention or detection of crime, the investigation of offences or the conduct of prosecutions are set out above.

PACE 1984, Code D, NfG 5B

When it would not be practicable to obtain the appropriate consent

The circumstances in which it would not be practicable to obtain the appropriate consent for a search, examination or the taking of a photograph of an identifying mark include:

PACE 1984, Code D, NfG 5D

(a) when the suspect is drunk or otherwise unfit to give consent;

(b) when there are reasonable grounds to suspect that if the person became aware a search or examination was to take place or an identifying mark was to be photographed, they would take steps to prevent this happening, *e.g.* by violently resisting, covering or concealing the mark, etc. and it would not otherwise be possible to carry out the search or examination or to photograph any identifying mark;

(c) in the case of a juvenile, if the parent or guardian cannot be contacted in sufficient time to allow the search or examination to be carried out or the photograph to be taken.

SEARCHES AND EXAMINATION TO ASCERTAIN IDENTITY—PRACTICAL GUIDANCE

Are the conditions satisfied?

The police have wide powers to search and examine a suspect for marks to establish identity or to identify the person as responsible for a crime. These powers extend to taking photographs of such a mark and the use of reasonable force if necessary so to do.

The adviser should be aware of the conditions which apply before the powers can be exercised and ensure that they exist before advising the suspect whether to consent to the procedure. Representations should be made to the custody officer if it is felt that the conditions are not made out even if authorisation has previously been given. For example, the police should be pressed on why they do not believe the suspect is who he says he is and whether there are any other methods of ascertaining his identity, *e.g.* from documentation in his possession on arrest. The adviser should keep a careful note of their representations and advice in these circumstances.

Ultimately if such an examination is to take place without consent the suspect should be advised that reasonable force may be used and that to actively resist may lead to a charge of obstruction or assaulting a police officer.

Volunteers

If the suspect is a volunteer, the search for, examination of and photographing of any marks can only be undertaken with consent. The statute specifically refers to "a person who is detained in a police station" and a suspect attending a police station voluntarily is not "detained". If such a suspect refuses to co-operate with the procedure, it may precipitate their arrest. If a volunteer agrees to the procedure and has a photograph taken, they should be advised as to the destruction requirements. If the volunteer gives consent for a photograph to be retained, it is not clear whether that consent can subsequently be withdrawn. There are no specific provisions in statute or the Codes of Practice concerning photographs unlike those for fingerprints.

Health of Suspect

DUTIES OF THE ADVISER

It is the duty of the legal adviser to look after the interests of the suspect. The Codes of Practice state that the legal adviser's only role in the police station is to protect and advance the legal rights of their client. The adviser may have concerns about the physical or mental health of the suspect and as to whether he is fit to be detained and interviewed. Subject to the instructions of the suspect, the adviser should consider bringing any concerns he may have about the health of the suspect to the attention of the custody officer.

PACE 1984, Code C, NfG 6D

DUTIES OF THE CUSTODY OFFICER

The custody officer is responsible for the welfare of the suspect in police detention. The custody officer must complete a risk assessment for the suspect on his arrival in the custody suite in order to determine whether the detainee is, or might be, in need of medical treatment or attention or requires an appropriate adult, help to check documentation or an interpreter. A record of this determination must be made.

PACE 1984, Code C, para. 3.5

The custody officer is responsible for initiating an assessment as to whether the suspect is likely to present specific risks to custody staff or themselves which will include a check on the Police National Computer as soon as is practicable. Others may be consulted in this process and if there is any delay in carrying out the assessment, the reasons for the delay must be recorded.

PACE 1984, Code C, para. 3.6

The risk assessment must be structured clearly defining the categories of risk to be considered and the result must be incorporated into the custody record. If no specific risks are identified, that should also be noted in the custody record.

PACE 1984, Code C, para. 3.8

Risk assessment is an ongoing process and should be reviewed if circumstances change during the detention of the suspect in the police station.

PACE 1984, Code C, para. 3.10

More detailed guidance on risk assessments is provided in Home Office Circular 32/2000.

PACE 1984, Code C, NfG 3E

The custody officer is responsible for implementing the response to any specific risk assessment by, for example, reducing the opportunities for self-harm, calling a health care professional or increasing the levels of monitoring or observation.

PACE 1984, Code C, para. 3.9

PACE 1984, Code C, para. 9.1

The responsibilities for the care and treatment of detained persons are set out in para. 9 of Code C. However, nothing in this section of the Code prevents the police from calling the police surgeon or, if appropriate, some other health care professional, to examine a suspect for the purposes of obtaining evidence relating to any offence in which he is suspected of being involved.

PACE 1984, Code C, para. 9.5

The custody officer is under a duty to ensure that the suspect receives appropriate clinical attention as soon as reasonably practicable if the suspect:

(a) appears to be suffering from physical illness; or

(b) is injured; or

(c) appears to be suffering from a mental disorder; or

(d) appears to need clinical attention.

PACE 1984, Code C, para. 9.5A
PACE 1984, Code C, Annex H
PACE 1984, Code C, NfG 9C

This requirement applies even if no request is made by the suspect and whether or not the suspect has received clinical attention elsewhere. If the need for attention appears urgent, the nearest available health care professional or an ambulance must be called immediately.

However, it does not apply to minor ailments or injuries which do not need attention. However, all such ailments or injuries must be recorded in the custody record and any doubt must be resolved in favour of calling the appropriate health care professional.

PACE 1984, Code C, para. 9.3

Detained suspects should be visited at least every hour. If no reasonably foreseeable risk was identified in a risk assessment, there is no need to wake a sleeping detainee. Those suspected of being intoxicated through drink or drugs or whose level of consciousness causes concern must, subject to any clinical directions given by the appropriate health care professional, be visited and roused at least every half hour, have their condition assessed as in Code C Annex H and have clinical treatment arranged if appropriate.

PACE 1984, Code C, Annex H

Annex H to Code C provides a list of observations whereby if a suspect fails to meet any of the criteria, an appropriate health care professional or an ambulance must be called. The observations include "rousability", appropriate response to simple questions and appropriate response to simple commands or requests.

PACE 1984, Code C, NfG 9H

The purpose of recording a person's responses when attempting to rouse them using the procedure in Annex H is to enable any change in the individual's consciousness level to be noted and clinical treatment arranged if appropriate.

When arrangements are made to secure clinical attention for a suspect, the custody officer must make sure all relevant information which might assist in the treatment of the suspect's condition is made available to the responsible health care professional. This applies whether or not the health care professional asks for such information. Any officer or police staff with relevant information must inform the custody officer as soon as practicable.

PACE 1984, Code C, para. 9.4

The custody officer must also consider the need for clinical attention in relation to those suffering the effects of alcohol or drugs. A suspect who appears drunk or behaves abnormally may be suffering from illness, the effects of drugs or may have sustained injury, particularly a head injury which is not apparent. A suspect needing or dependent on certain drugs, including alcohol, may experience harmful effects within a short time of being deprived of their supply. In these circumstances, when there is any doubt, police should always act urgently to call an appropriate health care professional or an ambulance.

PACE 1984, Code C, para. 9.5B

PACE 1984, Code C, NfG 9C

If it appears to the custody officer, or they are told, that the suspect may be suffering from an infectious disease or condition, the custody officer must take reasonable steps to safeguard the health of the suspect and others at the station. In deciding what action to take, advice must be sought from an appropriate health care professional. The custody officer has discretion to isolate the person and their property until clinical directions have been obtained.

PACE 1984, Code C, para. 9.7

However, the Codes state that it is important to respect a person's right to privacy and information about their health must be kept confidential and only disclosed with their consent or in accordance with clinical advice when it is necessary to protect the suspect's health or that of others who come into contact with them.

PACE 1984, Code C, NfG 9E

If the suspect requests a clinical examination, an appropriate health care professional must be called as soon as practicable to assess his clinical needs. If a safe and appropriate care plan cannot be provided, the police surgeon's advice must be sought. The suspect may also be examined by a medical practitioner of their choice at their expense.

PACE 1984, Code C, para. 9.8

A "health care professional" means a clinically qualified person working within the scope of practice as determined by their relevant professional body. Whether a health care professional is "appropriate" depends on the circumstances of the duties they carry out at the time.

PACE 1984, Code C, NfG 9A

PACE 1984, Code C, para. 9.9

If a suspect is required to take or apply any medication in compliance with clinical directions prescribed before their detention, the custody officer must consult the appropriate health care professional before the use of the medication. The custody officer is responsible for the safekeeping of any medication and for making sure the suspect is given the opportunity to take or apply prescribed or approved medication. Any such consultation and its outcome shall be noted in the custody record.

PACE 1984, Code C, para. 9.10

However, no police officer may administer or supervise the self-administration of controlled drugs of the types and forms listed in the Misuse of Drugs Regulations 2001, Sch. 1, 2 or 3. A suspect may only self-administer such drugs under the personal supervision of the registered medical practitioner authorising their use. Drugs listed in Sch. 4 or 5 may be distributed by the custody officer for self-administration if they have consulted the registered medical practitioner authorising their use (which may be done by telephone) and both parties are satisfied self-administration will not expose the suspect, police officers or anyone else to the risk of harm or injury.

PACE 1984, Code C, para. 9.11

When an appropriate health care professional administers drugs or other medications, or supervises their self-administration, it must be within current medicines legislation and the scope of practice as determined by their relevant professional body.

PACE 1984, Code C, para. 9.12

If a suspect has in their possession, or claims to need, medication relating to a heart condition, diabetes, epilepsy or a condition of comparable potential seriousness then, the advice of the appropriate health care professional must be obtained.

PACE 1984, Code C, para. 9.13

Whenever the appropriate health care professional is called in accordance with this section to examine or treat a suspect, the custody officer shall ask for their opinion about any risks or problems which police need to take into account when making decisions about the suspect's continued detention, when to carry out an interview if applicable, and the need for safeguards.

PACE 1984, Code C, para. 9.14

When clinical directions are given by the appropriate health care professional, whether orally or in writing, and the custody officer has any doubts or is in any way uncertain about any aspect of the directions, the custody officer shall ask for clarification. It is particularly important that directions concerning the frequency of visits are clear, precise and capable of being implemented.

PACE 1984, Code C, NfG 9F

The custody officer should always seek to clarify directions that the suspect requires constant observation or supervision and should ask the appropriate health care professional to explain precisely what action needs to be taken to implement such directions.

COMPLAINTS

If a complaint is made by, or on behalf of, a suspect about their treatment since their arrest, or it comes to notice that a suspect may have been treated improperly, a report must be made as soon as practicable to an officer of inspector rank or above who is not connected with the investigation. If the matter concerns a possible assault or the possibility of the unnecessary or unreasonable use of force, an appropriate health care professional must also be called as soon as practicable.

PACE 1984, Code C, para. 9.2

DOCUMENTATION

A record must be made in the custody record of:

PACE 1984, Code C, para. 9.15

(a) the arrangements made for an examination by an appropriate health care professional as a result of a complaint by the suspect and of any complaint reported together with any relevant remarks by the custody officer;

(b) any arrangements made for the suspect to receive clinical attention;

(c) any request for a clinical examination and any arrangements made in response;

(d) the injury, ailment, condition or other reason which made it necessary to make the arrangements in (a) to (c);

(e) any clinical directions and advice, including any further clarifications, given to police by a health care professional concerning the care and treatment of the detainee in connection with any of the arrangements made in (a) to (c);

(f) if applicable, the responses received when attempting to rouse a person using the procedure in Annex H.

There is no requirement to record any information about the cause of any injury, ailment or condition on the custody record if it appears capable of providing evidence of an offence.

PACE 1984, Code C, NfG 9G

If a health care professional does not record their clinical findings in the custody record, the record must show where they are recorded.

PACE 1984, Code C, para. 9.16

Any information about the cause of any injury, ailment or condition are not required to be recorded on the custody record if it appears capable of providing evidence of an offence.

PACE 1984, Code C, NfG 9G

PACE 1984, Code C, para. 9.16

However, information which is necessary to custody staff to ensure the effective ongoing care and well being of the suspect must be recorded openly in the custody record.

PACE 1984, Code C, para. 9.17

The custody record shall include a record of all medication a detainee has in their possession on arrival at the police station and a note of any such medication they claim to need but do not have with them.

ASSESSMENT OF FITNESS FOR INTERVIEW

PACE 1984, Code C, Annex G

The Codes of Practice provide general guidance to help police officers and health care professionals assess whether a suspect might be at risk in an interview.

A suspect may be at risk in an interview if it is considered that conducting the interview could significantly harm his physical or mental state or anything the suspect says in the interview about their involvement or suspected involvement in the offence about which they are being interviewed might be considered unreliable in subsequent court proceedings because of their physical or mental state.

In assessing whether the suspect should be interviewed, the following must be considered:

(a) how the suspect's physical or mental state might affect their ability to understand the nature and purpose of the interview, to comprehend what is being asked and to appreciate the significance of any answers given and make rational decisions about whether they want to say anything;

(b) the extent to which the suspect's replies may be affected by their physical or mental condition rather than representing a rational and accurate explanation of their involvement in the offence;

(c) how the nature of the interview, which could include particularly probing questions, might affect the suspect.

Health care professionals must consider the functional ability of the suspect rather than simply relying on a medical diagnosis, *e.g.* it is possible for a person with severe mental illness to be fit for interview.

Health care professionals should advise on the need for an appropriate adult to be present, whether reassessment of the person's fitness for interview may be necessary if the interview lasts beyond a specified time, and whether a further specialist opinion may be required.

When health care professionals identify risks they should be asked to quantify the risks. They should inform the custody officer whether the person's condition is likely to improve, whether it will require or be amenable to treatment, and indicate how long it may take for such improvement to take effect.

The role of the health care professional is to consider the risks and advise the custody officer of the outcome of that consideration. The health care professional's determination and any advice or recommendations should be made in writing and form part of the custody record.

Once the health care professional has provided that information, it is a matter for the custody officer to decide whether or not to allow the interview to go ahead and if the interview is to proceed, to determine what safeguards are needed. Nothing prevents safeguards being provided in addition to those required under the Code. An example might be to have an appropriate health care professional present during the interview, in addition to an appropriate adult, in order constantly to monitor the person's condition and how it is being affected by the interview.

The adviser will also find some assistance in this Annex of the Code and should make their own initial assessment of the fitness of the suspect to be detained and interviewed at the initial meeting with the suspect.

If the adviser forms the opinion that the suspect is unfit to be interviewed by police, he should object to any proposed interview and request that the objection be noted on the custody record. A separate record should be made in the adviser's own notes of the objection, the reasons for it and the police response to it.

If the police insist on going ahead with an interview, the suspect should be advised not to answer questions and a note of the reasons for the advice made in the adviser's notes. As specifically set out in this Annex to the Code, it is for the police to decide if the suspect is fit to be interviewed, although if the adviser raises the issue one would expect the custody officer to seek the advice of a health care professional.

R. v Crampton (1991) 92 Cr. App.R. 369

Any suspect who appears unable to appreciate the significance of questions and their answers or to understand what is happening because of the effects of drink, drugs or any illness, ailment or condition may not be interviewed unless an

PACE 1984, Code C, para.11.18

officer of superintendent rank or above considers delay will lead to:

PACE 1984, Code C, para. 11.1

- interference with, or harm to, evidence connected with an offence; or
- interference with, or physical harm to, other people; or
- serious loss of, or damage to, property; or
- alerting other people suspected of committing an offence but not yet arrested for it; or
- hinder the recovery of property obtained in consequence of the commission of an offence.

PACE 1984, Code C, para. 11.18

The officer must also be satisfied that the interview would not significantly harm the person's physical or mental state (see Annex G).

PACE 1984, Code C, para. 11.19
PACE 1984, Code C, para. 11.20

An interview in these circumstances may not continue once sufficient information has been obtained to avert the above consequences and a record shall be made of the grounds for any decision to interview a person in such circumstances.

PRACTICAL GUIDANCE

(1) Fitness for interview

PACE 1984, Code C, para. 12.2
PACE 1984, Code C, para. 9.8

A suspect may be unfit for a variety of reasons such as stress, anxiety for the safety of his children or tiredness. The suspect will be entitled to a period of eight hours' continuous rest in any 24-hour period and, if he is tired, he may prefer to take advantage of this provision by taking his rest at that time, leaving him more refreshed for interview at a later stage. If stress is an issue, the suspect could be advised to request a medical examination, following which request a health care professional will have to be called as soon as practicable.

The adviser will find some assistance in Annex G of Code C and should make their own initial assessment of the fitness of the suspect to be detained and interviewed at the initial meeting with the suspect.

PACE 1984, Code C, para. 11.18

If the suspect appears unable to appreciate the significance of questions put to him and their answers or to understand what is happening because of the effects of drink, drugs, any illness, ailment or condition, he may not be interviewed unless an officer of superintendent rank authorises it in the specific restricted conditions outlined above. The adviser should be aware of this and bring it to the attention of police if appropriate.

If the adviser forms the opinion that the suspect is unfit to be interviewed by police, he should object to any proposed interview and request that the objection be noted on the custody record. A separate record should be made in the adviser's own notes of the objection, the reasons for it and the police response to it.

If the police insist on going ahead with an interview, the suspect should be advised not to answer questions and a note of the reasons for the advice made in the adviser's notes. The adviser should consider repeating the objection at the start of the interview on tape but should be wary of stating that he has advised the suspect not to answer questions on that basis as this may waive privilege.

As specifically set out in Annex G to Code C, it is for the police to decide if the suspect is fit to be interviewed, although if the adviser raises the issue one would expect the custody officer to seek the advice of a health care professional.

R. v Crampton (1991) 92 Cr. App.R. 369

(2) Mental disorder

A suspect may also be unfit as a result of a mental condition. If the suspect appears to be mentally disordered or otherwise mentally vulnerable, the adviser should, subject to the suspect's instructions, inform the custody officer. Having been told in good faith that the suspect appears to be mentally disordered, the suspect must then be treated as if he were mentally disordered and all the safeguards for such suspects must be applied (refer to the **Mentally Disordered Suspects** index heading).

PACE, 1984, Code C, para. 1.4

(3) Physical injuries

If the suspect has physical injuries, subject to the suspect's instructions, the police should be asked to note the injuries, take photographs of them and have the suspect examined by a health care professional as they may be relevant to a defence such as self-defence or a complaint of police maltreatment. Whether or not the police comply with that request, the adviser should make notes of the injuries, with diagrams if appropriate, and advise the suspect to see his own doctor and take his own photographs immediately after release from the police station if the suspect is to be bailed.

PACE 1984, Code C, para. 9.2

If the police do not co-operate with such a request and it is obvious that the injuries will be relevant to a potential defence

PACE 1984, Code C, para. 9.8

and that the suspect is unlikely to be given bail, the adviser should consider arranging for the suspect to be seen by an independent doctor (which may be a legitimate legal aid disbursement—refer to the **Public Funding** index heading).

PACE 1984, Code C, para. 9.2 and 9.5

Situations in which it will be necessary to do this should be very rare indeed, given the duty of the custody officer to call a health care professional whenever a suspect appears to be suffering from a physical illness or injury, or when any complaint of police maltreatment is made.

Identification Procedures

INTRODUCTION

Visual identification procedures (as opposed to forensic identification by way of samples, fingerprints, *etc.*) are governed by PACE 1984, Code D but are not dealt with in the Act itself.

This chapter deals with the following forms of visual identification procedures:

(a) video identification;

(b) identification parades;

(c) group identification;

(d) confrontation; and

(e) identification by photograph.

These procedures are designed to test the witness' ability to identify the person they saw on a previous occasion and to provide safeguards against mistaken identification.

PACE 1984, Code D, para. 1.2

The first four of these procedures are to be used when the suspect is known to police and effectively form a hierarchy. The preferred method of identification is the video identification procedure which will be offered to the suspect unless it is not practicable or an identification parade is both practicable and more suitable than a video identification. A group identification may initially be offered if the officer in charge of the investigation considers it is more suitable than a video identification or an identification parade and the identification officer considers it practicable to arrange. The identification officer may arrange for the suspect to be confronted by the witness if none of the other options are practicable.

PACE 1984, Code D, para. 3.14

PACE 1984, Code D, para. 3.16

PACE 1984, Code D, para. 3.23

Identification from photographs should only be used where the police do not have a known suspect. Where the suspect is known but not available for whatever reason it may still be possible to hold a video identification procedure or a similar procedure with still photographs.

While PACE 1984 Code D concentrates on visual identification procedures, it does not preclude the police making use of aural identification procedures such as a "voice identification parade", where they judge such a procedure to be appropriate.

PACE 1984, Code D, para. 1.2

Recognition or identification?

Brown and Isaac v The State 67 J.C.L. 469, P.C.

The Codes apply to identification evidence not to the situation where a witness recognises a suspect in so far as the witness knows the suspect from previous dealings with him. An identification procedure is not necessary, and may be positively undesirable, when it is accepted that the suspect is a person well known to the identifying witness. In such a case, the procedure would establish the uncontroversial fact that the witness is able to identify the person he knows, but will not advance the question of whether that person committed the offence.

However, if the recognition is less certain, for instance if the witness claims only slight acquaintance with the suspect or the suspect denies that he is the person whom the witness claims to know, an identification procedure may serve a useful purpose and should be held.

R. v Fergus [1992] Crim. L.R. 363

In a case where the witness claimed only to have seen the suspect once before and had been told his name by a third party, an identification procedure should have been held.

IDENTIFICATION PROCEDURES—PRACTICE AND PROCEDURE

General

First Description

PACE 1984, Code D, para. 3.1

A record must be made of the description of the suspect as first given by a potential witness. This record must:

- be made and kept in a form which enables details of that description to be accurately produced from it;
- be in a visible and legible form which can be given to the suspect or his legal adviser; and
- unless otherwise specified, be made before the witness takes part in any identification procedure.

A copy of the record shall, where practicable, be given to the suspect or his legal adviser before any identification procedure is carried out.

PACE 1984, Code D, NfG 3E, Annex E, para. 1

When it is proposed to show photographs to a witness in accordance with PACE 1984, Code D, Annex E (see below), it is the responsibility of the officer in charge of the investigation to confirm to the officer responsible for supervising and directing the showing of photographs, that the first description given by that witness has been recorded. If this description has not been recorded, the showing of the photographs must be postponed.

The identification officer

The "identification officer" must not be below inspector rank or involved with the investigation. He is responsible for:

PACE 1984, Code D, para. 3.11

- arrangements for a video identification, an identification parade or a group identification procedure;
- the conduct of such a procedure; and
- the circumstances in which an identification procedure must be held.

Unless otherwise specified, the identification officer may allow another officer or police staff to make arrangements for and conduct any of these identification procedures. In delegating these procedures, the identification officer must be able to supervise effectively and either intervene or be contacted for advice.

No officer or any other person involved with the investigation of the case against the suspect, beyond the extent required by these procedures, may take any part in these procedures or act as the identification officer. However, the identification officer may consult the officer in charge of the investigation to determine which identification procedure to use.

When an identification procedure is required, in the interest of fairness to suspects and witnesses, it must be held as soon as practicable. However, often suspects are bailed from police custody for such a procedure to take place. In these circumstances, the duties of the identification officer to provide the explanations, warnings and the written notice of those matters to the suspect before an identification procedure may be performed by the custody officer or other officer not involved in the investigation if an inspector is not available to act as the identification officer before the suspect leaves the station. The officer concerned shall inform the identification officer of the action taken and give them the signed copy of the notice. This provision is designed to avoid or reduce delay in arranging identification procedures by enabling the required information and warnings to be given at the earliest opportunity.

PACE 1984, Code D, paras 3.19, 3.17

PACE 1984, Code D, NfG 3C

Documentation

PACE 1984, Code D, para. 3.25

A record shall be made of the video identification, identification parade, group identification or confrontation on forms provided for the purpose.

PACE 1984, Code D, para. 3.26

If the identification officer considers it is not practicable to hold a video identification or identification parade requested by the suspect, the reasons shall be recorded and explained to the suspect.

PACE 1984, Code D, para. 3.27

A record shall also be made of the failure or refusal of a suspect to co-operate in a video identification, identification parade or group identification and, if applicable, of the grounds for obtaining images before the notice is given to the suspect as above.

Showing films and photographs of incidents and information released to the media

PACE 1984, Code D, para. 3.28

The police may show films or photographs to the public through the national or local media, or to police officers for the purposes of recognition and tracing suspects.

However, when such material is shown to potential witnesses, including police officers, to obtain identification evidence, it shall be shown to them individually to avoid any possibility of collusion, and, as far as possible, the procedure must follow the principles for video identification if the suspect is known or identification by photographs if the suspect is not known.

PACE 1984, Code D, para. 3.29

When a broadcast or publication is made, a copy of the relevant material released to the media for the purposes of recognising or tracing the suspect, shall be kept. The suspect or his legal adviser shall be allowed to view such material before any identification procedure, provided it is practicable and would not unreasonably delay the investigation.

Each witness involved in the procedure shall be asked, after they have taken part, whether they have seen any broadcast or published films or photographs relating to the offence or any description of the suspect and their replies shall be recorded.

Destruction and retention of photographs and images taken or used in identification procedures

PACE 1984, s.64A; PACE 1984, Code D, para. 3.30

The police may take photographs of suspects detained at police stations and these photographs may be used or disclosed only for purposes related to the prevention or detection of crime, the investigation of offences or the conduct of prosecutions by, or on behalf of, police or other law enforcement and prosecuting authorities inside and outside the United Kingdom. After being so used or disclosed, they may be retained but can only be used or disclosed for the same purposes.

Subject to any separate requirement under the CPIA 1996 to retain material in connection with criminal investigations, the photographs (and all negatives and copies) of suspects not detained and any moving images (and copies) of suspects whether or not they have been detained which are taken for the purposes of, or in connection with, any identification procedure must be destroyed unless the suspect:

PACE 1984, Code D, para. 3.31 and 3.33

(a) is charged with, or informed they may be prosecuted for, a recordable offence;

(b) is prosecuted for a recordable offence;

(c) is cautioned for a recordable offence or given a warning or reprimand in accordance with the CDA 1998 for a recordable offence; or

(d) gives informed consent, in writing, for the photograph or images to be retained for the above purposes.

When the destruction of any photograph or image is required as above, the person must be given an opportunity to witness the destruction or to have a certificate confirming the destruction if they request one within five days of being informed that the destruction is required.

PACE 1984, Code D, para. 3.32

Juvenile suspects

If consent is required for a particular identification procedure, that consent must be obtained from the juvenile and his parent or guardian and not the appropriate adult, if the juvenile is aged 14 or over. With a suspect aged under 14, only the consent of the parent or guardian is required. The "parent or guardian" includes any local authority or voluntary organisation in the care of which the juvenile is placed.

PACE 1984, Code D, para. 2.12

PACE 1984, Code D, NfG 2A

The parent, guardian or representative of a local authority or voluntary organisation need not be present to give their consent, unless they are acting as the appropriate adult. However, a parent or guardian who is not present must be fully informed before being asked to consent to the identification procedure. They must be given the same information about the procedure and the juvenile's suspected involvement in the offence as the juvenile and appropriate adult. The parent or guardian must also be allowed to speak to the juvenile and the appropriate adult

PACE 1984, Code D, NfG 2A

if they wish. Provided the consent is fully informed and is not withdrawn, it may be obtained at any time before the procedure takes place.

Consent is required for identification parades, group identifications and video identifications.

PACE 1984, Code D, para. 2.14

If any identification procedure requires information to be given to or sought from a juvenile suspect, it must be given or sought in the presence of the appropriate adult. If the appropriate adult is not present when the information is first given or sought, the procedure must be repeated in the presence of the appropriate adult when they arrive.

PACE 1984, Code D, para. 2.15

Any identification procedure involving the participation of a juvenile, must take place in the presence of the appropriate adult. However, the adult must not be allowed to prompt any identification of a suspect by a witness.

Mentally disordered suspects

PACE 1984, Code D, para. 2.12

For those identification procedures that require the consent of the suspect, consent is only valid if given in the presence of the appropriate adult. Consent cannot be given by the appropriate adult on behalf of the suspect.

Consent is required for identification parades, group identifications and video identifications.

PACE 1984, Code D, para. 2.14

If any identification procedure requires information to be given to or sought from a mentally vulnerable suspect, it must be given or sought in the presence of the appropriate adult. If the appropriate adult is not present when the information is first given or sought, the procedure must be repeated in the presence of the appropriate adult when they arrive.

PACE 1984, Code D, para. 2.15

Any identification procedure involving the participation of a mentally vulnerable suspect, must take place in the presence of the appropriate adult. However, the adult must not be allowed to prompt any identification of a suspect by a witness.

Effect of a refusal to co-operate with an identification procedure

PACE 1984, Code D, para. 3.21

If the suspect refuses to co-operate with a video identification procedure, the police may use covertly taken video images (*e.g.* from the CCTV in the custody suite) to create a video film to show to the witnesses without the consent of the suspect. The police may also use still images instead of video images in such a situation. The images obtained in this way and the film ultimately compiled may not be as fair to the suspect as one with which he consents to co-operate.

If the suspect refuses to co-operate with a group identification or a confrontation, the procedure can be done covertly without the suspect's consent although force cannot be used to effect either form of identification procedure.

R. v Jones and Nelson, The Times, April, 21, 1999

If the suspect refuses to co-operate with an identification parade, such a parade cannot be formed covertly.

However, if the suspect does not consent to and co-operate in a video identification, identification parade or group identification, his refusal may be given in evidence in any subsequent trial and police may make other arrangements to test whether a witness can identify him which may not be as fair to the suspect. There is no provision in PACE 1984 or the CJPOA 1994 for an adverse inference to be drawn from the refusal but the fact finding tribunal at trial may draw their own conclusions.

PACE 1984, Code D, para. 3.17(v)

If a suspect is to refuse to co-operate the adviser should note the reasons for the refusal. It may well be justifiable to refuse to co-operate if there is little or no supporting evidence of involvement in the offence and the witnesses' descriptions are vague or do not resemble the suspect. No proper advice can be given as to whether to co-operate until the descriptions are obtained. Lack of information generally from the police may also be a reason to refuse to co-operate at that stage.

Once a decision to co-operate has been made and a video image taken, the suspect cannot effectively withdraw that consent as the police can proceed without it and use the image they have already taken.

Post-charge identification procedures

Although the police are limited in questioning a suspect post-charge, there is no reference in Code D to post-charge identification procedures. It would appear that the police have the ability to request co-operation in such a procedure post charge as much as they have pre-charge.

PACE 1984, Code C, para. 16.1

It may well be arguable that the analogy with interviewing is perfectly valid and that, if co-operation with a post-charge identification procedure is requested and refused, nothing adverse to the defendant should flow from that at a later stage. In order to charge the suspect the police reasonably believe that they have sufficient evidence to provide a realistic prospect of a conviction for the offence. It is inherently unfair that after that stage has been reached the defendant is asked to co-operate with police potentially to bolster the prosecution case on pain of a potential adverse evidential finding at a stage where the investigation procedure should have ceased.

It is, of course, possible that the request is made because there are doubts about the evidence and that a non-identification would lead to charges being dropped. It may also be the case that post-charge the defendant wishes to have the benefit of an identification procedure and it may not have been clear to the police previously that identification was in dispute.

PACE 1984, Code C, para. 16.5

If the defendant is identified in a post-charge procedure, the police may seek to interview him. This could only conceivably be justified as being in the interests of justice to put to him and give him an opportunity to comment on information concerning the offence which has come to light since he was charged, *i.e.* the identification. If the police seek to interview in such circumstances, no adverse inference can be drawn from silence and the shorter version of the caution is appropriate.

When such requests are made, it is always a difficult decision whether to co-operate or not. For publicly funded defendants, any post-charge identification procedure is funded additionally as part of the investigation stage of a case rather than the proceedings stage.

Effect of a breach of Code D

A breach of the Code of Practice may occur because the police have failed to hold an identification procedure where they should have done so or have failed to follow the requirements of Code D in the identification procedure.

R. v Popat [1998] Crim. L.R. 825

A breach of the Code will not automatically lead to evidence of identification being excluded by the court under s.78 of PACE 1984. The court will consider whether the overall purpose of the Code (to ensure that fair identification procedures are observed so that reliable identification evidence is obtained) has been upheld. The Court of Appeal considers that, whilst it is of the greatest importance that the Codes of Practice are complied with, evidence obtained in breach of a Code will not automatically be excluded. In a borderline case, the question whether there has been a breach is of less importance than the question whether it was fair for the disputed evidence to be admitted.

R. v Haynes (2004) 148 S.J. 181, CA

It is, therefore, important for the adviser to intervene if the Code is breached to the detriment of the suspect or the procedure appears to be in any way unfair.

1. Cases when the suspect's identity is not known

In cases when the suspect's identity is not known, a witness may be taken to a particular area or place to see whether they can identify the person they saw. Although the number, age, sex, race, general description and style of clothing of other people present at the location and the way in which any identification is made cannot be controlled, the principles applicable to the formal identification procedures (see below) shall be followed as far as practicable.

PACE 1984, Code D, para. 3.2

This means that, where it is practicable to do so, a record should be made of the first description of the suspect given by the witness before asking the witness to make an identification and care must be taken not to direct the attention of the witness to any individual unless, taking into account all the circumstances, this cannot be avoided. However, this does not prevent a witness being asked to look carefully at the people around at the time or to look towards a group or in a particular direction, if this appears necessary to make sure that the witness does not overlook a possible suspect simply because the witness is looking in another direction. This may also be done to enable the witness to make comparisons between any suspect and others who are in the area.

PACE 1984, Code D, para. 3.2(a)

PACE 1984, Code D, para. 3.2(b)

Where there is more than one witness, they should be taken to see whether they can identify a person independently and every effort should be made to keep them apart throughout. Once there is sufficient information to justify the arrest of a particular individual for suspected involvement in the offence, *e.g.* after a witness makes a positive identification, the formal identification procedure provisions apply for any other witnesses in relation to that individual.

PACE 1984, Code D, para. 3.2(c)

PACE 1984, Code D, para. 3.2(d)

The officer or police staff accompanying the witness must record, in their pocket book, the action taken as soon as, and in as much detail, as possible. The record should include:

PACE 1984, Code D, para. 3.2(e)

- the date, time and place of the relevant occasion the witness claims to have previously seen the suspect;
- where any identification was made;
- how it was made and the conditions at the time (*e.g.* the distance the witness was from the suspect, the weather and light);
- if the attention of the witness was drawn to the suspect, the reason for this; and
- anything said by the witness or the suspect about the identification or the conduct of the procedure.

The admissibility and value of identification evidence obtained from this procedure may be compromised if, before a person is

PACE 1984, Code D, NfG 3F

identified, the attention of the witness is specifically drawn to that person, or the identity of the suspect becomes known before the procedure takes place.

PACE 1984, Code D, para. 3.3

A witness may only be shown photographs, computerised or artist's composite likenesses or similar likenesses or pictures (including "E-fit" images) if the identity of the suspect is not known to the police. This must be done in accordance with Annex E (see below).

2. Cases when the suspect is known and available

PACE 1984, Code D, para. 3.4

If the suspect's identity is known to the police and they are available a video identification, identification parade or group identification may be used. A suspect is "known" if there is sufficient information known to the police to justify his arrest for suspected involvement in the offence. A suspect is "available" if they are immediately available (or will be within a reasonably short time) and are willing to take an effective part in at least one of the identification procedures which it is practicable to arrange.

When is an identification procedure required?

PACE 1984, Code D, para. 3.12

Firstly, an identification procedure must be held in the following circumstances:

- whenever a witness has identified a suspect or purported to have identified them; or
- there is a witness available, who expresses an ability to identify the suspect, or where there is a reasonable chance of the witness being able to do so; or
- they have not been given an opportunity to identify the suspect in any identification procedure; and
- the suspect disputes being the person the witness claims to have seen.

Even in the above circumstances an identification procedure may not be held if it is not practicable to do so or it would serve no useful purpose in proving or disproving whether the suspect was involved in committing the offence. For example, when it is not disputed that the suspect is already well known to the witness who claims to have seen them commit the crime.

PACE 1984, Code D, para. 3.13

Secondly, an identification procedure may be held if the officer in charge of the investigation considers it would be useful.

(i) The witness has already identified the suspect

It may be the case that a witness has already identified the suspect before the suspect was known to police by way of a "street" identification (as above) or by viewing photographs. In these circumstances an identification procedure would still be required. The police may consider that no useful purpose would be served in such circumstances and the adviser will need to consider with the suspect whether this is the case in the particular circumstances.

PACE 1984, Code D, paras 3.2, 3.3; PACE 1984, Code D, para. 3.12

(ii) The witness expresses an ability to identify the suspect

A witness may believe that they would or might be able to identify the person they saw on the earlier occasion. Of course, this person may or may not have been the arrested suspect.

Equally an identification procedure would be required (if the other conditions are satisfied) if the witness does not say that they may be able to make a positive identification but where it is judged that there is a reasonable chance that they might be able to do so.

R. v Nolan [2002] EWCA Crim 464

(iii) The suspect disputes being the person concerned

The suspect may make it known to police in interview that he disputes being the person described as responsible for the offence. Equally he may make no comment in interview but indicate that he is willing to co-operate with an identification procedure. In these circumstances it will be obvious that identity is disputed.

Identity may also be disputed where the suspect admits presence at the scene but denies participation in the offence. The situation in such circumstances is, however, much more complicated. The Court of Appeal has held that there does not necessarily have to be a positive dispute as to identification raised by the particular suspect as it is sufficient if the circumstances are such that it is clear to the police that there is an identification issue. However, it may be reasonable for the police to conclude in a case that participation and not identification is the issue albeit that it is perfectly possible for there still to be a serious identification issue notwithstanding that presence at the scene is admitted.

R. v Lambert and others [2004] EWCA Crim 154

The question of whether a suspect disputes an identification made or purported to have been made by a witness, such as to require an identification procedure, is to be considered at the time that the police are investigating the offence.

R. v Lambert and others [2004] EWCA Crim 154

R. v McCartney, Hamlett and others [2003], 6 *Archbold News* 2, CA

If the suspect does dispute the purported identification by the witness, even if admitting presence at the scene, it may be helpful to make some positive assertion in order to put identification into dispute and so trigger the provisions of the Code. However, one needs to be careful that in so doing, the suspect does not provide the police with evidence of his presence at the scene which they would otherwise not have.

Karia v DPP [2002] EWHC 2175; (200) 166 J.P. 753

It is often the case that identification procedures are carried out after charge. It may be that the suspect would prefer not to make any comment until charge and once charged suggest through his legal adviser that identification is an issue (in a defence statement or by letter) and invite an identification procedure. If identification is raised as an issue only at trial, there is a risk of the court allowing a "dock identification" which is of course much problematic for the accused.

(iv) an identification procedure is impracticable

With the increase in the use of video procedures, it is much more difficult for the police to claim that an identification procedure is not practicable. It may be that a suspect has a distinguishing feature which is not easily disguised, but even that can be addressed in most cases by pixilation of images in a video procedure. If the feature is not easily disguised in such a way, it may be more practicable to hold an identification parade or to film volunteers wearing hats or other objects such as sticking plasters.

R. v Marcus, The Times, December 3, 2004, CA

Pixilation of images to obscure unusual features is relatively easily done by police in video procedures. If the suspect agrees to a video procedure on the basis that certain distinguishing facial features will be obscured, it is blatantly unfair for the police to conduct a parallel procedure with no obscuring of the images and for the suspect to be told of this at a stage when it was too late to pull out. This is a deliberate device to avoid the protection of Code D and the evidence of identification should be excluded.

R. v Britton and Richards [1989] Crim. L.R. 144

The police have to take a decision on impracticability on reasonable grounds and must take all reasonable steps to investigate the possibility of holding a parade before moving on to another form of identification. This case was decided before the advent of video identification procedures but would apply to the impracticability of all identification procedures and also to the decision as to which type of procedure to use.

(v) the procedure would not serve a useful purpose

If an identification procedure would serve no useful purpose in proving or disproving whether the suspect was involved in committing the offence, no such procedure is required. The Code gives the example of when it is not disputed that the suspect is already well known to the witness who claims to have seen them commit the crime.

Whether an identification procedure would not serve a useful purpose is likely to be an extremely difficult question to answer. The most likely situation where the police may consider that an identification procedure would serve no useful purpose may be where there has already been a street identification. However, the Code specifically allows for an identification procedure to take place in such circumstances. It is of course possible that if a formal identification procedure takes place after a street identification, the witness may be identifying the person he has previously identified on the street rather than the person he saw committing the offence. However, if the suspect wishes to take part in an identification procedure in such circumstances, the adviser should inform the police and seek to persuade them that it would serve a useful purpose.

PACE 1984, Code D, para. 3.12(i)

In a case where the victim of an offence had identified the defendant in the street (after he had been stopped by the police, when he passed by the scene of the crime, as matching the general description that had been given by the victim) by his clothing, and not by recognition of his features, the Court of Appeal considered that an identification parade would have been of little assistance.

R. v Haynes (2004) 148 S.J. 181, CA

Recognition or identification?

The Codes apply to identification evidence not to the situation where a witness recognises a suspect in so far as the witness knows the suspect from previous dealings with him. An identification procedure is not necessary, and may be positively undesirable, when it is accepted that the suspect is a person well known to the identifying witness. In such a case, the procedure would establish the uncontroversial fact that the witness is able to identify the person he knows, but will not advance the question of whether that person committed the offence.

Brown and Isaac v The State, 67 J.C.L. 469, P.C.

In a case where an identifying witness described the suspects as "well known to him" but the suspects disputed the identification or recognition and agreed to a video identification

R. and others v Director of

Public Prosecutions, [2003] EWHC 3074 (Admin)

procedure, such a procedure was not held. The Court held that in such circumstances it would probably have achieved no more than to test whether or not the witness did know the defendants well and would be less effective, if at all, in testing whether he was truthful or accurate as to what they had done.

Brown and Isaac v The State, 67 J.C.L. 469, P.C.

However, in a situation where the witness claims to know the suspect, an identification may still serve a useful purpose. If the recognition is less certain, for instance if the witness claims only slight acquaintance with the suspect or the suspect denies that he is the person whom the witness claims to know, an identification procedure may serve a useful purpose and should be held.

R. v Fergus [1992] Crim. L.R. 363; *R. v Harris* [2003] EWCA Crim 174

In a case where the witness claimed only to have seen the suspect once before and had been told his name by a third party, an identification procedure should have been held. In a case where the witness claimed to recognise the suspect as having been to the same school but where the suspect denied involvement in the offence and had not been at the school for two years, there was a useful purpose in the identification procedure as there was a real possibility that the witness would not have identified the suspect.

Which procedure is to be used?

PACE 1984, Code D, para. 3.14

The suspect must initially be offered a video identification procedure unless:

PACE 1984, Code D, para. 3.16

- it is not practicable;
- an identification parade is practicable and more suitable; or
- the officer in charge of the investigation considers a group identification to be more suitable than a video identification or an identification parade and the identification officer considers a group identification practicable to arrange.

PACE 1984, Code D, para. 3.14

The identification officer and the officer in charge of the investigation shall consult each other to determine which option is to be offered.

PACE 1984, Code D, para. 3.15

If the suspect refuses the identification procedure first offered, he must be asked to state his reason for refusing and may get advice from his solicitor and/or, if present, the appropriate adult.

PACE 1984, Code D, para. 3.15

The suspect, his legal adviser and/or the appropriate adult must be allowed to make representations about why another procedure should be used. A record should be made of the reasons for refusal and any representations made. After considering any reasons given and representations made, the identification officer shall arrange for the suspect to be offered an alternative suitable and practicable procedure, if it is appropriate to do so. If he decides it is not suitable and practicable to offer an alternative identification procedure, the reasons for that decision shall be recorded.

Information to be provided to the suspect

Before a video identification, an identification parade or group identification is arranged, the identification officer (or other officer—see below) must explain to the suspect:

PACE 1984, Code D, para. 3.17

(i) the purposes of the video identification, identification parade or group identification;

(ii) the suspect's entitlement to free legal advice;

(iii) the procedures for holding it, including the right to have a solicitor or friend present;

(iv) that the suspect does not have to consent to or co-operate in a video identification, identification parade or group identification;

(v) that if the suspect does not consent to, and co-operate in, a video identification, identification parade or group identification, their refusal may be given in evidence in any subsequent trial and police may proceed covertly without their consent or make other arrangements to test whether a witness can identify them;

(vi) whether, for the purposes of the video identification procedure, images of them have previously been obtained, and if so, that they may co-operate in providing further, suitable images to be used instead;

(vii) if appropriate, the special arrangements for juveniles;

(viii) if appropriate, the special arrangements for mentally disordered or otherwise mentally vulnerable people;

(ix) that if the suspect significantly alters his appearance between being offered an identification procedure and any attempt to hold an identification procedure, this may be given in evidence if the case comes to trial, and the identification officer may then consider other forms of identification;

(x) that a moving image or photograph may be taken of them when they attend for any identification procedure;

(xi) whether, before their identity became known, the witness was shown photographs, a computerised or artist's composite likeness or similar likeness or image by the police;

(xii) that if the suspect changes his appearance before an identification parade, it may not be practicable to arrange one on the day or subsequently and, because of the appearance change, the identification officer may consider alternative methods of identification;

(xiii) that the suspect or his legal adviser will be provided with details of the description of the suspect as first given by any witnesses who are to attend the video identification, identification parade, group identification or confrontation.

PACE 1984, Code D, para. 3.18

This information must be recorded in a written notice which must be handed to the suspect. He must be given a reasonable opportunity to read the notice, after which, he should be asked to sign a second copy to indicate if he is willing to co-operate with the making of a video or to take part in the identification parade or group identification. The signed copy shall be retained by the identification officer.

PACE 1984, Code D, para. 3.19

The above duties of the identification officer may be performed by the custody officer or other officer not involved in the investigation if it is proposed to hold an identification procedure at a later date and an inspector is not available to act as the identification officer before the suspect leaves the station. The officer concerned shall inform the identification officer of the action taken and give them the signed copy of the notice.

PACE 1984, Code D, para. 3.20

This information may be delayed pending the identification officer arranging for suitable images of the suspect for use in a video identification procedure to be obtained, if the identification officer and officer in charge of the investigation suspect, on reasonable grounds, that the suspect would take steps to avoid being seen by a witness in any identification procedure if given the information beforehand.

If the suspect's images are obtained in these circumstances, the suspect may, for the purposes of a video identification procedure, co-operate in providing suitable new images to be used instead.

3. Cases where the suspect is known but not available

When a known suspect is not available or has ceased to be available, the identification officer may make arrangements for a video identification. This applies when:

PACE 1984, Code D, para. 3.21

- a known suspect deliberately makes himself "unavailable" in order to delay or frustrate arrangements for obtaining identification evidence;
- a suspect refuses or fails to take part in a video identification, an identification parade or a group identification, or
- refuses or fails to take part in the only practicable options from that list.

PACE 1984, Code D, NfG 3D

If necessary, the identification officer may use still images but follow the video identification procedures. Any suitable moving or still images may be used and these may be obtained covertly if necessary. Alternatively, the identification officer may make arrangements for a group identification. These provisions may also be applied to juveniles where the consent of their parent or guardian is either refused or reasonable efforts to obtain that consent have failed.

PACE 1984, Code D, para. 3.21

Any covert activity should be strictly limited to that necessary to test the ability of the witness to identify the suspect.

PACE 1984, Code D, para. 3.22

The identification officer may arrange for the suspect to be confronted by the witness if none of the other identification procedures are practicable. A "confrontation" is when the suspect is directly confronted by the witness. A confrontation does not require the suspect's consent. Confrontations must be carried out in accordance with Annex D (see below).

PACE 1984, Code D, para. 3.23

Requirements for information to be given to, or sought from, a suspect or for the suspect to be given an opportunity to view images before they are shown to a witness, do not apply if the suspect's lack of co-operation prevents the necessary action.

PACE 1984, Code D, para. 3.24

THE FORMAL IDENTIFICATION PROCEDURES

A. VIDEO IDENTIFICATION

A "video identification" is when the witness is shown moving images of a known suspect, together with similar images of others who resemble the suspect. Where the suspect is known

PACE 1984, Code D, para. 3.5

PACE 1984, Code D, para. 3.6

but not available (see above) still images may be used. Video identifications must be carried out in accordance with PACE 1984, Code D, Annex A.

General

PACE 1984, Code D, Annex A, para. 1; PACE 1984, Code D, Annex A, para. 2

An identification officer, who has no direct involvement with the case, is responsible for making arrangements to obtain and to ensure the availability of a suitable set of images to be used in a video identification. The set of images must include the suspect and at least eight other people who, so far as possible, resemble the suspect in age, height, general appearance and position in life. Only one suspect shall appear in any set unless there are two suspects of roughly similar appearance, in which case they may be shown together with at least 12 other people.

PACE 1984, Code D, Annex A, para. 3

The images used to conduct a video identification shall, as far as possible, show the suspect and other people in the same positions or carrying out the same sequence of movements. They shall also show the suspect and other people under identical conditions unless the identification officer reasonably believes:

- because of the failure or refusal of the suspect to co-operate or other reasons, it is not practicable for the conditions to be identical; and
- any difference in the conditions would not direct the attention of a witness to any individual image.

PACE 1984, Code D, Annex A, para. 4

A record must be made of the reasons why it was not considered practicable for the conditions to be identical.

PACE 1984, Code D, Annex A, paras 5 and 6

Each person must be identified by number and, if police officers are shown, any numerals or other identifying badges must be concealed. If a prison inmate is shown as a suspect or volunteer either all or none of the people shown should be in prison clothing.

PACE 1984, Code D, Annex A, para. 7

The suspect or his legal adviser, friend, or appropriate adult must be given a reasonable opportunity to see the complete set of images before it is shown to any witness. If the suspect has a reasonable objection to the set of images or any of the participants, the suspect shall be asked to state the reasons for the objection. Steps shall, if practicable, be taken to remove the grounds for objection. If this is not practicable, the suspect and/or their representative shall be told why their objections cannot be met and the objection, the reason given for it and why it cannot be met shall be recorded on forms provided for the purpose.

Before the images are shown as above, the suspect or his legal adviser must be provided with details of the first description of the suspect by any witnesses who are to attend the video identification.

PACE 1984, Code D, Annex A, para. 8

When a broadcast or publication is made, the suspect or his legal adviser must also be allowed to view any material released to the media by the police for the purpose of recognising or tracing the suspect, provided it is practicable and would not unreasonably delay the investigation.

PACE 1984, Code D, Annex A, para. 8

The suspect's legal adviser, if practicable, shall be given reasonable notification of the time and place the video identification is to be conducted so a representative may attend on behalf of the suspect. If the suspect is unrepresented, this information shall be given to him directly but, for obvious reasons, he may not be present when the images are shown to the witnesses. In the absence of a representative for the suspect, the viewing itself shall be recorded on video. No unauthorised people may be present.

PACE 1984, Code D, Annex A, para. 9

Conducting the video identification

The identification officer is responsible for making the arrangements to ensure that prior to viewing the video the witnesses are not able to communicate with each other about the case or overhear a witness who has already seen the video. The identification officer must not discuss the composition of the set of images with the witness and no witness can be told whether a previous witness has made any identification.

PACE 1984, Code D, Annex A, para. 10

The witnesses must view the video individually. Immediately before the video is shown to the witness, he must be told that the person he saw on a specified earlier occasion may, or may not, appear in the video and that if he cannot make a positive identification, he should say so. The witness shall be advised that at any point, he may ask to see a particular part of the set of images or to have a particular image frozen for them to study. Furthermore, it should be pointed out to the witness that there is no limit on how many times they can view the whole set of images or any part of them. However, they should be asked not to make any decision as to whether the person they saw is on the set of images until they have seen the whole set at least twice.

PACE 1984, Code D, Annex A, para. 11

PACE 1984, Code D, Annex A, para. 12

Once the witness has seen the whole set of images at least twice and has indicated that they do not want to view the images, or any part of them, again, the witness shall be asked to say whether the individual they saw in person on a specified earlier occasion has been shown and, if so, to identify them by number of the image. The witness will then be shown that image to confirm the identification.

PACE 1984, Code D, Annex A, para. 13

The identification officer (and any other person present) must take care not to direct the attention of the witness to any one individual image or to give any indication of the suspect's identity.

PACE 1984, Code D, Annex A, para. 13

Where a witness has previously made an identification by photographs, or a computerised or artist's composite or similar likeness, the witness must not be reminded of such a photograph or composite likeness once a suspect is available for a formal identification procedure. The witness must not be reminded of any description of the suspect.

PACE 1984, Code D, Annex A, para. 14

After the procedure, each witness shall be asked whether they have seen any broadcast or published films or photographs, or any descriptions of suspects relating to the offence and their reply shall be recorded.

Image security and destruction

PACE 1984, Code D, Annex A, para. 15

Arrangements shall be made for all relevant material containing sets of images used for specific identification procedures to be kept securely and their movements accounted for. In particular, no-one involved in the investigation shall be permitted to view the material prior to it being shown to any witness.

PACE 1984, Code D, paras 3.31, 3.32, Annex A, para. 16

The destruction or retention of relevant sets of images is dealt with above.

Documentation

PACE 1984, Code D, Annex A, para. 17

A record must be made of:

- all those participating in, or seeing, the set of images whose names are known to the police;

PACE 1984, Code D, Annex A, para. 18

- the conduct of the video identification which shall include anything said by the witness about any identifications or the conduct of the procedure and any reasons it was not practicable to comply with any of the provisions of the Code governing the conduct of video identifications.

VIDEO IDENTIFICATION—PRACTICAL GUIDANCE

(1) Should the video identification take place?

Whenever a suspect disputes an identification, an identification procedure should be held if he consents and the procedure is both practicable and would serve a useful purpose. A video identification procedure is the preferred option although the decision is for the police.

It will normally be clear when identification is in dispute and the suspect will be asked by the police to agree to an identification procedure. However, there may be situations when the suspect will want to request that he be allowed to take part in such a procedure when the police do not themselves consider it necessary. In these circumstances the procedure must be held if it is practicable to do so unless the police believe that it will serve no useful purpose. In such circumstances the adviser should inform the police that the suspect wishes such a procedure to take place.

Advising on whether the suspect should positively request an identification procedure is not an easy task, as there is always the possibility that he will be identified and thus the case against him will be strengthened. On the other hand, if he is not identified, it may be of great assistance to his case or may even result in no further action being taken.

The adviser should consider:

(a) the description given by the witness;

(b) the nature of the identification evidence;

(c) the number of identification witnesses; and

(d) whether any witness has seen the suspect previously

before advising on whether the suspect should request an identification procedure. The above list is not exhaustive and the adviser should seek as much information as possible from the police before any advice is given.

If an identification procedure is to take place, it is most likely that it will be a video procedure unless such a procedure is impracticable. If the adviser feels that another form of identification procedure is preferable, he should make representations to the identification officer who should consider them before deciding on the type of procedure to use.

In fact, there are some advantages to a video identification over the other forms of identification procedure. For instance, a video procedure uses just a head and shoulders shot of the suspect. This means that the witness will not easily be able to gauge the height, build or general physique of the suspect. In addition, in a video procedure, the concern about a suspect being asked to take a certain posture or speak is removed.

(2) Appropriateness of video procedure images

The adviser must be given the opportunity to attend the video identification procedure and to view the completed film before it is seen by any witness. In fact, the adviser, if instructed at the appropriate stage, and the suspect will be given the opportunity to help select the appropriate images from the database.

The adviser should ensure that all the persons on the film are of broadly similar appearance and that nothing marks out the suspect as being different from the others. This may not be as a result of his appearance but because of other considerations, such as the background of the video, the lighting or other such factors.

PACE 1984, Code D, Annex A, para. 7

Any representations should be noted and the identification officer will be obliged to cater for those objections or to explain why it is not practicable to do so. For instance it may be that the suspect has an unusual feature which cannot be replicated in the other images and needs to be obscured (see below).

The police will compile nine versions of the film with the suspect at a different position in each film. The adviser will be able to choose which film is shown to each witness (and therefore select the position of the suspect).

(3) Unusual appearance of the suspect

If the suspect has a particular unusual identifying feature, a video procedure can generally still be practical.

It is a legitimate tactic to request that the unusual feature be disguised. This is most likely to involve the pixilating of the images to obscure the feature. In certain cases, it may involve the police obtaining volunteers to be filmed using sticking plaster to cover a tattoo or scar, or a hat to hide an unusual hairstyle, although this is likely to be a less common occurrence. In the case of an unusual hairstyle such a procedure may be the most appropriate way to deal with the situation other than conducting an identification parade using similar measures. The purpose is to avoid the suspect being identified purely as a result of the striking feature.

The fact that a witness has identified the perpetrator of the crime as having such a distinguishing feature may be enough in itself for the suspect to be charged with the offence, notwithstanding that he has not been identified on an identification procedure.

(4) Requesting that the image be seen without the pixilation

It may be possible that a witness may wish to view an image of an individual on the film without the obscuring element. It will depend on the technology used as to whether such a request can be met. One would expect that if there is a video with pixilation, it will have been produced from a video without the images pixilated. Whether that film is available to show to the witness is another matter.

If there is pixilation or another obscuring element used, the adviser should check with the identification officer prior to the witness viewing the film what his response will be if the witness makes such a request. If the technology or facilities are available for the witness to see the image without the obscuring element, the adviser should consider making representations to the officer at that point that he should not allow the witness to see an unobscured image whether it be the suspect or a "volunteer". For the witness to see whether there is or is not something under the obscured part of the film, may have an undue influence on his decision as to whether the image is the person he saw on a previous occasion or not. It would not be helpful to make the objection at the time that the witness makes the request as it may draw attention to the suspect.

The adviser may be assisted in these representations by the fact that there is no mention in Annex A of allowing the witness to see an image in a different form to that which appears on the video. This is in contrast to provisions in Annex B concerning identification parades where an individual is asked to speak or remove an obscuring item such as a hat.

(5) Consequences of refusing an identification procedure

The suspect will be informed by the police that evidence may be given of his refusal to co-operate with an identification procedure. However, it is not specified in PACE 1984 or CJPOA 1994 that an adverse inference can be drawn from refusal to co-operate.

PACE 1984, Code D, para. 3.17

It is, of course, entirely possible that a jury or magistrate will draw their own conclusions from such a refusal and the suspect should be so warned. However, any prejudicial evidential effects of refusal to consent to an identification procedure may not be as devastating to the defence case as a positive identification.

If the suspect refuses to co-operate with a video identification procedure, the police may proceed with a video procedure without consent using an image taken covertly to compile a video film to show to the witness. In such a film the images may not be identical and the film may not be as fair as one to which the suspect had consented. The suspect can volunteer to replace the covert image with another image at that time and it is certainly arguable that the police ought to allow this.

PACE 1984, Code D, para. 3.17 (vi)

The police may also consider other forms of identification procedure which may not be as fair to the suspect. Ultimately, the position may be reached where a confrontation is held without the consent of the suspect. The adviser should warn the suspect of these possibilities before the suspect decides whether or not to consent to the video identification procedure.

(6) Notes

The adviser must take careful notes of all that happens, including the identity of the persons present, the time taken by the witness viewing the individuals on the film and anything said by any of the parties present.

The adviser should note what is said to and by the witness and the actions of the witness, including how he views the film and whether he asks for any of the frames to be paused or to view certain individuals again.

B. IDENTIFICATION PARADES

PACE 1984, Code D, paras 3.7, 3.8

An "identification parade" is when the witness sees the suspect in a line of others who resemble the suspect. Identification parades must be carried out in accordance with PACE 1984, Code D, Annex B.

General

PACE 1984, Code D, Annex B, para. 1

A suspect must be given a reasonable opportunity to have a legal adviser or friend present, and the suspect shall be asked to indicate on a second copy of the notice whether or not they wish to do so.

An identification parade may take place either in a normal room or one equipped with a screen permitting witnesses to see members of the identification parade without being seen. The procedures for the composition and conduct of the identification parade are the same in both cases, except that an identification parade involving a screen may take place only when the suspect's legal adviser, friend or appropriate adult is present or the identification parade is recorded on video.

PACE 1984, Code D, Annex B, para. 2

PACE 1984, Code D, Annex B, para. 8

Before the identification parade takes place, the suspect or his legal adviser must be provided with details of the first description of the suspect by any witnesses who are attending the identification parade. When a broadcast or publication is made the suspect or his legal adviser should also be allowed to view any material released to the media by the police for the purpose of recognising or tracing the suspect, provided it is practicable to do so and would not unreasonably delay the investigation.

PACE 1984, Code D, Annex B, para. 3

Identification parades involving prison inmates

If a prison inmate is required for identification, and there are no security problems about the person leaving the establishment, they may be asked to participate in an identification parade or video identification.

PACE 1984, Code D, Annex B, para. 4

An identification parade may be held in a prison establishment but shall be conducted, as far as practicable under normal identification parade rules. Members of the public shall make up the identification parade unless there are serious security or control objections to their admission to the establishment. In such cases, or if a group or video identification is arranged within the establishment, other inmates may participate. If an inmate is the suspect, they are not required to wear prison clothing for the identification parade unless the other people taking part are other inmates in similar clothing, or are members of the public who are prepared to wear prison clothing for the occasion.

PACE 1984, Code D, Annex B, para. 5

Conduct of the identification parade

Immediately before the identification parade, the suspect must be reminded of the procedures governing its conduct and given the appropriate caution.

PACE 1984, Code D, Annex B, para. 6

All unauthorised people must be excluded from the place where the identification parade is held. Once the identification parade has been formed, everything afterwards, in respect of it, shall take place in the presence and hearing of the suspect and any interpreter, legal adviser, friend or appropriate adult who is present. If the identification parade involves a screen, everything

PACE 1984, Code D, Annex B, para. 7

PACE 1984, Code D, Annex B, para. 8

said to or by any witness at the place where the identification parade is held, must be said in the hearing and presence of the suspect's legal adviser, friend or appropriate adult or be recorded on video.

PACE 1984, Code D, Annex B, para. 9

The identification parade shall consist of the suspect plus at least eight people who, so far as possible, resemble the suspect in age, height, general appearance and position in life. Only one suspect shall be included in an identification parade unless there are two suspects of roughly similar appearance, in which case they may be paraded together with at least 12 other people. In no circumstances shall more than two suspects be included in one identification parade and where two suspects have separate identification parades, the parades shall be made up of different volunteers.

PACE 1984, Code D, Annex B, para. 10

If the suspect has an unusual physical feature (such as a facial scar, tattoo or distinctive hairstyle or hair colour) which cannot be replicated on other members of the identification parade, steps may be taken to conceal the location of that feature on the suspect and the other members of the identification parade so that all members of the parade resemble each other in general appearance. This may be done by way of a sticking plaster or a hat.

PACE 1984, Code D, Annex B, para. 11

When all members of a similar group are possible suspects, separate identification parades shall be held for each unless there are two suspects of similar appearance when they may appear on the same identification parade with at least 12 other members of the group who are not suspects. When police officers in uniform form an identification parade any numerals or other identifying badges shall be concealed.

PACE 1984, Code D, Annex B, para. 12

When the suspect is brought to the place where the identification parade is to be held, he shall be asked if he has any objection to the arrangements for the identification parade or to any of the other participants in it and to state the reasons for the objection. The suspect may obtain advice from their legal adviser or friend, if present, before the identification parade proceeds.

PACE 1984, Code D, Annex B, para. 12

If the suspect has a reasonable objection to the arrangements or any of the participants, steps shall, if practicable, be taken to remove the grounds for objection. When it is not practicable to do so, the suspect shall be told why the objections cannot be met and the objection, the reason given for it and why it cannot be met, shall be recorded.

PACE 1984, Code D,

The suspect may select his own position in the line, but may not otherwise interfere with the order of the people forming the line. When there is more than one witness, the suspect must be told, after each witness has left the room, that he can, if he wishes, change position in the line. Each position in the line must be clearly numbered, whether by means of a number laid on the floor in front of each identification parade member or by other means.

Annex B, para. 13

Appropriate arrangements must be made to make sure, before witnesses attend the identification parade, they are not able to:

PACE 1984, Code D, Annex B, para. 14

(i) communicate with each other about the case or overhear a witness who has already seen the identification parade;

(ii) see any member of the identification parade;

(iii) see, or be reminded of, any photograph or description of the suspect or be given any other indication as to the suspect's identity; or

(iv) see the suspect before or after the identification parade.

The person conducting a witness to an identification parade must not discuss with them the composition of the identification parade and, in particular, must not disclose whether a previous witness has made any identification.

PACE 1984, Code D, Annex B, para. 15

Witnesses shall be brought in one at a time. Immediately before the witness inspects the identification parade, the conducting officer must tell him that the person he saw on a specified earlier occasion may, or may not, be present and if he cannot make a positive identification, he should say so. The witness must also be told that they should not make any decision about whether the person they saw is on the identification parade until they have looked at each member at least twice.

PACE 1984, Code D, Annex B, para. 16

When the conducting officer is satisfied the witness has properly looked at each member of the identification parade, they shall ask the witness whether the person they saw on a specified earlier occasion is on the identification parade and, if so, to indicate the number of the person concerned.

PACE 1984, Code D, Annex B, para. 17

If the witness wishes to hear any identification parade member speak, adopt any specified posture or move, they shall first be asked whether they can identify any person on the identification parade on the basis of appearance only. When the request is to hear members of the identification parade speak, the witness shall be reminded that the participants in the

PACE 1984, Code D, Annex B, para. 18

identification parade have been chosen on the basis of physical appearance only. Members of the identification parade may then be asked to comply with the request to speak, move or adopt any specified posture.

PACE 1984, Code D, Annex B, para. 19

If the witness requests that the person they have indicated remove anything used to conceal an unusual physical feature, that person may be asked to remove it.

PACE 1984, Code D, Annex B, para. 20

If the witness makes an identification after the identification parade has ended, the suspect and, if present, his legal adviser, interpreter or friend shall be informed. In such a situation, consideration should be given to allowing the witness a second opportunity to identify the suspect.

PACE 1984, Code D, Annex B, para. 21

After the procedure, each witness shall be asked whether they have seen any broadcast or published films or photographs or any descriptions of suspects relating to the offence and their reply shall be recorded.

PACE 1984, Code D, Annex B, para. 22

When the last witness has left, the suspect shall be asked whether they wish to make any comments on the conduct of the identification parade.

Documentation

PACE 1984, Code D, Annex B, para. 23

The identification parade should be video recorded but, if it is impracticable to do so, a colour photograph must be taken of the parade. A copy of the video recording or photograph shall be supplied, on request, to the suspect or his legal adviser within a reasonable time.

PACE 1984, Code D, paras 3.31, 3.32, Annex B, para. 24

The destruction or retention of any photograph or video taken is dealt with above.

A record must be made of:

PACE 1984, Code D, Annex B, para. 25

- the circumstances in which any person is asked to leave an identification parade because they are interfering with its conduct;

PACE 1984, Code D, Annex B, para. 26

- all those present at an identification parade whose names are known to the police;

PACE 1984, Code D, Annex B, para. 27

- the circumstances in which any prison inmates make up an identification parade;

PACE 1984, Code D, Annex B, para. 28

- the conduct of any identification parade (on forms provided for the purpose) which includes anything said by the witness or the suspect about any identifications or the conduct of the procedure, and any reasons it was not practicable to comply with any provisions of the Code.

IDENTIFICATION PARADES—PRACTICAL GUIDANCE

Much of the advice and guidance which applies to video identification procedures also applies to identification parades.

(1) Should a parade be held?

An identification parade will generally only be held if a video identification procedure is impracticable. In some circumstances, a parade may be preferable perhaps as a result of an unusual feature of the suspect which cannot easily be disguised on a video, such as an unusual hair colour or style.

(2) Forming the parade

Normally, the police gather a number of volunteers together, from which the suspect and his adviser choose the best eight. The volunteers are never going to be identical to the suspect but the adviser should assist in choosing those that appear most similar to the suspect and to the description given by the witness.

The adviser and the suspect should object to volunteers who are unsuitable but should bear in mind that a parade may be considered impracticable if too many volunteers are rejected. The adviser should consider whether he could assist in finding suitable volunteers and let the police know if this may be possible.

It is important that all the persons on the parade are dressed in similar clothes. Clothing can be swapped amongst members of the parade or provided by the police.

(3) Unusual appearance of suspect

If the suspect has a particular unusual identifying feature, a parade can generally still be practical.

It is a legitimate tactic to request that the unusual feature be disguised. This may involve using sticking plaster to cover a tattoo or scar, or a hat to hide an unusual hairstyle: obviously, all of the volunteers on the parade will have to wear the sticking plaster in the same position or a similar type of hat. This will avoid the suspect being identified purely as a result of the striking feature.

The fact that a witness has identified the perpetrator of the crime as having such a distinguishing feature may be enough in itself for the suspect to be charged with the offence, notwithstanding that he has not been identified on a parade.

(4) Demeanour during the parade

The suspect should be told to act in the same manner as the volunteers. He should adopt the same posture and try not to appear nervous or anxious. Generally, the suspect should be told to look straight ahead and to remain as still as possible.

If the suspect is asked to speak or strike a particular pose during the parade, he should be told to do so and to leave any objection to the adviser (refer to point (7) below).

(5) Consequences of refusing a parade

PACE 1984, Code D, para. 3.17

The suspect will be informed by the police that evidence may be given of his refusal to stand on an identification parade. However, it is not specified in PACE 1984 or CJPOA 1994 that an adverse inference can be drawn from refusal to stand on a parade.

It is of course entirely possible that a jury or magistrate will draw their own conclusions from such a refusal and the suspect should be so warned. However, any prejudicial evidential effects of refusal to consent to an identification parade may not be as devastating to the defence case as a positive identification.

If the suspect does refuse to stand on an identification parade, the police may consider other forms of identification procedure which may not be as fair to the suspect as a parade. Ultimately, the position may be reached where a confrontation is held without the consent of the suspect. The adviser should warn the suspect of these possibilities before the suspect decides whether or not to consent to the identification parade.

(6) Notes

It is vitally important that the adviser takes a note of everything that happens during an identification parade even where the parade is recorded on videotape.

The adviser should note what is said to and by the witness and the actions of the witness, including how he views the parade and whether he pauses at any particular member of the parade. It is helpful to record the movements of the witness in diagrammatical form.

A note should also be made of the identity of the police officer bringing the witness to the parade, to ensure he is not involved in the investigation.

(7) Requests for a member of the parade to speak or move

PACE 1984, Code D,

If the witness makes such a request, the adviser should consider whether to object. Such a request can be acceded to by the identification officer. However, the parade has been formed on the basis of physical appearance and not voice or movement. The identification officer will have to remind the witness of this and any objection should be made at this stage by the adviser only if it is possible to do so without identifying the suspect in any way. If, however, the request is acceded to by the identification officer and the person who is requested to speak or move is the suspect, he should do so immediately. Further objection can be made after the parade if the suspect is identified.

Annex B, para. 18

(8) Photograph or video recording

The parade will either have to be recorded on videotape or in a colour photograph. The adviser should ensure that these provisions are complied with by the police.

PACE 1984, Code D, Annex B, para. 23

C. GROUP IDENTIFICATION

A "group identification" is when the witness sees the suspect in an informal group of people. Such procedures must be carried out in accordance with PACE 1984, Code D, Annex C.

PACE 1984, Code D, paras 3.9, 3.10

General

A group identification should follow the principles and procedures for identification parades in order that the conditions are fair to the suspect in the way the ability of the witness to make an identification is tested. Group identifications may take place either:

PACE 1984, Code D, Annex C, para. 1

- with the consent and cooperation of the suspect; or
- covertly, *i.e.* without the consent of the suspect.

PACE 1984, Code D, Annex C, para. 2

The identification officer decides on the location of the group identification, although he may take account of any representations made by the suspect, his legal adviser, appropriate adult or friend.

PACE 1984, Code D, Annex C, para. 3

The group identification should be held in a place where other people are either passing by or waiting around informally in groups so that the suspect can join them and be seen by the witness at the same time as others in the group. The Code gives the following examples: people leaving an escalator, pedestrians walking through a shopping centre, passengers on railway and bus stations, waiting in queues or groups or where people are standing or sitting in groups in other public places.

PACE 1984, Code D, Annex C, para. 4

PACE 1984, Code D, Annex C, para. 5

The choice of location for a covert group identification will be limited by the places where the suspect can be found and the number of other people present at that time. In these cases, suitable locations might be along regular routes taken by the suspect, including buses or trains or public places frequented by the suspect.

PACE 1984, Code D, Annex C, para. 6

PACE 1984, Code D, Annex C, para. 7

Although the identification officer cannot control the number, age, sex, race and general description and style of clothing of other people present at the location, in selecting the location he must consider the general appearance and numbers of people likely to be present at that location. In particular, he must reasonably expect that during the observation, the witness will be able to see, from time to time, a number of others whose appearance is broadly similar to that of the suspect. If the identification officer believes that none of the available locations would contain sufficient people of a similar appearance to the suspect because of his unusual appearance, a group identification need not be held as any identification may not be fair.

PACE 1984, Code D, Annex C, para. 8

PACE 1984, Code D, Annex C, para. 9

Immediately after a group identification procedure has taken place (with or without the consent of the suspect), a colour photograph or video should be taken of the general scene, if practicable, to give a general impression of the scene and the number of people present. Alternatively, if it is practicable, the group identification may be video recorded. If it is not practicable to take a photograph or video of the scene at the time, one should be taken later at a time determined by the identification officer if the officer considers it practicable to do so.

PACE 1984, Code D, Annex C, para. 10

If the suspect was on his own rather than in a group at the time he was seen by the witness, it still constitutes a group identification.

PACE 1984, Code D, Annex C, para. 11

PACE 1984, Code D, Annex C, para. 12

The suspect or his legal adviser must be provided with details of the first descriptions by any witnesses who are to attend the identification procedure before it takes place. The suspect or his legal adviser must also be allowed to view any material released by the police to the media for the purposes of recognising or tracing the suspect, provided that it is practicable and would not unreasonably delay the investigation. After the procedure, each witness must be asked whether they have seen any broadcast or published films or photographs or any descriptions of suspects relating to the offence and a record made of their reply.

Identification with the consent of the suspect

PACE 1984, Code D, Annex C, para. 13

The suspect must be given a reasonable opportunity to have a legal adviser or friend present and he must be asked to indicate on a second copy of the notice whether or not he wishes to do so.

The witness, the person carrying out the procedure and the suspect's legal adviser, appropriate adult, friend or any interpreter for the witness, may be concealed from the sight of the individuals in the group they are observing, if the person carrying out the procedure considers this assists the conduct of the identification.

PACE 1984, Code D, Annex C, para. 14

The person taking a witness to a group identification must not discuss with them the forthcoming group identification and, in particular, must not disclose whether a previous witness has made any identification.

PACE 1984, Code D, Annex C, para. 15

Anything said to or by the witness during the procedure about the identification should be said in the presence and hearing of those present at the procedure.

PACE 1984, Code D, Annex C, para. 16

Appropriate arrangements must be made to ensure that before witnesses attend the group identification, they are not able to:

PACE 1984, Code D, Annex C, para. 17

- communicate with each other about the case or overhear a witness who has already been given an opportunity to see the suspect in the group;
- see the suspect; or
- see or be reminded of any photographs or description of the suspect or be given any other indication of his identity.

The witnesses must be brought to the place where they are to observe the group individually. Immediately before the witness is asked to look at the group, the person conducting the procedure shall tell them that the person they saw may or may not be in the group and that if they cannot make a positive identification, they should say so. The witness shall be asked to observe the group in which the suspect is to appear. The way in which the witness should do this depends on whether it is a moving or stationary group.

PACE 1984, Code D, Annex C, para. 18

(i) Moving group

When the group in which the suspect is to appear is moving, *e.g.* leaving an escalator, the following provisions must be adhered to:

PACE 1984, Code D, Annex C, para. 19

- If two or more suspects consent to a group identification, each should be the subject of separate identification

PACE 1984, Code D, Annex C, para. 20

procedures which may be conducted consecutively on the same occasion.

PACE 1984, Code D, Annex C, para. 21

- The person conducting the procedure shall tell the witness to observe the group and ask them to point out any person they think they saw on the specified earlier occasion.

PACE 1984, Code D, Annex C, para. 22

- The suspect should then be allowed to take whatever position in the group he wishes.

PACE 1984, Code D, Annex C, para. 23

- When the witness points out a person they shall, if practicable, be asked to take a closer look at the person to confirm the identification. If this is not practicable, or they cannot confirm the identification, they shall be asked how sure they are that the person they have indicated is the relevant people.

PACE 1984, Code D, Annex C, para. 24

- The witness should continue to observe the group for the period which the person conducting the procedure reasonably believes is necessary in the circumstances for them to be able to make comparisons between the suspect and other individuals of broadly similar appearance.

(ii) Stationary groups

PACE 1984, Code D, Annex C, para. 25

When the group in which the suspect is to appear is stationary, *e.g.* people waiting in a queue, the following provisions must be adhered to:

PACE 1984, Code D, Annex C, para. 26

- If two or more suspects consent to a group identification, each should be subject to separate identification procedures unless they are of broadly similar appearance when they may appear in the same group. When separate group identifications are held, the groups must be made up of different people.

PACE 1984, Code D, Annex C, para. 27

- The suspect may take whatever position in the group they wish. If there is more than one witness, the suspect must be told, out of the sight and hearing of any witness, that they can, if they wish, change their position in the group.

PACE 1984, Code D, Annex C, para. 28

- The witness shall be asked to pass along, or amongst, the group and to look at each person in the group at least twice, taking as much care and time as possible according to the circumstances, before making an identification. The witness shall then be asked whether the person they saw on the specified earlier occasion is in the group and to indicate any such person by whatever means the person conducting the procedure considers appropriate in the circumstances. If this is not practicable, the witness shall be asked to point out any person they think they saw on the earlier occasion.

- When the witness makes an indication, arrangements shall be made, if practicable, for the witness to take a closer look at the person to confirm the identification. If this is not practicable, or the witness is unable to confirm the identification, they shall be asked how sure they are that the person they have indicated is the relevant person.

PACE 1984, Code D, Annex C, para. 29

(iii) All cases

The following points apply to all types of group identification procedure:

- If the suspect unreasonably delays joining the group, or having joined the group, deliberately conceals himself from the sight of the witness, he may be treated as having refused to co-operate in the group identification.

PACE 1984, Code D, Annex C, para. 30

- If the witness identifies a person other than the suspect, that person should be informed what has happened and asked if they are prepared to give their name and address. There is no obligation upon any member of the public to give these details. There is no duty to record any details of any other member of the public present in the group or at the place where the procedure is conducted.

PACE 1984, Code D, Annex C, para. 31

- When the group identification has been completed, the suspect shall be asked whether they wish to make any comments on the conduct of the procedure.

PACE 1984, Code D, Annex C, para. 32

- If the suspect has not been previously informed, they shall be told of any identifications made by the witnesses.

PACE 1984, Code D, Annex C, para. 33

Identification without the suspect's consent

Group identifications held covertly without the consent of the suspect should, as far as practicable, follow the rules for conduct of group identification by consent.

PACE 1984, Code D, Annex C, para. 34

However, the suspect has no right to have a legal adviser, appropriate adult or friend present as the identification will take

PACE 1984, Code D,

Annex C, paras 35, 36

place without his knowledge and in such circumstances any number of suspects may be identified at the same time.

Identifications in police stations

PACE 1984, Code D, Annex C, paras 37, 38, 39

Group identifications should only take place in police stations for reasons of safety, security or because it is not practicable to hold them elsewhere. In such situations the group identification may take place either in a room equipped with a screen permitting witnesses to see members of the group without being seen, or anywhere else in the police station that the identification officer considers appropriate. Any of the additional safeguards applicable to identification parades should be followed if the identification officer considers it is practicable to do so in the circumstances.

Identifications involving prison inmates

PACE 1984, Code D, Annex C, paras 40, 41

A group identification involving a prison inmate may only be arranged in the prison or at a police station. In such circumstances, the arrangements should follow those for identifications in a police station (see above). If a group identification takes place in a prison, other inmates may participate and if the suspect is an inmate, he does not have to wear prison clothing unless the other participants are wearing such clothing.

Documentation

PACE 1984, Code D, Annex C, para. 42

When a photograph or video is taken of the scene, a copy of the photograph or video shall be supplied on request to the suspect or his legal adviser within a reasonable time.

PACE 1984, Code D, paras 3.31, 3.32, Annex C, para. 43

The destruction or retention of any such photograph or video which includes the suspect is dealt with above.

PACE 1984, Code D, Annex C, para. 44

A record of the conduct of any group identification must be made on forms provided for the purpose which includes anything said by the witness or suspect about any identifications or the conduct of the procedure and any reasons why it was not practicable to comply with any of the provisions of the Code governing the conduct of group identifications.

GROUP IDENTIFICATION—PRACTICAL GUIDANCE

Much of the advice and guidance which applies to video identification procedures and identification parades also applies to group identification procedures.

(1) Should the group identification take place?

A group identification can take place in preference to any other form of procedure if the officer in charge of the investigation considers it more satisfactory than a video procedure or identification parade and the identification officer considers it practicable to arrange.

PACE 1984, Code D, para. 3.16

Generally, however, a video identification procedure must be offered to the suspect as a first choice and the suspect can make representations on the type of procedure to be used. If the police wish to use a group identification as a first preference, they should be asked to explain why they consider it more satisfactory than the other type of procedure.

(2) Type of group identification

Group identifications can take place in a number of different situations and places, they can be moving or stationary.

The adviser should be prepared to make representations about the suitability of the proposed venue for the group identification. It may be that the adviser believes that the area in which the police propose to hold the group identification is unlikely to contain sufficient persons of similar appearance to the suspect and that another area may be more suitable. If this is the case, the adviser should inform the identification officer of his concerns and suggested location.

(3) Without consent

A group identification can be held covertly without consent if the suspect is not "available" (see above).

(4) Can force be used?

Force cannot be used to effect a group identification. The case law on this issue relates to a confrontation but the same principles apply to a group identification.

R. v Jones and Nelson, *The Times*, April 21, 1999

(5) Notes

Group identifications cannot be conducted in as controlled a fashion as identification parades, so the adviser must be especially vigilant in noting important aspects of the scene, in particular the number of other people in the area and their appearance relative to the suspect, the position of the witness and anything said by him and the duration of the procedure.

The police are under an obligation to take a photograph or video film of the scene and, if possible, the adviser should

PACE 1984, Code D, Annex C, paras 8, 9

ensure that the film or photograph taken accurately reflects the scene at the time of the identification procedure.

D. CONFRONTATIONS

PACE 1984, Code D, para. 3.23

A "confrontation" is when the suspect is directly confronted by the witness. A confrontation does not require the consent of the suspect but must be carried out in accordance with PACE 1984, Code D, Annex D.
Before the confrontation takes place:

PACE 1984, Code D, Annex D, para. 1

- the witness must be told that the person they saw may or may not be the person they are to confront and that if it is not that person, then the witness should say so;

PACE 1984, Code D, Annex D, para. 2

- the suspect or his legal adviser shall be provided with details of the first description given by any witness who is to attend;

PACE 1984, Code D, Annex D, para. 3

- the suspect or his legal adviser should be allowed to view any material released to the media for the purposes of recognising or tracing the suspect, provided it is practicable to do so and would not unreasonably delay the investigation.

The police may not use force to make the face of the suspect visible to the witness.

PACE 1984, Code D, Annex D, para. 4

The confrontation must take place in the presence of the suspect's legal adviser, interpreter or friend unless this would cause unreasonable delay.

PACE 1984, Code D, Annex D, para. 5

The suspect shall be confronted independently by each witness, who shall be asked "Is this the person?" If the witness identifies the person but is unable to confirm the identification, they shall be asked how sure they are that the person is the one they saw on the earlier occasion.

PACE 1984, Code D, Annex D, para. 6

The confrontation should normally take place in the police station, either in a normal room or one equipped with a screen permitting a witness to see the suspect without being seen. In both cases, the procedures are the same except that a room equipped with a screen may be used only when the suspect's legal adviser, friend or appropriate adult is present or the confrontation is recorded on video.

PACE 1984, Code D, Annex D, para. 7

After the procedure, each witness shall be asked whether they have seen any broadcast or published films or photographs or any descriptions of suspects relating to the offence and a record made of their reply.

CONFRONTATION—PRACTICAL GUIDANCE

(1) Notes

The adviser must, as always, make a full note of the identity of the persons present and everything that is said by any of those persons.

(2) Should the confrontation take place?

A confrontation can only be held where all other forms of identification are considered to be impracticable.

PACE 1984, Code D, para. 3.23

Such a procedure is inherently unfair to the suspect, as the witness will know that the person who he is being asked to look at is a suspect and, therefore, the risk of a false identification is dramatically increased. The adviser should ensure that where the police are to conduct a confrontation, they do so in accordance with the PACE 1984 Codes of Practice and that no other form of identification procedure is in fact practicable.

If the adviser believes another form of identification is practicable, representations must be made to the identification officer and a note made of those representations and the response to them.

(3) Reasonable force cannot be used

Whilst it is clear that a confrontation can take place without the consent of the suspect, the PACE 1984 Codes of Practice are silent on the use of force in such a procedure.

However, the Court of Appeal held that it is not permissible for the police to use reasonable force to bring about a confrontation. If the police make it clear that they will use force, the adviser should strongly object and refer the identification officer to the judgment of the Court of Appeal in *R. v Jones and Nelson*. The adviser should note his objection in his own notes and request that it also be noted on the custody record.

R. v Jones and Nelson, The Times, April 21, 1999

A subsequent civil action against the police for assault may well be successful in these circumstances.

E. IDENTIFICATION FROM PHOTOGRAPHS

Only where the identity of the suspect is not known to the police, may a witness be shown photographs, computerised or artist's composite likenesses or similar likenesses or pictures (including "E-fit" images). This must be done in accordance with PACE 1984, Code D, Annex E. When a known suspect is not available or has ceased to be available, the identification officer may make

PACE 1984, Code D, para. 3.3

PACE 1984, Code D, para. 3.21

arrangements for a "video" identification which may include using suitable still images. In such situations, the police must follow the video identification procedures.

Procedure

PACE 1984, Code D, Annex E, para. 1

The officer responsible for supervising and directing the showing of photographs must be of sergeant rank or above, although the actual showing of the photographs may be done by another officer or member of police staff.

PACE 1984, Code D, Annex E, para. 2, NfG 3E

Before the witness is shown any photographs, the supervising officer must confirm that the first description given by the witness has been recorded and if he is unable to confirm this, he shall postpone showing of the photographs. It is the responsibility of the officer in charge of the investigation to confirm to the supervising officer that the first description has been recorded.

PACE 1984, Code D, Annex E, paras 3, 4

Only one witness shall be shown photographs at a time. Each witness shall be given as much privacy as practicable and shall not be allowed to communicate with any other witness in the case. The witness must be shown at least 12 photographs at a time, which must be of a similar type as far as that is possible.

PACE 1984, Code D, Annex E, para. 5

When the witness is shown the photographs, they shall be told the photograph of the person they saw may or may not be there and, if they cannot make a positive identification, they should say so. The witness shall also be told they should not make a decision until they have seen at least 12 photographs. The witness must not be prompted or guided in any way but must be left to make any selection without help.

PACE 1984, Code D, Annex E, para. 6

If a witness makes a positive identification, unless the person identified is otherwise eliminated from enquiries or is not available, other witnesses shall not be shown photographs. However, all witnesses including the one who has made the identification, shall be asked to attend a formal identification procedure unless there is no dispute about the suspect's identification.

PACE 1984, Code D, Annex E, para. 7

If the witness makes a selection but is unable to confirm the identification, the person showing the photographs shall ask them how sure they are that the photograph they have indicated is the person they saw on the specified earlier occasion.

PACE 1984, Code D, Annex E, para. 8

If a computerised or artist's composite or similar likeness has led to a suspect becoming known to police and he can be asked to participate in a formal identification procedure, that likeness must not be shown to other potential witnesses.

When a witness attending a formal identification procedure has previously been shown photographs or computerised or artist's composite or similar likeness, the suspect and his legal adviser must be informed before the identification procedure takes place. It is the responsibility of the officer in charge of the investigation to make the identification officer aware that this is the case.

PACE 1984, Code D, Annex E, para. 9, NfG 3B

No photographs shown to a witness can be destroyed, whether or not an identification has been made, as they may be required for court purposes. The photographs shall be numbered and a separate photograph taken of the frame or part of the album from which the witness made an identification as an aid to reconstituting it.

PACE 1984, Code D, Annex E, para. 10

Documentation

Whether an identification is made or not, a record shall be kept of the showing of photographs on forms provided for the purpose which shall include:

PACE 1984, Code D, Annex E, para. 11

- anything said by the witness about any identification or the conduct of the procedure;
- any reasons why it was not practicable to comply with any of the provisions of the Code governing the showing of photographs; and
- the name and rank of the supervising officer.

The supervising officer shall inspect and sign the record as soon as practicable.

PACE 1984, Code D, Annex E, para. 12

IDENTIFICATION FROM PHOTOGRAPHS—PRACTICAL GUIDANCE

As this procedure can only take place where the identity of the suspect is unknown to the police, it is not going to take place in the presence of the legal adviser. However, the legal adviser should be aware of whether any witness has been shown photographs prior to any other identification procedure and should specifically ask the identification officer whether this has occurred.

The adviser should also be aware of the relevant procedures and seek to establish if they were followed, as this may lead to the identification evidence being ruled inadmissible at any subsequent trial.

VOICE IDENTIFICATION—PRACTICAL GUIDANCE

PACE 1984, Code D, para. 1.2

PACE 1984, Code D deals with the visual identification of a suspect not the identification of a suspect by his voice. However, the Code does not preclude the police making use of aural identification procedures such as a "voice identification parade", where they judge that appropriate.

R. v Hersey [1998] Crim. L.R. 281

There may be occasions when the voice is the only medium of potential identification available and the police request a "voice identification parade". Such a "parade" in which 11 volunteers and the suspect read out a piece of text has been held to be admissible by the Court of Appeal.

Refusal to co-operate with such a parade will not lead to an adverse inference under CJPOA 1994. However, it is not so clear as to whether evidence of the refusal to co-operate would be admissible and, if so, the court may draw its own conclusions.

The fairness of such a "parade" is very difficult for the adviser to judge. It is submitted that any such "parade" should mirror as far as possible the provisions of Code D in relation to visual identification procedures. The volunteers should have a similar accent to the suspect, be of a similar age and as articulate as the suspect. Any objections to the "parade" should be carefully noted.

Immigration Aspects

INTRODUCTION

Immigration law is often unfamiliar to police station advisers but they will have to deal with it on occasion. This chapter is intended to be of assistance to the adviser by providing an overview of the more common areas of immigration law encountered whilst advising persons detained at police stations.

The adviser may be asked to represent a suspect with immigration problems at the police station because:

- he has been arrested for a non-immigration criminal offence and then he is suspected of an immigration offence;
- he has been arrested for an immigration offence; or
- he is being held in administrative detention (where the Immigration Service is using the police station because no other place is available for detention).

Previously, the most common reasons for detention of a suspect on immigration matters were that he was believed to be an illegal entrant, an overstayer or acting in breach of the conditions attached to his permission to enter/remain in the country. Although these are all criminal offences, administrative powers of arrest, detention, removal or deportation were more usually used. However, more serious immigration offences have been introduced and such practice may change.

IA 1971, s.24

THE LAW, PRACTICE AND PROCEDURE

Illegal entrants

An illegal entrant is defined as someone who:

- is unlawfully entering or seeking to enter the UK in breach of a deportation order or of the immigration laws; or
- is entering or seeking to enter by means which include deception by them or another person, or
- has entered in either of the above ways.

IA 1971, s.33(1) as amended by AIA 1996, s.12(1), Sch. 2, para. 4(1)

IA 1971, s.24(4)(b)

The burden of proving illegal entry is on the prosecution except where the suspect is shown to have entered the UK within six months before the date when the proceedings were commenced. Although a criminal offence an illegal entrant is more likely to be removed from the country than prosecuted.

It is important to be aware when advising suspects in this situation of which factors will cause the suspect to be regarded as an illegal entrant.

For a suspected illegal entrant by whom the immigration service are alleging deception on entry, it is important to establish whether the original purpose for which the person entered the country was genuinely and truthfully declared to the immigration officer at the time of entry. If it was but has since changed, the suspect would not be an illegal entrant. For example, someone entering as a student but subsequently meeting and marrying a British national would not have entered illegally if, at the time of his entry to the United Kingdom, he intended only to study and to leave the United Kingdom at the end of his studies.

There is no right of appeal while the suspect remains in the UK against a decision to treat the suspect as an illegal entrant and he will be removed from the country.

An illegal entrant may have a limited appeal against the destination of the removal. He will have to prove in writing that he will be accepted in a third country, which is extremely difficult.

IA 1971, Sch. 2, para. 16

An illegal entrant who has been served with a notice of removal can be held in detention under the administrative provisions of the Immigration Acts, on which there is no time limit.

Although there is no right to bail, the Home Office may on rare occasions agree to a temporary release from custody.

In addition, the Home Office will consider representations to allow the detainee to remain in the country if there are exceptional compassionate circumstances. The suspect should be referred to a specialist immigration firm of solicitors or an appropriate advice agency. Representations from the local Member of Parliament may also be of assistance.

Overstayers and those in breach of entry conditions

Overstayers are those who entered the country legitimately and were given leave to enter or remain in the country for a defined period, but who have remained in the country in excess of that period without obtaining leave to extend the length of their stay. If an application has been made to extend leave, he can stay until his application has been considered even if the existing leave has expired.

On arrival in the country, a person's stay may be made subject to certain conditions, a common one being that the person does not take up any form of employment or claim benefit. If that person subsequently starts working or claiming benefit, he is liable to arrest and administrative deportation or criminal prosecution. It is not an offence as such for an overstayer to work, because any conditions will cease to apply when permission to remain in the country lapses.

The immigration officer has discretion to allow the suspect temporary release, usually on conditions of residence and a requirement that he report to the authorities. Often, however, the suspect will be detained in a police station until taken to a detention centre. Thereafter, under the administrative provisions of the Immigration Acts, there is no limit to the time he may spend in custody.

Refugees/asylum seekers

If the suspect is unwilling to return to his country owing to a well-founded fear of persecution for reasons of race, religion, nationality, membership of a particular social group or political opinion, he may be able to support an application for asylum in the United Kingdom under the provisions of the UN Convention and Protocol Relating to the Status of Refugees. The scope for asylum is not fixed and has been held to include people who are persecuted for their sexuality.

The Home Office will have to consider the application for asylum and would either allow the asylum seeker temporary release or detain him while a decision is made. Detention is reviewed weekly and a temporary release is often granted to asylum seekers. If the asylum seeker has arrived from a third country, he may be returned to that country to make his application for asylum.

If asylum is refused, there is a limited right of appeal against the decision. It may be possible to renew an asylum claim once appeal rights have been exhausted, if evidence that was not available at the time subsequently becomes available.

Human Rights applications

An application to remain in the country may also be made on human rights grounds. This is similar to an asylum application and may result in leave to remain being granted. When an application on human rights grounds is made, the suspect cannot be removed until it is considered. The main human rights considered in such applications are the right to life (*e.g.* if the suspect were returned home, his life would be in danger and his home state is unable or unwilling to provide protection), prohibition of torture, right to liberty, right to a fair trial, right to respect for private and family life (if the suspect has established ties to this country *e.g.* wife and/or children legitimately living here), freedom of thought, conscience and religion, freedom of expression and freedom of association and assembly.

Powers of arrest

(a) Power of arrest without warrant

IA 1971, s.28A

A police officer or an immigration officer may arrest without warrant anyone who has committed or attempted to commit or whom they have reasonable grounds to suspect has committed or attempted to commit one of the following offences:

IA 1971, s.24(1)(a)

- knowingly entering the UK in breach of a deportation order or without leave;

IA 1971, s.24(1)(b)

- having only a limited leave to enter or remain in the UK, knowingly either remains beyond the time limited by the leave, or fails to observe a condition of the leave;

IA 1971, s.24(1)(c)

- having lawfully entered the UK without leave as a seaman or crew member, he remains without leave beyond the time allowed;

IA 1971, s.24(1)(e)

- failing, without reasonable excuse, to observe any restriction imposed on him as to residence, his employment or occupation or reporting to the police or immigration service;

IA 1971, s.24(1)(f)

- disembarking in the UK from a ship or aircraft after being placed on board with a view to his removal from the UK;

IA 1971, s.24(1)(g)

- embarking in contravention of a restriction imposed by or under an Order in Council;

IA 1971, s.24A(1)(a)

- obtaining or seeking to obtain leave to enter or remain in the UK by deception;

IA 1971, s.24A(1)(b)

- securing or seeking to secure the avoidance, postponement or revocation of enforcement action against him by deception;

IA 1971, s.25

- facilitating the commission of a breach of immigration law by an individual who is not a citizen of the European Union, knowing or having reasonable cause for believing that the act done facilitates the breach and that the individual is not a citizen of the European Union;

- knowingly and for gain facilitating the arrival in the UK an individual who he knows or has reasonable cause to believe is an asylum-seeker; IA 1971, s.25A
- assisting entry to the UK in breach of a deportation or exclusion order; IA 1971, s.25B
- obstructing an immigration officer or other person lawfully acting in the execution of the Immigration Act without reasonable excuse where it is impractical to serve a summons because of a lack of certainty about the suspect's identity or address, or where the arrest is necessary to prevent him from causing or suffering physical injury or causing loss or damage to property; IA 1971, s.26(1)(g); IA 1971, s.28A(6)–(8)
- making a false registration card; altering a registration card with intent to deceive or to enable another to deceive; having a false or altered registration card in his possession without reasonable excuse; using or attempting to use a false registration card for a purpose for which a registration card is issued; using or attempting to use an altered registration card with intent to deceive; making an article designed to be used in making a false registration card; making an article designed to be used in altering a registration card with intent to deceive or to enable another to deceive, or having such an article in his possession without reasonable excuse; or IA 1971, s.26A
- having in his possession an immigration stamp or replica immigration stamp without reasonable excuse. IA 1971, s.26B

In addition, a power to arrest without warrant exists where an immigration officer in the course of exercising a function under the Immigration Acts forms a reasonable suspicion that a person has committed or attempted to commit any of the following offences: AI(TC)A 2004, s.14

- conspiracy at common law (in relation to conspiracy to defraud),
- bigamy;
- making a false statements under ss 3, 4 or 7 of Perjury Act 1911;

- theft;
- obtaining property by deception;
- obtaining pecuniary advantage by deception;
- false accounting;
- handling stolen goods;
- obtaining services, or evading liability, by deception;
- forgery;
- copying false instrument;
- using false instrument;
- using copy of false instrument;
- trafficking for sexual exploitation; or
- trafficking people for exploitation.

IA 1971, s.28C

The following provisions would also apply to immigration officers in these circumstances (see below):

IA 1971, s.28E, s.28F
IA 1971, s.28G, s.28H
IA 1971, s.28I

- search and arrest without warrant;
- entry and search of premises following arrest;
- searching arrested persons;
- access to and copying of seized material.

Prior to this new provision, immigration officers only had the power to deal with offences under the Immigration Acts now however immigration officers can arrest for a new range of criminal offences but their powers are limited to when they suspect the commission of offences during the course of exercising a function under the Immigration Acts. In other words immigration officers must uncover the evidence of the offences in the course of their usual duties investigating immigration matters.

(b) Power of arrest with warrant

IA 1971, s.28AA; IA 1971, s.24(1)(d)

An immigration officer may arrest a person, after having obtained a warrant from the magistrates' court if there are reasonable grounds for suspecting that a person has committed an offence of failing to comply with any requirement to report to a medical officer, or to attend, or submit to a test or examination, as required by such an officer without reasonable excuse or committed an employment offence.

Powers to Search premises

(a) Power to search and arrest without warrant

An immigration officer may enter and search any premises for the purpose of arresting a person for any of the following offences if he has reasonable grounds for believing that the person whom he is seeking is on the premises and only to the extent that entry and search is reasonably required for that purpose:

IA 1971, s.28C(21), (2)

- facilitating the commission of a breach of immigration law by an individual who is not a citizen of the European Union, knowing or having reasonable cause for believing that the act done facilitates the breach and that the individual is not a citizen of the European Union; — IA 1971, s.25
- knowingly and for gain facilitating the arrival in the UK of an individual who he knows or has reasonable cause to believe is an asylum-seeker; — IA 1971, s.25A
- assisting entry to the UK in breach of a deportation or exclusion order. — IA 1971, s.25B

(b) Power to search and arrest with warrant

An immigration or police officer has the power to enter any premises named in a warrant issued by a magistrates' court, with force if necessary, for the purpose of searching for and arresting anyone suspected of one of the following offences:

IA 1971, s.28B

- knowingly entering the UK in breach of a deportation order or without leave; — IA 1971, s.24(1)(a)
- having only a limited leave to enter or remain in the UK, knowingly either remains beyond the time limited by the leave, or fails to observe a condition of the leave; — IA 1971, s.24(1)(b)
- having lawfully entered the UK without leave as a seaman or crew member, he remains without leave beyond the time allowed; — IA 1971, s.24(1)(c)
- failing, without reasonable excuse, to observe any restriction imposed on him as to residence, his employment or — IA 1971, s.24(1)(e)

occupation or reporting to the police or immigration service;

IA 1971, s.24(1)(f)

- disembarking in the UK from a ship or aircraft after being placed on board with a view to his removal from the UK;

IA 1971, s.24A(1)(a)

- obtaining or seeking to obtain leave to enter or remain in the UK by deception;

IA 1971, s.24A(1)(b)

- securing or seeking to secure the avoidance, postponement or revocation of enforcement action against him by deception;

IA 1971, s.26A

- the above registration card offences; or

IA 1971, s.26B

- having in his possession an immigration stamp or replica immigration stamp without reasonable excuse.

(c) Business premises: entry to arrest

IA 1971, s.28CA

A police or immigration officer may enter and search any business premises for the purpose of arresting a person if he has reasonable grounds for believing that the person whom he is seeking is on the premises and only to the extent that the entry and search is reasonably required.

This power exists for all offences under Immigration Act 1971 ss 24 and 24A (see above) and for those subject to request for examination or removal.

The authority of the Secretary of State or Chief Superintendent is required.

(d) Entry and search of premises

IA 1971, s.28D(1), (2)

An immigration officer may enter and search premises with a warrant if there are reasonable grounds for believing that:

- a relevant offence has been committed;
- there is material on the premises which is likely to be of substantial value (whether by itself or together with other material to the investigation of the offence);
- the material is likely to be relevant evidence;
- the material does not consist of or include items subject to legal privilege, excluded material or special procedure material; and either
- it is not practicable to communicate with any person entitled to grant entry to the premises;

- it is practicable to communicate with a person entitled to grant entry to the premises but it is not practicable to communicate with any person entitled to grant access to the evidence;
- entry to the premises will not be granted unless a warrant is produced; or
- the purpose of a search may be frustrated or seriously prejudiced unless an immigration officer arriving at the premises can secure immediate entry to them.

The relevant offences are those under Immigration Act 1971 ss 24(1)(a)–(f), 24A, 25, 25A, 25B, 26A and 26B (see above).

(e) Entry and search of premises following arrest

If the suspect is arrested for an offence and is at a place other than at a police station, an immigration officer may enter and search any premises in which person was when he was arrested, or in which he was immediately before his arrest for evidence relating to the offence for which the arrest was made.

IA 1971, s.28E

The immigration officer must have reasonable grounds for believing that there is relevant evidence on the premises and the search can only extend so far as it is reasonably required for the purpose of discovering relevant evidence, which he may then seize and retain.

If the suspect is arrested for an offence of:

- facilitating the commission of a breach of immigration law by an individual who is not a citizen of the European Union;
- knowingly and for gain facilitating the arrival in the UK of an individual who he knows or has reasonable cause to believe is an asylum-seeker; or
- assisting entry to the UK in breach of a deportation or exclusion order,

IA 1971, s.28F; IA 1971, s.25, 25A, 25B

an immigration officer may enter and search any premises occupied or controlled by the person arrested if the officer has reasonable grounds for suspecting that there is relevant evidence on the premises.

The search can extend only in so far as it is reasonably required for the purpose of discovering relevant evidence and must be authorised by a senior officer in writing.

IA 1971, s.28F (3),(4)

Such a search can take place before taking the arrested person to a place where he is to be detained without obtaining the authorisation, if the presence of that person at a place other than one where he is to be detained is necessary for the effective investigation of the offence and a senior officer is informed as soon as is practicable.

IA 1971, s.28F(5)

A written record must be made of the grounds for the search and the nature of the evidence that was sought.

IA 1971, s.28F(6)
IA 1971, s.28F(7)

An officer searching premises under this section may seize and retain anything he finds which he has reasonable grounds for suspecting is relevant evidence which excludes items subject to legal privilege.

(f) Search for personnel records—warrant unnecessary

Where a person has been arrested or is reasonably believed to be liable to arrest for an offence under Immigration Act 1971 s.24(1) or 24A(1) (see above) or as a person liable to be detained for examination or removal, a police or immigration officer may search business premises where the arrest was made or where the person liable to arrest is, if they reasonably believe that an immigration employment offence has been committed in relation to that person and that employee records will be found on the premises and will be of substantial value on their own or together with other material in the investigation of the immigration employment offence.

IA 1971, s.28FA(3)

A police or immigration officer searching the premises may seize and retain employee records, other than items subject to legal privilege, which he reasonably suspects will be of substantial value (whether on their own or together with other material) in the investigation of an immigration employment offence or an offence of fraud relating to a claim for support for an Asylum Seeker.

IA 1971, s.28FA(4)

The power may be exercised only to the extent that it is reasonably required for the purpose of discovering the employee records, if the police or immigration officer produces identification and if the police or immigration officer reasonably believes that either:

IA 1971, s.28FA(5)

- it is not practicable to communicate with the person entitled to grant access to the records; or
- permission to search has been refused; or
- permission to search would be refused if requested; or

- the purpose of a search would be frustrated or seriously prejudiced if it is not carried out in reliance of this provision.

Powers to search persons

(a) Searching arrested persons not in police custody

If the suspect is arrested for an offence and is at a place other than at a police station, an immigration officer may search him if he has reasonable grounds for believing that he may present a danger to himself or others.

IA 1971, s.28G(2)

An immigration officer may search the arrested person for anything which he might use to assist his escape from lawful custody or anything which might be evidence relating to the offence for which he has been arrested.

IA 1971, s.28G(3)

Such a search can only take place if the officer has reasonable grounds for believing that the arrested person may have concealed on him anything of a kind mentioned above and the search can extend only as far as it is reasonably required for the purpose of discovering any such thing.

IA 1971, s.28G(4)

There is no power to require a person to remove any of his clothing in public other than an outer coat, jacket or glove, although a search of a person's mouth is permissible.

IA 1971, s.28G(5)

An officer may seize and retain anything he finds if he has reasonable grounds for believing that the person might use it to cause physical injury to himself or to another person, that it might be used to assist escape from lawful custody, or that it is evidence that relates to the offence in question.

IA 1971, s.28G(6), (7)

(b) Searching persons in police custody

If the suspect has been arrested and is in custody at a police station or in police detention at a place other than a police station, an immigration officer may at any time search the arrested person in order to see whether he has with him anything which may cause physical injury to himself or others, damage property, interfere with evidence or assist his escape, or which the officer has reasonable grounds for believing is evidence relating to the offence in question.

IA 1971, s.28H (1), (2)

This power may be exercised only to the extent that the custody officer concerned considers it necessary for the purposes set out above.

IA 1971, s.28H (3)

An officer may seize anything he finds, if he has reasonable grounds for believing that the person might use it for one or more of the above purposes (in which case it may be retained by

IA 1971, s.28H (4), (5), (6)

police) or that it is evidence relating to the offence in question (in which case it may be retained by the immigration officer).

IA 1971, s.28H (7)

The person from whom something is seized must be told the reason for the seizure unless he is violent or appears likely to become violent or is incapable of understanding what is said to him.

IA 1971, s.28H (8)

An intimate search must not be conducted under this section.

IA 1971, s.28H (9)

The person carrying out a search under this section must be of the same sex as the person searched.

Powers of detention

The immigration service can detain persons in the following circumstances:

IA 1971, Sch. 2, para. 16

- arriving in the UK pending a decision on whether to grant leave to enter;

IA 1971, Sch. 2, para. 16(1A)

- arriving with leave but whose leave has been suspended pending further examination;

IA 1971, Sch. 2, para. 16(2)

- refused leave to enter but pending a decision on removal;
- illegal entrants (or suspected illegal entrants) pending a decision on removal;
- in breach of leave conditions, overstayers or those who have obtained or are suspected of having obtained leave to enter by deception;

ACSA 2001, s.23(2)

- suspected of being international terrorists who cannot be removed due to a point of law under an international treaty or a practical difficulty.

In addition, the Secretary of State can detain persons relating to a decision to deport in the following circumstances:

IA 1971, Sch. 3, para. 2(1)

- where a recommendation for deportation made by a court is in force and that person is not detained in pursuance of the sentence or order of any court, he may be detained pending the making of a deportation order in pursuance of the recommendation, unless the Secretary of State directs him to be released pending further consideration of his case or he is released on bail;

IA 1971, Sch. 3, para. 2(2)

- where notice has been given to a person of a decision to make a deportation order against him, he may be detained pending the making of the deportation order;

- where a deportation order is in force against any person, he may be detained pending his removal or departure from the UK.

IA 1971, Sch. 3, para. 2(3)

Other immigration related offences

As well as the offences set out briefly above, there are a number of immigration related offences for which a suspect may be under arrest. It is beyond the scope of this chapter to deal with these offences in total or in detail but the adviser should be aware of the general nature of the newer and more common offences which are listed below:

IA 1971, s.26(1)

- failure to submit to immigration examination without reasonable excuse;
- failure or refusal to provide information or documents as required at such an examination without reasonable excuse;
- making false statements at such an examination without reasonable excuse;
- altering official documents without reasonable excuse;
- failure to complete or produce landing cards without reasonable excuse;
- failure to comply with police registration without reasonable excuse;
- obstruction of an immigration officer or other person lawfully acting in the execution of his duty;
- entering UK without a passport—a person commits an offence if at a leave or asylum interview he does not have with him an immigration document which is in force and satisfactorily establishes his identity and nationality or citizenship or satisfactorily establishes the same for any child travelling with him. No offence is committed if the interview takes place after entry into the UK and within 3 days beginning with the date of the interview those documents are provided to the Immigration Service. In addition, it is a defence if there is a reasonable excuse for not being in possession of the document, he produces a false immigration document which he used for travel to the UK or he travelled to the UK without being in possession of an immigration document;

AI(TC)A 2004, s.2

FCA 1981, s.5. as amended by AI(TC)A 2004, s.3

- forgery of immigration documents which means a card, adhesive label or a document if it is designed to be given in the exercise of a function under the Immigration Acts to a person who has been granted leave to enter or remain in the UK and carries information (whether or not wholly or partly electronically) about the leave granted;

AI(TC)A 2004, s.4

- trafficking people for exploitation—an either way offence is committed if a person arranges or facilitates the arrival in the UK or the departure from the UK of an individual and either he or another intends to exploit him or he believes that such an offence may have been committed;

AIA 1996, s.8 as amended by AI(TC)A 2004, s.6

- employment of people subject to immigration control.

Fingerprints

PACE 1984, s.61(9)

The provisions of PACE 1984 do not apply to a person detained for immigration enquiries.

PACE 1984, Code D, para. 4.10
PACE 1984, Code D, para. 4.11

A person's fingerprints may be taken for the purposes of Immigration Service enquiries. In these circumstances, fingerprints can only be taken with consent in writing or without consent if the following conditions apply:

IA 1971, Sch. 2, para. 16, 18(2)

(a) when it is reasonably necessary for the purposes of identifying a person detained as liable to examination or removal;

IAA 1999, s.141(7)(a)

(b) from a person who fails to produce, on arrival, a valid passport with a photograph or some other document satisfactorily establishing their identity and nationality if an immigration officer does not consider the person has a reasonable excuse for the failure;

IAA 1999, s.141(7)(b)

(c) from a person who has been refused entry to the UK but has been temporarily admitted if an immigration officer reasonably suspects the person might break a condition imposed on them relating to residence or reporting to a police or immigration officer, and their decision is confirmed by a chief immigration officer;

IAA 1999, s.141(7)(c)

(d) when directions are given to remove a person as an illegal entrant, liable to removal under the Immigration and Asylum Act 1999, s.10, or who is the subject of a deportation order from the UK;

(e) from a person arrested under UK immigration laws under the Immigration Act 1971, Sch. 2, para. 17;

IAA 1999, s.141(7)(d)

(f) from a person who has made a claim for asylum or under Art. 3 of the European Convention on Human Rights; or

IAA 1999, s.141(7)(e)

(g) from a person who is a dependant of someone who falls into (b) to (f) above.

IAA 1999, s.141(7)(f)

Police and immigration officers have the power to arrest, without warrant, a person who fails to comply with a requirement imposed by the Secretary of State to attend a specified place for fingerprinting.

IAA 1999, s.142(3); PACE 1984, Code D, para. 4.12

Before any fingerprints are taken, with or without consent, the person must be informed:

PACE 1984, Code D, para. 4.13

(a) of the reason their fingerprints are to be taken;

(b) the fingerprints, and all copies of them, will be destroyed as soon as practicable if the person from whom they were taken proves they are a British or Commonwealth citizen who has the right of abode in the UK or is a dependent of such a person, or in any event within ten years of being taken or within such period specified by the Secretary of State.

PACE 1984, Code D, Annex F, Pt B
IAA 1999, s.143.

Reasonable force may be used, if necessary, to take a person's fingerprints without their consent.

PACE 1984, Code D, para. 4.14

Codes of Practice

An immigration officer exercising any specified power to arrest, question, search or take fingerprints from a person, enter and search premises or seize property found on persons or premises must have regard to such provisions of the PACE 1984 Codes of Practice as may be specified.

IAA 1999, s.145(1)

The Codes of Practice have been held to apply to immigration officers exercising administrative powers in relation to illegal entrants and overstayers, at least if a criminal offence was potentially involved. However, they are statutorily obliged to have regard to certain specified provisions of the Codes of Practice:

R. v SS HD Ex p. Ibrahim [1993] Imm. A.R. 124 QBD

IAA 1999, ss 145 and 146

- on arresting without warrant (for criminal offences of illegal entry, overstaying, obtaining leave to enter or remain by deception, securing or seeking to secure the avoidance, postponement or revocation of enforcement action by deception, breach of landing conditions, or observing conditions such as residence or reporting, facilitating illegal entry, harbouring immigration offenders, obstruction of immigration officer); and

- during detention of such a suspect at a police station;
- when conducting interviews in respect of an immigration related criminal offence, they should not refuse access to solicitors, and questioning should be under caution and contemporaneously recorded. Such interview should be in compliance with PACE and Codes of Practice.

When arresting under the administrative provisions, the provisions of PACE 1984, Code C would not apply. In practice, however, immigration officers will adhere to the Codes of Practice and the adviser should argue that they should apply.

At present it seems that where interviews are conducted at Immigration Service offices or places other than police stations the Codes of Practice do not apply. However if there is any issue or suspicion that a criminal offence has been committed then the person should be taken to the police station when PACE and the Codes of Practice will apply.

Legal Aid

GCC 2004, Pt B, para. 3.6

Under the General Criminal Contract where the adviser gives Police Station Advice and Assistance on an own client case and it is apparent, or becomes apparent, that an immigration offence (breach of immigration rules) may have been committed or that an immigration issue arises (where an individual is arrested or attends the police station as volunteer in relation to alleged criminal conduct and becomes clear that an immigration offence may have been committed), the adviser shall give advice and assistance to the client up until the point where the immigration authorities take over conduct of the investigation.

The firm may continue to advise after this point if the client remains in detention and requires advice, however the firm should consider whether it is practicable to refer the immigration offence to a supplier with a contract in the Immigration Category of Work in the local area. If it is not practicable the firm can continue to act, provided a full note of the relevant circumstances is on the file.

A firm with no immigration contract may not act under the General Criminal Contract if:

- an individual is detained after entry and is served with illegal entry papers or a notice of intention to deport;
- an individual is detained by the immigration authorities on entry;
- an individual is arrested by police on behalf of the immigration authorities where no criminal allegations are made and is detained under the immigration authorities' administrative powers.

A duty solicitor is expected to advise a suspect at the police station on immigration matters. The General Criminal Contract covers cases where police station advice is required by clients being held in connection with the investigation of an immigration offence. The requirement for duty solicitors to accept all rota calls whilst being paid standby includes the acceptance of such immigration cases referred to them by the Duty Solicitor Call Centre.

Duty Solicitor Manual (June 2004), para. 6.16

Useful contacts

The following may be of use in dealing with more complex immigration related issues:

- Refugee Council, 3 Bondway, London, SW8 1SJ, Tel: 0207 820 3000, Fax: 0207 582 9929.
- Immigration Law Practitioners (ILPA), Lindsey House, 40/42 Charterhouse Street, London, EC1 6N, Tel: 0207 251 8343, Fax: 0207 251 8384.
- Joint Council for the Welfare of Immigrants (JCWI), 115 Old Street, London, EC1V 9RT Tel: 0207 251 8707, Fax: 0207 251 8707.
- Refugee Legal Centre, Nelson House, 153–7 Commercial Rd, London, E1 2EB, Tel: 0207 803 2000, Fax: 0207 7803 2001.
- Immigration Advisory Service, 3rd Floor, County House, 190 Great Dover Street, London, SE1 4YB, Tel: 0207 967 1330.

- Institute of Linguists—National Register of Public Service Interpreters, Saxon House, 48 Southwark Street, London, SE1 1UN, Tel: 0207 940 5150, Fax: 0207 940 3101.

PRACTICAL GUIDANCE

(1) Information from the immigration officer

It is essential that the adviser clarifies with the immigration officer whether the suspect is thought to be an illegal entrant, an overstayer or in breach of entry conditions or which other potential offences are alleged. Obviously, the view of the immigration officer could change as a result of the interview.

The immigration officer should be asked about any Home Office documentation or items seized from the suspect's premises and whether questions will be asked about them in interview. The adviser should ask to see any documentation, whether it will be relied upon or not, as it may have some bearing on the suspect's case.

In this way the adviser will be able to assess and establish the basis of the suspect's detention and may be able to obtain an indication as to the likely immigration disposal from the immigration officer, although this officer is likely to be liaising with a chief immigration officer usually on the telephone.

The adviser should establish the potential criminal offences alleged and try to obtain a view on likely disposal of the criminal matters in the event of removal papers being served. It may also be helpful to speak to the custody officer in this regard.

(2) Advising the suspect

It is generally unrealistic for a suspect in these circumstances to exercise his right to silence, since the manner in which immigration officers make and implement their decisions is discretionary and it is likely that, in the absence of any explanation from the suspect, he will be treated as an illegal entrant, overstayer or in breach of his entry conditions. This will not be the case in relation to some of the other immigration related criminal offences.

As full instructions as possible should be taken and clear advice given about the legal issues involved and the sort of questions which may be asked. The adviser should obtain instructions on the suspect's personal background and should check that the details on the custody record are correct as often they are completed without the assistance of an interpreter and mistakes made.

The adviser should obtain from the suspect his full name, date and place of birth, nationality, details of any identity documents and passport, date of last arrival in the UK, basis of arrival in the UK, leave given, reason for coming to and remaining in the UK and any previous visits to the UK.

It is likely that the suspect will be asked in detail about what he said to immigration officers on entering the country. The interviewing immigration officer will usually have with him a copy of the notes made by the immigration officer who interviewed the suspect on arrival, sight of which should be requested by the adviser prior to the interview. It is important that the suspect attempts to recall as accurately as possible what was said, albeit that entry to the United Kingdom could have been many years before.

It is important that the suspect understands the reason for the questions he will be asked and that the immigration officer interviewing him at the police station may try to use anything said in the interview to allege that the suspect deceived the immigration service on entry to the country.

The adviser should bear in mind that a change in the intentions of the suspect since arrival and the initial entry interview would not mean that entry had been gained by deception.

The suspect should be advised on the basis of his detention under immigration and criminal law and the possible disposal options open to the police and immigration service.

Instructions should be taken to ascertain whether he can take advantage of any applications or appeals. If the suspect wishes to claim asylum, it should be raised in the interview and another more detailed interview ought then to be arranged at a subsequent date.

If there are compelling compassionate circumstances which may form the basis of later representations, the suspect should be advised to raise them in the interview.

Sometimes such a suspect will wish to arrange his own departure rather than face removal or deportation. Often he will be given the option of such a supervised voluntary departure.

(3) Recommendation to deport

If the suspect is subsequently convicted of a serious criminal offence or if he is a regular offender, it is possible that, regardless of his status in the country, the sentencing court will recommend that he be deported at the end of his sentence. Such a recommendation can be appealed as part of the sentence imposed.

The Home Office will subsequently decide whether to act on the recommendation in due course but it is usual for them to follow such recommendations. Although, often a long way off when in the police station, it may be helpful for the suspect to be aware of such a possibility and the fact that he may be served with the necessary initiating documentation even at the police station stage.

(4) Interpreters

The adviser should ensure that the interpreter is appropriate and speaks the correct language and dialect. Some interpreters may be unsympathetic to certain ethnic groups and may not interpret accurately: this may be a particular problem if issues of asylum are to be raised. Payment may be obtained from the Legal Services Commission for the adviser to provide an interpreter if there is good reason. Although this may delay matters in the short term, it may have longer-term advantages. (See the **Interpreters** index heading.)

(5) In the interview

It is imperative that the suspect understands the nature of the questions being asked and their purpose. Language may be a problem and the adviser should be ready to intervene when necessary. This is particularly true in deception cases.

The adviser should intervene if a question is misleading or ambiguous. A full record of the questions and answers should also be made.

(6) After the interview

The adviser should ask the immigration officer what his intentions are and make any appropriate representations about how the suspect is to be considered. The suspect should be advised about any notices served and as to the position on appeal and bail.

Referral to a specialist agency or firm of solicitors is essential.

Information Gathering

INTRODUCTION

Before meeting and advising the suspect, it is essential that the adviser obtains as much information as possible from the police (or other investigating body). This is not always easy, as there is no **right** to be given such information.

R. v Imran and Hussein [1997] Crim. L.R. 754

The adviser should attempt to obtain the information in order not only to be in the best position to advise the suspect on how to deal with any subsequent interview but also with a view to advising if necessary on requests for samples, fingerprints, identification and other such procedures.

SOURCES OF INFORMATION

There are three main sources from which the adviser can seek to obtain information: the custody record, the custody officer and the investigating officer/officer in the case.

(1) Custody record

The adviser has the right to inspect the custody record on his arrival at the police station and it is essential that this is done. Much of the information that the adviser could request from the custody officer will be recorded on the custody record and it may save time if the adviser inspects it before speaking to the custody officer: thus, the basic information will not need to be extracted personally from the custody officer. Any questions arising or matters which are not immediately apparent from inspection of the custody record can then be put to the custody officer.

PACE 1984, Code C, para. 2.4

The custody record is an important document and must be read carefully. Detailed notes should be made of the information contained in the record including:

(a) the custody number;

(b) the name and address of the suspect or whether he is noted as of no fixed abode;

(c) the time of and reason for the arrest;

(d) the time of arrival at the police station and the time detention was authorised (so that the maximum period of detention and the review times can be calculated);

(e) the grounds of detention;

(f) the time that his rights were administered and the request made for a solicitor;

(g) whether the suspect is a juvenile or mentally vulnerable and, if so, what steps have been taken to contact the appropriate adult and a health care professional where appropriate;

(h) whether there is any doubt about the fitness of the suspect to be further detained or interviewed as a result of his consumption of drink or drugs, or for any other reason; and, if so, whether a health care professional has been called and, if he has already attended, what his opinion was and whether any medication has been prescribed or administered;

(i) what property was found on the suspect at the time of arrest and authorisation of detention and whether the suspect has signed the custody record in confirmation;

(j) whether any search of property has been or is to be carried out and on what legal authority and, if a search has been carried out, what if anything was found;

(k) whether admissions or any unsolicited comments have been made and/or pertinent questions met with silence;

(l) whether the suspect has already been interviewed and, if so, on what authority;

(m) any other authorities have been given for various samples, fingerprints and photographs and whether they have already been taken.

(2) Custody officer

As the officer responsible for all persons in detention at the police station, the custody officer should be aware of the basic features of the arrest and the grounds for suspected involvement in an offence.

There may have been a change of shift from when the suspect was first arrested but the incoming custody officer will have been fully briefed by the outgoing custody officer and the detention of the suspect is, of course, kept under regular review.

Any of the above information not obtained from the custody record should be obtained from the custody officer. In addition, the custody officer should be asked for the following specific information:

(a) any specific information they have about the circumstances of the arrest and the offence suspected;

(b) any information obtained from the risk assessment which is not contained in the custody record;

(c) whether the suspect is to be interviewed and when that interview is likely to take place; and

(d) whether anyone else has been arrested or is being sought in relation to the same offence.

(3) Officer in the case and interviewing officer

The officer who is going to interview the suspect or the arresting officer may not be the officer in charge of the case and may only have a limited brief on the case itself. This is particularly so in larger and more complex investigations. Therefore, where possible, the adviser should seek to establish what knowledge the interviewing officer has of the investigation as a whole and speak to the officer in charge of the investigation, if he is a different person and is available. Obviously in the more straightforward cases, the interviewing officer will be in control of the investigation.

Police duty of disclosure

The police do not have a general obligation to disclose material prior to charge which, according to the Divisional Court, would be "impracticable in many cases and highly undesirable in some". Equally, the Court of Appeal does not consider that the police are required to disclose all material to a legal representative before the interview with a suspect commences although they do accept that there is a duty on the police not actively to mislead any suspect. However, the Court of Appeal has recognised that a lack of disclosure may be a relevant consideration in deciding whether an adverse inference should be drawn from silence in interview.

DPP v Ara [2001] 4 All E.R. 559

R. v Imran and Hussein [1997] Crim. L.R. 754

R. v Roble [1997] Crim. L.R. 449

In some circumstances disclosure is clearly necessary. For instance, the question as to whether a suspect should accept a caution requires the adviser to know accurately the terms of an earlier interview on the basis of which the police were prepared to offer the caution. In such circumstances the record of the previous interview should be disclosed otherwise it would be impossible

DPP v Ara [2001] 4 All E.R. 559

for the adviser to give informed advice as to whether to consent to a caution.

Why is disclosure by police important?

R. v Roble [1997] Crim. L.R. 449

If the police do not provide any information about the case against the suspect or provide very limited information, it becomes extremely difficult for the adviser to advise the suspect effectively (which was recognised in *Roble*).

The advice which an adviser provides to a suspect is more likely to be correct if it is based on full knowledge of the facts available at the time. It will be very difficult, if not impossible, to judge which facts a suspect may be relying upon should the matter proceed to trial and, therefore, which facts he ought reasonably to mention in an interview if only limited disclosure has been provided.

Staged disclosure

In many cases, the police use staged disclosure techniques, especially in more complex and serious enquiries. The interviewing officer will provide the adviser with written disclosure and is rarely willing to provide any additional information. Indeed there is often a "disclosure officer" monitoring what information is provided to the suspect and when that is done. This has the advantage of clarifying exactly what has been disclosed to the adviser and when that information was disclosed.

However, the purpose would appear to be to keep certain matters back from the suspect but to disclose enough to encourage him to start answering questions. Once he has committed himself to an account, the police would hope to reveal further information which may contradict that account. Furthermore, the police would hope to disclose just enough to invite an adverse inference at trial if certain facts are not mentioned in interview.

It may not always be obvious that such a technique is being employed. It is helpful, if it is suspected that staged disclosure is being used, to ask the officer directly if this is the case and whether they have further information which they are not disclosing at that time. If staged disclosure is being used or suspected by the adviser, the client should be informed. Often the most prudent course in such situations is to remain silent until further disclosure has been made. However, it is extremely difficult to judge when sufficient disclosure has been made for the suspect to put forward an account.

What information should be sought from the officer?

(a) Facts/evidence against the suspect

The officer in the case should be asked for as much information as it is possible to obtain about the facts of the case and the evidence which the police have that may tend to implicate the suspect. The adviser will have to use his own questioning skills to elicit this information from the officer concerned and to assess the reliability of the information given.

The officer may not be as forthcoming about the evidence as the adviser would wish: the adviser should always treat with caution the information given by police officers in these circumstances. The officer may wish to conceal from the suspect certain key elements of the case so that he can surprise the suspect with them in interview. Equally, the officer may exaggerate the strength of the case against the suspect in the hope of obtaining a confession. Considerations for the adviser should include the following.

(i) Potential inadmissibility of evidence

The adviser should consider whether the evidence outlined by the police officer is potentially inadmissible or unlikely ever to be given in court proceedings (perhaps because the witness will be reluctant to give evidence or is not competent to do so). The adviser should be familiar with the hearsay provisions of the Criminal Justice Act 2003 which came into force on April 4, 2005.

CJA 2003, s.114

If a co-suspect has implicated the suspect, that evidence is unlikely to be admissible against the suspect unless the co-suspect subsequently gives evidence for the Crown at trial. The officer in the case should therefore be asked whether anyone else is being sought or has been arrested in connection with the same offence and whether they have implicated the suspect.

If any admissions have been made to the police by the suspect or relevant questions met with silence prior to or on arrest, after arrest *en route* to or at the police station (whether in formal interview or not), or during any search or any other procedure, the adviser should consider whether the circumstances in which the admissions/silences were obtained could render them arguably inadmissible in later court proceedings. The suspect will be given the opportunity in interview to comment on any significant statements or silences.

(ii) Insufficient information

If the officer does not provide the adviser with enough information about the evidence to be able to advise the suspect effectively, the adviser is left with little choice but to advise the suspect not to answer any questions.

R. v Roble [1997] Crim. L.R. 449

A refusal by the officer to provide adequate information before an interview may amount to circumstances in which it would be reasonable for the suspect not to answer questions in interview, preventing any adverse inference being drawn in later court proceedings.

In order to deal with the situation where the officer in the case is reluctant to give sufficient information about the case, it may be helpful to refer him to the case of *R. v Roble* in which the Court of Appeal indicated that lack of or insufficient disclosure by the police may amount to a good reason why no inference should be drawn under s.34 of the CJPOA 1994 if the suspect refused to comment.

It may be of use for the solicitor to state at the start of the interview that he has been given no or insufficient information on which to advise the suspect properly and that, as a result, he is advising that the suspect not answer any questions in the interview. It is important that the present tense is used on the tape so that the advice is effectively being given at that instance. This ought to maintain privilege in relation to the consultation before the interview.

The information that one would normally expect to be given before the interview may well emerge during the course of the interview. Once the suspect is aware of the basis of the allegations, he can be advised if necessary to request a second interview at which his version can be given in the light of the information obtained in the first interview. As there is no right to be given a second interview the adviser could submit a written statement by the suspect to the police as an alternative.

Alternatively, as new material is disclosed in the interview, the adviser may wish to stop the interview and advise the suspect on the information obtained. Whether the suspect comments at that stage or waits until the interviews have finished is a difficult judgement to make and will depend on the circumstances of the case and the information obtained.

(iii) Passing information on to the suspect

Principle 16.06, *Guide to*

The adviser must not be led into any sort of collusion with police whereby the officer provides information to the adviser on the basis that it is not passed on to the suspect. There is no duty of confidentiality between the adviser and the police and the suspect is generally entitled to all the information supplied to the adviser. It is advisable to inform the officer that information cannot be accepted under such conditions.

Professional Conduct of Solicitors (Law Society) 2004

However, the Law Society recognises that there may be certain circumstances where passing on certain information could be harmful to the client's mental or physical condition. Consequently, it will be necessary for the adviser to decide whether to disclose such information to the suspect.

Principle 16.06, *Guide to Professional Conduct of Solicitors (Law Society)* 2004

In addition, the adviser cannot pass on information to the suspect which is likely to prejudice an investigation concerning recovery of the proceeds of crime—the offence "tipping off" under the Proceeds of Crime Act 2002 or other similar legislation—subject to the possible defence that the disclosure was in connection with giving legal advice.

POCA 2002, s.333; Principle 16.07, *Guide to Professional Conduct of Solicitors (Law Society)* 2004

(b) Other information

In addition to information about the evidence against the suspect, the officer in the case should also be asked for the following further information:

(a) the time of and reason for the arrest, or whether the suspect is a volunteer;

(b) whether a search of any property has been or is to be conducted and, if so, the grounds for the search: if a search has taken place, the officer should be asked if anything of evidential value was discovered;

(c) whether the police are considering carrying out any other procedure, such as an identification procedure, a request for samples or an intimate search: if such a procedure is to be carried out, the reasons and the legal authority for it should be requested;

(d) whether the suspect is to be interviewed and, if so, when that is likely to take place and what the purpose of the interview is;

(e) whether the suspect has already been spoken to and what, if anything, was said by him;

(f) whether any significant comments or silences are to be put to the suspect;

(g) whether any questions have been or are to be put concerning the suspect's presence at a place, or whether any comment is or has been invited as to any items, substances or marks on the suspect;

(h) whether the suspect is wanted or suspected of involvement in any other offence and, if so, whether he is to be rearrested for it; and

(i) whether the officer considers there is sufficient evidence to charge to suspect at that stage and what is envisaged after the interview.

CONCLUSION

Once the adviser is satisfied that he has obtained as much relevant information from the police as possible, he will be in a position to advise the suspect in private. The issues involved when advising a suspect before interview are dealt with under the **Advising the Suspect—Preparation for Interview** index heading.

Interpreters

INTRODUCTION

Interpreters may be required not only for those suspects who have difficulty understanding and communicating in English because of language difficulties but also for those suspects who have difficulty in communicating as a result of speech problems, deafness or other hearing difficulties.

The police are responsible for making sure that appropriate arrangements are in place for providing suitably qualified interpreters who, wherever possible, should be drawn from the National Register of Public Service Interpreters.

PACE 1984, Code C, para. 13.1

ARRIVAL AT THE POLICE STATION

If there is doubt about the ability of the suspect properly to hear, speak or understand English and the custody officer cannot establish effective communication with the suspect in order to provide the suspect with the required information about his rights whilst in custody and the reason for detention, he must call an interpreter as soon as practicable. The information must then be given to the suspect with the assistance of the interpreter.

PACE 1984, Code C, para. 3.12

The notice of entitlements required to be given to the suspect should be available at the police station in a number of different languages and in an audio version.

PACE 1984, Code C, NfG 3B

All reasonable attempts should be made to make it clear to the suspect that an interpreter will be provided at public expense.

PACE 1984, Code C, para. 13.8

A record must be made of any action to call an interpeter.

PACE 1984, Code C, para. 13.11

INTERVIEWS

General rule

No suspect who is believed to have communication difficulties which require the services of an interpreter should be interviewed in the absence of a person capable of acting as an interpreter if, in the case of those suspects with difficulty understanding English, the interviewer does not speak the suspect's own language and the suspect requests an interpreter to be present.

PACE 1984, Code C, para. 13.2

A police officer may interpret only if he first obtains the suspect's written agreement (and that of any appropriate adult)

PACE 1984, Code C, para. 13.9

or if the interview is tape or visually recorded in accordance with Codes E and F of the PACE 1984 Codes of Practice.

PACE 1984, Code C, para. 13.5

If there is doubt as to the suspect's hearing or speaking ability, he must not be interviewed in the absence of an interpreter unless he agrees in writing to be interviewed without one or one of the exceptions below applies.

PACE 1984, Code C, para. 13.6

An interpreter will also be required if a juvenile is to be interviewed and the parent or guardian present as the appropriate adult appears to be deaf or there is doubt about his hearing or speaking ability. An interpreter need not be called in these circumstances if the appropriate adult agrees in writing or the interview is to be conducted under one of the exceptions below.

PACE 1984, Code C, para. 13.11

A record must be made of any agreement to be interviewed in the absence of an interpreter.

PACE 1984, Code E, para. 4.7

PACE 1984, Code C, para. 11.11

If the suspect is deaf or hearing impaired and the interview is tape-recorded, the interviewer shall make a written note of the interview at the same time as it is recording. The suspect must be given an opportunity to read the interview record.

Exceptions

An interview can take place without an interpreter in the following circumstances:

PACE 1984, Code C, para. 11.1

(a) following the suspect's arrest, the delay in taking him to a police station or other authorised place of detention would be likely to lead to:

- interference with or harm to evidence or other people;
- the alerting of other unarrested suspects; or
- the hindrance of the recovery of property obtained as a result of the offence.

Interviewing in these circumstances shall cease when the relevant risk has been averted or the necessary questions to attempt to avert the risk have been put to the suspect.

PACE 1984, Code C, para. 11.18

(b) if the suspect is in a police station or other authorised place of detention and a superintendent or above considers that the delay in having an interpreter attend would lead to:

- interference with or harm to evidence or other people;
- the alerting of other unarrested suspects; or

- the hindrance of the recovery of property obtained as a result of the offence; and
- the superintendent is satisfied that the interview would not significantly harm the suspect's physical or mental state.

Such questioning can only continue until sufficient information has been obtained to avert the consequences.

PACE 1984, Code C, para. 11.19

A record shall be made of the grounds for any decision to interview a person under Code C, para. 11.18.

PACE 1984, Code C, para. 11.20

WRITTEN INTERVIEWS

In relation to interviews other than those conducted on tape, the interviewing officer must ensure that the interpreter makes a contemporaneous note of the interview in the suspect's language and certifies its accuracy. The suspect must be given the opportunity to read the record of interview or have it read to them and to sign it as correct or indicate what the respects in which he considers it to be inaccurate.

PACE 1984, Code C, para. 13.3

STATEMENTS

If a statement is made to a police officer or other police staff in a language other than English, the interpreter shall take down the statement in that language and the maker of the statement be invited to sign it, after which an official translation into English shall be made.

PACE 1984, Code C, para. 13.4

OBTAINING LEGAL ADVICE

Where a suspect is exercising his right to legal advice (whether in person, in writing or on the telephone) and it becomes apparent that there are difficulties of communication which require the services of an interpreter, the police must call an interpreter. In these circumstances, where the interpreter is required to facilitate legal advice, that interpreter may not be a police officer or other police staff.

PACE 1984, Code C, para. 13.9

ON CHARGE

When a suspect appears to have communication difficulties and is to be charged with an offence, the custody officer, if he cannot establish effective communication, must call an interpreter to

PACE 1984, Code C, para. 13.10

explain the offence concerned and any other information given by the custody officer.

IDENTIFICATION PROCEDURES

PACE 1984, Code D, para. 2.14

In relation to identification procedures, if information is to be given to or required from the suspect and there is doubt as to the suspect's ability to communicate, the information must be given or sought through an interpreter.

PACE 1984, Code D, Annex B, para. 8

Once an identification parade has been formed, the whole parade must take place in the presence and hearing of an interpreter. If the witness makes an identification after an identification parade, the suspect and his interpreter must be informed.

PACE 1984, Code D, Annex B, para. 20

If an identification is made by a witness after the parade has ended, the suspect and his interpreter must be informed.

RECORDS

PACE 1984, Code C, para. 13.11

Any action taken to call an interpreter and any agreement to be interviewed in the absence of an interpreter must be recorded.

PRACTICAL GUIDANCE

(1) Is an interpreter required?

If, during the course of a private consultation with the suspect, the adviser forms the view that the suspect appears to have language, hearing or speech difficulties, he should consider advising the suspect to allow the adviser to bring the problem to the attention of the custody officer, who will then have to obtain the services of an interpreter. The custody officer is so obliged if the suspect appears to come within any of these categories.

The suspect may not wish the adviser to take this course of action, as he may fear that it may alert the authorities to problems with his immigration status or that the police will contact the embassy or consulate of a country on behalf of a suspect who has claimed political asylum from that country. Regarding the latter fear, the police are prohibited from contacting an asylum seeker's embassy and the adviser should make it clear to the police that no such contact should be made.

PACE 1984, Code C, para. 7.4

It may also be that the suspect does not want to delay matters by waiting for an interpreter to arrive. However, as the provisions are intended to protect the suspect, it would be normal to advise the suspect that the police ought to be informed and an interpreter called.

(2) Is the interpreter suitable?

The Law Society has issued guidance on the use of interpreters in the police station. It was suggested that the adviser use a separate interpreter for the consultation with the suspect than the interpreter used for the interview with police. The cost of using another interpreter can be claimed as a disbursement under the General Criminal Contract.

"Operational Guidance: Interpreters" (2001) *Criminal Practitioners' Newsletter*, October p.2

Whilst the Law Society guidance is good practice, it is not always going to be practical to arrange for a separate interpreter especially late at night, at weekends, with unusual languages or in more rural areas. Therefore, the adviser may have to rely on the same interpreter.

It may be possible to use friends, family or members of the local community to assist in interpeting for the suspect in consultation. However, the adviser should be aware that the suspect may feel constrained in talking freely in the presence of certain people and that the "casual" interpreter may not always provide an accurate interpretation if they feel it may not assist the suspect.

Clearly with the police arranging the interpreter (as they are obliged to do), it is likely that the same interpreters will be called on a regular basis to the same police station and therefore be on good terms with the police. This may cause problems for the adviser especially if the interpreter gives the suspect the impression that he is other than independent of the police.

The adviser should satisfy himself that the interpreter is competent to interpret for the particular suspect. Although the interpreter and the suspect may have the same country of origin, they may not speak the same language or dialect. It may also be that the interpreter comes from a different ethnic group to the suspect and that the difference in ethnic origin could be a source of conflict within that country.

If the adviser has doubts as to the suitability of the interpreter, he should object to the use of that interpreter, such objection to be noted on the custody record if possible and by the adviser independently.

(3) Privilege and confidentiality

Although the interpreter may have no duty of confidentiality to the suspect, the adviser should ensure that the interpreter understands that communications between the suspect and the adviser as facilitated by the interpreter are subject to legal privilege and the content of those discussions must not under any circumstances be divulged to the police or to any third party.

It is advisable to obtain an undertaking from the interpreter that no information obtained during a consultation will be passed on to the police. If the interpreter refuses to give such an undertaking, it may be that objection can be made as to their suitability. Certainly most competent registered interpreters will understand this issue and have no difficulty in giving such an undertaking.

Interviews under Caution

INTRODUCTION

The adviser will have already met the suspect and advised him regarding how to deal with the interview under caution, as discussed under the **Advising the Suspect** index heading. This heading deals with the police interview itself.

DEFINITION AND FORMALITIES

An "interview" is defined as the "questioning of a person regarding their involvement or suspected involvement in a criminal offence or offences". If questioning amounts to an interview, certain formalities have to be observed:

PACE 1984, Code C, para. 11.1A

(a) the suspect must be cautioned;

(b) the suspect should be reminded of the right to free legal advice and that the interview can be delayed to obtain that advice; and

PACE 1984, Code C, para. 11.2

(c) an accurate record of the interview must be made.

PACE 1984, Code C, para. 11.7

Most interviews at which legal advisers are present will fall within the definition of an interview and will take place in a police station or other establishment of a similar nature. In most cases interviews are audiotape recorded; some are videotape recorded, whilst others may be recorded contemporaneously in writing.

WHEN SHOULD QUESTIONING CEASE?

The interview or further interview of a person about an offence with which that person has not been charged or for which they have not been informed they may be prosecuted, must cease when:

PACE 1984, Code C, para. 11.6

(a) the officer in charge of the investigation is satisfied all the questions they consider relevant to obtaining accurate and reliable information about the offence have been put to the suspect which includes allowing the suspect an opportunity to give an innocent explanation and asking questions to test if the explanation is accurate and reliable, *e.g.* to clear up ambiguities or clarify what the suspect said;

(b) the officer in charge of the investigation has taken account of any other available evidence; and

(c) the officer in charge of the investigation, or in the case of a detained suspect, the custody officer reasonably believes there is sufficient evidence to provide a realistic prospect of conviction for that offence.

AUDIOTAPE—RECORDED INTERVIEWS

PACE 1984, Code E, para. 3.2

The tape recording of interviews is governed by Code E except for suspects interviewed under the Terrorism Act 2000 Sch. 7 or arrested under s.41 of that Act for which there is a separate Code of Practice.

PACE 1984, Code E, para. 3.1

Tape recording is mandatory for any interview:

(a) with a person cautioned under Code C, para. 10 in respect of any indictable offence, including an offence triable either way;

(b) which takes place as a result of an interviewer exceptionally putting further questions to a suspect about such an offence after they have been charged with, or told they may be prosecuted for, that offence;

(c) when an interviewer wants to tell a person, after they have been charged with, or informed they may be prosecuted for such an offence about any written statement or interview with another person.

PACE 1984, Code E, para. 3.5

The whole of the interview must be recorded including the taking or reading back of any statement.

PACE 1984, Code E, para. 3.3

The custody officer may authorise an interview not to be tape-recorded where it is not reasonably practicable to do so as a result of equipment failure or the unavailability of a suitable interview room or recorder and where he reasonably considers that the interview should not be delayed, or where it is clear that no prosecution will ensue. A note of the reasons for the interview not being tape recorded must be made. If the interview is not tape recorded in these circumstances, it must be recorded in writing.

PACE 1984, Code E, NfG 3A

Interviews conducted in circumstances other than those mentioned above may also be tape-recorded and, indeed, generally are tape-recorded.

If a suspect refuses to go into or remain in a suitable interview room and the custody officer considers, on reasonable grounds, that the interview should not be delayed, the interview may, at the custody officer's discretion, be conducted in a cell using portable recording equipment or, if none is available, recorded in writing. The reasons for this shall be recorded.

PACE 1984, Code E, para. 3.4

If the suspect objects to the interview being tape-recorded at the outset, during the interview or during a break, the interview must be recorded in writing. The suspect should be invited to have his objections to being interviewed on tape recorded on tape and, if he refuses to do so, the officer may turn off the tape after having given his reasons for so doing. The officer may also continue to put questions to the suspect with the tape recorder on if he considers it reasonable to do so.

PACE 1984, Code E, para. 4.8

Procedure

(a) Introductions

At the start of a tape-recorded interview, the police officer should open the tapes in the presence of the suspect and load them into the machine. The officer should then tell the suspect that the interview is being tape-recorded, identify himself and any other interviewer, ask the suspect and any other party present to identify themselves, state the date, time of commencement and place of the interview and inform the suspect that he will be given a notice at the end of the interview about what will happen to the tapes.

PACE 1984, Code E, para. 4.3

PACE 1984, Code E, para. 4.4

(b) Caution

The interviewing officer must, first of all, caution the suspect in the following terms:

PACE 1984, Code E, para. 4.5

> You do not have to say anything. But it may harm your defence if you do not mention when questioned something which you later rely on in court. Anything you do say may be given in evidence.

PACE 1984, Code C, para. 10.5

PACE 1984, Code C, para. 10.7

A minor deviation will not constitute a breach of the requirement to caution, provided that the sense of the caution is preserved. If the caution is not understood by the suspect, the police officer should explain it in his own words.

PACE 1984, Code C, NfG 10D

(c) Legal advice

PACE 1984, Code E, para. 4.5

The suspect should then be reminded that he has the right to free legal advice and that the interview can be delayed for legal advice to be obtained.

PACE 1984, Code C, para. 11.2

(d) Previous statements or silences

PACE 1984, Code E, para. 4.6

PACE 1984, Code C, para. 11.4

PACE 1984, Code C, NfG 11A

PACE 1984, Code C, para. 11.4

PACE 1984, Code C, para. 11.4A

At the beginning of the interview, the interviewer must put to the suspect any significant statement or silence occurring in the presence and hearing of a police officer or other police staff before the interview and which has not been put to the suspect in the course of any other interview. The same statements and silences may be put to the suspect again at a later stage or in a further interview.

The interviewer shall ask the suspect whether they confirm or deny that earlier statement or silence and if they want to add anything.

A significant statement is one which appears capable of being used in evidence against the suspect, in particular a direct admission of guilt. A significant silence is a failure or refusal to answer a question or answer satisfactorily when under caution, which might, allowing for the restriction on drawing adverse inferences from silence, give rise to an inference under the Criminal Justice and Public Order Act 1994, Pt III.

(e) Breaks

PACE 1984, Code E, para. 4.12

PACE 1984, Code E, para. 4.12A

PACE 1984, Code E, para. 4.13

If there is a break in an interview, the fact of the break, the reasons for it and the time shall be recorded. If the suspect leaves the interview room during the break, the tapes should then be removed from the machine, sealed and signed as they would be under the procedure which is followed at the end of the interview.

If the break is short and both the suspect and a police officer remain in the room, the reason for the break and the time should be recorded. The machine can be turned off and the interview recommenced on the same tapes with the time recorded at which the interview recommences.

If there is a break in the interview, the adviser should ensure that the full reasons for the break are recorded (*e.g.* "for refreshments *and* legal advice" rather than just for legal advice).

PACE 1984, Code E, para. 4.14

The suspect should be reminded by the interviewing officer of the fact that he is still under caution and of the right to free legal advice before the interview recommences.

(f) Changing tapes

PACE 1984, Code E, para. 4.11

When the recorder shows the tapes have only a short time left, the interviewer shall tell the suspect the tapes are coming to an end and round off that part of the interview. The interviewer will remove the tapes from the tape recorder and insert the new tapes which shall be unwrapped or opened in the suspect's presence.

If the interviewer has to leave the room to get a second set of tapes, the suspect shall not be left unattended.

In order to avoid confusion between the tapes, the interviewer shall mark the tapes with an identification number immediately they are removed from the tape recorder.

The tape recorder should then be set to record on the new tapes.

(h) Removing tapes from the recorder

When tapes are removed from the recorder during the interview, they shall be retained and the procedures for dealing with the conclusion of the interview (see below) followed.

PACE 1984, Code E, para. 4.16

(i) Failure of recording equipment

If there is an equipment failure which can be rectified quickly, *e.g.* by inserting new tapes, the interviewer shall follow the tape changing procedures above. When the recording is resumed the interviewer shall explain what happened and record the time that the interview recommences.

PACE 1984, Code E, para. 4.15

If, however, it is not possible to continue recording on that tape recorder and no replacement recorder is readily available, the interview may continue without being tape recorded. The interviewing officer shall seek the custody officer's authority and the interview be recorded in writing.

PACE 1984, Code E, para. 4.15
PACE 1984, Code E, para. 3.3

(j) Conclusion

At the conclusion of the interview, the suspect shall be offered the opportunity to clarify anything he has said and asked if there is anything he wants to add.

PACE 1984, Code E, para. 4.17

The time that the interview concluded shall be recorded and the tape recorder switched off. The interviewer shall seal the master tape with a master tape label and treat it as an exhibit. The interviewer shall sign the label and ask the suspect and any third party present during the interview to sign it. If the suspect or third party refuse to sign the label an officer of at least inspector rank, or if not available the custody officer, shall be called into the interview room and asked to sign it.

PACE 1984, Code E, para. 4.18

The suspect shall be handed a notice which explains how the tape-recording will be used, the arrangements for access to it and that, if he is charged or informed he will be prosecuted, a copy of the tape will be supplied as soon as practicable or as otherwise agreed between the suspect and the police.

PACE 1984, Code E, para. 4.19

Tape security

PACE 1984, Code E, para. 6.1

The officer in charge of each police station at which interviews with suspects are recorded shall make arrangements for master tapes to be kept securely and their movements accounted for on the same basis as material which may be used for evidential purposes.

PACE 1984, Code E, para. 6.2

A police officer has no authority to break the seal on a master tape required for a criminal trial or appeal proceedings. If it is necessary to gain access to the master tape, the police officer shall arrange for its seal to be broken in the presence of a representative of the Crown Prosecution Service. The defendant or their legal adviser should be informed and given a reasonable opportunity to be present. If the defendant or their legal representative is present they shall be invited to reseal and sign the master tape. If either refuses or neither is present this should be done by the representative of the Crown Prosecution Service.

PACE 1984, Code E, para. 6.4

When the master tape seal is broken, a record must be made of the procedure followed, including the date, time, place and persons present.

(k) Interviews with deaf persons

PACE 1984, Code E, para. 4.7

If the suspect is deaf or is suspected of having impaired hearing, the interviewing officer shall make a contemporaneous written note of the interview at the same time as tape-recording it.

PACE 1984, Code E, NfG 4B

This is to give a person who is deaf or has impaired hearing equivalent rights of access to the full interview record as far as this is possible using audio recording.

VIDEOTAPED INTERVIEWS

There is no statutory requirement to visually record interviews but if an interviewing officer decides to make a visual recording with sound of an interview with a suspect, he should consider the contents of PACE 1984, Code F.

An interviewing officer may consider it appropriate to make a visual recording in the following circumstances:

PACE 1984, Code F, para. 3.1

(a) an interview with a suspect in respect of an indictable offence (including an offence triable either way);

(b) an interview which takes place as a result of an interviewer exceptionally putting further questions to a suspect about such an offence after they have been charged with, or informed they may be prosecuted for, that offence;

(c) an interview in which an interviewer wishes to bring to the notice of a person, after that person has been charged with, or informed they may be prosecuted for such an offence, any written statement made by another person, or the content of an interview with another person;

(d) an interview with, or in the presence of, a deaf or deaf/blind or speech impaired person who uses sign language to communicate;

(e) an interview with, or in the presence of anyone who requires an "appropriate adult"; or

(f) an interview in any case where the suspect or their representative requests that the interview be recorded visually.

The provisions of Code F do not apply to interviews of those detained under Terrorism Act 2000 Sch. 7 or s.41.

PACE 1984, Code F, para. 3.2

The custody officer may authorise the interviewing officer not to record the interview visually:

PACE 1984, Code F, para. 3.3

(a) where it is not reasonably practicable to do so because of failure of the equipment, or the non-availability of a suitable interview room, or recorder, and the authorising officer considers on reasonable grounds that the interview should not be delayed until the failure has been rectified or a suitable room or recorder becomes available. In such cases the custody officer may authorise the interviewing officer to audio record the interview in accordance with the guidance set out in Code E;

(b) where it is clear from the outset that no prosecution will ensue; or

(c) where it is not practicable to do so because at the time the person resists being taken to a suitable interview room or other location which would enable the interview to be recorded, or otherwise fails or refuses to go into such a room or location, and the authorising officer considers on reasonable grounds that the interview should not be delayed until these conditions cease to apply.

In all cases the custody officer shall make a note in the custody records of the reasons for not taking a visual record.

The whole of each interview shall be recorded visually, including the taking and reading back of any statement.

PACE 1984, Code F, para. 3.5

The provisions for conducting the interview largely mirror those in Code E and will not be repeated here.

INTERVIEWS RECORDED IN WRITING

PACE 1984, Code C, para. 11.7(a)

It is rare for interviews to be recorded in writing rather than tape-recorded but if the interview is to be so recorded an accurate record must be made of each such interview, whether or not the interview takes place at a police station.

PACE 1984, Code C, para. 11.7(b)

The record must state the place of interview, the time it begins and ends, any breaks and the names of all those present: it must be made on the forms provided for this purpose or in the interviewer's pocket book or in accordance with the Codes of Practice E or F.

PACE 1984, Code C, para. 11.7(c)

Any written record must be made and completed during the interview, unless this would not be practicable or would interfere with the conduct of the interview, and must constitute either a verbatim record of what has been said or, failing this, an account of the interview which adequately and accurately summarises it.

PACE 1984, Code C, para. 11.8

PACE 1984, Code C, para. 11.9

If a written record is not made during the interview, it must be made as soon as practicable after its completion, be timed and signed by the maker and the reason why it was not completed during the interview must be recorded in the interview record.

PACE 1984, Code C, para. 11.10

PACE 1984, Code C, para. 11.11

Unless it is impracticable, the suspect shall be given the opportunity to read the interview record and to sign it as correct or to indicate how they consider it to be inaccurate. If the person interviewed cannot read or refuses to read the record or sign it, the senior interviewer present shall read it to them and ask whether they would like to sign it as correct or make their mark or to indicate how they consider it to be inaccurate. The interviewer shall certify on the interview record itself what has occurred.

PACE 1984, Code C, para. 11.12

If the appropriate adult or the suspect's solicitor is present during the interview, they should also be given an opportunity to read and sign the interview record or any written statement taken down during the interview.

PACE 1984, Code C, para. 11.13

A written record shall be made of any comments made by a suspect, including unsolicited comments, which are outside the context of an interview but which might be relevant to the offence. Any such record must be timed and signed by the maker. When practicable the suspect shall be given the opportunity to read that record and to sign it as correct or to indicate how they consider it to be inaccurate.

Any refusal by a person to sign an interview record when asked must itself be recorded.

PACE 1984, Code C, para. 11.14

It may be necessary for the adviser to refer to his own notes of the interview if a dispute as to accuracy arises. When the adviser is given the opportunity to read and sign the record, he should obviously read it but there is not normally any positive reason why he should sign it.

EXCLUSION OF LEGAL ADVISER

Reasons

A legal adviser can only be excluded from an interview in extreme circumstances where his conduct is such that the interviewing officer is unable properly to put questions to the suspect. This means that the adviser has gone well beyond interrupting or intervening to protect the interests of the suspect or requesting that the interview be stopped for further advice to be given, all of which is perfectly acceptable.

PACE 1984, Code C, para. 6.9

PACE 1984, Code C, NfG 6D

The conduct of the legal adviser would have to be such that the interviewing officer is prevented or unreasonably obstructed from putting proper questions to the suspect or from having the answers recorded. Such behaviour would include answering questions on behalf of the suspect or providing written responses for him to quote.

PACE 1984, Code C, NfG 6D

Procedure

If the interviewing officer believes that the adviser is acting in such a way as to warrant his exclusion from the interview, he must consult an officer of at least the rank of superintendent, if available, or inspector if a superintendent is not readily available. This officer must be unconnected with the investigation and can only make a decision after speaking to the adviser. The officer must be able to satisfy a court that the decision was properly made and therefore may need to witness the conduct for himself.

PACE 1984, Code C, para. 6.10

PACE 1984, Code C, NfG 6E

If the adviser is excluded from the remainder of the interview, the suspect must be given the opportunity of consulting another legal adviser before the interview continues and of having the new adviser present in the interview.

PACE 1984, Code C, para. 6.10

If a legal adviser has been excluded from an interview, a superintendent making the decision or to whom the decision has been reported will have to consider reporting the matter to the Law Society and, in the case of a duty solicitor, the Legal Services Commission.

PACE 1984, Code C, para. 6.11

PACE 1984, Code C, NfG 6F

If an officer of at least inspector rank considers that a particular solicitor or firm is persistently sending unsuitable probationary representatives to the police station, they should inform an officer of at least the rank of superintendent who may wish to take the matter up with the Law Society.

Any adviser who is excluded from an interview should make a careful note of what happened as soon as possible, as this may be relevant either at trial or in any disciplinary hearing.

PRACTICAL GUIDANCE

(1) The role and tactics of the interviewing officer

The purpose of an interview is not to obtain a confession, nor to prove that the suspect is guilty. The purpose of an interview is to attempt to obtain accurate and reliable information from the suspect in order to discover the truth about the matters under investigation.

In theory, the interview should be approached with an open mind. However, in practice many police officers approach the interview in a closed frame of mind and appear to treat it as a means of obtaining evidence against the suspect to prove his guilt.

The police employ a number of tactics which vary from officer to officer and from case to case. It is impossible to anticipate exactly what officers will do in interview and what methods will be employed to get the suspect to talk or confess: some specific examples of possible tactics are given below.

(2) The role of the legal adviser

PACE 1984, Code C, NfG 6D

The adviser is not simply an observer; he has a specific and very important role. It is the duty of the legal adviser to protect and advance the legal rights of the suspect. The adviser should be ready to intervene during the interview for a variety of purposes, including challenging improper questions and providing further legal advice. The adviser should seek to protect the suspect from the inevitable pressures and stresses of detention in a police station and to ensure that the police comply with PACE 1984 and the Codes of Practice at all times.

It is essential that the adviser keeps as full a note as possible of what is said in the interview. There are a number of reasons why that note may become important, for example it can be used to correct police officers who have inaccurately remembered an earlier part of the interview. It may also be a useful tool at any bail application or application for a warrant of further detention.

(3) Before the interview

The police are on their home territory and will try to capitalise on this by assuming as much control over proceedings as they possibly can. As a counterbalance, the adviser should always be smartly dressed (as this tends to lend authority to a person) and act in a confident and properly assertive manner. The adviser should not allow the police officer to introduce him to the suspect but should affect the introductions himself.

In the interview room, the police may try to place the adviser in a location that appears to undermine his status and to exclude him from the interview. The adviser should not allow this to happen and should take control of the situation by telling the suspect where to sit and positioning himself next to the suspect and in the interviewing officer's line of vision. This may seem a small matter but unless the adviser is correctly positioned he will find it difficult to take an active part in the interview.

If the adviser is not happy with his original position once the interview has commenced, he should not be afraid to move to a better position.

(4) Introductions in interview

PACE 1984, Code C, NfG 6D

At the start of the interview, the adviser will be asked to introduce himself for the purposes of the tape recording. It is suggested that the adviser should take this opportunity to explain in a few words the role which he is performing by his presence in the interview, namely that he is there to protect the interests of the suspect. Advisers can make specific reference to the provision in the PACE 1984 Codes of Practice dealing with this issue: thus making it clear to the police that he is not just going to sit meekly in the corner throughout the interview.

If the adviser is not a solicitor, it is suggested that it is good practice at this point to make it clear what position he holds. This should have already been explained to the suspect before the interview and will negate any attempt by the police to undermine the confidence of the suspect in his legal adviser by making patronising references to his status during the interview.

R. v Bowden [1999] 2 Cr. App.R. 176; [1999] 4 All E.R. 43

If the interview is to be one in which comment is declined for a reason, such as non-disclosure of the evidence or the vulnerability of the suspect, the adviser should be careful not to inadvertently waive privilege by stating on the tape the reasons for the intended "no comment" interview. It may be necessary to give the suspect the advice on tape in the present tense which should not amount to a waiver of privilege as it would not refer to a previous privileged conversation.

R. v Fitzgerald [1998] 4 *Archbold News* 2, CA

The adviser should also be aware that anything said by them on the tape will be admissible in evidence in future proceedings.

(5) Intervening during the interview

The adviser must be ready to intervene during the course of the interview if it becomes necessary to do so. Intervention will become necessary if the interview is not conducted in accordance with PACE 1984 or the Codes of Practice or is otherwise conducted in an unfair manner.

The adviser will be aware that the courts are less likely to exclude evidence obtained in an interview conducted in the presence of legal representation, notwithstanding any breaches of PACE 1984 or the Codes of Practice which may have taken place. This highlights the need to intervene at the time, rather than relying on the courts to correct the results of any malpractice at a later stage.

If any breach of PACE 1984 or the Codes of Practice becomes apparent to the adviser, he must intervene, even if that breach appears minor.

PACE 1984, s.58

PACE 1984, Code C, NfG 6D

If the suspect has decided before the interview not to answer questions but during the interview starts to do so, the adviser should intervene immediately to remind him of the earlier decision or request that the interview be suspended for further advice. If the suspect continues to answer questions, the adviser should consider requesting that the interview be suspended to enable him to give further legal advice to the suspect. The suspect has the right to free legal advice in private at any time, which includes during an interview. This may be considered by the police to be the right of the suspect and not the adviser. However, the adviser clearly does have the right to interrupt an interview and request that he be able to advise the suspect further which is recognised in the Codes.

The police may use certain tactics to get a silent suspect to talk during interview. Whilst the police are entitled to ask questions even when it is obvious that the suspect does not wish to answer them, there will come a point where continued questioning in the face of silence will become oppressive. It is difficult to know when this point has been reached but the adviser should be ready to intervene and point out to the interviewing officers when he believes that that point has been reached.

(a) Examples of police tactics when faced with a silent suspect

Some common tactics to get a silent suspect talking follow.

(i) Starting with background questions

This involves the police officer asking the suspect questions in relation to his background at the start of an interview with a view to getting the suspect talking.

This ploy should be objected to, as the suspect's background can rarely be relevant to the offence about which the suspect is being interviewed. The Codes of Practice state that an "interview is the questioning of a person regarding their involvement or suspected involvement in a criminal offence".

PACE 1984, Code C, para. 11.1A

Such antecedent details should only be taken after charge and, if the police persist in questioning of this nature, the suspect should be advised to remain silent.

(ii) Silence on legal advice

Police officers sometimes ask the suspect if he is remaining silent on the advice of his legal representative. This information is subject to legal privilege and objection should be taken to the question.

(iii) Suspect's decision

The police may point out to a suspect who is refusing to answer questions that to remain silent on legal advice will not prevent an adverse inference being drawn and it is their decision whether to answer questions not the legal adviser's. Again, what advice the suspect may or may not have had is subject to privilege. However, it may be best to warn the suspect of this tactic before the interview starts to take the sting out of it if this tactic is used.

Indeed this sort of statement by the police is not strictly accurate. The fact that the suspect has been advised not to say anything will not of itself prevent an adverse inference being drawn. However, it is one factor for the court to consider in deciding whether to draw an adverse inference. If the reason for the advice is explained at trial, the court may well consider the silence in interview to have been reasonable and hence no inference may be drawn.

R. v Condron [1997] 1 Cr. App.R. 185

It may be helpful to intervene in such circumstances and remind the interviewing officer that should the matter proceed to trial, it will be for the court to decide whether an adverse inference should be drawn.

(iv) The suspect's opportunity to give his side of the story

Every legal adviser will have experienced police officers saying to silent suspects that the interview is the suspect's opportunity to tell his side of the story.

The best way to deal with this tactic is to warn the suspect of it before interview, which ought to nullify the effect. Otherwise, the suspect may feel that he will not have any other opportunity to put forward his version of events.

(b) Unfair questions

The adviser should intervene if the police use any questions which do not appear to be fair to the suspect. A question can be unfair for a number of reasons:

(i) Ambiguous

Objection should be taken to questions which are ambiguous and to which the answer could be taken to mean something other than what the suspect intended it to mean.

(ii) Co-suspects

A statement by a co-suspect implicating the suspect for whom the adviser acts will generally not be admissible at trial unless that co-suspect gives evidence at trial as a prosecution witness.

Whilst no objection can necessarily be made about police officers introducing questions arising from a co-suspect's interview, the suspect should have been advised previously of the likely evidential status of a co-suspect's comments. The suspect should have been told that he should not begin answering questions because he does not agree with what has been said by a co-suspect. If such advice has not been given, the adviser can interrupt the interview to advise the suspect further in private before the suspect answers such a question.

(iii) Hypothetical

Objection should be taken to questions which are hypothetical and the suspect should be advised not to answer such questions if they are asked.

(iv) Inducement

Any question containing either implied or express inducements to the suspect to answer in a certain way must be the subject of an objection by the adviser. The inducement may be blatant or much more subtle, such as an expression of apparent concern on behalf of the officer about the welfare of the suspect or someone the suspect is worried about.

(v) Irrelevant

An interview is the questioning of a suspect concerning his involvement in a criminal offence and, as such, objection should be taken to any questions which do not appear relevant to the offence for which the suspect has been arrested and detained and about which he is being interviewed.

The adviser may not always be able to tell whether a question is relevant, as he will only know what he has been told by the police and the suspect, but if a question does appear irrelevant an intervention may provoke the police officer to give some indication as to why that particular question is considered relevant to the alleged offence.

Questions in relation to offences other than those for which the suspect has been arrested should also be objected to as irrelevant. It may be that the suspect will be arrested in relation to other offences at a later stage: it is only at that point that such questions will become relevant.

(vi) Multiple questions

If a police officer asks more than one question at a time, the adviser should ask the officer to split the question into individual parts so that the suspect can answer each question in turn. In this way, the answer to part of a multiple question cannot be taken to be the answer to another part of it.

(c) Oppressive questioning

It is obviously vitally important for the adviser to object if questioning becomes aggressive, offensive, insulting, threatening or otherwise "oppressive".

Oppression can result from continued repetition of questions which have already been answered or to which a "no comment" answer has been given, from an officer raising his voice or becoming angry or from continued interruptions of the suspect by the officer.

The adviser should be alert to the tone of the interview and intervene if he believes the interview is becoming oppressive. If such behaviour persists, the adviser should consider interrupting the interview to advise the suspect in private or to make a complaint (refer to the **Complaints** index heading).

(d) The interview should cease

PACE 1984, Code C, para. 11.6

As stated above the interview must cease when the officer in charge of the investigation is satisfied that all the questions they consider relevant to obtaining accurate and reliable information about the offence have been put to the suspect, he has taken account of any other available evidence, and the custody officer reasonably believes there is sufficient evidence to provide a realistic prospect of conviction for that offence.

PACE 1984, s.37(1)

However, PACE 1984 states that the custody officer shall determine whether there is sufficient evidence to charge the suspect and, if he believes there is, he should charge him. Arguably, the statutory test of "sufficient evidence to charge" is lower than that of "sufficient evidence to provide a realistic prospect of conviction" as set out in the Code.

If the adviser feels that it is in the best interests of the suspect for the interviewing to cease and for him to be charged, it may be useful to intervene and terminate the interview so that instructions can be taken from the suspect and, if he is in agreement, representations made to the custody officer on his obligations to charge under PACE 1984.

CPIA 1996, Code, 3.4

PACE 1984, Code C, NfG 11B

This is a very difficult argument as the Codes of Practice both for PACE 1984 and the CPIA 1996 give the police a lot of latitude in when they should cease questioning. The police are reminded specifically to keep in mind that they should pursue all reasonable lines of enquiry, whether these point towards or away from the suspect. This enables them to justify continuing to ask questions about possible defences when they may otherwise have concluded the interview. This may be particularly damaging if a suspect is not answering questions as it may well assist the court to draw an inference in due course.

It is very difficult indeed for an adviser to assess when the stage has been reached that questioning should cease as they will not know the extent of the evidence that the police have in their possession.

(6) End of the interview

Once the interview has come to an end, the adviser should keep a note of anything said between the parties after the tape has been turned off.

The adviser should find out from the police what the intended course of action is and advise the suspect in private as to the likely future course of events. It may be that a further interview is required or that the police are considering bailing the suspect for further inquiries, charging him or releasing him without charge.

If the suspect has raised issues in the interview which warrant further police investigation, and the suspect agrees with this course of action, it can be useful to ask the police what investigations they are going to make as a result of what the suspect has said. The police can be reminded of their obligation to pursue all reasonable lines of enquiry, whether these point towards or away from the suspect. It may become relevant at trial if such lines of enquiry are not pursued by police so a careful note should be kept of these discussions.

CPIA 1996, Code 3.4

The suspect should also be advised of the continued right to free legal advice at any time and warned against any conversations with police officers if he is to remain in custody.

Juvenile Suspects

INTRODUCTION

Juvenile suspects have the same basic rights as other suspects. However, there are a number of special rules which apply when the suspect is a juvenile. This heading deals with those considerations particular to juveniles.

Juvenile suspects are generally considered to be vulnerable and therefore the adviser should be aware of the purpose of the protection afforded to this particular type of suspect. Whilst juvenile suspects can provide reliable evidence, they may also be prone to giving information that is unreliable, misleading or self-incriminating without knowing or wishing to do so. (PACE 1984, Code C, NfG 11C)

The PACE 1984 Codes of Practice remind the police that special care is required when questioning such suspects and that corroborative evidence of any admissions made should be sought wherever possible. (PACE 1984, Code C, NfG 11C)

Under the CDA 1998, local authorities have an obligation in co-operation with police, probation and health authorities to ensure that certain services and schemes are available in their area. Prior to a juvenile appearing in court these include "appropriate adult" services, a final warning scheme and related services, bail support and placement of those remanded to local authority accommodation. (CDA 1998, s.38)

Furthermore local authorities must publish youth justice plans and appoint youth offending teams to co-ordinate and provide youth justice services in their area. The adviser must be familiar with the arrangements in their locality. (CDA 1998, ss 39 and 40)

THE LAW

Definition

(PACE 1984, s.37(15))

The police are under a duty to treat as a juvenile any suspect who appears to be under the age of 17, unless there is clear evidence to show that he is older. (PACE 1984, Code C, para. 1.5)

A suspect who is or appears to be 17 years of age is to be treated as though he were an adult whilst in detention at the police station. However, if that suspect is charged or summonsed, he will be dealt with by the Youth Court and he is treated as a young person for the purposes of reprimands and final warnings. (PACE 1984, Code D, para. 2.4) (CYPA 1933, ss 31, 34; CJA 1991, Sch. 8)

CYPA 1933, s.50

As the age of criminal responsibility is 10 years, no child who is younger than 10 should ever be arrested or held in detention at a police station or elsewhere. However, the police do have some additional powers in relation to persons under the age of 18 including those under the age of 10:

CA 1989, s.46(1)

CA 1989, s.46(3)(f)

(i) A child under the age of 10 may be held at a police station as a place of safety if the police have reasonable cause to believe that he would be likely to suffer significant harm if not removed to suitable accommodation. A child can be kept under such protection for up to 72 hours but must be removed to local authority or other suitable accommodation as soon as reasonably practicable;

CDA 1998, s.11

(ii) A court will be able to make a child safety order in respect of a child under 10 years who has committed an act which would have constituted an offence if the child had been 10 years or over, although the police have no powers of arrest in relation to such orders;

CDA 1998, s.14

CDA 1998, s.15

(iii) A local authority can establish local child curfew schemes applicable to children under 10 years. If a police constable has reasonable grounds to believe that a child is in breach of a ban imposed by such a curfew order, he can take the child home unless he has reasonable grounds to believe that the child would be likely to suffer significant harm there, in which case the child could be removed to a place of safety;

CDA 1998, s.16

(iv) If a police officer has reasonable grounds to believe that a child or young person of compulsory school age found by him in a specified area during a specified period is absent from school without lawful authority, he may remove the child to the local authority designated premises or the school from which he is absent.

Intimation of arrest

CYPA 1933, s.34(9); PACE 1984, ss 57, 56(1)

The police have a duty to inform certain persons of the arrest of a juvenile, in addition to their obligation to allow the juvenile suspect to contact one friend, relative or other person known to him who is likely to take an interest in his welfare.

(a) Person responsible for the welfare of the juvenile

CYPA 1933, s.34(2); PACE 1984, s.57

When a juvenile is in police detention, the police have to take such steps as are practicable to ascertain the identity of a person responsible for his welfare.

Once the identity of the person responsible for the welfare of the juvenile in detention has been established, that person shall be informed that the juvenile has been arrested, why he has been arrested and where he is being detained. This information should be given as soon as practicable.

CYPA 1933, s.34(3),(4); PACE 1984, s.57; PACE 1984, Code C, para. 3.13

The person responsible for the welfare of the juvenile will be:

PACE 1984, Code C, para. 3.13

(a) a parent or guardian;

(b) if the juvenile is in local authority or voluntary organisation care, or is otherwise being looked after under the Children Act 1989, a person appointed by that authority or organisation to have responsibility for the juvenile's welfare; or

(c) any other person who has for the time being assumed responsibility for his welfare.

(b) Person responsible for the supervision of the juvenile

If a juvenile is known to be subject to a court order under which a person or organisation is given any degree of statutory responsibility to supervise or otherwise monitor them, reasonable steps must also be taken to notify that person or organisation (the "responsible officer"). The responsible officer will normally be a member of a Youth Offending Team, except for a curfew order which involves electronic monitoring when the contractor providing the monitoring will normally be the responsible officer.

CYPA 1933, s.34(7); PACE 1984, s.57; PACE 1984, Code C, para. 3.14

(c) Appropriate adult

The appropriate adult (see below) must also be informed as soon as practicable of the grounds and place of detention and asked to come to the police station. This cannot be delayed even if the suspect is being held incommunicado.

PACE 1984, Code C, para. 3.15
PACE 1984, Code C, Annex B, NfG B 1

Detention or bail after charge

If a juvenile has been charged with an offence, the custody officer will have to consider whether he is to be released on bail or kept in police custody, taking into account the same considerations as apply for an adult. However, there is an additional ground on which a juvenile can be kept in custody, namely if the custody officer has reasonable grounds for believing that he ought to be detained in his "own interests" which is not a defined term.

PACE 1984, s.38(1)(b)

PACE 1984, s.38(6); PACE 1984, Code C, para. 16.7

If the juvenile suspect who has been charged with an offence is to be refused bail from the police station, the custody officer must arrange for the juvenile to be moved to local authority accommodation, unless:

(a) the custody officer certifies, for reasons which he must specify, that it is impracticable for him to do so; or

(b) if the juvenile is 12 years old or over, the custody officer certifies that no secure accommodation is available and that keeping him in other local authority accommodation would not be adequate to protect the public from serious harm from him.

PACE 1984, Code C, NfG 16D

Neither a juvenile's behaviour nor the nature of the offence provides grounds for the custody officer to decide it is impracticable to arrange the juvenile's transfer to local authority care. Similarly, the lack of secure local authority accommodation does not make it impracticable to transfer the juvenile. The availability of secure accommodation is only a factor in relation to a juvenile aged 12 or over when the local authority accommodation would not be adequate to protect the public from serious harm from the juvenile.

PACE 1984, s.36(6A)

If the offence is violent or sexual, protecting the public from serious harm should be construed as protecting the public from death or serious personal injury, whether physical or psychological, occasioned by further such offences committed by the juvenile.

HOC 78/1992

Impractical should only mean where it proves to be physically impossible to transfer the juvenile to local authority accommodation, for instance because the local authority cannot be contacted despite efforts to do so or because of extremely adverse weather conditions which render travel dangerous.

PACE 1984, s.46

The obligation to transfer a juvenile to local authority accommodation applies as much to a juvenile charged during the daytime as to a juvenile to be held overnight, subject to a requirement to bring the juvenile before a court as soon as practicable.

PACE 1984, s.38(7); PACE 1984, Code C, para. 16.10

The certificate made out by the custody officer must be produced to the court before which the juvenile is first brought.

Once a juvenile has been placed with a local authority under the above provisions, that local authority may decide to hold him in secure accommodation for up to 72 hours within any

28-day period, if it appears that non-secure accommodation is inappropriate because the juvenile is likely to abscond from other accommodation or injure himself or other people if kept in other accommodation.

C(SA)R 1991, SI 1991/1505, regs 10(1), 6

Detention in a cell

A juvenile must not be held in a police cell unless no other secure accommodation is available and the custody officer considers that it is not practicable to supervise him unless he is placed in a cell or that a cell is the most comfortable secure accommodation in the police station. In any event, a juvenile must not be placed in a cell with a detained adult.

CYPA 1933, s.31

PACE 1984, Code C, para. 8.8

PRACTICE AND PROCEDURE

Duties of the police

If the suspect appears to be under the age of 17, then the police must treat him as if he were a juvenile, unless there is clear evidence to indicate that he is in fact 17 years of age or older.

PACE 1984, Code C, para. 1.5

The police must notify the person responsible for the juvenile suspect's welfare and supervision (if appropriate) that he has been arrested, the reason for the arrest and where he is being detained. An appropriate adult (if a different person from those mentioned above) must also be informed of the grounds for and place of his detention and asked to come to the police station.

PACE 1984, Code C, paras 3.13,3.14

PACE 1984, Code C, para. 3.15

APPROPRIATE ADULT

(a) Definition

There is a hierarchy of persons who can act as an appropriate adult:

(i) the parent, guardian or, if the juvenile is in local authority or voluntary organisation care, or is otherwise being looked after under the Children Act 1989, a person representing that authority or organisation; failing which

PACE 1984, Code C, para. 1.7(a), Code D, para. 2.6

(ii) a social worker of a local authority social services department; failing which

(iii) some other responsible adult aged 18 or over who is not a police officer or employed by the police.

(b) Inappropriate persons

PACE 1984, Code C, NfG 1B

No person should act as an appropriate adult if he:

(a) is suspected of being involved in the offence;

(b) is the victim of the offence;

(c) is a witness to the offence;

(d) is involved in the investigation of the offence; or

(e) has received admissions before attending the police station.

PACE 1984, Code C, NfG 1B

If the juvenile expressly and specifically objects to the presence of a parent from whom he is estranged, that parent should not be asked to act as the appropriate adult.

PACE 1984, Code C, NfG 1C

If a juvenile admits an offence to, or in the presence of, a social worker or member of a youth offending team other than during the time that person is acting as the juvenile's appropriate adult, another appropriate adult should be appointed in the interest of fairness.

PACE 1984, Code C, NfG 1F

A legal adviser or an independent custody visitor present at the police station in that capacity may not act as an appropriate adult.

R. v Morse [1991] Crim. L.R. 195; *R. v Palmer*, Sept 1991, *Legal Action* 21

Other inappropriate persons would include a parent or guardian (or other person) who is unlikely to be capable of appreciating the seriousness of the situation. This may arise, for example, because of low intelligence, literacy difficulties or mental health problems. A person under the age of 18 cannot be an appropriate adult.

Role of the appropriate adult

PACE 1984, Code C, para. 3.18

The suspect should be informed by the custody officer that the appropriate adult is there to assist and advise him and can be consulted privately at any time.

PACE 1984, Code C, para. 2.4

The appropriate adult can also inspect the custody record on arrival at the police station and subsequently be supplied with a copy on request.

PACE 1984, Code C, NfG 1E

Appropriate adults are not bound by confidentiality or privilege and there is nothing to prevent them passing on information they have received during a consultation with the suspect to the police. Initial advice ought therefore to be given in the absence of the appropriate adult, such advice to include the risk of disclosure of information by the appropriate adult. Indeed the Code specifically provides for such a situation.

The role of the appropriate adult is to ensure that the suspect understands what is happening to them and why. The appropriate adult should support, advise and assist the suspect, observe whether the police are acting fairly and object if he considers that they are not, assist with communication between the suspect and police, and ensure the suspect understands their rights. It is not part of the role of the appropriate adult to provide legal advice.

Home Office Guidance for Appropriate Adults, Annex A

Notification of detention

The appropriate adult must be informed of the grounds for detention of the juvenile suspect and his whereabouts as soon as practicable. He should then be asked to come to the police station.

PACE 1984, Code C, para. 3.15

There is no provision which allows for delay in informing the appropriate adult (or indeed the person responsible for the welfare of the juvenile, if a different person) even if the juvenile would otherwise be delayed the right of intimation of arrest or access to legal advice. In effect this means that there can be no circumstances in which access to legal advice should be delayed.

PACE 1984, Code C, Annex B, NfG B 1

Notification and exercise of rights

The appropriate adult must be present when the juvenile suspect is told of the reasons for his detention and his rights to legal advice, to have someone informed of his arrest and to consult the PACE 1984 Codes of Practice, and when handed the written notice of these rights. This may mean that the suspect is provided with this information on two occasions.

PACE 1984, Code C, para. 3.17

The appropriate adult can exercise the right to legal advice on behalf of the juvenile suspect, although the suspect cannot be forced to see the legal adviser if they do not wish to do so. If, however, the suspect has requested access to legal advice on arrival at the police station, there should be no delay to await the arrival of the appropriate adult. Indeed, the suspect should be given the opportunity to consult privately with the legal adviser in the absence of the appropriate adult, if he wishes to do so.

PACE 1984, Code C, para. 3.19

PACE 1984, Code C, para. 6.5A

PACE 1984, Code C, NfG 1E

Interviews

The Codes of Practice recognise the particular difficulties in interviewing juvenile suspects who are often capable of providing reliable evidence but may, without knowing or wishing to do so, be prone in certain circumstances to provide information

PACE 1984, Code C, NfG 11C

that may be unreliable, misleading or self-incriminating. Special care should always be taken when questioning a juvenile suspect and the police are reminded that it is important to obtain corroboration of any facts admitted whenever possible.

PACE 1984, Code C, para. 11.15
PACE 1984, Code C, para. 11.18

A juvenile suspect must not be interviewed or asked to provide or sign a written statement under caution or to sign a record of interview in the absence of the appropriate adult unless an officer of superintendent rank or above considers delay will:

PACE 1984, Code C, para. 11.1

- lead to interference with or harm to evidence connected with an offence;
- lead to interference with, or physical harm to, other people;
- lead to serious loss of, or damage to, property;
- alert other people suspected of committing an offence but not yet arrested for it; or
- hinder the recovery of property obtained in consequence of the commission of an offence; and

the officer is satisfied the interview would not significantly harm the suspect's physical or mental state.

PACE 1984, Code C, paras 11.1 and 11.19

Interviewing in any of these circumstances shall cease once sufficient information has been obtained to avert the above consequences

PACE 1984, Code C, para. 11.20

A record shall be made of the grounds for any decision to interview a juvenile suspect without an appropriate adult.

PACE 1984, Code C, para. 11.17

Before any interview, the appropriate adult must be reminded that his role is not simply to act as an observer but to facilitate communication with the interviewee, to advise that person and to ensure that the interview is being conducted fairly and properly.

Interviews at school premises

PACE 1984, Code C, para. 11.16

Such interviews should only take place in exceptional circumstances and only with the agreement of the principal of the school or his nominee. Every effort must be made to notify the parent(s) or other person responsible for the welfare of the child and the appropriate adult, if a different person, that the police want to interview the juvenile and a reasonable time allowed to enable the appropriate adult to be present at the interview. If the delay in awaiting the arrival of the appropriate adult is unreasonable, the principal or nominee can act as appropriate adult unless the offence suspected is one committed against the educational establishment.

Juveniles should not be arrested at their place of education unless this is unavoidable. When a juvenile is arrested at their place of education, the principal or their nominee must be informed.

PACE 1984, Code C, NfG 11D

Although legal advice is available in the normal way, as the juvenile is a volunteer, he is not at a police station and therefore does not have to be told of the right to such advice.

Reviews of detention

If the detention of a juvenile suspect is to be reviewed, the appropriate adult, if available at the time, must be permitted to make representations about the continued detention of the suspect.

PACE 1984, Code C, para. 15.3

Detaining a juvenile for longer than 24 hours will be dependent on the circumstances of the case and with regard to the suspect's:

PACE 1984, Code C, para. 15.2A
PACE 1984, s.42(1)

(a) special vulnerability;

(b) the legal obligation to provide an opportunity for representations to be made prior to a decision about extending detention;

(c) the need to consult and consider the views of any appropriate adult; and

(d) any alternatives to police custody.

Charge

If a juvenile suspect is to be charged with an offence or other action as deemed appropriate by the custody officer is to be taken, this must be done in the presence of the appropriate adult.

PACE 1984, Code C, para. 16.1

When a juvenile suspect is charged the appropriate adult shall be given a written notice showing particulars of the offence and the officer's name and the case reference number.

PACE 1984, Code C, para. 16.3

If, after a juvenile suspect has been charged with or informed they may be prosecuted for an offence, an officer wants to tell them about any written statement or interview with another person relating to such an offence, the suspect and the appropriate adult shall either be handed a copy of the written statement or the content of the interview record brought to their attention. No reply or comment should be invited but the suspect

PACE 1984, Code C, paras 16.4 and 4A

should be cautioned (no inference can be drawn) and reminded of their right to legal advice.

PACE 1984, Code C, paras 16.5 and 16.6

If any interview after charge is to take place in the restricted circumstances that such an interview is permissible, the interview must take place in the presence of the appropriate adult.

Searches

A search on initial detention can take place in the absence of the appropriate adult.

PACE 1984, Code C, Annex A, para. 11(c)

A **strip search** which involves exposure of intimate body parts can only take place in the absence of an appropriate adult in urgent cases where there is a risk of serious harm to the suspect or others. Except in such urgent cases, a search of a juvenile may take place in the absence of the appropriate adult only if the juvenile signifies in the presence of the appropriate adult that they do not want the adult to be present during the search and the adult agrees. A record shall be made of the juvenile's decision and signed by the appropriate adult.

PACE 1984, Code C, Annex A, para. 5

An **intimate search** must take place in the presence of an appropriate adult of the same sex unless the suspect specifically requests the presence of a particular adult of the opposite sex who is readily available. Such a search may take place in the absence of the appropriate adult only if the juvenile signifies in the presence of the appropriate adult they do not want the adult present during the search and the adult agrees. A record shall be made of the juvenile's decision and signed by the appropriate adult.

Identification procedures

PACE 1984, Code D, para. 2.12

If consent is required for a particular identification procedure, that consent must be obtained from the juvenile and his parent or guardian and not the appropriate adult, if the juvenile is aged 14 or over. With a suspect aged under 14, only the consent of the parent or guardian is required. The "parent or guardian" includes any local authority or voluntary organisation in the care of which the juvenile is placed.

PACE 1984, Code D, NfG 2A

PACE 1984, Code D, NfG 2A

The parent, guardian or representative of a local authority or voluntary organisation need not be present to give their consent, unless they are acting as the appropriate adult. However, a parent or guardian who is not present must be fully informed before being asked to consent to the identification procedure. They must be given the same information about the procedure and the juvenile's suspected involvement in the offence as the juvenile and appropriate adult. The parent or guardian must also be allowed to speak to the juvenile and the appropriate adult if they wish. Provided the consent is fully informed and is not withdrawn, it may be obtained at any time before the procedure takes place.

Consent (as above) is required for fingerprints, photographs, non-intimate samples and searches and examinations to ascertain identity (all with exceptions in certain circumstances), intimate samples, identification parades, group identifications and video identifications. It would not be practicable for a sample of handwriting to be taken without the consent of the suspect, although neither PACE 1984 nor the Codes of Practice deal specifically with such samples.

If any identification procedure requires information to be given to or sought from a juvenile suspect, it must be given or sought in the presence of the appropriate adult. If the appropriate adult is not present when the information is first given or sought, the procedure must be repeated in the presence of the appropriate adult when they arrive.

PACE 1984, Code D, para. 2.14

Any identification procedure involving the participation of a juvenile, must take place in the presence of the appropriate adult. However, the adult must not be allowed to prompt any identification of a suspect by a witness.

PACE 1984, Code D, para. 2.15

Alternatives to charge

A system of police "reprimands" and "final warnings" was introduced by the CDA 1998 in order to reduce the likelihood of young offenders re-offending and ensuring a consistent approach by the police when dealing with young offenders. Extensive guidance on the system is contained in the Home Office publications: *Final Warning Scheme: Guidance for the Police and Youth Offending Teams* and *Further Guidance for the Police and Youth Offending Teams.*

Reprimands are to be available for first-time minor offences. Any re-offending will result in either a final warning or charge. A final warning may also be given for more serious offences without there having been a prior reprimand. Only in exceptional cases will further offending after a final warning result in any police action other than a charge.

CDA 1998, ss 65–66

For a full explanation of the system refer to the **Charging and Alternatives** index heading.

Youth Offending Team

Before a decision is taken as to whether a juvenile is to be charged or otherwise dealt with by way of reprimand, final warning or whether no further action is to be taken, the custody officer may refer the case to the Youth Offending Team ("YOT") for an assessment. This is very often likely to be the case if consideration is being given to administering a final warning.

While those inquiries are pursued, the juvenile will have been released on police bail to return to the police station.

PRACTICAL GUIDANCE

(1) Vulnerability

PACE 1984, Code C, NfG 11C

The PACE 1984 Codes of Practice contain a warning to police officers about dealing with juveniles, which the adviser would do well to have in mind when advising a juvenile suspect. Although juveniles are capable of providing reliable evidence, they may, without knowing or wishing to do so, be particularly prone in certain circumstances to provide information which is unreliable, misleading or self-incriminating. Special care should be exercised in interviewing juveniles and corroboration sought of any facts admitted wherever possible. If the police are aware of the difficulties presented by juvenile suspects, so should the adviser be.

The adviser may need to work hard to dispel the image of being another adult in authority who cannot be trusted. Juveniles may be more nervous, frightened and generally vulnerable than adult suspects and may require a different approach from the adviser.

Conversely, some juvenile suspects are highly experienced in the police station. If this is the case, it may be that the suspect fails to appreciate the gravity of the situation.

When dealing with juvenile suspects it may be appropriate for the adviser to adapt his language and to take longer than would otherwise be the case with the suspect to ascertain precisely what his understanding is and what he has to say about the situation. The adviser should be particularly alert to indictors of learning disability, such as the nature of the school attended and whether they have any particular help with reading or other activities at school.

The adviser should take special care to ensure that, as far as is possible, the juvenile suspect understands the caution and its implications.

The adviser should be ready as always to intervene in interview if the situation becomes oppressive. This may arise more easily than with an adult suspect.

(2) The suspect appears to be a juvenile

If a suspect appears to be a juvenile but is claiming to be an adult, the adviser should consider strong advice to the suspect to reveal his true age, as the provisions in relation to juveniles are protective. Failure to accede to the advice may give the adviser ethical problems particularly if he knows that the suspect is a juvenile claiming to be an adult.

(3) Appropriate adults

Problems may arise in relation to dealing with appropriate adults. Parents are sometimes angry with their children for having been arrested and can be hostile towards them. If the appropriate adult is hostile towards the suspect, the adviser should consider requesting that the adult be excluded on the grounds that he is no longer suitable in the role of appropriate adult. The same situation could arise if the appropriate adult is hostile towards the adviser chosen by their child.

It is advisable to speak initially to the suspect in the absence of the appropriate adult. The suspect can request that the consultation be in the absence of the appropriate adult.

PACE 1984, Code C, NfG 1E

Appropriate adults, whether parents or social workers, are not bound by any duty of confidentiality or legal privilege. It is possible that anything said to them by the suspect or during the course of advising the suspect may be passed on to the police. Indeed, guidance issued to social workers advises that they may disclose information if they consider the juvenile represents a danger to other persons and evidence has been given as part of the prosecution case by a social worker appropriate adult as to admissions made by a suspect to her in the absence of his solicitor.

R. v Brown (Marcus), May 21, 1999, unreported, CA

The appropriate adult could be asked to undertake not to pass on any such information to the police, but this would not be enforceable against them. If there is any doubt about the security of the advice session, consideration must be given to advising the suspect in the absence of the appropriate adult, such a decision should be taken in consultation with the suspect and the appropriate adult where possible.

The adviser should remember that the juvenile suspect is his client and not the appropriate adult. However, in the rare circumstances where the appropriate adult has exercised the right to legal advice against the wishes of the juvenile, the adviser may be justified in treating the adult as the client, rather than forcing advice on an unwilling juvenile client.

Mentally Disordered Suspects

INTRODUCTION

Persons with a mental disorder or limited understanding as a result of mental incapacity are particularly vulnerable. Therefore the adviser must be aware of the provisions which apply to this category of suspect in the PACE 1984 Codes of Practice which are helpfully summarised at Code C, Annex E.

PACE 1984, Code C, Annex E

Mentally vulnerable suspects can provide reliable evidence but they may also be prone to giving information that is unreliable, misleading or self-incriminating without knowing or wishing to do so. Special care is required when questioning such suspects and corroborative evidence of any admissions made should be sought wherever possible.

PACE 1984, Code C, NfG 11C

If an officer has any suspicion or is told in good faith or suspects that a suspect, regardless of age, may be suffering from mental disorder or be otherwise mentally vulnerable, then, in the absence of clear evidence to dispel that suspicion, he shall be treated as a mentally vulnerable. Therefore if the custody officer has any doubt about the mental state or capacity of a suspect, he should be treated as mentally vulnerable and an appropriate adult called.

PACE 1984, Code C, 1.4 and NfG 1G

THE LAW

Definition

"Mental disorder" is defined as "mental illness, arrested or incomplete development of mind, psychopathic disorder and any other disorder or disability of the mind" by MHA 1983.

MHA 1983, s.1(2)

PACE 1984 refers to suspects who are "mentally handicapped" which is considered to be a congenital and incurable mental state and is defined as "arrested or incomplete development of mind which includes significant impairment of intelligence and social functioning".

PACE 1984, s.77

A suspect is considered "mentally vulnerable" if, because of their mental state or capacity, they may not understand the significance of what is said, of questions or of their replies.

PACE 1984, Code C, NfG 1G

Although the terms have different meanings, they are treated identically for the purposes of the PACE 1984 Codes of Practice for the purposes of treatment and detention at the police station and any identification procedures.

Place of safety

The adviser should establish initially whether the suspect has been arrested in relation to a criminal offence or is being detained under MHA 1983, s.136 which provides a police officer with powers to remove a person from a public place to a place of safety if he considers that the person is suffering from a mental disorder and is in immediate need of care and control: the police can exercise this power whether or not the person is suspected of having committed a criminal offence.

MHA 1983, s.136

Once detained in this manner, the person can be held for up to 72 hours, during which time he must be assessed by a registered medical practitioner and interviewed by an approved social worker so that suitable arrangements can be made for treatment or care. As soon as the assessment and arrangements for treatment or care have been made, he can no longer be held under the section.

PACE 1984, Code C, para. 3.16

When an assessment under this section takes place at a police station, the custody officer must consider whether an appropriate health care professional should be called to conduct an initial clinical check on the suspect particularly when there is likely to be any significant delay in the arrival of a suitably qualified medical practitioner.

PACE 1984, Code C, para. 9.6

A detainee under this section must be immediately released, if the registered medical practitioner, having examined him, concludes that he is not mentally disordered within the meaning of the MHA.

PACE 1984, Code C, para. 3.16

Although a police station can be a place of safety, wherever practicable, arrangements should be made for the person to be taken to a hospital. There is no power under the MHA to transfer a person detained under s.136 from one place of safety to another place of safety for assessment.

HOC66/1990, para. 4(i)
PACE 1984, Code C, NfG 9D

Code C (with the exception of the review and extension provisions in para.15) applies to persons detained under s.136.

PACE 1984, Code C, para. 1.10

PRACTICE AND PROCEDURE

Duties of the police

If an officer has any suspicion or is told in good faith or suspects that a suspect, regardless of age, may be suffering from mental disorder or be otherwise mentally vulnerable, then, in the absence of clear evidence to dispel that suspicion, he shall be treated as a mentally vulnerable. If the custody officer has any doubt as to the mental state or capacity of a suspect, he should

PACE 1984, Code C, para. 1.4 and NfG 1G

treat the suspect as mentally vulnerable and call an appropriate adult.

On arrival at the police station the custody officer must carry out a risk assessment and act upon any risks identified, including calling a health care professional if necessary. The risk assessment is an ongoing duty. For more detail see the **Health of Suspect** index heading.

PACE 1984, Code C, paras 3.6–3.10

If the suspect appears to be suffering from a mental disorder, the custody officer must make sure he receives appropriate clinical attention as soon as reasonably practicable even if the suspect makes no request for clinical attention and whether or not they have already received clinical attention elsewhere. If the need for attention appears urgent, the nearest available health care professional or an ambulance must be called immediately.

PACE 1984, Code C, paras 9.5 and 9.5A

Whenever the appropriate health care professional is to examine or treat a suspect in such circumstances, the custody officer shall ask for their opinion about any risks or problems which police need to take into account when making decisions about the suspect's continued detention, when to carry out an interview, if applicable, and the need for any safeguards.

PACE 1984, Code C, para. 9.13

Appropriate adult

(a) Definition

The persons capable of acting as an appropriate adult for a mentally disordered or mentally vulnerable suspect are:

PACE 1984, Code C, para. 1.7(b)

(a) a relative, guardian or some other person responsible for his care or custody;

(b) someone who has experience of dealing with mentally disordered or mentally vulnerable persons but who is not a police officer or employed by the police; or

(c) failing either of the above, some other responsible adult aged 18 or over who is not a police officer or employed by the police.

Although the above list is a hierarchy of persons suitable to act as an appropriate adult, in certain circumstances it may be more satisfactory for all concerned if the appropriate adult is someone who has experience or training in the care of mentally disordered or mentally vulnerable persons rather than a less qualified relative. However, the wishes of the suspect should, if

PACE 1984, Code C, NfG 1D

practicable, be respected if he prefers a relative to a more qualified stranger or objects to a particular person.

(b) Inappropriate persons

PACE 1984, Code C, NfG 1B

No person should act as an appropriate adult if he:

(a) is suspected of being involved in the offence;

(b) is the victim of the offence;

(c) is a witness to the offence;

(d) is involved in the investigation of the offence; or

(e) has received admissions before attending the police station.

PACE 1984, Code C, NfG 1F

A legal adviser present at the police station in his professional capacity may not act as an appropriate adult; nor may an independent custody visitor.

Role of the appropriate adult

PACE 1984, Code C, para. 3.18

The suspect should be informed by the custody officer that the appropriate adult is there to assist and advise him and can be consulted privately at any time.

PACE 1984, Code C, para. 2.4

The appropriate adult can also inspect the custody record on arrival at the police station and subsequently be supplied with a copy on request.

Appropriate adults are not bound by confidentiality or privilege and there is nothing to prevent them passing on information they have received during a consultation with the suspect to the police. Initial advice ought therefore to be given in the absence of the appropriate adult, such advice to include the risk of disclosure of information by the appropriate adult. Indeed the Code specifically provides for such a situation.

PACE 1984, Code C, NfG 1E

Home Office Guidance for Appropriate Adults, Annex A

The role of the appropriate adult is to ensure that the suspect understands what is happening to them and why. The appropriate adult should support, advise and assist the suspect, observe whether the police are acting fairly and object if he considers that they are not, assist with communication between the suspect and police, and ensure the suspect understands their rights. It is not part of the role of the appropriate adult to provide legal advice.

Notification of detention

PACE 1984, Code C, para. 3.15

The appropriate adult must be informed of the grounds for detention of the mentally disordered or mentally vulnerable suspect and his whereabouts as soon as practicable. He should then be asked to come to the police station.

This notification cannot be delayed under any circumstances even if the suspect is being held incommunicado.

PACE 1984, Code C, Annex B, NfG B1

Notification and exercise of rights

The appropriate adult must be present when the mentally disordered suspect is told of the reasons for his detention and his rights to legal advice, to have someone informed of his arrest and to consult the PACE 1984 Codes of Practice, and when handed the written notice of these rights. This may mean that the suspect is provided with this information on two occasions.

PACE 1984, Code C, para. 3.17

The appropriate adult can exercise the right to legal advice on behalf of the mentally disordered suspect, although the suspect cannot be forced to see the legal adviser if they do not wish to do so. If, however, the suspect has requested access to legal advice on arrival at the police station, there should be no delay to await the arrival of the appropriate adult. Indeed, the suspect should be given the opportunity to consult privately with the legal adviser in the absence of the appropriate adult, if he wishes to do so.

PACE 1984, Code C, para. 3.19

PACE 1984, Code C, NfG 1E

Interviews

A mentally disordered or mentally vulnerable suspect must not be interviewed or asked to provide or sign a written statement under caution or to sign a record of interview in the absence of the appropriate adult unless an officer of superintendent rank or above considers delay will:

PACE 1984, Code C, para. 11.15

PACE 1984, Code C, para. 11.18

- lead to interference with or harm to evidence connected with an offence;
- lead to interference with, or physical harm to, other people;
- lead to serious loss of, or damage to, property;
- alert other people suspected of committing an offence but not yet arrested for it; or
- hinder the recovery of property obtained in consequence of the commission of an offence; and

PACE 1984, Code C, para. 11.1

the officer is satisfied the interview would not significantly harm the suspect's physical or mental state.

PACE 1984, Code C, para. 11.1 and 11.19

Interviewing in any of these circumstances shall cease once sufficient information has been obtained to avert the above consequences.

PACE 1984, Code C, para. 11.20

A record shall be made of the grounds for any decision to interview a mentally disordered or mentally vulnerable suspect without an appropriate adult.

PACE 1984, s.77(1)

PACE 1984 states that where the case against the accused depends wholly or substantially on a confession made otherwise than in the presence of an independent person and the court is satisfied that he is mentally handicapped, there is a special need for caution before convicting on that confession. Although the Act does not appear to apply to mentally disordered or mentally vulnerable suspects, as the definition is not the same, the principles are the same and the judge has a discretion to give such a warning or exclude the evidence of the confession under either s.76 or 78 of PACE 1984.

PACE 1984, Code C, para. 11.17

Before any interview, the appropriate adult must be reminded that his role is not simply to act as an observer but to facilitate communication with the interviewee, to advise that person and to ensure that the interview is being conducted fairly and properly.

Reviews of detention

PACE 1984, Code C, para. 15.3

If the detention of a mentally disordered suspect is to be reviewed, the appropriate adult, if available at the time, must be permitted to make representations about the continued detention of the suspect.

PACE 1984, Code C, para. 15.2A

Detaining a mentally vulnerable person for longer than 24 hours will be dependent on the circumstances of the case and with regard to the suspect's:

PACE 1984, s.42(1)

(a) special vulnerability;

(b) the legal obligation to provide an opportunity for representations to be made prior to a decision about extending detention;

(c) the need to consult and consider the views of any appropriate adult; and

(d) any alternatives to police custody.

Charge

PACE 1984, Code C, para. 16.1

If a mentally disordered suspect is to be charged with an offence or other action as deemed appropriate by the custody officer is to be taken, this must be done in the presence of the appropriate adult.

When a mentally disordered suspect is charged the appropriate adult shall be given a written notice showing particulars of the offence and the officer's name and the case reference number.

PACE 1984, Code C, para. 16.3

If, after a mentally disordered suspect has been charged with or informed they may be prosecuted for an offence, an officer wants to tell them about any written statement or interview with another person relating to such an offence, the suspect and the appropriate adult shall either be handed a copy of the written statement or the content of the interview record brought to their attention. No reply or comment should be invited but the suspect should be cautioned (no inference can be drawn) and reminded of their right to legal advice.

PACE 1984, Code C, para. 16.4 and 4A

If any interview after charge is to take place in the restricted circumstances that such an interview is permissible, the interview must take place in the presence of the appropriate adult.

PACE 1984, Code C, paras 16.5 and 16.6

Searches

A search on initial detention can take place in the absence of the appropriate adult.

A **strip search** can only take place in the absence of an appropriate adult in urgent cases where there is a risk of serious harm to the suspect or others.

PACE 1984, Code C, Annex A, para. 11(c)

An **intimate search** must take place in the presence of an appropriate adult of the same sex unless the suspect specifically requests the presence of a particular adult of the opposite sex who is readily available. No intimate search can take place in the absence of an appropriate adult where a mentally disordered or mentally vulnerable suspect is concerned.

PACE 1984, Code C, Annex A, para. 5

Identification procedures

For those identification procedures that require the consent of the suspect, consent is only valid if given in the presence of the appropriate adult. Consent cannot be given by the appropriate adult on behalf of the suspect.

PACE 1984, Code D, para. 2.12

Consent (as above) is required for fingerprints, photographs, non-intimate samples (all with exceptions in certain circumstances), intimate samples, identification parades, group identifications and video identifications. It would not be practicable for a sample of handwriting to be taken without the consent of the suspect, although neither PACE 1984 nor the Codes of Practice deal specifically with such samples.

PACE 1984, Code D, para. 2.14

If any identification procedure requires information to be given to or sought from a mentally vulnerable suspect, it must be given or sought in the presence of the appropriate adult. If the appropriate adult is not present when the information is first given or sought, the procedure must be repeated in the presence of the appropriate adult when they arrive.

PACE 1984, Code D, para. 2.15

Any identification procedure involving the participation of a mentally vulnerable suspect, must take place in the presence of the appropriate adult. However, the adult must not be allowed to prompt any identification of a suspect by a witness.

Bail or detention after charge

HOC 66/1990, para. 4(v)

A mentally disordered suspect who has been charged with an offence has the same right to bail as any other type of suspect. However, there may be particular problems associated with the suspect's mental state which would justify the custody officer in refusing bail on the grounds of the suspect's own protection, to prevent injury or damage or for fear of the suspect failing to appear at court.

HOC 66/1990, para. 4(v)

The police are encouraged to liaise where possible on a voluntary basis with the probation, health and social services to make bail arrangements for such suspects charged with offences but, in practice, such arrangements are rare.

Cautions and alternatives to prosecution

HOC 66/1990, para. 4(iii)

A mentally disordered suspect is as much a candidate for a police caution as any other type of suspect. Indeed, HOC 66/1990 specifies that, wherever possible, such suspects should be dealt with other than by prosecution.

A caution is one way in which a mentally disordered suspect can be diverted from the prosecution process. Obviously the normal cautioning criteria must apply.

Consideration should also be given to taking no action against such a suspect if a caution is not appropriate, or to seeking informal assistance from social services instead of a prosecution.

One final possible option to prosecution is to seek admission to hospital or guardianship under MHA 1983.

PRACTICAL GUIDANCE

(1) Home Office Circular on mentally disordered offenders

Any adviser attending at a police station should be familiar with and have a copy of HOC 66/1990 as well as HOC 12/1995

Mentally Disordered Offenders: Inter-agency Working which supplements the earlier Circular.

The circular summarises the legal powers available and is specifically designed to highlight:

HOC 66/1990, para. 1(b)

> the desirability of ensuring effective co-operation between agencies to ensure that the best use is made of resources and that mentally disordered persons are not prosecuted where this is not required in the public interest.

It can be a useful tool for the adviser in attempting to persuade police officers not to prosecute or the Crown Prosecution Service not to continue with a prosecution if the suspect has been charged with an offence.

(2) Disclosing that the suspect may be mentally disordered

The provisions in the PACE 1984 Codes of Practice are protective of the mentally disordered suspect. As a general rule, if the adviser fears that a suspect may have problems of this nature, the suspect should be encouraged to reveal this to the custody officer. The custody officer must then treat the suspect as mentally disordered, as he has been told in good faith that this may be the case.

PACE 1984, Code C, para. 1.4

Despite this general rule, the question of whether to disclose such suspicions to the police is an extremely delicate and difficult one for the adviser. Although each case will have to be judged on its own individual circumstances, it is argued that no such disclosure should be made without having discussed the matter with the suspect and obtained his consent. Of course, there may be times when the adviser feels that even discussion of the issues may not be prudent.

If the suspect is known to the adviser to be mentally disordered through previous contact or a disclosure is made during the course of discussions with the suspect at the police station, the information is likely to be covered by the duty of confidentiality and should not be disclosed without the consent of the suspect. However, if the suspicion is based on mere observation of the suspect at the police station, confidentiality may not attach but it is still argued that the adviser ought to have the consent of the suspect before any disclosure is made to the police.

The adviser should be aware of some basic signs that the suspect may be mentally vulnerable such as agitation, anger, unpredictable behaviour, incoherence, lack of understanding or reference to medication, periods of hospitalisation, or mental health workers.

If during the course of an interview it becomes apparent to the adviser that the suspect is having difficulty understanding the significance of the questions asked or his answers to those questions, he should stop the interview to discuss in private with the suspect whether the police should be informed that the suspect appears to fall within the definition of somebody requiring special treatment under the PACE 1984 Codes of Practice.

(3) Appropriate adults

It may not always be easy or even possible for the adviser to build a rapport with such suspects but assistance may be forthcoming from the appropriate adult, particularly if he is known to the suspect and has the relevant training or experience in dealing with mentally disordered persons.

PACE 1984, Code C, NfG 1E

However, the adviser should remember that appropriate adults do not have the same duty of confidentiality as the adviser. There is a danger of information being passed to the police by the appropriate adult. Initial advice should be given to the suspect in the absence of the appropriate adult. In addition the adviser should impress upon the appropriate adult the need for confidentiality and the appropriate adult should be asked to undertake not to pass any information on to the police although such an undertaking would not be enforceable.

PACE 1984, Code C, para. 6.5A

The adviser should always remember that the suspect and not the appropriate adult is the client. However, in the rare circumstances where the appropriate adult has exercised the right to legal advice on behalf of the suspect and the suspect is hostile to the adviser, he may well be justified in treating the appropriate adult as the client, as the suspect cannot be made to see the adviser against his will.

Public Funding

POLICE STATION ADVICE AND ASSISTANCE

Eligibility

Public funding is available through the Legal Service Commission's General Criminal Contract (GCC 2004) for police station "advice and assistance" where the adviser is attending a person at a police station (or other place of detention) who:

AJA 1999, s.13(1); CDS(G)R 2001, reg.4; GCC 2004, Contract Spec., Pt A, para. 2.2(c)

(a) is under arrest and held in custody; or

(b) is being interviewed in connection with a serious service offence; or

(c) is a volunteer; or

(d) is detained under Sch. 7 of the Terrorism Act 2000; or

(e) is the subject of an identification procedure carried out by means of video recordings who is not present at a police station at the time the procedure is carried out.

The funding is available to persons of any age and without them having to undergo any financial means testing.

CDS(G)R 2001, reg. 5(1)

A "serious service offence" is defined in as an offence under either the Army Act 1955, the Air Force Act 1955, or the Naval Discipline Act 1957 which cannot be dealt with summarily or which appears to the interviewing services police to be serious.

GCC 2004, Contract Standard Terms, Pt A, para. 1

A "volunteer" is any person who attends voluntarily at a police station or customs office, or at any other place where a constable or customs officer is present, "for the purpose of assisting with an investigation" but who has not been arrested. He remains a "volunteer" "during his period of voluntary attendance".

PACE 1984, s.29; CDS(G)R 2001, reg. 5(1)

In situations where "advice and assistance" is given over the telephone but there is no attendance by the adviser at the police station, funding is also available in all of the above circumstances apart from (e).

GCC 2004, Contract Spec., Pt A, para. 2.2(b)

As the funding is not subject to any means test, the adviser need only be sure that the client falls into one of the eligible categories and that the "sufficient benefits test" is satisfied in order for the scheme to become operative.

CDS(G)R 2001, reg. 5(1)

The "sufficient benefits test" limits "advice and assistance" to legal issues concerning English law where there is sufficient

GCC 2004, Contract Spec.,

Pt B, para. 2.5

benefit to the client, having regard to all the circumstances, to justify the work. The test will be automatically satisfied for all initial advice given under the "police station advice and assistance" scheme (as defined above). However, the test must still be consciously applied by the adviser to determining the extent of the "advice and assistance" which is required after this initial advice (including, for example, whether initial telephone advice should be followed by a personal attendance at the police station; and the length of time which should be spent on a client's particular matter).

GCC 2004, Contract Spec., Pt B, para. 3.5; CDS(G)R 2001, regs 4 and 5(4)

If the adviser attends with a volunteer at an interview conducted by investigators who are neither police nor customs officers, and there is no constable present, the advice falls outside of the police station scheme. Publicly funded remuneration for such advice can be provided under the means tested "advice and assistance" scheme but only if the volunteer "may" be subject to criminal charges as a result of the investigation.

Police station representatives

GCC 2004, Contract Spec., Pt B, para. 3.3

Public funding is not available for police station "advice and assistance" by a solicitor's representative unless the representative has been accredited under the scheme, or is registered with the Legal Aid Board as a probationary representative.

This applies to any non-solicitor representative including trainee solicitors.

For further details, refer to the **Solicitor's Representatives** index heading.

Scope of the advice and assistance

GCC 2004, Contract Spec., Pt A, paras 2.1, 2.2

Police station "advice and assistance" includes all **work properly undertaken** for a qualifying client during the criminal investigation of a matter (*i.e.* up to the point at which the client is charged or summoned for the matter under investigation, or the investigation is otherwise terminated).

GCC 2004, Contract Spec., Pt A, para. 2.2

It will include all post-charge police station "advice and assistance" work on the same matter which is necessary to complete the attendance at the police station immediately following charge, and post-charge police station "advice and assistance" work where the client is being represented in the "criminal proceedings class" of work and in the same matter or case:

- the client is arrested for breach of bail conditions or on a warrant for failing to appear at the magistrates' or Crown Court; or

- the client is required to attend a post-charge interview or identification procedure or is the subject of an identification procedure carried out by video recordings who is not present at a police station at the time; or
- the client is recharged following discontinuance or dismissal of proceedings; or
- the client is required to attend the police station for a reprimand, warning or caution.

Time spent **travelling** to and from a client and **waiting** on arrival is covered, subject to the time so spent being deemed "reasonable". **Travel disbursements** properly incurred can be claimed, also subject to the costs being "reasonable". These requirements of reasonableness may mean that these elements of the claim are disallowed in "own solicitor" cases if the Legal Aid Board is of the view that a local agent or duty solicitor should have been instructed.

GCC 2004, Contract Spec., Pt B, paras 2.4 and 7.9

One '**police station telephone advice fixed fee**' may be claimed per investigation provided that at least once telephone call is undertaken during the course of the investigation. No further fixed fee may be claimed if any further arrest of the same client takes place any time at a police station or other place of detention whilst the investigation continues.

GCC 2004, Contract Spec., Pt E, para. 2.2

Only one such telephone fee may be claimed per investigation, irrespective of the number of telephone attendances on the client, police or other parties during the course of the investigation. If a client is bailed to return to the police station, that is a continuation of the same investigation and no further fixed fee may be claimed.

If telephone advice is given to more than one client during the course of a single investigation, one telephone fee may be claimed for each client who receives such advice.

Telephone fixed fees cannot be claimed if the adviser accepts a matter whilst already in attendance at the same police station unless the investigation has not concluded following that attendance.

Any **disbursements** incurred by the adviser can be claimed where it is in the best interests of the client to have incurred them. Any disbursement must have been actually and reasonably incurred and must be for a reasonable amount. Disbursements may include the fees of an interpreter, doctor, photographer or other expert.

GCC 2004, Contract Spec., Pt C, para. 1.18

Special stand-by payments are paid for a **police station duty solicitor** who is on duty and "available" during a duty

GCC 2004, Contract Spec., Pt E, para. 2.2

period. **Hotel expenses** actually and reasonably incurred may be claimed as a disbursement by a duty solicitor whilst on a police station duty solicitor rota.

For further details, refer to the **Duty Solicitors** index heading.

Rates of payment

GCC 2004, Contract Spec., Pt E, paras 1 and 2.2

Standard rates of payment apply for all own client work irrespective of the day or time that the "advice and assistance" is given, although slightly higher rates are paid to firms situated within the Legal Services Commission's London region.

GCC 2004, Contract Spec., Pt E, paras 1 and 2.2

For duty solicitor work, different rates apply for normal and "unsocial" hours. "Unsocial hours" are defined as the hours between 5.30 pm and 9.30 am on weekdays and at all times on weekends, Christmas Day, Good Friday and bank holidays.

The rates are reviewed annually and published in a number of journals, including the Law Society Gazette.

Costs limits

The Criminal Defence Service can only pay for "advice and assistance" if the supplier holds a General Criminal Contract.

GCC 2004, Contract Spec., Pt B, para. 2.11(a)

All police station "advice and assistance" provided to one client is counted as a single matter and a "unique file number" (UFN) must be allocated to each separate matter. At the proceedings stage, a lead UFN must be assigned to all charges that will form a "case" for standard fee purposes.

GCC 2004, Contract Spec., Pt C, para. 1.13

All costs claimed must have been actually and reasonably incurred.

GCC 2004, Contract Spec., Pt B, para 2.8

Each claim is subject to an upper costs limit which, at the date of publication, stands at £300 (+ vat). This limit covers all costs and disbursements other than duty solicitor standby claims and hotel expenses.

GCC 2004, Contract Spec., Pt B, para 2.9

The upper limit cannot be exceeded unless it has been extended by the Regional Director. The "sufficient benefit test" must be reapplied before any extension is sought and, if an extension is granted, claims are made at the appropriate rate for all work actually and reasonably carried out up to the maximum amount authorised.

GCC 2004, Contract Spec., Pt C, para. 1.11

A claim which is not met in full may be the subject of an appeal to the Costs Committee provided that the appeal is:

(a) made within 28 days (or such longer period as may be agreed) of the notification of the Regional Director's decision; and

(b) is in writing setting out the grounds of appeal; and

(c) is accompanied by the relevant file.

Making a claim

Claims are made by the completion and submission of a "Contract Work Report Form". If the claim relates to "advice and assistance" or "further advice and assistance" on the same matter, the same "unique file number" (UFN) must be used.

GCC 2004, Contract Spec., Pt C, paras 1.5 and 1.9

When "advice and assistance" has been given to more than one client in the same investigation, a UFN must be allocated to each client and a separate claim for each must be submitted. The time spent must be apportioned between each claim. A breakdown of the total time spent and the work undertaken for each client must be retained.

Forms must be submitted within three months of the date on which the work was done. If a claim is submitted out of time the amount paid may be reduced on a sliding scale basis by up to 100 per cent. If the claim form is not properly completed it will be rejected, however, the original submission date remains the relevant date.

GCC 2004, Contract Spec., Pt C, para.1.2

The form must always be signed by a qualified solicitor who has had overall conduct or supervision of the matter.

ADVOCACY ASSISTANCE

Eligibility

Public funding is available for such "advice and assistance" as is considered appropriate for individuals who are arrested and held in custody at a police station or other premises and for individuals involved in criminal investigations. This includes "advocacy assistance" done on behalf of a suspect for court work undertaken in relation to either the obtaining of warrants of further detention or custody hearings for Armed Forces personnel.

AJA 1999, s.13; GCC 2004, Contract Spec., Pt A, paras 1.2 and 1.4, and Pt B, para. 4.6

Rates of payment

Rates of payment are similar to those paid for non-standard fee magistrates' court legal aid work, with slightly higher rates paid to firms situated within the Legal Services Commission's London region and enhanced rates paid for work undertaken by Duty Solicitors in "unsocial hours" (*i.e.* between 5.30 pm and 9.30 am on weekdays and at all times on weekends, Christmas Day, Good Friday and bank holidays).

GCC 2004, Contract Spec., Pt E, para. 2.3

PRACTICAL GUIDANCE

(1) Competitive Tendering

On January 28, 2005 the Legal Services Commission published proposals to introduce competitive tendering for law firms in the London area undertaking publicly funded work in police stations and magistrates' courts.

At the time of writing it remains unclear as to precisely how any such scheme will operate, but the proposals are for the tender process to commence in August 2005 and that the earliest date envisaged for the new contracts to start is January 2006.

It is undoubtedly the case that if these proposals come to fruition, and if the new system is deemed a success (in that the government's expenditure on this type of legal work is reduced), the system of competitive tendering the government will look to extend to all other areas.

(2) Forms

Advisers should always ensure that they carry a stock of LSC application and claim forms. These are available from the LSC who supply a free master-pack to all solicitor account holders. The pack contains a hard copy of all the necessary forms for copying as and when required.

The forms can also be downloaded from the LSC's website at *www.legalservices.gov.uk.*

The LSC forms are also produced by many software companies, in various packages, for purchase by legal suppliers. A list containing some of these software suppliers is available from the Legal Software Suppliers Association website at: *www.legaltechnology.org*.

(3) Billing

It is good practice to submit claims for work done immediately the work covered by the relevant scheme has been completed. This ensures that time limits are not exceeded, as well as assisting with the firm's cash flow.

(4) Private clients

Practice Rule 15, para. 5.01, The Law Society's Guide to the Professional Conduct of Solicitors

Solicitors are under a professional duty to consider whether a client may be eligible for public funding and to advise accordingly. Therefore, if a client is eligible for police station "advice and assistance" but chooses to instruct on a private basis, it is advisable to have these instructions confirmed in writing. This will prevent any future misunderstandings arising.

Samples—Intimate, Non-intimate and Handwriting

INTIMATE SAMPLES—THE LAW

Definition

An intimate sample is defined as:

(a) a sample of blood, semen or any other tissue fluid, urine or pubic hair;

PACE 1984, s.65

(b) a dental impression; or

(c) a swab from a body orifice other than the mouth.

Police powers when suspect in police detention

The police have the power to take intimate samples from a person who is in police detention only if:

PACE 1984, s.62 (1)

(a) the appropriate consent is obtained; and

(b) the action is authorised by an officer of at least the rank of inspector.

The appropriate consent is the consent of the suspect if he has attained the age of 17, the consent of the suspect and his parent or guardian if he is over 14 but less than 17 years of age and the consent of the suspect's parent or guardian if the suspect is less than 14 years of age. In the case of a mentally disordered or otherwise mentally vulnerable person the consent must be given in the presence of the appropriate adult. The appropriate consent must be given in writing.

PACE 1984, s.65(1), Code D, para. 2.12

Authorisation can only be given if there are reasonable grounds for:

PACE 1984, s.62(4)

(a) suspecting the involvement of the person from whom the sample is to be taken in a recordable offence; and

PACE 1984, s.62(2)

(b) believing that the sample would tend to confirm or disprove his involvement in that offence.

The authorisation can be oral but must be confirmed in writing as soon as practicable. A record must be made of the authorisation

PACE 1984, s.62(3)

PACE 1984, s.62(7)
PACE 1984, s.62(8)

including the name and rank of the authorising officer, the grounds for giving the authorisation and the fact that the appropriate consent was given. This should be entered on the custody record if the suspect is detained at the police station.

Police powers when suspect not in police detention

If the person is not in police detention then the police can take intimate samples if:

PACE 1984, s.62(1A)

(a) during the course of the investigation of an offence, two or more non-intimate samples suitable for the same means of analysis have been taken but proved insufficient;

(b) a police officer of at least the rank of inspector authorises the taking of the sample; and

(c) the appropriate consent is given.

PACE 1984, s.63A (3)

Where an intimate sample can be taken, it may also be taken in prison or other establishment to which the Prison Act 1952 applies.

PACE 1984, s.63A(4); PRA 2000, Sch. 4, para. 32
PACE 1984, s.63A(5)
PACE 1984, s.63A(6)
PACE 1984, s.63A(7)

A constable or designated civilian may require a person not in police detention or in custody to attend a police station for a sample to be taken where that person has been charged with, reported for or convicted of a recordable offence and no sample was taken in the investigation of that offence or the sample was unsuitable or insufficient for analysis. The request must be made within one month of the date of charge, notification of report for summons, conviction or from when the appropriate officer was informed that the sample was unsuitable or insufficient. The person shall be given at least 7 days to attend and can be arrested without warrant should he fail to comply with the requirement. This is only a power to enforce attendance at the police station not to take an intimate sample in the absence of consent or the other conditions of PACE 1984, s.62(1) or 62(1A).

Speculative searches

PACE 1984, s.63A(1), (1A) and (1B)

Where a person has been arrested on suspicion of being involved in a recordable offence, has been charged or informed that he will be reported for summons for such an offence, any samples or information derived from samples taken from him may be checked against other samples held by a law enforcement agency (which includes international agencies) or held in connection with or as a result of an investigation of an offence.

Samples taken improperly

The taking of samples in circumstances other than those outlined above could amount to an assault or trespass to the person and render any evidence obtained inadmissible in future court proceedings.

Recordable offences

A recordable offence is an offence for which a conviction, caution, reprimand or warning is recordable on the police national computer. These offences, *inter alia*, are:

PACE, Code D, NfG 4A
NPR(RO)(A)R 2003

(a) all offences punishable by imprisonment;

(b) offences under SOA 1959, s.1 (loitering or soliciting for the purposes of prostitution);

(c) offences under TA 1984, s.43 (improper use of a public telecommunications system);

(d) offences under RTA 1988, s.25 (tampering with motor vehicles);

(e) offences under MCA 1988, s.1 (sending letters, *etc.* with intent to cause anxiety or distress);

(f) other offences as set out in the National Police Records (Recordable Offences) Regulations 2000 as amended by the National Police Records (Recordable Offences) (Amendment) Regulations 2003.

Information to the suspect before the sample is taken

Before an intimate sample is taken, the suspect must be informed that authorisation has been given and told the grounds for such authorisation. The suspect must also be told of the nature of the offence in which it is suspected he is involved.

PACE 1984, s.62(5) and (6)

In addition, the suspect must be informed that the sample may be the subject of a speculative search and the fact that he has been so informed noted on the custody record as soon as practicable after the sample has been taken.

PACE 1984, s.62(7A) and (8)

Failure to provide this information to the suspect could render the taking of the sample unlawful and may amount to an assault or trespass to the person, as well as the results there from being inadmissible as evidence at a later trial.

Who takes the sample?

PACE 1984, s.62(9A) as amended by PRA 2002, s.65
PACE 1984, s.62(9)

Samples other than samples of urine must be taken by a registered medical practitioner, registered nurse or registers paramedic. A dental impression must be taken by a registered dentist; otherwise the taking of such a sample could be unlawful.

Effect of refusal

PACE 1984, s.62(10)

If the suspect withholds his consent for such a sample to be taken without good cause, the court, in deciding whether to commit or dismiss the case, whether there is a case to answer or in determining guilt, may draw such inferences from the refusal as appear proper.

Destruction of samples

PACE 1984, s.64(1A)

Where samples are taken in connection with the investigation of an offence they may be retained after they have fulfilled the purposes for which they were taken but shall not be used except for purposes related to the prevention or detection of crime, the investigation of an offence or the conduct of a prosecution.

PACE 1984, s.64(3), (3AA) and (3AC)

Samples must be destroyed if taken from someone other than a suspect once the purpose has been fulfilled unless they were taken for the purposes of an investigation of an offence for which someone has been convicted and a sample was also taken from the convicted person. Consent can be given for the retention of samples taken from non-suspects, such consent once given being irrevocable.

R. (on the application of Marper and Another) v Chief Constable of South Yorkshire [2002] 1 W.L.R. 3223; [2003] 1 All E.R. 148

This means that samples from a suspect whether arrested or attending voluntarily do not have to be destroyed even if that person is never charged or, if charged, is subsequently acquitted. These provisions have survived a challenge under the Human Rights Act 1998.

Road Traffic Act 1988

PACE 1984, s.62(11)

The powers of the police to take blood or urine samples under RTA 1988, ss 4–11 are not affected by PACE 1984 or of ss 26 to 38 of the Transport and Works Act 1992.

Terrorist Offences

TA 2000, Sch. 7, s.41 and Sch. 8;
PACE 1984, s.62(12)

Intimate samples can be taken from persons detained under the terrorism legislation in similar circumstances to those outlined in PACE 1984. For further details of these provisions, see the **Terrorist Suspects** index heading.

INTIMATE SAMPLES—PRACTICE AND PROCEDURE

The relevant PACE 1984 Code of Practice mirrors the provisions for the taking of such samples in the statute.

PACE 1984, Code D, para. 6

Warning of consequences of refusal

Any suspect from whom an intimate sample is requested must be warned that a refusal to provide the sample may harm his defence at any subsequent trial. A record must be made that such a warning has been given. The suggested form of wording for the warning is:

PACE 1984, Code D, para. 6.3

PACE 1984, Code D, para. 6.11

> You do not have to provide this sample/allow this swab or impression to be taken but I must warn you that if you refuse without good cause, your refusal may harm your case if it comes to trial.

PACE 1984, Code D, NfG 6D

Reminder of entitlement to free legal advice

A suspect should be reminded of his entitlement to free legal advice and the reminder noted on the custody record. If the suspect refuses such advice, the custody officer should inform the suspect that he can speak to a legal adviser on the telephone. If the suspect waives his right to legal advice, the custody officer should ask his reasons for so doing and note any reasons given on the custody record. A suspect does not have to give his reasons and should not be pressed to do so once his wishes have become clear.

PACE 1984, Code D, para. 6.3

PACE 1984, Code C, para. 6.5

PACE 1984, Code C, NfG 6K

Grounds for authorisation

The suspect must be informed before the sample is taken of the reason for taking the sample and the grounds on which the relevant authority has been given. A record of the reasons for taking the sample must be made as soon as practicable, together with a note that written consent has been given.

PACE 1984, Code D, para. 6.8

PACE 1984, Code D, para. 6.10

Speculative search

The suspect must be informed that the sample or information derived from it may be retained and subject of a speculative search. This means that they may be checked against other DNA records held by, or on behalf of, the police and other law enforcement authorities in or outside the UK or held in connection with, or as a result of, an investigation of an offence inside or outside the UK.

PACE 1984, Code D, para. 6.8

PACE 1984, Code D, NfG 6E

PACE 1984, Code D, NfG 6E

Samples taken from a person suspected of committing a recordable offence but who has not been arrested, charged or informed they will be reported for it, may be subject to a speculative search only if the person consents in writing. The following is an example of a basic form of words:

PACE 1984, Code D, NfG 6E

> I consent to my DNA sample and information derived from it being retained and used only for purposes related to the prevention and detection of a crime, the investigation of an offence or the conduct of a prosecution either nationally or internationally. I understand that this sample may be checked against other DNA records held by or on behalf of relevant law enforcement authorities, either nationally or internationally. I understand that once I have given my consent for the sample to be retained and used I cannot withdraw this consent.

PACE 1984, Code D, para. 6.10

The fact that the suspect has been warned that the sample may be used in such a speculative search must be recorded.

Insufficiency of previous non-intimate samples

PACE 1984, Code D, para. 6.2

If two non-intimate samples have previously been taken from someone in the course of an investigation of an offence but have proved insufficient or unsuitable for a particular form of analysis, an intimate sample may be taken from him even if he is not in police detention, if an inspector or above authorises it and the suspect consents in writing.

PACE 1984, Code D, NfG 6B

A sample can be insufficient, either in quantity or quality, for a particular type of analysis, such as DNA analysis or may be insufficient if enough information cannot be obtained from it by analysis because of loss, destruction, damage or contamination of the sample or as a result of an earlier, unsuccessful attempt at analysis. Alternatively, a sample may be unsuitable by its very nature for a particular type of analysis.

PACE 1984, Code D, para. 6.3 and Code C, para. 3.21

A person from whom samples are requested in these circumstances and who has attended the police station voluntarily should be told of his entitlement to free legal advice and that such right includes the right to speak to a legal adviser on the telephone.

Destruction of samples

PACE 1984, Code D, Annex F, para. 1

When samples are taken from a person in connection with an investigation and the person is not suspected of having committed the offence, they must be destroyed as soon as they have fulfilled the purpose for which they were taken unless:

(a) they were taken for the purposes of an investigation of an offence for which a person has been convicted; and

(b) fingerprints or samples were also taken from the convicted person for the purposes of that investigation.

However the samples, and the information derived from them, may not be used in the investigation of any offence or in evidence against the person who is, or would be, entitled to the destruction of the samples.

It follows, therefore, that samples taken from a suspect for an offence whether arrested or attending voluntarily, do not have to be destroyed even if that person is never charged or, if charged, is acquitted.

The above requirement to destroy samples, and information derived from them, and restrictions on their retention and use do not apply if the person gives their written consent for their sample to be retained and used after they have fulfilled the purpose for which they were taken.

PACE 1984, Code D, Annex F, para. 2

When a person's samples are to be destroyed neither the samples or any information derived from them may be used in the investigation of any offence or in evidence against the person who is, or would be, entitled to its destruction.

PACE 1984, Code D, Annex F, para. 3

Samples and the information derived from samples, taken in connection with the investigation of an offence which are not required to be destroyed, may be retained after they have fulfilled the purposes for which they were taken but may be used only for purposes related to the prevention or detection of crime, the investigation of an offence or the conduct of a prosecution in, as well as outside, the UK and may also be subject to a speculative search. This includes checking them against other DNA records held by, or on behalf of, the police and other law enforcement authorities in, as well as outside, the UK.

PACE 1984, Code D, Annex F, para. 4

As far as volunteers are concerned the Code makes it clear that it is important to make sure "innocent volunteers" are not deterred from participating and their consent to their DNA being used for the purposes of a specific investigation is fully informed and voluntary. If the police or volunteer seek to have the sample retained for use after the specific investigation ends, it is important the volunteer's consent to this is also fully

PACE 1984, Code D, Annex F, NfG F1

informed and voluntary. Examples of consent for the various consents are given in the Code.

Removal of clothes

PACE 1984, Code D, para. 6.9

If the taking of the sample requires that a suspect removes clothing in circumstances that would be likely to cause embarrassment, no person of the opposite sex who is not a registered medical practitioner or registered healthcare professional shall be present; nor shall anyone be present whose attendance is unnecessary.

If the suspect is a juvenile or mentally disordered, he can specifically request the presence of a particular adult of the opposite sex who is readily available.

The removal of clothing from a juvenile may take place in the absence of the appropriate adult only if the juvenile signifies, whilst the appropriate adult is present, that he would prefer the sample be taken in the adult's absence and the appropriate adult agrees.

INTIMATE SAMPLES—PRACTICAL GUIDANCE

There are a number of key areas to consider when formulating advice to a suspect from whom an intimate sample is requested.

(1) Recordable offence

The adviser must be satisfied that the offence under investigation is in fact a recordable offence. Given the number of offences that are within the definition and the type of offence for which such samples are normally requested, this is unlikely to be a contentious issue.

(2) Confirm or disprove involvement

The sample can only be requested if it would tend to confirm or disprove the involvement of the suspect in a recordable offence. The officer should therefore be asked pertinent questions about the nature of the police inquiry, for example if the police are not in possession of any forensic samples which could be readily compared with the sample requested, representations as to whether the taking of the sample would fulfil this requirement should be made or consideration given to advising the suspect to withhold consent.

Alternatively, the taking of an intimate sample may not take matters any further, for example if the suspect has been arrested for an offence of rape and has already admitted in interview that intercourse had taken place but has maintained that the alleged victim consented to intercourse: in such circumstances the provision of a sample would be unlikely to have any probative value.

(3) Adverse inference

In advising a suspect from whom an intimate sample has been requested, the adviser should have firmly in mind the fact that a court, in deciding if there is a case to answer or at trial, would be allowed to draw such inferences from any refusal as appear proper. This will always be a difficult area, as the adviser is unlikely to be fully informed of the prosecution case at the time at which the sample is requested.

A careful note should be made of advice given at this particular stage and the reasons for that advice, as it may be necessary to give evidence on the matter at a subsequent trial, subject of course to professional privilege being waived by the client.

The adviser should always be aware of the possibility that a refusal of a suspect to give consent to the taking of such a sample may pose little danger at any trial particularly if there is very weak evidence against him, whereas providing a sample may bolster the prosecution case.

(4) Good cause

If the suspect gives a reason for not wanting to provide a sample, the adviser will have to consider whether it is likely to amount to a good cause.

Some assistance may be derived from the case law concerning the defence of "reasonable excuse" under RTA 1988, s.7. A refusal to provide a sample of blood based on genuine religious grounds is unlikely to amount to good cause. A fear of AIDS is not a reasonable excuse. However, a genuine phobia, *e.g.* of needles may be successful if supported by medical evidence.

R. v Harding [1974] R.T.R. 325; *Fountain v DPP* [1988] Crim. L.R. 123; *De Freitas v DPP* [1993] R.T.R. 98

A careful note of the reasons given by the suspect should be made and the suspect warned that the court may not consider that the reasons amount to good cause. It may be advisable, subject to instructions for the suspect, to inform the police of the reasons for the refusal in these circumstances and ask for it to be noted on the custody record.

(5) Attendance to provide a further sample

If the person is at the police station to provide an intimate sample having been requested to attend or arrested following a failure to attend to provide an intimate sample under PACE 1984 s.63A, the adviser must consider carefully whether the police actually have the power to take the intimate sample. The request to attend must have been made within the required time period.

In these circumstances, the provisions of s.62 (1A) must apply as the person is not in police detention because he has not been arrested for an offence. Therefore, two non-intimate samples must have previously been taken and proved to be insufficient. If the police had previously taken only an intimate sample or one non-intimate sample there is no power to take a further intimate sample.

NON-INTIMATE SAMPLES—THE LAW

Definition

A non-intimate sample is:

PACE 1984, s.65

(a) a sample of hair other than pubic hair;

(b) a sample taken from a nail or from under a nail;

(c) a swab from any part of the body including the mouth but not from any other body orifice;

(d) saliva; or

(e) a skin impression which is any record (other than a fingerprint) of the skin pattern and other physical characteristics or features of the whole or any part of the foot or any other part of the body.

Police powers to take samples without consent

A non-intimate sample can be taken without the appropriate consent in the following circumstances:

PACE 1984, s.63 (2A),(2B) and (2C) as amended by CJA 2003, s.10

(a) if the suspect is in police detention as a result of his arrest for a recordable offence and he has not had a non-intimate sample of the same type and from the same part of the body taken in the course of the investigation of the offence by the police or he has had such a sample taken but it proved insufficient. No authorisation is necessary.

(b) if the suspect in police custody on the authority of a court and an officer of at least the rank of inspector authorises the taking of the sample because he has reasonable grounds for:

(i) suspecting the involvement of the suspect in a recordable offence; and

(ii) believing that the sample would tend to disprove or confirm the involvement of the suspect in that offence;

PACE 1984, s.63(3) as amended by CJA 2003, s.10

PACE 1984, s.63(4) as amended by CJA 2003, s.10

(c) whether or not the suspect is in police detention or held on the authority of a court, if he has been charged with a recordable offence or informed that he will be reported for such an offence; and:

PACE 1984, s.63(3A) as amended by CJA 2003, s.10

(i) he has not had a non-intimate sample taken from him in the course of the investigation of the offence by the police; or

(ii) he has had such a sample taken but it was unsuitable or insufficient for a particular means of analysis; or

if he has been convicted of a recordable offence

PACE 1984, s.63(3B)

(e) if he is detained following acquittal on grounds of insanity or finding of unfitness to plead.

PACE 1984, s.63(3C); CE(A)A 1997, s.2

Appropriate consent is the consent of the suspect if 17 years of age or over, the consent of the suspect and his parent or guardian if the suspect is over 14 but not yet 17 years of age and the consent of the parent or guardian if the suspect is not yet 14 years of age. In the case of a mentally disordered or otherwise mentally vulnerable person the consent must be given in the presence of the appropriate adult.

PACE 1984 s.65(1), Code D, para. 2.12

The **authorisation** of the inspector will no longer be required in most cases where non-intimate samples are requested. However, where the authorisation is still required it may be given orally but must be confirmed in writing as soon as practicable. A record of the authorisation by virtue of which a non-intimate sample is taken and the grounds for the giving of that authorisation must be made as soon as practicable after the sample has been taken and if the suspect is detained at a police station then these matters must be recorded in the custody record.

PACE 1984, s.63(5)

PACE 1984, s.63(8)

PACE 1984, s.63(9)

Police powers to take samples with consent

A non-intimate sample can be taken in any circumstances if the appropriate consent is given. The consent should be in writing.

PACE 1984, s.63(1) and (2)

Recordable offences

PACE Code D, NfG 4A; NPR(RO)(A)R 2003

Recordable offences are defined as for intimate samples (refer to the section above).

Information to the suspect

PACE 1984, s.63(6) and (7)

Where authorisation has been given for the taking of a non-intimate sample, the suspect must be informed that the authorisation has been given and the grounds for which it was given, which must include a statement as to the nature of the offence in which it is believed the suspect is involved.

PACE 1984, s.63(8B) and (9)

In addition, the suspect must be informed that the sample may be the subject of a speculative search and the fact that he has been so informed noted on the custody record as soon as practicable after the sample has been taken.

Failure to provide this information to the suspect could render the taking of the sample unlawful and may amount to an assault or trespass to the person. The result could be inadmissible as evidence at a later trial.

Speculative searches

PACE 1984, s.63A(1), (1A) and (1B)

Where a person has been arrested on suspicion of being involved in a recordable offence, has been charged or informed that he will be reported for summons for such an offence, any samples or information derived from samples taken from him may be checked against other samples held by a law enforcement agency (which includes international agencies) or held in connection with or as a result of an investigation of an offence.

Hair samples

PACE 1984, s.63A(2)

If a sample of non-pubic hair is to be taken, it can be done either by cutting or plucking the hair with its roots. No more hair should be plucked than the person taking the sample considers reasonably necessary for a sufficient sample.

Effect of refusal

If a suspect withholds consent, there are no provisions specified in PACE 1984 for the court to draw an adverse inference from that refusal. However, the adviser should be aware that, in the wide-ranging circumstances described above, non-intimate samples can be taken without consent and by force if necessary.

Attendance requirement for the taking of non-intimate samples

A person not in police custody may be required to attend a police station to have a non-intimate sample taken in the following circumstances:

(a) where he has been charged with or informed that he will be reported for a recordable offence and either he has not had a sample taken from him during the investigation, or the sample was unsuitable or insufficient for the same means of analysis; or

PACE 1984, s.63A(4)

(b) where he has been convicted of a recordable offence and either has not had a sample taken since conviction, or the sample was unsuitable or insufficient for the same means of analysis.

A person can be required to attend the police station in the above circumstances within a period of one month from either the date of charge, the date of conviction or the date on which the appropriate officer was informed that the sample was unsuitable or insufficient, whichever is the relevant event.

PACE 1984, s.63A(5)

The person will be given seven days to attend and may be given specific times within which he should attend. There is a power to arrest without warrant anyone who fails to comply with the requirement.

PACE 1984, s.63A(6) and (7)

Destruction of samples

Where samples are taken in connection with the investigation of an offence they may be retained after they have fulfilled the purposes for which they were taken but shall not be used except for purposes related to the prevention or detection of crime, the investigation of an offence or the conduct of a prosecution.

PACE 1984, s.64 (1A)

Samples must be destroyed if taken from someone other than a suspect once the purpose has been fulfilled unless they were taken for the purposes of an investigation of an offence for which someone has been convicted and a sample was also taken from the convicted person. Consent can be given for the retention of samples taken from non-suspects, such consent once given being irrevocable.

PACE 1984, s.64 (3), (3AA) and (3AC)

This means that samples from a suspect whether arrested or attending voluntarily do not have to be destroyed even if that person is never charged or, if charged, is subsequently acquitted.

R. (on the application of Marper and

Another) v Chief Constable of South Yorkshire [2002] 1 W.L.R. 3223; [2003] 1 All E.R. 148

These provisions have survived a challenge under the Human Rights Act 1998.

NON-INTIMATE SAMPLES—PRACTICE AND PROCEDURE

The relevant PACE 1984 Code of Practice mirrors the provisions for the taking of such samples in the statute.

Is Authorisation required?

PACE 1984, Code D, para. 6.6

Authorisation is not necessary if the suspect is in police detention for a recordable offence and has not had a non-intimate sample of the same type and from the same part of the body taken previously or, if he has, that sample proved insufficient.

PACE 1984, Code D, para. 6.8

If the sample is being requested under the section for which authorisation is required (where he is held in custody by the police on the authority of a court), the suspect must be informed before the sample is taken of the grounds on which the relevant authority has been given. A record of the reasons for taking the sample must be made as soon as practicable, together with a note that written consent has been given.

Speculative search

PACE 1984, Code D, para. 6.8; PACE 1984, Code D, NfG 6E

The suspect must be informed that the sample or information derived from it may be retained and subject of a speculative search. This means that they may be checked against other DNA records held by, or on behalf of, the police and other law enforcement authorities in or outside the UK or held in connection with, or as a result of, an investigation of an offence inside or outside the UK. More detail is provided under intimate samples above.

Insufficiency or unsuitability of previous non-intimate sample

PACE 1984, Code D, NfG 6B

A sample can be insufficient, either in quantity or quality, to provide information for a particular type of analysis, such as DNA analysis or may be insufficient if enough information cannot be obtained from it by analysis because of loss, destruction, damage or contamination of the sample or as a result of an earlier, unsuccessful attempt at analysis. Alternatively a sample may be unsuitable for a particular type of analysis.

Destruction of samples

The circumstances in which samples may be retained or destroyed is dealt with above under intimate samples.

Removal of clothes

If the taking of the sample requires that a suspect removes clothing in circumstances that would be likely to cause embarrassment, no person of the opposite sex who is not a medical practitioner or registered healthcare professional shall be present; nor shall anyone be present whose attendance is unnecessary.

PACE 1984, Code D, para. 6.9

If the suspect is a juvenile or mentally disordered, he can specifically request the presence of a particular adult of the opposite sex who is readily available.

The removal of clothing from a juvenile may take place in the absence of the appropriate adult only if the juvenile signifies, whilst the appropriate adult is present, that he would prefer the sample to be taken in the adult's absence and the appropriate adult agrees.

Hair samples

If hair samples are to be taken for the purpose of DNA analysis, the suspect should be allowed a reasonable choice as to the body part from which the sample is to be taken. If the hair is to be plucked it should be done so individually unless the suspect prefers otherwise and no more than the person taking the sample considers sufficient should be taken.

PACE 1984, Code D, NfG 6A

Reasonable force

Reasonable force may be used if necessary to take a non-intimate sample in circumstances where the sample can be taken without consent. If force is used, a record should be made of the circumstances and those present when the sample is taken.

PACE 1984, Code D, para. 6.7 and 6.10

NON-INTIMATE SAMPLES—PRACTICAL GUIDANCE

As with intimate samples, there are a number of points to consider when advising a suspect from whom a non-intimate sample is requested:

(1) Recordable offence

It is important to be ready to make representations as to whether the offence is in fact recordable: if it is not a recordable offence then a non-intimate sample cannot be taken without consent. Given the number of offences that are within the definition, this is unlikely to be a contentious issue.

(2) No requirement for authorisation

Non-intimate samples can now be taken without consent without the requirement for authorisation when a suspect is in police detention under arrest for a recordable offence and he has not had a previous sample of the same type taken in the investigation or, if he has, it has proved insufficient. This removes any requirement for there to be consideration as to whether the taking of the sample will tend to prove or disprove the suspect's involvement in a recordable offence.

The provision remains if the suspect is in police custody on the authority of a court. In such a case, the adviser should also be mindful of whether the taking of the non-intimate sample would actually tend to confirm or disprove the suspect's involvement in a recordable offence.

It may be necessary to request further information from the police as to what their inquiries have revealed thus far, for example if no forensic evidence has been found the taking of non-intimate samples may not be appropriate.

(3) Consequences of refusal

Although no adverse inferences from a refusal to provide a non-intimate sample should be drawn by a court in subsequent proceedings, the suspect should be advised that if any of the grounds on which the sample could be taken without consent are satisfied then that sample can be taken without consent and by reasonable force if necessary.

Attempting to prevent the taking of the sample other than by passive non-co-operation could lead to the suspect being charged with obstruction or assault on police officers.

In reality, it would appear that police can now take non-intimate samples in every case where a suspect is under arrest for a recordable offence whether or not the taking of the sample might assist the investigation. This is particularly concerning given the fact that in most cases samples taken during an investigation will now be retained rather than destroyed.

HANDWRITING—THE LAW

There is no provision in PACE 1984 relating to the taking of handwriting samples.

It is unclear whether a refusal to co-operate with a request for a handwriting sample could lead to an adverse inference being drawn at trial or whether that refusal could amount to corroboration of other relevant evidence. It is, of course, impossible for a reliable sample to be taken without the consent of the suspect.

The fact that there are no specific provisions in PACE 1984 concerning handwriting samples provides strong support for the argument that no adverse inference should be drawn from a refusal to provide handwriting samples: if Parliament had intended the courts to be able to draw such adverse inferences, the legislation should have specifically included a section to that effect, as indeed it did for the refusal to provide intimate samples and in relation to the right of silence provisions in the CJPOA 1994.

In the absence of any post-PACE 1984 case, the situation remains unclear. In a case which was decided before PACE 1984 came into force, it was held that a refusal in the presence of a solicitor of a police request for a sample of head hair was capable of amounting to corroboration of other evidence against the defendant. The particular issue in *Smith* would now be covered by s.63 of PACE 1984, as the sample requested was a non-intimate sample and reasonable force could have been used if the relevant circumstances were satisfied.

R. v Smith (Robert William) (1985) 81 Cr. App.R. 286, CA

However, it has been suggested that this case provides authority for the courts to hold that a refusal of a request by police for a sample or a specimen of handwriting may be capable of amounting to corroboration of other evidence against the suspect, if that refusal were made in the presence of a solicitor. The issue of whether a refusal to provide samples could be capable of amounting to corroboration was specifically included in PACE 1984 in relation to intimate samples but PACE 1984 is silent on whether the same is true for non-intimate samples. One must therefore be in a strong position to argue that no adverse inference should be drawn and the refusal should not be capable of amounting to corroboration; otherwise, Parliament would have so enacted. *Smith* may therefore be of limited assistance to the court but one should always be wary of the case in advising in relation to handwriting samples.

HANDWRITING—PRACTICAL GUIDANCE

Having considered the potential problems of *Smith* when advising a suspect from whom a sample of handwriting has been requested, the dangers of providing the sample should be considered very carefully. These dangers often tend to outweigh any adverse affect that a refusal may have on subsequent proceedings and the suspect is, therefore, usually best advised to refuse to provide the sample.

DRUG TEST FOLLOWING CHARGE

Adults

PACE 1984, s.63B

Where an adult suspect is detained under PACE 1984 and is charged with certain offences, the police have the power to request a sample of urine or a non-intimate sample in order to test for the presence of a specified class A drug. Such a sample can only be taken by consent but failure without good cause to give a sample amounts to a summary offence punishable by a maximum sentence of three months' imprisonment and/or a level 4 fine.

PACE 1984, s.63B(8) and 63C(1)

Bail can be delayed for up to six hours from the time of charge to enable a sample to be taken if the custody officer has reasonable grounds for believing that detention is necessary for this purpose.

PACE 1984, s.38(1)(a)(iiia)

The "trigger" offences are:

PACE 1984, s.63C(6); PACE, Code C, NfG17E

- theft;
- burglary or aggravated burglary;
- taking without consent or aggravated taking without consent;
- going equipped for theft etc;
- obtaining property by deception;
- producing, supplying, possessing or possessing with intent to supply as class A drug;
- handling stolen goods; (CJCSA 2000)
- begging and persitent begging;
- attempted theft, robbery, burglary, handling stolen goods or obtaining by deception.

PACE 1984, s.63B(2)–(5)

Before a sample can be taken the following criteria must be met:

- the person must have been charged with a trigger offence or any other offence where an inspector or above has reasonable grounds for believing that the misuse by that person of any specified class A drug caused or contributed to the offence, authorises a sample to be taken;

- the person is aged 18 or over;
- a police officer has requested that the sample be taken;
- before requesting the sample the officer must inform the person of the purpose of taking the sample and that authorisation has been given (if relevant), warn them that failure without good cause will render them liable to prosecution, remind them of their right to legal advice, to inform someone of their arrest and to consult the codes of practice.

Where authorisation is given it can be oral or in writing. If oral it must be confirmed in writing as soon as practicable. The authorisation and the grounds for suspicion shall be recorded on the custody record as soon as practicable after the sample is taken.

PACE 1984, s.63C(2)

PACE 1984, s.63C(3)

PACE 1984, s.63C(4)

The information derived from the sample can not be used in evidence or for identification purposes but it can be disclosed to inform a decision on bail, prior to conviction to inform any decision as to the supervision of the person in police detention, in custody or on bail, following conviction to inform any decision about sentence, supervision or release and to ensure that appropriate advice and treatment is made available to the person concerned.

PACE 1984, s.63B(7)

Youths

In the following police areas the provisions for testing for class A drugs after charge are extended to include those persons aged 14 to 17:

CJA 2003, s.5, SI 2004/1867, Art. 2

- Cleveland
- Greater Manchester
- Humberside
- Merseyside
- Metropolitan Police District
- Nottinghamshire
- West Yorkshire

PACE 1984, s.63B(5A) as amended by CJA 2003, s.5(3)

The making of the request for such a sample, the giving of the warning as to potential prosecution for failure to provide the sample without good cause, the giving of the information as to the authorisation the grounds for it and the taking of the sample may not take place except in the presence of an appropriate adult.

Search of Person

SEARCHES AND THE RIGHT OF SILENCE

Adverse inferences may be drawn from a suspect's silence in certain circumstances. These include instances where an arrested suspect fails or refuses, on a constable's request, to account for the presence of any object, substance or mark on or about him, or in his possession, or found in any place at which he was at the time of his arrest, the presence of which the constable reasonably believes to be attributable to his participation in an offence.

CJPOA 1994, s.36

For further details of this provision refer to the **Advising the Suspect—Right of Silence** index heading.

SEARCHES BEFORE ARREST

The police have various powers to search a suspect before an arrest. These are primarily governed by Pt I (Powers to stop and search) and Pt II (Powers of entry, search and seizure) of PACE 1984 and Code A. In using these powers, it is unlawful for police officers to discriminate on the grounds of race, colour, ethnic origin or nationality.

PACE 1984, Code A, para. 1.1 and RR(A)A 2000, s.1

An officer may search any person or vehicle for stolen or "prohibited" articles and may detain a person or vehicle for the purpose of such a search. The officer must have reasonable grounds for suspecting that he will find stolen or prohibited items. For further details on searches of a vehicle refer to the **Search of Property** index heading.

PACE 1984, s.1 (1)–(9) and Code A, paras 2.2–2.11

An article is prohibited if it is an offensive weapon or an article made or adapted for use in connection with burglary, theft, "TDA", criminal damage or any other of the specified offences.

PACE 1984, s.1(7)–(8) [as amended by CJA 2003 s.1(2)]

Failure by a person to answer questions put to him by a police officer cannot in itself turn what was an unreasonable suspicion into reasonable suspicion.

Samuels v Commissioner of Police for the Metropolis (unreported), March 3, 1999, CA

The searching officer inform the suspect of relevant information including his name, police station, object of the search and the grounds for proposing to make the search. A failure by an officer to provide this information will render the search unlawful.

PACE 1984, s.2(3), *Osman v DPP The Times*, September, 28, 1999

The police powers to search are significantly restricted if the suspect is within the grounds of a dwelling, unless he is not the occupier and is there without the occupier's permission.

PACE 1984, s.1 (1), (4)–(5)

PACE 1984, s.2(9), and Code A, para. 3.5–3.6

If a search requires the suspect to remove more than a coat, jacket or gloves then it should be conducted in private (which may be in a nearby police van or police station) and may only be made by an officer of the same sex as the suspect (without any person of the opposite sex present, unless the suspect specifically requests it).

PACE 1984, s.1(6)–(9)

A constable can seize any article found during any such search if he has reasonable grounds for suspecting that the article has been stolen, or is an offensive weapon, or is an article for use in the commission of an offence.

As well as their general powers under PACE 1984, the police have various other statutory powers to search a suspect prior to arrest. These include:

CJPOA 1994, s.60

(a) Occasions when a senior officer authorises for a period of up to 24 hours the stopping and searching of persons (and vehicles) for offensive weapons or bladed or sharply pointed instruments. Such authorisation can be given if the officer either reasonably anticipates incidents involving serious violence in his locality or reasonably believes that persons are carrying dangerous instruments or offensive weapons in his locality.

CJPOA 1994, s.60(4A) and PACE 1984, Code A, para. 3.5

Additional powers exist to require a suspect to remove any item of clothing, and for its seizure, if it is reasonably believed that it is being worn to conceal the suspect's identity.

TA 2000, s.45(3) and PACE 1984, Code A, para. 3.5

(b) Occasions when special stop and search powers are authorised in order to prevent acts of terrorism.

Additional powers exist to not only require the suspect to remove his coat, jacket or gloves in public but also his shoes and headgear.

For further details refer to the **Terrorist Suspects** index heading.

SEARCHES AFTER ARREST PRIOR TO ARRIVAL AT A POLICE STATION

The police have the power to search a suspect after an arrest but before arrival at a police station if:

PACE 1984, s.32(1)

(a) they have reasonable grounds to believe that the suspect may present a danger to himself or others; or

(b) it is for the purpose of seizing any article which may be used to assist an escape or which may be relevant evidence.

PACE 1984, s.32(2)(a)

Such searches may only be conducted to the extent that they are reasonably required for either of these purposes.

PACE 1984, s.32(3)

In conducting such a search, the suspect cannot be required to remove clothing in public other than his coat, jacket or gloves. If this is required then the search should be conducted in private (which may be in a nearby police van or police station) and by an officer of the same sex (without any person of the same sex present, unless the suspect specifically requests it).

PACE 1984, s.32(4) and Code A, para. 3.5

A constable cannot conduct such a search unless he has reasonable grounds for believing that the suspect has concealed items of a type for which such a search is permitted.

PACE 1984, s.32(5)

Any items found may be seized by the police provided that they are not subject to legal privilege and provided that they may either be used to cause physical injury or to assist an escape, or may be relevant evidence.

PACE 1984, s.32(8)–(9)

SEARCHES AFTER ARREST AT A POLICE STATION

General searches—the law

When a suspect under arrest arrives at a police station or when a suspect is arrested at a police station, the custody officer must ascertain everything that the suspect has with him and may record or cause to be recorded all or any of these items. Any such record may be made as part of his custody record.

PACE 1984, s.54(1)–(2)

General searches—practice and procedure

The custody officer may authorise that the suspect be searched if of the view that this is necessary: such a search must be limited in extent to that which is required to fulfil the s.54(1) requirement.

PACE 1984, s.54(6)

This provision is likely to come into operation when either the suspect refuses to comply with the standard request to "empty your pockets" or the custody officer believes that the suspect is only partially complying with such a request in an attempt to conceal relevant items of property.

A suspect under arrest remains liable to search at any time during his detention for the purposes of ascertaining whether he has any item which may be used to cause injury, damage property or interfere with evidence, or to assist in an escape.

PACE 1984, s.54(6a)

PACE 1984, ss 54(8)–(9), 117

Any such searches must be carried out by a police officer of the same sex as the suspect and, if resistance is met, reasonable force may be used in effecting a properly authorised search.

Searches and examination to ascertain identity—the law

PACE 1984, s.54A (1)

If an officer of at least the rank of inspector authorises it, a person who is detained in a police station may be searched and/or examined:

(a) for the purpose of ascertaining whether he has any mark that would tend to identify him as a person involved in the commission of an offence; or

(b) for the purpose of facilitating the ascertainment of his identity.

Searches and examination to ascertain identity—practice and procedure

PACE 1984, s.54A (2)–(3)

The officer may only give his authorisation if the suspect has refused to identify himself or the officer has reasonable grounds for suspecting that he is not who he claims to be. The suspect must also have withheld his consent to the search or it is not practicable to obtain such consent.

PACE 1984, s.54A (5), (9)

Any identifying mark found during the search or examination may be photographed with or without the suspect's consent. Such a photograph may be used by, or disclosed to, any person for any purpose related to the prevention or detection of crime, the investigation of an offence or the conduct of a prosecution.

PACE 1984, s.54A (12)

It is an "identifying mark" if its existence facilitates the ascertainment of the suspect's identification in the commission of an offence and can include features and injuries.

PACE 1984, s.54A (7)

An officer of the opposite sex to the suspect may not carry out the search or examination nor take any photograph of any part of the suspect's body.

Strip searches—the law

PACE 1984, s.54(6) and Code C, para. 4.1

In complying with his general obligations, a custody officer can authorise a strip search of the suspect if he considers it necessary to remove any article which the suspect would not otherwise be allowed to keep (see the **Seizure of property** heading below).

PACE 1984, Code C, Annex A, para. 9

A strip search is defined as "a search involving the removal of more than outer clothing" but must not involve any element of an **"intimate search"** (see below).

Strip searches—practice and procedure

A strip search may only take place if it is considered **necessary to remove an article** which the suspect would not be allowed to keep and the officer reasonably considers that the suspect might have concealed such an article.

PACE 1984, Code C, Annex A, para. 10

The reasons for, the results of and details of those present during a strip search must be **recorded** by the custody officer as part of the custody record.

PACE 1984, Code C, Annex A, para. 12

Any such search must not only be carried out by a **police officer of the same sex** as the suspect but no person of the opposite sex, nor anyone whose presence is unnecessary, shall be present (other than an appropriate adult whose presence has been specifically requested by the suspect).

PACE 1984, s.54(8)–(9) and Code C, Annex A, para. 11(a)–(b)

Other than in cases of urgency (where there is risk of serious harm), there must be at least **two persons present** other than the suspect if the search involves exposure of **intimate parts** of the body. One of these must be the appropriate adult if the suspect is a juvenile or mentally disordered person (unless a juvenile, but not a mentally disordered suspect, requests otherwise and the appropriate adult agrees). No more than two other persons should be present, other than an appropriate adult, other than in the "most exceptional circumstances".

PACE 1984, Code C, Annex A, para. 11(c)

The search must be effected with due regard to the suspect's **sensitivity and vulnerability**, including a requirement that the suspect, should not normally be required to remove all his clothes at once.

PACE 1984, Code C, Annex A, para. 11(d)

To assist the search, the suspect may be required to hold his **arms in the air**, or to stand with his **legs apart** and bending forward. However, there must be no physical contact with any body orifice.

PACE 1984, Code C, Annex A, para. 11(e)

If any articles are detected within a body orifice (other than the mouth) and the suspect refuses to hand them over voluntarily then they can only be removed by way of an **intimate search** (see below).

PACE 1984, Code C, Annex A, para. 11(f)

The search must be **conducted as quickly as possible** and the suspect be allowed to dress as soon as it has finished.

PACE 1984, Code C, Annex A, para. 11(g)

The police are entitled to use **reasonable force** in effecting a properly authorised strip search.

PACE 1984, s.117

Intimate searches—the law

An "intimate search" is a search which involves the physical examination of any of the suspect's body orifices other than the

PACE 1984, s.65(1) and

Code C, Annex A, para. 1

R. v Hughes, *The Times*, November 12, 1993

mouth. The examination involves some physical intrusion into the body orifice and is more than mere visual examination.

An intimate search can only be performed upon a suspect who is under arrest and in police detention.

PACE 1984, s.55(1), (2) and Code C, Annex A, para. 2

An intimate search must be authorised by an officer of the rank of inspector or above. The authorising officer must have reasonable grounds for believing that the item(s) being searched for cannot be found without an intimate search, and:

(a) the suspect may have concealed on him anything which could be used to cause physical injury to himself or another, and might be so used whilst in police detention or the custody of a court; or

(b) the suspect may have a Class A drug concealed on him and was in possession of it with the appropriate criminal intent before arrest either to supply or to export the drug.

PACE 1984, s.55(3)

Authorisation for such a search may be given orally or in writing. However, if given orally then it should be subsequently confirmed in writing as soon as is practicable.

Intimate searches—practice and procedure

PACE 1984, Code C, Annex A, para. 2A

The **reasons** why an intimate search is considered necessary must be explained to the suspect before the search takes place.

PACE 1984, s.55(4)–(7) and Code C, Annex A, para. 3–3A

The search should only be carried out by a **registered medical practitioner or registered nurse** unless an officer of the rank of inspector or above considers this impractical and the search is for an object that could cause injury. In these circumstances, the search must be carried out by a constable of the same sex as the suspect. If the search relates to a drug offence, then it must be conducted by a registered medical practitioner or registered nurse.

PACE 1984, s.55(8)–(9)

Searches relating to **drug offences** must be carried out in a hospital or surgery or other **medical premises**.

PACE 1984, s.55(8)–(9)

Searches for **articles which may cause injury** may be carried out at a **police station** or hospital, surgery or other **medical premises**.

PACE 1984, s.55(7) and Code C, Annex A, para. 6

Other than a registered medical practitioner or registered nurse, **no person of the opposite sex** to the suspect should be present during an intimate search; nor should anyone whose presence is unnecessary be present.

Code C, Annex A, para. 6

A minimum of **two persons** should be present other than the suspect, and the search must be conducted with due regard to the suspect's **sensitivity and vulnerability**.

If the suspect is a **juvenile or mentally disordered**, the search must be in the presence of an appropriate adult of the same sex (unless the suspect has specifically requested an appropriate adult of the opposite sex). A juvenile (but not a mentally disordered suspect) may request that the appropriate adult's presence be excused but the appropriate adult must also agree to this.

Code C, Annex A, para. 5

Once properly authorised, an intimate search can be affected with the use of reasonable force by the police but not by a registered medical practitioner or registered nurse.

PACE 1984, s.117

After an intimate search has been carried out, the **custody record shall be noted** as soon as practicable with the details of the parts of the body searched, why they were searched, who carried out the search, who was present and the results of the search. If the search was carried out by a police officer, there must also be a note of why it was impracticable for a suitably qualified medical person to conduct it.

PACE 1984, s.55(10)–(11) and Code C, Annex A, paras 7–8

Distinction between searches and the taking of samples

Strip searches and intimate searches are separate and distinct from those procedures followed by the police or their agents when taking "intimate samples" (refer to the **Samples** index heading). The key distinctions are as follows.

Although a search may involve the **physical examination** of a body orifice, intimate samples are **taken** from parts of the body (which may or may not be orifices).

The suspect must **consent** to the taking of an intimate sample, whereas no such consent is necessary for the performance of a search.

It should always be remembered that an intimate sample cannot be taken under the guise of an intimate search.

Seizure of property

In carrying out any **search other than an intimate search**, the custody officer is free to seize any item other than clothes and personal effects. Clothes and personal effects may only be seized if the officer:

PACE 1984, s.54(3)–(4), (6b)–(6c) and Code C, para. 4.2

(a) believes that the suspect may use them:

  (i) to cause physical injury to himself or another;
  (ii) to damage property;
  (iii) to interfere with evidence; or
  (iv) to assist in an escape; or

(b) has reasonable grounds for believing that they may be evidence.

PACE 1984, Code C, para. 4.3

"Personal effects" are items which the suspect may lawfully need or use or refer to whilst in detention; this definition excludes cash or other items of value.

PACE 1984, s.55(12)

In effecting an **intimate search**, the custody officer can only seize any item which satisfies the same criteria as (a) or (b) above.

PACE 1984, ss 54(5), 55(13)

When items of property are seized, the suspect must be **told of the reasons** for the seizure unless he is violent, likely to become violent or incapable of understanding what is being said.

PACE 1984, Code C, para. 4.4, 4.5

It is for the custody officer to decide whether a **record** should be made of the property a detainee has with him or had taken from him on arrest. Any record made is not required to be kept as part of the custody record but the custody record should be noted as to where such a record exists. Whenever a record is made the detainee shall be allowed to check and sign the record of property as being correct and a refusal to do so will be recorded. If a detainee is not allowed to keep any article of clothing or personal effects, the reason for this must be recorded.

PRACTICAL GUIDANCE

(1) Adviser to be present during search

Whenever possible, the legal adviser should be present during any search of the suspect.

If there is to be a strip search or an intimate search and the suspect is of a different sex than the adviser, consideration should be given to arranging the attendance of a colleague of the appropriate sex.

PACE 1984, s.58(1)
PACE 1984, Code C, Note for Guidance 6D

If the police object to the adviser being present, they should be reminded that an arrested suspect held in custody is entitled to consult their solicitor "at any time", and that the PACE 1984 Codes of Practice recognise that it is the adviser's role "to protect . . . the legal rights of his client".

(2) Searches conducted other than in the adviser's presence

There will be occasions when it is not possible for the adviser to be present during a search, for example when the search was conducted prior to the suspect's arrival at the police station.

PACE 1984, s.54(1), (6)

The adviser should inquire of the custody officer as to what searches have been carried out and what items seized immediately upon arrival at the police station. The suspect's instructions should then be taken to seek confirmation as to whether he agrees with the police information.

If there is a dispute then consideration should be given to registering a complaint either formally or informally (refer to the **Complaints** index heading).

(3) No search at police station necessary

It is normally the case that when an arrested suspect arrives at a police station the custody officer will seek to identify the property he holds and, if necessary, do so by way of a search.

However, this is not an absolute requirement. If the custody officer is of the view that the suspect is only to be detained for a short period and is not to be placed in a cell, they may decide that there is no need to identify the property he holds.

PACE 1984, Code C, Note for Guidance 4A

In such circumstances the custody record should be endorsed "not searched" and the suspect be invited to sign the entry. If the suspect refuses to so sign then the custody officer will return to the normal search procedures.

(4) Objections to a search

Any search of a suspect which is improperly authorised or otherwise unlawful is likely to be a criminal and/or civil assault.

If appropriate, this can be pointed out to the police if the suspect objects to a search, particularly when this is to be either a strip search or an intimate search.

In the case of an intimate search, the police should be asked to explain why they consider it appropriate to conduct such a search and argument against these reasons should be made if such exist. Although the police are under no obligation to hear such representations, it will invariably be the case that they will be prepared to justify their reasons, particularly given that these will have to be recorded in any event.

Regardless of any objections which may be made, if the requisite officer provides the requisite authorisation for a search, it should then be allowed to proceed.

The suspect should be advised that whilst he may object to the search he should not actively resist, as to do so may give rise to a prosecution for an assault upon or an obstruction of the police. Although there is authority for the contention that a suspect is entitled to use force in resisting an unlawful search, it would be inadvisable to rely upon this, particularly given that a definitive ruling on whether a proposed search is unlawful can only be made by a court at a later date.

R. v Churchill [1989] Crim. L.R. 226

Search of Premises

INTRODUCTION

The police have a variety of statutory powers to enter and search premises either with or without a warrant. Many of these are governed by Pt II (Powers of entry, search and seizure) of PACE 1984 and Code B. In addition, a new system for the authorisation and regulation of covert surveillance (which may involve entry into a person's premises or other interference with his property) has been introduced under Pt II of RIPA 2000.

It would be too lengthy to refer in detail to all such powers in this book. Rather, attention will be given to those issues which are most likely to arise for the adviser whilst attending upon a suspect at a police station.

In addition to their statutory powers, the police always have the right to search premises with the "consent" of any person entitled to grant access to the premises. Indeed, specific consent is not even required in circumstances where it is reasonable to assume that the seeking of it would cause "disproportionate inconvenience" to the persons concerned (*e.g.* where the suspect is believed to be hiding in the gardens of innocent householders).

R. v Sanghera [2001] 1 Cr. App.R. 20; PACE 1984, Code B, para. 5

SEARCHES AND THE RIGHT OF SILENCE

Adverse inferences may be drawn from a suspect's silence in certain circumstances. These include instances where an arrested suspect fails or refuses, on a constable's request, to account for the presence of any object, substance or mark on or about him, or in his possession, or found in any place at which he was at the time of his arrest, the presence of which the constable reasonably believes to be attributable to his participation in an offence.

CJPOA 1994, s.36

For further details of this provision, refer to the **Advising the Suspect—Right of Silence** index heading.

SEARCHES ON OR PRIOR TO AN ARREST—THE LAW

When a suspect is arrested at a place other than a police station, a constable may enter and search without a warrant any premises in which the suspect was situated when arrested or "*immediately*

PACE 1984, s.32(2)(b); *R. v Commissioner*

of Police of the Metropolis Ex p. Rottman [2002] 2 All E.R. 865; *Hewitson v Chief Constable of Dorset Police, The Times*, January 6, 2004
PACE 1984, s.23
PACE 1984, s.32(7)
PACE 1984, s.32(3), (6) Code B, para. 6.9

before" arrest. The search must be for evidence relating to the offence (including extradition offences) for which the suspect was arrested.

"Premises" include any vehicle, vessel, aircraft, tent or movable structure. Where premises are subject to multiple occupations, they are defined as those parts occupied by the suspect and parts to which he has joint access.

Any such search must be limited to the extent that it is reasonably required for the purpose of discovering evidence, and the constable must have reasonable grounds for believing that there is evidence on the premises for which a search is permitted.

CJA 2003, s.2

There will be occasions, prior to the arrest of a suspect, when the police (and appropriately authorised civilians) are empowered to enter and search premises pursuant to the granting of a warrant. The rules and safeguards for the grant of such warrants are contained within ss 8 to 16 of PACE 1984.

PACE 1984, s.8(2)

The police station adviser will rarely be involved in such procedures, unless the circumstances have allowed him to be called out to attend premises whilst a search is still underway, but he should be aware that a constable may only enter premises and seize and retain material for which the search has been authorised under the warrant.

SEARCHES ON ARREST—PRACTICE AND PROCEDURE

The **definition** of premises does not necessarily involve legal ownership or control. Thus, if a suspect is arrested at premises owned by another or in public premises, the premises may be searched provided that the other requirements are satisfied.

R. v Beckford (1991) 94 Cr.App.R. 43; *Hewitson v Chief Constable of Dorset Police, The Times*, January 6, 2004

Some confusion may arise as to the meaning of premises where the suspect was present "immediately before" he was arrested. In one case, "immediately" was defined as premises "recently" left by the suspect. It would appear that the normal meaning is to be given to the word and that premises vacated some hours earlier will not be covered by the s.32 powers.

PACE 1984, s.117 and Code B, paras 6.4, 6.6

The police are entitled to use **reasonable force** to carry out the entry and search of premises if certain criteria are satisfied; such as the premises being known to be unoccupied, or the person entitled to grant access having refused a request to allow entry.

PACE 1984, ss 19(2)–(3)

Unlike searches under warrant, any item found during such a search on arrest may be **seized** if the police believe that it is evidence, even if it is evidence of a crime other than the one for which the suspect has been arrested.

Before conducting a search, the police should normally provide the occupier of the premises (who may or may not be the suspect) with a **notice** specifying, *inter alia*, the occupier's rights and the rights of the owner of any property seized.

PACE 1984, Code B, paras 6.7–6.8

SEARCHES AFTER ARREST—THE LAW

When a suspect has been arrested for an arrestable offence, a constable may enter and search any premises occupied or controlled by him if there are reasonable grounds for suspecting that there is evidence on the premises (other than items subject to legal privilege) that relates either:

PACE 1984, s.18(1)

(a) to that offence; or

(b) to some other arrestable offence connected with or similar to that offence.

Premises are defined in the same way as for s.32 searches on arrest (see above).

It is important to note that, unlike s.32 searches on arrest, s.18 searches can only take place when the suspect has been arrested for "an arrestable offence" and the relevant premises must either be in the occupation of or be under the control of the suspect.

Any such search may only be conducted to the extent that it is reasonably required for the purpose of discovering evidence as defined.

PACE 1984, s.18(3) and Code B, para. 6.9

Such searches must be authorised in writing by an officer of the rank of inspector or above, unless the search is conducted before the suspect has been taken to a police station (or released on bail instead of being taken to the police station) and the suspect's presence at a place other than a police station is necessary for the effective investigation of the offence. In such cases, an officer of the rank of inspector or above must be informed of the search as soon as practicable after it has been made.

PACE 1984, s.18(4)–(5) and Code B, para. 4.3

SEARCHES AFTER ARREST—PRACTICE AND PROCEDURE

The police may **seize** and retain any items found during the search which relate to the purpose of the search.

PACE 1984, s.18(2)

PACE 1984, s.18(7) and Code B, para. 4.3

The officer who authorises a s.18 search or the officer who is informed of such a search after the event shall make a **written record** of the grounds for the search and the nature of the evidence sought. This record should be included in the custody record, where there is one.

PACE 1984, s.18(8)

If the occupier or controller of the premises searched is in police detention then the written record must be part of the custody record.

PACE 1984, s.117 and Code B, paras 6.4, 6.6

The police are entitled to use **reasonable force** to carry out a properly authorised entry and search of premises if the same criteria are met as for a search "on arrest" (see above).

PACE 1984, Code B, paras 6.7–6.8

Before conducting a search, the police should provide the occupier of the premises (who will usually be the suspect) with a **notice** specifying, *inter alia*, the occupier's rights and the rights of the owner of any property seized.

PRACTICAL GUIDANCE

(1) Adviser to be present during search

It is usually the case that, subject to instructions from the suspect, the adviser should seek to be present during any search of premises. This is only likely to be practical for a s.18 search conducted after the adviser's arrival at a police station.

PACE 1984, Code B, para. 6.11

If the police object to the adviser's attendance and the premises to be searched are occupied by the suspect then they should be reminded that the "occupier" has the right to request a friend, neighbour or other person to witness the search and that this must be allowed unless the officer in charge has reasonable grounds for believing that this would "seriously hinder the investigation or endanger" any persons.

When the suspect is not the "occupier", the point should be made that the adviser's presence may minimise the risks of any subsequent allegations being made that evidence was planted or that the search was otherwise conducted improperly.

If the police are not persuaded to allow the adviser's attendance then this refusal should be noted by the adviser and the custody officer asked to note the same on the custody record.

The adviser should be aware that if they are present during a search and if any aspect of the conduct of the search subsequently becomes an issue, the adviser may become liable to be called as a witness of fact during the trial. Some argue that this is a reason why advisers should not be present during searches.

(2) Procedure when present during a search

If present during a search of premises, the adviser should take careful contemporaneous notes of all police movements and make a schedule of all property seized.

Representations should be made to the police that only one room or area should be searched at a time, thereby allowing the adviser to be present. Reference can be made (as described in point (1) above) to the advantage that this will minimise the risk of any subsequent complaint being made as to the manner in which the search was conducted.

(3) Suspect to be present during search

Suspects have no right to be present during a s.18 search. However, in practice, it is often the case that they are taken with the police when such a search is to be carried out.

If a suspect wishes to be present but the police do not initially agree to this then representations should be made by the adviser (similar to those described in point (1) above) that the suspect's presence will minimise the risk of any subsequent complaint being made.

The suspect must be fully advised in advance of any such attendance on how to respond to any questions which may be put to him by the police during a search.

(4) Travelling in police vehicles

Before travelling to premises about to be searched under s.18, the police will often refuse to take the adviser with them on the grounds that their insurance does not cover passengers.

The adviser may wish to accompany the police either due to simple convenience or because they have no other means of transport. If the suspect is being transported in the police vehicle then it is even more desirable that the adviser also be so carried, to ensure that no police questioning occurs *en route*.

The adviser should be aware of the terms of his employer's insurance policies and, in particular, whether they cover the employee's business travel in third parties' vehicles. If such cover exists then this should be explained to the police and, if requested, a declaration given to this effect.

If no such insurance exists then the adviser should suggest to his employer that it be obtained, to prevent this becoming an issue in the future.

(5) Searches conducted other than in the adviser's presence

There will be many occasions when it is not possible for the adviser to be present during a search of premises. This is invariably the case when a s.32 search on arrest was conducted prior to the adviser having been instructed, or there was a search on warrant prior to arrest.

In such circumstances, the adviser should inquire of the custody officer immediately upon arrival at the police station as to what searches have been carried out and what items seized. The suspect's instructions should then be taken to seek confirmation as to whether he agrees with the police information.

If there is a dispute then consideration should be given to registering a complaint either formally or informally (refer to the **Complaints** index heading).

(6) Objections to improper searches

A search of premises which was improperly authorised or otherwise unlawful is likely to be a criminal and/or civil trespass.

If appropriate, this can be pointed out to the police if it is proposed to conduct a search which, in the adviser's opinion, cannot be justified under the appropriate statutory provisions.

R. v Fennelley [1989] Crim.L.R. 142; *Chapman v DPP* (1988) 89 Cr.App.R. 190

It may also be arguable that property seized as a result of an improper search will be inadmissible as evidence in any future criminal proceedings. Although experience suggests that such arguments usually fail, it is recommended that the suspect be advised not to comment upon items of property seized if it is believed that they were seized during an improper search since, if comment is made, this may assist a future prosecution argument *vis-à-vis* the admissibility of the evidence.

(7) Items subject to legal privilege

PACE 1984, ss 8(1)–(2) and s.19(6); *R. v Chesterfield Justices Ex p. Bramley* (2000) 2 W.L.R. 409

The police are prohibited from seizing any item which is reasonably believed to be the subject of legal privilege.

Such items are defined as to include communications between a legal adviser and his client relating to legal advice or connected to actual or contemplated legal proceedings. However any item held with the intention of furthering a criminal offence cannot be subject to legal privilege.

PACE 1984, s.10

If there is any dispute between the adviser and an investigating officer as to whether material seized or about to be seized is subject to legal privilege, it should be suggested that the normal practice is to have the items sealed before any inspection of them and should remain so sealed until a court ruling can be obtained upon the issue.

Solicitors' Representatives

DEFINITION OF A "SOLICITOR"

PACE 1984 provides the suspect with the right to advice from a solicitor. A "solicitor" is defined in the PACE 1984 Codes of Practice to include any person who is:

PACE 1984, s.58

(a) a solicitor who holds a valid practising certificate;

(b) an accredited or probationary representative included on the register of representatives maintained by the Legal Services Commission.

PACE 1984, Code C, para. 6.12

Trainee solicitors who wish to attend the police station must be accredited or probationary representatives.

THE POLICE STATION REPRESENTATIVE ACCREDITATION SCHEME

The Legal Services Commission will not pay for advice given by a solicitors' representative in a police station unless that representative is registered as an accredited or probationary representative. A representative can apply for probationary status for up to one year and will only be paid for advice on cases which are not indictable only.

The accreditataion process has three parts to it: submission of a detailed portfolio of cases, a written test and a "critical incidents" test. Full details of the scheme are available from the Law Society on *www.lawsociety.org.uk.*

The purpose of the accreditation scheme is to ensure that solicitors' representatives have the required knowledge, competence and skills to represent suspects effectively in the police station.

Qualified solicitors who do not hold the Police Station Qualification will be required to undergo the accreditation process before undertaking police station work. They must register before November 1, 2005, have passed the portfolio or critical incidents test by May 1, 2006 and both tests by November 1, 2006. They are exempt from the written test. This will not apply to a firm on the Serious Fraud Panel if the client is arrested for a fraud offence.

REFUSAL OF ADMISSION

PACE 1984, Code C, para. 6.12A

The admission to a police station of an accredited or probationary representative can only be refused if a police officer of the rank of inspector or above considers that such a visit will hinder the investigation which does not include giving proper legal advice to a suspect.

In exercising this discretion, the inspector should take into account the following:

PACE 1984, Code C, para. 6.13

(a) whether the identity and status of an accredited or probationary representative have been satisfactorily established;

(b) whether the accredited or probationary representative is of suitable character to provide legal advice: a person with a criminal record is unlikely to be deemed to be a suitable person unless the conviction is minor and not recent;

(c) any other matters contained in any letter of authorisation provided by the solicitor on whose behalf such representative is attending the police station.

PACE 1984, Code C, para. 6.12A and NfG 6D

An accredited or probationary representative cannot be considered to be unsuitable by reason of lack of experience or qualifications, nor as a result of giving proper legal advice to a suspect in accordance with the defined role of a solicitor.

PACE 1984, Code C, para. 6.14

If an inspector refuses access to an accredited or probationary representative or a decision is taken not to allow such a person to remain in an interview, he must notify the solicitor on whose behalf the representative was acting and give him the opportunity to make alternative arrangements. The suspect must also be told and a note made on the custody record.

PACE 1984, Code C, NfG 6F

PACE 1984, Code C, para. 6.12A

If an officer of at least the rank of inspector considers that an individual solicitor or firm of solicitors is persistently sending unsuitable probationary representatives to the police station, he should inform an officer of at least the rank of superintendent, who may take the matter up with the Law Society.

PACE 1984, Code C, para. 6.9 and NfG 6D and 6E

Once admitted to the police station the accredited or probationary representative is to be treated as a solicitor and can only be removed from the police station if their conduct is such that the interviewer is unable properly to put questions to the suspect.

DUTY SOLICITORS AND THEIR REPRESENTATIVES

Only if a duty solicitor has personally advised the suspect initially on the telephone may he send an accredited representative to the police station. In addition, a solicitor who is not a duty solicitor can only attend on behalf of the duty solicitor is he has also passed the police station accreditation scheme or is otherwise treated as accredited (*e.g.* a solicitor who was previously a duty solicitor and is deemed to be accredited). The suspect must have been informed of the status of the person attending.

Duty Solicitor Manual, para. 9.4

GCC 2004, Pt B, para. 8.2.12

A duty solicitor's representative may not give advice to a Services person unless that representative is a solicitor in certain circumstances.

GCC 2004, Pt B, para. 8.2.9–11

FREELANCE REPRESENTATIVES

If a freelance representative is to be instructed to give "own solicitor" advice, the solicitor instructing the freelance representative must be satisfied that the representative is competent to do the work, *i.e.* has the necessary skill, knowledge and experience. The representative must be a solicitor or currently registered as a probationary or accredited representative.

GCC 2004, Pt B, para. 3.3

The General Criminal Contract sets out instructions for the use of freelance representatives which if not followed may lead to payment for the police station attendance being refused.

The instructions are as follows:

(a) Before attending the Police station, the representative must have the telephone number of the conducting solicitor (including an out of hours number if appropriate);

GCC 2004, Pt B, para. 3.3

(b) The representative must be able to contact the conducting solicitor (or another solicitor in the firm with sufficient experience of police station work) in case the representative requires guidance as to how to proceed with the case when advising and assisting at the police station;

(c) A written report on the case must be submitted to the conducting solicitor by the representative once the attendance at the police station has concluded and at the latest by the next working day.

The travel time which can be claimed under the General Criminal Contract is limited to 45 minutes each way where a freelance represtentative is used.

GCC 2004, Pt B, para. 3.3

PRACTICAL GUIDANCE

(1) Refusal of access

If an accredited or probationary representative sent to the police station on behalf of a solicitor is refused access or is excluded from the police station, the solicitor should seek confirmation of the reasons for such a refusal or exclusion in writing and consider taking the matter up with an officer of higher rank.

Obviously, once an accredited or probationary representative has been refused access to the police station on one occasion, he may well be refused access in the future.

(2) Police tactics/information to suspect

It is a relatively common police practice to attempt to undermine the authority of the adviser in the police station. If that adviser is a non-solicitor, the police may refer to that fact at the start of or during any interview.

It is essential that, if the adviser is not a solicitor, the suspect be informed of this fact by the adviser when the parties initially meet and before the police interview, as this will reduce or negate the impact of the tactic if employed by the police. Indeed, not to do so is contrary to the General Criminal Contract and Law Society guidance and could be considered deception of the suspect.

GCC 2004, Pt B, para. 8.2.12

If the police do use this tactic, it is without doubt contrary to the spirit of Code C, para. 6.12, if not to its letter, and the solicitor on whose behalf the representative is acting should consider taking the matter up with a higher police authority.

Statements under Caution

THE LAW

The right to make a statement

The police are empowered to accept a written statement under caution from a suspect as well as subjecting him to interview under caution. Such statements must be prepared in the form specified in Annex D of PACE 1984, Code C.

PACE 1984, Code C, para. 12.13
PACE 1984, Code C, para. 12.14

Statements written by the suspect

The suspect should first be invited to write his own statement. The statement should start with one of the following prescribed declarations, depending upon the circumstances.

PACE 1984, Code C, Annex D, para. 1

If the restriction on drawing adverse inference from silence does not apply and the statement is made either;

(a) prior to the suspect being charged with, or informed that he may be prosecuted for, the offence to which the statement relates, or

PACE 1984, Code C, Annex D, para. 2(a)

(b) on the occasion of being charged with, or informed he may be prosecuted for, the offence to which the statement relates.

PACE 1984, Code C, Annex D, para. 3(a)

The following declaration should be written and signed by the suspect before he writes the statement:

> I make this statement of my own free will. I understand that I do not have to say anything but that it may harm my defence if I do not mention when questioned something which I later rely on in court. This statement may be given in evidence.

If the restriction on drawing adverse inferences from silence does apply and the statement is made either;

(a) prior to the suspect being charged with, or informed that he may be prosecuted for, the offence to which the statement relates, or

PACE 1984, Code C, Annex D, para. 2(b)

(b) on the occasion of being charged with, or informed he may be prosecuted for, the offence to which the statement relates.

PACE 1984, Code C,

Annex D, para. 3(b)

The following declaration should be written and signed by the suspect before he writes the statement:

> I make this statement of my own free will. I understand that I do not have to say anything. This statement may be given in evidence.

PACE 1984, Code C, Annex D, para. 4

Once a suspect has been charged with, or informed that he may be prosecuted for, any offence but subsequently asks to make a statement relating to the offence, the following declaration should be written and signed by the suspect before he writes the statement:

> I make this statement of my own free will. I understand that I do not have to say anything. This statement may be given in evidence.

PACE 1984, Code C, Annex D, para. 5

The police officer or other police staff should not prompt the suspect whilst he writes his statement, but they may indicate matters which are material and seek to clarify any ambiguities in the statement.

Statements written by the police

PACE 1984, Code C, Annex D, para. 6

If the suspect does not wish to write the statement himself then a police officer or other police staff shall write it. The statement should start with one of the following prescribed declarations, depending upon the circumstances.

If the restriction on drawing adverse inferences from silence does not apply and the statement is made either:

PACE 1984, Code C, Annex D, para. 7(a)

(a) prior to the suspect being charged with, or informed that he may be prosecuted for, the offence to which the statement relates, or

PACE 1984, Code C, Annex D, para. 8(a)

(b) on the occasion of being charged with, or informed he may be prosecuted for, the offence to which the statement relates.

The suspect should be asked to sign, or make his mark, to the following declaration:

> I (suspect's name), wish to make a statement. I want someone to write down what I say. I understand that I do not have to say anything but that it may harm my defence

> if I do not mention when questioned something which I later rely on in court. This statement may be given in evidence.

If the restriction on drawing adverse inferences from silence does apply and the statement is written either:

(a) prior to the suspect being charged with, or informed that he may be prosecuted for, the offence to which the statement relates, or

PACE 1984, Code C, Annex D, para. 7(b)

(b) on the occasion of being charged or informed he may be prosecuted for the offence to which the statement relates, then the suspect should be asked to sign, or make his mark, to the following declaration:

PACE 1984, Code C, Annex D, para. 8(b)

> I (suspect's name), wish to make a statement. I want someone to write it down what I say. This statement may be given in evidence.

Once a suspect has been charged with, or informed that he may be prosecuted for, any offence but subsequently asks to have a statement written for him relating to the offence, then the suspect should be asked to sign, or make his mark, to the following declaration:

PACE 1984, Code C, Annex D, para. 9

> I (suspect's name), wish to make a statement. I want someone to write it down what I say. This statement may be given in evidence.

The person writing the statement must take down the suspect's exact words. Questions should only be asked if necessary; for example to make the wording more intelligible. Any such questions and their answers must be recorded verbatim in the statement.

PACE 1984, Code C, Annex D, para. 10

At the conclusion of the statement the suspect should read it (or have it read to him), correct it and then sign (or append his "mark" to) this final declaration:

PACE 1984, Code C, Annex D, paras 11–12

> I have read the above statement, and I have been able to correct, alter or add anything I wish. This statement is true. I have made it of my own free will.

PRACTICE AND PROCEDURE

Advantages and admissibility

A statement under caution has the advantage over an interview that potential areas of weakness in the suspect's account cannot be explored by police questioning.

R. v Pearce (1979) 69 Cr.App.R. 365; *R. v Longman* (1988) 88 Cr.App.R. 148

On the other hand, the manner in which the statement is given may affect the weight that a court attaches to it in any future criminal proceedings. In particular, a statement which is solely exculpatory may be held to be inadmissible on the grounds that it is merely "self serving".

Use to avoid adverse comment/inferences

R. v Turner (2004) 1 All E. R. 1025; *R. v Ali* (2001) EWCA Crim. 863; *R v. McGarry* (1999) Crim. L.R. 316

The submission of a statement under caution which deals with all of the pertinent points that are to be relied on in any future criminal proceedings may avoid adverse comments being made or inferences being drawn under s.34 of CJPOA 1994 if the suspect makes a "no comment" interview (refer to the ***Advising the Suspect—Right of Silence*** index heading). In addition, such a statement will provide material for the defence advocate; for example when making a closing speech to the jury.

This use of the statement under caution is commonplace, and there will rarely be any harm in submitting such a statement in cases where the suspect has given clear and unequivocal instructions that he will not be answering questions in interview under any circumstances but does wish to put on the record key aspects of his defence. However, it must always be remembered that the making of a statement does not in itself provide automatic immunity against adverse inferences being drawn and certainly will not if, for example, the statement is incomplete in a key material regard or inconsistent with the suspect's subsequent account at trial.

R. v Knight (2004) 1 W.L.R. 340

How to introduce a statement

If it is felt advisable to tender a written statement under caution then this should be proposed to the police by the adviser. However, the suspect has no right as such to insist upon such a course being followed.

If the police initially refuse to be parties to the preparation of a statement (either by inviting the suspect to write one or offering to write it on his behalf), there is nothing to prevent the adviser from handing in a statement made by or on behalf of the suspect in the appropriate form.

The police will have to accept the statement under their general duty to preserve any material that may be relevant evidence.

Preparation of a statement by the adviser or a 3rd party

Although PACE 1984, Code C refers only to statements written either by the suspect, the police or other police staff, there is no prohibition against them being written by another third party on the suspect's behalf. The declaration which heads a statement which is to be "written by a police officer or other police staff" refers to the suspect's wish to have "someone" write it for them and does not specify that it must be the police or other police staff.

There is therefore no reason why the adviser cannot write the statement if the suspect would like someone else to and either the police are not prepared to do so or it is thought inadvisable to allow them any role in its compilation.

If the adviser is to write the statement on the suspect's behalf, it should follow the same format and include the same opening and closing declarations as for "statements written by the police" (see above).

The adviser must ensure that, whilst he may assist in the preparation of the statement and may personally write it, he must always be acting upon the suspect's instructions. Nothing should be done that involves the adviser in assisting in the preparation of a fictionalised or otherwise inaccurate account.

PRACTICAL GUIDANCE

(1) When to hand in the statement

If a statement under caution is to be used as an alternative to answering questions in interview, the timing of its submission to the police may be critical in maximising the prospects of it preventing adverse comment/inferences being drawn.

The statement can be handed to the police at any point during their investigation; including at the start of an interview, at the end of an interview, when the suspect is charged, or after the suspect has been charged. The preferable option will usually be at the start of the first interview, thus preventing any future police argument that the statement was deliberately tailored only after the detailed police questions were put. However, there may be occasions when a later submission will be the best option.

(2) Further details

For further discussion of the use of statements under caution as a tactic to avoid comment/inferences being drawn when a suspect is to answer "no comment" to questions put in interview, refer to the **Advising the Suspect—The Right of Silence** index heading.

Suspect's Rights

INTRODUCTION

PACE 1984 and its accompanying Codes of Practice provide the suspect with various rights at each stage of the investigative process.

This chapter is not a definitive list of these rights but details those that are of most relevance to the legal adviser assisting a suspect in detention and, when appropriate, should be read together with the specific index headings for suspects who fall into any of the special categories (such as **Juvenile Suspects**, **Terrorist Suspects,** *etc*).

RIGHTS UPON ARREST—THE LAW

PACE 1984, s.28(1), (5); *Wilson v The Chief Constable of Lancashire Constabulary* (2001) 2 W.L.R. 302

A suspect must be informed of the fact that he is under arrest either upon arrest or as soon as is practicable after the arrest. A failure to do so renders the arrest unlawful unless it was not reasonably practicable because the suspect escaped from arrest before the information was given.

PACE 1984, s.28(3)–(5) *Edwards v DPP* (1993) 97 Cr.App.R. 301 *Harbhajan Singh Dhesi v Chief Constable of the West Midlands Police, The Times,* May 9, 2000

A suspect must be informed of the grounds for the arrest either upon arrest or as soon as is practicable after the arrest. A failure to inform the suspect of the grounds will also render the arrest unlawful, subject to the same exception when a suspect escapes from an arrest. The grounds do not necessarily have to be given by the arresting officer.

PACE 1984, s.30A, s.30(1); *R. v Keane* [1992] Crim. L.R. 306

PACE 1984, s.30(10)

If the suspect is arrested away from a police station then he must be taken to a police station as soon as is practicable after the arrest or be granted 'street bail'. This can be delayed if the suspect's presence is needed whilst the police carry out investigations which are reasonably required to be conducted immediately, such as a search of premises or the person.

PACE 1984, s.30(7), (7A)

If a suspect has been arrested but, before he arrives at a police station, the police are satisfied that there are no grounds for continuing the arrest, the suspect must be released immediately.

RIGHTS UPON ARREST—PRACTICE AND PROCEDURE

DPP v Hawkins (1988) 88

If an arrest is unlawful for any reason (which will include a failure to advise the suspect either that he is under arrest or of

Cr.App.R. 166; *Edwards v DPP* (1993) 97 Cr.App.R. 301; *Castorina v Chief Constable of Surrey, The Times*, June 15, 1988

the grounds for it) then any resulting detention of the suspect will also be unlawful.

This may not only give rise to a civil action against the police but also provide the adviser with an argument that the suspect be released immediately on the grounds that any continuing detention will be unlawful.

RIGHTS UPON ARRIVAL AT A POLICE STATION

PACE 1984, Code C, paras 3.1, 3.2

Upon arrival at a police station, a suspect under arrest must be advised by the custody officer orally and in writing of his various rights whilst in detention. These rights are:

(a) to have someone informed of his arrest and detention;

(b) to have access to free legal advice and details of the arrangements for this;

(c) to consult the PACE 1984 Codes of Practice;

(d) to be given a copy of the custody record on leaving police detention or on being taken before a court;

(e) to be given a copy of the caution; and

(f) notification of the suspect's other entitlements whilst in custody (such as the rights to visits, refreshments, washing facilities, *etc*).

PACE 1984, Code C, para. 3.2

The suspect will be asked to sign the custody record in acknowledgement of receipt of these notices and any refusal to sign must be recorded on the custody record.

PACE 1984, Code C, Note for Guidance 3B

These notices should be available in English, Welsh, the main ethnic minority languages and the principal European languages "whenever they are likely to be helpful". Audio versions of the notice should also be made available.

PACE 1984, Code C, para. 3.1

A person attending at a police station voluntarily who is subsequently arrested is entitled to the same oral and written notices at the time of arrest.

The right to have another informed of the detention—the law

PACE 1984, s.56(1)

Upon arrest and arrival at a police station, a suspect is entitled to have one friend or relative (or other person who is known to him or who is likely to take an interest in his welfare) informed of his arrest and detention as soon as is practicable upon the request of the suspect.

This right may be delayed if the suspect has been detained for a serious arrestable offence and an officer of the rank of inspector or above authorises the delay: though any such delay must not exceed 36 hours.

PACE 1984, s.56(2)–(3)

A delay may only be authorised if the officer has reasonable grounds for believing that by letting the nominated person be contacted this will:

PACE 1984, s.56(5) and Code C, Annex B

(a) lead to interference with or harm to either evidence connected with a serious arrestable offence or other persons;

(b) lead to the alerting of other suspects not yet arrested;

(c) hinder the recovery of any property obtained as a result of an offence;

(d) for drug-trafficking offences, hinder the recovery of the suspect's proceeds from drug-trafficking;

(e) for other offences where a confiscation order may be made under CJA 1988, hinder the recovery of the suspect's proceeds from such crime; or

(f) for serious arrestable offences where the officer has reasonable grounds for believing the suspect has benefited from his conduct, hinder the recovery of the value of the property constituting the benefit (for further details of drug-trafficking offences and confiscation orders, refer to the **Financial Interviews** index heading).

PACE 1984, s.56(5A)

When a delay is authorised, the suspect must be advised of the reasons: these must also be noted in the custody record.

PACE 1984, s.56(6)

Once the reasons for delay have ceased to exist, the normal right becomes immediately operative.

PACE 1984, s.56(9)

The right to have another informed of the detention—practice and procedure

If the person first nominated by the suspect is unavailable then up to two **alternatives** can be nominated as of right. Further nominations are allowable at the discretion of the custody officer.

PACE 1984, Code C, para. 5.1

If a friend, relative or other person interested in the suspect's welfare **inquires** of the police **as to the suspect's whereabouts** then he must be given this information subject to the suspect

PACE 1984, Code C, para. 5.5

agreeing and none of the reasons for delay (as defined above) existing.

PACE 1984, Code C, para. 5.4 and Note for Guidance 5B

A suspect may receive **visits** at the custody officer's discretion. As a rule, these should be allowed, subject to sufficient manpower being available to supervise the visit and there being no perceived risk of hindrance of the investigation.

The right to legal advice—the law

PACE 1984, s.58(1), (2) *Brennan v United Kingdom* (2002) 34 E.H.R.R. 507

A suspect who is under arrest and in detention is entitled to consult a solicitor privately at any time upon request. Any such request must be noted in the custody record.

PACE 1984, s.58(4) and Code C, para. 6.5

Once a request has been made, the suspect must be allowed to consult a solicitor as soon as is practicable and the custody officer must "act without delay to secure the provision of such advice".

PACE 1984, s.58(5)–(6)

This right may be delayed if the suspect has been detained for a serious arrestable offence and an officer of the rank of superintendent or above authorises the delay: though such a delay must not exceed 36 hours.

PACE 1984, s.58(8)–(8A) and Code C, Annex B *R. v Alladice* (1988) 87 Cr.App.R. 380

The delay may only be authorised if the officer has reasonable grounds for believing that if a solicitor is contacted, the same risks exist as described in the previous section for justifying the delay of access to another third party. The Court of Appeal has confirmed that such authorisation must only be given in the specified circumstances and that these will be strictly defined.

PACE 1984, s.58(9)

When a delay is authorised, the suspect must be advised of the reasons: these must also be noted in the custody record.

PACE 1984, s.58(11)

Once the reasons for delay have ceased to exist, the normal right becomes immediately operative.

The right to legal advice—practice and procedure

PACE 1984, Code C, para. 3.1

There are various times at which a suspect must be **advised as to his right to free legal advice**. These are:

PACE 1984, Code C, para. 3.5

(a) upon arrival at a police station under arrest;

(b) upon arrest, if already at a police station;

PACE 1984, Code C, para. 11.2

(c) immediately before the beginning or restart of an interview;

PACE 1984, Code C, para. 15.4

(d) before a review of detention;

PACE 1984, Code C, para. 16.4

(e) on being notified of any statement or interview with another after charge or notification of possible prosecution;

(f) before any questioning in the limited circumstances allowed after charge or notification of possible prosecution;

PACE 1984, Code C, para. 16.5

(g) before a request for an intimate sample; and

PACE 1984, Code D, para. 6.3

(h) before an identification parade or group or video identification.

PACE 1984, Code D, para 3.17(ii)

On the first occasion that the suspect is advised of his right to legal advice (usually on arrival at the police station), he should be asked to **sign the custody record** confirming his decision on whether to request such advice. On subsequent occasions, the fact that such **reminders** have been given **should be noted** on the custody record or interview record as appropriate.

PACE 1984, Code C, paras 3.5, 6.5

If, on any of these occasions, the **suspect declines to speak to a solicitor** in person, the officer must point out that he has the right to speak with a solicitor by telephone. The suspect must then be asked if he wishes to do so. If he declines, the officer must ask him the reasons for doing so and **note any reasons** given on either the custody record or interview record, as appropriate.

PACE 1984, Code C, para. 6.5

Once it is clear that a suspect does not wish to speak to a solicitor in person or by phone, he should cease to be asked his reasons.

PACE 1984, Code C, para. 6.5

Once the **suspect has requested legal advice, he cannot be interviewed,** or any current interview be allowed to continue, until he has received such advice. There are a number of exceptions to this rule:

PACE 1984, Code C, para. 6.6

(a) when an officer of the rank of superintendent or above has reasonable grounds for believing that a delay might lead to: interference with or harm to evidence or persons; serious loss of, or damage to, property; the alerting of other people suspected of having committed an offence but not yet arrested for it; or the hindering of the recovery of property obtained from the offence;

PACE 1984, Code C, para 6.6(b), Annex B

(b) when a solicitor has been contacted and has agreed to attend but an officer of the rank of superintendent or above has reasonable grounds for believing that waiting for his arrival will cause unreasonable delay to the investigation;

PACE 1984, Code C, para. 6.6(b)

(c) when the nominated solicitor or solicitor selected from a list cannot be contacted or has previously indicated that

PACE 1984, Code C, para. 6.6(c)

he does not wish to be contacted or has declined to attend and the suspect has declined the use of a duty solicitor: in such circumstances the authority from an officer of the rank of inspector or above must also be obtained;

PACE 1984, Code C, para. 6.6(d); *R. v Hughes* [1988] Crim. L.R. 519

(d) when the suspect changes his mind and confirms either in writing or on tape his wish to be interviewed without legal advice: in such circumstances, authority from an officer of the rank of inspector or above must also be obtained and the full details of events be recorded at the start of the taped or written interview record;

PACE 1984, Code C, Annex B, para. 2(i)

(e) when the suspect is arrested for a serious arrestable offence and the officer of the rank of superintendent or above has reasonable grounds for believing that the suspect has benefited from drug trafficking, and the recovery of the value of the suspect's proceeds from drug trafficking will be hindered by the provision of legal advice; or

PACE 1984, Code C, Annex B, para. 2(ii)

(f) when the suspect is arrested for a serious arrestable offence where a confiscation order may be made under CJA 1988 and the officer has reasonable grounds for believing the suspect has benefited for the offence and the provision of legal advise will hinder the recovery of the suspect's proceeds from such crime (for further details of drug-trafficking offences and confiscation orders, refer to the **Financial Interviews** index heading).

PACE 1984, Code C, para. 6.8

The general embargo against a suspect being interviewed until he has received advice once requested should be read together with the provision that a **suspect be allowed** to have his **solicitor present** during interview.

PACE 1984, Code C, Note for Guidance 6B

The suspect is entitled to request the assistance of the **solicitor of his choice** or of a duty solicitor. The solicitor of choice is defined as including any solicitor from the chosen solicitor's firm; alternatively, the police must provide a **list of solicitors** willing to provide legal advice.

If the first solicitor nominated is unavailable, the suspect is entitled to nominate up to two alternatives as of right. Further nominations may be made at the custody officer's discretion.

These provisions apart, the police must not advise the suspect about any particular firm of solicitors.

PACE 1984, Code C, para. 6.4

The **police are forbidden** to do or say anything at any time which is intended **to dissuade** the suspect from obtaining legal advice and, once a solicitor arrives at a police station, the suspect must be **informed of his arrival** and asked whether he would like to see him (unless it has been determined that one of the grounds for denying access to legal advice applies).

PACE 1984, Code C, para. 6.15

A **"solicitor" is defined** for all purposes under the PACE 1984 Codes of Practice as a solicitor holding a current practising certificate or a Legal Services Commission accredited or probationary representative (refer to the **Solicitors' Representatives** index heading).

PACE 1984, Code C, para. 6.12

The right to legal advice—practical guidance

(a) Privacy

A suspect is entitled to consult a solicitor "privately" at any time. Although this is not defined, the normal meaning of privacy should be applied and, in particular, the suspect's consultation with his legal adviser must be out of the sight and hearing of the police.

PACE 1984, s.58(1)

The PACE 1984 Codes of Practice also specify that when a suspect chooses to consult with a solicitor by phone he should be allowed to do so "in private" unless this is impractical due to the design of the custody area or the location of the phones.

PACE 1984, Code C, Note for Guidance 6J

(b) Representations against denial of access

The police are under no obligation to consider representations regarding any decision they have taken to delay the suspect's access to a solicitor, interested relative, friend or third party.

However, this is not to say that representations should not be made: such representations invariably will and, if necessary, should be put in written form and delivered by hand or facsimile to the custody officer.

Representations should cover any relevant issue which is or may be in dispute, for example:

(a) whether the offence for which the suspect has been detained is indeed a "serious arrestable offence";

(b) whether the suspect has requested access to a solicitor and/or another third party and what has been noted on the custody record in this regard; and

(c) whether any of the strictly defined grounds that may give rise to a reasonable belief that access will adversely affect the investigation can be said to truly exist.

A careful contemporaneous note should be made of all such representations and each and every attempt to gain access. These notes may be relevant to an argument in subsequent proceedings that evidence obtained from the suspect whilst he was held incommunicado is inadmissible.

The right to clinical treatment and attention

PACE 1984, Code C, para. 9.5

The custody officer must ensure a suspect receives appropriate clinical attention as soon as reasonably practicable if the suspect:

(a) appears to be suffering from a physical illness;
(b) is injured;
(c) appears to be suffering from a mental disorder; or
(d) appears to need clinical attention.

PACE 1984, Code C, para. 9.8

If the suspect requests a medical examination in circumstances other than the above then an appropriate health care professional must be called as soon as practicable. The suspect is also entitled to be seen by a medical practitioner of his own choice but at his own expense.

PACE 1984, Code C, paras 9.9–9.12

The custody officer is also responsible for the safe keeping and dispensing of medication properly required by the suspect, in consultation with an appropriate health care professional where appropriate.

The right to rest

PACE 1984, Code C, para. 12.2

In any period of 24 hours, a suspect must be allowed a continuous period of at least eight hours for uninterrupted rest.

This period should normally be at night and must not be interrupted or delayed other than at the request of the suspect or his representative, unless there are reasonable grounds for believing it would:

(a) involve a risk of harm to persons or serious loss of, or damage to, property;
(b) delay unnecessarily the suspect's release from custody; or
(c) otherwise prejudice the outcome of the investigation.

The right to write letters and make telephone calls

PACE 1984, Code C, para. 5.6

A suspect in police custody is entitled to writing materials upon request and the right to speak on the telephone to one person for a reasonable time.

These rights can only be denied if an officer of the rank of inspector or above is satisfied that one of the consequences as defined in Code C, Annex B may result.

PACE 1984, Code C, para. 5.6 and Annex B

The suspect must be advised that any letter or message sent or telephone call made by him may be read or listened to and may be given in evidence. This does not apply to privileged communications with a solicitor.

PACE 1984, Code C, para. 5.7

Other rights during detention

If a suspect is **blind or illiterate**, the custody officer must ensure that the solicitor, relative or appropriate adult is available to assist the suspect in checking documentation. Whenever the suspect is required to sign a document then the person assisting may be asked to sign on his behalf.

PACE 1984, Code C, para. 3.20

A suspect who is a **foreign national** must be advised as to his right to communicate with his high commission, embassy or consulate.

PACE 1984, Code C, paras 3.3, 7.1–7.5

Suspects should be detained in **cells** singly, so far as is practicable. Cells must be adequately heated, clean, ventilated and lit. No additional restraints should be used in locked cells, other than suitable handcuffs when "absolutely necessary".

PACE 1984, Code C, paras 8.1, 8.2

Suspects in detention shall be **visited** every hour, and those who are drunk at least every half hour. A suspect who is drunk should be roused and spoken to on each visit.

PACE 1984, Code C, para. 9.3

Bedding should be of a reasonable standard and in a clean and sanitary condition.

PACE 1984, Code C, para. 8.3

Access to **toilets** and washing facilities must be provided.

PACE 1984, Code C, para. 8.4

If a suspect's clothing is seized then suitable **replacement clothing** must be provided.

PACE 1984, Code C, para. 8.5

At least two light **meals** and one main meal must be offered in any 24-hour period of detention. So far as practicable, meals should be served at "recognised meal times". Special dietary needs or religious beliefs should be accommodated, as far as practicable. The suspect's family or friends may also provide meals but at their own expense.

PACE 1984, Code C, para. 8.6 and Note for Guidance 8B

Drinks should be provided with meals and upon reasonable request between meals.

PACE 1984, Code C, para. 8.6

Brief outdoor **exercise** should be offered daily, as far as it is practicable to do so.

PACE 1984, Code C, para. 8.7

Terrorist Suspects

INTRODUCTION

Many of the provisions introduced by PACE 1984 and its accompanying Codes of Practice, together with the relevant sections of the CJPOA 1994, apply to the investigation of offences and the treatment of suspects arrested under anti-terrorist legislation. Therefore, this section will only deal with the special rules and procedures that apply when the adviser's client is a terrorist suspect.

The special provisions that do apply are governed by the Terrorism Act 2000 as amended by the Anti-Terrorism, Crime and Security Act 2001. This new statutory regime came into force in December 2001.

TA 2000 provides a number exceptional powers to search, arrest, detain and question persons who are suspected of "terrorism". The act defines "terrorism" as the use or threat of "action" designed to influence the government or to intimidate the public for the purpose of advancing a political, religious or ideological cause.

TA 2000, ss 1(1)–(2)

It is important to note that the suspected acts of terrorism could have been committed in another country, or to the detriment of another country's government or its public.

TA 2000, s.1(4)

A "terrorist" is defined as a person who has been concerned in the commission, preparation or instigation of acts of terrorism—including the following specific offences:

TA 2000, s.40(1)

(a) membership or support of an organisation proscribed by TA 2000;
(b) involvement in directing the activities of such an organisation;
(c) any financial support or assistance to such an organisation; and
(d) any weapons training not wholly disassociated with terrorism.

TA 2000, ss 11–12, 15–18, 54, 56

DETENTION, SEARCH AND EXAMINATION AT PORTS OF ENTRY—THE LAW

Special powers exist to detain and examine suspects at a port or in a border area of Great Britain and Northern Ireland.

TA 2000, s.53 and Sch. 7

TA 2000, Sch. 7, para. 1(1)

These powers may be operated by an "examining officer", defined as constables, immigration officers and customs officers acting as immigration officers.

TA 2000, Sch. 7, paras 2(1)–(3) and s.40(1)(b) *R. v Hundal* (2004)2 Cr. App.R. 19

An examining officer may question any person, if he believes that person is entering or leaving Great Britain or Northern Ireland, or travelling by air within one of the two countries, for the purposes of determining whether that person has been concerned in an act of terrorism.

TA 2000, Sch. 7, paras 5, 6, 18

The examining officer may stop any person or vehicle and detain any person in the process of the examination. Once detained, the suspect is obliged to furnish all such information as is required by the examining officer. This is a specific exception to the common law right of silence. It is wider in scope than the provisions of CJPOA 1994, in that it makes it an offence to remain silent, rather than merely allowing an adverse inference to be drawn.

DETENTION, SEARCH AND EXAMINATION AT PORTS OF ENTRY—PRACTICE AND PROCEDURE

TA 2000, Sch. 7, para. 6(4)

Detention for the purposes of examination may not exceed 9 hours, timed from the start of the examination, unless authorised through any other power.

TA 2000, s.41

In order for any extension in the detention period to be authorised, a suspect needs to be arrested under TA 2000 (see **Powers of Arrest** heading below).

TA 2000, Sch. 7, para. 6(3);

TA 2000, Sch. 14, para. 6

Persons detained at port for examination are not treated as being in police detention, and the PACE Codes of Practice do not apply. Their treatment is governed by Pt I of Sch. 8 to TA 2000 (see **Suspect's Rights** heading below). The conduct of the examining officers is governed by para. 6 in Sch. 14 to TA 2000 and the separate Code of Practice for Examining Officers Under the Terrorism Act 2000.

TA 2000, Sch. 7, paras 7–9

An examining officer may search any person or anything recently found in or on any ship, aircraft or vehicle; but only for the purpose of determining whether there are persons or things concerned with terrorism. Any search of the suspect must be conducted by someone of the same sex.

TA 2000, Sch. 7, para. 1(3)

A person detained under these special provisions may be taken in custody to any place where his attendance is required for his examination, establishing his citizenship or arranging for his deportation.

The examining officer is authorised to seize and retain anything obtained from a search which he believes may be useful in criminal proceedings.

TA 2000, Sch. 11, para. 11

A person commits an offence if he wilfully fails to comply with a duty or obstructs a search or investigation under these special provisions.

TA 2000, Sch. 7, para. 18

STOP AND SEARCH OF SUSPECTS—THE LAW

In addition to the right to search suspects detained at a port of entry, there are other specific powers enabling the stop and search of persons suspected of being involved in terrorist activities.

TA 2000, s.43

The most commonly used provision entitles a constable, on the basis of a reasonable suspicion, to stop and search a suspect to ascertain whether he possesses anything which may constitute evidence that he is a terrorist.

TA 2000, s.43(1)

Subject to the appropriate authorisation having been given, further powers exist to stop and search vehicle drivers, their vehicles and their passengers, and to stop a pedestrian and search anything carried by him, in order to prevent acts of terrorism.

TA 2000, ss 44–46

These powers enable any constable to affect a search for articles that could be used in connection with an act of terrorism whether or not "he has any grounds for suspecting the presence of articles of that kind". The geographical scope of the authorisation can be wide; for example extending to the whole London Metropolitan district.

TA 2000, s.45(1)
R. (on application of G) v Metropolitan Police Commissioner, The Times, November, 5, 2003, DC

Any authorisation granted must be submitted to the Secretary of State for him to confirm or alter within 48 hours of the grant.

TA 2000, s.46(4)

STOP AND SEARCH OF SUSPECTS—PRACTICE AND PROCEDURE

Searches under s.43 of TA 2000 must be carried out by a person of the same sex as the suspect.

TA 2000, s.43(3)

Searches under s.44 of TA 2000 may not require a person to remove any item of clothing in public, except for headgear, footwear, an outer coat, a jacket or gloves.

TA 2000, s.45(3)

If searching a person under s.43 of TA 2000, a constable may seize and retain anything that he discovers in the course of a search and which he reasonably suspects may constitute evidence that he is a terrorist. If searching a person under s.44 of TA 2000, a constable may seize and retain only articles he

TA 2000, ss 43(4), 45(2)

reasonably suspects are intended to be used in connection with terrorism.

PACE 1984, Code A, para. 2.1

Searches of persons not detained at port are also subject to the PACE 1984 safeguards, as defined in Code A.

For further details, refer to the **Search of Person** index heading.

SEARCH OF PREMISES AND SEIZURE OF MATERIAL—THE LAW

TA 2000, s.42(1), Sch. 5, para. 1(1)

Special procedures operate under TA 2000 for the issuing of search warrants for premises either occupied by those suspected of certain terrorism offences or where it is believed material exists that relates to a terrorist investigation.

TA 2000, Sch. 5, para. 1(2)

Such warrants authorise the entry and search of premises, the search of any person found on the premises and the seizure of relevant material.

TA 2000, Sch. 5, para. 5

There are particular powers attached to orders issued for discovery of "excluded" or "special procedure" material.

TA 2000, Sch. 5, para. 4; PACE 1984, ss 11, 14

In general terms, "excluded" and "special procedure" material is defined as including records created in the course of any business, human tissue or tissue fluid taken for medical purposes and journalistic material.

TA 2000, Sch. 5, para. 15

In urgent cases of great emergency, a search for "excluded" or "special procedure" material may be authorised by an officer of the rank of superintendent or above, rather than the normal requirement that an order be obtained from a circuit judge.

SEARCH OF PREMISES AND SEIZURE OF MATERIAL—PRACTICE AND PROCEDURE

PACE 1984, ss 15, 16; Code B, Note for Guidance 2A

The PACE 1984 provisions in ss 15 and 16 dealing with the issue and execution of warrants and Code B dealing with the search of premises apply to warrants issued and searches affected under s.42 and Sch. 5 to the TA 2000.

PACE 1984, ss 21, 22; TA 2000, Sch. 5, para. 17

The PACE 1984 provisions in ss 21 and 22 for access to, copying, seizure and retention of property apply in addition to the other provisions specified in TA 2000.

For further details, refer to the **Search of Premises** index heading.

POWERS OF DETENTION AND ARREST

There are two special powers of detention and arrest created by TA 2000.

(a) Detention by an examining officer (Sch. 7)

As detailed above, suspects at a port of entry are liable to detention under Sch. 7 to TA 2000 by an examining officer.

TA 2000, s.53, Sch. 7, para. 2

(b) Arrest on suspicion of terrorism (s.41)

A constable may arrest without warrant a suspect when there are reasonable grounds for suspecting he is a terrorist. A "terrorist" is a person who has committed certain offences or has been concerned in the commission, preparation or instigation of acts of terrorism.

TA 2000, s.41(1)

A constable may search a person detained under s.41 of TA 2000 and retain anything that he discovers in the course of a search and which he reasonably suspects may constitute evidence of that the person is a terrorist. Such a search must be conducted by a person of the same sex as the suspect.

TA 2000, s.43(2)

DETENTION AFTER ARREST—THE LAW

Under TA 2000, a person may be detained for specific purposes in accordance with:

(a) Schedule 7 (detention at a port or border control);
(b) Section 43 (stop and search of the person);
(c) Section 44 (stop and search of a vehicle); and
(d) Section 41 (arrest as a suspected terrorist).

TA 2000, ss 41, 43, 44, Schs 7 and 8

Under Sch. 7 of TA 2000, a suspect may be detained for no more than 9 hours after the start of the examination. Any further detention under TA 2000 must be by way of an authorised arrest in accordance with s.41.

TA 2000, s.41, Sch. 7, para. 6(4)

The Secretary of State shall designate places at which persons may be detained under Sch. 7 and s.41 of TA 2000.

TA 2000, Sch. 8, para. 1(1)

A constable who arrests a person under s.41 of TA 2000 must take that person as soon as practicable to the police station that the constable considers the most appropriate.

TA 2000, Sch. 8, para. 1(4)

A person held under s.41 of TA 2000 must be released after no longer than 48 hours beginning with either his s.41 arrest or the start of his Sch. 7 examination, unless detained under a warrant of further detention or any other power. The release may be delayed pending the conclusion of an application for a warrant of further detention or, if a police officer intends to do so, the making of the application.

TA 2000, s.41(3)

TA 2000, ss 41(5)–(6)

DETENTION AFTER ARREST—PRACTICE AND PROCEDURE

Reviews of detention without warrant

TA 2000, s.41(2)

Detention powers exercised under s.41 of TA 2000 are subject to the rules and procedures laid down in Pt II of Sch. 8 to the Act.

TA 2000, Sch. 8, paras 21(1)–(3), 22

Reviews of the detention must be carried out as soon as practicable after the beginning of detention and thereafter at intervals of no more than 12 hours. Reviews may be postponed if the suspect is being questioned, no review officer is readily available, or it is not practicable for any other reason.

TA 2000, Sch. 8, para. 24

Reviews within the first 24 hours must be by an officer of the rank of inspector or above and thereafter by an officer of the rank of superintendent or above. The reviewing officer must be independent of the investigation.

Continued detention will be authorised only if the reviewing officer is satisfied that it is necessary either:

TA 2000, Sch. 8, paras 23(1)(a)–(f), (4)

(a) to obtain or preserve evidence relevant to the detained person's involvement with acts of terrorism;

(b) pending the decision to apply for a deportation notice, the making or concluding of an application for a deportation notice; or

(c) pending a decision whether the detained person should be charged with an offence.

TA 2000, Sch. 8, paras 24(2)–(3)

In any of the above circumstances, the reviewing officer must also be satisfied that the investigation or consideration is being carried out diligently and expeditiously.

TA 2000, Sch. 8, para. 22

A review may be postponed if an interview is in progress and an interruption of it will prejudice the matter; if no review officer is readily available; or it is not practicable at the time for any other reason. When a review is postponed, it shall carried out as soon as is reasonably practicable.

TA 2000, Sch. 8, para. 26

The suspect or his solicitor is entitled to make representations to the reviewing officer either orally or in writing. A review officer may refuse to hear oral representations from a detained person who he deems unfit to make representations because of his condition or behaviour.

TA 2000, Sch. 8, para. 27

When a reviewing officer authorises continued detention, he must make the detained person aware of his rights to inform someone of his whereabouts and consult a solicitor, if those rights have not been exercised. If either of these rights is being delayed, the reviewing officer must consider whether the reasons for the delay continue to subsist. If he believes the reasons have ceased to exist, he must inform the officer who authorised the delay (unless he was that officer).

The reviewing officer shall make a full written record of the outcome of the review. This should be in the presence of the detained person unless the detainee is incapable of understanding, violent, likely to become violent or in urgent need of medical attention.

TA 2000, Sch. 8, para. 28

Warrants of further detention

Reviews cease to take place once a warrant extending detention has been issued under Pt III of Sch. 8 to TA 2000.

TA 2000, Sch. 8, para. 21(4)

A superintendent may apply to a "judicial authority" for a warrant authorising further detention for a specified period of not more than **7 days** from the suspect's arrest or examination. In England and Wales the appropriate "judicial authority" is the Senior District Judge, his deputy or any other specially designated District Judge.

TA 2000, Sch. 8, para. 29

Such an application must be made during the first 48 from the start of detention, or within the following 6 hours provided the judicial authority considers it was not reasonably practicable to apply earlier.

TA 2000, Sch. 8, para. 30

An application for a warrant may not be heard unless the person to whom it relates has been given notice of the time at which the application was made, when it is to be heard and the grounds upon which further detention is sought.

TA 2000, Sch. 8, para. 31

The judicial authority may issue a warrant only if satisfied that further detention is necessary to obtain or preserve evidence of the detained person's involvement with acts of terrorism (through his questioning or otherwise) and that the investigation is being conducted diligently and expeditiously.

TA 2000, Sch. 8, para. 32

The person to whom an application relates is entitled to be legally represented, even if this necessitates the interruption of an application, and he must be given the opportunity to make oral or written representations to the judicial authority. Such a hearing may be conducted via a live television link or similar device. However, the judicial authority has the right to exclude from any part of the hearing the person to whom the application relates or anyone representing him.

TA 2000, Sch. 8, para. 33

Upon an application for a warrant, the judicial authority may order that specified information be withheld from the detained person or his representative, provided it believes that either:

(a) evidence that the detained person has committed a terrorist offence would be interfered with or harmed;

TA 2000, Sch. 8, paras 34(2)(a–g), 34(3)(a)

(b) the recovery of property obtained as a result of such a terrorist offence, or which could otherwise be forfeit, would be hindered;

(c) the apprehension or conviction of a person suspected of involvement in acts of terrorism would be made more difficult;

(d) the prevention or gathering of information about an act of terrorism would be interfered with;

(e) a person would be interfered with or physically injured; or

(f) the detained person has benefited from his criminal conduct, and the recovery of the benefit, or a comparative value of property, would be compromised by sharing the information with the detained person.

TA 2000, Sch. 8, para. 34(4)

An application that specified information be withheld from the detained person or his representative must itself be made out of the presence of the detained person or his representative.

TA 2000, Sch. 8, para. 36 CJA 2003, s.306

Once a warrant has been granted, an officer of the rank of superintendent or above may apply to a judicial authority for further extensions of the specified period. The same procedural regulations as set out above apply to all such further application and the cumulative total time of all extensions must not exceed **14 days** from the start of the suspect's examination (Sch. 7) or arrest (s.41).

TA 2000, Sch. 8, para. 37

Any person detained by virtue of a warrant must be released immediately if the officer having custody of him becomes aware either: that the detention is not necessary to safeguard evidence of that person's involvement with terrorism; or the investigation is not being conducted diligently and expeditiously.

Once the detention period has ended, the suspect must be released, bailed, charged or made subject to a deportation order.

FINGERPRINTS AND SAMPLES—THE LAW

Fingerprints and non-intimate samples

PACE 1984, s.65(1)

A "non-intimate" sample is a sample of hair (other than pubic hair), a sample of a nail or taken from under a nail, a swab taken of any part of the body including the mouth (but not any other orifice), saliva, or a skin impression.

Fingerprints and non-intimate samples may be taken from the detained person only if either:

(a) they are taken by a constable with "appropriate consent" (see definition below) given in writing; TA 2000, Sch. 8, paras 10(2)(a), (3)(a)

(b) he is detained at a police station and an officer of at least the rank of superintendent authorises the sample; TA 2000, Sch. 8, para. 10(4)(a)

(c) he has been convicted of a recordable offence at any time (in the case of fingerprints) or after April 10, 1995 (in the case of non-intimate samples); or TA 2000, Sch. 8, para. 10(4)(b)

(d) in the case of fingerprints only, the officer is satisfied that the fingerprints will facilitate the ascertainment of that person's identity and the officer reasonably suspects that he person has refused to identify himself truthfully. TA 2000, Sch. 8, paras 10(6A)-(6B)

"Appropriate consent" is defined as the consent of the detained person (if older than 17), the consent of a parent or guardian (if younger than 14), or the consent of both (if between 14 and 17). PACE 1984, s.65(1)

A superintendent may authorise the taking of a sample only if he believes it will assist in confirming or disproving whether the detained person is a terrorist. TA 2000, Sch. 8, para. 6

Intimate samples

An intimate sample is a sample of any body or tissue fluid (blood, semen, urine), pubic hair, a dental impression, or a swab taken from a body orifice other than the mouth. PACE 1984, s.65(1)

An intimate sample may be taken from the detained person only if: TA 2000, Sch. 8, paras 10(5), 13(2)

(a) he is detained at the police station;

(b) the appropriate consent (see definition above) is given in writing;

(c) a police officer of at least the rank of superintendent authorises the sample; and

(d) a constable or medical practitioner (where appropriate) takes the sample.

A superintendent may authorise the taking of a sample only if he believes it will assist in confirming or disproving whether the detained person is a terrorist. TA 2000, Sch. 8, para. 6

FINGERPRINTS AND SAMPLES—PRACTICE AND PROCEDURE

TA 2000, Sch. 8, para. 11(1)

Before any prints or samples are taken from a suspect, he must be informed that they may be used for identification under PACE 1984. In addition he must be given the reason for the sample or print being taken where a non-intimate sample or print is taken with appropriate consent, or where the detained person has been convicted of a recordable offence.

TA 2000, Sch. 8, para. 11(2)

Before any prints or samples are taken on the authority of a superintendent without consent the detained person must be informed that authorisation has been given, the grounds upon which it was given and the nature of the suspected offence.

TA 2000, Sch. 8, para. 12

If two or more non-intimate samples suitable for the same means of analysis were taken from a detained person and have proved insufficient, an intimate sample may be taken at a later time even though that person has been released from detention. The usual procedural safeguards governing the taking of intimate samples will apply.

TA 2000, Sch. 8, para. 13

Where "appropriate consent" to the taking of an intimate sample is refused without good cause, inferences may be drawn from the refusal in any proceedings against that person for an offence.

TA 2000, Sch. 8, para. 14

Prints or samples, or any information derived from them, may be retained or checked against others but only for the purposes of a terrorist investigation or the prevention, detection or prosecution of a criminal offence.

SUSPECTS' RIGHTS

General

TA 2000, Sch. 8 para. 1(6)

Part I of Sch. 8 to TA 2000 regulates the treatment of suspects arrested and detained under the Act's special provisions (*i.e.* detention at a port or border control under Sch. 7 or an arrest on suspicion of being a terrorist under s.41).

PACE 1984, s.67(9)

However, if a suspect is in the detention of an examining officer who is not a police constable then the examining officer must still "have regard to" the relevant PACE 1984 codes.

PACE 1984, Code C, para. 1.11

Once a suspect has been moved to and detained in police custody then the normal procedures as governed by PACE 1984 Code C are applicable in respect of their detention, treatment and questioning; subject to those special provisions described below.

Identification

An authorised person, including a constable or prison officer, may take any steps as may be reasonably necessary for photographing, measuring or otherwise identifying the detained person. This does not include the taking of fingerprints or body samples (for which refer to **Fingerprints and Samples** heading above).

TA 2000, Sch. 8, para. 2

Interviews

When a constable interviews a person detained under TA 2000 within a police station or any other place designated for detention under s.41 of TA 2000, the interview must be audio recorded in accordance with the special Code of Practice on Audio Recordings of Interviews 2001.

TA 2000, Sch. 8, paras 3(1)(a), (2)(b)

TA 2000 provides for codes of practice to be introduced for the video recording of such interviews and the special Code of Practice on Video Recording of Interviews (Northern Ireland) 2003 is now in force.

TA 2000, Sch.8, para. 3(2)

Right to have another informed

A person detained at a police station under TA 2000 has the right, if he so requests, to have one named person informed as soon as is reasonably practicable that he is being detained there. This named person must be a friend, relative, person known to the detained person or person likely to take an interest in his welfare. The right may be exercised again if the detained person is moved between police stations. The right may be delayed for up to 48 hours in certain circumstances (see **Delaying the right to inform someone or consult a solicitor** heading below).

TA 2000, Sch. 8, para. 6

A detained suspect who is not a citizen of the United Kingdom must be informed of his right to communicate at any time with the High Commission, embassy or consulate of his own country, and to have them informed of his whereabouts and the reason for the detention. The exercise of this right may not be delayed.

PACE 1984, Code C, para. 7, Note for Guidance 7A

Access to legal advice

A person detained at a police station under TA 2000 is entitled to consult a solicitor as soon as is practicable and at any time. When such a request for legal advice is made, the time and date must be recorded.

TA 2000, Sch. 8, para. 7

When a solicitor is present at a police station to advise the suspect, an officer of the rank of commander or assistant chief

TA 2000, Sch. 8, para. 9(1)

constable or above may direct that any consultations be in the sight and hearing of a "qualified officer".

TA 2000, Sch. 8, para. 9(4)

A "qualified officer" is a member of the uniformed branch of the same force as the directing officer, but with no connection to the case, and must be of the rank of inspector or above.

TA 2000, Sch. 8, para. 9(3)

Such a direction can only be given when the directing officer has reasonable grounds for believing that any of the reasons for which access to legal advice could be delayed are in existence (see **Delaying the right to inform someone or consult a solicitor** heading below).

R. v Davison (1988) Crim. L.R. 442

It will be very hard for the police to justify a delay in access to a legal representative if another person has already been informed of the detention.

TA 2000, Sch. 8, para. 9(5)

Once the reason for giving the direction has ceased to exist then the normal right to consult in private becomes immediately operative.

Delaying the right to inform someone or consult a solicitor

An officer of the rank of superintendent or above may authorise a delay for up to 48 hours in the suspect's rights to have someone informed of his detention and/or to consult a solicitor. The officer may authorise the delay only if he believes a failure to do so will either:

TA 2000, Sch. 8, paras 8(1)–(5)

(a) interfere with or harm evidence of a serious arrestable offence;

(b) interfere with or physically injure any person;

(c) alert a person suspected of having committed a serious arrestable offence who has not yet been arrested;

(d) lead to interference with the gathering of information about the commission, preparation or instigation of acts of terrorism;

(e) alert a person and thereby make it more difficult to prevent an act of terrorism;

(f) alert a person and thereby make it more difficult to secure a person's apprehension, prosecution or conviction in connection with an act of terrorism;

(g) hinder the recovery of property obtained as a result of a serious arrestable offence or in respect of which a forfeiture order could be made under s.23; or

(h) hinder the recovery of the value of the property constituting the benefit the detained person has benefited from as a result of his criminal conduct.

When a delay is authorised the suspect must be advised of the reasons, which must also be recorded as soon as practicable.

TA 2000, Sch. 8, para. 8(7)

Once the reason for delay has ceased to exist then the normal rights become immediately operative.

TA 2000, Sch. 8, para. 8(8)

PRACTICAL GUIDANCE

(1) Access to a copy of the Terrorism Act 2000

This section only highlights those provisions of TA 2000 which are most likely to give rise to concern for the adviser representing a suspect detained during a terrorism investigation.

If the adviser knows in advance that a suspected terrorist is in detention then he should ensure that he has a current copy of TA 2000 (as amended), the Code of Practice on Audio Recordings of Interviews 2001 and the Code of Practice on Video Recording of Interviews (Northern Ireland) 2003, where appropriate, before leaving for the police station. If the adviser is attending a suspect detained at a port of entry then he will also require the Code of Practice for Examining Officers Under the Terrorism Act 2000.

(2) Need to take particular care

TA 2000, s.39

Advisers should take particular care when dealing with suspects who are subject to a terrorism investigation. It is an offence to disclose any information, which is likely to prejudice the investigation of terrorism or to interfere with any relevant material—if the person disclosing the information knew or had reasonable cause to suspect it could affect a terrorist investigation. While this does not apply to legal advice in connection with actual or contemplated legal proceedings, the adviser could unwittingly become involved in the passing on of a coded message, which subsequently renders him open to an allegation of committing such an offence.

(3) Treatment in accordance with the PACE 1984 Codes of Practice

TA 2000 prescribes very specific circumstances where the normal protections afforded by the PACE 1984 Codes of Practice to persons in police custody, such as private communication with a legal representative, can be lost. However, unless informed of the specific legal authority for any such loss, the adviser should always demand the same treatment for his client as would normally be afforded to suspects in police custody.

(4) Remuneration

GCC 2004, Pt A, para. 2.2.1(c)(iv)

Although a suspect detained for examination under TA 2000, Sch. 7 is technically neither in police custody nor under arrest, legal advice can be given under the General Criminal Contract.

Volunteers

INTRODUCTION

There will be occasions when the adviser is asked to assist a person at a police station who is neither under arrest nor changed with an offence. Such "volunteers" may either be persons from whom the police are seeking assistance or suspects who have yet to be arrested. In the latter case, an arrest has usually been delayed because the police consider that they have insufficient evidence with which to affect an arrest.

However, it may be the case that such evidence does exist but the police are deliberately delaying an arrest in order to postpone the triggering of the "relevant time" which governs the period an arrested suspect can be detained against his will without charge. When a suspect attends a police station voluntarily but is subsequently placed under arrest, the "relevant time" is the time of arrest and not the time of arrival at the police station.

PACE 1984, s.41(2)(c)

FREEDOM TO LEAVE

A volunteer who attends a police station, or any other place where a constable is present, is free to leave that place at any time unless he is placed under arrest.

PACE 1984, s.29(a) and Code C, para. 3.21

A volunteer may remain at a police station indefinitely: the detention time limits applying only to those who are under arrest.

If a volunteer is placed under arrest then he must be immediately informed of this and given details of his rights as for other detainees. Thereafter, the normal PACE 1984 provisions relating to the detention, treatment and questioning of suspects come into operation.

PACE 1984, s.29(b) and Code C, para. 3.21

POLICE TREATMENT OF VOLUNTEERS

The police are under instructions that any volunteer present at their station should be treated with no less consideration than a suspect in detention (*e.g.* by offering refreshments at appropriate times). In particular, volunteers must be allowed to enjoy an absolute right to obtain legal advice or communicate

PACE 1984, Code C, Note for Guidance 1A

with anyone outside of the police station as and when they require.

LEGAL ADVICE

PACE 1984, Code C, para. 3.22

If a volunteer enquires at any time as to his right to legal advice then he should be given a copy of the standard written notice explaining the arrangements for obtaining such advice.

PACE 1984, Code C, para. 6.1 and Note for Guidance 1A

There is no provision to enable the police to delay a volunteer's access to legal advice once this has been requested. Such provisions applying only to suspects in "detention", *i.e.* under arrest.

VOLUNTEERS QUESTIONED UNDER CAUTION

PACE 1984, Code C, para. 10.1

If a volunteer is a suspect and the police wish to conduct an interview or otherwise speak to him in order to obtain evidence, the police must caution the suspect. This situation may arise in the course of questioning if it is the volunteer's previous answers that have given rise to the grounds for now treating him as a suspect.

PACE 1984, Code C, para. 10.1

Even if the volunteer is viewed as a suspect, he need not be cautioned if the questions are for a purpose other than obtaining evidence; for example solely to establish his identity or his ownership of a vehicle.

PACE 1984, Code C, paras 3.21, 10.2

If a suspect is cautioned then he must be reminded that he is not under arrest and is free to leave, and that if he remains he may obtain free and independent legal advice, which includes the right to speak to a solicitor on the telephone. He must then be asked if he wishes to exercise this right.

REMUNERATION

CDS(G)R 2001, regs 2 and 4(j)

The Police Station Advice and Assistance scheme will fund the provision of legal advice to a volunteer at a police station, customs office, or any other place where a constable or customs officer is present, if he is attending for the purpose of assisting with an investigation.

CDS(G)R 2001, reg. 4(i)

The scheme is also available to volunteers who are witnesses in criminal proceedings and require advice regarding self-incrimination.

GCC 2004, Pt B, s.3.5

In all other circumstances remuneration may be available under the freestanding Advice and Assistance scheme, if the volunteer is financially eligible, otherwise he must pay on a private basis

PRACTICAL GUIDANCE

(1) Volunteers unwilling to co-operate

Advisers may be asked to assist a volunteer who is not viewed as a suspect but as someone who has information which could assist the police in their inquiries. Often the volunteer will not wish to assist, maybe because the suspect is a close relative or simply due to a reluctance to "become involved".

Whilst each case must be assessed individually and on its own facts, it may be appropriate to confirm to the volunteer that there is no legal obligation upon him to answer police questions or otherwise provide assistance but that to provide false information deliberately will put him at risk of being prosecuted for wasting police time or attempting to pervert the course of justice.

(2) Suspects yet to be cautioned

It can be extremely difficult when advising a volunteer who is seen as a potential suspect by the police but has yet to be interviewed under caution.

On the one hand, by co-operating voluntarily this may strengthen the police case and lead to a cautioned interview and/or an arrest. On the other hand, a refusal to co-operate will inevitably increase police suspicions and may in itself lead to such a result. There is no straightforward solution to this dilemma.

The adviser should endeavour to obtain as much information as possible from the police, including an indication as to their likely attitude if the volunteer does not assist. Thereafter, full instructions must be taken from the volunteer and the options considered with him. This exercise is similar to, and should be as detailed as, advising an arrested suspect who is about to be interviewed (refer to the **Advising the Suspect—Preparation for Interview** index heading).

If a volunteer continues to hold significant doubts as to whether to co-operate then he should be advised to consider the option of seeking to leave the police station. This will resolve the matter to the extent that he will either be allowed to leave or be arrested. Even in the latter case, there are a number of benefits to be gained: the suspect will now know how he is viewed by the police; his status looses any ambiguity; and the "relevant time" will be triggered, thereby limiting the period he can be further detained and questioned.

Warrants of Further Detention

THE LAW

Periods of detention

Other than those under investigation for terrorism offences, the maximum period a suspect may be detained without charge upon the appropriate police authorisation is 36 hours from the commencement of the "relevant time" (refer to the **Detention Periods and Reviews** index heading).

PACE 1984, s.42(1)(10)

Any further detention will only be lawful when a magistrates' court issues a "warrant of further detention".

Grounds for issue of a warrant

A warrant will only be issued if the court is satisfied that there are reasonable grounds for believing that the suspect's further detention is justified.

PACE 1984, s.43(1)

Legal representation

The suspect is entitled to legal representation before the court and, if necessary, the court shall adjourn the hearing to enable him to obtain such representation. During any such adjournment, the suspect will remain in police detention.

PACE 1984, s.43(3)

Duration and extension of the warrant

A warrant may be for any period, up to a maximum of 36 hours. The period must be stated in the warrant and shall be such period as the court thinks fit, having regard to the evidence placed before it.

PACE 1984, s.43(11)–(12)

Once a warrant has been issued, it may be extended by further application, provided that the extended period of detention does not exceed 36 hours nor end later than 96 hours from the commencement of the "relevant time". Hence, 96 hours is the maximum period a suspect can be detained in police custody without charge.

PACE 1984, s.44(1)–(4)

Unlawful prior detention

A warrant cannot be issued in circumstances where the suspect's prior detention was unlawful; for example because the original arrest was without good reason, or the police decision to detain the suspect beyond 24 hours was made improperly, or the original arrest was itself unlawful.

Re an Application for a Warrant of Further Detention (1988) Crim. L.R. 296

PRACTICE AND PROCEDURE

Time limits

PACE 1984, s.43(5)(a)

A warrant of further detention may normally be applied for at any time before the expiry of 36 hours from the "relevant time".

R. v Slough Justices Ex p. Stirling (1987) Crim. L.R. 576

The time that the application is made is deemed to be the point at which the constable makes the application under oath and commences the giving of evidence.

PACE 1984, s.43(5)(b), (6)

If it is not practicable for the appropriate magistrates' court to sit at the expiry of 36 hours from the "relevant time" but it will sit within the six-hour period thereafter, the application may be made within this 6-hour period. The suspect may be detained in police custody awaiting such an application, although the custody record must be noted with the reasons why a detention beyond the normal 36-hour period is being enforced.

PACE 1984, s.43(7)

Despite the above provision, if an application is made after the expiry of 36 hours from the "relevant time" it will be automatically dismissed if the court is of the view that it would have been reasonable for the police to have made it before the expiry of that period.

PACE 1984, Code C, Note for Guidance 15D

The application should be made between 10 am and 9 pm and, if possible, during normal court hours.

The application

PACE 1984, s.43(1)

Warrants are sought by an application on oath by a constable supported by written information. The information must detail:

PACE 1984, s.43(14)

(a) the nature of the offence for which the suspect was arrested;

(b) the general nature of the evidence on which the suspect was arrested;

(c) what inquiries relating to the offence have been made and what further inquiries are proposed; and

(d) the reasons for believing that the suspect's continued detention is necessary for the further inquiries.

PACE 1984, s.43(2)

The suspect must be provided with a copy of the information prior to the hearing and must be present at the hearing.

PACE 1984, s.45(1)

The court shall consist of two or more justices of the peace (or a District Judge) and shall sit *in camera*.

Grounds for a warrant

A warrant may only be issued or extended if the court is satisfied that there are reasonable grounds for believing that the further detention of the suspect is "justified". Justification will only arise if:

PACE 1984, s.43(1), 44(1)

(a) the suspect's detention without charge is necessary to secure or preserve evidence relating to an offence for which he is under arrest or to obtain such evidence by questioning him; and

(b) an offence for which he is under arrest is a serious arrestable offence; and

PACE 1984, s.43(4)

(c) the investigation is being conducted diligently and expeditiously.

It will be noted that (a) above is the same requirement as that which applies at the time that the suspect's initial detention is authorised by the custody officer; hence the same principles apply in relation to it when making representations to the court as are discussed under the **Detention Periods and Reviews** index heading.

The hearing

The hearing of the application will be in private before the magistrates or District Judge.

The suspect will normally be represented; by a solicitor or barrister with rights of audience.

The police may themselves be represented; if they are, it is usually by a member of the Crown Prosecution Service with rights of audience.

There may be preliminary argument on points of law such as:

(a) whether the suspect's detention has been lawful;

(b) whether the necessary prerequisites have been complied with, such as the provision of the written information to the suspect; and

(c) whether the application has been made within time.

If there are no such points or the points are argued unsuccessfully on behalf of the suspect, the police officer will then make the application by giving evidence on oath.

It is for the police to satisfy the court that proper grounds for the issue of a warrant exist and, once the evidence has been given in chief, the suspect's advocate has the opportunity to cross-examine.

Once the evidence has concluded, closing submissions can be made to the court. On behalf of the suspect, these should include argument as to the period of duration of the warrant, remembering that, whilst the court can authorise a period of further detention of up to 36 hours, this is the maximum period and a shorter length of time is often more appropriate.

The grant of a warrant

PACE 1984, s.43(1)
PACE 1984, s.43(11)–(12)

If the magistrates are satisfied that reasonable grounds for justifying the suspect's further detention exist then a warrant may be issued. The warrant should be for such period as the court thinks fit, having regard to the evidence placed before it, but for no longer than 36 hours.

PACE 1984, s.44(1)–(3)

The warrant may be extended by way of further application(s) but subject to the limits that the suspect's total time in detention without charge be no longer than 96 hours from the commencement of the "relevant time" and that no single extension be for a period of more than 36 hours.

PACE 1984, s.34(2)

A suspect detained under a warrant continues to have his detention "reviewed" and must still be released if the grounds for detention cease to apply even if the warrant has yet to expire.

Refusal of a warrant

PACE 1984, s.43(8)

If the magistrates are not satisfied that reasonable grounds exist then they must either refuse the application or adjourn the hearing until a time no later than 36 hours after the commencement of the "relevant time".

PACE 1984, s.43(9)

If the hearing is adjourned, the suspect can be kept in police custody during the period of the adjournment.

PACE 1984, s.43(7)

If the application is refused, a new application can be made only if relevant evidence has come to light since the refusal.

PRACTICAL GUIDANCE

(1) Advisers without rights of audience

Police station advisers without rights of audience before the magistrates' court must be particularly alert to the possibility of the police seeking a warrant of further detention.

As soon as it becomes clear that an application may be made, the adviser should contact his office and ensure that arrangements are in hand for a qualified (and suitably experienced) solicitor or barrister to be available to attend the court at short notice.

(2) Duty solicitors and remuneration

Under the General Criminal Contract police station duty solicitors are obliged to represent suspects who become subject to an application for a warrant of further detention.

GCC 2004, Pt B, para. 8.2.6(g)

Otherwise, an own solicitor can represent his client under the Contract without having to apply the sufficient benefit test as the suspect is deemed to be in police custody even when appearing before the magistrates.

GCC 2004, Pt A, para. 2.2.1(d), Pt B, para. 2.5.9

(3) Custody records

When a suspect either leaves a police station or is taken before a court, he or his legal adviser is entitled upon request to a copy of the custody record as soon as practicable.

PACE 1984, Code C, para. 2.4A

It is important to insist upon being supplied with such a copy before the hearing of an application for a warrant, as it may reveal that relevant parts of PACE 1984 and/or the Codes of Practice have been breached, rendering the detention unlawful. An unlawful detention automatically prevents the application from succeeding.

(4) Arguments for resisting the police's application

Although the burden rests with the police to establish that the requisite conditions exist to justify a warrant being issued, the suspect's advocate should always be prepared to argue strongly that any one or any combination of the conditions have not been satisfied. For example it may be possible to demonstrate that the investigation has not been conducted "diligently and expeditiously', or that there is no good reason why the police cannot continue with their investigation whilst the suspect is on bail, even if this is to mean a future return to the police station for further interview.

(5) A suspect who has already been charged

Occasions may arise whereby a suspect has been charged with one offence but remains detained by the police under an investigation into other offence(s).

PACE 1984, ss 38(1), 46(1)

In such circumstances, it is not proper for a warrant of further detention to be sought in respect of the outstanding offence(s);

MCA 1980, s.128(7)

rather, the suspect must either be bailed or brought before a magistrates' court in respect of the charged offence. In the latter case, the police may seek a remand in police custody for a period of up to three days, thereby enabling further investigations to continue in relation to the outstanding offence(s).

Appendix 1

Police and Criminal Evidence Act 1984, Codes of Practice Revised Edition (Code A–E with effect August 1, 2004)

POLICE AND CRIMINAL EVIDENCE ACT 1984 (PACE), CODE A: CODE OF PRACTICE FOR THE EXERCISE BY: POLICE OFFICERS OF STATUTORY POWERS OF STOP AND SEARCH POLICE OFFICERS AND POLICE STAFF OF REQUIREMENTS TO RECORD PUBLIC ENCOUNTERS

CONTENTS

Commencement—Transitional Arrangements

This code applies to any search by a police officer which commences after midnight on 31 July 2004.
Recording of public encounters must be implemented in all force areas by 1 April 2005. Prior to that date, it is up to individual forces to decide when they implement paragraphs 4.11 to 4.20 of this Code.

General

This code of practice must be readily available at all police stations for consultation by police officers, police staff, detained persons and members of the public.

The notes for guidance included are not provisions of this code, but are guidance to police officers and others about its application and interpretation. Provisions in the annexes to the code are provisions of this code.

This code governs the exercise by police officers of statutory powers to search a person or a vehicle without first making an arrest. The main stop and search powers to which this code applies are set out in Annex A, but that list should not be regarded as definitive. [See *Note 1*] In addition, it covers requirements on police officers and police staff to record encounters not governed by statutory powers.This code does not apply to:

(a) the powers of stop and search under;
  (i) Aviation Security Act 1982, section 27(2);
  (ii) Police and Criminal Evidence Act 1984, section 6(1) (which relates specifically to powers of constables employed by statutory undertakers on the premises of the statutory undertakers).
(b) searches carried out for the purposes of examination under Schedule 7 to the Terrorism Act 2000 and to which the Code of Practice issued under paragraph 6 of Schedule 14 to the Terrorism Act 2000 applies.

1 Principles governing stop and search

1.1 Powers to stop and search must be used fairly, responsibly, with respect for people being searched and without unlawful discrimination. The Race Relations (Amendment)

Act 2000 makes it unlawful for police officers to discriminate on the grounds of race, colour, ethnic origin, nationality or national origins when using their powers.

1.2 The intrusion on the liberty of the person stopped or searched must be brief and detention for the purposes of a search must take place at or near the location of the stop.

1.3 If these fundamental principles are not observed the use of powers to stop and search may be drawn into question. Failure to use the powers in the proper manner reduces their effectiveness. Stop and search can play an important role in the detection and prevention of crime, and using the powers fairly makes them more effective.

1.4 The primary purpose of stop and search powers is to enable officers to allay or confirm suspicions about individuals without exercising their power of arrest. Officers may be required to justify the use or authorisation of such powers, in relation both to individual searches and the overall pattern of their activity in this regard, to their supervisory officers or in court. Any misuse of the powers is likely to be harmful to policing and lead to mistrust of the police. Officers must also be able to explain their actions to the member of the public searched. The misuse of these powers can lead to disciplinary action.

1.5 An officer must not search a person, even with his or her consent, where no power to search is applicable. Even where a person is prepared to submit to a search voluntarily, the person must not be searched unless the necessary legal power exists, and the search must be in accordance with the relevant power and the provisions of this Code. The only exception, where an officer does not require a specific power, applies to searches of persons entering sports grounds or other premises carried out with their consent given as a condition of entry.

2 Explanation of powers to stop and search

2.1 This code applies to powers of stop and search as follows:

(a) powers which require reasonable grounds for suspicion, before they may be exercised; that articles unlawfully obtained or possessed are being carried, or under Section 43 of the Terrorism Act 2000 that a person is a terrorist;

(b) authorised under section 60 of the Criminal Justice and Public Order Act 1994, based upon a reasonable belief that incidents involving serious violence may take place or that people are carrying dangerous instruments or offensive weapons within any locality in the police area;

(c) authorised under section 44(1) and (2) of the Terrorism Act 2000 based upon a consideration that the exercise of one or both powers is expedient for the prevention of acts of terrorism;

(d) powers to search a person who has not been arrested in the exercise of a power to search premises (see Code B paragraph 2.3a).

Searches requiring reasonable grounds for suspicion

2.2 Reasonable grounds for suspicion depend on the circumstances in each case. There must be an objective basis for that suspicion based on facts, information, and/or intelligence which are relevant to the likelihood of finding an article of a certain kind or, in the case of searches under section 43 of the Terrorism Act 2000, to the likelihood that the person is a terrorist. Reasonable suspicion can never be supported on the basis of personal factors alone without reliable supporting intelligence or information or some specific behaviour by the person concerned. For example, a person's race, age, appearance, or the fact that the person is known to have a previous conviction, cannot be used alone or in combination with each other as the reason for searching that person. Reasonable suspicion cannot be based on generalisations or stereotypical images of certain groups or categories of people as more likely to be involved in criminal activity.

2.3 Reasonable suspicion can sometimes exist without specific information or intelligence and on the basis of some level of generalisation stemming from the behaviour of a person. For example, if an officer encounters someone on the street at night who is obviously trying to hide something, the officer may (depending on the other surrounding circumstances) base such suspicion on the fact that this kind of behaviour is often linked to stolen or prohibited articles being carried. Similarly, for the purposes of section 43 of the Terrorism Act 2000, suspicion that a person is a terrorist may arise from the person's behaviour at or near a location which has been identified as a potential target for terrorists.

2.4 However, reasonable suspicion should normally be linked to accurate and current intelligence or information, such as information describing an article being carried, a suspected offender, or a person who has been seen carrying a type of article known to have been stolen recently from premises in the area. Searches based on accurate and current intelligence or information are more likely to be effective. Targeting searches in a particular area at specified crime problems increases their effectiveness and minimises inconvenience to law-abiding members of the public. It also helps in justifying the use of searches both to those who are searched and to the public. This does not however prevent stop and search powers being exercised in other locations where such powers may be exercised and reasonable suspicion exists.

2.5 Searches are more likely to be effective, legitimate, and secure public confidence when reasonable suspicion is based on a range of factors. The overall use of these powers is more likely to be effective when up to date and accurate intelligence or information is communicated to officers and they are well-informed about local crime patterns.

2.6 Where there is reliable information or intelligence that members of a group or gang habitually carry knives unlawfully or weapons or controlled drugs, and wear a distinctive item of clothing or other means of identification to indicate their membership of the group or gang, that distinctive item of clothing or other means of identification may provide reasonable grounds to stop and search a person. [See *Note 9*]

2.7 A police officer may have reasonable grounds to suspect that a person is in innocent possession of a stolen or prohibited article or other item for which he or she is empowered to search. In that case the officer may stop and search the person even though there would be no power of arrest.

2.8 Under section 43(1) of the Terrorism Act 2000 a constable may stop and search a person whom the officer reasonably suspects to be a terrorist to discover whether the person is in possession of anything which may constitute evidence that the person is a terrorist. These searches may only be carried out by an officer of the same sex as the person searched.

2.9 An officer who has reasonable grounds for suspicion may detain the person concerned in order to carry out a search. Before carrying out a search the officer may ask questions about the person's behaviour or presence in circumstances which gave rise to the suspicion. As a result of questioning the detained person, the reasonable grounds for suspicion necessary to detain that person may be confirmed or, because of a satisfactory explanation, be eliminated. [See *Notes 2* and *3*] Questioning may also reveal reasonable grounds to suspect the possession of a different kind of unlawful article from that originally suspected. Reasonable grounds for suspicion however cannot be provided retrospectively by such questioning during a person's detention or by refusal to answer any questions put.

2.10 If, as a result of questioning before a search, or other circumstances which come to the attention of the officer, there cease to be reasonable grounds for suspecting that an article is being carried of a kind for which there is a power to stop and search, no search may take place. [See *Note 3*] In the absence of any other lawful power to detain, the person is free to leave at will and must be so informed.

2.11 There is no power to stop or detain a person in order to find grounds for a search. Police officers have many encounters with members of the public which do not involve detaining people against their will. If reasonable grounds for suspicion emerge during such an encounter, the officer may search the person, even though no grounds existed when the encounter began. If an officer is detaining someone for the purpose of a search, he or she should inform the person as soon as detention begins.

Searches authorised under section 60 of the Criminal Justice and Public Order Act 1994

2.12 Authority for a constable in uniform to stop and search under section 60 of the Criminal Justice and Public Order Act 1994 may be given if the authorising officer reasonably believes:

(a) that incidents involving serious violence may take place in any locality in the officer's police area, and it is expedient to use these powers to prevent their occurrence, or

(b) that persons are carrying dangerous instruments or offensive weapons without good reason in any locality in the officer's police area.

2.13 An authorisation under Section 60 may only be given by an officer of the rank of inspector or above, in writing, specifying the grounds on which it was given, the locality in which the powers may be exercised and the period of time for which they are in force. The period authorised shall be no longer than appears reasonably necessary to prevent, or seek to prevent incidents of serious violence, or to deal with the problem of carrying dangerous instruments or offensive weapons. It may not exceed 24 hours. [See *Notes 10–13*]

2.14 If an inspector gives an authorisation, he or she must, as soon as practicable, inform an officer of or above the rank of superintendent. This officer may direct that the authorisation shall be extended for a further 24 hours, if violence or the carrying of dangerous instruments or offensive weapons has occurred, or is suspected to have occurred, and the continued use of the powers is considered necessary to prevent or deal with further such activity. That direction must also be given in writing at the time or as soon as practicable afterwards. [See *Note 12*]

Powers to require removal of face coverings

2.15 Section 60AA of the Criminal Justice and Public Order Act 1994 also provides a power to demand the removal of disguises. The officer exercising the power must reasonably believe that someone is wearing an item wholly or mainly for the purpose of concealing identity. There is also a power to seize such items where the officer believes that a person intends to wear them for this purpose. There is no power to stop and search for disguises. An officer may seize any such item which is discovered when exercising a power of search for something else, or which is being carried, and which the officer reasonably believes is intended to be used for concealing anyone's identity. This power can only be used if an authorisation under section 60 or an authorisation under section 60AA is in force.

2.16 Authority for a constable in uniform to require the removal of disguises and to seize them under section 60AA may be given if the authorising officer reasonably believes that activities may take place in any locality in the officer's police area that are likely to involve the commission of offences and it is expedient to use these powers to prevent or control these activities.

2.17 An authorisation under section 60AA may only be given by an officer of the rank of inspector or above, in writing, specifying the grounds on which it was given, the locality in which the powers may be exercised and the period of time for which they are in force. The period authorised shall be no longer than appears reasonably necessary to prevent, or seek to prevent the commission of offences. It may not exceed 24 hours. [See *Notes 10–13*]

2.18 If an inspector gives an authorisation, he or she must, as soon as practicable, inform an officer of or above the rank of superintendent. This officer may direct that the authorisation shall be extended for a further 24 hours, if crimes have been committed, or is suspected to have been committed, and the continued use of the powers is considered necessary to prevent or deal with further such activity. This direction must also be given in writing at the time or as soon as practicable afterwards. [See *Note 12*]

Searches authorised under section 44 of the Terrorism Act 2000

2.19 An officer of the rank of assistant chief constable (or equivalent) or above, may give authority for the following powers of stop and search under section 44 of the Terrorism Act 2000 to be exercised in the whole or part of his or her police area if the officer considers it is expedient for the prevention of acts of terrorism:

(a) under section 44(1) of the Terrorism Act 2000, to give a constable in uniform power to stop and search any vehicle, its driver, any passenger in the vehicle and anything in or on the vehicle or carried by the driver or any passenger; and

(b) under section 44(2) of the Terrorism Act 2000, to give a constable in uniform power to stop and search any pedestrian and anything carried by the pedestrian.

An authorisation under section 44(1) may be combined with one under section 44(2).

2.20 If an authorisation is given orally at first, it must be confirmed in writing by the officer who gave it as soon as reasonably practicable.

2.21 When giving an authorisation, the officer must specify the geographical area in which the power may be used, and the time and date that the authorisation ends (up to a maximum of 28 days from the time the authorisation was given). [See *Notes 12* and *13*]

2.22 The officer giving an authorisation under section 44(1) or (2) must cause the Secretary of State to be informed, as soon as reasonably practicable, that such an authorisation has been given. An authorisation which is not confirmed by the Secretary of State within 48 hours of its having been given, shall have effect up until the end of that 48 hour period or the end of the period specified in the authorisation (whichever is the earlier). [See *Note 14*]

2.23 Following notification of the authorisation, the Secretary of State may:
- (i) cancel the authorisation with immediate effect or with effect from such other time as he or she may direct;
- (ii) confirm it but for a shorter period than that specified in the authorisation; or
- (iii) confirm the authorisation as given.

2.24 When an authorisation under section 44 is given, a constable in uniform may exercise the powers:
- (a) only for the purpose of searching for articles of a kind which could be used in connection with terrorism (see paragraph 2.25);
- (b) whether or not there are any grounds for suspecting the presence of such articles.

2.24A When a Community Support Officer on duty and in uniform has been conferred powers under Section 44 of the Terrorism Act 2000 by a Chief Officer of their force, the exercise of this power must comply with the requirements of this Code of Practice, including the recording requirements.

2.25 The selection of persons stopped under section 44 of Terrorism Act 2000 should reflect an objective assessment of the threat posed by the various terrorist groups active in Great Britain. The powers must not be used to stop and search for reasons unconnected with terrorism. Officers must take particular care not to discriminate against members of minority ethnic groups in the exercise of these powers. There may be circumstances, however, where it is appropriate for officers to take account of a person's ethnic origin in selecting persons to be stopped in response to a specific terrorist threat (for example, some international terrorist groups are associated with particular ethnic identities). [See *Notes 12* and *13*]

2.26 The powers under sections 43 and 44 of the Terrorism Act 2000 allow a constable to search only for articles which could be used for terrorist purposes. However, this would not prevent a search being carried out under other powers if, in the course of exercising these powers, the officer formed reasonable grounds for suspicion.

Powers to search in the exercise of a power to search premises

2.27 The following powers to search premises also authorise the search of a person, not under arrest, who is found on the premises during the course of the search:
- (a) section 139B of the Criminal Justice Act 1988 under which a constable may enter school premises and search the premises and any person on those premises for any bladed or pointed article or offensive weapon; and
- (b) under a warrant issued under section section 23(3) of the Misuse of Drugs Act 1971 to search premises for drugs or documents but only if the warrant specifically authorises the search of persons found on the premises.

2.28 Before the power under section 139B of the Criminal Justice Act 1988 may be exercised, the constable must have reasonable grounds to believe that an offence under section 139A of the Criminal Justice Act 1988 (having a bladed or pointed article or offensive weapon on school premises) has been or is being committed. A warrant to search premises and persons found therein may be issued under section section 23(3) of the Misuse of Drugs Act 1971 if there are reasonable grounds to suspect that controlled drugs or certain documents are in the possession of a person on the premises.

2.29 The powers in paragraph 2.27(a) or (b) do not require prior specific grounds to suspect that the person to be searched is in possession of an item for which there is an existing power to search. However, it is still necessary to ensure that the selection and treatment of those searched under these powers is based upon objective factors connected with the search of the premises, and not upon personal prejudice.

3 Conduct of searches

3.1 All stops and searches must be carried out with courtesy, consideration and respect for the person concerned. This has a significant impact on public confidence in the police. Every reasonable effort must be made to minimise the embarrassment that a person being searched may experience. [See *Note 4*]

3.2 The co-operation of the person to be searched must be sought in every case, even if the person initially objects to the search. A forcible search may be made only if it has been established that the person is unwilling to co-operate or resists. Reasonable force may be used as a last resort if necessary to conduct a search or to detain a person or vehicle for the purposes of a search.

3.3 The length of time for which a person or vehicle may be detained must be reasonable and kept to a minimum. Where the exercise of the power requires reasonable suspicion, the thoroughness and extent of a search must depend on what is suspected of being carried, and by whom. If the suspicion relates to a particular article which is seen to be slipped into a person's pocket, then, in the absence of other grounds for suspicion or an opportunity for the article to be moved elsewhere, the search must be confined to that pocket. In the case of a small article which can readily be concealed, such as a drug, and which might be concealed anywhere on the person, a more extensive search may be necessary. In the case of searches mentioned in paragraph 2.1(b), (c), and (d), which do not require reasonable grounds for suspicion, officers may make any reasonable search to look for items for which they are empowered to search. [See *Note 5*]

3.4 The search must be carried out at or near the place where the person or vehicle was first detained. [See *Note 6*]

3.5 There is no power to require a person to remove any clothing in public other than an outer coat, jacket or gloves except under section 45(3) of the Terrorism Act 2000 (which empowers a constable conducting a search under section 44(1) or 44(2) of that Act to require a person to remove headgear and footwear in public) and under section 60AA of the Criminal Justice and Public Order Act 1994 (which empowers a constable to require a person to remove any item worn to conceal identity). [See *Notes 4* and *6*] A search in public of a person's clothing which has not been removed must be restricted to superficial examination of outer garments. This does not, however, prevent an officer from placing his or her hand inside the pockets of the outer clothing, or feeling round the inside of collars, socks and shoes if this is reasonably necessary in the circumstances to look for the object of the search or to remove and examine any item reasonably suspected to be the object of the search. For the same reasons, subject to the restrictions on the removal of headgear, a person's hair may also be searched in public (see paragraphs 3.1 and 3.3).

3.6 Where on reasonable grounds it is considered necessary to conduct a more thorough search (*e.g.* by requiring a person to take off a T-shirt), this must be done out of public view, for example, in a police van unless paragraph 3.7 applies, or police station if there is one nearby. [See *Note 6*] Any search involving the removal of more than an outer coat, jacket, gloves, headgear or footwear, or any other item concealing identity, may only be made by an officer of the same sex as the person searched and may not be made in the presence of anyone of the opposite sex unless the person being searched specifically requests it. [See *Notes 4, 7* and *8*]

3.7 Searches involving exposure of intimate parts of the body must not be conducted as a routine extension of a less thorough search, simply because nothing is found in the course of the initial search. Searches involving exposure of intimate parts of the body may be carried out only at a nearby police station or other nearby location which is out of public view (but not a police vehicle). These searches must be conducted in accordance with paragraph 11 of Annex A to Code C except that an intimate search mentioned in paragraph 11(f) of Annex A to Code C may not be authorised or carried out under any stop and search powers. The other provisions of Code C do not apply to the conduct and recording of searches of persons detained at police stations in the exercise of stop and search powers. [See *Note 7*]

Steps to be taken prior to a search

3.8 Before any search of a detained person or attended vehicle takes place the officer must take reasonable steps to give the person to be searched or in charge of the vehicle the following information:

- (a) that they are being detained for the purposes of a search
- (b) the officer's name (except in the case of enquiries linked to the investigation of terrorism, or otherwise where the officer reasonably believes that giving his or her name might put him or her in danger, in which case a warrant or other identification number shall be given) and the name of the police station to which the officer is attached;
- (c) the legal search power which is being exercised; and
- (d) a clear explanation of:
    - (i) the purpose of the search in terms of the article or articles for which there is a power to search; and
    - (ii) in the case of powers requiring reasonable suspicion (see paragraph 2.1(a)), the grounds for that suspicion; or
    - (iii) in the case of powers which do not require reasonable suspicion (see paragraph 2.1(b), and (c)), the nature of the power and of any necessary authorisation and the fact that it has been given.

3.9 Officers not in uniform must show their warrant cards. Stops and searches under the powers mentioned in paragraphs 2.1(b), and (c) may be undertaken only by a constable in uniform.

3.10 Before the search takes place the officer must inform the person (or the owner or person in charge of the vehicle that is to be searched) of his or her entitlement to a copy of the record of the search, including his entitlement to a record of the search if an application is made within 12 months, if it is wholly impracticable to make a record at the time. If a record is not made at the time the person should also be told how a copy can be obtained (see section 4). The person should also be given information about police powers to stop and search and the individual's rights in these circumstances.

3.11 If the person to be searched, or in charge of a vehicle to be searched, does not appear to understand what is being said, or there is any doubt about the person's ability to understand English, the officer must take reasonable steps to bring information regarding the person's rights and any relevant provisions of this Code to his or her attention. If the person is deaf or cannot understand English and is accompanied by someone, then the officer must try to establish whether that person can interpret or otherwise help the officer to give the required information.

4 Recording requirements

4.1 An officer who has carried out a search in the exercise of any power to which this Code applies, must make a record of it at the time, unless there are exceptional circumstances which would make this wholly impracticable (*e.g.* in situations involving public disorder or when the officer's presence is urgently required elsewhere). If a record is not made at the time, the officer must do so as soon as practicable afterwards. There may be situations in which it is not practicable to obtain the information necessary to complete a record, but the officer should make every reasonable effort to do so.

4.2 A copy of a record made at the time must be given immediately to the person who has been searched. The officer must ask for the name, address and date of birth of the person searched, but there is no obligation on a person to provide these details and no power of detention if the person is unwilling to do so.

4.3 The following information must always be included in the record of a search even if the person does not wish to provide any personal details:

- (i) the name of the person searched, or (if it is withheld) a description;
- (ii) a note of the person's self-defined ethnic background; [See *Note 18*]
- (iii) when a vehicle is searched, its registration number; [See *Note 17*]
- (iv) the date, time, and place that the person or vehicle was first detained;
- (v) the date, time and place the person or vehicle was searched (if different from (iv));
- (vi) the purpose of the search;
- (vii) the grounds for making it, or in the case of those searches mentioned in paragraph 2.1(b) and (c), the nature of the power and of any necessary authorisation and the fact that it has been given; [See *Note 17*]
- (viii) its outcome (*e.g.* arrest or no further action);
- (ix) a note of any injury or damage to property resulting from it;
- (x) subject to paragraph 3.8(a), the identity of the officer making the search. [See *Note 15*]

4.4 Nothing in paragraph 4.3 (x) requires the names of police officers to be shown on the search record or any other record required to be made under this code in the case of enquiries linked to the investigation of terrorism or otherwise where an officer reasonably believes that recording names might endanger the officers. In such cases the record must show the officers' warrant or other identification number and duty station.

4.5 A record is required for each person and each vehicle searched. However, if a person is in a vehicle and both are searched, and the object and grounds of the search are the same, only one record need be completed. If more than one person in a vehicle is searched, separate records for each search of a person must be made. If only a vehicle is searched, the name of the driver and his or her self-defined ethnic background must be recorded, unless the vehicle is unattended.

4.6 The record of the grounds for making a search must, briefly but informatively, explain the reason for suspecting the person concerned, by reference to the person's behaviour and/or other circumstances.

4.7 Where officers detain an individual with a view to performing a search, but the search is not carried out due to the grounds for suspicion being eliminated as a result of questioning the person detained, a record must still be made in accordance with the procedure outlined above.

4.8 After searching an unattended vehicle, or anything in or on it, an officer must leave a notice in it (or on it, if things on it have been searched without opening it) recording the fact that it has been searched.

4.9 The notice must include the name of the police station to which the officer concerned is attached and state where a copy of the record of the search may be obtained and where any application for compensation should be directed.

4.10 The vehicle must if practicable be left secure.

Recording of encounters not governed by Statutory Powers

4.11 It is up to individual forces to decide when they implement paragraphs 4.12 to 4.20 of this Code. However, there must be full implementation across every force prior to 1st April 2005. Consequently, if an officer requests a person in a public place to account for themselves prior to 1st April 2005 and in an area where the force has not at that time implemented these provisions, no record will be completed.

4.12 When an officer requests a person in a public place to account for themselves, *i.e.* their actions, behaviour, presence in an area or possession of anything, a record of the encounter must be completed at the time and a copy given to the person who has been questioned. The record must identify the name of the officer who has made the stop and conducted the encounter. This does not apply under the exceptional circumstances outlined in paragraph 4.1 of this code.

4.13 This requirement does not apply to general conversations such as when giving directions to a place, or when seeking witnesses. It also does not include occasions on which an officer is seeking general information or questioning people to establish background to incidents which have required officers to intervene to keep the peace or resolve a dispute.

4.14 When stopping a person in a vehicle, a separate record need not be completed when an HORT/1 form, a Vehicle Defect Rectification Scheme Notice, or an Endorsable Fixed Penalty ticket is issued. It also does not apply when a specimen of breath is required under Section 6 of the Road Traffic Act 1988.

4.15 Officers must inform the person of their entitlement to a copy of a record of the encounter.

4.16 The provisions of paragraph 4.4 of this code apply equally when the encounters described in 4.12 and 4.13 are recorded.

4.17 The following information must be included in the record

- (i) the date, time and place of the encounter;
- (ii) if the person is in a vehicle, the registration number;
- (iii) the reason why the officer questioned that person; [See *Note 18*]
- (iv) a note of the person's self-defined ethnic background; [See *Note 19*]
- (v) the outcome of the encounter.

4.18 There is no power to require the person questioned to provide personal details. If a person refuses to give their self-defined ethnic background, a form must still be completed, which includes a description of the person's ethnic background. [See *Note 19*]

4.19 A record of an encounter must always be made when a person requests it, regardless of whether the officer considers that the criteria set out in 4.12 have been met. If the form was requested when the officer does not believe the criteria were met, this should be recorded on the form.

4.20 All references to officers in this section include police staff designated as Community Support Officers under section 38 of the Police Reform Act 2002.

5 Monitoring and supervising the use of stop and search powers

5.1 Supervising officers must monitor the use of stop and search powers and should consider in particular whether there is any evidence that they are being exercised on the basis of stereotyped images or inappropriate generalisations. Supervising officers should satisfy themselves that the practice of officers under their supervision in stopping, searching and recording is fully in accordance with this Code. Supervisors must also examine whether the records reveal any trends or patterns which give cause for concern, and if so take appropriate action to address this

5.2 Senior officers with area or force-wide responsibilities must also monitor the broader use of stop and search powers and, where necessary, take action at the relevant level.

5.3 Supervision and monitoring must be supported by the compilation of comprehensive statistical records of stops and searches at force, area and local level. Any apparently disproportionate use of the powers by particular officers or groups of officers or in relation to specific sections of the community should be identified and investigated.

5.4 In order to promote public confidence in the use of the powers, forces in consultation with police authorities must make arrangements for the records to be scrutinised by representatives of the community, and to explain the use of the powers at a local level. [See *Note 19*].

Notes for Guidance

Officers exercising stop and search powers

1 This code does not affect the ability of an officer to speak to or question a person in the ordinary course of the officer's duties without detaining the person or exercising any element of compulsion. It is not the purpose of the code to prohibit such encounters between the police and the community with the co-operation of the person concerned and neither does it affect the principle that all citizens have a duty to help police officers to prevent crime and discover offenders. This is a civic rather than a legal duty; but when a police officer is trying to discover whether, or by whom, an offence has been committed he or she may question any person from whom useful information might be obtained, subject to the restrictions imposed by Code C. A person's unwillingness to reply does not alter this entitlement, but in the absence of a power to arrest, or to detain in order to search, the person is free to leave at will and cannot be compelled to remain with the officer.

2 In some circumstances preparatory questioning may be unnecessary, but in general a brief conversation or exchange will be desirable not only as a means of avoiding unsuccessful

searches, but to explain the grounds for the stop/search, to gain co-operation and reduce any tension there might be surrounding the stop/search.

3 Where a person is lawfully detained for the purpose of a search, but no search in the event takes place, the detention will not thereby have been rendered unlawful.

4 Many people customarily cover their heads or faces for religious reasons—for example, Muslim women, Sikh men, Sikh or Hindu women, or Rastarfarian men or women. A police officer cannot order the removal of a head or face covering except where there is reason to believe that the item is being worn by the individual wholly or mainly for the purpose of disguising identity, not simply because it disguises identity. Where there may be religious sensitivities about ordering the removal of such an item, the officer should permit the item to be removed out of public view. Where practicable, the item should be removed in the presence of an officer of the same sex as the person and out of sight of anyone of the opposite sex.

5 A search of a person in public should be completed as soon as possible.

6 A person may be detained under a stop and search power at a place other than where the person was first detained, only if that place, be it a police station or elsewhere, is nearby. Such a place should be located within a reasonable travelling distance using whatever mode of travel (on foot or by car) is appropriate. This applies to all searches under stop and search powers, whether or not they involve the removal of clothing or exposure of intimate parts of the body (see paragraphs 3.6 and 3.7) or take place in or out of public view. It means, for example, that a search under the stop and search power in section 23 of the Misuse of Drugs Act 1971 which involves the compulsory removal of more than a person's outer coat, jacket or gloves cannot be carried out unless a place which is both nearby the place they were first detained and out of public view, is available. If a search involves exposure of intimate parts of the body and a police station is not nearby, particular care must be taken to ensure that the location is suitable in that it enables the search to be conducted in accordance with the requirements of paragraph 11 of Annex A to Code C.

7 A search in the street itself should be regarded as being in public for the purposes of paragraphs 3.6 and 3.7 above, even though it may be empty at the time a search begins. Although there is no power to require a person to do so, there is nothing to prevent an officer from asking a person voluntarily to remove more than an outer coat, jacket or gloves (and headgear or footwear under section 45(3) of the Terrorism Act 2000) in public.

8 Where there may be religious sensitivities about asking someone to remove headgear using a power under section 45(3) of the Terrorism Act 2000, the police officer should offer to carry out the search out of public view (for example, in a police van or police station if there is one nearby).

9 Other means of identification might include jewellery, insignias, tattoos or other features which are known to identify members of the particular gang or group.

Authorising officers

10 The powers under section 60 are separate from and additional to the normal stop and search powers which require reasonable grounds to suspect an individual of carrying an offensive weapon (or other article). Their overall purpose is to prevent serious violence and the widespread carrying of weapons which might lead to persons being seriously

injured by disarming potential offenders in circumstances where other powers would not be sufficient. They should not therefore be used to replace or circumvent the normal powers for dealing with routine crime problems. The purpose of the powers under section 60AA is to prevent those involved in intimidatory or violent protests using face coverings to disguise identity.

11 Authorisations under section 60 require a reasonable belief on the part of the authorising officer. This must have an objective basis, for example: intelligence or relevant information such as a history of antagonism and violence between particular groups; previous incidents of violence at, or connected with, particular events or locations; a significant increase in knife-point robberies in a limited area; reports that individuals are regularly carrying weapons in a particular locality; or in the case of section 60AA previous incidents of crimes being committed while wearing face coverings to conceal identity.

12 It is for the authorising officer to determine the period of time during which the powers mentioned in paragraph 2.1 (b) and (c) may be exercised. The officer should set the minimum period he or she considers necessary to deal with the risk of violence, the carrying of knives or offensive weapons, or terrorism. A direction to extend the period authorised under the powers mentioned in paragraph 2.1(b) may be given only once. Thereafter further use of the powers requires a new authorisation. There is no provision to extend an authorisation of the powers mentioned in paragraph 2.1(c); further use of the powers requires a new authorisation.

13 It is for the authorising officer to determine the geographical area in which the use of the powers is to be authorised. In doing so the officer may wish to take into account factors such as the nature and venue of the anticipated incident, the number of people who may be in the immediate area of any possible incident, their access to surrounding areas and the anticipated level of violence. The officer should not set a geographical area which is wider than that he or she believes necessary for the purpose of preventing anticipated violence, the carrying of knives or offensive weapons, acts of terrorism, or, in the case of section 60AA, the prevention of commission of offences. It is particularly important to ensure that constables exercising such powers are fully aware of where they may be used. If the area specified is smaller than the whole force area, the officer giving the authorisation should specify either the streets which form the boundary of the area or a divisional boundary within the force area. If the power is to be used in response to a threat or incident that straddles police force areas, an officer from each of the forces concerned will need to give an authorisation.

14 An officer who has authorised the use of powers under section 44 of the Terrorism Act 2000 must take immediate steps to send a copy of the authorisation to the National Joint Unit, Metropolitan Police Special Branch, who will forward it to the Secretary of State. The Secretary of State should be informed of the reasons for the authorisation. The National Joint Unit will inform the force concerned, within 48 hours of the authorisation being made, whether the Secretary of State has confirmed or cancelled or altered the authorisation.

Recording

15 Where a stop and search is conducted by more than one officer the identity of all the officers engaged in the search must be recorded on the record. Nothing prevents an officer who is present but not directly involved in searching from completing the record during the course of the encounter.

16 Where a vehicle has not been allocated a registration number (*e.g.* a rally car or a trials motorbike) that part of the requirement under 4.3(iii) does not apply.

17 It is important for monitoring purposes to specify whether the authority for exercising a stop and search power was given under section 60 of the Criminal Justice and Public Order Act 1994, or under section 44(1) or 44(2) of the Terrorism Act 2000.

18 Officers should record the self-defined ethnicity of every person stopped according to the categories used in the 2001 census question listed in Annex B. Respondents should be asked to select one of the five main categories representing broad ethnic groups and then a more specific cultural background from within this group. The ethnic classification should be coded for recording purposes using the coding system in Annex B. An additional "Not stated" box is available but should not be offered to respondents explicitly. Officers should be aware and explain to members of the public, especially where concerns are raised, that this information is required to obtain a true picture of stop and search activity and to help improve ethnic monitoring, tackle discriminatory practice, and promote effective use of the powers. If the person gives what appears to the officer to be an "incorrect" answer (*e.g.* a person who appears to be white states that they are black), the officer should record the response that has been given. Officers should also record their own perception of the ethnic background of every person stopped and this must be done by using the PNC/Phoenix classification system. If the "Not stated" category is used the reason for this must be recorded on the form.

19 Arrangements for public scrutiny of records should take account of the right to confidentiality of those stopped and searched. Anonymised forms and/or statistics generated from records should be the focus of the examinations by members of the public.

ANNEX A SUMMARY OF MAIN STOP AND SEARCH POWERS

Power	Object of Search	Extent of Search	Where Exercisable
Unlawful articles general			
1. Public Stores Act 1875, s.6	HM Stores stolen or unlawfully obtained	Persons, vehicles and vessels	Anywhere where the constabulary powers are exercisable
2. Firearms Act 1968, s.47	Firearms	Persons and vehicles	A public place, or anywhere in the case of reasonable suspicion of offences of carrying firearms with criminal intent or trespassing with firearms
3. Misuse of Drugs Act 1971, s.23	Controlled drugs	Persons and vehicles	Anywhere
4. Customs and Excise Management Act 1979, s.163	Goods: (a) on which duty has not been paid; (b) being unlawfully removed, imported or exported; (c) otherwise liable to forfeiture to HM Customs and Excise	Vehicles and vessels only	Anywhere
5. Aviation Security Act 1982, s.27(1)	Stolen or unlawfully obtained goods	Airport employees and vehicles carrying airport employees or aircraft or any vehicle in a cargo area whether or not carrying an employee	Any designated airport
6. Police and Criminal Evidence Act 1984, s.1	Stolen goods; articles for use in certain Theft Act offences; offensive weapons, including bladed or sharply-pointed articles (except folding pocket knives with a bladed cutting edge not exceeding 3 inches)	Persons and vehicles	Where there is public access

ANNEX A—*Contd*

Power	**Object of Search**	**Extent of Search**	**Where Exercisable**
	Criminal Damage: Articles made, adapted or intended for use in destroying or damaging property	Persons and vehicles	Where there is public access
Police and Criminal Evidence Act 1984, s.6(3) (by a constable of the United Kingdom Atomic Energy Authority Constabulary in respect of property owned or controlled by British Nuclear Fuels plc	HM Stores (in the form of goods and chattels belonging to British Nuclear Fuels plc)	Persons, vehicles and vessels	Anywhere where the constabulary powers are exercisable
7. Sporting events (Control of Alcohol *etc.*) Act 1985, s.7	Intoxicating liquor	Persons, coaches and trains	Designated sports grounds or coaches and trains travelling to or from a designated sporting event
8. Crossbows Act 1987, s.4	Crossbows or parts of crossbows (except crossbows with a draw weight of less than 1.4 kilograms)	Persons and vehicles	Anywhere except dwellings
9. Criminal Justice Act 1988 s.139B	Offensive weapons, bladed or sharply pointed article	Persons	School premises
Evidence of game and wildlife offences			
10. Poaching Prevention Act 1862, s.2	Game or poaching equipment	Persons and vehicles	A public place
11. Deer Act 1991, s.12	Evidence of offences under the Act	Persons and vehicles	Anywhere except dwellings

ANNEX A—*Contd*

Power	Object of Search	Extent of Search	Where Exercisable
12. Conservation of Seals Act 1970, s.4	Seals or hunting equipment	Vehicles only	Anywhere
13. Badgers Act 1992, s.11	Evidence of offences under the Act	Persons and vehicles	Anywhere
14. Wildlife and Countryside Act 1981, s.19	Evidence of wildlife offences	Persons and vehicles	Anywhere except dwellings
Other			
15. Terrorism Act 2000, s.43	Evidence of liability to arrest under section 14 of the Act	Persons	Anywhere
16. Terrorism Act 2000, s.44(1)	Articles which could be used for a purpose connected with the commission, preparation or instigation of acts of terrorism	Vehicles, driver and passengers	Anywhere within the area or locality authorised under subsection (1)
17. Terrorism Act 2000, s.44(2)	Articles which could be used for a purpose connected with the commission, preparation or instigation of acts of terrorism	Pedestrians	Anywhere within the area of locality authorised
18. Paragraphs 7 and 8 of Schedule 7 to the Terrorism Act 2000	Anything relevant to determining if a person being examined falls within paragraph 2(1)(a) to (c) of Schedule 5	Persons, vehicles, vessels *etc.*	Ports and airports
19. Section 60 Criminal Justice and Public Order Act 1994, as amended by s.8 of the Knives Act 1997	Offensive weapons or dangerous instruments to prevent incidents of serious violence or to deal with the carrying of such items	Persons and vehicles	Anywhere within a locality authorised under subsection (1)

ANNEX B SELF-DEFINED ETHNIC CLASSIFICATION CATEGORIES

White	**W**
A. White—British	W1
B. White—Irish	W2
C. Any other White background	W9
Mixed	**M**
D. White and Black Caribbean	M1
E. White and Black African	M2
F. White and Asian	M3
G. Any other Mixed Background	M9
Asian/Asian—British	**A**
H. Asian—Indian	A1
I. Asian—Pakistani	A2
J. Asian—Bangladeshi	A3
K. Any other Asian background	A9
Black/Black—British	**B**
L. Black—Caribbean	B 1
M. Black African	B 2
N. Any other Black background	B 9
Other	**O**
O. Chinese	O1
P. Any other	O9
Not Stated	**NS**

POLICE AND CRIMINAL EVIDENCE ACT 1984, (PACE) CODE B: CODE OF PRACTICE FOR SEARCHES OF PREMISES BY POLICE OFFICERS AND THE SEIZURE OF PROPERTY FOUND BY POLICE OFFICERS ON PERSONS OR PREMISES

CONTENTS

Commencement—Transitional Arrangements

This Code applies to applications for warrants made after 31 July 2004 and to searches and seizures taking place after midnight on 31 July 2004.

1 Introduction

1.1 This Code of Practice deals with police powers to:

- search premises
- seize and retain property found on premises and persons

1.1A These powers may be used to find:

- property and material relating to a crime
- wanted persons
- children who abscond from local authority accommodation where they have been remanded or committed by a court

1.2 A justice of the peace may issue a search warrant granting powers of entry, search and seizure, *e.g.* warrants to search for stolen property, drugs, firearms and evidence of serious offences. Police also have powers without a search warrant. The main ones provided by the Police and Criminal Evidence Act 1984 (PACE) include powers to search premises:

- to make an arrest
- after an arrest

1.3 The right to privacy and respect for personal property are key principles of the Human Rights Act 1998. Powers of entry, search and seizure should be fully and clearly justified before use because they may significantly interfere with the occupier's privacy. Officers should consider if the necessary objectives can be met by less intrusive means.

1.4 In all cases, police should:

- exercise their powers courteously and with respect for persons and property
- only use reasonable force when this is considered necessary and proportionate to the circumstances

1.5 If the provisions of PACE and this Code are not observed, evidence obtained from a search may be open to question.

2 General

2.1 This Code must be readily available at all police stations for consultation by:

- police officers
- police staff
- detained persons
- members of the public

2.2 The *Notes for Guidance* included are not provisions of this Code.
2.3 This Code applies to searches of premises:

(a) by police for the purposes of an investigation into an alleged offence, with the occupier's consent, other than:
  - routine scene of crime searches;
  - calls to a fire or burglary made by or on behalf of an occupier or searches following the activation of fire or burglar alarms or discovery of insecure premises;
  - searches when *paragraph 5.4* applies;
  - bomb threat calls;

(b) under powers conferred on police officers by PACE, sections 17, 18 and 32;
(c) undertaken in pursuance of search warrants issued to and executed by constables in accordance with PACE, sections 15 and 16. See *Note 2A*;
(d) subject to paragraph *2.6*, under any other power given to police to enter premises with or without a search warrant for any purpose connected with the investigation into an alleged or suspected offence. See *Note 2B*.

For the purposes of this Code, "premises" as defined in PACE, section 23, includes any place, vehicle, vessel, aircraft, hovercraft, tent or movable structure and any offshore installation as defined in the Mineral Workings (Offshore Installations) Act 1971, section 1. See *Note 2D*

2.4 A person who has not been arrested but is searched during a search of premises should be searched in accordance with Code A. See *Note 2C*

2.5 This Code does not apply to the exercise of a statutory power to enter premises or to inspect goods, equipment or procedures if the exercise of that power is not dependent on the existence of grounds for suspecting that an offence may have been committed and the person exercising the power has no reasonable grounds for such suspicion.

2.6 This Code does not affect any directions of a search warrant or order, lawfully executed in England or Wales that any item or evidence seized under that warrant or order be handed over to a police force, court, tribunal, or other authority outside England or Wales. For example, warrants and orders issued in Scotland or Northern Ireland, see *Note 2B(f)* and search warrants issued under the Criminal Justice (International Co-operation) Act 1990, section 7.

2.7 When this Code requires the prior authority or agreement of an officer of at least inspector or superintendent rank, that authority may be given by a sergeant or chief inspector authorised to perform the functions of the higher rank under PACE, section 107.

2.8 Written records required under this Code not made in the search record shall, unless otherwise specified, be made:

- in the recording officer's pocket book ("pocket book" includes any official report book issued to police officers) or
- on forms provided for the purpose

2.9 Nothing in this Code requires the identity of officers, or anyone accompanying them during a search of premises, to be recorded or disclosed:

(a) in the case of enquiries linked to the investigation of terrorism; or
(b) if officers reasonably believe recording or disclosing their names might put them in danger.

In these cases officers should use warrant or other identification numbers and the name of their police station. Police staff should use any identification number provided to them by the police force. See *Note 2E*

2.10 The "officer in charge of the search" means the officer assigned specific duties and responsibilities under this Code. Whenever there is a search of premises to which this Code applies one officer must act as the officer in charge of the search. See *Note 2F*

2.11 In this Code:

(a) "designated person" means a person other than a police officer, designated under the Police Reform Act 2002, Part 4 who has specified powers and duties of police officers conferred or imposed on them;
(b) any reference to a police officer includes a designated person acting in the exercise or performance of the powers and duties conferred or imposed on them by their designation.
(c) a person authorised to accompany police officers or designated persons in the execution of a warrant has the same powers as a constable in the execution of the warrant and the search and seizure of anything related to the warrant. These powers must be exercised in the company and under the supervision of a police officer

2.12 If a power conferred on a designated person:

(a) allows reasonable force to be used when exercised by a police officer, a designated person exercising that power has the same entitlement to use force;
(b) includes power to use force to enter any premises, that power is not exercisable by that designated person except:
    (i) in the company and under the supervision of a police officer; or
    (ii) for the purpose of:
        - saving life or limb; or
        - preventing serious damage to property.

2.13 Designated persons must have regard to any relevant provisions of the Codes of Practice.

Notes for guidance

2A PACE sections 15 and 16 apply to all search warrants issued to and executed by constables under any enactment, *e.g.* search warrants issued by a:

(a) justice of the peace under the:
    - Theft Act 1968, section 26—stolen property;
    - Misuse of Drugs Act 1971, section 23—controlled drugs;

- PACE, section 8—evidence of serious arrestable offence;
- Terrorism Act 2000, Schedule 5, paragraph 1;

(b) circuit judge under the:

- PACE, Schedule 1;
- Terrorism Act 2000, Schedule 5, paragraph 11.

2B Examples of the other powers in paragraph 2.3(d) include:

(a) Road Traffic Act 1988 giving police power to enter premises:

(i) under section 4(7) to:

- arrest a person for driving or being in charge of a vehicle when unfit;

(ii) under section 6(6) to:

- require a person to provide a specimen of breath; or
- arrest a person following:
  - a positive breath test;
  - failure to provide a specimen of breath;

(b) Transport and Works Act 1992, sections 30(3) and 30(4) giving police powers to enter premises mirroring the powers in (a) in relation to specified persons working on transport systems to which the Act applies;

(c) Criminal Justice Act 1988, section 139B giving police power to enter and search school premises for offensive weapons, bladed or pointed articles;

(d) Terrorism Act 2000, Schedule 5, paragraphs 3 and 15 empowering a superintendent in urgent cases to give written authority for police to enter and search premises for the purposes of a terrorist investigation;

(e) Explosives Act 1875, section 73(b) empowering a superintendent to give written authority for police to enter premises, examine and search them for explosives;

(f) search warrants and production orders or the equivalent issued in Scotland or Northern Ireland endorsed under the Summary Jurisdiction (Process) Act 1881 or the Petty Sessions (Ireland) Act 1851 respectively for execution in England and Wales.

2C The Criminal Justice Act 1988, section 139B provides that a constable who has reasonable grounds to believe an offence under the Criminal Justice Act 1988, section 139A has or is being committed may enter school premises and search the premises and any persons on the premises for any bladed or pointed article or offensive weapon. Persons may be searched under a warrant issued under the Misuse of Drugs Act 1971, section 23(3) to search premises for drugs or documents only if the warrant specifically authorises the search of persons on the premises.

2D The Immigration Act 1971, Part III and Schedule 2 gives immigration officers powers to enter and search premises, seize and retain property, with and without a search warrant. These are similar to the powers available to police under search warrants issued by a justice of the peace and without a warrant under PACE, sections 17, 18, 19 and 32 except they only apply to specified offences under the Immigration Act 1971 and immigration control powers. For certain types of investigations and enquiries these powers avoid the need for the Immigration Service to rely on police officers becoming directly involved. When exercising these powers, immigration officers are required by the Immigration and Asylum Act 1999, section 145 to have regard to this Code's corresponding provisions.When immigration officers are dealing with persons or property at police stations, police officers should give appropriate assistance to help them discharge their specific duties and responsibilities.

2E The purpose of paragraph 2.9(b) is to protect those involved in serious organised crime investigations or arrests of particularly violent suspects when there is reliable information that those arrested or their associates may threaten or cause harm to the officers or anyone accompanying them during a search of premises. In cases of doubt, an officer of inspector rank or above should be consulted.

2F For the purposes of paragraph 2.10, the officer in charge of the search should normally be the most senior officer present. Some exceptions are:

(a) a supervising officer who attends or assists at the scene of a premises search may appoint an officer of lower rank as officer in charge of the search if that officer is:
- more conversant with the facts;
- a more appropriate officer to be in charge of the search;

(b) when all officers in a premises search are the same rank. The supervising officer if available must make sure one of them is appointed officer in charge of the search, otherwise the officers themselves must nominate one of their number as the officer in charge;

(c) a senior officer assisting in a specialist role. This officer need not be regarded as having a general supervisory role over the conduct of the search or be appointed or expected to act as the officer in charge of the search.

Except in (c), nothing in this Note diminishes the role and responsibilities of a supervisory officer who is present at the search or knows of a search taking place.

3 Search warrants and production orders

(a) Before making an application

3.1 When information appears to justify an application, the officer must take reasonable steps to check the information is accurate, recent and not provided maliciously or irresponsibly. An application may not be made on the basis of information from an anonymous source if corroboration has not been sought. See *Note 3A*

3.2 The officer shall ascertain as specifically as possible the nature of the articles concerned and their location.

3.3 The officer shall make reasonable enquiries to:

(i) establish if:
- anything is known about the likely occupier of the premises and the nature of the premises themselves;
- the premises have been searched previously and how recently;

(ii) obtain any other relevant information.

3.4 An application:

(a) to a justice of the peace for a search warrant or to a circuit judge for a search warrant or production order under PACE, Schedule 1
must be supported by a signed written authority from an officer of inspector rank or above:
Note: If the case is an urgent application to a justice of the peace and an inspector or above is not readily available, the next most senior officer on duty can give the written authority.

(b) to a circuit judge under the Terrorism Act 2000, Schedule 5 for
- a production order;
- search warrant; or

- an order requiring an explanation of material seized or produced under such a warrant or production order

must be supported by a signed written authority from an officer of superintendent rank or above.

3.5 Except in a case of urgency, if there is reason to believe a search might have an adverse effect on relations between the police and the community, the officer in charge shall consult the local police/community liaison officer:

- before the search; or
- in urgent cases, as soon as practicable after the search

(b) Making an application

3.6 A search warrant application must be supported in writing, specifying:

(a) the enactment under which the application is made, see *Note 2A;*

(b) the premises to be searched;

(c) the object of the search, see *Note 3B;*

(d) the grounds for the application, including, when the purpose of the proposed search is to find evidence of an alleged offence, an indication of how the evidence relates to the investigation;

(e) there are no reasonable grounds to believe the material to be sought, when making application to a:

(i) justice of the peace or a circuit judge, consists of or includes items subject to legal privilege;

(ii) justice of the peace, consists of or includes excluded material or special procedure material;

Note: this does not affect the additional powers of seizure in the Criminal Justice and Police Act 2001, Part 2 covered in paragraph 7.7, see Note 3B;

(f) if applicable, a request for the warrant to authorise a person or persons to accompany the officer who executes the warrant, see *Note 3C.*

3.7 A search warrant application under PACE, Schedule 1, paragraph 12(a), shall if appropriate indicate why it is believed service of notice of an application for a production order may seriously prejudice the investigation. Applications for search warrants under the Terrorism Act 2000, Schedule 5, paragraph 11 must indicate why a production order would not be appropriate.

3.8 If a search warrant application is refused, a further application may not be made for those premises unless supported by additional grounds.

Notes for guidance

3A The identity of an informant need not be disclosed when making an application, but the officer should be prepared to answer any questions the magistrate or judge may have about:

- the accuracy of previous information from that source
- any other related matters

3B The information supporting a search warrant application should be as specific as possible, particularly in relation to the articles or persons being sought and where in the premises it is suspected they may be found.The meaning of “items subject to legal privilege", "special procedure material" and "excluded material" are defined by PACE, sections 10, 11 and 14 respectively.

3C Under PACE, section 16(2), a search warrant may authorise persons other than police officers to accompany the constable who executes the warrant. This includes, *e.g.* any suitably qualified or skilled person or an expert in a particular field whose presence is needed to help accurately identify the material sought or to advise where certain evidence is most likely to be found and how it should be dealt with. It does not give them any right to force entry, but it gives them the right to be on the premises during the search and to search for or seize property without the occupier's permission.

4 Entry without warrant—particular powers

(a) Making an arrest etc

4.1 The conditions under which an officer may enter and search premises without a warrant are set out in PACE, section 17. It should be noted that this section does not create or confer any powers of arrest. See other powers in *Note 2B(a)*.

(b) Search of premises where arrest takes place or the arrested person was immediately before arrest

4.2 The powers of an officer to search premises where that officer arrested a person or where the person was immediately before being arrested are set out in PACE, section 32.

(c) Search of premises occupied or controlled by the arrested person

4.3 The specific powers to search premises occupied or controlled by an arrested person are set out in PACE, section 18. They may not be exercised, except if section 18 (5) applies, unless an officer of inspector rank or above has given written authority. That authority should only be given when the authorising officer is satisfied the necessary grounds exist. If possible the authorising officer should record the authority on the Notice of Powers and Rights and, subject to paragraph 2.9, sign the Notice. The record of the grounds for the search and the nature of the evidence sought as required by section 18(7) of the Act should be made in:

- the custody record if there is one, otherwise
- the officer's pocket book, or
- the search record

5 Search with consent

5.1 Subject to *paragraph 5.4*, if it is proposed to search premises with the consent of a person entitled to grant entry the consent must, if practicable, be given in writing on the Notice of Powers and Rights before the search. The officer must make any necessary enquiries to be satisfied the person is in a position to give such consent. See *Notes 5A* and *5B*

5.2 Before seeking consent the officer in charge of the search shall state the purpose of the proposed search and its extent. This information must be as specific as possible, particularly regarding the articles or persons being sought and the parts of the premises to be searched. The person concerned must be clearly informed they are not obliged to consent and anything seized may be produced in evidence. If at the time the person is not suspected of an offence, the officer shall say this when stating the purpose of the search.

5.3 An officer cannot enter and search or continue to search premises under *paragraph 5.1* if consent is given under duress or withdrawn before the search is completed.

5.4 It is unnecessary to seek consent under *paragraphs 5.1* and *5.2* if this would cause disproportionate inconvenience to the person concerned. See *Note 5C*

Notes for guidance

5A In a lodging house or similar accommodation, every reasonable effort should be made to obtain the consent of the tenant, lodger or occupier. A search should not be made solely on the basis of the landlord's consent unless the tenant, lodger or occupier is unavailable and the matter is urgent.

5B If the intention is to search premises under the authority of a warrant or a power of entry and search without warrant, and the occupier of the premises co-operates in accordance with paragraph 6.4, there is no need to obtain written consent.

5C Paragraph 5.4 is intended to apply when it is reasonable to assume innocent occupiers would agree to, and expect, police to take the proposed action, *e.g.* if:

- a suspect has fled the scene of a crime or to evade arrest and it is necessary quickly to check surrounding gardens and readily accessible places to see if the suspect is hiding
- police have arrested someone in the night after a pursuit and it is necessary to make a brief check of gardens along the pursuit route to see if stolen or incriminating articles have been discarded

6 Searching premises—general considerations

(a) Time of searches

6.1 Searches made under warrant must be made within one calendar month of the date of the warrant's issue.

6.2 Searches must be made at a reasonable hour unless this might frustrate the purpose of the search.

6.3 A warrant authorises an entry on one occasion only. When the extent or complexity of a search mean it is likely to take a long time, the officer in charge of the search may consider using the seize and sift powers referred to in *section 7*.

(b) Entry other than with consent

6.4 The officer in charge of the search shall first try to communicate with the occupier, or any other person entitled to grant access to the premises, explain the authority under which entry is sought and ask the occupier to allow entry, unless:

(i) the search premises are unoccupied;
(ii) the occupier and any other person entitled to grant access are absent;
(iii) there are reasonable grounds for believing that alerting the occupier or any other person entitled to grant access would frustrate the object of the search or endanger officers or other people.

6.5 Unless *sub-paragraph 6.4(iii)* applies, if the premises are occupied the officer, subject to *paragraph 2.9*, shall, before the search begins:

(i) identify him or herself, show their warrant card (if not in uniform) and state the purpose of and grounds for the search;

(ii) identify and introduce any person accompanying the officer on the search (such persons should carry identification for production on request) and briefly describe that person's role in the process.

6.6 Reasonable and proportionate force may be used if necessary to enter premises if the officer in charge of the search is satisfied the premises are those specified in any warrant, or in exercise of the powers described in *paragraphs 4.1* to *4.3*, and if:

(i) the occupier or any other person entitled to grant access has refused entry;
(ii) it is impossible to communicate with the occupier or any other person entitled to grant access; or
(iii) any of the provisions of *paragraph 6.4* apply.

(c) Notice of Powers and Rights

6.7 If an officer conducts a search to which this Code applies the officer shall, unless it is impracticable to do so, provide the occupier with a copy of a Notice in a standard format:

(i) specifying if the search is made under warrant, with consent, or in the exercise of the powers described in *paragraphs 4.1* to *4.3*. Note: the notice format shall provide for authority or consent to be indicated, see *paragraphs 4.3* and *5.1;*
(ii) summarising the extent of the powers of search and seizure conferred by PACE;
(iii) explaining the rights of the occupier, and the owner of the property seized;
(iv) explaining compensation may be payable in appropriate cases for damages caused entering and searching premises, and giving the address to send a compensation application, see *Note 6A;*
(v) stating this Code is available at any police station.

6.8 If the occupier is:

- present, copies of the Notice and warrant shall, if practicable, be given to them before the search begins, unless the officer in charge of the search reasonably believes this would frustrate the object of the search or endanger officers or other people
- not present, copies of the Notice and warrant shall be left in a prominent place on the premises or appropriate part of the premises and endorsed, subject to *paragraph 2.9* with the name of the officer in charge of the search, the date and time of the search

The warrant shall be endorsed to show this has been done.

(d) Conduct of searches

6.9 Premises may be searched only to the extent necessary to achieve the object of the search, having regard to the size and nature of whatever is sought.

6.9A A search may not continue under:

- a warrant's authority once all the things specified in that warrant have been found
- any other power once the object of that search has been achieved

6.9B No search may continue once the officer in charge of the search is satisfied whatever is being sought is not on the premises. See *Note 6B*. This does not prevent a further search of the same premises if additional grounds come to light supporting a further application for a search warrant or exercise or further exercise of another power. For example, when, as a result of new information, it is believed articles previously not found or additional articles are on the premises.

6.10 Searches must be conducted with due consideration for the property and privacy of the occupier and with no more disturbance than necessary. Reasonable force may be used only when necessary and proportionate because the co-operation of the occupier cannot be obtained or is insufficient for the purpose. See *Note 6C*

6.11 A friend, neighbour or other person must be allowed to witness the search if the occupier wishes unless the officer in charge of the search has reasonable grounds for believing the presence of the person asked for would seriously hinder the investigation or endanger officers or other people. A search need not be unreasonably delayed for this purpose. A record of the action taken should be made on the premises search record including the grounds for refusing the occupier's request.

6.12 A person is not required to be cautioned prior to being asked questions that are solely necessary for the purpose of furthering the proper and effective conduct of a search, see Code C, *paragraph 10.1(c)*. For example, questions to discover the occupier of specified premises, to find a key to open a locked drawer or cupboard or to otherwise seek co-operation during the search or to determine if a particular item is liable to be seized.

6.12A If questioning goes beyond what is necessary for the purpose of the exemption in Code C, the exchange is likely to constitute an interview as defined by Code C, *paragraph 11.1A* and would require the associated safeguards included in Code C, *section 10*.

(e) Leaving premises

6.13 If premises have been entered by force, before leaving the officer in charge of the search must make sure they are secure by:

- arranging for the occupier or their agent to be present
- any other appropriate means

(f) Searches under PACE Schedule 1 or the Terrorism Act 2000, Schedule 5

6.14 An officer shall be appointed as the officer in charge of the search, see *paragraph 2.10*, in respect of any search made under a warrant issued under PACE Act 1984, Schedule 1 or the Terrorism Act 2000, Schedule 5. They are responsible for making sure the search is conducted with discretion and in a manner that causes the least possible disruption to any business or other activities carried out on the premises.

6.15 Once the officer in charge of the search is satisfied material may not be taken from the premises without their knowledge, they shall ask for the documents or other records concerned. The officer in charge of the search may also ask to see the index to files held on the premises, and the officers conducting the search may inspect any files which, according to the index, appear to contain the material sought. A more extensive search of the premises may be made only if:

- the person responsible for them refuses to:
  - produce the material sought, or
  - allow access to the index
- it appears the index is:
  - inaccurate, or
  - incomplete
- for any other reason the officer in charge of the search has reasonable grounds for believing such a search is necessary in order to find the material sought

Notes for guidance

6A Whether compensation is appropriate depends on the circumstances in each case. Compensation for damage caused when effecting entry is unlikely to be appropriate if the search was lawful, and the force used can be shown to be reasonable, proportionate and necessary to effect entry. If the wrong premises are searched by mistake everything possible should be done at the earliest opportunity to allay any sense of grievance and there should normally be a strong presumption in favour of paying compensation.

6B It is important that, when possible, all those involved in a search are fully briefed about any powers to be exercised and the extent and limits within which it should be conducted.

6C In all cases the number of officers and other persons involved in executing the warrant should be determined by what is reasonable and necessary according to the particular circumstances.

7 Seizure and retention of property

(a) Seizure

7.1 Subject to *paragraph 7.2*, an officer who is searching any person or premises under any statutory power or with the consent of the occupier may seize anything:

(a) covered by a warrant

(b) the officer has reasonable grounds for believing is evidence of an offence or has been obtained in consequence of the commission of an offence but only if seizure is necessary to prevent the items being concealed, lost, disposed of, altered, damaged, destroyed or tampered with

(c) covered by the powers in the Criminal Justice and Police Act 2001, Part 2 allowing an officer to seize property from persons or premises and retain it for sifting or examination elsewhere

See *Note 7B*

7.2 No item may be seized which an officer has reasonable grounds for believing to be subject to legal privilege, as defined in PACE, section 10, other than under the Criminal Justice and Police Act 2001, Part 2.

7.3 Officers must be aware of the provisions in the Criminal Justice and Police Act 2001, section 59, allowing for applications to a judicial authority for the return of property seized and the subsequent duty to secure in section 60, see *paragraph 7.12(iii)*.

7.4 An officer may decide it is not appropriate to seize property because of an explanation from the person holding it but may nevertheless have reasonable grounds for believing it was obtained in consequence of an offence by some person. In these circumstances, the officer should identify the property to the holder, inform the holder of their suspicions and explain the holder may be liable to civil or criminal proceedings if they dispose of, alter or destroy the property.

7.5 An officer may arrange to photograph, image or copy, any document or other article they have the power to seize in accordance with *paragraph 7.1*. This is subject to specific restrictions on the examination, imaging or copying of certain property seized under the Criminal Justice and Police Act 2001, Part 2. An officer must have regard to their statutory obligation to retain an original document or other article only when a photograph or copy is not sufficient.

7.6 If an officer considers information stored in any electronic form and accessible from the premises could be used in evidence, they may require the information to be produced in a form:

- which can be taken away and in which it is visible and legible; or
- from which it can readily be produced in a visible and legible form

(b) Criminal Justice and Police Act 2001: Specific procedures for seize and sift powers

7.7 The Criminal Justice and Police Act 2001, Part 2 gives officers limited powers to seize property from premises or persons so they can sift or examine it elsewhere. Officers must be careful they only exercise these powers when it is essential and they do not remove any more material than necessary. The removal of large volumes of material, much of which may not ultimately be retainable, may have serious implications for the owners, particularly when they are involved in business or activities such as journalism or the provision of medical services. Officers must carefully consider if removing copies or images of relevant material or data would be a satisfactory alternative to removing originals. When originals are taken, officers must be prepared to facilitate the provision of copies or images for the owners when reasonably practicable. See *Note 7C*

7.8 Property seized under the Criminal Justice and Police Act 2001, sections 50 or 51 must be kept securely and separately from any material seized under other powers. An examination under section 53 to determine which elements may be retained must be carried out at the earliest practicable time, having due regard to the desirability of allowing the person from whom the property was seized, or a person with an interest in the property, an opportunity of being present or represented at the examination.

7.8A All reasonable steps should be taken to accommodate an interested person's request to be present, provided the request is reasonable and subject to the need to prevent harm to, interference with, or unreasonable delay to the investigatory process. If an examination proceeds in the absence of an interested person who asked to attend or their representative, the officer who exercised the relevant seizure power must give that person a written notice of why the examination was carried out in those circumstances. If it is necessary for security reasons or to maintain confidentiality officers may exclude interested persons from decryption or other processes which facilitate the examination but do not form part of it. See *Note 7D*

7.9 It is the responsibility of the officer in charge of the investigation to make sure property is returned in accordance with sections 53 to 55. Material which there is no power to retain must be:

- separated from the rest of the seized property
- returned as soon as reasonably practicable after examination of all the seized property

7.9A Delay is only warranted if very clear and compelling reasons exist, *e.g.* the:

- unavailability of the person to whom the material is to be returned
- need to agree a convenient time to return a large volume of material

7.9B Legally privileged, excluded or special procedure material which cannot be retained must be returned:

- as soon as reasonably practicable
- without waiting for the whole examination

7.9C As set out in section 58, material must be returned to the person from whom it was seized, except when it is clear some other person has a better right to it. See *Note 7E*

7.10 When an officer involved in the investigation has reasonable grounds to believe a person with a relevant interest in property seized under section 50 or 51 intends to make an application under section 59 for the return of any legally privileged, special procedure or excluded material, the officer in charge of the investigation should be informed as soon as practicable and the material seized should be kept secure in accordance with section 61. See *Note 7C*

7.11 The officer in charge of the investigation is responsible for making sure property is properly secured. Securing involves making sure the property is not examined, copied, imaged or put to any other use except at the request, or with the consent, of the applicant or in accordance with the directions of the appropriate judicial authority. Any request, consent or directions must be recorded in writing and signed by both the initiator and the officer in charge of the investigation. See *Notes 7F* and *7G*

7.12 When an officer exercises a power of seizure conferred by sections 50 or 51 they shall provide the occupier of the premises or the person from whom the property is being seized with a written notice:

- (i) specifying what has been seized under the powers conferred by that section;
- (ii) specifying the grounds for those powers;
- (iii) setting out the effect of sections 59 to 61 covering the grounds for a person with a relevant interest in seized property to apply to a judicial authority for its return and the duty of officers to secure property in certain circumstances when an application is made;
- (iv) specifying the name and address of the person to whom:
  - notice of an application to the appropriate judicial authority in respect of any of the seized property must be given;
  - an application may be made to allow attendance at the initial examination of the property.

7.13 If the occupier is not present but there is someone in charge of the premises, the notice shall be given to them. If no suitable person is available, so the notice will easily be found it should either be:

- left in a prominent place on the premises
- attached to the exterior of the premises

(c) Retention

7.14 Subject to *paragraph 7.15*, anything seized in accordance with the above provisions may be retained only for as long as is necessary. It may be retained, among other purposes:

- (i) for use as evidence at a trial for an offence;
- (ii) to facilitate the use in any investigation or proceedings of anything to which it is inextricably linked, see *Note 7H*;
- (iii) for forensic examination or other investigation in connection with an offence;
- (iv) in order to establish its lawful owner when there are reasonable grounds for believing it has been stolen or obtained by the commission of an offence.

7.15 Property shall not be retained under *paragraph 7.14(i), (ii)* or *(iii)* if a copy or image would be sufficient.

(d) Rights of owners etc

7.16 If property is retained, the person who had custody or control of it immediately before seizure must, on request, be provided with a list or description of the property within a reasonable time.

7.17 That person or their representative must be allowed supervised access to the property to examine it or have it photographed or copied, or must be provided with a photograph or copy, in either case within a reasonable time of any request and at their own expense, unless the officer in charge of an investigation has reasonable grounds for believing this would:

(i) prejudice the investigation of any offence or criminal proceedings; or
(ii) lead to the commission of an offence by providing access to unlawful material such as pornography;

A record of the grounds shall be made when access is denied.

Notes for guidance

7A Any person claiming property seized by the police may apply to a magistrates' court under the Police (Property) Act 1897 for its possession and should, if appropriate, be advised of this procedure.

7B The powers of seizure conferred by PACE, sections 18(2) and 19(3) extend to the seizure of the whole premises when it is physically possible to seize and retain the premises in their totality and practical considerations make seizure desirable. For example, police may remove premises such as tents, vehicles or caravans to a police station for the purpose of preserving evidence.

7C Officers should consider reaching agreement with owners and/or other interested parties on the procedures for examining a specific set of property, rather than awaiting the judicial authority's determination. Agreement can sometimes give a quicker and more satisfactory route for all concerned and minimise costs and legal complexities.

7D What constitutes a relevant interest in specific material may depend on the nature of that material and the circumstances in which it is seized. Anyone with a reasonable claim to ownership of the material and anyone entrusted with its safe keeping by the owner should be considered.

7E Requirements to secure and return property apply equally to all copies, images or other material created because of seizure of the original property.

7F The mechanics of securing property vary according to the circumstances; "bagging up", *i.e.* placing material in sealed bags or containers and strict subsequent control of access is the appropriate procedure in many cases.

7G When material is seized under the powers of seizure conferred by PACE, the duty to retain it under the Code of Practice issued under the Criminal Procedure and Investigations Act 1996 is subject to the provisions on retention of seized material in PACE, section 22.

7H Paragraph 7.14 (ii) applies if inextricably linked material is seized under the Criminal Justice and Police Act 2001, sections 50 or 51. Inextricably linked material is material it is not reasonably practicable to separate from other linked material without prejudicing the use of that other material in any investigation or proceedings. For example, it may not be possible to separate items of data held on computer disk without damaging their evidential integrity. Inextricably linked material must not be examined, imaged, copied or used for any purpose other than for proving the source and/or integrity of the linked material.

8 Action after searches

8.1 If premises are searched in circumstances where this Code applies, unless the exceptions in *paragraph 2.3(a)* apply, on arrival at a police station the officer in charge of the search shall make or have made a record of the search, to include:

(i) the address of the searched premises;
(ii) the date, time and duration of the search;
(iii) the authority used for the search:
- if the search was made in exercise of a statutory power to search premises without warrant, the power which was used for the search:
- if the search was made under a warrant or with written consent;
  - a copy of the warrant and the written authority to apply for it, see paragraph 3.4; or
  - the written consent;
- shall be appended to the record or the record shall show the location of the copy warrant or consent.

(iv) subject to *paragraph 2.9*, the names of:
- the officer(s) in charge of the search;
- all other officers and any authorised persons who conducted the search;

(v) the names of any people on the premises if they are known;
(vi) any grounds for refusing the occupier's request to have someone present during the search, see *paragraph 6.11;*
(vii) a list of any articles seized or the location of a list and, if not covered by a warrant, the grounds for their seizure;
(viii) whether force was used, and the reason;
(ix) details of any damage caused during the search, and the circumstances;
(x) if applicable, the reason it was not practicable;
(a) to give the occupier a copy of the Notice of Powers and Rights, see *paragraph 6.7*;
(b) before the search to give the occupier a copy of the Notice, see *paragraph 6.8*;
(xi) when the occupier was not present, the place where copies of the Notice of Powers and Rights and search warrant were left on the premises, see *paragraph 6.8*.

8.2 When premises are searched under warrant, the warrant shall be endorsed to show:

(i) if any articles specified in the warrant were found;
(ii) if any other articles were seized;
(iii) the date and time it was executed;
(iv) subject to *paragraph 2.9*, the names of the officers who executed it and any authorised persons who accompanied them;
(v) if a copy, together with a copy of the Notice of Powers and Rights was:
- handed to the occupier; or
- endorsed as required by *paragraph 6.8*; and left on the premises and where.

8.3 Any warrant shall be returned within one calendar month of its issue, if it was issued by a:

- justice of the peace, to the clerk to the justices for the petty sessions area concerned
- judge, to the appropriate officer of the court concerned

9 Search registers

9.1 A search register will be maintained at each sub-divisional or equivalent police station. All search records required under *paragraph 8.1* shall be made, copied, or referred to in the register. See *Note 9A.*

Note for guidance

9A Paragraph 9.1 also applies to search records made by immigration officers. In these cases, a search register must also be maintained at an immigration office. See also Note 2D.

POLICE AND CRIMINAL EVIDENCE ACT 1984 (PACE), CODE C: CODE OF PRACTICE FOR THE DETENTION, TREATMENT AND QUESTIONING OF PERSONS BY POLICE OFFICERS

CONTENTS

Commencement—Transitional Arrangements

This Code applies to people in police detention after midnight on 31 July 2004, notwithstanding that their period of detention may have commenced before that time.

1 General

1.1 All persons in custody must be dealt with expeditiously, and released as soon as the need for detention no longer applies.

1.1A A custody officer must perform the functions in this Code as soon as practicable. A custody officer will not be in breach of this Code if delay is justifiable and reasonable steps are taken to prevent unnecessary delay. The custody record shall show when a delay has occurred and the reason. See *Note 1H*

1.2 This Code of Practice must be readily available at all police stations for consultation by:

- police officers
- police staff
- detained persons
- members of the public.

1.3 The provisions of this Code:

- include the *Annexes*
- do not include the *Notes for Guidance*.

1.4 If an officer has any suspicion, or is told in good faith, that a person of any age may be mentally disordered or otherwise mentally vulnerable, in the absence of clear evidence to dispel that suspicion, the person shall be treated as such for the purposes of this Code. See *Note 1G*

1.5 If anyone appears to be under 17, they shall be treated as a juvenile for the purposes of this Code in the absence of clear evidence that they are older.

1.6 If a person appears to be blind, seriously visually impaired, deaf, unable to read or speak or has difficulty orally because of a speech impediment, they shall be treated as such for the purposes of this Code in the absence of clear evidence to the contrary.

1.7 "The appropriate adult" means, in the case of a:

(a) juvenile:
  (i) the parent, guardian or, if the juvenile is in local authority or voluntary organisation care, or is otherwise being looked after under the Children Act 1989, a person representing that authority or organisation;
  (ii) a social worker of a local authority social services department;
  (iii) failing these, some other responsible adult aged 18 or over who is not a police officer or employed by the police.

(b) person who is mentally disordered or mentally vulnerable: See *Note 1D*
  (i) a relative, guardian or other person responsible for their care or custody;
  (ii) someone experienced in dealing with mentally disordered or mentally vulnerable people but who is not a police officer or employed by the police;
  (iii) failing these, some other responsible adult aged 18 or over who is not a police officer or employed by the police.

1.8 If this Code requires a person be given certain information, they do not have to be given it if at the time they are incapable of understanding what is said, are violent or may become violent or in urgent need of medical attention, but they must be given it as soon as practicable.

1.9 References to a custody officer include those performing the functions of a custody officer.

1.9A When this Code requires the prior authority or agreement of an officer of at least inspector or superintendent rank, that authority may be given by a sergeant or chief inspector authorised to perform the functions of the higher rank under the Police and Criminal Evidence Act 1984 (PACE), section 107.

1.10 Subject to paragraph 1.12, this Code applies to people in custody at police stations in England and Wales, whether or not they have been arrested, and to those removed to a police station as a place of safety under the Mental Health Act 1983, sections 135 and 136. Section 15 applies solely to people in police detention, *e.g.* those brought to a police station under arrest or arrested at a police station for an offence after going there voluntarily.

1.11 People in police custody include anyone detained under the Terrorism Act 2000, Schedule 8 and section 41, having been taken to a police station after being arrested under the Terrorism Act 2000, section 41. In these cases, reference to an offence in this Code includes the commission, preparation and instigation of acts of terrorism.

1.12 This Code's provisions do not apply to people in custody:

(i) arrested on warrants issued in Scotland by officers under the Criminal Justice and Public Order Act 1994, section 136(2), or arrested or detained without warrant by officers from a police force in Scotland under section 137(2). In these cases, police powers and duties and the person's rights and entitlements whilst at a police station in England or Wales are the same as those in Scotland;

(ii) arrested under the Immigration and Asylum Act 1999, section 142(3) in order to have their fingerprints taken;

(iii) whose detention is authorised by an immigration officer under the Immigration Act 1971;

(iv) who are convicted or remanded prisoners held in police cells on behalf of the Prison Service under the Imprisonment (Temporary Provisions) Act 1980;

(v) detained for examination under the Terrorism Act 2000, Schedule 7 and to whom the Code of Practice issued under that Act, Schedule 14, paragraph 6 applies;

(vi) detained for searches under stop and search powers except as required by Code A.

The provisions on conditions of detention and treatment in sections 8 and 9 must be considered as the minimum standards of treatment for such detainees.

1.13 In this Code:

(a) "designated person" means a person other than a police officer, designated under the Police Reform Act 2002, Pt 4 who has specified powers and duties of police officers conferred or imposed on them;

(b) reference to a police officer includes a designated person acting in the exercise or performance of the powers and duties conferred or imposed on them by their designation.

1.14 If a power conferred on a designated person:

(a) allows reasonable force to be used when exercised by a police officer, a person exercising that power has the same entitlement to use force; or

(b) includes power to use force to enter any premises, that power is not exercisable by that designated person except:

  (i) in the company, and under the supervision, of a police officer;

  (ii) for the purpose of:

  - saving life or limb; or
  - preventing serious damage to property.

1.15 Nothing in this Code prevents the custody officer, or other officer given custody of the detainee from allowing police staff who are not designated persons to carry out individual procedures or tasks at the police station if the law allows. However, the officer remains responsible for making sure the procedures and tasks are carried out correctly in accordance with the Codes of Practice. Any such person must be:

(a) a person employed by a police authority maintaining a police force and under the control and direction of the Chief Officer of that force;

(b) employed by a person with whom a police authority has a contract for the provision of services relating to persons arrested or otherwise in custody.

1.16 Designated persons and other police staff must have regard to any relevant provisions of the Codes of Practice.

1.17 References to pocket books include any official report book issued to police officers or other police staff.

Notes for guidance

1A Although certain sections of this Code apply specifically to people in custody at police stations, those there voluntarily to assist with an investigation should be treated with no less consideration, *e.g.* offered refreshments at appropriate times, and enjoy an absolute right to obtain legal advice or communicate with anyone outside the police station.

1B A person, including a parent or guardian, should not be an appropriate adult if they:

- are
  - suspected of involvement in the offence
  - the victim
  - a witness
  - involved in the investigation
- received admissions prior to attending to act as the appropriate adult.

Note: If a juvenile's parent is estranged from the juvenile, they should not be asked to act as the appropriate adult if the juvenile expressly and specifically objects to their presence.

1C If a juvenile admits an offence to, or in the presence of, a social worker or member of a youth offending team other than during the time that person is acting as the juvenile's appropriate adult, another appropriate adult should be appointed in the interest of fairness.

1D In the case of people who are mentally disordered or otherwise mentally vulnerable, it may be more satisfactory if the appropriate adult is someone experienced or trained in their care rather than a relative lacking such qualifications. But if the detainee prefers a relative to a better qualified stranger or objects to a particular person their wishes should, if practicable, be respected.

1E A detainee should always be given an opportunity, when an appropriate adult is called to the police station, to consult privately with a solicitor in the appropriate adult's absence if they want.

1F A solicitor or independent custody visitor (formerly a lay visitor) present at the police station in that capacity may not be the appropriate adult.

1G "Mentally vulnerable" applies to any detainee who, because of their mental state or capacity, may not understand the significance of what is said, of questions or of their replies. "Mental disorder" is defined in the Mental Health Act 1983, section 1(2) as "mental illness, arrested or incomplete development of mind, psychopathic disorder and any other disorder or disability of mind". When the custody officer has any doubt about the mental state or capacity of a detainee, that detainee should be treated as mentally vulnerable and an appropriate adult called.

1H paragraph 1.1A is intended to cover delays which may occur in processing detainees *e.g.* if:

- a large number of suspects are brought into the station simultaneously to be placed in custody;
- interview rooms are all being used;
- there are difficulties contacting an appropriate adult, solicitor or interpreter.

1I The custody officer must remind the appropriate adult and detainee about the right to legal advice and record any reasons for waiving it in accordance with section 6.

2 Custody records

2.1A When a person is brought to a police station:

- under arrest;
- is arrested at the police station having attended there voluntarily; or
- attends a police station to answer bail

they should be brought before the custody officer as soon as practicable after their arrival at the station or, if appropriate, following arrest after attending the police station voluntarily. This applies to designated and non-designated police stations. A person is deemed to be "at a police station" for these purposes if they are within the boundary of any building or enclosed yard which forms part of that police station.

2.1 A separate custody record must be opened as soon as practicable for each person brought to a police station under arrest or arrested at the station having gone there voluntarily or attending a police station in answer to street bail. All information recorded under this Code must be recorded as soon as practicable in the custody record unless otherwise specified. Any audio or video recording made in the custody area is not part of the custody record.

2.2 If any action requires the authority of an officer of a specified rank, subject to paragraph 2.6A, their name and rank must be noted in the custody record.

2.3 The custody officer is responsible for the custody record's accuracy and completeness and for making sure the record or copy of the record accompanies a detainee if they are transferred to another police station. The record shall show the:

- time and reason for transfer;
- time a person is released from detention.

2.4 A solicitor or appropriate adult must be permitted to consult a detainee's custody record as soon as practicable after their arrival at the station and at any other time whilst the person is detained. Arrangements for this access must be agreed with the custody officer and may not unreasonably interfere with the custody officer's duties.

2.4A When a detainee leaves police detention or is taken before a court they, their legal representative or appropriate adult shall be given, on request, a copy of the custody record as soon as practicable. This entitlement lasts for 12 months after release.

2.5 The detainee, appropriate adult or legal representative shall be permitted to inspect the original custody record after the detainee has left police detention provided they give reasonable notice of their request. Any such inspection shall be noted in the custody record.

2.6 Subject to paragraph 2.6A, all entries in custody records must be timed and signed by the maker. Records entered on computer shall be timed and contain the operator's identification.

2.6A Nothing in this Code requires the identity of officers or other police staff to be recorded or disclosed:
- (a) in the case of enquiries linked to the investigation of terrorism; or
- (b) if the officer or police staff reasonably believe recording or disclosing their name might put them in danger.

In these cases, they shall use their warrant or other identification numbers and the name of their police station. See *Note 2A*

2.7 The fact and time of any detainee's refusal to sign a custody record, when asked in accordance with this Code, must be recorded.

Note for guidance

2A The purpose of paragraph 2.6A(b) is to protect those involved in serious organised crime investigations or arrests of particularly violent suspects when there is reliable information that those arrested or their associates may threaten or cause harm to those involved. In cases of doubt, an officer of inspector rank or above should be consulted.

3 Initial action

(a) Detained persons—normal procedure

3.1 When a person is brought to a police station under arrest or arrested at the station having gone there voluntarily, the custody officer must make sure the person is told clearly about the following continuing rights which may be exercised at any stage during the period in custody:
- (i) the right to have someone informed of their arrest as in section 5;
- (ii) the right to consult privately with a solicitor and that free independent legal advice is available;
- (iii) the right to consult these Codes of Practice. See *Note 3D*

3.2 The detainee must also be given:
- a written notice setting out:
  - the above three rights;
  - the arrangements for obtaining legal advice;
  - the right to a copy of the custody record as in paragraph 2.4A;
  - the caution in the terms prescribed in section 10.
- an additional written notice briefly setting out their entitlements while in custody, see *Notes 3A* and *3B*.

Note: The detainee shall be asked to sign the custody record to acknowledge receipt of these notices. Any refusal must be recorded on the custody record.

3.3 A citizen of an independent Commonwealth country or a national of a foreign country, including the Republic of Ireland, must be informed as soon as practicable about their rights of communication with their High Commission, Embassy or Consulate. See section 7

3.4 The custody officer shall:
- note on the custody record any comment the detainee makes in relation to the arresting officer's account but shall not invite comment. If the arresting officer is not physically present when the detainee is brought to a police station, the

arresting officer's account must be made available to the custody officer remotely or by a third party on the arresting officer's behalf. If the custody officer authorises a person's detention the detainee must be informed of the grounds as soon as practicable and before they are questioned about any offence;
- note any comment the detainee makes in respect of the decision to detain them but shall not invite comment;
- not put specific questions to the detainee regarding their involvement in any offence, nor in respect of any comments they may make in response to the arresting officer's account or the decision to place them in detention. Such an exchange is likely to constitute an interview as in paragraph 11.1A and require the associated safeguards in section 11.

See paragraph 11.13 in respect of unsolicited comments.

3.5 The custody officer shall:
- (a) ask the detainee, whether at this time, they:
  - (i) would like legal advice, see paragraph 6.5;
  - (ii) want someone informed of their detention, see section 5;
- (b) ask the detainee to sign the custody record to confirm their decisions in respect of *(a)*;
- (c) determine whether the detainee:
  - (i) is, or might be, in need of medical treatment or attention, see section 9;
  - (ii) requires:
    - an appropriate adult;
    - help to check documentation;
    - an interpreter;
- (d) record the decision in respect of *(c)*.

3.6 When determining these needs the custody officer is responsible for initiating an assessment to consider whether the detainee is likely to present specific risks to custody staff or themselves. Such assessments should always include a check on the Police National Computer, to be carried out as soon as practicable, to identify any risks highlighted in relation to the detainee. Although such assessments are primarily the custody officer's responsibility, it may be necessary for them to consult and involve others, *e.g.* the arresting officer or an appropriate health care professional, see paragraph 9.13. Reasons for delaying the initiation or completion of the assessment must be recorded.

3.7 Chief Officers should ensure that arrangements for proper and effective risk assessments required by paragraph 3.6 are implemented in respect of all detainees at police stations in their area.

3.8 Risk assessments must follow a structured process which clearly defines the categories of risk to be considered and the results must be incorporated in the detainee's custody record. The custody officer is responsible for making sure those responsible for the detainee's custody are appropriately briefed about the risks. If no specific risks are identified by the assessment, that should be noted in the custody record. See *Note 3E* and paragraph 9.14

3.9 The custody officer is responsible for implementing the response to any specific risk assessment, *e.g.*:
- reducing opportunities for self harm;
- calling a health care professional;
- increasing levels of monitoring or observation.

3.10 Risk assessment is an ongoing process and assessments must always be subject to review if circumstances change.

3.11 If video cameras are installed in the custody area, notices shall be prominently displayed showing cameras are in use. Any request to have video cameras switched off shall be refused.

(b) Detained persons—special groups

3.12 If the detainee appears deaf or there is doubt about their hearing or speaking ability or ability to understand English, and the custody officer cannot establish effective communication, the custody officer must, as soon as practicable, call an interpreter for assistance in the action under paragraphs 3.1–3.5. See section 13

3.13 If the detainee is a juvenile, the custody officer must, if it is practicable, ascertain the identity of a person responsible for their welfare. That person:

- may be:
  - the parent or guardian;
  - if the juvenile is in local authority or voluntary organisation care, or is otherwise being looked after under the Children Act 1989, a person appointed by that authority or organisation to have responsibility for the juvenile's welfare;
  - any other person who has, for the time being, assumed responsibility for the juvenile's welfare.
- must be informed as soon as practicable that the juvenile has been arrested, why they have been arrested and where they are detained. This right is in addition to the juvenile's right in section 5 not to be held incommunicado. See *Note 3C*

3.14 If a juvenile known to be subject to a court order under which a person or organisation is given any degree of statutory responsibility to supervise or otherwise monitor them, reasonable steps must also be taken to notify that person or organisation (the "responsible officer"). The responsible officer will normally be a member of a Youth Offending Team, except for a curfew order which involves electronic monitoring when the contractor providing the monitoring will normally be the responsible officer.

3.15 If the detainee is a juvenile, mentally disordered or otherwise mentally vulnerable, the custody officer must, as soon as practicable:

- inform the appropriate adult, who in the case of a juvenile may or may not be a person responsible for their welfare, as in paragraph 3.13, of:
  - the grounds for their detention;
  - their whereabouts.
- ask the adult to come to the police station to see the detainee.

3.16 It is imperative a mentally disordered or otherwise mentally vulnerable person, detained under the Mental Health Act 1983, section 136, be assessed as soon as possible. If that assessment is to take place at the police station, an approved social worker and a registered medical practitioner shall be called to the station as soon as possible in order to interview and examine the detainee. Once the detainee has been interviewed, examined and suitable arrangements made for their treatment or care, they can no longer be detained under section 136. A detainee must be immediately discharged from detention under section 136 if a registered medical practitioner, having examined them, concludes they are not mentally disordered within the meaning of the Act.

3.17 If the appropriate adult is:
- already at the police station, the provisions of paragraphs 3.1 to 3.5 must be complied with in the appropriate adult's presence;
- not at the station when these provisions are complied with, they must be complied with again in the presence of the appropriate adult when they arrive.

3.18 The detainee shall be advised that:
- the duties of the appropriate adult include giving advice and assistance;
- they can consult privately with the appropriate adult at any time.

3.19 If the detainee, or appropriate adult on the detainee's behalf, asks for a solicitor to be called to give legal advice, the provisions of section 6 apply.

3.20 If the detainee is blind, seriously visually impaired or unable to read, the custody officer shall make sure their solicitor, relative, appropriate adult or some other person likely to take an interest in them and not involved in the investigation is available to help check any documentation. When this Code requires written consent or signing the person assisting may be asked to sign instead, if the detainee prefers. This paragraph does not require an appropriate adult to be called solely to assist in checking and signing documentation for a person who is not a juvenile, or mentally disordered or otherwise mentally vulnerable (see paragraph 3.15).

(c) Persons attending a police station voluntarily

3.21 Anybody attending a police station voluntarily to assist with an investigation may leave at will unless arrested. If it is decided they shall not be allowed to leave, they must be informed at once that they are under arrest and brought before the custody officer, who is responsible for making sure they are notified of their rights in the same way as other detainees. If they are not arrested but are cautioned as in section 10, the person who gives the caution must, at the same time, inform them they are not under arrest, they are not obliged to remain at the station but if they remain at the station they may obtain free and independent legal advice if they want. They shall be told the right to legal advice includes the right to speak with a solicitor on the telephone and be asked if they want to do so.

3.22 If a person attending the police station voluntarily asks about their entitlement to legal advice, they shall be given a copy of the notice explaining the arrangements for obtaining legal advice. See paragraph 3.2

(d) Documentation

3.23 The grounds for a person's detention shall be recorded, in the person's presence if practicable.

3.24 Action taken under paragraphs 3.12 to 3.20 shall be recorded.

(e) Persons answering street bail

3.25 When a person is answering street bail, the custody officer should link any documentation held in relation to arrest with the custody record. Any further action shall be recorded on the custody record in accordance with paragraphs 3.23 and 3.24 above.

Notes for guidance

3A The notice of entitlements should:

- list the entitlements in this Code, including:
  - visits and contact with outside parties, including special provisions for Commonwealth citizens and foreign nationals;
  - reasonable standards of physical comfort;
  - adequate food and drink;
  - access to toilets and washing facilities, clothing, medical attention, and exercise when practicable.
- mention the:
  - provisions relating to the conduct of interviews;
  - circumstances in which an appropriate adult should be available to assist the detainee and their statutory rights to make representation whenever the period of their detention is reviewed.

3B In addition to notices in English, translations should be available in Welsh, the main minority ethnic languages and the principal European languages, whenever they are likely to be helpful. Audio versions of the notice should also be made available.

3C If the juvenile is in local authority or voluntary organisation care but living with their parents or other adults responsible for their welfare, although there is no legal obligation to inform them, they should normally be contacted, as well as the authority or organisation unless suspected of involvement in the offence concerned. Even if the juvenile is not living with their parents, consideration should be given to informing them.

3D The right to consult the Codes of Practice does not entitle the person concerned to delay unreasonably any necessary investigative or administrative action whilst they do so. Examples of action which need not be delayed unreasonably include:

- procedures requiring the provision of breath, blood or urine specimens under the Road Traffic Act 1988 or the Transport and Works Act 1992
- searching detainees at the police station
- taking fingerprints or non-intimate samples without consent for evidential purposes.

3E Home Office Circular 32/2000 provides more detailed guidance on risk assessments and identifies key risk areas which should always be considered.

4 Detainee's property

(a) Action

4.1 The custody officer is responsible for:

(a) ascertaining what property a detainee:

(i) has with them when they come to the police station, whether on:

- arrest or re-detention on answering to bail;
- commitment to prison custody on the order or sentence of a court;
- lodgement at the police station with a view to their production in court from prison custody;
- transfer from detention at another station or hospital;
- detention under the Mental Health Act 1983, section 135 or 136;

(ii) might have acquired for an unlawful or harmful purpose while in custody;

(b) the safekeeping of any property taken from a detainee which remains at the police station.

The custody officer may search the detainee or authorise their being searched to the extent they consider necessary, provided a search of intimate parts of the body or involving the removal of more than outer clothing is only made as in *Annex A*. A search may only be carried out by an officer of the same sex as the detainee. See *Note 4A*

4.2 Detainees may retain clothing and personal effects at their own risk unless the custody officer considers they may use them to cause harm to themselves or others, interfere with evidence, damage property, effect an escape or they are needed as evidence. In this event the custody officer may withhold such articles as they consider necessary and must tell the detainee why.

4.3 Personal effects are those items a detainee may lawfully need, use or refer to while in detention but do not include cash and other items of value.

(b) Documentation

4.4 It is a matter for the custody officer to determine whether a record should be made of the property a detained person has with him or had taken from him on arrest. Any record made is not required to be kept as part of the custody record but the custody record should be noted as to where such a record exists. Whenever a record is made the detainee shall be allowed to check and sign the record of property as correct. Any refusal to sign shall be recorded.

4.5 If a detainee is not allowed to keep any article of clothing or personal effects, the reason must be recorded.

Notes for guidance

4A PACE, Section 54(1) and paragraph 4.1 require a detainee to be searched when it is clear the custody officer will have continuing duties in relation to that detainee or when that detainee's behaviour or offence makes an inventory appropriate. They do not require every detainee to be searched, *e.g.* if it is clear a person will only be detained for a short period and is not to be placed in a cell, the custody officer may decide not to search them. In such a case the custody record will be endorsed "not searched", paragraph 4.4 will not apply, and the detainee will be invited to sign the entry. If the detainee refuses, the custody officer will be obliged to ascertain what property they have in accordance with paragraph 4.1.

4B Paragraph 4.4 does not require the custody officer to record on the custody record property in the detainee's possession on arrest if, by virtue of its nature, quantity or size, it is not practicable to remove it to the police station.

4C Paragraph 4.4 does not require items of clothing worn by the person be recorded unless withheld by the custody officer as in paragraph 4.2.

5 Right not to be held incommunicado

(a) Action

5.1 Any person arrested and held in custody at a police station or other premises may, on request, have one person known to them or likely to take an interest in their welfare informed at public expense of their whereabouts as soon as practicable. If the person cannot be contacted the detainee may choose up to two alternatives. If they cannot be contacted, the person in charge of detention or the investigation has discretion to allow further attempts until the information has been conveyed. See *Notes 5C* and *5D*

5.2 The exercise of the above right in respect of each person nominated may be delayed only in accordance with *Annex B*.

5.3 The above right may be exercised each time a detainee is taken to another police station.

5.4 The detainee may receive visits at the custody officer's discretion. See *Note 5B*

5.5 If a friend, relative or person with an interest in the detainee's welfare enquires about their whereabouts, this information shall be given if the suspect agrees and *Annex B* does not apply. See *Note 5D*

5.6 The detainee shall be given writing materials, on request, and allowed to telephone one person for a reasonable time, see *Notes 5A* and *5E*. Either or both these privileges may be denied or delayed if an officer of inspector rank or above considers sending a letter or making a telephone call may result in any of the consequences in:

- (a) *Annex B* paragraphs 1 and 2 and the person is detained in connection with an arrestable or serious arrestable offence; or
- (b) *Annex B* paragraphs 8 and 9 and the person is detained under the Terrorism Act 2000, Schedule 7 or section 41

For the purposes of this paragraph, any reference to a serious arrestable offence in *Annex B* includes an arrestable offence. However, nothing in this paragraph permits the restriction or denial of the rights in paragraphs 5.1 and 6.1.

5.7 Before any letter or message is sent, or telephone call made, the detainee shall be informed that what they say in any letter, call or message (other than in a communication to a solicitor) may be read or listened to and may be given in evidence. A telephone call may be terminated if it is being abused. The costs can be at public expense at the custody officer's discretion.

(b) Documentation

5.8 A record must be kept of any:

- (a) request made under this section and the action taken;
- (b) letters, messages or telephone calls made or received or visit received;
- (c) refusal by the detainee to have information about them given to an outside enquirer. The detainee must be asked to countersign the record accordingly and any refusal recorded.

Notes for guidance

5A A person may request an interpreter to interpret a telephone call or translate a letter.

5B At the custody officer's discretion, visits should be allowed when possible, subject to having sufficient personnel to supervise a visit and any possible hindrance to the investigation.

5C If the detainee does not know anyone to contact for advice or support or cannot contact a friend or relative, the custody officer should bear in mind any local voluntary bodies or other organisations who might be able to help. Paragraph 6.1 applies if legal advice is required.

5D In some circumstances it may not be appropriate to use the telephone to disclose information under paragraphs 5.1 and 5.5.

5E The telephone call at paragraph 5.6 is in addition to any communication under paragraphs 5.1 and 6.1.

6 Right to legal advice

(a) Action

6.1 Unless *Annex B* applies, all detainees must be informed that they may at any time consult and communicate privately with a solicitor, whether in person, in writing or by telephone, and that free independent legal advice is available from the duty solicitor. See paragraph 3.1, *Note 6B* and *Note 6J*

6.2 Not Used

6.3 A poster advertising the right to legal advice must be prominently displayed in the charging area of every police station. See *Note 6H*

6.4 No police officer should, at any time, do or say anything with the intention of dissuading a detainee from obtaining legal advice.

6.5 The exercise of the right of access to legal advice may be delayed only as in *Annex B*. Whenever legal advice is requested, and unless *Annex B* applies, the custody officer must act without delay to secure the provision of such advice. If, on being informed or reminded of this right, the detainee declines to speak to a solicitor in person, the officer should point out that the right includes the right to speak with a solicitor on the telephone. If the detainee continues to waive this right the officer should ask them why and any reasons should be recorded on the custody record or the interview record as appropriate. Reminders of the right to legal advice must be given as in paragraphs 3.5, 11.2, 15.4, 16.4 and 16.5 and Code D, paragraphs 3.17(ii) and 6.3. Once it is clear a detainee does not want to speak to a solicitor in person or by telephone they should cease to be asked their reasons. See *Note 6K*

6.5A In the case of a juvenile, an appropriate adult should consider whether legal advice from a solicitor is required. If the juvenile indicates that they do not want legal advice, the appropriate adult has the right to ask for a solicitor to attend if this would be in the best interests of the person. However, the detained person cannot be forced to see the solicitor if he is adamant that he does not wish to do so.

6.6 A detainee who wants legal advice may not be interviewed or continue to be interviewed until they have received such advice unless:

(a) *Annex B* applies, when the restriction on drawing adverse inferences from silence in *Annex C* will apply because the detainee is not allowed an opportunity to consult a solicitor; or

(b) an officer of superintendent rank or above has reasonable grounds for believing that:

  (i) the consequent delay might:

  - lead to interference with, or harm to, evidence connected with an offence;
  - lead to interference with, or physical harm to, other people;
  - lead to serious loss of, or damage to, property;

- lead to alerting other people suspected of having committed an offence but not yet arrested for it;
- hinder the recovery of property obtained in consequence of the commission of an offence.

(ii) when a solicitor, including a duty solicitor, has been contacted and has agreed to attend, awaiting their arrival would cause unreasonable delay to the process of investigation.

Note: In these cases the restriction on drawing adverse inferences from silence in *Annex C* will apply because the detainee is not allowed an opportunity to consult a solicitor;

(c) the solicitor the detainee has nominated or selected from a list:

(i) cannot be contacted;

(ii) has previously indicated they do not wish to be contacted; or

(iii) having been contacted, has declined to attend; and

- the detainee has been advised of the Duty Solicitor Scheme but has declined to ask for the duty solicitor.
- In these circumstances the interview may be started or continued without further delay provided an officer of inspector rank or above has agreed to the interview proceeding.

Note: The restriction on drawing adverse inferences from silence in *Annex C* will not apply because the detainee is allowed an opportunity to consult the duty solicitor;

(d) the detainee changes their mind, about wanting legal advice.

In these circumstances the interview may be started or continued without delay provided that:

(i) the detainee agrees to do so, in writing or on tape; and

(ii) an officer of inspector rank or above has inquired about the detainee's reasons for their change of mind and gives authority for the interview to proceed.

Confirmation of the detainee's agreement, their change of mind, the reasons for it if given and, subject to paragraph 2.6A, the name of the authorising officer shall be recorded in the taped or written interview record. See *Note 6I*

Note: In these circumstances the restriction on drawing adverse inferences from silence in *Annex C* will not apply because the detainee is allowed an opportunity to consult a solicitor if they wish.

6.7 If paragraph 6.6(b)(i) applies, once sufficient information has been obtained to avert the risk, questioning must cease until the detainee has received legal advice unless paragraph 6.6(a), (b)(ii), (c) or (d) applies.

6.8 A detainee who has been permitted to consult a solicitor shall be entitled on request to have the solicitor present when they are interviewed unless one of the exceptions in paragraph 6.6 applies.

6.9 The solicitor may only be required to leave the interview if their conduct is such that the interviewer is unable properly to put questions to the suspect. See *Notes 6D and 6E*

6.10 If the interviewer considers a solicitor is acting in such a way, they will stop the interview and consult an officer not below superintendent rank, if one is readily available, and otherwise an officer not below inspector rank not connected with the investigation. After speaking to the solicitor, the officer consulted will decide if the interview should continue in the presence of that solicitor. If they decide it should not, the suspect will be given the opportunity to consult another solicitor before the interview continues and that solicitor given an opportunity to be present at the interview. See *Note 6E*

6.11 The removal of a solicitor from an interview is a serious step and, if it occurs, the officer of superintendent rank or above who took the decision will consider if the incident should be reported to the Law Society. If the decision to remove the solicitor has been taken by an officer below superintendent rank, the facts must be reported to an officer of superintendent rank or above who will similarly consider whether a report to the Law Society would be appropriate. When the solicitor concerned is a duty solicitor, the report should be both to the Law Society and to the Legal Services Commission.

6.12 "Solicitor" in this Code means:
- a solicitor who holds a current practising certificate
- an accredited or probationary representative included on the register of representatives maintained by the Legal Services Commission.

6.12A An accredited or probationary representative sent to provide advice by, and on behalf of, a solicitor shall be admitted to the police station for this purpose unless an officer of inspector rank or above considers such a visit will hinder the investigation and directs otherwise. Hindering the investigation does not include giving proper legal advice to a detainee as in *Note 6D*. Once admitted to the police station, paragraphs 6.6 to 6.10 apply.

6.13 In exercising their discretion under paragraph 6.12A, the officer should take into account in particular:
- whether:
  - the identity and status of an accredited or probationary representative have been satisfactorily established;
  - they are of suitable character to provide legal advice, *e.g.* a person with a criminal record is unlikely to be suitable unless the conviction was for a minor offence and not recent.
- any other matters in any written letter of authorisation provided by the solicitor on whose behalf the person is attending the police station. See *Note 6F*

6.14 If the inspector refuses access to an accredited or probationary representative or a decision is taken that such a person should not be permitted to remain at an interview, the inspector must notify the solicitor on whose behalf the representative was acting and give them an opportunity to make alternative arrangements. The detainee must be informed and the custody record noted.

6.15 If a solicitor arrives at the station to see a particular person, that person must, unless *Annex B* applies, be so informed whether or not they are being interviewed and asked if they would like to see the solicitor. This applies even if the detainee has declined legal advice or, having requested it, subsequently agreed to be interviewed without receiving advice.The solicitor's attendance and the detainee's decision must be noted in the custody record.

(b) Documentation

6.16 Any request for legal advice and the action taken shall be recorded.

6.17 A record shall be made in the interview record if a detainee asks for legal advice and an interview is begun either in the absence of a solicitor or their representative, or they have been required to leave an interview.

Notes for guidance

6A In considering if paragraph 6.6(b) applies, the officer should, if practicable, ask the solicitor for an estimate of how long it will take to come to the station and relate this to the time detention is permitted, the time of day (*i.e.* whether the rest period under paragraph 12.2 is imminent) and the requirements of other investigations. If the solicitor is on their way or is to set off immediately, it will not normally be appropriate to begin an interview before they arrive. If it appears necessary to begin an interview before the solicitor's arrival, they should be given an indication of how long the police would be able to wait before 6.6(b) applies so there is an opportunity to make arrangements for someone else to provide legal advice.

6B A detainee who asks for legal advice should be given an opportunity to consult a specific solicitor or another solicitor from that solicitor's firm or the duty solicitor. If advice is not available by these means, or they do not want to consult the duty solicitor, the detainee should be given an opportunity to choose a solicitor from a list of those willing to provide legal advice. If this solicitor is unavailable, they may choose up to two alternatives. If these attempts are unsuccessful, the custody officer has discretion to allow further attempts until a solicitor has been contacted and agrees to provide legal advice. Apart from carrying out these duties, an officer must not advise the suspect about any particular firm of solicitors.

6C Not Used

6D A detainee has a right to free legal advice and to be represented by a solicitor. The solicitor's only role in the police station is to protect and advance the legal rights of their client. On occasions this may require the solicitor to give advice which has the effect of the client avoiding giving evidence which strengthens a prosecution case. The solicitor may intervene in order to seek clarification, challenge an improper question to their client or the manner in which it is put, advise their client not to reply to particular questions, or if they wish to give their client further legal advice. Paragraph 6.9 only applies if the solicitor's approach or conduct prevents or unreasonably obstructs proper questions being put to the suspect or the suspect's response being recorded. Examples of unacceptable conduct include answering questions on a suspect's behalf or providing written replies for the suspect to quote.

6E An officer who takes the decision to exclude a solicitor must be in a position to satisfy the court the decision was properly made. In order to do this they may need to witness what is happening.

6F If an officer of at least inspector rank considers a particular solicitor or firm of solicitors is persistently sending probationary representatives who are unsuited to provide legal advice, they should inform an officer of at least superintendent rank, who may wish to take the matter up with the Law Society.

6G Subject to the constraints of *Annex B*, a solicitor may advise more than one client in an investigation if they wish. Any question of a conflict of interest is for the solicitor under their professional code of conduct. If, however, waiting for a solicitor to give advice to one client may lead to unreasonable delay to the interview with another, the provisions of paragraph 6.6(b) may apply.

6H In addition to a poster in English, a poster or posters containing translations into Welsh, the main minority ethnic languages and the principal European languages should be displayed wherever they are likely to be helpful and it is practicable to do so.

6I Paragraph 6.6(d) requires the authorisation of an officer of inspector rank or above to the continuation of an interview when a detainee who wanted legal advice changes their mind. It is permissible for such authorisation to be given over the telephone, if the authorising officer is able to satisfy themselves about the reason for the detainee's change of mind and is satisfied it is proper to continue the interview in those circumstances.

6J Whenever a detainee exercises their right to legal advice by consulting or communicating with a solicitor, they must be allowed to do so in private. This right to consult or communicate in private is fundamental. Except as allowed by the Terrorism Act 2000, Schedule 8, paragraph 9, if the requirement for privacy is compromised because what is said or written by the detainee or solicitor for the purpose of giving and receiving legal advice is overheard, listened to, or read by others without the informed consent of the detainee, the right will effectively have been denied. When a detainee chooses to speak to a solicitor on the telephone, they should be allowed to do so in private unless this is impractical because of the design and layout of the custody area or the location of telephones. However, the normal expectation should be that facilities will be available, unless they are being used, at all police stations to enable detainees to speak in private to a solicitor either face to face or over the telephone.

6K A detainee is not obliged to give reasons for declining legal advice and should not be pressed to do so.

7 Citizens of independent Commonwealth countries or foreign nationals

(a) Action

7.1 Any citizen of an independent Commonwealth country or a national of a foreign country, including the Republic of Ireland, may communicate at any time with the appropriate High Commission, Embassy or Consulate. The detainee must be informed as soon as practicable of:

- this right;
- their right, upon request, to have their High Commission, Embassy or Consulate told of their whereabouts and the grounds for their detention. Such a request should be acted upon as soon as practicable.

7.2 If a detainee is a citizen of a country with which a bilateral consular convention or agreement is in force requiring notification of arrest, the appropriate High Commission, Embassy or Consulate shall be informed as soon as practicable, subject to paragraph 7.4. The countries to which this applies as at 1st April 2003 are listed in *Annex F*.

7.3 Consular officers may visit one of their nationals in police detention to talk to them and, if required, to arrange for legal advice. Such visits shall take place out of the hearing of a police officer.

7.4 Notwithstanding the provisions of consular conventions, if the detainee is a political refugee whether for reasons of race, nationality, political opinion or religion, or is seeking political asylum, consular officers shall not be informed of the arrest of one of their nationals or given access or information about them except at the detainee's express request.

(b) Documentation

7.5 A record shall be made when a detainee is informed of their rights under this section and of any communications with a High Commission, Embassy or Consulate.

Notes for guidance

7A The exercise of the rights in this section may not be interfered with even though *Annex B* applies.

8 Conditions of detention

(a) Action

8.1 So far as it is practicable, not more than one detainee should be detained in each cell.

8.2 Cells in use must be adequately heated, cleaned and ventilated. They must be adequately lit, subject to such dimming as is compatible with safety and security to allow people detained overnight to sleep. No additional restraints shall be used within a locked cell unless absolutely necessary and then only restraint equipment, approved for use in that force by the Chief Officer, which is reasonable and necessary in the circumstances having regard to the detainee's demeanour and with a view to ensuring their safety and the safety of others. If a detainee is deaf, mentally disordered or otherwise mentally vulnerable, particular care must be taken when deciding whether to use any form of approved restraints.

8.3 Blankets, mattresses, pillows and other bedding supplied shall be of a reasonable standard and in a clean and sanitary condition. See *Note 8A*

8.4 Access to toilet and washing facilities must be provided.

8.5 If it is necessary to remove a detainee's clothes for the purposes of investigation, for hygiene, health reasons or cleaning, replacement clothing of a reasonable standard of comfort and cleanliness shall be provided. A detainee may not be interviewed unless adequate clothing has been offered.

8.6 At least two light meals and one main meal should be offered in any 24 hour period. See *Note 8B*. Drinks should be provided at meal times and upon reasonable request between meals. Whenever necessary, advice shall be sought from the appropriate health care professional, see *Note 9A*, on medical and dietary matters. As far as practicable, meals provided shall offer a varied diet and meet any specific dietary needs or religious beliefs the detainee may have. The detainee may, at the custody officer's discretion, have meals supplied by their family or friends at their expense. See *Note 8A*

8.7 Brief outdoor exercise shall be offered daily if practicable.

8.8 A juvenile shall not be placed in a police cell unless no other secure accommodation is available and the custody officer considers it is not practicable to supervise them if they are not placed in a cell or that a cell provides more comfortable accommodation than other secure accommodation in the station. A juvenile may not be placed in a cell with a detained adult.

(b) Documentation

8.9 A record must be kept of replacement clothing and meals offered.

8.10 If a juvenile is placed in a cell, the reason must be recorded.

8.11 The use of any restraints on a detainee whilst in a cell, the reasons for it and, if appropriate, the arrangements for enhanced supervision of the detainee whilst so restrained, shall be recorded. See paragraph 3.9

Notes for guidance

8A The provisions in paragraph 8.3 and 8.6 respectively are of particular importance in the case of a person detained under the Terrorism Act 2000, immigration detainees and others likely to be detained for an extended period. In deciding whether to allow meals to be supplied by family or friends, the custody officer is entitled to take account of the risk of items being concealed in any food or package and the officer's duties and responsibilities under food handling legislation.

8B Meals should, so far as practicable, be offered at recognised meal times, or at other times that take account of when the detainee last had a meal.

9 Care and treatment of detained persons

(a) General

9.1 Nothing in this section prevents the police from calling the police surgeon or, if appropriate, some other health care professional, to examine a detainee for the purposes of obtaining evidence relating to any offence in which the detainee is suspected of being involved. See *Note 9A*

9.2 If a complaint is made by, or on behalf of, a detainee about their treatment since their arrest, or it comes to notice that a detainee may have been treated improperly, a report must be made as soon as practicable to an officer of inspector rank or above not connected with the investigation. If the matter concerns a possible assault or the possibility of the unnecessary or unreasonable use of force, an appropriate health care professional must also be called as soon as practicable.

9.3 Detainees should be visited at least every hour. If no reasonably foreseeable risk was identified in a risk assessment, see paragraphs 3.6–3.10, there is no need to wake a sleeping detainee. Those suspected of being intoxicated through drink or drugs or whose level of consciousness causes concern must, subject to any clinical directions given by the appropriate health care professional, see paragraph 9.13:

- be visited and roused at least every half hour
- have their condition assessed as in *Annex H*
- and clinical treatment arranged if appropriate

See *Notes 9B, 9C* and *9H*

9.4 When arrangements are made to secure clinical attention for a detainee, the custody officer must make sure all relevant information which might assist in the treatment of the detainee's condition is made available to the responsible health care professional. This applies whether or not the health care professional asks for such information. Any officer or police staff with relevant information must inform the custody officer as soon as practicable.

(b) Clinical treatment and attention

9.5 The custody officer must make sure a detainee receives appropriate clinical attention as soon as reasonably practicable if the person:

(a) appears to be suffering from physical illness; or
(b) is injured; or
(c) appears to be suffering from a mental disorder;
(d) appears to need clinical attention.

9.5A This applies even if the detainee makes no request for clinical attention and whether or not they have already received clinical attention elsewhere. If the need for attention appears urgent, *e.g.* when indicated as in *Annex H*, the nearest available health care professional or an ambulance must be called immediately.

9.5B The custody officer must also consider the need for clinical attention as set out in Note for Guidance 9C in relation to those suffering the effects of alcohol or drugs.

9.6 Paragraph 9.5 is not meant to prevent or delay the transfer to a hospital if necessary of a person detained under the Mental Health Act 1983, section 136. See *Note 9D*. When an assessment under that Act takes place at a police station, see paragraph 3.16, the custody officer must consider whether an appropriate health care professional should be called to conduct an initial clinical check on the detainee. This applies particularly when there is likely to be any significant delay in the arrival of a suitably qualified medical practitioner.

9.7 If it appears to the custody officer, or they are told, that a person brought to a station under arrest may be suffering from an infectious disease or condition, the custody officer must take reasonable steps to safeguard the health of the detainee and others at the station. In deciding what action to take, advice must be sought from an appropriate health care professional. See *Note 9E*. The custody officer has discretion to isolate the person and their property until clinical directions have been obtained.

9.8 If a detainee requests a clinical examination, an appropriate health care professional must be called as soon as practicable to assess the detainee's clinical needs. If a safe and appropriate care plan cannot be provided, the police surgeon's advice must be sought. The detainee may also be examined by a medical practitioner of their choice at their expense.

9.9 If a detainee is required to take or apply any medication in compliance with clinical directions prescribed before their detention, the custody officer must consult the appropriate health care professional before the use of the medication. Subject to the restrictions in paragraph 9.10, the custody officer is responsible for the safekeeping of any medication and for making sure the detainee is given the opportunity to take or apply prescribed or approved medication. Any such consultation and its outcome shall be noted in the custody record.

9.10 No police officer may administer or supervise the self-administration of controlled drugs of the types and forms listed in the Misuse of Drugs Regulations 2001, Schedule1, 2 or 3. A detainee may only self-administer such drugs under the personal supervision of the registered medical practitioner authorising their use. Drugs listed in Schedule 4 or 5 may be distributed by the custody officer for self-administration if they have consulted the registered medical practitioner authorising their use, this may be done by telephone, and both parties are satisfied self-administration will not expose the detainee, police officers or anyone else to the risk of harm or injury.

9.11 When appropriate health care professionals administer drugs or other medications, or supervise their self-administration, it must be within current medicines legislation and the scope of practice as determined by their relevant professional body.

9.12 If a detainee has in their possession, or claims to need, medication relating to a heart condition, diabetes, epilepsy or a condition of comparable potential seriousness then, even though paragraph 9.5 may not apply, the advice of the appropriate health care professional must be obtained.

9.13 Whenever the appropriate health care professional is called in accordance with this section to examine or treat a detainee, the custody officer shall ask for their opinion about:

- any risks or problems which police need to take into account when making decisions about the detainee's continued detention;
- when to carry out an interview if applicable; and
- the need for safeguards.

9.14 When clinical directions are given by the appropriate health care professional, whether orally or in writing, and the custody officer has any doubts or is in any way uncertain about any aspect of the directions, the custody officer shall ask for clarification. It is particularly important that directions concerning the frequency of visits are clear, precise and capable of being implemented. See *Note 9F*.

(c) Documentation

9.15 A record must be made in the custody record of:

(a) the arrangements made for an examination by an appropriate health care professional under paragraph 9.2 and of any complaint reported under that paragraph together with any relevant remarks by the custody officer;
(b) any arrangements made in accordance with paragraph 9.5;
(c) any request for a clinical examination under paragraph 9.8 and any arrangements made in response;
(d) the injury, ailment, condition or other reason which made it necessary to make the arrangements in (*a*) to (*c*), see *Note 9G;*
(e) any clinical directions and advice, including any further clarifications, given to police by a health care professional concerning the care and treatment of the detainee in connection with any of the arrangements made in (*a*) to (*c*), see *Note 9F;*
(f) if applicable, the responses received when attempting to rouse a person using the procedure in *Annex H,* see *Note 9H.*

9.16 If a health care professional does not record their clinical findings in the custody record, the record must show where they are recorded. See *Note 9G*. However, information which is necessary to custody staff to ensure the effective ongoing care and well being of the detainee must be recorded openly in the custody record, see paragraph 3.8 and *Annex G,* paragraph 7.

9.17 Subject to the requirements of section 4, the custody record shall include:

- a record of all medication a detainee has in their possession on arrival at the police station;
- a note of any such medication they claim to need but do not have with them.

Notes for guidance

9A A "health care professional" means a clinically qualified person working within the scope of practice as determined by their relevant professional body. Whether a health care professional is "appropriate" depends on the circumstances of the duties they carry out at the time.

9B Whenever possible juveniles and mentally vulnerable detainees should be visited more frequently.

9C A detainee who appears drunk or behaves abnormally may be suffering from illness, the effects of drugs or may have sustained injury, particularly a head injury which is not apparent. A detainee needing or dependent on certain drugs, including alcohol, may experience harmful effects within a short time of being deprived of their supply. In these circumstances, when there is any doubt, police should always act urgently to call an appropriate health care professional or an ambulance. Paragraph 9.5 does not apply to minor ailments or injuries which do not need attention. However, all such ailments or injuries must be recorded in the custody record and any doubt must be resolved in favour of calling the appropriate health care professional.

9D Whenever practicable, arrangements should be made for persons detained for assessment under the Mental Health Act 1983, section 136 to be taken to a hospital. There is no power under that Act to transfer a person detained under section 136 from one place of safety to another place of safety for assessment.

9E It is important to respect a person's right to privacy and information about their health must be kept confidential and only disclosed with their consent or in accordance with clinical advice when it is necessary to protect the detainee's health or that of others who come into contact with them.

9F The custody officer should always seek to clarify directions that the detainee requires constant observation or supervision and should ask the appropriate health care professional to explain precisely what action needs to be taken to implement such directions.

9G Paragraphs 9.15 and 9.16 do not require any information about the cause of any injury, ailment or condition to be recorded on the custody record if it appears capable of providing evidence of an offence.

9H The purpose of recording a person's responses when attempting to rouse them using the procedure in *Annex H* is to enable any change in the individual's consciousness level to be noted and clinical treatment arranged if appropriate.

10 Cautions

(a) When a caution must be given

10.1 A person whom there are grounds to suspect of an offence, see *Note 10A*, must be cautioned before any questions about an offence, or further questions if the answers provide the grounds for suspicion, are put to them if either the suspect's answers or silence, (*i.e.* failure or refusal to answer or answer satisfactorily) may be given in evidence to a court in a prosecution. A person need not be cautioned if questions are for other necessary purposes, *e.g.*:

- (a) solely to establish their identity or ownership of any vehicle;
- (b) to obtain information in accordance with any relevant statutory requirement, see paragraph 10.9;
- (c) in furtherance of the proper and effective conduct of a search, *e.g.* to determine the need to search in the exercise of powers of stop and search or to seek co-operation while carrying out a search;
- (d) to seek verification of a written record as in paragraph 11.13;
- (e) when examining a person in accordance with the Terrorism Act 2000, Schedule 7 and the Code of Practice for Examining Officers issued under that Act, Schedule 14, paragraph 6.

10.2 Whenever a person not under arrest is initially cautioned, or reminded they are under caution, that person must at the same time be told they are not under arrest and are free to leave if they want to. See *Note 10C*

10.3 A person who is arrested, or further arrested, must be informed at the time, or as soon as practicable thereafter, that they are under arrest and the grounds for their arrest, see *Note 10B*.

10.4 A person who is arrested, or further arrested, must also be cautioned unless:
(a) it is impracticable to do so by reason of their condition or behaviour at the time;
(b) they have already been cautioned immediately prior to arrest as in paragraph 10.1.

(b) Terms of the cautions

10.5 The caution which must be given on:
(a) arrest;
(b) all other occasions before a person is charged or informed they may be prosecuted, see section 16,

should, unless the restriction on drawing adverse inferences from silence applies, see *Annex C*, be in the following terms:

> "You do not have to say anything. But it may harm your defence if you do not mention when questioned something which you later rely on in Court. Anything you do say may be given in evidence."

See *Note 10G*

10.6 *Annex C,* paragraph 2 sets out the alternative terms of the caution to be used when the restriction on drawing adverse inferences from silence applies.

10.7 Minor deviations from the words of any caution given in accordance with this Code do not constitute a breach of this Code, provided the sense of the relevant caution is preserved. See *Note 10D*

10.8 After any break in questioning under caution, the person being questioned must be made aware they remain under caution. If there is any doubt the relevant caution should be given again in full when the interview resumes. See *Note 10E*

10.9 When, despite being cautioned, a person fails to co-operate or to answer particular questions which may affect their immediate treatment, the person should be informed of any relevant consequences and that those consequences are not affected by the caution. Examples are when a person's refusal to provide:
- their name and address when charged may make them liable to detention;
- particulars and information in accordance with a statutory requirement, *e.g.* under the Road Traffic Act 1988, may amount to an offence or may make the person liable to a further arrest.

(c) Special warnings under the Criminal Justice and Public Order Act 1994, sections 36 and 37

10.10 When a suspect interviewed at a police station or authorised place of detention after arrest fails or refuses to answer certain questions, or to answer satisfactorily, after due warning, see *Note 10F*, a court or jury may draw such inferences as appear proper under the Criminal Justice and Public Order Act 1994, sections 36 and 37. Such inferences may only be drawn when:
(a) the restriction on drawing adverse inferences from silence, see *Annex C*, does not apply; and

(b) the suspect is arrested by a constable and fails or refuses to account for any objects, marks or substances, or marks on such objects found:
- on their person;
- in or on their clothing or footwear;
- otherwise in their possession; or
- in the place they were arrested;

(c) the arrested suspect was found by a constable at a place at or about the time the offence for which that officer has arrested them is alleged to have been committed, and the suspect fails or refuses to account for their presence there.

When the restriction on drawing adverse inferences from silence applies, the suspect may still be asked to account for any of the matters in (*b*) or (*c*) but the special warning described in paragraph 10.11 will not apply and must not be given.

10.11 For an inference to be drawn when a suspect fails or refuses to answer a question about one of these matters or to answer it satisfactorily, the suspect must first be told in ordinary language:

(a) what offence is being investigated;
(b) what fact they are being asked to account for;
(c) this fact may be due to them taking part in the commission of the offence;
(d) a court may draw a proper inference if they fail or refuse to account for this fact;
(e) a record is being made of the interview and it may be given in evidence if they are brought to trial.

(d) Juveniles and persons who are mentally disordered or otherwise mentally vulnerable

10.12 If a juvenile or a person who is mentally disordered or otherwise mentally vulnerable is cautioned in the absence of the appropriate adult, the caution must be repeated in the adult's presence.

(e) Documentation

10.13 A record shall be made when a caution is given under this section, either in the interviewer's pocket book or in the interview record.

Notes for guidance

10A There must be some reasonable, objective grounds for the suspicion, based on known facts or information which are relevant to the likelihood the offence has been committed and the person to be questioned committed it.

10B An arrested person must be given sufficient information to enable them to understand they have been deprived of their liberty and the reason they have been arrested, *e.g.* when a person is arrested on suspicion of committing an offence they must be informed of the suspected offence's nature, when and where it was committed. If the arrest is made under the general arrest conditions in PACE, section 25, the grounds for arrest must include an explanation of the conditions which make the arrest necessary. Vague or technical language should be avoided.

10C The restriction on drawing inferences from silence, see *Annex C*, paragraph 1, does not apply to a person who has not been detained and who therefore cannot be prevented from seeking legal advice if they want, see paragraph 3.21.

10D If it appears a person does not understand the caution, the person giving it should explain it in their own words.

10E It may be necessary to show to the court that nothing occurred during an interview break or between interviews which influenced the suspect's recorded evidence. After a break in an interview or at the beginning of a subsequent interview, the interviewing officer should summarise the reason for the break and confirm this with the suspect.

10F The Criminal Justice and Public Order Act 1994, sections 36 and 37 apply only to suspects who have been arrested by a constable or Customs and Excise officer and are given the relevant warning by the police or customs officer who made the arrest or who is investigating the offence. They do not apply to any interviews with suspects who have not been arrested.

10G Nothing in this Code requires a caution to be given or repeated when informing a person not under arrest they may be prosecuted for an offence. However, a court will not be able to draw any inferences under the Criminal Justice and Public Order Act 1994, section 34, if the person was not cautioned.

11 Interviews—general

(a) Action

11.1A An interview is the questioning of a person regarding their involvement or suspected involvement in a criminal offence or offences which, under paragraph 10.1, must be carried out under caution. Whenever a person is interviewed they must be informed of the nature of the offence, or further offence. Procedures under the Road Traffic Act 1988, section 7 or the Transport and Works Act 1992, section 31 do not constitute interviewing for the purpose of this Code.

11.1 Following a decision to arrest a suspect, they must not be interviewed about the relevant offence except at a police station or other authorised place of detention, unless the consequent delay would be likely to:

(a) lead to:
   - interference with, or harm to, evidence connected with an offence;
   - interference with, or physical harm to, other people; or
   - serious loss of, or damage to, property;

(b) lead to alerting other people suspected of committing an offence but not yet arrested for it; or

(c) hinder the recovery of property obtained in consequence of the commission of an offence.

Interviewing in any of these circumstances shall cease once the relevant risk has been averted or the necessary questions have been put in order to attempt to avert that risk.

11.2 Immediately prior to the commencement or re-commencement of any interview at a police station or other authorised place of detention, the interviewer should remind the suspect of their entitlement to free legal advice and that the interview can be delayed for legal advice to be obtained, unless one of the exceptions in paragraph 6.6 applies. It is the interviewer's responsibility to make sure all reminders are recorded in the interview record.

11.3 Not Used

11.4 At the beginning of an interview the interviewer, after cautioning the suspect, see section 10, shall put to them any significant statement or silence which occurred in the presence and hearing of a police officer or other police staff before the start of the interview and which have not been put to the suspect in the course of a previous interview. See *Note 11A*. The interviewer shall ask the suspect whether they confirm or deny that earlier statement or silence and if they want to add anything.

11.4A A significant statement is one which appears capable of being used in evidence against the suspect, in particular a direct admission of guilt. A significant silence is a failure or refusal to answer a question or answer satisfactorily when under caution, which might, allowing for the restriction on drawing adverse inferences from silence, see *Annex C*, give rise to an inference under the Criminal Justice and Public Order Act 1994, Pt III.

11.5 No interviewer may try to obtain answers or elicit a statement by the use of oppression. Except as in paragraph 10.9, no interviewer shall indicate, except to answer a direct question, what action will be taken by the police if the person being questioned answers questions, makes a statement or refuses to do either. If the person asks directly what action will be taken if they answer questions, make a statement or refuse to do either, the interviewer may inform them what action the police propose to take provided that action is itself proper and warranted.

11.6 The interview or further interview of a person about an offence with which that person has not been charged or for which they have not been informed they may be prosecuted, must cease when:

(a) the officer in charge of the investigation is satisfied all the questions they consider relevant to obtaining accurate and reliable information about the offence have been put to the suspect, this includes allowing the suspect an opportunity to give an innocent explanation and asking questions to test if the explanation is accurate and reliable, *e.g.* to clear up ambiguities or clarify what the suspect said;

(b) the officer in charge of the investigation has taken account of any other available evidence; and

(c) the officer in charge of the investigation, or in the case of a detained suspect, the custody officer, see paragraph 16.1, reasonably believes there is sufficient evidence to provide a realistic prospect of conviction for that offence. See *Note 11B*

This paragraph does not prevent officers in revenue cases or acting under the confiscation provisions of the Criminal Justice Act 1988 or the Drug Trafficking Act 1994 from inviting suspects to complete a formal question and answer record after the interview is concluded.

(b) Interview records

11.7 (a) An accurate record must be made of each interview, whether or not the interview takes place at a police station

(b) The record must state the place of interview, the time it begins and ends, any interview breaks and, subject to paragraph 2.6A, the names of all those present; and must be made on the forms provided for this purpose or in the interviewer's pocket book or in accordance with the Codes of Practice E or F;

(c) Any written record must be made and completed during the interview, unless this would not be practicable or would interfere with the conduct of the interview, and must constitute either a verbatim record of what has been said or, failing this, an account of the interview which adequately and accurately summarises it.

11.8 If a written record is not made during the interview it must be made as soon as practicable after its completion.

11.9 Written interview records must be timed and signed by the maker.

11.10 If a written record is not completed during the interview the reason must be recorded in the interview record.

11.11 Unless it is impracticable, the person interviewed shall be given the opportunity to read the interview record and to sign it as correct or to indicate how they consider it inaccurate. If the person interviewed cannot read or refuses to read the record or sign it, the senior interviewer present shall read it to them and ask whether they would like to sign it as correct or make their mark or to indicate how they consider it inaccurate. The interviewer shall certify on the interview record itself what has occurred. See *Note 11E*

11.12 If the appropriate adult or the person's solicitor is present during the interview, they should also be given an opportunity to read and sign the interview record or any written statement taken down during the interview.

11.13 A written record shall be made of any comments made by a suspect, including unsolicited comments, which are outside the context of an interview but which might be relevant to the offence. Any such record must be timed and signed by the maker. When practicable the suspect shall be given the opportunity to read that record and to sign it as correct or to indicate how they consider it inaccurate. See *Note 11E*

11.14 Any refusal by a person to sign an interview record when asked in accordance with this Code must itself be recorded.

(c) Juveniles and mentally disordered or otherwise mentally vulnerable people

11.15 A juvenile or person who is mentally disordered or otherwise mentally vulnerable must not be interviewed regarding their involvement or suspected involvement in a criminal offence or offences, or asked to provide or sign a written statement under caution or record of interview, in the absence of the appropriate adult unless paragraphs 11.1, 11.18 to 11.20 apply. See *Note 11C*

11.16 Juveniles may only be interviewed at their place of education in exceptional circumstances and only when the principal or their nominee agrees. Every effort should be made to notify the parent(s) or other person responsible for the juvenile's welfare and the appropriate adult, if this is a different person, that the police want to interview the juvenile and reasonable time should be allowed to enable the appropriate adult to be present at the interview. If awaiting the appropriate adult would cause unreasonable delay, and unless the juvenile is suspected of an offence against the educational establishment, the principal or their nominee can act as the appropriate adult for the purposes of the interview.

11.17 If an appropriate adult is present at an interview, they shall be informed:

- they are not expected to act simply as an observer; and
- the purpose of their presence is to:
  - advise the person being interviewed;
  - observe whether the interview is being conducted properly and fairly;
  - facilitate communication with the person being interviewed.

(d) Vulnerable suspects—urgent interviews at police stations

11.18 The following persons may not be interviewed unless an officer of superintendent rank or above considers delay will lead to the consequences in paragraph 11.1(a) to (c), and is satisfied the interview would not significantly harm the person's physical or mental state (see *Annex G*):

(a) a juvenile or person who is mentally disordered or otherwise mentally vulnerable if at the time of the interview the appropriate adult is not present;
(b) anyone other than in (*a*) who at the time of the interview appears unable to:
- appreciate the significance of questions and their answers; or
- understand what is happening because of the effects of drink, drugs or any illness, ailment or condition;

(c) a person who has difficulty understanding English or has a hearing disability, if at the time of the interview an interpreter is not present.

11.19 These interviews may not continue once sufficient information has been obtained to avert the consequences in paragraph 11.1(a) to (c).

11.20 A record shall be made of the grounds for any decision to interview a person under paragraph 11.18.

Notes for guidance

11A Paragraph 11.4 does not prevent the interviewer from putting significant statements and silences to a suspect again at a later stage or a further interview.

11B The Criminal Procedure and Investigations Act 1996 Code of Practice, paragraph 3.4 states "In conducting an investigation, the investigator should pursue all reasonable lines of enquiry, whether these point towards or away from the suspect. What is reasonable will depend on the particular circumstances." Interviewers should keep this in mind when deciding what questions to ask in an interview.

11C Although juveniles or people who are mentally disordered or otherwise mentally vulnerable are often capable of providing reliable evidence, they may, without knowing or wishing to do so, be particularly prone in certain circumstances to provide information that may be unreliable, misleading or self-incriminating. Special care should always be taken when questioning such a person, and the appropriate adult should be involved if there is any doubt about a person's age, mental state or capacity. Because of the risk of unreliable evidence it is also important to obtain corroboration of any facts admitted whenever possible.

11D Juveniles should not be arrested at their place of education unless this is unavoidable. When a juvenile is arrested at their place of education, the principal or their nominee must be informed.

11E Significant statements described in paragraph 11.4 will always be relevant to the offence and must be recorded. When a suspect agrees to read records of interviews and other comments and sign them as correct, they should be asked to endorse the record with, *e.g.* "I agree that this is a correct record of what was said" and add their signature. If the suspect does not agree with the record, the interviewer should record the details of any disagreement and ask the suspect to read these details and sign them to the effect that they accurately reflect their disagreement. Any refusal to sign should be recorded.

12 Interviews in police stations

(a) Action

12.1 If a police officer wants to interview or conduct enquiries which require the presence of a detainee, the custody officer is responsible for deciding whether to deliver the detainee into the officer's custody.

12.2 Except as below, in any period of 24 hours a detainee must be allowed a continuous period of at least 8 hours for rest, free from questioning, travel or any interruption in connection with the investigation concerned. This period should normally be at night or other appropriate time which takes account of when the detainee last slept or rested. If a detainee is arrested at a police station after going there voluntarily, the period of 24 hours runs from the time of their arrest and not the time of arrival at the police station. The period may not be interrupted or delayed, except:

- (a) when there are reasonable grounds for believing not delaying or interrupting the period would:
  - (i) involve a risk of harm to people or serious loss of, or damage to, property;
  - (ii) delay unnecessarily the person's release from custody;
  - (iii) otherwise prejudice the outcome of the investigation;
- (b) at the request of the detainee, their appropriate adult or legal representative;
- (c) when a delay or interruption is necessary in order to:
  - (i) comply with the legal obligations and duties arising under section 15;
  - (ii) to take action required under section 9 or in accordance with medical advice.

If the period is interrupted in accordance with *(a)*, a fresh period must be allowed. Interruptions under *(b)* and *(c)*, do not require a fresh period to be allowed.

12.3 Before a detainee is interviewed the custody officer, in consultation with the officer in charge of the investigation and appropriate health care professionals as necessary, shall assess whether the detainee is fit enough to be interviewed. This means determining and considering the risks to the detainee's physical and mental state if the interview took place and determining what safeguards are needed to allow the interview to take place. See *Annex G*. The custody officer shall not allow a detainee to be interviewed if the custody officer considers it would cause significant harm to the detainee's physical or mental state. Vulnerable suspects listed at paragraph 11.18 shall be treated as always being at some risk during an interview and these persons may not be interviewed except in accordance with paragraphs 11.18 to 11.20.

12.4 As far as practicable interviews shall take place in interview rooms which are adequately heated, lit and ventilated.

12.5 A suspect whose detention without charge has been authorised under PACE, because the detention is necessary for an interview to obtain evidence of the offence for which they have been arrested, may choose not to answer questions but police do not require the suspect's consent or agreement to interview them for this purpose. If a suspect takes steps to prevent themselves being questioned or further questioned, *e.g.* by refusing to leave their cell to go to a suitable interview room or by trying to leave the interview room, they shall be advised their consent or agreement to interview is not required. The suspect shall be cautioned as in section 10, and informed if they fail or refuse to co-operate, the interview may take place in the cell and that their failure or refusal to co-operate may be given in evidence. The suspect shall then be invited to co-operate and go into the interview room.

12.6 People being questioned or making statements shall not be required to stand.

12.7 Before the interview commences each interviewer shall, subject to paragraph 2.6A, identify themselves and any other persons present to the interviewee.

12.8 Breaks from interviewing should be made at recognised meal times or at other times that take account of when an interviewee last had a meal. Short refreshment breaks shall be provided at approximately two hour intervals, subject to the interviewer's discretion to delay a break if there are reasonable grounds for believing it would:

(i) involve a:
  - risk of harm to people;
  - serious loss of, or damage to, property;

(ii) unnecessarily delay the detainee's release;

(iii) otherwise prejudice the outcome of the investigation.

See *Note 12B*

12.9 If during the interview a complaint is made by or on behalf of the interviewee concerning the provisions of this Code, the interviewer should:

(i) record it in the interview record;

(ii) inform the custody officer, who is then responsible for dealing with it as in section 9.

(b) Documentation

12.10 A record must be made of the:

- time a detainee is not in the custody of the custody officer, and why
- reason for any refusal to deliver the detainee out of that custody

12.11 A record shall be made of:

(a) the reasons it was not practicable to use an interview room; and

(b) any action taken as in paragraph 12.5.

The record shall be made on the custody record or in the interview record for action taken whilst an interview record is being kept, with a brief reference to this effect in the custody record.

12.12 Any decision to delay a break in an interview must be recorded, with reasons, in the interview record.

12.13 All written statements made at police stations under caution shall be written on forms provided for the purpose.

12.14 All written statements made under caution shall be taken in accordance with *Annex D*. Before a person makes a written statement under caution at a police station they shall be reminded about the right to legal advice. See *Note 12A*

Notes for guidance

12A It is not normally necessary to ask for a written statement if the interview was recorded or taped at the time and the record signed by the interviewee in accordance with paragraph 11.11. Statements under caution should normally be taken in these circumstances only at the person's express wish. A person may however be asked if they want to make such a statement.

12B Meal breaks should normally last at least 45 minutes and shorter breaks after two hours should last at least 15 minutes. If the interviewer delays a break in accordance with paragraph 12.8 and prolongs the interview, a longer break should be provided. If there is a short interview, and another short interview is contemplated, the length of the break may be reduced if there are reasonable grounds to believe this is necessary to avoid any of the consequences in paragraph 12.8(i) to (iii).

13 Interpreters

(a) General

13.1 Chief officers are responsible for making sure appropriate arrangements are in place for provision of suitably qualified interpreters for people who:

- are deaf;
- do not understand English.

Whenever possible, interpreters should be drawn from the National Register of Public Service Interpreters (NRPSI).

(b) Foreign languages

13.2 Unless paragraphs 11.1, 11.18 to 11.20 apply, a person must not be interviewed in the absence of a person capable of interpreting if:

(a) they have difficulty understanding English;
(b) the interviewer cannot speak the person's own language;
(c) the person wants an interpreter present.

13.3 The interviewer shall make sure the interpreter makes a note of the interview at the time in the person's language for use in the event of the interpreter being called to give evidence, and certifies its accuracy. The interviewer should allow sufficient time for the interpreter to note each question and answer after each is put, given and interpreted. The person should be allowed to read the record or have it read to them and sign it as correct or indicate the respects in which they consider it inaccurate. If the interview is tape-recorded or visually recorded, the arrangements in Code E or F apply.

13.4 In the case of a person making a statement to a police officer or other police staff other than in English:

(a) the interpreter shall record the statement in the language it is made;
(b) the person shall be invited to sign it;
(c) an official English translation shall be made in due course.

(c) Deaf people and people with speech difficulties

13.5 If a person appears to be deaf or there is doubt about their hearing or speaking ability, they must not be interviewed in the absence of an interpreter unless they agree in writing to being interviewed without one or paragraphs 11.1, 11.18 to 11.20 apply.

13.6 An interpreter should also be called if a juvenile is interviewed and the parent or guardian present as the appropriate adult appears to be deaf or there is doubt about their hearing or speaking ability, unless they agree in writing to the interview proceeding without one or paragraphs 11.1, 11.18 to 11.20 apply.

13.7 The interviewer shall make sure the interpreter is allowed to read the interview record and certify its accuracy in the event of the interpreter being called to give evidence. If the interview is tape-recorded or visually recorded, the arrangements in Code E or F apply.

(d) Additional rules for detained persons

13.8 All reasonable attempts should be made to make the detainee understand that interpreters will be provided at public expense.

13.9 If paragraph 6.1 applies and the detainee cannot communicate with the solicitor because of language, hearing or speech difficulties, an interpreter must be called. The interpreter may not be a police officer or any other police staff when interpretation is needed for the purposes of obtaining legal advice. In all other cases a police officer or other police staff may only interpret if the detainee and the appropriate adult, if applicable, give their agreement in writing or if the interview is tape-recorded or visually recorded as in Code E or F.

13.10 When the custody officer cannot establish effective communication with a person charged with an offence who appears deaf or there is doubt about their ability to hear, speak or to understand English, arrangements must be made as soon as practicable for an interpreter to explain the offence and any other information given by the custody officer.

(e) Documentation

13.11 Action taken to call an interpreter under this section and any agreement to be interviewed in the absence of an interpreter must be recorded.

14 Questioning—special restrictions

14.1 If a person is arrested by one police force on behalf of another and the lawful period of detention in respect of that offence has not yet commenced in accordance with PACE, section 41 no questions may be put to them about the offence while they are in transit between the forces except to clarify any voluntary statement they make.

14.2 If a person is in police detention at a hospital they may not be questioned without the agreement of a responsible doctor. See *Note 14A*

Note for guidance

14A If questioning takes place at a hospital under paragraph 14.2, or on the way to or from a hospital, the period of questioning concerned counts towards the total period of detention permitted.

15 Reviews and extensions of detention

(a) Persons detained under PACE

15.1 The review officer is responsible under PACE, section 40 for periodically determining if a person's detention, before or after charge, continues to be necessary. This requirement continues throughout the detention period and except as in paragraph 15.10, the review officer must be present at the police station holding the detainee. See *Notes 15A* and *15B*

15.2 Under PACE, section 42, an officer of superintendent rank or above who is responsible for the station holding the detainee may give authority any time after the second review to extend the maximum period the person may be detained without charge by up to 12 hours. Further detention without charge may be authorised only by a magistrates' court in accordance with PACE, sections 43 and 44. See *Notes 15C*, *15D* and *15E*

15.2A Section.42(1) of PACE as amended extends the maximum period of detention for arrestable offences from 24 hours to 36 hours. Detaining a juvenile or mentally vulnerable person for longer than 24 hours will be dependent on the circumstances of the case and with regard to the person's:

(a) special vulnerability;
(b) the legal obligation to provide an opportunity for representations to be made prior to a decision about extending detention;
(c) the need to consult and consider the views of any appropriate adult; and
(d) any alternatives to police custody.

15.3 Before deciding whether to authorise continued detention the officer responsible under paragraphs 15.1 or 15.2 shall give an opportunity to make representations about the detention to:

(a) the detainee, unless in the case of a review as in paragraph 15.1, the detainee is asleep;
(b) the detainee's solicitor if available at the time; and
(c) the appropriate adult if available at the time.

15.3A Other people having an interest in the detainee's welfare may also make representations at the authorising officer's discretion.

15.3B Subject to paragraph 15.10, the representations may be made orally in person or by telephone or in writing. The authorising officer may, however, refuse to hear oral representations from the detainee if the officer considers them unfit to make representations because of their condition or behaviour. See *Note 15C*

15.3C The decision on whether the review takes place in person or by telephone or by video conferencing (see Note 15G) is a matter for the review officer. In determining the form the review may take, the review officer must always take full account of the needs of the person in custody. The benefits of carrying out a review in person should always be considered, based on the individual circumstances of each case with specific additional consideration if the person is:

(a) a juvenile (and the age of the juvenile); or
(b) mentally vulnerable; or
(c) has been subject to medical attention for other than routine minor ailments; or
(d) there are presentational or community issues around the person's detention.

15.4 Before conducting a review or determining whether to extend the maximum period of detention without charge, the officer responsible must make sure the detainee is reminded of their entitlement to free legal advice, see paragraph 6.5, unless in the case of a review the person is asleep.

15.5 If, after considering any representations, the officer decides to keep the detainee in detention or extend the maximum period they may be detained without charge, any comment made by the detainee shall be recorded. If applicable, the officer responsible under paragraph 15.1 or 15.2 shall be informed of the comment as soon as practicable. See also paragraphs 11.4 and 11.13

15.6 No officer shall put specific questions to the detainee:

- regarding their involvement in any offence; or
- in respect of any comments they may make:
  - when given the opportunity to make representations; or
  - in response to a decision to keep them in detention or extend the maximum period of detention.

Such an exchange could constitute an interview as in paragraph 11.1A and would be subject to the associated safeguards in section 11 and, in respect of a person who has been charged, paragraph 16.5. See also paragraph 11.13

15.7 A detainee who is asleep at a review, see paragraph 15.1, and whose continued detention is authorised must be informed about the decision and reason as soon as practicable after waking.

(b) Persons detained under the Terrorism Act 2000

15.8 In terrorism cases:

(a) the powers and duties of the review officer are in the Terrorism Act 2000, Schedule 8, Pt II;
(b) a police officer of at least superintendent rank may apply to a judicial authority for a warrant of further detention under the Terrorism Act 2000, Schedule 8, Pt III.

(c) Telephone review of detention

15.9 PACE, section 40A provides that the officer responsible under section 40 for reviewing the detention of a person who has not been charged, need not attend the police station holding the detainee and may carry out the review by telephone.

15.9A PACE, section 45A(2) provides that the officer responsible under section 40 for reviewing the detention of a person who has not been charged, need not attend the police station holding the detainee and may carry out the review by video conferencing facilities (See *Note 15G*).

15.9B A telephone review is not permitted where facilities for review by video conferencing exist and it is practicable to use them.

15.9C The review officer can decide at any stage that a telephone review or review by video conferencing should be terminated and that the review will be conducted in person. The reasons for doing so should be noted in the custody record.

See *Note 15F*

15.10 When a telephone review is carried out, an officer at the station holding the detainee shall be required by the review officer to fulfil that officer's obligations under PACE, section 40 or this Code by:

(a) making any record connected with the review in the detainee's custody record;
(b) if applicable, making a record in *(a)* in the presence of the detainee; and
(c) giving the detainee information about the review.

15.11 When a telephone review is carried out, the requirement in paragraph 15.3 will be satisfied:

(a) if facilities exist for the immediate transmission of written representations to the review officer, *e.g.* fax or email message, by giving the detainee an opportunity to make representations:
    (i) orally by telephone; or
    (ii) in writing using those facilities; and
(b) in all other cases, by giving the detainee an opportunity to make their representations orally by telephone.

(d) Documentation

15.12 It is the officer's responsibility to make sure all reminders given under paragraph 15.4 are noted in the custody record.

15.13 The grounds for, and extent of, any delay in conducting a review shall be recorded.

15.14 When a telephone review is carried out, a record shall be made of:
- (a) the reason the review officer did not attend the station holding the detainee;
- (b) the place the review officer was;
- (c) the method representations, oral or written, were made to the review officer, see paragraph 15.11.

15.15 Any written representations shall be retained.

15.16 A record shall be made as soon as practicable about the outcome of each review or determination whether to extend the maximum detention period without charge or an application for a warrant of further detention or its extension. If paragraph 15.7 applies, a record shall also be made of when the person was informed and by whom. If an authorisation is given under PACE, section 42, the record shall state the number of hours and minutes by which the detention period is extended or further extended. If a warrant for further detention, or extension, is granted under section 43 or 44, the record shall state the detention period authorised by the warrant and the date and time it was granted.

Notes for guidance

15A Review officer for the purposes of:
- PACE, sections 40 and 40A means, in the case of a person arrested but not charged, an officer of at least inspector rank not directly involved in the investigation and, if a person has been arrested and charged, the custody officer;
- the Terrorism Act 2000, means an officer not directly involved in the investigation connected with the detention and of at least inspector rank, for reviews within 24 hours of the detainee's arrest or superintendent for all other reviews.

15B The detention of persons in police custody not subject to the statutory review requirement in paragraph 15.1 should still be reviewed periodically as a matter of good practice. Such reviews can be carried out by an officer of the rank of sergeant or above. The purpose of such reviews is to check the particular power under which a detainee is held continues to apply, any associated conditions are complied with and to make sure appropriate action is taken to deal with any changes. This includes the detainee's prompt release when the power no longer applies, or their transfer if the power requires the detainee be taken elsewhere as soon as the necessary arrangements are made. Examples include persons:
- (a) arrested on warrant because they failed to answer bail to appear at court or failed to answer street bail;
- (b) arrested under the Bail Act 1976, section 7(3) for breaching a condition of bail granted after charge;
- (c) in police custody for specific purposes and periods under the Crime (Sentences) Act 1997, Schedule 1;
- (d) convicted, or remand prisoners, held in police stations on behalf of the Prison Service under the Imprisonment (Temporary Provisions) Act 1980, section 6;
- (e) being detained to prevent them causing a breach of the peace;
- (f) detained at police stations on behalf of the Immigration Service.

The detention of persons remanded into police detention by order of a court under the Magistrates' Courts Act 1980, section 128 is subject to a statutory requirement to review that detention. This is to make sure the detainee is taken back to court no later than the end of the period authorised by the court or when the need for their detention by police ceases, whichever is the sooner.

15C In the case of a review of detention, but not an extension, the detainee need not be woken for the review. However, if the detainee is likely to be asleep, *e.g.* during a period of rest allowed as in paragraph 12.2, at the latest time a review or authorisation to extend detention may take place, the officer should, if the legal obligations and time constraints permit, bring forward the procedure to allow the detainee to make representations. A detainee not asleep during the review must be present when the grounds for their continued detention are recorded and must at the same time be informed of those grounds unless the review officer considers the person is incapable of understanding what is said, violent or likely to become violent or in urgent need of medical attention.

15D An application to a Magistrates' Court under PACE, sections 43 or 44 for a warrant of further detention or its extension should be made between 10am and 9pm, and if possible during normal court hours. It will not usually be practicable to arrange for a court to sit specially outside the hours of 10am to 9pm. If it appears a special sitting may be needed outside normal court hours but between 10am and 9pm, the clerk to the justices should be given notice and informed of this possibility, while the court is sitting if possible.

15E In paragraph 15.2, the officer responsible for the station holding the detainee includes a superintendent or above who, in accordance with their force operational policy or police regulations, is given that responsibility on a temporary basis whilst the appointed long-term holder is off duty or otherwise unavailable.

15F The provisions of PACE, section 40A allowing telephone reviews do not apply to reviews of detention after charge by the custody officer or to reviews under the Terrorism Act 2000, Schedule 8, Pt II in terrorism cases. When video conferencing is not required, they allow the use of a telephone to carry out a review of detention before charge. The procedure under PACE, section 42 must be done in person.

15G The use of video conferencing facilities for decisions about detention under section 45A of PACE is subject to the introduction of regulations by the Secretary of State.

16 Charging detained persons

(a) Action

16.1 When the officer in charge of the investigation reasonably believes there is sufficient evidence to provide a realistic prospect of conviction for the offence (see paragraph 11.6), they shall without delay, and subject to the following qualification, inform the custody officer who will be responsible for considering whether the detainee should be charged. See *Notes 11B and 16A*. When a person is detained in respect of more than one offence it is permissible to delay informing the custody officer until the above conditions are satisfied in respect of all the offences, but see paragraph 11.6. If the detainee is a juvenile, mentally disordered or otherwise mentally vulnerable, any resulting action shall be taken in the presence of the appropriate adult if they are present at the time. See *Notes 16B and 16C*

16.1A Where guidance issued by the Director of Public Prosecutions under section 37A is in force the custody officer must comply with that Guidance in deciding how to act in dealing with the detainee. See *Note 16AB*

16.1B Where in compliance with the DPP's Guidance the custody officer decides that the case should be immediately referred to the CPS to make the charging decision, consultation should take place with a Crown Prosecutor as soon as is reasonably practicable. Where the Crown Prosecutor is unable to make the charging decision on the information available at that time, the detainee may be released without charge and on bail (with conditions if necessary) under section 37(7)(a). In such circumstances, the detainee should be informed that they are being released to enable the Director of Public Prosecutions to make a decision under section 37B.

16.2 When a detainee is charged with or informed they may be prosecuted for an offence, see *Note 16B*, they shall, unless the restriction on drawing adverse inferences from silence applies, see *Annex C*, be cautioned as follows:

> "You do not have to say anything. But it may harm your defence if you do not mention now something which you later rely on in court. Anything you do say may be given in evidence."

Annex C, paragraph 2 sets out the alternative terms of the caution to be used when the restriction on drawing adverse inferences from silence applies.

16.3 When a detainee is charged they shall be given a written notice showing particulars of the offence and, subject to paragraph 2.6A, the officer's name and the case reference number. As far as possible the particulars of the charge shall be stated in simple terms, but they shall also show the precise offence in law with which the detainee is charged. The notice shall begin:

> "*You are charged with the offence(s) shown below.*" Followed by the caution.

If the detainee is a juvenile, mentally disordered or otherwise mentally vulnerable, the notice should be given to the appropriate adult.

16.4 If, after a detainee has been charged with or informed they may be prosecuted for an offence, an officer wants to tell them about any written statement or interview with another person relating to such an offence, the detainee shall either be handed a true copy of the written statement or the content of the interview record brought to their attention. Nothing shall be done to invite any reply or comment except to:

(a) caution the detainee, "*You do not have to say anything, but anything you do say may be given in evidence.*"; and

(b) remind the detainee about their right to legal advice.

16.4A If the detainee:

- cannot read, the document may be read to them
- is a juvenile, mentally disordered or otherwise mentally vulnerable, the appropriate adult shall also be given a copy, or the interview record shall be brought to their attention.

16.5 A detainee may not be interviewed about an offence after they have been charged with, or informed they may be prosecuted for it, unless the interview is necessary:

- to prevent or minimise harm or loss to some other person, or the public
- to clear up an ambiguity in a previous answer or statement

- in the interests of justice for the detainee to have put to them, and have an opportunity to comment on, information concerning the offence which has come to light since they were charged or informed they might be prosecuted

Before any such interview, the interviewer shall:

(a) caution the detainee, "*You do not have to say anything, but anything you do say may be given in evidence.*";

(b) remind the detainee about their right to legal advice.

See *Note 16B*

16.6 The provisions of paragraphs 16.2 to 16.5 must be complied with in the appropriate adult's presence if they are already at the police station. If they are not at the police station then these provisions must be complied with again in their presence when they arrive unless the detainee has been released.

See *Note 16C*

16.7 When a juvenile is charged with an offence and the custody officer authorises their continued detention after charge, the custody officer must try to make arrangements for the juvenile to be taken into the care of a local authority to be detained pending appearance in court unless the custody officer certifies it is impracticable to do so or, in the case of a juvenile of at least 12 years old, no secure accommodation is available and there is a risk to the public of serious harm from that juvenile, in accordance with PACE, section 38(6). See *Note 16D*

(b) Documentation

16.8 A record shall be made of anything a detainee says when charged.

16.9 Any questions put in an interview after charge and answers given relating to the offence shall be recorded in full during the interview on forms for that purpose and the record signed by the detainee or, if they refuse, by the interviewer and any third parties present. If the questions are tape recorded or visually recorded the arrangements in Code E or F apply.

16.10 If it is not practicable to make arrangements for a juvenile's transfer into local authority care as in paragraph 16.7, the custody officer must record the reasons and complete a certificate to be produced before the court with the juvenile. See *Note 16D*

Notes for guidance

16A The custody officer must take into account alternatives to prosecution under the Crime and Disorder Act 1998, reprimands and warning applicable to persons under 18, and in national guidance on the cautioning of offenders, for persons aged 18 and over.

16AB Where Guidance issued by the Director of Public Prosecutions under section 37B is in force, custody officers are entitled (notwithstanding section 37(1)) to take reasonable time to apply that Guidance in deciding how a detained person is to be dealt with in accordance with section 37(7), as amended by Schedule 2 of the Criminal Justice Act 2003, including where appropriate consultation with a Duty Prosecutor. Where in accordance with the Guidance the case is referred to the CPS for decision, the custody officer should ensure that an officer involved in the investigation sends to the CPS such information as is specified in the Guidance.

16B The giving of a warning or the service of the Notice of Intended Prosecution required by the Road Traffic Offenders Act 1988, section 1 does not amount to informing a detainee they may be prosecuted for an offence and so does not preclude further questioning in relation to that offence.

16C There is no power under PACE to detain a person and delay action under paragraphs 16.2 to 16.5 solely to await the arrival of the appropriate adult. After charge, bail cannot be refused, or release on bail delayed, simply because an appropriate adult is not available, unless the absence of that adult provides the custody officer with the necessary grounds to authorise detention after charge under PACE, section 38.

16D Except as in paragraph 16.7, neither a juvenile's behaviour nor the nature of the offence provides grounds for the custody officer to decide it is impracticable to arrange the juvenile's transfer to local authority care. Similarly, the lack of secure local authority accommodation does not make it impracticable to transfer the juvenile. The availability of secure accommodation is only a factor in relation to a juvenile aged 12 or over when the local authority accommodation would not be adequate to protect the public from serious harm from them. The obligation to transfer a juvenile to local authority accommodation applies as much to a juvenile charged during the daytime as to a juvenile to be held overnight, subject to a requirement to bring the juvenile before a court under PACE, section 46.

17 Testing persons for the presence of specified Class A drugs

(a) Action

17.1 A sample of urine or a non-intimate sample may be taken from a person in police detention for the purpose of ascertaining whether he has any specified Class A drug in his body if:

- (a) he has been charged with a trigger offence, or
- (b) he has been charged with an offence and a police officer of inspector rank or above, who has reasonable grounds for suspecting that the misuse by him of any specified Class A drug caused or contributed to the offence, has authorised the sample to be taken.

17.2 The person from whom the sample is taken must have attained the minimum age for drug testing under the provisions in force in the police area or police station concerned (14 or 18 years of age). See *Note 17F*

17.3 A police officer must have requested the person concerned to give the sample.

17.4 Before requesting a sample from the person concerned, an officer must:

- (a) inform him that the purpose of taking the sample is for drug testing under PACE. This is to ascertain whether he has a specified Class A drug present in his body;
- (b) warn him that if, when so requested, he fails without good cause to provide a sample he may be liable to prosecution;
- (c) where the taking of the sample has been authorised by an inspector or above in accordance with paragraph 17.1(b) of this Code, inform him that the authorisation has been given and the grounds for giving it;
- (d) remind him of the following rights, which may be exercised at any stage during the period in custody:
  - (i) the right to have someone informed of his arrest [see section 5];
  - (ii) the right to consult privately with a solicitor and that free independent legal advice is available [see section 6]; and
  - (iii) the right to consult these Codes of Practice [see section 3].

17.5 In the case of a person who has not attained the age of 17—
- (a) the making of the request for a sample under paragraph 17.3 above;
- (b) the giving of the warning and the information under paragraph 17.4 above; and
- (c) the taking of the sample, may not take place except in the presence of an appropriate adult. (see *Note 17G*)

17.6 Authorisation by an officer of the rank of inspector or above within paragraph 17.1 (b) may be given orally or in writing but, if it is given orally, it must be confirmed in writing as soon as practicable.

17.7 Custody officers may authorise continued detention for up to six hours from the time of charge to enable a sample to be taken.

(b) Documentation

17.8 If a sample is taken following authorisation by an officer of the rank of inspector or above, the authorisation and the grounds for suspicion must be recorded in the custody record.

17.9 The giving of a warning of the consequences of failure to provide a specimen must be recorded in the custody record.

17.10 The time of charge and the time at which the sample was given must be recorded in the custody record.

(c) General

17.11 A sample may only be taken by a prescribed person. See *Note 17C*

17.12 Force may not be used to take any sample for the purpose of drug testing.

17.13 The terms "Class A drug" and "misuse" have the same meanings as in the Misuse of Drugs Act 1971. "Specified" (in relation to a Class A drug) and "trigger offence" have the same meanings as in Pt III of the Criminal Justice and Court Services Act 2000.

17.14 Any sample taken:
- (a) may not be used for any purpose other than to ascertain whether the person concerned has a specified Class A drug present in his body; and
- (b) must be retained until the person concerned has made his first appearance before the court.

Notes for guidance

17A When warning a person who is asked to provide a urine or non-intimate sample in accordance with paragraph 17.1, the following form of words may be used:

> "You do not have to provide a sample, but I must warn you that if you fail or refuse without good cause to do so, you will commit an offence for which you may be imprisoned, or fined, or both".

17B A sample has to be sufficient and suitable. A sufficient sample is sufficient in quantity and quality to enable drug-testing analysis to take place. A suitable sample is one which by its nature, is suitable for a particular form of drug analysis.

17C A prescribed person in paragraph 17.11 is one who is prescribed in regulations made by the Secretary of State under section 63B(6) of the Police and Criminal Evidence Act

1984. [The regulations are currently contained in regulation SI 2001 No. 2645, the Police and Criminal Evidence Act 1984 (Drug Testing Persons in Police Detention) (Prescribed Persons) Regulations 2001.]

17D The retention of the sample in paragraph 17.14(b) allows for the sample to be sent for confirmatory testing and analysis if the detainee disputes the test. But such samples, and the information derived from them, may not be subsequently used in the investigation of any offence or in evidence against the persons from whom they were taken.

17E Trigger offences include: from the Theft Act 1968—theft, robbery, burglary, aggravated burglary, taking a motor vehicle (or other conveyance) without authority, aggravated vehicle-taking, obtaining property by deception, going equipped for stealing *etc.*; and from the Misuse of Drugs Act 1971(but only if committed in respect of a specified Class A drug)—producing and supplying a controlled drug, possessing a controlled drug, and possessing a controlled drug with intent to supply.

17F Section.17 is applicable only within certain police areas, where the relevant provisions for drug testing under section 63B of PACE have been brought into force. The areas where testing for persons aged 18 or over has been introduced are listed at *Annex I*. The minimum age of 14 will apply only in those police areas where:

- new provisions introduced by section 5 of the Criminal Justice Act 2003 to test persons aged 14 or over have been brought into force

AND

- the relevant chief officer of police has been notified by the Secretary of State that arrangements for the taking of samples from persons under the age of 18 have been made for the police area as a whole, or for a particular police station within that area and the notice has not been withdrawn.

The police areas where section 5 of the Criminal Justice Act 2003 is in force and where drug testing of persons aged 14–17 applies, if such notification is in force, are set out in *Annex J*.

17G Appropriate adult in paragraph 17.5 means the person's—

(a) parent or guardian or, if he is in the care of a local authority or voluntary organisation, a person representing that authority or organisation; or
(b) a social worker of a local authority social services department; or
(c) if no person falling within (*a*) or (*b*) above is available, any responsible person aged 18 or over who is not a police officer or a person employed by the police.

Annex A—Intimate and strip searches

A Intimate search

1. An intimate search consists of the physical examination of a person's body orifices other than the mouth. The intrusive nature of such searches means the actual and potential risks associated with intimate searches must never be underestimated.

(a) Action

2. Body orifices other than the mouth may be searched only if authorised by an officer of inspector rank or above who has reasonable grounds for believing that:

(a) the person may have concealed on themselves:
  (i) anything which they could and might use to cause physical injury to themself or others at the station; or
  (ii) a Class A drug which they intended to supply to another or to export; and

(b) an intimate search is the only means of removing those items.

2A. The reasons an intimate search is considered necessary shall be explained to the person before the search begins.

3. An intimate search may only be carried out by a registered medical practitioner or registered nurse, unless an officer of at least inspector rank considers this is not practicable and the search is to take place under paragraph 2(a)(i), in which case a police officer may carry out the search. See *Notes A1* to *A5*

3A. Any proposal for a search under paragraph 2(a)(i) to be carried out by someone other than a registered medical practitioner or registered nurse must only be considered as a last resort and when the authorising officer is satisfied the risks associated with allowing the item to remain with the detainee outweigh the risks associated with removing it. See *Notes A1* to *A5*

4. An intimate search under:
- paragraph 2(a)(i) may take place only at a hospital, surgery, other medical premises or police station
- paragraph 2(a)(ii) may take place only at a hospital, surgery or other medical premises and must be carried out by a registered medical practitioner or a registered nurse.

5. An intimate search at a police station of a juvenile or mentally disordered or otherwise mentally vulnerable person may take place only in the presence of an appropriate adult of the same sex, unless the detainee specifically requests a particular adult of the opposite sex who is readily available. In the case of a juvenile the search may take place in the absence of the appropriate adult only if the juvenile signifies in the presence of the appropriate adult they do not want the adult present during the search and the adult agrees. A record shall be made of the juvenile's decision and signed by the appropriate adult.

6. When an intimate search under paragraph 2(a)(i) is carried out by a police officer, the officer must be of the same sex as the detainee. A minimum of two people, other than the detainee, must be present during the search. Subject to paragraph 5, no person of the opposite sex who is not a medical practitioner or nurse shall be present, nor shall anyone whose presence is unnecessary.The search shall be conducted with proper regard to the sensitivity and vulnerability of the detainee.

(b) Documentation

7. In the case of an intimate search the custody officer shall as soon as practicable, record:
- which parts of the detainee's body were searched
- who carried out the search
- who was present
- the reasons for the search including the reasons to believe the article could not otherwise be removed
- the result.

8. If an intimate search is carried out by a police officer, the reason why it was impracticable for a registered medical practitioner or registered nurse to conduct it must be recorded.

B Strip search

9. A strip search is a search involving the removal of more than outer clothing. In this Code, outer clothing includes shoes and socks.

(a) Action

10. A strip search may take place only if it is considered necessary to remove an article which a detainee would not be allowed to keep, and the officer reasonably considers the detainee might have concealed such an article. Strip searches shall not be routinely carried out if there is no reason to consider that articles are concealed.

The conduct of strip searches

11. When strip searches are conducted:
   (a) a police officer carrying out a strip search must be the same sex as the detainee;
   (b) the search shall take place in an area where the detainee cannot be seen by anyone who does not need to be present, nor by a member of the opposite sex except an appropriate adult who has been specifically requested by the detainee;
   (c) except in cases of urgency, where there is risk of serious harm to the detainee or to others, whenever a strip search involves exposure of intimate body parts, there must be at least two people present other than the detainee, and if the search is of a juvenile or mentally disordered or otherwise mentally vulnerable person, one of the people must be the appropriate adult. Except in urgent cases as above, a search of a juvenile may take place in the absence of the appropriate adult only if the juvenile signifies in the presence of the appropriate adult that they do not want the adult to be present during the search and the adult agrees. A record shall be made of the juvenile's decision and signed by the appropriate adult. The presence of more than two people, other than an appropriate adult, shall be permitted only in the most exceptional circumstances;
   (d) the search shall be conducted with proper regard to the sensitivity and vulnerability of the detainee in these circumstances and every reasonable effort shall be made to secure the detainee's co-operation and minimise embarrassment. Detainees who are searched shall not normally be required to remove all their clothes at the same time, *e.g.* a person should be allowed to remove clothing above the waist and redress before removing further clothing;
   (e) if necessary to assist the search, the detainee may be required to hold their arms in the air or to stand with their legs apart and bend forward so a visual examination may be made of the genital and anal areas provided no physical contact is made with any body orifice;
   (f) if articles are found, the detainee shall be asked to hand them over. If articles are found within any body orifice other than the mouth, and the detainee refuses to hand them over, their removal would constitute an intimate search, which must be carried out as in *Pt A*;
   (g) a strip search shall be conducted as quickly as possible, and the detainee allowed to dress as soon as the procedure is complete.

(b) Documentation

12. A record shall be made on the custody record of a strip search including the reason it was considered necessary, those present and any result.

Notes for guidance

A1 Before authorising any intimate search, the authorising officer must make every reasonable effort to persuade the detainee to hand the article over without a search. If the detainee agrees, a registered medical practitioner or registered nurse should whenever possible be asked to assess the risks involved and, if necessary, attend to assist the detainee.

A2 If the detainee does not agree to hand the article over without a search, the authorising officer must carefully review all the relevant factors before authorising an intimate search. In particular, the officer must consider whether the grounds for believing an article may be concealed are reasonable.

A3 If authority is given for a search under paragraph 2(a)(i), a registered medical practitioner or registered nurse shall be consulted whenever possible. The presumption should be that the search will be conducted by the registered medical practitioner or registered nurse and the authorising officer must make every reasonable effort to persuade the detainee to allow the medical practitioner or nurse to conduct the search.

A4 A constable should only be authorised to carry out a search as a last resort and when all other approaches have failed. In these circumstances, the authorising officer must be satisfied the detainee might use the article for one or more of the purposes in paragraph 2(a)(i) and the physical injury likely to be caused is sufficiently severe to justify authorising a constable to carry out the search.

A5 If an officer has any doubts whether to authorise an intimate search by a constable, the officer should seek advice from an officer of superintendent rank or above.

Annex B—Delay in notifying arrest or allowing access to legal advice

A Persons detained under PACE

1. The exercise of the rights in Section 5 or Section 6, or both, may be delayed if the person is in police detention, as in PACE, section 118(2), in connection with a serious arrestable offence, has not yet been charged with an offence and an officer of superintendent rank or above, or inspector rank or above only for the rights in Section 5, has reasonable grounds for believing their exercise will:
   (i) lead to:
      - interference with, or harm to, evidence connected with a serious arrestable offence; or
      - interference with, or physical harm to, other people; or
   (ii) lead to alerting other people suspected of having committed a serious arrestable offence but not yet arrested for it; or
   (iii) hinder the recovery of property obtained in consequence of the commission of such an offence.

2. These rights may also be delayed if the serious arrestable offence is:
   (i) a drug trafficking offence and the officer has reasonable grounds for believing the detainee has benefited from drug trafficking, and the recovery of the value of the detainee's proceeds from drug trafficking will be hindered by the exercise of either right;
   (ii) an offence to which the Criminal Justice Act 1988, Pt VI (confiscation orders) applies and the officer has reasonable grounds for believing the detainee has benefited from the offence, and the exercise of either right will hinder the recovery of the value of the:
      - property obtained by the detainee from or in connection with the offence
      - pecuniary advantage derived by the detainee from or in connection with it.

3. Authority to delay a detainee's right to consult privately with a solicitor may be given only if the authorising officer has reasonable grounds to believe the solicitor the detainee wants to consult will, inadvertently or otherwise, pass on a message from the detainee or act in some other way which will have any of the consequences specified under paragraphs 1 or 2. In these circumstances the detainee must be allowed to choose another solicitor. See *Note B3*

4. If the detainee wishes to see a solicitor, access to that solicitor may not be delayed on the grounds they might advise the detainee not to answer questions or the solicitor was initially asked to attend the police station by someone else. In the latter case the detainee must be told the solicitor has come to the police station at another person's request, and must be asked to sign the custody record to signify whether they want to see the solicitor.

5. The fact the grounds for delaying notification of arrest may be satisfied does not automatically mean the grounds for delaying access to legal advice will also be satisfied.

6. These rights may be delayed only for as long as grounds exist and in no case beyond 36 hours after the relevant time as in PACE, section 41. If the grounds cease to apply within this time, the detainee must, as soon as practicable, be asked if they want to exercise either right, the custody record must be noted accordingly, and action taken in accordance with the relevant section of the Code.

7. A detained person must be permitted to consult a solicitor for a reasonable time before any court hearing.

B Persons detained under the Terrorism Act 2000

8. The rights as in sections 5 or 6, may be delayed if the person is detained under the Terrorism Act 2000, section 41 or Schedule 7, has not yet been charged with an offence and an officer of superintendent rank or above has reasonable grounds for believing the exercise of either right will:
- (i) lead to:
  - interference with, or harm to, evidence connected with a serious arrestable offence;
  - interference with, or physical harm to, other people; or
- (ii) lead to the alerting of other people suspected of having committed a serious arrestable offence but not yet arrested for it; or
- (iii) hinder the recovery of property:
  - obtained in consequence of the commission of such an offence; or
  - in respect of which a forfeiture order could be made under that Act, section 23;
- (iv) lead to interference with the gathering of information about the commission, preparation or instigation of acts of terrorism; or
- (v) by alerting any person, make it more difficult to prevent an act of terrorism or secure the apprehension, prosecution or conviction of any person in connection with the commission, preparation or instigation of an act of terrorism.

9. These rights may also be delayed if the officer has reasonable grounds for believing:
- (a) the detainee:
  - (i) has committed an offence to which the Criminal Justice Act 1988, Pt VI (confiscation orders) applies;

    (ii) has benefited from the offence; and
  (b) the exercise of either right will hinder the recovery of the value of that benefit.

10. In these cases paragraphs 3 (with regards to the consequences specified at paragraphs 8 and 9), 4 and 5 apply.

11. These rights may be delayed only for as long as is necessary but not beyond 48 hours from the time of arrest if arrested under section 41, or if detained under the Terrorism Act 2000, Schedule 7 when arrested under section 41, from the beginning of their examination. If the above grounds cease to apply within this time the detainee must as soon as practicable be asked if they wish to exercise either right, the custody record noted accordingly, and action taken in accordance with the relevant section of this Code.

12. In this case paragraph 7 applies.

C Documentation

13. The grounds for action under this *Annex* shall be recorded and the detainee informed of them as soon as practicable.

14. Any reply given by a detainee under paragraphs 6 or 11 must be recorded and the detainee asked to endorse the record in relation to whether they want to receive legal advice at this point.

D Cautions and special warnings

When a suspect detained at a police station is interviewed during any period for which access to legal advice has been delayed under this Annex, the court or jury may not draw adverse inferences from their silence.

Notes for guidance

B 1 Even if *Annex B* applies in the case of a juvenile, or a person who is mentally disordered or otherwise mentally vulnerable, action to inform the appropriate adult and the person responsible for a juvenile's welfare if that is a different person, must nevertheless be taken as in paragraph 3.13 and 3.15.

B 2 In the case of Commonwealth citizens and foreign nationals, see *Note 7A*.

B 3 A decision to delay access to a specific solicitor is likely to be a rare occurrence and only when it can be shown the suspect is capable of misleading that particular solicitor and there is more than a substantial risk that the suspect will succeed in causing information to be conveyed which will lead to one or more of the specified consequences.

Annex C—Restriction on drawing adverse inferences from silence and terms of the caution when the restriction applies

(a) The restriction on drawing adverse inferences from silence

1. The Criminal Justice and Public Order Act 1994, sections 34, 36 and 37 as amended by the Youth Justice and Criminal Evidence Act 1999, section 58 describe the conditions under which adverse inferences may be drawn from a person's failure or refusal to say anything about their involvement in the offence when interviewed, after being charged or informed they may be prosecuted. These provisions are subject to an overriding

restriction on the ability of a court or jury to draw adverse inferences from a person's silence. This restriction applies:

(a) to any detainee at a police station, see *Note 10C* who, before being interviewed, see section 11 or being charged or informed they may be prosecuted, see section 16, has:
   (i) asked for legal advice, see section 6, paragraph 6.1;
   (ii) not been allowed an opportunity to consult a solicitor, including the duty solicitor, as in this Code; and
   (iii) not changed their mind about wanting legal advice, see section 6, paragraph 6.6(d)

   Note the condition in (ii) will
   - apply when a detainee who has asked for legal advice is interviewed before speaking to a solicitor as in section 6, paragraph 6.6(a) or (b).
   - not apply if the detained person declines to ask for the duty solicitor, see section 6, paragraphs 6.6(c) and (d).

(b) to any person charged with, or informed they may be prosecuted for, an offence who:
   (i) has had brought to their notice a written statement made by another person or the content of an interview with another person which relates to that offence, see section 16, paragraph 16.4;
   (ii) is interviewed about that offence, see section 16, paragraph 16.5;or
   (iii) makes a written statement about that offence, see *Annex D* paragraphs 4 and 9.

(b) Terms of the caution when the restriction applies

2. When a requirement to caution arises at a time when the restriction on drawing adverse inferences from silence applies, the caution shall be:

"You do not have to say anything, but anything you do say may be given in evidence."

3. Whenever the restriction either begins to apply or ceases to apply after a caution has already been given, the person shall be re-cautioned in the appropriate terms. The changed position on drawing inferences and that the previous caution no longer applies shall also be explained to the detainee in ordinary language. See *Note C2*

Notes for guidance

C1 The restriction on drawing inferences from silence does not apply to a person who has not been detained and who therefore cannot be prevented from seeking legal advice if they want to, see paragraphs 10.2 and 3.15.

C2 The following is suggested as a framework to help explain changes in the position on drawing adverse inferences if the restriction on drawing adverse inferences from silence:

(a) begins to apply:

   "The caution you were previously given no longer applies. This is because after that caution:

   (i) you asked to speak to a solicitor but have not yet been allowed an opportunity to speak to a solicitor. See paragraph 1(a); or
   (ii) you have been charged with/informed you may be prosecuted.' See paragraph 1(b).

   "This means that from now on, adverse inferences cannot be drawn at court and your defence will not be harmed just because you choose to say nothing. Please listen carefully to the caution I am about to give you because it will apply from now on. You will see that it does not say anything about your defence being harmed."

(b) ceases to apply before or at the time the person is charged or informed they may be prosecuted, see paragraph 1(a);

"The caution you were previously given no longer applies. This is because after that caution you have been allowed an opportunity to speak to a solicitor. Please listen carefully to the caution I am about to give you because it will apply from now on. It explains how your defence at court may be affected if you choose to say nothing."

Annex D—Written statements under caution

(a) Written by a person under caution

1. A person shall always be invited to write down what they want to say.

2. A person who has not been charged with, or informed they may be prosecuted for, any offence to which the statement they want to write relates, shall:

(a) unless the statement is made at a time when the restriction on drawing adverse inferences from silence applies, see *Annex C*, be asked to write out and sign the following before writing what they want to say:

"I make this statement of my own free will. I understand that I do not have to say anything but that it may harm my defence if I do not mention when questioned something which I later rely on in court. This statement may be given in evidence.";

(b) if the statement is made at a time when the restriction on drawing adverse inferences from silence applies, be asked to write out and sign the following before writing what they want to say;

"I make this statement of my own free will. I understand that I do not have to say anything. This statement may be given in evidence."

3. When a person, on the occasion of being charged with or informed they may be prosecuted for any offence, asks to make a statement which relates to any such offence and wants to write it they shall:

(a) unless the restriction on drawing adverse inferences from silence, see *Annex C*, applied when they were so charged or informed they may be prosecuted, be asked to write out and sign the following before writing what they want to say:

"I make this statement of my own free will. I understand that I do not have to say anything but that it may harm my defence if I do not mention when questioned something which I later rely on in court. This statement may be given in evidence.";

(b) if the restriction on drawing adverse inferences from silence applied when they were so charged or informed they may be prosecuted, be asked to write out and sign the following before writing what they want to say:

"I make this statement of my own free will. I understand that I do not have to say anything. This statement may be given in evidence."

4. When a person, who has already been charged with or informed they may be prosecuted for any offence, asks to make a statement which relates to any such offence and wants to write it they shall be asked to write out and sign the following before writing what they want to say:

> "I make this statement of my own free will. I understand that I do not have to say anything. This statement may be given in evidence.";

5. Any person writing their own statement shall be allowed to do so without any prompting except a police officer or other police staff may indicate to them which matters are material or question any ambiguity in the statement.

(b) Written by a police officer or other police staff

6. If a person says they would like someone to write the statement for them, a police officer, or other police staff shall write the statement.

7. If the person has not been charged with, or informed they may be prosecuted for, any offence to which the statement they want to make relates they shall, before starting, be asked to sign, or make their mark, to the following:

(a) unless the statement is made at a time when the restriction on drawing adverse inferences from silence applies, see *Annex C*:

> "I, ..., wish to make a statement. I want someone to write down what I say. I understand that I do not have to say anything but that it may harm my defence if I do not mention when questioned something which I later rely on in court. This statement may be given in evidence.";

(b) if the statement is made at a time when the restriction on drawing adverse inferences from silence applies:

> "I, ..., wish to make a statement. I want someone to write down what I say. I understand that I do not have to say anything. This statement may be given in evidence."

8. If, on the occasion of being charged with or informed they may be prosecuted for any offence, the person asks to make a statement which relates to any such offence they shall before starting be asked to sign, or make their mark to, the following:

(a) unless the restriction on drawing adverse inferences from silence applied, see *Annex C*, when they were so charged or informed they may be prosecuted:

> "I, ..., wish to make a statement. I want someone to write down what I say. I understand that I do not have to say anything but that it may harm my defence if I do not mention when questioned something which I later rely on in court. This statement may be given in evidence.";

(b) if the restriction on drawing adverse inferences from silence applied when they were so charged or informed they may be prosecuted:

> "I, ..., wish to make a statement. I want someone to write down what I say. I understand that I do not have to say anything. This statement may be given in evidence."

9. If, having already been charged with or informed they may be prosecuted for any offence, a person asks to make a statement which relates to any such offence they shall before starting, be asked to sign, or make their mark to:

> "I, ..., wish to make a statement. I want someone to write down what I say. I understand that I do not have to say anything. This statement may be given in evidence."

10. The person writing the statement must take down the exact words spoken by the person making it and must not edit or paraphrase it. Any questions that are necessary, *e.g.* to make it more intelligible, and the answers given must be recorded at the same time on the statement form.

11. When the writing of a statement is finished the person making it shall be asked to read it and to make any corrections, alterations or additions they want. When they have finished reading they shall be asked to write and sign or make their mark on the following certificate at the end of the statement:

> "I have read the above statement, and I have been able to correct, alter or add anything I wish. This statement is true. I have made it of my own free will."

12. If the person making the statement cannot read, or refuses to read it, or to write the above mentioned certificate at the end of it or to sign it, the person taking the statement shall read it to them and ask them if they would like to correct, alter or add anything and to put their signature or make their mark at the end. The person taking the statement shall certify on the statement itself what has occurred.

Annex E—Summary of provisions relating to mentally disordered and otherwise mentally vulnerable people

1. If an officer has any suspicion, or is told in good faith, that a person of any age may be mentally disordered or otherwise mentally vulnerable, or mentally incapable of understanding the significance of questions or their replies that person shall be treated as mentally disordered or otherwise mentally vulnerable for the purposes of this Code. See paragraph 1.4

2. In the case of a person who is mentally disordered or otherwise mentally vulnerable, "the appropriate adult" means:

(a) a relative, guardian or other person responsible for their care or custody;
(b) someone experienced in dealing with mentally disordered or mentally vulnerable people but who is not a police officer or employed by the police;
(c) failing these, some other responsible adult aged 18 or over who is not a police officer or employed by the police.

See paragraph 1.7(b) and *Note 1D*

3. If the custody officer authorises the detention of a person who is mentally vulnerable or appears to be suffering from a mental disorder, the custody officer must as soon as practicable inform the appropriate adult of the grounds for detention and the person's whereabouts, and ask the adult to come to the police station to see them. If the appropriate adult:

- is already at the station when information is given as in paragraphs 3.1 to 3.5 the information must be given in their presence
- is not at the station when the provisions of paragraph 3.1 to 3.5 are complied with these provisions must be complied with again in their presence once they arrive.

See paragraphs 3.15 to 3.17

4. If the appropriate adult, having been informed of the right to legal advice, considers legal advice should be taken, the provisions of section 6 apply as if the mentally disordered or otherwise mentally vulnerable person had requested access to legal advice. See paragraph 3.19 and *Note E1*

5. The custody officer must make sure a person receives appropriate clinical attention as soon as reasonably practicable if the person appears to be suffering from a mental disorder or in urgent cases immediately call the nearest health care professional or an ambulance. It is not intended these provisions delay the transfer of a detainee to a place of safety under the Mental Health Act 1983, section 136 if that is applicable. If an assessment under that Act is to take place at a police station, the custody officer must consider whether an appropriate health care professional should be called to conduct an initial clinical check on the detainee. See paragraph 9.5 and 9.6

6. It is imperative a mentally disordered or otherwise mentally vulnerable person detained under the Mental Health Act 1983, section 136 be assessed as soon as possible. If that assessment is to take place at the police station, an approved social worker and registered medical practitioner shall be called to the station as soon as possible in order to interview and examine the detainee. Once the detainee has been interviewed, examined and suitable arrangements been made for their treatment or care, they can no longer be detained under section 136. A detainee should be immediately discharged from detention if a registered medical practitioner having examined them, concludes they are not mentally disordered within the meaning of the Act. See paragraph 3.16

7. If a mentally disordered or otherwise mentally vulnerable person is cautioned in the absence of the appropriate adult, the caution must be repeated in the appropriate adult's presence. See paragraph 10.12

8. A mentally disordered or otherwise mentally vulnerable person must not be interviewed or asked to provide or sign a written statement in the absence of the appropriate adult unless the provisions of paragraphs 11.1 or 11.18 to 11.20 apply. Questioning in these circumstances may not continue in the absence of the appropriate adult once sufficient information to avert the risk has been obtained. A record shall be made of the grounds for any decision to begin an interview in these circumstances. See paragraphs 11.1, 11.15 and 11.18 to 11.20

9. If the appropriate adult is present at an interview, they shall be informed they are not expected to act simply as an observer and the purposes of their presence are to:

- advise the interviewee
- observe whether or not the interview is being conducted properly and fairly
- facilitate communication with the interviewee

See paragraph 11.17

10. If the detention of a mentally disordered or otherwise mentally vulnerable person is reviewed by a review officer or a superintendent, the appropriate adult must, if available at the time, be given an opportunity to make representations to the officer about the need for continuing detention. See paragraph 15.3

11. If the custody officer charges a mentally disordered or otherwise mentally vulnerable person with an offence or takes such other action as is appropriate when there is sufficient evidence for a prosecution this must be done in the presence of the appropriate adult. The written notice embodying any charge must be given to the appropriate adult. See paragraphs 16.1 to 16.4A

12. An intimate or strip search of a mentally disordered or otherwise mentally vulnerable person may take place only in the presence of the appropriate adult of the same sex, unless the detainee specifically requests the presence of a particular adult of the opposite sex. A strip search may take place in the absence of an appropriate adult only in cases of urgency when there is a risk of serious harm to the detainee or others. See *Annex A*, paragraphs 5 and 11(c)

13. Particular care must be taken when deciding whether to use any form of approved restraints on a mentally disordered or otherwise mentally vulnerable person in a locked cell. See paragraph 8.2

Notes for guidance

E1 The purpose of the provision at paragraph 3.19 is to protect the rights of a mentally disordered or otherwise mentally vulnerable detained person who does not understand the significance of what is said to them. If the detained person wants to exercise the right to legal advice, the appropriate action should be taken and not delayed until the appropriate adult arrives. A mentally disordered or otherwise mentally vulnerable detained person should always be given an opportunity, when an appropriate adult is called to the police station, to consult privately with a solicitor in the absence of the appropriate adult if they want.

E2 Although people who are mentally disordered or otherwise mentally vulnerable are often capable of providing reliable evidence, they may, without knowing or wanting to do so, be particularly prone in certain circumstances to provide information that may be unreliable, misleading or self-incriminating. Special care should always be taken when questioning such a person, and the appropriate adult should be involved if there is any doubt about a person's mental state or capacity. Because of the risk of unreliable evidence, it is important to obtain corroboration of any facts admitted whenever possible.

E3 Because of the risks referred to in *Note E2*, which the presence of the appropriate adult is intended to minimise, officers of superintendent rank or above should exercise their discretion to authorise the commencement of an interview in the appropriate adult's absence only in exceptional cases, if it is necessary to avert an immediate risk of serious harm. See paragraphs 11.1, 11.18 to 11.20

Annex F—Countries with which bilateral consular conventions or agreements requiring notification of the arrest and detention of their nationals are in force as at 1 April 2003

Armenia
Austria
Azerbaijan
Belarus
Belgium
Bosnia-Herzegovina
Bulgaria
China*
Croatia
Cuba
Czech Republic
Denmark
Kazakhstan
Macedonia
Mexico
Moldova
Mongolia
Norway
Poland
Romania
Russia
Slovak Republic
Slovenia
Spain

Egypt
France
Georgia
German Federal Republic
Greece
Hungary
Italy
Japan
Sweden
Tajikistan
Turkmenistan
Ukraine
USA
Uzbekistan
Yugoslavia

* Police are required to inform Chinese officials of arrest/detention in the Manchester consular district only. This comprises Derbyshire, Durham, Greater Manchester, Lancashire, Merseyside, North South and West Yorkshire, and Tyne and Wear.

Annex G—Fitness to be interviewed

1. This Annex contains general guidance to help police officers and health care professionals assess whether a detainee might be at risk in an interview.

2. A detainee may be at risk in an interview if it is considered that:
   (a) conducting the interview could significantly harm the detainee's physical or mental state;
   (b) anything the detainee says in the interview about their involvement or suspected involvement in the offence about which they are being interviewed might be considered unreliable in subsequent court proceedings because of their physical or mental state.

3. In assessing whether the detainee should be interviewed, the following must be considered:
   (a) how the detainee's physical or mental state might affect their ability to understand the nature and purpose of the interview, to comprehend what is being asked and to appreciate the significance of any answers given and make rational decisions about whether they want to say anything;
   (b) the extent to which the detainee's replies may be affected by their physical or mental condition rather than representing a rational and accurate explanation of their involvement in the offence;
   (c) how the nature of the interview, which could include particularly probing questions, might affect the detainee.

4. It is essential health care professionals who are consulted consider the functional ability of the detainee rather than simply relying on a medical diagnosis, *e.g.* it is possible for a person with severe mental illness to be fit for interview.

5. Health care professionals should advise on the need for an appropriate adult to be present, whether reassessment of the person's fitness for interview may be necessary if the interview lasts beyond a specified time, and whether a further specialist opinion may be required.

6. When health care professionals identify risks they should be asked to quantify the risks. They should inform the custody officer:
- whether the person's condition:
  - is likely to improve
  - will require or be amenable to treatment; and
- indicate how long it may take for such improvement to take effect

7. The role of the health care professional is to consider the risks and advise the custody officer of the outcome of that consideration. The health care professional's determination and any advice or recommendations should be made in writing and form part of the custody record.

8. Once the health care professional has provided that information, it is a matter for the custody officer to decide whether or not to allow the interview to go ahead and if the interview is to proceed, to determine what safeguards are needed. Nothing prevents safeguards being provided in addition to those required under the Code. An example might be to have an appropriate health care professional present during the interview, in addition to an appropriate adult, in order constantly to monitor the person's condition and how it is being affected by the interview.

Annex H—Detained person: observation list

1. If any detainee fails to meet any of the following criteria, an appropriate health care professional or an ambulance must be called.

2. When assessing the level of rousability, consider:
   Rousability—can they be woken?
   - go into the cell
   - call their name
   - shake gently

   Response to questions—can they give appropriate answers to questions such as:
   - What's your name?
   - Where do you live?
   - Where do you think you are?

   Response to commands—can they respond appropriately to commands such as:
   - Open your eyes!
   - Lift one arm, now the other arm!

3. Remember to take into account the possibility or presence of other illnesses, injury, or mental condition, a person who is drowsy and smells of alcohol may also have the following:
   - Diabetes
   - Epilepsy
   - Head injury
   - Drug intoxication or overdose
   - Stroke

Annex I—Police areas where the power to test persons aged 18 and over for specified Class A drugs under section 63B of PACE has been brought into force*

Avon and Somerset
Bedfordshire
Cambridgeshire
Cleveland
Devon and Cornwall
Greater Manchester
Humberside
Lancashire

Leicestershire
Merseyside
Metropolitan Police District
North Wales
Northumbria
Nottinghamshire
South Yorkshire
Staffordshire
Thames Valley
West Midlands
West Yorkshire

* The provisions are being implemented in selected police stations within these police areas.

Annex J—Police areas where the power to test persons aged 14 and over for specified Class A drugs under section 63B of PACE (as amended by section 5 of the Criminal Justice Act 2003) has been brought into force*

Cleveland
Humberside
Greater Manchester
Metropolitan Police District
Nottinghamshire
Merseyside
West Yorkshire

This power is subject to notification by the Secretary of State that arrangements for the taking of samples from persons who have not attained the age of 18 (*i.e.* persons aged 14–17) are available in the police area as a whole or in the particular police station concerned. The minimum age of 14 will apply only following that notification and if the notice has not been withdrawn.

Testing in the case of those aged 14–17 cannot be carried out unless such notification is in force.

* The provisions are being implemented in selected police stations within these police areas.

POLICE AND CRIMINAL EVIDENCE ACT 1984 (PACE), CODE D: CODE OF PRACTICE FOR THE IDENTIFICATION OF PERSONS BY POLICE OFFICERS

CONTENTS

Commencement—Transitional Arrangements

This code has effect in relation to any identification procedure carried out after midnight on 31 July 2004.

1 Introduction

1.1 This Code of Practice concerns the principal methods used by police to identify people in connection with the investigation of offences and the keeping of accurate and reliable criminal records.

1.2 Identification by witnesses arises, *e.g.*, if the offender is seen committing the crime and a witness is given an opportunity to identify the suspect in a video identification, identification parade or similar procedure. The procedures are designed to:

- test the witness' ability to identify the person they saw on a previous occasion
- provide safeguards against mistaken identification.

While this Code concentrates on visual identification procedures, it does not preclude the police making use of aural identification procedures such as a "voice identification parade", where they judge that appropriate.

1.3 Identification by fingerprints applies when a person's fingerprints are taken to:

- compare with fingerprints found at the scene of a crime
- check and prove convictions
- help to ascertain a person's identity.

1.4 Identification by body samples and impressions includes taking samples such as blood or hair to generate a DNA profile for comparison with material obtained from the scene of a crime, or a victim.

1.5 Taking photographs of arrested people applies to recording and checking identity and locating and tracing persons who:

- are wanted for offences
- fail to answer their bail.

1.6 Another method of identification involves searching and examining detained suspects to find, *e.g.*, marks such as tattoos or scars which may help establish their identity or whether they have been involved in committing an offence.

1.7 The provisions of the Police and Criminal Evidence Act 1984 (PACE) and this Code are designed to make sure fingerprints, samples, impressions and photographs are taken, used and retained, and identification procedures carried out, only when justified and necessary for preventing, detecting or investigating crime. If these provisions are not observed, the application of the relevant procedures in particular cases may be open to question.

2 General

2.1 This Code must be readily available at all police stations for consultation by:

- police officers and police staff
- detained persons
- members of the public

2.2 The provisions of this Code:

- include the *Annexes*
- do not include the *Notes for guidance*.

2.3 Code C, paragraph 1.4, regarding a person who may be mentally disordered or otherwise mentally vulnerable and the *Notes for guidance* applicable to those provisions apply to this Code.

2.4 Code C, paragraph 1.5, regarding a person who appears to be under the age of 17 applies to this Code.

2.5 Code C, paragraph 1.6, regarding a person who appears blind, seriously visually impaired, deaf, unable to read or speak or has difficulty orally because of a speech impediment applies to this Code.

2.6 In this Code:

- "appropriate adult" means the same as in Code C, paragraph 1.7,
- "solicitor" means the same as in Code C, paragraph 6.12 and the *Notes for guidance* applicable to those provisions apply to this Code.

2.7 References to custody officers include those performing the functions of custody officer.

2.8 When a record of any action requiring the authority of an officer of a specified rank is made under this Code, subject to paragraph 2.18, the officer's name and rank must be recorded.

2.9 When this Code requires the prior authority or agreement of an officer of at least inspector or superintendent rank, that authority may be given by a sergeant or chief inspector who has been authorised to perform the functions of the higher rank under PACE, section 107.

2.10 Subject to paragraph 2.18, all records must be timed and signed by the maker.

2.11 Records must be made in the custody record, unless otherwise specified. References to "pocket book" include any official report book issued to police officers or police staff.

2.12 If any procedure in this Code requires a person's consent, the consent of a:

- mentally disordered or otherwise mentally vulnerable person is only valid if given in the presence of the appropriate adult
- juvenile, is only valid if their parent's or guardian's consent is also obtained unless the juvenile is under 14, when their parent's or guardian's consent is sufficient in its own right. If the only obstacle to an identification procedure in section 3 is that a juvenile's parent or guardian refuses consent or reasonable efforts to obtain it have failed, the identification officer may apply the provisions of paragraph 3.21. See *Note 2A*.

2.13 If a person is blind, seriously visually impaired or unable to read, the custody officer or identification officer shall make sure their solicitor, relative, appropriate adult or some other person likely to take an interest in them and not involved in the investigation is available to help check any documentation. When this Code requires written consent or signing, the person assisting may be asked to sign instead, if the detainee prefers. This paragraph does not require an appropriate adult to be called solely to assist in checking and signing documentation for a person who is not a juvenile, or mentally disordered or otherwise mentally vulnerable (see Note 2B and Code C paragraph 3.15).

2.14 If any procedure in this Code requires information to be given to or sought from a suspect, it must be given or sought in the appropriate adult's presence if the suspect is mentally disordered, otherwise mentally vulnerable or a juvenile. If the appropriate adult is not present when the information is first given or sought, the procedure must be repeated in the presence of the appropriate adult when they arrive. If the suspect appears deaf or there is doubt about their hearing or speaking ability or ability to understand English, and effective communication cannot be established, the information must be given or sought through an interpreter.

2.15 Any procedure in this Code involving the participation of a person (whether as a suspect or a witness) who is mentally disordered, otherwise mentally vulnerable or a juvenile, must take place in the presence of the appropriate adult. However, the adult must not be allowed to prompt any identification of a suspect by a witness.

2.16 References to:

- "taking a photograph", include the use of any process to produce a single, still, visual image
- "photographing a person", should be construed accordingly
- "photographs", "films", "negatives" and "copies" include relevant visual images recorded, stored, or reproduced through any medium
- "destruction" includes the deletion of computer data relating to such images or making access to that data impossible.

2.17 Except as described, nothing in this Code affects the powers and procedures:

(i) for requiring and taking samples of breath, blood and urine in relation to driving offences, etc, when under the influence of drink, drugs or excess alcohol under the:
  - Road Traffic Act 1988, sections 4 to 11
  - Road Traffic Offenders Act 1988, sections 15 and 16
  - Transport and Works Act 1992, sections 26 to 38;

(ii) under the Immigration Act 1971, Schedule 2, paragraph 18, for taking photographs and fingerprints from persons detained under that Act, Schedule 2, paragraph 16 (Administrative Controls as to Control on Entry *etc.*); for taking fingerprints in accordance with the Immigration and Asylum Act 1999; sections 141 and 142(3), or other methods for collecting information about a person's external physical characteristics provided for by regulations made under that Act, section 144;

(iii) under the Terrorism Act 2000, Schedule 8, for taking photographs, fingerprints, skin impressions, body samples or impressions from people:
- arrested under that Act, section 41,
- detained for the purposes of examination under that Act, Schedule 7, and to whom the Code of Practice issued under that Act, Schedule 14, paragraph 6, applies ("the terrorism provisions")

See *Note 2C*;

(iv) for taking photographs, fingerprints, skin impressions, body samples or impressions from people who have been:
- arrested on warrants issued in Scotland, by officers exercising powers under the Criminal Justice and Public Order Act 1994, section 136(2)
- arrested or detained without warrant by officers from a police force in Scotland exercising their powers of arrest or detention under the Criminal Justice and Public Order Act 1994, section 137(2), (Cross Border powers of arrest *etc.*).

Note: In these cases, police powers and duties and the person's rights and entitlements whilst at a police station in England and Wales are the same as if the person had been arrested in Scotland by a Scottish police officer.

2.18 Nothing in this Code requires the identity of officers or police staff to be recorded or disclosed:

(a) in the case of enquiries linked to the investigation of terrorism;

(b) if the officers or police staff reasonably believe recording or disclosing their names might put them in danger.

In these cases, they shall use warrant or other identification numbers and the name of their police station. See *Note 2D*

2.19 In this Code:

(a) "designated person" means a person other than a police officer, designated under the Police Reform Act 2002, Part 4, who has specified powers and duties of police officers conferred or imposed on them;

(b) any reference to a police officer includes a designated person acting in the exercise or performance of the powers and duties conferred or imposed on them by their designation.

2.20 If a power conferred on a designated person:

(a) allows reasonable force to be used when exercised by a police officer, a designated person exercising that power has the same entitlement to use force;

(b) includes power to use force to enter any premises, that power is not exercisable by that designated person except:

(i) in the company, and under the supervision, of a police officer; or

(ii) for the purpose of:
- saving life or limb; or
- preventing serious damage to property.

2.21 Nothing in this Code prevents the custody officer, or other officer given custody of the detainee, from allowing police staff who are not designated persons to carry out individual procedures or tasks at the police station if the law allows. However, the officer remains responsible for making sure the procedures and tasks are carried out correctly in accordance with the Codes of Practice. Any such civilian must be:

(a) a person employed by a police authority maintaining a police force and under the control and direction of the Chief Officer of that force;

(b) employed by a person with whom a police authority has a contract for the provision of services relating to persons arrested or otherwise in custody.

2.22 Designated persons and other police staff must have regard to any relevant provisions of the Codes of Practice.

Notes for guidance

2A For the purposes of paragraph 2.12, the consent required from a parent or guardian may, for a juvenile in the care of a local authority or voluntary organisation, be given by that authority or organisation. In the case of a juvenile, nothing in paragraph 2.12 requires the parent, guardian or representative of a local authority or voluntary organisation to be present to give their consent, unless they are acting as the appropriate adult under paragraphs 2.14 or 2.15. However, it is important that a parent or guardian not present is fully informed before being asked to consent. They must be given the same information about the procedure and the juvenile's suspected involvement in the offence as the juvenile and appropriate adult. The parent or guardian must also be allowed to speak to the juvenile and the appropriate adult if they wish. Provided the consent is fully informed and is not withdrawn, it may be obtained at any time before the procedure takes place.

2B People who are seriously visually impaired or unable to read may be unwilling to sign police documents. The alternative, *i.e.* their representative signing on their behalf, seeks to protect the interests of both police and suspects.

2C Photographs, fingerprints, samples and impressions may be taken from a person detained under the terrorism provisions to help determine whether they are, or have been, involved in terrorism, as well as when there are reasonable grounds for suspecting their involvement in a particular offence.

2D The purpose of paragraph 2.18(b) is to protect those involved in serious organised crime investigations or arrests of particularly violent suspects when there is reliable information that those arrested or their associates may threaten or cause harm to the officers. In cases of doubt, an officer of inspector rank or above should be consulted.

3 Identification by witnesses

3.1 A record shall be made of the suspect's description as first given by a potential witness. This record must:

(a) be made and kept in a form which enables details of that description to be accurately produced from it, in a visible and legible form, which can be given to the suspect or the suspect's solicitor in accordance with this Code; and

(b) unless otherwise specified, be made before the witness takes part in any identification procedures under paragraphs 3.5 to 3.10, 3.21 or 3.23.

A copy of the record shall where practicable, be given to the suspect or their solicitor before any procedures under paragraphs 3.5 to 3.10, 3.21 or 3.23 are carried out. See *Note 3E*

(a) Cases when the suspect's identity is not known

3.2 In cases when the suspect's identity is not known, a witness may be taken to a particular neighbourhood or place to see whether they can identify the person they saw. Although the number, age, sex, race, general description and style of clothing of other people present at the location and the way in which any identification is made cannot be controlled, the principles applicable to the formal procedures under paragraphs 3.5 to 3.10 shall be followed as far as practicable. For example:

(a) where it is practicable to do so, a record should be made of the witness' description of the suspect, as in paragraph 3.1(a), before asking the witness to make an identification;

(b) care must be taken not to direct the witness' attention to any individual unless, taking into account all the circumstances, this cannot be avoided. However, this does not prevent a witness being asked to look carefully at the people around at the time or to look towards a group or in a particular direction, if this appears necessary to make sure that the witness does not overlook a possible suspect simply because the witness is looking in the opposite direction and also to enable the witness to make comparisons between any suspect and others who are in the area; See *Note 3F*

(c) where there is more than one witness, every effort should be made to keep them separate and witnesses should be taken to see whether they can identify a person independently;

(d) once there is sufficient information to justify the arrest of a particular individual for suspected involvement in the offence, *e.g.*, after a witness makes a positive identification, the provisions set out from paragraph 3.4 onwards shall apply for any other witnesses in relation to that individual. Subject to paragraphs 3.12 and 3.13, it is not necessary for the witness who makes such a positive identification to take part in a further procedure;

(e) the officer or police staff accompanying the witness must record, in their pocket book, the action taken as soon as, and in as much detail, as possible. The record should include: the date, time and place of the relevant occasion the witness claims to have previously seen the suspect; where any identification was made; how it was made and the conditions at the time (*e.g.*, the distance the witness was from the suspect, the weather and light); if the witness's attention was drawn to the suspect; the reason for this; and anything said by the witness or the suspect about the identification or the conduct of the procedure.

3.3 A witness must not be shown photographs, computerised or artist's composite likenesses or similar likenesses or pictures (including "E-fit" images) if the identity of the suspect is known to the police and the suspect is available to take part in a video identification, an identification parade or a group identification. If the suspect's identity is not known, the showing of such images to a witness to obtain identification evidence must be done in accordance with *Annex E.*

(b) Cases when the suspect is known and available

3.4 If the suspect's identity is known to the police and they are available, the identification procedures set out in paragraphs 3.5 to 3.10 may be used. References in this section to a suspect being "known" mean there is sufficient information known to the police to justify the arrest of a particular person for suspected involvement in the offence. A suspect being "available" means they are immediately available or will be within a reasonably short time and willing to take an effective part in at least one of the following which it is practicable to arrange:

- video identification;
- identification parade; or
- group identification.

Video identification

3.5 A "video identification" is when the witness is shown moving images of a known suspect, together with similar images of others who resemble the suspect. See paragraph 3.21 for circumstances in which still images may be used.

3.6 Video identifications must be carried out in accordance with *Annex A*.

Identification parade

3.7 An "identification parade" is when the witness sees the suspect in a line of others who resemble the suspect.

3.8 Identification parades must be carried out in accordance with *Annex B*.

Group identification

3.9 A "group identification" is when the witness sees the suspect in an informal group of people.

3.10 Group identifications must be carried out in accordance with *Annex C*.

Arranging identification procedures

3.11 Except for the provisions in paragraph 3.19, the arrangements for, and conduct of, the identification procedures in paragraphs 3.5 to 3.10 and circumstances in which an identification procedure must be held shall be the responsibility of an officer not below inspector rank who is not involved with the investigation, "the identification officer". Unless otherwise specified, the identification officer may allow another officer or police staff, see paragraph 2.21, to make arrangements for, and conduct, any of these identification procedures. In delegating these procedures, the identification officer must be able to supervise effectively and either intervene or be contacted for advice. No officer or any other person involved with the investigation of the case against the suspect, beyond the extent required by these procedures, may take any part in these procedures or act as the identification officer. This does not prevent the identification officer from consulting the officer in charge of the investigation to determine which procedure to use. When an identification procedure is required, in the interest of fairness to suspects and witnesses, it must be held as soon as practicable.

Circumstances in which an identification procedure must be held

3.12 Whenever:

(i) a witness has identified a suspect or purported to have identified them prior to any identification procedure set out in paragraphs 3.5 to 3.10 having been held; or

(ii) there is a witness available, who expresses an ability to identify the suspect, or where there is a reasonable chance of the witness being able to do so, and they have not been given an opportunity to identify the suspect in any of the procedures set out in paragraphs 3.5 to 3.10, and the suspect disputes being the person the witness claims to have seen, an identification procedure shall be held unless it is not practicable or it would serve no useful purpose in proving or disproving whether the suspect was involved in committing the offence. For example, when it is not disputed that the suspect is already well known to the witness who claims to have seen them commit the crime.

3.13 Such a procedure may also be held if the officer in charge of the investigation considers it would be useful.

Selecting an identification procedure

3.14 If, because of paragraph 3.12, an identification procedure is to be held, the suspect shall initially be offered a video identification unless:

a) a video identification is not practicable; or
b) an identification parade is both practicable and more suitable than a video identification; or
c) paragraph 3.16 applies.

The identification officer and the officer in charge of the investigation shall consult each other to determine which option is to be offered. An identification parade may not be practicable because of factors relating to the witnesses, such as their number, state of health, availability and travelling requirements. A video identification would normally be more suitable if it could be arranged and completed sooner than an identification parade.

3.15 A suspect who refuses the identification procedure first offered shall be asked to state their reason for refusing and may get advice from their solicitor and/or if present, their appropriate adult. The suspect, solicitor and/or appropriate adult shall be allowed to make representations about why another procedure should be used. A record should be made of the reasons for refusal and any representations made. After considering any reasons given, and representations made, the identification officer shall, if appropriate, arrange for the suspect to be offered an alternative which the officer considers suitable and practicable. If the officer decides it is not suitable and practicable to offer an alternative identification procedure, the reasons for that decision shall be recorded.

3.16 A group identification may initially be offered if the officer in charge of the investigation considers it is more suitable than a video identification or an identification parade and the identification officer considers it practicable to arrange.

Notice to suspect

3.17 Unless paragraph 3.20 applies, before a video identification, an identification parade or group identification is arranged, the following shall be explained to the suspect:

(i) the purposes of the video identification, identification parade or group identification;
(ii) their entitlement to free legal advice; see Code C, paragraph 6.5;
(iii) the procedures for holding it, including their right to have a solicitor or friend present;
(iv) that they do not have to consent to or co-operate in a video identification, identification parade or group identification;
(v) that if they do not consent to, and co-operate in, a video identification, identification parade or group identification, their refusal may be given in evidence in any subsequent trial and police may proceed covertly without their consent or

make other arrangements to test whether a witness can identify them, see paragraph 3.21;

(vi) whether, for the purposes of the video identification procedure, images of them have previously been obtained, see paragraph 3.20, and if so, that they may co-operate in providing further, suitable images to be used instead;

(vii) if appropriate, the special arrangements for juveniles;

(viii) if appropriate, the special arrangements for mentally disordered or otherwise mentally vulnerable people;

(ix) that if they significantly alter their appearance between being offered an identification procedure and any attempt to hold an identification procedure, this may be given in evidence if the case comes to trial, and the identification officer may then consider other forms of identification, see paragraph 3.21 and *Note 3C*;

(x) that a moving image or photograph may be taken of them when they attend for any identification procedure;

(xi) whether, before their identity became known, the witness was shown photographs, a computerised or artist's composite likeness or similar likeness or image by the police, see *Note 3B;*

(xii) that if they change their appearance before an identification parade, it may not be practicable to arrange one on the day or subsequently and, because of the appearance change, the identification officer may consider alternative methods of identification, see *Note 3C;*

(xiii) that they or their solicitor will be provided with details of the description of the suspect as first given by any witnesses who are to attend the video identification, identification parade, group identification or confrontation, see paragraph 3.1.

3.18 This information must also be recorded in a written notice handed to the suspect. The suspect must be given a reasonable opportunity to read the notice, after which, they should be asked to sign a second copy to indicate if they are willing to co-operate with the making of a video or take part in the identification parade or group identification. The signed copy shall be retained by the identification officer.

3.19 The duties of the identification officer under paragraphs 3.17 and 3.18 may be performed by the custody officer or other officer not involved in the investigation if:

(a) it is proposed to hold an identification procedure at a later date, *e.g.*, if the suspect is to be bailed to attend an identification parade; and

(b) an inspector is not available to act as the identification officer, see paragraph 3.11, before the suspect leaves the station.

The officer concerned shall inform the identification officer of the action taken and give them the signed copy of the notice. See *Note 3C*

3.20 If the identification officer and officer in charge of the investigation suspect, on reasonable grounds that if the suspect was given the information and notice as in paragraphs 3.17 and 3.18, they would then take steps to avoid being seen by a witness in any identification procedure, the identification officer may arrange for images of the suspect suitable for use in a video identification procedure to be obtained before giving the information and notice. If suspect's images are obtained in these circumstances, the suspect may, for the purposes of a video identification procedure, co-operate in providing suitable new images to be used instead, see paragraph 3.17(vi).

(c) Cases when the suspect is known but not available

3.21 When a known suspect is not available or has ceased to be available, see paragraph 3.4, the identification officer may make arrangements for a video identification (see *Annex A*). If necessary, the identification officer may follow the video identification procedures but using **still** images. Any suitable moving or still images may be used and these may be obtained covertly if necessary. Alternatively, the identification officer may make arrangements for a group identification. See *Note 3D*. These provisions may also be applied to juveniles where the consent of their parent or guardian is either refused or reasonable efforts to obtain that consent have failed (see paragraph 2.12).

3.22 Any covert activity should be strictly limited to that necessary to test the ability of the witness to identify the suspect.

3.23 The identification officer may arrange for the suspect to be confronted by the witness if none of the options referred to in paragraphs 3.5 to 3.10 or 3.21 are practicable. A "confrontation" is when the suspect is directly confronted by the witness. A confrontation does not require the suspect's consent. Confrontations must be carried out in accordance with *Annex D*.

3.24 Requirements for information to be given to, or sought from, a suspect or for the suspect to be given an opportunity to view images before they are shown to a witness, do not apply if the suspect's lack of co-operation prevents the necessary action.

(d) Documentation

3.25 A record shall be made of the video identification, identification parade, group identification or confrontation on forms provided for the purpose.

3.26 If the identification officer considers it is not practicable to hold a video identification or identification parade requested by the suspect, the reasons shall be recorded and explained to the suspect.

3.27 A record shall be made of a person's failure or refusal to co-operate in a video identification, identification parade or group identification and, if applicable, of the grounds for obtaining images in accordance with paragraph 3.20.

(e) Showing films and photographs of incidents and information released to the media

3.28 Nothing in this Code inhibits showing films or photographs to the public through the national or local media, or to police officers for the purposes of recognition and tracing suspects. However, when such material is shown to potential witnesses, including police officers, see *Note 3A*, to obtain identification evidence, it shall be shown on an individual basis to avoid any possibility of collusion, and, as far as possible, the showing shall follow the principles for video identification if the suspect is known, see *Annex A*, or identification by photographs if the suspect is not known, see *Annex E*.

3.29 When a broadcast or publication is made, see paragraph 3.28, a copy of the relevant material released to the media for the purposes of recognising or tracing the suspect, shall be kept. The suspect or their solicitor shall be allowed to view such material before any procedures under paragraphs 3.5 to 3.10, 3.21 or 3.23 are carried out, provided it is practicable and would not unreasonably delay the investigation. Each witness involved in the procedure shall be asked, after they have taken part, whether they have seen any broadcast or published films or photographs relating to the offence or any description of the suspect and their replies shall be recorded. This paragraph does not affect any separate requirement under the Criminal Procedure and Investigations Act 1996 to retain material in connection with criminal investigations.

(f) Destruction and retention of photographs and images taken or used in identification procedures

3.30 PACE, section 64A, provides powers to take photographs of suspects detained at police stations and allows these photographs to be used or disclosed only for purposes related to the prevention or detection of crime, the investigation of offences or the conduct of prosecutions by, or on behalf of, police or other law enforcement and prosecuting authorities inside and outside the United Kingdom. After being so used or disclosed, they may be retained but can only be used or disclosed for the same purposes.

3.31 Subject to paragraph 3.33, the photographs (and all negatives and copies), of suspects not detained and any moving images, (and copies), of suspects whether or not they have been detained which are taken for the purposes of, or in connection with, the identification procedures in paragraphs 3.5 to 3.10, 3.21 or 3.23 must be destroyed unless the suspect:

- (a) is charged with, or informed they may be prosecuted for, a recordable offence;
- (b) is prosecuted for a recordable offence;
- (c) is cautioned for a recordable offence or given a warning or reprimand in accordance with the Crime and Disorder Act 1998 for a recordable offence; or
- (d) gives informed consent, in writing, for the photograph or images to be retained for purposes described in paragraph 3.30.

3.32 When paragraph 3.31 requires the destruction of any photograph or images, the person must be given an opportunity to witness the destruction or to have a certificate confirming the destruction if they request one within five days of being informed that the destruction is required.

3.33 Nothing in paragraph 3.31 affects any separate requirement under the Criminal Procedure and Investigations Act 1996 to retain material in connection with criminal investigations.

Notes for guidance

3A Except for the provisions of *Annex E*, paragraph 1, a police officer who is a witness for the purposes of this part of the Code is subject to the same principles and procedures as a civilian witness.

3B When a witness attending an identification procedure has previously been shown photographs, or been shown or provided with computerised or artist's composite likenesses, or similar likenesses or pictures, it is the officer in charge of the investigation's responsibility to make the identification officer aware of this.

3C The purpose of paragraph 3.19 is to avoid or reduce delay in arranging identification procedures by enabling the required information and warnings, see sub-paragraphs 3.17(ix) and 3.17(xii), to be given at the earliest opportunity.

3D Paragraph 3.21 would apply when a known suspect deliberately makes themself "unavailable" in order to delay or frustrate arrangements for obtaining identification evidence. It also applies when a suspect refuses or fails to take part in a video identification, an identification parade or a group identification, or refuses or fails to take part in the only practicable options from that list. It enables any suitable images of the suspect, moving or still, which are available or can be obtained, to be used in an identification procedure.

3E When it is proposed to show photographs to a witness in accordance with *Annex E*, it is the responsibility of the officer in charge of the investigation to confirm to the officer responsible for supervising and directing the showing, that the first description of the suspect given by that witness has been recorded. If this description has not been recorded, the procedure under *Annex E* must be postponed. See *Annex E* paragraph 2

3F The admissibility and value of identification evidence obtained when carrying out the procedure under paragraph 3.2 may be compromised if:

(a) before a person is identified, the witness' attention is specifically drawn to that person; or
(b) the suspect's identity becomes known before the procedure.

4 Identification by fingerprints

(A) Taking fingerprints in connection with a criminal investigation

(a) General

4.1 References to "fingerprints" means any record, produced by any method, of the skin pattern and other physical characteristics or features of a person's:

(i) fingers; or
(ii) palms.

(b) Action

4.2 A person's fingerprints may be taken in connection with the investigation of an offence only with their consent or if paragraph 4.3 applies. If the person is at a police station consent must be in writing.

4.3 PACE, section 61, provides powers to take fingerprints without consent from any person over the age of ten years:

(a) under section 61(3), from a person detained at a police station in consequence of being arrested for a recordable offence, see Note 4A, if they have not had their fingerprints taken in the course of the investigation of the offence unless those previously taken fingerprints are not a complete set or some or all of those fingerprints are not of sufficient quality to allow satisfactory analysis, comparison or matching.
(b) under section 61(4), from a person detained at a police station who has been charged with a recordable offence, see Note 4A, or informed they will be reported for such an offence if they have not had their fingerprints taken in the course of the investigation of the offence unless those previously taken fingerprints are not a complete set or some or all of those fingerprints are not of sufficient quality to allow satisfactory analysis, comparison or matching.
(c) under section 61(4A), from a person who has been bailed to appear at a court or police station if the person:
    (i) has answered to bail for a person whose fingerprints were taken previously and there are reasonable grounds for believing they are not the same person; or

(ii) who has answered to bail claims to be a different person from a person whose fingerprints were previously taken;

and in either case, the court or an officer of inspector rank or above, authorises the fingerprints to be taken at the court or police station;

(d) under section 61(6), from a person who has been:
  (i) convicted of a recordable offence;
  (ii) given a caution in respect of a recordable offence which, at the time of the caution, the person admitted; or
  (iii) warned or reprimanded under the Crime and Disorder Act 1998, section 65, for a recordable offence.

4.4 PACE, section 27, provides power to:

(a) require the person as in paragraph 4.3(d) to attend a police station to have their fingerprints taken if the:
  (i) person has not been in police detention for the offence and has not had their fingerprints taken in the course of the investigation of that offence; or
  (ii) fingerprints that were taken from the person in the course of the investigation of that offence, do not constitute a complete set or some, or all, of the fingerprints are not of sufficient quality to allow satisfactory analysis, comparison or matching; and

(b) arrest, without warrant, a person who fails to comply with the requirement.

Note: The requirement must be made within one month of the date the person is convicted, cautioned, warned or reprimanded and the person must be given a period of at least 7 days within which to attend. This 7 day period need not fall during the month allowed for making the requirement.

4.5 A person's fingerprints may be taken, as above, electronically.

4.6 Reasonable force may be used, if necessary, to take a person's fingerprints without their consent under the powers as in paragraphs 4.3 and 4.4.

4.7 Before any fingerprints are taken with, or without, consent as above, the person must be informed:

(a) of the reason their fingerprints are to be taken;
(b) of the grounds on which the relevant authority has been given if the powers mentioned in paragraph 4.3 (c) applies;
(c) that their fingerprints may be retained and may be subject of a speculative search against other fingerprints, see *Note 4B*, unless destruction of the fingerprints is required in accordance with *Annex F, Part (a)*; and
(d) that if their fingerprints are required to be destroyed, they may witness their destruction as provided for in *Annex F, Part (a)*.

(c) Documentation

4.8 A record must be made as soon as possible, of the reason for taking a person's fingerprints without consent. If force is used, a record shall be made of the circumstances and those present.

4.9 A record shall be made when a person has been informed under the terms of paragraph 4.7(c), of the possibility that their fingerprints may be subject of a speculative search.

(B) Taking fingerprints in connection with immigration enquiries

Action

4.10 A person's fingerprints may be taken for the purposes of Immigration Service enquiries in accordance with powers and procedures other than under PACE and for which the Immigration Service (not the police) are responsible, only with the person's consent in writing or if paragraph 4.11 applies.

4.11 Powers to take fingerprints for these purposes without consent are given to police and immigration officers under the:

(a) Immigration Act 1971, Schedule 2, paragraph 18(2), when it is reasonably necessary for the purposes of identifying a person detained under the Immigration Act 1971, Schedule 2, paragraph 16 (Detention of person liable to examination or removal);

(b) Immigration and Asylum Act 1999, section 141(7)(a), from a person who fails to produce, on arrival, a valid passport with a photograph or some other document satisfactorily establishing their identity and nationality if an immigration officer does not consider the person has a reasonable excuse for the failure;

(c) Immigration and Asylum Act 1999, section 141(7)(b), from a person who has been refused entry to the UK but has been temporarily admitted if an immigration officer reasonably suspects the person might break a condition imposed on them relating to residence or reporting to a police or immigration officer, and their decision is confirmed by a chief immigration officer;

(d) Immigration and Asylum Act 1999, section 141(7)(c), when directions are given to remove a person:
- as an illegal entrant,
- liable to removal under the Immigration and Asylum Act 1999, section 10,
- who is the subject of a deportation order from the UK;

(e) Immigration and Asylum Act 1999, section 141(7)(d), from a person arrested under UK immigration laws under the Immigration Act 1971, Schedule 2, paragraph 17;

(f) Immigration and Asylum Act 1999, section 141(7)(e), from a person who has made a claim:
- for asylum
- under Article 3 of the European Convention on Human Rights; or

(g) Immigration and Asylum Act 1999, section 141(7)(f), from a person who is a dependant of someone who falls into (b) to (f) above.

4.12 The Immigration and Asylum Act 1999, section 142(3), gives a police and immigration officer power to arrest, without warrant, a person who fails to comply with a requirement imposed by the Secretary of State to attend a specified place for fingerprinting.

4.13 Before any fingerprints are taken, with or without consent, the person must be informed:

(a) of the reason their fingerprints are to be taken;

(b) the fingerprints, and all copies of them, will be destroyed in accordance with *Annex F, Pt B*.

4.14 Reasonable force may be used, if necessary, to take a person's fingerprints without their consent under powers as in paragraph 4.11.

4.15 Paragraphs 4.1 and 4.8 apply.

Notes for guidance

4A References to "recordable offences" in this Code relate to those offences for which convictions, cautions, reprimands and warnings may be recorded in national police records. See PACE, section 27(4). The recordable offences current at the time when this Code was prepared, are any offences which carry a sentence of imprisonment on conviction (irrespective of the period, or the age of the offender or actual sentence passed) as well as the non-imprisonable offences under the Street Offences Act 1959, section 1 (loitering or soliciting for purposes of prostitution), the Telecommunications Act 1984, section 43 (improper use of public telecommunications systems), the Road Traffic Act 1988, section 25 (tampering with motor vehicles), the Malicious Communications Act 1988, section 1 (sending letters, *etc.* with intent to cause distress or anxiety) and others listed in the National Police Records (Recordable Offences) Regulations 2000.

4B Fingerprints or a DNA sample (and the information derived from it) taken from a person arrested on suspicion of being involved in a recordable offence, or charged with such an offence, or informed they will be reported for such an offence, may be subject of a speculative search. This means the fingerprints or DNA sample may be checked against other fingerprints and DNA records held by, or on behalf of, the police and other law enforcement authorities in, or outside, the UK, or held in connection with, or as a result of, an investigation of an offence inside or outside the UK. Fingerprints and samples taken from a person suspected of committing a recordable offence but not arrested, charged or informed they will be reported for it, may be subject to a speculative search only if the person consents in writing. The following is an example of a basic form of words:

> "I consent to my fingerprints and DNA sample and information derived from it being retained and used only for purposes related to the prevention and detection of a crime, the investigation of an offence or the conduct of a prosecution either nationally or internationally.
>
> I understand that my fingerprints or this sample may be checked against other fingerprint and DNA records held by or on behalf of relevant law enforcement authorities, either nationally or internationally.
>
> I understand that once I have given my consent for the sample to be retained and used I cannot withdraw this consent."

See *Annex F* regarding the retention and use of fingerprints taken with consent for elimination purposes.

5 Examinations to establish identity and the taking of photographs

(A) Detainees at police stations

(a) Searching or examination of detainees at police stations

5.1 PACE, section 54A (1), allows a detainee at a police station to be searched or examined or both, to establish:

- (a) whether they have any marks, features or injuries that would tend to identify them as a person involved in the commission of an offence and to photograph any identifying marks, see paragraph 5.5;or
- (b) their identity, see *Note 5A*.

A person detained at a police station to be searched under a stop and search power, see Code A, is not a detainee for the purposes of these powers.

5.2 A search and/or examination to find marks under section 54A (1) (a) may be carried out without the detainee's consent, see paragraph 2.12, only if authorised by an officer of at least inspector rank when consent has been withheld or it is not practicable to obtain consent, see *Note 5D*.

5.3 A search or examination to establish a suspect's identity under section 54A (1) (b) may be carried out without the detainee's consent, see paragraph 2.12, only if authorised by an officer of at least inspector rank when the detainee has refused to identify themselves or the authorising officer has reasonable grounds for suspecting the person is not who they claim to be.

5.4 Any marks that assist in establishing the detainee's identity, or their identification as a person involved in the commission of an offence, are identifying marks. Such marks may be photographed with the detainee's consent, see paragraph 2.12; or without their consent if it is withheld or it is not practicable to obtain it, see *Note 5D*.

5.5 A detainee may only be searched, examined and photographed under section 54A, by a police officer of the same sex.

5.6 Any photographs of identifying marks, taken under section 54A, may be used or disclosed only for purposes related to the prevention or detection of crime, the investigation of offences or the conduct of prosecutions by, or on behalf of, police or other law enforcement and prosecuting authorities inside, and outside, the UK. After being so used or disclosed, the photograph may be retained but must not be used or disclosed except for these purposes, see *Note 5B*.

5.7 The powers, as in paragraph 5.1, do not affect any separate requirement under the Criminal Procedure and Investigations Act 1996 to retain material in connection with criminal investigations.

5.8 Authority for the search and/or examination for the purposes of paragraphs 5.2 and 5.3 may be given orally or in writing. If given orally, the authorising officer must confirm it in writing as soon as practicable. A separate authority is required for each purpose which applies.

5.9 If it is established a person is unwilling to co-operate sufficiently to enable a search and/or examination to take place or a suitable photograph to be taken, an officer may use reasonable force to:

(a) search and/or examine a detainee without their consent; and
(b) photograph any identifying marks without their consent.

5.10 The thoroughness and extent of any search or examination carried out in accordance with the powers in section 54A must be no more than the officer considers necessary to achieve the required purpose. Any search or examination which involves the removal of more than the person's outer clothing shall be conducted in accordance with Code C, *Annex A*, paragraph 11.

5.11 An intimate search may not be carried out under the powers in section 54A.

(b) Photographing detainees at police stations

5.12 Under PACE, section 64A, an officer may photograph a detainee at a police station:
- (a) with their consent; or
- (b) without their consent if it is:
  - (i) withheld; or
  - (ii) not practicable to obtain their consent.

See *Note 5E*
and paragraph 5.6 applies to the retention and use of photographs taken under this section as it applies to the retention and use of photographs taken under section 54A, see *Note 5B*.

5.13 The officer proposing to take a detainee's photograph may, for this purpose, require the person to remove any item or substance worn on, or over, all, or any part of, their head or face. If they do not comply with such a requirement, the officer may remove the item or substance.

5.14 If it is established the detainee is unwilling to co-operate sufficiently to enable a suitable photograph to be taken and it is not reasonably practicable to take the photograph covertly, an officer may use reasonable force:
- (a) to take their photograph without their consent; and
- (b) for the purpose of taking the photograph, remove any item or substance worn on, or over, all, or any part of, the person's head or face which they have failed to remove when asked.

5.15 For the purposes of this Code, a photograph may be obtained without the person's consent by making a copy of an image of them taken at any time on a camera system installed anywhere in the police station.

(c) Information to be given

5.16 When a person is searched, examined or photographed under the provisions as in paragraph 5.1 and 5.12, or their photograph obtained as in paragraph 5.15, they must be informed of the:
- (a) purpose of the search, examination or photograph;
- (b) grounds on which the relevant authority, if applicable, has been given; and
- (c) purposes for which the photograph may be used, disclosed or retained.

This information must be given before the search or examination commences or the photograph is taken, except if the photograph is:
- (i) to be taken covertly;
- (ii) obtained as in paragraph 5.15, in which case the person must be informed as soon as practicable after the photograph is taken or obtained.

(d) Documentation

5.17 A record must be made when a detainee is searched, examined, or a photograph of the person, or any identifying marks found on them, are taken. The record must include the:
- (a) identity, subject to paragraph 2.18, of the officer carrying out the search, examination or taking the photograph;
- (b) purpose of the search, examination or photograph and the outcome;
- (c) detainee's consent to the search, examination or photograph, or the reason the person was searched, examined or photographed without consent;

(d) giving of any authority as in paragraphs 5.2 and 5.3, the grounds for giving it and the authorising officer.

5.18 If force is used when searching, examining or taking a photograph in accordance with this section, a record shall be made of the circumstances and those present.

(B) Persons at police stations not detained

5.19 When there are reasonable grounds for suspecting the involvement of a person in a criminal offence, but that person is at a police station **voluntarily** and not detained, the provisions of paragraphs 5.1 to 5.18 should apply, subject to the modifications in the following paragraphs.

5.20 References to the "person being detained" and to the powers mentioned in paragraph 5.1 which apply only to detainees at police stations shall be omitted.

5.21 Force may not be used to:
- (a) search and/or examine the person to:
  - (i) discover whether they have any marks that would tend to identify them as a person involved in the commission of an offence; or
  - (ii) establish their identity, see *Note 5A*;
- (b) take photographs of any identifying marks, see paragraph 5.4;or
- (c) take a photograph of the person.

5.22 Subject to paragraph 5.24, the photographs or images, of persons not detained, or of their identifying marks, must be destroyed (together with any negatives and copies) unless the person:
- (a) is charged with, or informed they may be prosecuted for, a recordable offence;
- (b) is prosecuted for a recordable offence;
- (c) is cautioned for a recordable offence or given a warning or reprimand in accordance with the Crime and Disorder Act 1998 for a recordable offence; or
- (d) gives informed consent, in writing, for the photograph or image to be retained as in paragraph 5.6.

5.23 When paragraph 5.22 requires the destruction of any photograph or image, the person must be given an opportunity to witness the destruction or to have a certificate confirming the destruction provided they so request the certificate within five days of being informed the destruction is required.

5.24 Nothing in paragraph 5.22 affects any separate requirement under the Criminal Procedure and Investigations Act 1996 to retain material in connection with criminal investigations.

Notes for guidance

5A The conditions under which fingerprints may be taken to assist in establishing a person's identity, are described in section 4.

5B Examples of purposes related to the prevention or detection of crime, the investigation of offences or the conduct of prosecutions include:
- (a) checking the photograph against other photographs held in records or in connection with, or as a result of, an investigation of an offence to establish whether the person is liable to arrest for other offences;

(b) when the person is arrested at the same time as other people, or at a time when it is likely that other people will be arrested, using the photograph to help establish who was arrested, at what time and where;
(c) when the real identity of the person is not known and cannot be readily ascertained or there are reasonable grounds for doubting a name and other personal details given by the person, are their real name and personal details. In these circumstances, using or disclosing the photograph to help to establish or verify their real identity or determine whether they are liable to arrest for some other offence, *e.g.* by checking it against other photographs held in records or in connection with, or as a result of, an investigation of an offence;
(d) when it appears any identification procedure in section 3 may need to be arranged for which the person's photograph would assist;
(e) when the person's release without charge may be required, and if the release is:
 (i) on bail to appear at a police station, using the photograph to help verify the person's identity when they answer their bail and if the person does not answer their bail, to assist in arresting them; or
 (ii) without bail, using the photograph to help verify their identity or assist in locating them for the purposes of serving them with a summons to appear at court in criminal proceedings;
(f) when the person has answered to bail at a police station and there are reasonable grounds for doubting they are the person who was previously granted bail, using the photograph to help establish or verify their identity;
(g) when the person arrested on a warrant claims to be a different person from the person named on the warrant and a photograph would help to confirm or disprove their claim;
(h) when the person has been charged with, reported for, or convicted of, a recor able offence and their photograph is not already on record as a result of (a) to (f) or their photograph is on record but their appearance has changed since it was taken and the person has not yet been released or brought before a court.

5C There is no power to arrest a person convicted of a recordable offence solely to take their photograph. The power to take photographs in this section applies only where the person is in custody as a result of the exercise of another power, *e.g.* arrest for fingerprinting under PACE, section 27.

5D Examples of when it would not be practicable to obtain a detainee's consent, see paragraph 2.12, to a search, examination or the taking of a photograph of an identifying mark include:
(a) when the person is drunk or otherwise unfit to give consent;
(b) when there are reasonable grounds to suspect that if the person became aware a search or examination was to take place or an identifying mark was to be photographed, they would take steps to prevent this happening, *e.g.* by violently resisting, covering or concealing the mark *etc.* and it would not otherwise be possible to carry out the search or examination or to photograph any identifying mark;
(c) in the case of a juvenile, if the parent or guardian cannot be contacted in sufficient time to allow the search or examination to be carried out or the photograph to be taken.

5E Examples of when it would not be practicable to obtain the person's consent, see paragraph 2.12, to a photograph being taken include:

(a) when the person is drunk or otherwise unfit to give consent;
(b) when there are reasonable grounds to suspect that if the person became aware a photograph, suitable to be used or disclosed for the use and disclosure described in paragraph 5.6, was to be taken, they would take steps to prevent it being taken, *e.g.* by violently resisting, covering or distorting their face etc, and it would not otherwise be possible to take a suitable photograph;
(c) when, in order to obtain a suitable photograph, it is necessary to take it covertly; and
(d) in the case of a juvenile, if the parent or guardian cannot be contacted in sufficient time to allow the photograph to be taken.

6 Identification by body samples and impressions

(A) General

6.1 References to:

(a) an "intimate sample" mean a dental impression or sample of blood, semen or any other tissue fluid, urine, or pubic hair, or a swab taken from a person's body orifice other than the mouth;
(b) a "non-intimate sample" means:
    (i) a sample of hair, other than pubic hair, which includes hair plucked with the root, see *Note 6A*;
    (ii) a sample taken from a nail or from under a nail;
    (iii) a swab taken from any part of a person's body including the mouth but not any other body orifice;
    (iv) saliva;
    (v) a skin impression which means any record, other than a fingerprint, which is a record, in any form and produced by any method, of the skin pattern and other physical characteristics or features of the whole, or any part of, a person's foot or of any other part of their body.

(B) Action

(a) Intimate samples

6.2 PACE, section 62, provides that intimate samples may be taken under:

(a) section 62(1), from a person in police detention only:
    (i) if a police officer of inspector rank or above has reasonable grounds to believe such an impression or sample will tend to confirm or disprove the suspect's involvement in a recordable offence, see *Note 4A*, and gives authorisation for a sample to be taken; and
    (ii) with the suspect's written consent;
(b) section 62(1A), from a person not in police detention but from whom two or more non-intimate samples have been taken in the course of an investigation of an offence and the samples, though suitable, have proved insufficient if:
    (i) a police officer of inspector rank or above authorises it to be taken; and
    (ii) the person concerned gives their written consent. See *Notes 6B* and *6C*

6.3 Before a suspect is asked to provide an intimate sample, they must be warned that if they refuse without good cause, their refusal may harm their case if it comes to trial, see *Note 6D*. If the suspect is in police detention and not legally represented, they must also be reminded of their entitlement to have free legal advice, see Code C, paragraph 6.5, and the reminder noted in the custody record. If paragraph 6.2(b) applies and the person is attending a station voluntarily, their entitlement to free legal advice as in Code C, paragraph 3.21 shall be explained to them.

6.4 Dental impressions may only be taken by a registered dentist. Other intimate samples, except for samples of urine, may only be taken by a registered medical practitioner or registered nurse or registered paramedic.

(b) Non-intimate samples

6.5 A non-intimate sample may be taken from a detainee only with their written consent or if paragraph 6.6 applies.

6.6 (a) under section 63, a non-intimate sample may not be taken from a person without consent and the consent must be in writing

(aa) A non-intimate sample may be taken from a person without the appropriate consent in the following circumstances:

(i) under section 63(2A) where the person is in police detention as a consequence of his arrest for a recordable offence and he has not had a non-intimate sample of the same type and from the same part of the body taken in the course of the investigation of the offence by the police or he has had such a sample taken but it proved insufficient.

(ii) Under section 63(3) (a) where he is being held in custody by the police on the authority of a court and an officer of at least the rank of inspector authorises it to be taken.

(b) under section 63(3A), from a person charged with a recordable offence or informed they will be reported for such an offence: and

(i) that person has not had a non-intimate sample taken from them in the course of the investigation; or

(ii) if they have had a sample taken, it proved unsuitable or insufficient for the same form of analysis, see *Note 6B*;or

(c) under section 63(3B), from a person convicted of a recordable offence after the date on which that provision came into effect. PACE, s.63A, describes the circumstances in which a police officer may require a person convicted of a recordable offence to attend a police station for a non-intimate sample to be taken.

6.7 Reasonable force may be used, if necessary, to take a non-intimate sample from a person without their consent under the powers mentioned in paragraph 6.6.

6.8 Before any intimate sample is taken with consent or non-intimate sample is taken with, or without, consent, the person must be informed:

(a) of the reason for taking the sample;

(b) of the grounds on which the relevant authority has been given;

(c) that the sample or information derived from the sample may be retained and subject of a speculative search, see *Note 6E*, unless their destruction is required as in *Annex F*, Pt A.

6.9 When clothing needs to be removed in circumstances likely to cause embarrassment to the person, no person of the opposite sex who is not a registered medical practitioner or registered health care professional shall be present, (unless in the case of a juvenile, mentally disordered or mentally vulnerable person, that person specifically requests the presence of an appropriate adult of the opposite sex who is readily available) nor shall anyone whose presence is unnecessary. However, in the case of a juvenile, this is subject to the overriding proviso that such a removal of clothing may take place in the absence of the appropriate adult only if the juvenile signifies, in their presence, that they prefer the adult's absence and they agree.

(c) Documentation

6.10 A record of the reasons for taking a sample or impression and, if applicable, of its destruction must be made as soon as practicable. If force is used, a record shall be made of the circumstances and those present. If written consent is given to the taking of a sample or impression, the fact must be recorded in writing.

6.11 A record must be made of a warning given as required by paragraph 6.3.

6.12 A record shall be made of the fact that a person has been informed as in paragraph 6.8(c) that samples may be subject of a speculative search.

Notes for guidance

6A When hair samples are taken for the purpose of DNA analysis (rather than for other purposes such as making a visual match), the suspect should be permitted a reasonable choice as to what part of the body the hairs are taken from. When hairs are plucked, they should be plucked individually, unless the suspect prefers otherwise and no more should be plucked than the person taking them reasonably considers necessary for a sufficient sample.

6B (a) An insufficient sample is one which is not sufficient either in quantity or quality to provide information for a particular form of analysis, such as DNA analysis. A sample may also be insufficient if enough information cannot be obtained from it by analysis because of loss, destruction, damage or contamination of the sample or as a result of an earlier, unsuccessful attempt at analysis.

(b) An unsuitable sample is one which, by its nature, is not suitable for a particular form of analysis.

6C Nothing in paragraph 6.2 prevents intimate samples being taken for elimination purposes with the consent of the person concerned but the provisions of paragraph 2.12 relating to the role of the appropriate adult, should be applied. Paragraph 6.2(b) does not, however, apply where the non-intimate samples were previously taken under the Terrorism Act 2000, Schedule 8, paragraph 10.

6D In warning a person who is asked to provide an intimate sample as in paragraph 6.3, the following form of words may be used:

> "You do not have to provide this sample/allow this swab or impression to be taken, but I must warn you that if you refuse without good cause, your refusal may harm your case if it comes to trial."

6E Fingerprints or a DNA sample and the information derived from it taken from a person arrested on suspicion of being involved in a recordable offence, or charged with such an offence, or informed they will be reported for such an offence, may be subject of a speculative search. This means they may be checked against other fingerprints and DNA records held by, or on behalf of, the police and other law enforcement authorities in or outside the UK or held in connection with, or as a result of, an investigation of an offence inside or outside the UK. Fingerprints and samples taken from any other person, *e.g.* a person suspected of committing a recordable offence but who has not been arrested, charged or informed they will be reported for it, may be subject to a speculative search only if the person consents in writing to their fingerprints being subject of such a search. The following is an example of a basic form of words:

> "I consent to my fingerprints/DNA sample and information derived from it being retained and used only for purposes related to the prevention and detection of a crime, the investigation of an offence or the conduct of a prosecution either nationally or internationally.
>
> I understand that this sample may be checked against other fingerprint/DNA records held by or on behalf of relevant law enforcement authorities, either nationally or internationally.
>
> I understand that once I have given my consent for the sample to be retained and used I cannot withdraw this consent."

See *Annex F* regarding the retention and use of fingerprints and samples taken with consent for elimination purposes.

6F Samples of urine and non-intimate samples taken in accordance with sections 63B and 63C of PACE may not be used for identification purposes in accordance with this Code. See Code C note for guidance 17D.

ANNEX A—VIDEO IDENTIFICATION

(a) General

1. The arrangements for obtaining and ensuring the availability of a suitable set of images to be used in a video identification must be the responsibility of an identification officer, who has no direct involvement with the case.

2. The set of images must include the suspect and at least eight other people who, so far as possible, resemble the suspect in age, height, general appearance and position in life. Only one suspect shall appear in any set unless there are two suspects of roughly similar appearance, in which case they may be shown together with at least twelve other people.

3. The images used to conduct a video identification shall, as far as possible, show the suspect and other people in the same positions or carrying out the same sequence of movements. They shall also show the suspect and other people under identical conditions unless the identification officer reasonably believes:

(a) because of the suspect's failure or refusal to co-operate or other reasons, it is not practicable for the conditions to be identical; and
(b) any difference in the conditions would not direct a witness' attention to any individual image.

4. The reasons identical conditions are not practicable shall be recorded on forms provided for the purpose.

5. Provision must be made for each person shown to be identified by number.

6. If police officers are shown, any numerals or other identifying badges must be concealed. If a prison inmate is shown, either as a suspect or not, then either all, or none of, the people shown should be in prison clothing.

7. The suspect or their solicitor, friend, or appropriate adult must be given a reasonable opportunity to see the complete set of images before it is shown to any witness. If the suspect has a reasonable objection to the set of images or any of the participants, the suspect shall be asked to state the reasons for the objection. Steps shall, if practicable, be taken to remove the grounds for objection. If this is not practicable, the suspect and/or their representative shall be told why their objections cannot be met and the objection, the reason given for it and why it cannot be met shall be recorded on forms provided for the purpose.

8. Before the images are shown in accordance with paragraph 7, the suspect or their solicitor shall be provided with details of the first description of the suspect by any witnesses who are to attend the video identification. When a broadcast or publication is made, as in paragraph 3.28, the suspect or their solicitor must also be allowed to view any material released to the media by the police for the purpose of recognising or tracing the suspect, provided it is practicable and would not unreasonably delay the investigation.

9. The suspect's solicitor, if practicable, shall be given reasonable notification of the time and place the video identification is to be conducted so a representative may attend on behalf of the suspect. If a solicitor has not been instructed, this information shall be given to the suspect. The suspect may not be present when the images are shown to the witness(es). In the absence of the suspect's representative, the viewing itself shall be recorded on video. No unauthorised people may be present.

(b) Conducting the video identification

10. The identification officer is responsible for making the appropriate arrangements to make sure, before they see the set of images, witnesses are not able to communicate with each other about the case or overhear a witness who has already seen the material. There must be no discussion with the witness about the composition of the set of images and they must not be told whether a previous witness has made any identification.

11. Only one witness may see the set of images at a time. Immediately before the images are shown, the witness shall be told that the person they saw on a specified earlier occasion may, or may not, appear in the images they are shown and that if they cannot make a positive identification, they should say so. The witness shall be advised that at any point, they may ask to see a particular part of the set of images or to have a particular image frozen for them to study. Furthermore, it should be pointed out to the witness that there is no limit on how many times they can view the whole set of images or any part of them. However, they should be asked not to make any decision as to whether the person they saw is on the set of images until they have seen the whole set at least twice.

12. Once the witness has seen the whole set of images at least twice and has indicated that they do not want to view the images, or any part of them, again, the witness shall be asked to say whether the individual they saw in person on a specified earlier occasion has been shown and, if so, to identify them by number of the image. The witness will then be shown that image to confirm the identification, see paragraph 17.

13. Care must be taken not to direct the witness' attention to any one individual image or give any indication of the suspect's identity. Where a witness has previously made an identification by photographs, or a computerised or artist's composite or similar likeness, the witness must not be reminded of such a photograph or composite likeness once a suspect is available for identification by other means in accordance with this Code. Nor must the witness be reminded of any description of the suspect.

14. After the procedure, each witness shall be asked whether they have seen any broadcast or published films or photographs, or any descriptions of suspects relating to the offence and their reply shall be recorded.

(c) Image security and destruction

15. Arrangements shall be made for all relevant material containing sets of images used for specific identification procedures to be kept securely and their movements accounted for. In particular, no-one involved in the investigation shall be permitted to view the material prior to it being shown to any witness.

16. As appropriate, paragraph 3.30 or 3.31 applies to the destruction or retention of relevant sets of images.

(d) Documentation

17. A record must be made of all those participating in, or seeing, the set of images whose names are known to the police.

18. A record of the conduct of the video identification must be made on forms provided for the purpose. This shall include anything said by the witness about any identifications or the conduct of the procedure and any reasons it was not practicable to comply with any of the provisions of this Code governing the conduct of video identifications.

ANNEX B—IDENTIFICATION PARADES

(a) General

1. A suspect must be given a reasonable opportunity to have a solicitor or friend present, and the suspect shall be asked to indicate on a second copy of the notice whether or not they wish to do so.

2. An identification parade may take place either in a normal room or one equipped with a screen permitting witnesses to see members of the identification parade without being seen. The procedures for the composition and conduct of the identification parade are the same in both cases, subject to paragraph 8 (except that an identification parade involving a screen may take place only when the suspect's solicitor, friend or appropriate adult is present or the identification parade is recorded on video).

3. Before the identification parade takes place, the suspect or their solicitor shall be provided with details of the first description of the suspect by any witnesses who are attending the identification parade. When a broadcast or publication is made as in paragraph 3.28, the suspect or their solicitor should also be allowed to view any material released to the media by the police for the purpose of recognising or tracing the suspect, provided it is practicable to do so and would not unreasonably delay the investigation.

(b) Identification parades involving prison inmates

4. If a prison inmate is required for identification, and there are no security problems about the person leaving the establishment, they may be asked to participate in an identification parade or video identification.

5. An identification parade may be held in a Prison Department establishment but shall be conducted, as far as practicable under normal identification parade rules. Members of the public shall make up the identification parade unless there are serious security, or

control, objections to their admission to the establishment. In such cases, or if a group or video identification is arranged within the establishment, other inmates may participate. If an inmate is the suspect, they are not required to wear prison clothing for the identification parade unless the other people taking part are other inmates in similar clothing, or are members of the public who are prepared to wear prison clothing for the occasion.

(c) Conduct of the identification parade

6. Immediately before the identification parade, the suspect must be reminded of the procedures governing its conduct and cautioned in the terms of Code C, paragraphs 10.5 or 10.6, as appropriate.

7. All unauthorised people must be excluded from the place where the identification parade is held.

8. Once the identification parade has been formed, everything afterwards, in respect of it, shall take place in the presence and hearing of the suspect and any interpreter, solicitor, friend or appropriate adult who is present (unless the identification parade involves a screen, in which case everything said to, or by, any witness at the place where the identification parade is held, must be said in the hearing and presence of the suspect's solicitor, friend or appropriate adult or be recorded on video).

9. The identification parade shall consist of at least eight people (in addition to the suspect) who, so far as possible, resemble the suspect in age, height, general appearance and position in life. Only one suspect shall be included in an identification parade unless there are two suspects of roughly similar appearance, in which case they may be paraded together with at least twelve other people. In no circumstances shall more than two suspects be included in one identification parade and where there are separate identification parades, they shall be made up of different people.

10. If the suspect has an unusual physical feature, *e.g.*, a facial scar, tattoo or distinctive hairstyle or hair colour which cannot be replicated on other members of the identification parade, steps may be taken to conceal the location of that feature on the suspect and the other members of the identification parade if the suspect and their solicitor, or appropriate adult, agree. For example, by use of a plaster or a hat, so that all members of the identification parade resemble each other in general appearance.

11. When all members of a similar group are possible suspects, separate identification parades shall be held for each unless there are two suspects of similar appearance when they may appear on the same identification parade with at least twelve other members of the group who are not suspects. When police officers in uniform form an identification parade any numerals or other identifying badges shall be concealed.

12. When the suspect is brought to the place where the identification parade is to be held, they shall be asked if they have any objection to the arrangements for the identification parade or to any of the other participants in it and to state the reasons for the objection. The suspect may obtain advice from their solicitor or friend, if present, before the identification parade proceeds. If the suspect has a reasonable objection to the arrangements or any of the participants, steps shall, if practicable, be taken to remove the grounds for objection. When it is not practicable to do so, the suspect shall be told why their objections cannot be met and the objection, the reason given for it and why it cannot be met, shall be recorded on forms provided for the purpose.

13. The suspect may select their own position in the line, but may not otherwise interfere with the order of the people forming the line. When there is more than one witness, the suspect must be told, after each witness has left the room, that they can, if they wish, change position in the line. Each position in the line must be clearly numbered, whether by means of a number laid on the floor in front of each identification parade member or by other means.

14. Appropriate arrangements must be made to make sure, before witnesses attend the identification parade, they are not able to:
- (i) communicate with each other about the case or overhear a witness who has already seen the identification parade;
- (ii) see any member of the identification parade;
- (iii) see, or be reminded of, any photograph or description of the suspect or be given any other indication as to the suspect's identity; or
- (iv) see the suspect before or after the identification parade.

15. The person conducting a witness to an identification parade must not discuss with them the composition of the identification parade and, in particular, must not disclose whether a previous witness has made any identification.

16. Witnesses shall be brought in one at a time. Immediately before the witness inspects the identification parade, they shall be told the person they saw on a specified earlier occasion may, or may not, be present and if they cannot make a positive identification, they should say so. The witness must also be told they should not make any decision about whether the person they saw is on the identification parade until they have looked at each member at least twice.

17. When the officer or police staff (see paragraph 3.11) conducting the identification procedure is satisfied the witness has properly looked at each member of the identification parade, they shall ask the witness whether the person they saw on a specified earlier occasion is on the identification parade and, if so, to indicate the number of the person concerned, see paragraph 28.

18. If the witness wishes to hear any identification parade member speak, adopt any specified posture or move, they shall first be asked whether they can identify any person(s) on the identification parade on the basis of appearance only. When the request is to hear members of the identification parade speak, the witness shall be reminded that the participants in the identification parade have been chosen on the basis of physical appearance only. Members of the identification parade may then be asked to comply with the witness' request to hear them speak, see them move or adopt any specified posture.

19. If the witness requests that the person they have indicated remove anything used for the purposes of paragraph 10 to conceal the location of an unusual physical feature, that person may be asked to remove it.

20. If the witness makes an identification after the identification parade has ended, the suspect and, if present, their solicitor, interpreter or friend shall be informed. When this occurs, consideration should be given to allowing the witness a second opportunity to identify the suspect.

21. After the procedure, each witness shall be asked whether they have seen any broadcast or published films or photographs or any descriptions of suspects relating to the offence and their reply shall be recorded.

22. When the last witness has left, the suspect shall be asked whether they wish to make any comments on the conduct of the identification parade.

(d) Documentation

23. A video recording must normally be taken of the identification parade. If that is impracticable, a colour photograph must be taken. A copy of the video recording or photograph shall be supplied, on request, to the suspect or their solicitor within a reasonable time.

24. As appropriate, paragraph 3.30 or 3.31, should apply to any photograph or video taken as in paragraph 23.

25. If any person is asked to leave an identification parade because they are interfering with its conduct, the circumstances shall be recorded.

26. A record must be made of all those present at an identification parade whose names are known to the police.

27. If prison inmates make up an identification parade, the circumstances must be recorded.

28. A record of the conduct of any identification parade must be made on forms provided for the purpose. This shall include anything said by the witness or the suspect about any identifications or the conduct of the procedure, and any reasons it was not practicable to comply with any of this Code's provisions.

ANNEX C—GROUP IDENTIFICATION

(a) General

1. The purpose of this *Annex* is to make sure, as far as possible, group identifications follow the principles and procedures for identification parades so the conditions are fair to the suspect in the way they test the witness' ability to make an identification.

2. Group identifications may take place either with the suspect's consent and co-operation or covertly without their consent.

3. The location of the group identification is a matter for the identification officer, although the officer may take into account any representations made by the suspect, appropriate adult, their solicitor or friend.

4. The place where the group identification is held should be one where other people are either passing by or waiting around informally, in groups such that the suspect is able to join them and be capable of being seen by the witness at the same time as others in the group. For example people leaving an escalator, pedestrians walking through a shopping centre, passengers on railway and bus stations, waiting in queues or groups or where people are standing or sitting in groups in other public places.

5. If the group identification is to be held covertly, the choice of locations will be limited by the places where the suspect can be found and the number of other people present at that time. In these cases, suitable locations might be along regular routes travelled by the suspect, including buses or trains or public places frequented by the suspect.

6. Although the number, age, sex, race and general description and style of clothing of other people present at the location cannot be controlled by the identification officer, in selecting the location the officer must consider the general appearance and numbers of

people likely to be present. In particular, the officer must reasonably expect that over the period the witness observes the group, they will be able to see, from time to time, a number of others whose appearance is broadly similar to that of the suspect.

7. A group identification need not be held if the identification officer believes, because of the unusual appearance of the suspect, none of the locations it would be practicable to use satisfy the requirements of paragraph 6 necessary to make the identification fair.

8. Immediately after a group identification procedure has taken place (with or without the suspect's consent), a colour photograph or video should be taken of the general scene, if practicable, to give a general impression of the scene and the number of people present. Alternatively, if it is practicable, the group identification may be video recorded.

9. If it is not practicable to take the photograph or video in accordance with paragraph 8, a photograph or film of the scene should be taken later at a time determined by the identification officer if the officer considers it practicable to do so.

10. An identification carried out in accordance with this Code remains a group identification even though, at the time of being seen by the witness, the suspect was on their own rather than in a group.

11. Before the group identification takes place, the suspect or their solicitor shall be provided with details of the first description of the suspect by any witnesses who are to attend the identification. When a broadcast or publication is made, as in paragraph 3.28, the suspect or their solicitor should also be allowed to view any material released by the police to the media for the purposes of recognising or tracing the suspect, provided that it is practicable and would not unreasonably delay the investigation.

12. After the procedure, each witness shall be asked whether they have seen any broadcast or published films or photographs or any descriptions of suspects relating to the offence and their reply recorded.

(b) Identification with the consent of the suspect

13. A suspect must be given a reasonable opportunity to have a solicitor or friend present. They shall be asked to indicate on a second copy of the notice whether or not they wish to do so.

14. The witness, the person carrying out the procedure and the suspect's solicitor, appropriate adult, friend or any interpreter for the witness, may be concealed from the sight of the individuals in the group they are observing, if the person carrying out the procedure considers this assists the conduct of the identification.

15. The person conducting a witness to a group identification must not discuss with them the forthcoming group identification and, in particular, must not disclose whether a previous witness has made any identification.

16. Anything said to, or by, the witness during the procedure about the identification should be said in the presence and hearing of those present at the procedure.

17. Appropriate arrangements must be made to make sure, before witnesses attend the group identification, they are not able to:

- (i) communicate with each other about the case or overhear a witness who has already been given an opportunity to see the suspect in the group;

(ii) see the suspect; or
(iii) see, or be reminded of, any photographs or description of the suspect or be given any other indication of the suspect's identity.

18. Witnesses shall be brought one at a time to the place where they are to observe the group. Immediately before the witness is asked to look at the group, the person conducting the procedure shall tell them that the person they saw may, or may not, be in the group and that if they cannot make a positive identification, they should say so. The witness shall be asked to observe the group in which the suspect is to appear. The way in which the witness should do this will depend on whether the group is moving or stationary.

Moving group

19. When the group in which the suspect is to appear is moving, *e.g.* leaving an escalator, the provisions of paragraphs 20 to 24 should be followed.

20. If two or more suspects consent to a group identification, each should be the subject of separate identification procedures. These may be conducted consecutively on the same occasion.

21. The person conducting the procedure shall tell the witness to observe the group and ask them to point out any person they think they saw on the specified earlier occasion.

22. Once the witness has been informed as in paragraph 21 the suspect should be allowed to take whatever position in the group they wish.

23. When the witness points out a person as in paragraph 21 they shall, if practicable, be asked to take a closer look at the person to confirm the identification. If this is not practicable, or they cannot confirm the identification, they shall be asked how sure they are that the person they have indicated is the relevant person.

24. The witness should continue to observe the group for the period which the person conducting the procedure reasonably believes is necessary in the circumstances for them to be able to make comparisons between the suspect and other individuals of broadly similar appearance to the suspect as in paragraph 6.

Stationary groups

25. When the group in which the suspect is to appear is stationary, *e.g.* people waiting in a queue, the provisions of paragraphs 26 to 29 should be followed.

26. If two or more suspects consent to a group identification, each should be subject to separate identification procedures unless they are of broadly similar appearance when they may appear in the same group. When separate group identifications are held, the groups must be made up of different people.

27. The suspect may take whatever position in the group they wish. If there is more than one witness, the suspect must be told, out of the sight and hearing of any witness, that they can, if they wish, change their position in the group.

28. The witness shall be asked to pass along, or amongst, the group and to look at each person in the group at least twice, taking as much care and time as possible according to the circumstances, before making an identification. Once the witness has done this, they shall be asked whether the person they saw on the specified earlier occasion is in the group and to indicate any such person by whatever means the person conducting the procedure

considers appropriate in the circumstances. If this is not practicable, the witness shall be asked to point out any person they think they saw on the earlier occasion.

29. When the witness makes an indication as in paragraph 28, arrangements shall be made, if practicable, for the witness to take a closer look at the person to confirm the identification. If this is not practicable, or the witness is unable to confirm the identification, they shall be asked how sure they are that the person they have indicated is the relevant person.

All cases

30. If the suspect unreasonably delays joining the group, or having joined the group, deliberately conceals themselves from the sight of the witness, this may be treated as a refusal to co-operate in a group identification.

31. If the witness identifies a person other than the suspect, that person should be informed what has happened and asked if they are prepared to give their name and address. There is no obligation upon any member of the public to give these details. There shall be no duty to record any details of any other member of the public present in the group or at the place where the procedure is conducted.

32. When the group identification has been completed, the suspect shall be asked whether they wish to make any comments on the conduct of the procedure.

33. If the suspect has not been previously informed, they shall be told of any identifications made by the witnesses.

(c) Identification without the suspect's consent

34. Group identifications held covertly without the suspect's consent should, as far as practicable, follow the rules for conduct of group identification by consent.

35. A suspect has no right to have a solicitor, appropriate adult or friend present as the identification will take place without the knowledge of the suspect.

36 Any number of suspects may be identified at the same time.

(d) Identifications in police stations

37. Group identifications should only take place in police stations for reasons of safety, security or because it is not practicable to hold them elsewhere.

38. The group identification may take place either in a room equipped with a screen permitting witnesses to see members of the group without being seen, or anywhere else in the police station that the identification officer considers appropriate.

39. Any of the additional safeguards applicable to identification parades should be followed if the identification officer considers it is practicable to do so in the circumstances.

(e) Identifications involving prison inmates

40. A group identification involving a prison inmate may only be arranged in the prison or at a police station.

41. When a group identification takes place involving a prison inmate, whether in a prison or in a police station, the arrangements should follow those in paragraphs 37 to 39.If a group identification takes place within a prison, other inmates may participate. If an

inmate is the suspect, they do not have to wear prison clothing for the group identification unless the other participants are wearing the same clothing.

(f) Documentation

42. When a photograph or video is taken as in paragraph 8 or 9, a copy of the photograph or video shall be supplied on request to the suspect or their solicitor within a reasonable time.

43. Paragraph 3.30 or 3.31, as appropriate, shall apply when the photograph or film taken in accordance with paragraph 8 or 9 includes the suspect.

44. A record of the conduct of any group identification must be made on forms provided for the purpose. This shall include anything said by the witness or suspect about any identifications or the conduct of the procedure and any reasons why it was not practicable to comply with any of the provisions of this Code governing the conduct of group identifications.

ANNEX D—CONFRONTATION BY A WITNESS

1. Before the confrontation takes place, the witness must be told that the person they saw may, or may not, be the person they are to confront and that if they are not that person, then the witness should say so.

2. Before the confrontation takes place the suspect or their solicitor shall be provided with details of the first description of the suspect given by any witness who is to attend. When a broadcast or publication is made, as in paragraph 3.28, the suspect or their solicitor should also be allowed to view any material released to the media for the purposes of recognising or tracing the suspect, provided it is practicable to do so and would not unreasonably delay the investigation.

3. Force may not be used to make the suspect's face visible to the witness.

4. Confrontation must take place in the presence of the suspect's solicitor, interpreter or friend unless this would cause unreasonable delay.

5. The suspect shall be confronted independently by each witness, who shall be asked "Is this the person?". If the witness identifies the person but is unable to confirm the identification, they shall be asked how sure they are that the person is the one they saw on the earlier occasion.

6. The confrontation should normally take place in the police station, either in a normal room or one equipped with a screen permitting a witness to see the suspect without being seen. In both cases, the procedures are the same except that a room equipped with a screen may be used only when the suspect's solicitor, friend or appropriate adult is present or the confrontation is recorded on video.

7. After the procedure, each witness shall be asked whether they have seen any broadcast or published films or photographs or any descriptions of suspects relating to the offence and their reply shall be recorded.

ANNEX E—SHOWING PHOTOGRAPHS

(a) Action

1. An officer of sergeant rank or above shall be responsible for supervising and directing the showing of photographs. The actual showing may be done by another officer or police staff, see paragraph 3.11.

2. The supervising officer must confirm the first description of the suspect given by the witness has been recorded before they are shown the photographs. If the supervising officer is unable to confirm the description has been recorded they shall postpone showing the photographs.

3. Only one witness shall be shown photographs at any one time. Each witness shall be given as much privacy as practicable and shall not be allowed to communicate with any other witness in the case.

4. The witness shall be shown not less than twelve photographs at a time, which shall, as far as possible, all be of a similar type.

5. When the witness is shown the photographs, they shall be told the photograph of the person they saw may, or may not, be amongst them and if they cannot make a positive identification, they should say so. The witness shall also be told they should not make a decision until they have viewed at least twelve photographs. The witness shall not be prompted or guided in any way but shall be left to make any selection without help.

6. If a witness makes a positive identification from photographs, unless the person identified is otherwise eliminated from enquiries or is not available, other witnesses shall not be shown photographs. But both they, and the witness who has made the identification, shall be asked to attend a video identification, an identification parade or group identification unless there is no dispute about the suspect's identification.

7. If the witness makes a selection but is unable to confirm the identification, the person showing the photographs shall ask them how sure they are that the photograph they have indicated is the person they saw on the specified earlier occasion.

8. When the use of a computerised or artist's composite or similar likeness has led to there being a known suspect who can be asked to participate in a video identification, appear on an identification parade or participate in a group identification, that likeness shall not be shown to other potential witnesses.

9. When a witness attending a video identification, an identification parade or group identification has previously been shown photographs or computerised or artist's composite or similar likeness (and it is the responsibility of the officer in charge of the investigation to make the identification officer aware that this is the case), the suspect and their solicitor must be informed of this fact before the identification procedure takes place.

10. None of the photographs shown shall be destroyed, whether or not an identification is made, since they may be required for production in court. The photographs shall be numbered and a separate photograph taken of the frame or part of the album from which the witness made an identification as an aid to reconstituting it.

(b) Documentation

11. Whether or not an identification is made, a record shall be kept of the showing of photographs on forms provided for the purpose. This shall include anything said by the witness about any identification or the conduct of the procedure, any reasons it was not practicable to comply with any of the provisions of this Code governing the showing of photographs and the name and rank of the supervising officer.

12. The supervising officer shall inspect and sign the record as soon as practicable.

ANNEX F—FINGERPRINTS AND SAMPLES—DESTRUCTION AND SPECULATIVE SEARCHES

(a) Fingerprints and samples taken in connection with a criminal investigation

1. When fingerprints or DNA samples are taken from a person in connection with an investigation and the person is not suspected of having committed the offence, see *Note F1*, they must be destroyed as soon as they have fulfilled the purpose for which they were taken unless:

   (a) they were taken for the purposes of an investigation of an offence for which a person has been convicted; and
   (b) fingerprints or samples were also taken from the convicted person for the purposes of that investigation.

However, subject to paragraph 2, the fingerprints and samples, and the information derived from samples, may not be used in the investigation of any offence or in evidence against the person who is, or would be, entitled to the destruction of the fingerprints and samples, see *Note F2*.

2. The requirement to destroy fingerprints and DNA samples, and information derived from samples, and restrictions on their retention and use in paragraph 1 do not apply if the person gives their written consent for their fingerprints or sample to be retained and used after they have fulfilled the purpose for which they were taken, see *Note F1*.

3 When a person's fingerprints or sample are to be destroyed:

   (a) any copies of the fingerprints must also be destroyed;
   (b) the person may witness the destruction of their fingerprints or copies if they ask to do so within five days of being informed destruction is required;
   (c) access to relevant computer fingerprint data shall be made impossible as soon as it is practicable to do so and the person shall be given a certificate to this effect within three months of asking; and
   (d) neither the fingerprints, the sample, or any information derived from the sample, may be used in the investigation of any offence or in evidence against the person who is, or would be, entitled to its destruction.

4. Fingerprints or samples, and the information derived from samples, taken in connection with the investigation of an offence which are not required to be destroyed, may be retained after they have fulfilled the purposes for which they were taken but may be used only for purposes related to the prevention or detection of crime, the investigation of an offence or the conduct of a prosecution in, as well as outside, the UK and may also be subject to a speculative search. This includes checking them against other fingerprints and DNA records held by, or on behalf of, the police and other law enforcement authorities in, as well as outside, the UK.

(b) Fingerprints taken in connection with Immigration Service enquiries

5. Fingerprints taken for Immigration Service enquiries in accordance with powers and procedures other than under PACE and for which the Immigration Service, not the police, are responsible, must be destroyed as follows:

   (a) fingerprints and all copies must be destroyed as soon as practicable if the person from whom they were taken proves they are a British or Commonwealth citizen who has the right of abode in the UK under the Immigration Act 1971, section 2(1)(b);

(b) fingerprints taken under the power as in paragraph 4.11(g) from a dependant of a person in *4.11 (b)* to *(f)* must be destroyed when that person's fingerprints are to be destroyed;

(c) fingerprints taken from a person under any power as in paragraph 4.11 or with the person's consent which have not already been destroyed as above, must be destroyed within ten years of being taken or within such period specified by the Secretary of State under the Immigration and Asylum Act 1999, section 143(5).

Notes for guidance

F1 Fingerprints and samples given voluntarily for the purposes of elimination play an important part in many police investigations. It is, therefore, important to make sure innocent volunteers are not deterred from participating and their consent to their fingerprints and DNA being used for the purposes of a specific investigation is fully informed and voluntary. If the police or volunteer seek to have the sample or fingerprints retained for use after the specific investigation ends, it is important the volunteer's consent to this is also fully informed and voluntary.

Examples of consent for:

- DNA/fingerprints—to be used only for the purposes of a specific investigation;
- DNA/fingerprints—to be used in the specific investigation **and** retained by the police for future use.

To minimise the risk of confusion, each consent should be physically separate and the volunteer should be asked to sign one or the other, **not both**.

(a) DNA:

(i) DNA sample taken for the purposes of elimination or as part of an intelligence-led screen and to be used only for the purposes of that investigation and destroyed afterwards:
"I consent to my DNA/mouth swab being taken for forensic analysis. I understand that the sample will be destroyed at the end of the case and that my profile will only be compared to the crime stain profile from this enquiry. I have been advised that the person taking the sample may be required to give evidence and/or provide a written statement to the police in relation to the taking of it".

(ii) DNA sample to be retained on the National DNA database and used in the future:

"I consent to my DNA sample and information derived from it being retained and used only for purposes related to the prevention and detection of a crime, the investigation of an offence or the conduct of a prosecution either nationally or internationally."

"I understand that this sample may be checked against other DNA records held by, or on behalf of, relevant law enforcement authorities, either nationally or internationally".

"I understand that once I have given my consent for the sample to be retained and used I cannot withdraw this consent."

(b) Fingerprints:

(i) Fingerprints taken for the purposes of elimination or as part of an intelligence-led screen and to be used only for the purposes of that investigation and destroyed afterwards:

"I consent to my fingerprints being taken for elimination purposes. I understand that the fingerprints will be destroyed at the end of the case and that my fingerprints will only be compared to the fingerprints from this enquiry. I have been advised that the person taking the fingerprints may be required to give evidence and/or provide a written statement to the police in relation to the taking of it."

(ii) Fingerprints to be retained for future use:

"I consent to my fingerprints being retained and used only for purposes related to the prevention and detection of a crime, the investigation of an offence or the conduct of a prosecution either nationally or internationally".

"I understand that my fingerprints may be checked against other records held by, or on behalf of, relevant law enforcement authorities, either nationally or internationally."

"I understand that once I have given my consent for my fingerprints to be retained and used I cannot withdraw this consent."

F2 The provisions for the retention of fingerprints and samples in paragraph 1 allow for all fingerprints and samples in a case to be available for any subsequent miscarriage of justice investigation.

POLICE AND CRIMINAL EVIDENCE ACT 1984 (PACE), CODE E: CODE OF PRACTICE ON TAPE RECORDING INTERVIEWS WITH SUSPECTS

CONTENTS

Commencement—Transitional Arrangements

This code applies to interviews carried out after midnight on 31 July 2004, notwithstanding that the interview may have commenced before that time.

1 General

1.1 This Code of Practice must be readily available for consultation by:

- police officers
- police staff
- detained persons
- members of the public.

1.2 The *Notes for Guidance* included are not provisions of this Code.

1.3 Nothing in this Code shall detract from the requirements of Code C, the Code of Practice for the detention, treatment and questioning of persons by police officers.

1.4 This Code does not apply to those people listed in Code C, *paragraph 1.12*.

1.5 The term:

- "appropriate adult" has the same meaning as in Code C, *paragraph 1.7*
- "solicitor" has the same meaning as in Code C, *paragraph 6.12*.

1.6 In this Code:

(a) "designated person" means a person other than a police officer, designated under the Police Reform Act 2002, Part 4 who has specified powers and duties of police officers conferred or imposed on them;

(b) any reference to a police officer includes a designated person acting in the exercise or performance of the powers and duties conferred or imposed on them by their designation.

1.7 If a power conferred on a designated person:

(a) allows reasonable force to be used when exercised by a police officer, a designated person exercising that power has the same entitlement to use force;

(b) includes power to use force to enter any premises, that power is not exercisable by that designated person except:

(i) in the company, and under the supervision, of a police officer; or

(ii) for the purpose of:
- saving life or limb; or
- preventing serious damage to property.

1.8 Nothing in this Code prevents the custody officer, or other officer given custody of the detainee, from allowing police staff who are not designated persons to carry out individual procedures or tasks at the police station if the law allows. However, the officer remains responsible for making sure the procedures and tasks are carried out correctly in accordance with these Codes. Any such civilian must be:

(a) a person employed by a police authority maintaining a police force and under the control and direction of the Chief Officer of that force; or
(b) employed by a person with whom a police authority has a contract for the provision of services relating to persons arrested or otherwise in custody.

1.9 Designated persons and other police staff must have regard to any relevant provisions of the Codes of Practice.

1.10 References to pocket book include any official report book issued to police officers or police staff.

1.11 References to a custody officer include those performing the functions of a custody officer.

2 Recording and sealing master tapes

2.1 Tape recording of interviews shall be carried out openly to instil confidence in its reliability as an impartial and accurate record of the interview.

2.2 One tape, the master tape, will be sealed in the suspect's presence. A second tape will be used as a working copy. The master tape is either of the two tapes used in a twin deck machine or the only tape in a single deck machine. The working copy is either the second/third tape used in a twin/triple deck machine or a copy of the master tape made by a single deck machine. [See *Notes 2A* and *2B*]

2.3 Nothing in this Code requires the identity of officers or police staff conducting interviews to be recorded or disclosed:

(a) in the case of enquiries linked to the investigation of terrorism; or
(b) if the interviewer reasonably believes recording or disclosing their name might put them in danger.

In these cases interviewers should use warrant or other identification numbers and the name of their police station. [See *Note 2C*]

Notes for guidance

2A The purpose of sealing the master tape in the suspect's presence is to show the tape's integrity is preserved. If a single deck machine is used the working copy of the master tape must be made in the suspect's presence and without the master tape leaving their sight. The working copy shall be used for making further copies if needed.

2B Reference to "tapes" includes "tape", if a single deck machine is used.

2C The purpose of paragraph 2.3(b) is to protect those involved in serious organised crime investigations or arrests of particularly violent suspects when there is reliable information that those arrested or their associates may threaten or cause harm to those involved. In cases of doubt, an officer of inspector rank or above should be consulted.

3 Interviews to be tape recorded

3.1 Subject to *paragraphs 3.3* and *3.4*, tape recording shall be used at police stations for any interview:

(a) with a person cautioned under Code C, *section 10* in respect of any indictable offence, including an offence triable either way; [see *Note 3A*]

(b) which takes place as a result of an interviewer exceptionally putting further questions to a suspect about an offence described in *paragraph 3.1(a)* after they have been charged with, or told they may be prosecuted for, that offence, see Code C, *paragraph 16.5*

(c) when an interviewer wants to tell a person, after they have been charged with, or informed they may be prosecuted for, an offence described in *paragraph 3.1(a)*, about any written statement or interview with another person, see Code C, *paragraph 16.4.*

3.2 The Terrorism Act 2000 makes separate provision for a Code of Practice for the tape recording of interviews of those arrested under Section 41 or detained under Schedule 7 of the Act. The provisions of this Code do not apply to such interviews.

3.3 The custody officer may authorise the interviewer not to tape record the interview when it is:

(a) not reasonably practicable because of equipment failure or the unavailability of a suitable interview room or recorder and the authorising officer considers, on reasonable grounds, that the interview should not be delayed; or

(b) clear from the outset there will not be a prosecution.

Note: In these cases the interview should be recorded in writing in accordance with Code C, *section 11*. In all cases the custody officer shall record the specific reasons for not tape recording. [See *Note 3B*]

3.4 If a person refuses to go into or remain in a suitable interview room, see Code C *paragraph 12.5*, and the custody officer considers, on reasonable grounds, that the interview should not be delayed the interview may, at the custody officer's discretion, be conducted in a cell using portable recording equipment or, if none is available, recorded in writing as in Code C, *section 11*. The reasons for this shall be recorded.

3.5 The whole of each interview shall be tape recorded, including the taking and reading back of any statement.

Notes for guidance

3A Nothing in this Code is intended to preclude tape recording at police discretion of interviews at police stations with people cautioned in respect of offences not covered by paragraph 3.1, or responses made by persons after they have been charged with, or told they may be prosecuted for, an offence, provided this Code is complied with.

3B A decision not to tape record an interview for any reason may be the subject of comment in court. The authorising officer should be prepared to justify that decision.

4 The interview

(a) General

4.1 The provisions of Code C:

- *sections 10 and 11*, and the applicable *Notes for Guidance* apply to the conduct of interviews to which this Code applies
- *paragraphs 11.7 to 11.14* apply only when a written record is needed.

4.2 Code C, *paragraphs 10.10, 10.11* and Annex C describe the restriction on drawing adverse inferences from a suspect's failure or refusal to say anything about their involvement in the offence when interviewed or after being charged or informed they may be prosecuted, and how it affects the terms of the caution and determines if and by whom a special warning under sections 36 and 37 can be given.

(b) Commencement of interviews

4.3 When the suspect is brought into the interview room the interviewer shall, without delay but in the suspect's sight, load the recorder with new tapes and set it to record. The tapes must be unwrapped or opened in the suspect's presence.

4.4 The interviewer should tell the suspect about the tape recording. The interviewer shall:

(a) say the interview is being tape recorded
(b) subject to *paragraph 2.3*, give their name and rank and that of any other interviewer present
(c) ask the suspect and any other party present, *e.g.* a solicitor, to identify themselves
(d) state the date, time of commencement and place of the interview
(e) state the suspect will be given a notice about what will happen to the tapes. [See *Note 4A*]

4.5 The interviewer shall:

- caution the suspect, see Code C, *section 10*
- remind the suspect of their entitlement to free legal advice, see Code C, *paragraph 11.2.*

4.6 The interviewer shall put to the suspect any significant statement or silence; see Code C, *paragraph 11.4.*

(c) Interviews with deaf persons

4.7 If the suspect is deaf or is suspected of having impaired hearing, the interviewer shall make a written note of the interview in accordance with Code C, at the same time as tape recording it in accordance with this Code. [See *Notes 4B* and *4C*]

(d) Objections and complaints by the suspect

4.8 If the suspect objects to the interview being tape recorded at the outset, during the interview or during a break, the interviewer shall explain that the interview is being tape recorded and that this Code requires the suspect's objections be recorded on tape. When any objections have been tape recorded or the suspect has refused to have their objections recorded, the interviewer shall say they are turning off the recorder, give their reasons and turn it off. The interviewer shall then make a written record of the interview as in Code C, *section 11*. If, however, the interviewer reasonably considers they may proceed to question the suspect with the tape still on, the interviewer may do so. [See *Note 4D*]

4.9 If in the course of an interview a complaint is made by or on behalf of the person being questioned concerning the provisions of this Code or Code C, the interviewer shall act as in Code C, *paragraph 12.9*. [See *Notes 4E* and *4F*]

4.10 If the suspect indicates they want to tell the interviewer about matters not directly connected with the offence and they are unwilling for these matters to be tape recorded, the suspect should be given the opportunity to tell the interviewer at the end of the formal interview.

(e) Changing tapes

4.11 When the recorder shows the tapes have only a short time left, the interviewer shall tell the suspect the tapes are coming to an end and round off that part of the interview. If the interviewer leaves the room for a second set of tapes, the suspect shall not be left unattended. The interviewer will remove the tapes from the tape recorder and insert the new tapes which shall be unwrapped or opened in the suspect's presence. The tape recorder should be set to record on the new tapes. To avoid confusion between the tapes, the interviewer shall mark the tapes with an identification number immediately they are removed from the tape recorder.

(f) Taking a break during interview

4.12 When a break is taken, the fact that a break is to be taken, the reason for it and the time shall be recorded on tape.

4.12A When the break is taken and the interview room vacated by the suspect, the tapes shall be removed from the tape recorder and the procedures for the conclusion of an interview followed; see *paragraph 4.18*.

4.13 When a break is a short one and both the suspect and an interviewer remain in the interview room, the tape recorder may be turned off. There is no need to remove the tapes and when the interview recommences the tape recording should continue on the same tapes. The time the interview recommences shall be recorded on tape.

4.14 After any break in the interview the interviewer must, before resuming the interview, remind the person being questioned that they remain under caution or, if there is any doubt, give the caution in full again. [See *Note 4G*]

(g) Failure of recording equipment

4.15 If there is an equipment failure which can be rectified quickly, *e.g.* by inserting new tapes, the interviewer shall follow the appropriate procedures as in *paragraph 4.11*. When the recording is resumed the interviewer shall explain what happened and record the time the interview recommences. If, however, it will not be possible to continue recording on that tape recorder and no replacement recorder is readily available, the interview may continue without being tape recorded. If this happens, the interviewer shall seek the custody officer's authority as in *paragraph 3.3*. [See *Note 4H*]

(h) Removing tapes from the recorder

4.16 When tapes are removed from the recorder during the interview, they shall be retained and the procedures in *paragraph 4.18* followed.

(i) Conclusion of interview

4.17 At the conclusion of the interview, the suspect shall be offered the opportunity to clarify anything he or she has said and asked if there is anything they want to add.

4.18 At the conclusion of the interview, including the taking and reading back of any written statement, the time shall be recorded and the tape recorder switched off. The interviewer shall seal the master tape with a master tape label and treat it as an exhibit in accordance with force standing orders. The interviewer shall sign the label and ask the suspect and any third party present during the interview to sign it. If the suspect or third party refuse to sign the label an officer of at least inspector rank, or if not available the custody officer, shall be called into the interview room and asked, subject to *paragraph 2.3*, to sign it.

4.19 The suspect shall be handed a notice which explains:

- how the tape recording will be used
- the arrangements for access to it
- that if the person is charged or informed they will be prosecuted, a copy of the tape will be supplied as soon as practicable or as otherwise agreed between the suspect and the police.

Notes for guidance

4A For the purpose of voice identification the interviewer should ask the suspect and any other people present to identify themselves.

4B This provision is to give a person who is deaf or has impaired hearing equivalent rights of access to the full interview record as far as this is possible using audio recording.

4C The provisions of Code C, section 13 on interpreters for deaf persons or for interviews with suspects who have difficulty understanding English continue to apply. However, in a tape recorded interview the requirement on the interviewer to make sure the interpreter makes a separate note of the interview applies only to paragraph 4.7 (interviews with deaf persons).

4D The interviewer should remember that a decision to continue recording against the wishes of the suspect may be the subject of comment in court.

4E If the custody officer is called to deal with the complaint, the tape recorder should, if possible, be left on until the custody officer has entered the room and spoken to the person being interviewed. Continuation or termination of the interview should be at the interviewer's discretion pending action by an inspector under Code C, paragraph 9.2.

4F If the complaint is about a matter not connected with this Code or Code C, the decision to continue is at the interviewer's discretion. When the interviewer decides to continue the interview, they shall tell the suspect the complaint will be brought to the custody officer's attention at the conclusion of the interview. When the interview is concluded the interviewer must, as soon as practicable, inform the custody officer about the existence and nature of the complaint made.

4G The interviewer should remember that it may be necessary to show to the court that nothing occurred during a break or between interviews which influenced the suspect's recorded evidence. After a break or at the beginning of a subsequent interview, the interviewer should consider summarising on tape the reason for the break and confirming this with the suspect.

4H If one of the tapes snaps during the interview it should be sealed as a master tape in the suspect's presence and the interview resumed where it left off. The unbroken tape should be copied and the original sealed as a master tape in the suspect's presence, if necessary after the interview. If equipment for copying the unbroken tape is not readily available, both tapes should be sealed in the suspect's presence and the interview begun again. If the tape breaks when a single deck machine is being used and the machine is one where a broken tape cannot be copied on available equipment, the tape should be sealed as a master tape in the suspect's presence and the interview begun again.

5 After the interview

5.1 The interviewer shall make a note in their pocket book that the interview has taken place, was tape recorded, its time, duration and date and the master tape's identification number.

5.2 If no proceedings follow in respect of the person whose interview was recorded, the tapes must be kept securely as in *paragraph 6.1* and *Note 6A*.

Note for guidance

5A Any written record of a tape recorded interview should be made in accordance with national guidelines approved by the Secretary of State.

6 Tape security

6.1 The officer in charge of each police station at which interviews with suspects are recorded shall make arrangements for master tapes to be kept securely and their movements accounted for on the same basis as material which may be used for evidential purposes, in accordance with force standing orders. [See *Note 6A*]

6.2 A police officer has no authority to break the seal on a master tape required for criminal trial or appeal proceedings. If it is necessary to gain access to the master tape, the police officer shall arrange for its seal to be broken in the presence of a representative of the Crown Prosecution Service. The defendant or their legal adviser should be informed and given a reasonable opportunity to be present. If the defendant or their legal representative is present they shall be invited to reseal and sign the master tape. If either refuses or neither is present this should be done by the representative of the Crown Prosecution Service. [See *Notes 6B and 6C*]

6.3 If no criminal proceedings result or the criminal trial and, if applicable, appeal proceedings to which the interview relates have been concluded, the chief officer of police is responsible for establishing arrangements for breaking the seal on the master tape, if necessary.

6.4 When the master tape seal is broken, a record must be made of the procedure followed, including the date, time, place and persons present.

Notes for guidance

6A This section is concerned with the security of the master tape sealed at the conclusion of the interview. Care must be taken of working copies of tapes because their loss or destruction may lead to the need to access master tapes.

6B If the tape has been delivered to the crown court for their keeping after committal for trial the crown prosecutor will apply to the chief clerk of the crown court centre for the release of the tape for unsealing by the crown prosecutor.

6C Reference to the Crown Prosecution Service or to the crown prosecutor in this part of the Code should be taken to include any other body or person with a statutory responsibility for prosecution for whom the police conduct any tape recorded interviews.

POLICE AND CRIMINAL EVIDENCE ACT 1984 (PACE), CODE F: CODE OF PRACTICE ON VISUAL RECORDING WITH SOUND OF INTERVIEWS WITH SUSPECTS

CONTENTS

Commencement—Transitional Arrangements

The contents of this code should be considered if an interviewing officer decides to make a visual recording with sound of an interview with a suspect. There is no statutory requirement to visually record interviews.

1 August 2004

1 General

1.1 This code of practice must be readily available for consultation by police officers and other police staff, detained persons and members of the public.

1.2 The notes for guidance included are not provisions of this code. They form guidance to police officers and others about its application and interpretation.

1.3 Nothing in this code shall be taken as detracting in any way from the requirements of the Code of Practice for the Detention, Treatment and Questioning of Persons by Police Officers (Code C). [See *Note 1A*]

1.4 The interviews to which this Code applies are set out in paragraph 3.1–3.3.

1.5 In this code, the term "appropriate adult", "solicitor" and "interview" have the same meaning as those set out in Code C. The corresponding provisions and Notes for Guidance in Code C applicable to those terms shall also apply where appropriate.

1.6 Any reference in this code to visual recording shall be taken to mean visual recording with sound.

1.7 References to "pocket book" in this Code include any official report book issued to police officers.

Note for Guidance

1A As in Code C, references to custody officers include those carrying out the functions of a custody officer.

2 Recording and sealing of master tapes

2.1 The visual recording of interviews shall be carried out openly to instil confidence in its reliability as an impartial and accurate record of the interview. [See *Note 2A*]

2.2 The camera(s) shall be placed in the interview room so as to ensure coverage of as much of the room as is practicably possible whilst the interviews are taking place.

2.3 The certified recording medium will be of a high quality, new and previously unused. When the certified recording medium is placed in the recorder and switched on to record, the correct date and time, in hours, minutes and seconds, will be superimposed automatically, second by second, during the whole recording. [See *Note 2B*]

2.4 One copy of the certified recording medium, referred to in this code as the master copy, will be sealed before it leaves the presence of the suspect. A second copy will be used as a working copy. [See *Note 2C and 2D*]

2.5 Nothing in this code requires the identity of an officer to be recorded or disclosed if:

(a) the interview or record relates to a person detained under the Terrorism Act 2000; or

(b) otherwise where the officer reasonably believes that recording or disclosing their name might put them in danger.

In these cases, the officer will have their back to the camera and shall use their warrant or other identification number and the name of the police station to which they are attached. Such instances and the reasons for them shall be recorded in the custody record. [See *Note 2E*]

Notes for Guidance

2A Interviewing officers will wish to arrange that, as far as possible, visual recording arrangements are unobtrusive. It must be clear to the suspect, however, that there is no opportunity to interfere with the recording equipment or the recording media.

2B In this context, the certified recording media will be of either a VHS or digital CD format and should be capable of having an image of the date and time superimposed upon them as they record the interview.

2C The purpose of sealing the master copy before it leaves the presence of the suspect is to establish their confidence that the integrity of the copy is preserved.

2D The recording of the interview is not to be used for any identification purpose.

2E The purpose of the paragraph 2.5 is to protect police officers and others involved in the investigation of serious organised crime or the arrest of particularly violent suspects when there is reliable information that those arrested or their associates may threaten or cause harm to the officers, their families or their personal property.

3 Interviews to be visually recorded

3.1 Subject to paragraph 3.2 below, if an interviewing officer decides to make a visual recording these are the areas where it might be appropriate:

(a) with a suspect in respect of an indictable offence (including an offence triable either way) [see *Notes 3A and 3B*];

(b) which takes place as a result of an interviewer exceptionally putting further questions to a suspect about an offence described in sub-paragraph (a) above after they have been charged with, or informed they may be prosecuted for, that offence [see *Note 3C*];

(c) in which an interviewer wishes to bring to the notice of a person, after that person has been charged with, or informed they may be prosecuted for an offence described in sub-paragraph (a) above, any written statement made by another person, or the content of an interview with another person [see *Note 3D*];

(d) with, or in the presence of, a deaf or deaf/blind or speech impaired person who uses sign language to communicate;

(e) with, or in the presence of anyone who requires an "appropriate adult"; or

(f) in any case where the suspect or their representative requests that the interview be recorded visually.

3.2 The Terrorism Act 2000 makes separate provision for a code of practice for the video recording of interviews in a police station of those detained under Schedule 7 or s.41 of the Act. The provisions of this code do not therefore apply to such interviews [see *Note 3E*].

3.3 The custody officer may authorise the interviewing officer not to record the interview visually:

(a) where it is not reasonably practicable to do so because of failure of the equipment, or the non-availability of a suitable interview room, or recorder, and the authorising officer considers on reasonable grounds that the interview should not be delayed until the failure has been rectified or a suitable room or recorder becomes available. In such cases the custody officer may authorise the interviewing officer to audio record the interview in accordance with the guidance set out in Code E;

(b) where it is clear from the outset that no prosecution will ensue; or

(c) where it is not practicable to do so because at the time the person resists being taken to a suitable interview room or other location which would enable the interview to be recorded, or otherwise fails or refuses to go into such a room or location, and the authorising officer considers on reasonable grounds that the interview should not be delayed until these conditions cease to apply.

In all cases the custody officer shall make a note in the custody records of the reasons for not taking a visual record. [See *Note 3F*]

3.4 When a person who is voluntarily attending the police station is required to be cautioned in accordance with Code C prior to being interviewed, the subsequent interview shall be recorded, unless the custody officer gives authority in accordance with the provisions of paragraph 3.3 above for the interview not to be so recorded.

3.5 The whole of each interview shall be recorded visually, including the taking and reading back of any statement.

3.6 A visible illuminated sign or indicator will light and remain on at all times when the recording equipment is activated or capable of recording or transmitting any signal or information

Notes for Guidance

3A Nothing in the code is intended to preclude visual recording at police discretion of interviews at police stations with people cautioned in respect of offences not covered by paragraph 3.1, or responses made by interviewees after they have been charged with, or informed they may be prosecuted for, an offence, provided that this code is complied with.

3B Attention is drawn to the provisions set out in Code C about the matters to be considered when deciding whether a detained person is fit to be interviewed.

3C Code C sets out the circumstances in which a suspect may be questioned about an offence after being charged with it.

3D Code C sets out the procedures to be followed when a person's attention is drawn after charge, to a statement made by another person. One method of bringing the content of an interview with another person to the notice of a suspect may be to play him a recording of that interview.

3E When it only becomes clear during the course of an interview which is being visually recorded that the interviewee may have committed an offence to which paragraph 3.2 applies, the interviewing officer should turn off the recording equipment and the interview should continue in accordance with the provisions of the Terrorism Act 2000.

3F A decision not to record an interview visually for any reason may be the subject of comment in court. The authorising officer should therefore be prepared to justify their decision in each case.

4 The Interview

(a) General

4.1 The provisions of Code C in relation to cautions and interviews and the Notes for Guidance applicable to those provisions shall apply to the conduct of interviews to which this Code applies.

4.2 Particular attention is drawn to those parts of Code C that describe the restrictions on drawing adverse inferences from a suspect's failure or refusal to say anything about their involvement in the offence when interviewed, or after being charged or informed they may be prosecuted and how those restrictions affect the terms of the caution and determines whether a special warning under Sections 36 and 37 of the Criminal Justice and Public Order Act 1994 can be given.

(b) Commencement of interviews

4.3 When the suspect is brought into the interview room the interviewer shall without delay, but in sight of the suspect, load the recording equipment and set it to record. The recording media must be unwrapped or otherwise opened in the presence of the suspect. [See *Note 4A*]

4.4 The interviewer shall then tell the suspect formally about the visual recording. The interviewer shall:

- (a) explain the interview is being visually recorded;
- (b) subject to paragraph 2.5, give his or her name and rank, and that of any other interviewer present;
- (c) ask the suspect and any other party present (*e.g.* his solicitor) to identify themselves.
- (d) state the date, time of commencement and place of the interview; and
- (e) state that the suspect will be given a notice about what will happen to the recording.

4.5 The interviewer shall then caution the suspect, which should follow that set out in Code C, and remind the suspect of their entitlement to free and independent legal advice and that they can speak to a solicitor on the telephone.

4.6 The interviewer shall then put to the suspect any significant statement or silence (*i.e.* failure or refusal to answer a question or to answer it satisfactorily) which occurred before the start of the interview, and shall ask the suspect whether they wish to confirm or deny that earlier statement or silence or whether they wish to add anything. The definition of a "significant" statement or silence is the same as that set out in Code C.

(c) Interviews with the deaf

4.7 If the suspect is deaf or there is doubt about their hearing ability, the provisions of Code C on interpreters for the deaf or for interviews with suspects who have difficulty in understanding English continue to apply.

(d) Objections and complaints by the suspect

4.8 If the suspect raises objections to the interview being visually recorded either at the outset or during the interview or during a break in the interview, the interviewer shall explain the fact that the interview is being visually recorded and that the provisions of this code require that the suspect's objections shall be recorded. The suspect's objections shall be noted.

4.9 If in the course of an interview a complaint is made by the person being questioned, or on their behalf, concerning the provisions of this code or of Code C, then the interviewer shall act in accordance with Code C, record it in the interview record and inform the custody officer. [See *4B and 4C*]

4.10 If the suspect indicates that they wish to tell the interviewer about matters not directly connected with the offence of which they are suspected and that they are unwilling for these matters to be recorded, the suspect shall be given the opportunity to tell the interviewer about these matters after the conclusion of the formal interview.

(e) Changing the recording media

4.11 In instances where the recording medium is not of sufficient length to record all of the interview with the suspect, further certified recording medium will be used. When the recording equipment indicates that the recording medium has only a short time left to run, the interviewer shall advise the suspect and round off that part of the interview. If the interviewer wishes to continue the interview but does not already have further certified recording media with him, they shall obtain a set. The suspect should not be left unattended in the interview room. The interviewer will remove the recording media from the recording equipment and insert the new ones which have been unwrapped or otherwise opened in the suspect's presence. The recording equipment shall then be set to record. Care must be taken, particularly when a number of sets of recording media have been used, to ensure that there is no confusion between them. This could be achieved by marking the sets of recording media with consecutive identification numbers.

(f) Taking a break during the interview

4.12 When a break is to be taken during the course of an interview and the interview room is to be vacated by the suspect, the fact that a break is to be taken, the reason for it and the time shall be recorded. The recording equipment must be turned off and the recording media removed. The procedures for the conclusion of an interview set out in paragraph 4.19, below, should be followed.

4.13 When a break is to be a short one, and both the suspect and a police officer are to remain in the interview room, the fact that a break is to be taken, the reasons for it and the time shall be recorded on the recording media. The recording equipment may be turned off, but there is no need to remove the recording media. When the interview is recommenced the recording shall continue on the same recording media and the time at which the interview recommences shall be recorded.

4.14 When there is a break in questioning under caution, the interviewing officer must ensure that the person being questioned is aware that they remain under caution. If there is any doubt, the caution must be given again in full when the interview resumes. [See *Notes 4D and 4E*]

(g) Failure of recording equipment

4.15 If there is a failure of equipment which can be rectified quickly, the appropriate procedures set out in paragraph 4.12 shall be followed. When the recording is resumed the interviewer shall explain what has happened and record the time the interview recommences. If, however, it is not possible to continue recording on that particular recorder and no alternative equipment is readily available, the interview may continue without being recorded visually. In such circumstances, the procedures set out in paragraph 3.3 of this code for seeking the authority of the custody officer will be followed. [See *Note 4F*]

(h) Removing used recording media from recording equipment

4.16 Where used recording media are removed from the recording equipment during the course of an interview, they shall be retained and the procedures set out in paragraph 4.18 below followed.

(i) Conclusion of interview

4.17 Before the conclusion of the interview, the suspect shall be offered the opportunity to clarify anything he or she has said and asked if there is anything that they wish to add.

4.18 At the conclusion of the interview, including the taking and reading back of any written statement, the time shall be recorded and the recording equipment switched off. The master tape or CD shall be removed from the recording equipment, sealed with a master copy label and treated as an exhibit in accordance with the force standing orders. The interviewer shall sign the label and also ask the suspect and any appropriate adults or other third party present during the interview to sign it. If the suspect or third party refuses to sign the label, an officer of at least the rank of inspector, or if one is not available, the custody officer, shall be called into the interview room and asked to sign it.

4.19 The suspect shall be handed a notice which explains the use which will be made of the recording and the arrangements for access to it. The notice will also advise the suspect that a copy of the tape shall be supplied as soon as practicable if the person is charged or informed that he will be prosecuted.

Notes for Guidance

4A The interviewer should attempt to estimate the likely length of the interview and ensure that an appropriate quantity of certified recording media and labels with which to seal the master copies are available in the interview room.

4B Where the custody officer is called immediately to deal with the complaint, wherever possible the recording equipment should be left to run until the custody officer has entered the interview room and spoken to the person being interviewed. Continuation or termination of the interview should be at the discretion of the interviewing officer pending action by an inspector as set out in Code C.

4C Where the complaint is about a matter not connected with this code of practice or Code C, the decision to continue with the interview is at the discretion of the interviewing officer. Where the interviewing officer decides to continue with the interview, the person being interviewed shall be told that the complaint will be brought to the attention of the custody officer at the conclusion of the interview. When the interview is concluded, the interviewing officer must, as soon as practicable, inform the custody officer of the existence and nature of the complaint made.

4D In considering whether to caution again after a break, the officer should bear in mind that he may have to satisfy a court that the person understood that he was still under caution when the interview resumed.

4E The officer should bear in mind that it may be necessary to satisfy the court that nothing occurred during a break in an interview or between interviews which influenced the suspect's recorded evidence. On the re-commencement of an interview, the officer should consider summarising on the tape or CD the reason for the break and confirming this with the suspect.

4F If any part of the recording media breaks or is otherwise damaged during the interview, it should be sealed as a master copy in the presence of the suspect and the interview resumed where it left off. The undamaged part should be copied and the original sealed as a master tape in the suspect's presence, if necessary after the interview. If equipment for copying is not readily available, both parts should be sealed in the suspect's presence and the interview begun again.

5 After the Interview

5.1 The interviewer shall make a note in his or her pocket book of the fact that the interview has taken place and has been recorded, its time, duration and date and the identification number of the master copy of the recording media.

5.2 Where no proceedings follow in respect of the person whose interview was recorded, the recording media must nevertheless be kept securely in accordance with paragraph 6.1 and *Note* 6A.

Note for Guidance

5A Any written record of a recorded interview shall be made in accordance with national guidelines approved by the Secretary of State, and with regard to the advice contained in the Manual of Guidance for the preparation, processing and submission of files.

6 Tape Security

(a) General

6.1 The officer in charge of the police station at which interviews with suspects are recorded shall make arrangements for the master copies to be kept securely and their movements accounted for on the same basis as other material which may be used for evidential purposes, in accordance with force standing orders [see *Note 6A*].

(b) Breaking master copy seal for criminal proceedings

6.2 A police officer has no authority to break the seal on a master copy which is required for criminal trial or appeal proceedings. If it is necessary to gain access to the master copy, the police officer shall arrange for its seal to be broken in the presence of a representative of the Crown Prosecution Service. The defendant or their legal adviser shall be informed and given a reasonable opportunity to be present. If the defendant or their legal representative is present they shall be invited to reseal and sign the master copy. If either refuses or neither is present, this shall be done by the representative of the Crown Prosecution Service. [See *Notes 6B* and *6C*]

(c) Breaking master copy seal: other cases

6.3 The chief officer of police is responsible for establishing arrangements for breaking the seal of the master copy where no criminal proceedings result, or the criminal proceedings, to which the interview relates, have been concluded and it becomes necessary to break the seal. These arrangements should be those which the chief officer considers are reasonably necessary to demonstrate to the person interviewed and any other party who may wish to use or refer to the interview record that the master copy has not been tampered with and that the interview record remains accurate. [See *Note 6D*]

6.4 Subject to paragraph 6.6, a representative of each party must be given a reasonable opportunity to be present when the seal is broken, the master copy copied and resealed.

6.5 If one or more of the parties is not present when the master copy seal is broken because they cannot be contacted or refuse to attend or paragraph 6.6 applies, arrangements should be made for an independent person such as a custody visitor, to be present. Alternatively, or as an additional safeguard, arrangement should be made for a film or photographs to be taken of the procedure.

6.6 Paragraph 6.5 does not require a person to be given an opportunity to be present when:

(a) it is necessary to break the master copy seal for the proper and effective further investigation of the original offence or the investigation of some other offence; and

(b) the officer in charge of the investigation has reasonable grounds to suspect that allowing an opportunity might prejudice any such an investigation or criminal proceedings which may be brought as a result or endanger any person. [See *Note 6E*]

(d) Documentation

6.7 When the master copy seal is broken, copied and re-sealed, a record must be made of the procedure followed, including the date time and place and persons present.

Notes for Guidance

6A This section is concerned with the security of the master copy which will have been sealed at the conclusion of the interview. Care should, however, be taken of working copies since their loss or destruction may lead unnecessarily to the need to have access to master copies.

6B If the master copy has been delivered to the Crown Court for their keeping after committal for trial the Crown Prosecutor will apply to the Chief Clerk of the Crown Court Centre for its release for unsealing by the Crown Prosecutor.

6C Reference to the Crown Prosecution Service or to the Crown Prosecutor in this part of the code shall be taken to include any other body or person with a statutory responsibility for prosecution for whom the police conduct any recorded interviews.

6D The most common reasons for needing access to master copies that are not required for criminal proceedings arise from civil actions and complaints against police and civil actions between individuals arising out of allegations of crime investigated by police.

6E Paragraph 6.6 could apply, for example, when one or more of the outcomes or likely outcomes of the investigation might be: (i) the prosecution of one or more of the original suspects, (ii) the prosecution of someone previously not suspected, including someone who was originally a witness; and (iii) any original suspect being treated as a prosecution witness and when premature disclosure of any police action, particularly through contact with any parties involved, could lead to a real risk of compromising the investigation and endangering witnesses.

Appendix 2

Relevant Sections of the Police and criminal Evidence Act 1984

ARRANGEMENT OF SECTIONS

. . . . .

Part II Powers of Entry, Search and Seizure

. . . . .

Entry and search without search warrant

18 Entry and search after arrest

Seizure, etc.

19 General power of seizure, *etc.*

. . . . .

Part III Arrest

24 Arrest without warrant for arrestable offences
25 General arrest conditions
26 Repeal of statutory powers of arrest without warrant or order
27 Fingerprinting of certain offenders
28 Information to be given on arrest
29 Voluntary attendance at police station, *etc.*
30 Arrest elsewhere than at police station

. . . . .

Part IV Detention

Detention—conditions and duration

34 Limitations on police detention

. . . . .

37 Duties of custody officer before charge
38 Duties of custody officer after charge
39 Responsibilities in relation to person detained
40 Review of police detention
41 Limits on period of detention without charge
42 Authorisation of continued detention
43 Warrants of further detention
44 Extension of warrants of further detention

. . . . .

Detention—miscellaneous

46 Detention after charge
46A Power of arrest for failure to answer to police bail
47 Bail after arrest

. . . . .

Part V Questioning and Treatment of Persons by Police

. . . . .

54 Searches of detained persons
55 Intimate searches
56 Right to have someone informed when arrested

. . . . .

58 Acess to legal advice

. . . . .

61 Fingerprinting
62 Intimate samples
63 Other samples
63A Fingerprints and samples: supplementary provisions
64 Destruction of fingerprints and samples
65 Part V—supplementary

. . . . .

Part VIII Evidence in Criminal Proceedings—General

. . . . .

Confessions

76 Confessions

. . . . .

Part XI Miscellaneous and Supplementary

. . . . .

116 Meaning of "serious arrestable offence"

. . . . .

18 Entry and search after arrest

(1) Subject to the following provisions of this section, a constable may enter and search any premises occupied or controlled by a person who is under arrest for an arrestable offence, if he has reasonable grounds for suspecting that there is on the premises evidence, other than items subject to legal privilege, that relates—

(a) to that offence; or—

(b) to some other arrestable offence which is connected with or similar to that offence.

(2) A constable may seize and retain anything for which he may search under subsection (1) above.

(3) The power to search conferred by subsection (1) above is only a power to search to the extent that is reasonably required for the purpose of discovering such evidence.

(4) Subject to subsection (5) below, the powers conferred by this section may not be exercised unless an officer of the rank of inspector or above has authorised them in writing.

[(5) A constable may conduct a search under subsection (1)—

(a) before the person is taken to a police station or released on bail under section 30A, and

(b) without obtaining an authorisation under subsection (4),

if the condition in subsection (5A) is satisfied.

(5A) The condition is that the presence of the person at a place (other than a police station) is necessary for the effective investigation of the offence.[1]

(6) If a constable conducts a search by virtue of subsection (5) above, he shall inform an officer of the rank of inspector or above that he has made the search as soon as practicable after he has made it.

(7) An officer who—

(a) authorises a search; or

(b) is informed of a search under subsection (6) above, shall make a record in writing—

(i) of the grounds for the search; and

(ii) of the nature of the evidence that was sought.

(8) If the person who was in occupation or control of the premises at the time of the search is in police detention at the time the record is to be made, the officer shall make the record as part of his custody record.

[1] s.18(5)–(5A) Substituted for s.18.5 by Criminal Justice Act (2003).

19 General power of seizure etc

. . . . . .

(2) The constable may seize anything which is on the premises if he has reasonable grounds for believing—

(a) that it has been obtained in consequence of the commission of an offence; and

(b) that it is necessary to seize it in order to prevent it being concealed, lost, damaged, altered or destroyed.

(3) The constable may seize anything which is on the premises if he has reasonable grounds for believing—

(a) that it is evidence in relation to an offence which he is investigating or any other offence; and

(b) that it is necessary to seize it in order to prevent the evidence being concealed, lost, altered or destroyed.

. . . . . .

24 Arrest without warrant for arrestable offences

(1) The powers of summary arrest conferred by the following subsections shall apply—

(a) to offences for which the sentence is fixed by law;

(b) to offences for which a person of 21 years of age or over (not previously convicted) may be sentenced to imprisonment for a term of five years (or might be so sentenced but for the restrictions imposed by section 33 of the Magistrates' Courts Act 1980); and

(c) to the offences listed in Schedule 1A,

and in this Act "arrestable offence" means any such offence.

(2) Schedule 1A (which lists the offences referred to in subsection (1)(c)) shall have effect.

(3) Without prejudice to section 2 of the Criminal Attempts Act 1981, the powers of summary arrest conferred by the following subsections shall also apply to the offences of—

(a) conspiring to commit any of the offences listed in Schedule 1A;

(b) attempting to commit any such offence other than [one which is a summary offence][1];

(c) inciting, aiding, abetting, counselling or procuring the commission of any such offence;

and such offences are also arrestable offences for the purposes of this Act.

(4) Any person may arrest without a warrant—

(a) anyone who is in the act of committing an arrestable offence;

(b) anyone whom he has reasonable grounds for suspecting to be committing such an offence.

(5) Where an arrestable offence has been committed, any person may arrest without a warrant—

(a) anyone who is guilty of the offence;

(b) anyone whom he has reasonable grounds for suspecting to be guilty of it.

(6) Where a constable has reasonable grounds for suspecting that an arrestable offence has been committed, he may arrest without a warrant anyone whom he has reasonable grounds for suspecting to be guilty of the offence.

(7) A constable may arrest without a warrant—

(a) anyone who is about to commit an arrestable offence;

(b) anyone whom he has reasonable grounds for suspecting to be about to commit an arrestable offence.

[1] substituted by Police Reform Act (2002 c.30), Part 4 c. 2 section 48(4)(b).

25 General arrest conditions

(1) Where a constable has reasonable grounds for suspecting that any offence which is not an arrestable offence has been committed or attempted, or is being committed or attempted, he may arrest the relevant person if it appears to him that service of a summons is impracticable or inappropriate because any of the general arrest conditions is satisfied.

(2) In this section "the relevant person" means any person whom the constable has reasonable grounds to suspect of having committed or having attempted to commit the offence or of being in the course of committing or attempting to commit it.

(3) The general arrest conditions are—

(a) that the name of the relevant person is unknown to, and cannot be readily ascertained by, the constable;

(b) that the constable has reasonable grounds for doubting whether a name furnished by the relevant person as his name is his real name;

(c) that—

(i) the relevant person has failed to furnish a satisfactory address for service; or

(ii) the constable has reasonable grounds for doubting whether an address furnished by the relevant person is a satisfactory address for service;

(d) that the constable has reasonable grounds for believing that arrest is necessary to prevent the relevant person—

(i) causing physical injury to himself or any other person;

(ii) suffering physical injury;

(iii) causing loss of or damage to property;

(iv) committing an offence against public decency;

or

(v) causing an unlawful obstruction of the highway;

(e) that the constable has reasonable grounds for believing that arrest is necessary to protect a child or other vulnerable person from the relevant person.

(4) For the purposes of subsection (3) above an address is a satisfactory address for service if it appears to the constable—

(a) that the relevant person will be at it for a sufficiently long period for it to be possible to serve him with a summons; or

(b) that some other person specified by the relevant person will accept service of a summons for the relevant person at it.

(5) Nothing in subsection (3)(d) above authorises the arrest of a person under subparagraph (iv) of that paragraph except where members of the public going about their normal business cannot reasonably be expected to avoid the person to be arrested.

(6) This section shall not prejudice any power of arrest conferred apart from this section.

26 Repeal of statutory powers of arrest without warrant or order

(1) Subject to subsection (2) below, so much of any Act (including a local Act) passed before this Act as enables a constable—

(a) to arrest a person for an offence without a warrant; or

(b) to arrest a person otherwise than for an offence without a warrant or an order of a court,

shall cease to have effect.

(2) Nothing in subsection (1) above affects the enactments specified in Schedule 2 to this Act.

Notes:

Section 26 excluded by Representation of the People Act 1985 (c.50), s.25(1)

27 Fingerprinting of certain offenders

(1) If a person—

(a) has been convicted of a recordable offence;

(b) has not at any time been in police detention for the offence; and
(c) has not had his fingerprints taken—
(i) in the course of the investigation of the offence by the police; or
(ii) since the conviction,
any constable may at any time not later than one month after the date of the conviction require him to attend a police station in order that his fingerprints may be taken.

(1A) Where a person convicted of a recordable offence has already had his fingerprints taken as mentioned in paragraph (c) of subsection (1) above, that fact (together with any time when he has been in police detention for the offence) shall be disregarded for the purposes of that subsection if-
(a) the fingerprints taken on the previous occasion do not constitute a complete set of his fingerprints; or
(b) some or all of the fingerprints taken on the previous occasion are not of sufficient quality to allow satisfactory analysis, comparison or matching.

(1B) Subsections (1) and (1A) above apply-
(a) where a person has been given a caution in respect of a recordable offence which, at the time of the caution, he has admitted, or
(b) where a person has been warned or reprimanded under section 65 of the Crime and Disorder Act 1998 (c. 37) for a recordable offence,
as they apply where a person has been convicted of an offence, and references in this section to a conviction shall be construed accordingly.

(2) A requirement under subsection (1) above—
(a) shall give the person a period of at least 7 days within which he must so attend; and
(b) may direct him to so attend at a specified time of day or between specified times of day.

(3) Any constable may arrest without warrant a person who has failed to comply with a requirement under subsection (1) above.

(4) The Secretary of State may by regulations make provision for recording in national police records convictions for such offences as are specified in the regulations. [. . .][1]

(5) Regulations under this section shall be made by statutory instrument and shall be subject to annulment in pursuance of a resolution of either House of Parliament.

[1] repealed by Criminal Justice and Police Act (2001 c.16), Schedule 7 (2)(1) paragraph 1.

28 Information to be given on arrest

(1) Subject to subsection (5) below, where a person is arrested, otherwise than by being informed that he is under arrest, the arrest is not lawful unless the person arrested is informed that he is under arrest as soon as is practicable after his arrest.

(2) Where a person is arrested by a constable, subsection (1) above applies regardless of whether the fact of the arrest is obvious.

(3) Subject to subsection (5) below, no arrest is lawful unless the person arrested is informed of the ground for the arrest at the time of, or as soon as is practicable after, the arrest.

(4) Where a person is arrested by a constable, subsection (3) above applies regardless of whether the ground for the arrest is obvious.

(5) Nothing in this section is to be taken to require a person to be informed—

(a) that he is under arrest; or

(b) of the ground for the arrest,

if it was not reasonably practicable for him to be so informed by reason of his having escaped from arrest before the information could be given.

29 Voluntary attendance at police station etc.

Where for the purpose of assisting with an investigation a person attends voluntarily at a police station or at any other place where a constable is present or accompanies a constable to a police station or any such other place without having been arrested—

(a) he shall be entitled to leave at will unless he is placed under arrest;

(b) he shall be informed at once that he is under arrest if a decision is taken by a constable to prevent him from leaving at will.

30 Arrest elsewhere than at police station

(1) Subsection (1A) applies where a person is, at any place other than a police station—

(a) arrested by a constable for an offence, or

(b) taken into custody by a constable after being arrested for an offence by a person other than a constable.

. . . . . .

(6) If the first police station to which an arrested person is taken after his arrest is not a designated police station, he shall be taken to a designated police station not more than six hours after his arrival at the first police station unless he is released previously.

[(7) A person arrested by a constable at any place other than a police station must be released without bail if the condition in subsection (7A) is satisfied.]

. . . . . .

(10) Nothing in subsection (1A) or in section 30A prevents a constable delaying taking a person to a police station or releasing him on bail if the condition in subsection (10A) is satisfied.

. . . . . .

32 Search upon arrest

(1) A constable may search an arrested person, in any case where the person to be searched has been arrested at a place other than a police station, if the constable has reasonable grounds for believing that the arrested person may present a danger to himself or others.

(2) Subject to subsections (3) to (5) below, a constable shall also have power in any such case—

(a) to search the arrested person for anything—

(i) which he might use to assist him to escape from lawful custody; or

(ii) which might be evidence relating to an offence; and

(b) to enter and search any premises in which he was when arrested or immediately before he was arrested for evidence relating to the offence for which he has been arrested.

(3) The power to search conferred by subsection (2) above is only a power to search to the extent that is reasonably required for the purpose of discovering any such thing or any such evidence.

(4) The powers conferred by this section to search a person are not to be construed as authorising a constable to require a person to remove any of his clothing in public other than an outer coat, jacket or gloves but they do authorise a search of a person's mouth.

(5) A constable may not search a person in the exercise of the power conferred by subsection (2)(a) above unless he has reasonable grounds for believing that the person to be searched may have concealed on him anything for which a search is permitted under that paragraph.

(6) A constable may not search premises in the exercise of the power conferred by subsection (2)(b) above unless he has reasonable grounds for believing that there is evidence for which a search is permitted under that paragraph on the premises.

(7) In so far as the power of search conferred by subsection (2)(b) above relates to premises consisting of two or more separate dwellings, it is limited to a power to search—

(a) any dwelling in which the arrest took place or in which the person arrested was immediately before his arrest; and
(b) any parts of the premises which the occupier of any such dwelling uses in common with the occupiers of any other dwellings comprised in the premises.

(8) A constable searching a person in the exercise of the power conferred by subsection (1) above may seize and retain anything he finds, if he has reasonable grounds for believing that the person searched might use it to cause physical injury to himself or to any other person.

(9) A constable searching a person in the exercise of the power conferred by subsection (2)(a) above may seize and retain anything he finds, other than an item subject to legal privilege, if he has reasonable grounds for believing—

(a) that he might use it to assist him to escape from lawful custody; or
(b) that it is evidence of an offence or has been obtained in consequence of the commission of an offence.

(10) Nothing in this section shall be taken to affect the power conferred by [section 43 of the Terrorism Act 2000][1].

[1] words substituted by Terrorism Act (2000 c.11), Schedule 15 paragraph 5(3).

34 Limitations on police detention

(1) A person arrested for an offence shall not be kept in police detention except in accordance with the provisions of this Part of this Act.

(2) Subject to subsection (3) below, if at any time a custody officer—

(a) becomes aware, in relation to any person in police detention, that the grounds for the detention of that person have ceased to apply; and
(b) is not aware of any other grounds on which the continued detention of that person could be justified under the provisions of this Part of this Act,

it shall be the duty of the custody officer, subject to subsection (4) below, to order his immediate release from custody.

(3) No person in police detention shall be released except on the authority of a custody officer at the police station where his detention was authorised or, if it was authorised at more than one station, a custody officer at the station where it was last authorised.

(4) A person who appears to the custody officer to have been unlawfully at large when he was arrested is not to be released under subsection (2) above.

(5) A person whose release is ordered under subsection (2) above shall be released without bail unless it appears to the custody officer—

(a) that there is need for further investigation of any matter in connection with which he was detained at any time during the period of his detention; or

(b) that, in respect of any such matter, proceedings may be taken against him or he may be reprimanded or warned under section 65 of the Crime and Disorder Act 1998 and, if it so appears, he shall be released on bail.

(6) For the purposes of this Part of this Act a person arrested under [section 6D of the Road Traffic Act 1988][1] or section 30(2) of the Transport and Works Act 1992 (c. 42) is arrested for an offence.

(7) For the purposes of this Part a person who—

(a) attends a police station to answer to bail granted under section 30A,

(b) returns to a police station to answer to bail granted under this Part, or

(c) is arrested under section 30D or 46A, is to be treated as arrested for an offence and that offence is the offence in connection with which he was granted bail.

[1] words substituted by Railways and Transport Safety Act (2003 c.20), Schedule 7 paragraph 12.

37 Duties of custody officer before charge

(1) Where—

(a) a person is arrested for an offence—

(i) without a warrant; or

(ii) under a warrant not endorsed for bail,

the custody officer at each police station where he is detained after his arrest shall determine whether he has before him sufficient evidence to charge that person with the offence for which he was arrested and may detain him at the police station for such period as is necessary to enable him to do so.

(2) If the custody officer determines that he does not have such evidence before him, the person arrested shall be released either on bail or without bail, unless the custody officer has reasonable grounds for believing that his detention without being charged is necessary to secure or preserve evidence relating to an offence for which he is under arrest or to obtain such evidence by questioning him.

(3) If the custody officer has reasonable grounds for so believing, he may authorise the person arrested to be kept in police detention.

(4) Where a custody officer authorises a person who has not been charged to be kept in police detention, he shall, as soon as is practicable, make a written record of the grounds for the detention.

(5) Subject to subsection (6) below, the written record shall be made in the presence of the person arrested who shall at that time be informed by the custody officer of the grounds for his detention.

(6) Subsection (5) above shall not apply where the person arrested is, at the time when the written record is made—

(a) incapable of understanding what is said to him;

(b) violent or likely to become violent; or

(c) in urgent need of medical attention.

(7) Subject to section 41(7) below, if the custody officer determines that he has before him sufficient evidence to charge the person arrested with the offence for which he was arrested, the person arrested—

(a) shall be released without charge and on bail for the purpose of enabling the Director of Public Prosecutions to make a decision under section 37B below,
(b) shall be released without charge and on bail but not for that purpose,
(c) shall be released without charge and without bail, or
(d) shall be charged.

(7A) The decision as to how a person is to be dealt with under subsection (7) above shall be that of the custody officer.

(7B) Where a person is released under subsection (7)(a) above, it shall be the duty of the custody officer to inform him that he is being released to enable the Director of Public Prosecutions to make a decision under section 37B below.

(8) Where—
(a) a person is released under subsection (7)(b)[or (c)][1] above; and
(b) at the time of his release a decision whether he should be prosecuted for the offence for which he was arrested has not been taken,

it shall be the duty of the custody officer so to inform him.

(9) If the person arrested is not in a fit state to be dealt with under subsection (7) above, he may be kept in police detention until he is.

(10) The duty imposed on the custody officer under subsection (1) above shall be carried out by him as soon as practicable after the person arrested arrives at the police station or, in the case of a person arrested at the police station, as soon as practicable after the arrest.

(15) In this Part of this Act—

"arrested juvenile" means a person arrested with or without a warrant who appears to be under the age of 17;
"endorsed for bail" means endorsed with a direction for bail in accordance with section 117(2) of the Magistrates' Courts Act 1980.

[1] words inserted by Criminal Justice Act (2003 c.44), Schedule 2 paragraph 2 (4).

38 Duties of custody officer after charge

(1) Where a person arrested for an offence otherwise than under a warrant endorsed for bail is charged with an offence, the custody officer shall, subject to section 25 of the Criminal Justice and Public Order Act 1994, order his release from police detention, either on bail or without bail, unless—
(a) if the person arrested is not an arrested juvenile—
  (i) his name or address cannot be ascertained or the custody officer has reasonable grounds for doubting whether a name or address furnished by him as his name or address is his real name or address;
  (ii) the custody officer has reasonable grounds for believing that the person arrested will fail to appear in court to answer to bail;
  (iii) in the case of a person arrested for an imprisonable offence, the custody officer has reasonable grounds for believing that the detention of the person arrested is necessary to prevent him from committing an offence;
  (iiia) except in a case where (by virtue of subsection (9) of section 63B below) that section does not apply, the custody officer has reasonable grounds for believing that the detention of the person is necessary to enable a sample to be taken from him under that section;
  (iv) in the case of a person arrested for an offence which is not an imprisonable offence, the custody officer has reasonable grounds for believing that the

detention of the person arrested is necessary to prevent him from causing physical injury to any other person or from causing loss of or damage to property;

(v) the custody officer has reasonable grounds for believing that the detention of the person arrested is necessary to prevent him from interfering with the administration of justice or with the investigation of offences or of a particular offence; or

(vi) the custody officer has reasonable grounds for believing that the detention of the person arrested is necessary for his own protection;

(b) if he is an arrested juvenile—

(i) any of the requirements of paragraph (a) above is satisfied (but, in the case of paragraph (a)(iiia) above, only if the arrested juvenile has attained the minimum age); or

(ii) the custody officer has reasonable grounds for believing that he ought to be detained in his own interests.

(2) If the release of a person arrested is not required by subsection (1) above, the custody officer may authorise him to be kept in police detention but may not authorise a person to be kept in police detention by virtue of subsection (1)(a)(iiia) after the end of the period of six hours beginning when he was charged with the offence.

(2A) The custody officer, in taking the decisions required by subsection (1)(a) and (b) above (except (a)(i) and (vi) and (b)(ii)), shall have regard to the same considerations as those which a court is required to have regard to in taking the corresponding decisions under paragraph 2(1) of Part I of Schedule 1 to the Bail Act 1976 (disregarding paragraph 2(2) of that Part).

(3) Where a custody officer authorises a person who has been charged to be kept in police detention, he shall, as soon as practicable, make a written record of the grounds for the detention.

(4) Subject to subsection (5) below, the written record shall be made in the presence of the person charged who shall at that time be informed by the custody officer of the grounds for his detention.

(5) Subsection (4) above shall not apply where the person charged is, at the time when the written record is made—

(a) incapable of understanding what is said to him;

(b) violent or likely to become violent; or

(c) in urgent need of medical attention.

39 Responsibilities in relation to persons detained

(6) Where—

(a) an officer of higher rank than the custody officer gives directions relating to a person in police detention; and

(b) the directions are at variance—

(i) with any decision made or action taken by the custody officer in the performance of a duty imposed on him under this Part of this Act; or

(ii) with any decision or action which would but for the directions have been made or taken by him in the performance of such a duty,

the custody officer shall refer the matter at once to an officer of the rank of superintendent or above who is responsible for the police station for which the custody officer is acting as custody officer.

40 Review of police detention

(1) Reviews of the detention of each person in police detention in connection with the investigation of an offence shall be carried out periodically in accordance with the following provisions of this section—

(a) in the case of a person who has been arrested and charged, by the custody officer; and

(b) in the case of a person who has been arrested but not charged, by an officer of at least the rank of inspector who has not been directly involved in the investigation.

(2) The officer to whom it falls to carry out a review is referred to in this section as a "review officer".

(3) Subject to subsection (4) below—

(a) the first review shall be not later than six hours after the detention was first authorised;

(b) the second review shall be not later than nine hours after the first;

(c) subsequent reviews shall be at intervals of not more than nine hours.

(4) A review may be postponed—

(a) if, having regard to all the circumstances prevailing at the latest time for it specified in subsection (3) above, it is not practicable to carry out the review at that time;

(b) without prejudice to the generality of paragraph (a) above—

(i) if at that time the person in detention is being questioned by a police officer and the review officer is satisfied that an interruption of the questioning for the purpose of carrying out the review would prejudice the investigation in connection with which he is being questioned; or

(ii) if at that time no review officer is readily available.

(5) If a review is postponed under subsection (4) above it shall be carried out as soon as practicable after the latest time specified for it in subsection (3) above.

(6) If a review is carried out after postponement under subsection (4) above, the fact that it was so carried out shall not affect any requirement of this section as to the time at which any subsequent review is to be carried out.

(7) The review officer shall record the reasons for any postponement of a review in the custody record.

(8) Subject to subsection (9) below, where the person whose detention is under review has not been charged before the time of the review, section 37(1) to (6) above shall have effect in relation to him, but with the modifications specified in subsection (8A).

(8A) The modifications are—

(a) the substitution of references to the person whose detention is under review for references to the person arrested;

(b) the substitution of references to the review officer for references to the custody officer; and

(c) in subsection (6), the insertion of the following paragraph after paragraph (a)— "(aa) asleep;".

(9) Where a person has been kept in police detention by virtue of [section 37(9) or 37D(5)][1] above, section 37(1) to (6) shall not have effect in relation to him but it shall be the duty of the review officer to determine whether he is yet in a fit state.

(10) Where the person whose detention is under review has been charged before the time of the review, section 38(1) to (6B) above shall have effect in relation to him, but with the modifications specified in subsection (10A).

(10A) The modifications are—

(a) the substitution of a reference to the person whose detention is under review for any reference to the person arrested or to the person charged; and

(b) in subsection (5), the insertion of the following paragraph after paragraph (a)—

"(aa) asleep;".

(11) Where—

(a) an officer of higher rank than the review officer gives directions relating to a person in police detention; and

(b) the directions are at variance—

(i) with any decision made or action taken by the review officer in the performance of a duty imposed on him under this Part of this Act; or

(ii) with any decision or action which would but for the directions have been made or taken by him in the performance of such a duty.

the review officer shall refer the matter at once to an officer of the rank of superintendent or above who is responsible for the police station for which the review officer is acting as review officer in connection with the detention.

(12) Before determining whether to authorise a person's continued detention the review officer shall give—

(a) that person (unless he is asleep); or

(b) any solicitor representing him who is available at the time of the review,

an opportunity to make representations to him about the detention.

(13) Subject to subsection (14) below, the person whose detention is under review or his solicitor may make representations under subsection (12) above either orally or in writing.

(14) The review officer may refuse to hear oral representations from the person whose detention is under review if he considers that he is unfit to make such representations by reason of his condition or behaviour.

[1] words inserted by Criminal Justice Act (2003 c.44), Schedule 2 paragraph 4.

41 Limits on period of detention without charge

(1) Subject to the following provisions of this section and to ss 42 and 43 below, a person shall not be kept in police detention for more than 24 hours without being charged.

(2) The time from which the period of detention of a person is to be calculated (in this Act referred to as "the relevant time")—

(a) in the case of a person to whom this paragraph applies, shall be—

(i) the time at which that person arrives at the relevant police station; or

(ii) the time 24 hours after the time of that person's arrest,

whichever is the earlier;

(b) in the case of a person arrested outside England and Wales, shall be—

(i) the time at which that person arrives at the first police station to which he is taken in the police area in England or Wales in which the offence for which he was arrested is being investigated; or

(ii) the time 24 hours after the time of that person's entry into England and Wales,

whichever is the earlier;

(c) in the case of a person who—

(i) attends voluntarily at a police station; or

(ii) accompanies a constable to a police station without having been arrested, and is arrested at the police station, the time of his arrest;

[(ca) in the case of a person who attends a police station to answer to bail granted under section 30A, the time when he arrives at the police station;][1]

(d) in any other case, except where subsection (5) below applies, shall be the time at which the person arrested arrives at the first police station to which he is taken after his arrest.

(3) Subsection (2)(a) above applies to a person if—

(a) his arrest is sought in one police area in England and Wales;

(b) he is arrested in another police area; and

(c) he is not questioned in the area in which he is arrested in order to obtain evidence in relation to an offence for which he is arrested;

and in sub-paragraph (i) of that paragraph "the relevant police station" means the first police station to which he is taken in the police area in which his arrest was sought.

(4) Subsection (2) above shall have effect in relation to a person arrested under section 31 above as if every reference in it to his arrest or his being arrested were a reference to his arrest or his being arrested for the offence for which he was originally arrested.

(5) If—

(a) a person is in police detention in a police area in England and Wales ("the first area"); and

(b) his arrest for an offence is sought in some other police area in England and Wales ("the second area"); and

(c) he is taken to the second area for the purposes of investigating that offence, without being questioned in the first area in order to obtain evidence in relation to it,

the relevant time shall be—

(i) the time 24 hours after he leaves the place where he is detained in the first area; or

(ii) the time at which he arrives at the first police station to which he is taken in the second area,

whichever is the earlier.

(6) When a person who is in police detention is removed to hospital because he is in need of medical treatment, any time during which he is being questioned in hospital or on the way there or back by a police officer for the purpose of obtaining evidence relating to an offence shall be included in any period which falls to be calculated for the purposes of this Part of this Act, but any other time while he is in hospital or on his way there or back shall not be so included.

(7) Subject to subsection (8) below, a person who at the expiry of 24 hours after the relevant time is in police detention and has not been charged shall be released at that time either on bail or without bail.

(8) Subsection (7) above does not apply to a person whose detention for more than 24 hours after the relevant time has been authorised or is otherwise permitted in accordance with section 42 or 43 below.

(9) A person released under subsection (7) above shall not be re-arrested without a warrant for the offence for which he was previously arrested unless new evidence justifying a further arrest has come to light since his release; but this subsection does not prevent an arrest under section 46A below.

[1] added by Criminal Justice Act (2003 c.44), Schedule 1 paragraph 8.

42 Authorisation of continued detention

(1) Where a police officer of the rank of superintendent or above who is responsible for the police station at which a person is detained has reasonable grounds for believing that—

(a) the detention of that person without charge is necessary to secure or preserve evidence relating to an offence for which he is under arrest or to obtain such evidence by questioning him;

[(b) an offence for which he is under arrest is an arrestable offence; and][1]

(c) the investigation is being conducted diligently and expeditiously.

he may authorise the keeping of that person in police detention for a period expiring at or before 36 hours after the relevant time.

(2) Where an officer such as is mentioned in subsection (1) above has authorised the keeping of a person in police detention for a period expiring less than 36 hours after the relevant time, such an officer may authorise the keeping of that person in police detention for a further period expiring not more than 36 hours after that time if the conditions specified in subsection (1) above are still satisfied when he gives the authorisation.

(3) If it is proposed to transfer a person in police detention to another police area, the officer determining whether or not to authorise keeping him in detention under subsection (1) above shall have regard to the distance and the time the journey would take.

(4) No authorisation under subsection (1) above shall be given in respect of any person—

(a) more than 24 hours after the relevant time; or

(b) before the second review of his detention under section 40 above has been carried out.

(5) Where an officer authorises the keeping of a person in police detention under subsection (1) above, it shall be his duty—

(a) to inform that person of the grounds for his continued detention; and

(b) to record the grounds in that person's custody record.

(6) Before determining whether to authorise the keeping of a person in detention under subsection (1) or (2) above, an officer shall give—

(a) that person; or

(b) any solicitor representing him who is available at the time when it falls to the officer to determine whether to give the authorisation,

an opportunity to make representations to him about the detention.

(7) Subject to subsection (8) below, the person in detention or his solicitor may make representations under subsection (6) above either orally or in writing.

(8) The officer to whom it falls to determine whether to give the authorisation may refuse to hear oral representations from the person in detention if he considers that he is unfit to make such representations by reason of his condition or behaviour.

(9) Where—

(a) an officer authorises the keeping of a person in detention under subsection (1) above; and

(b) at the time of the authorisation he has not yet exercised a right conferred on him by section 56 or 58 below,

the officer—

(i) shall inform him of that right;

(ii) shall decide whether he should be permitted to exercise it;

(iii) shall record the decision in his custody record; and

(iv) if the decision is to refuse to permit the exercise of the right, shall also record the grounds for the decision in that record.

(10) Where an officer has authorised the keeping of a person who has not been charged in detention under subsection (1) or (2) above, he shall be released from detention, either on bail or without bail, not later than 36 hours after the relevant time, unless—

(a) he has been charged with an offence; or

(b) his continued detention is authorised or otherwise permitted in accordance with section 43 below.

(11) A person released under subsection (10) above shall not be re-arrested without a warrant for the offence for which he was previously arrested unless new evidence justifying a further arrest has come to light since his release; but this subsection does not prevent an arrest under section 46A below.

[1] substituted by Criminal Justice Act (2003 c.44), Part 1 section 7.

43 Warrants of further detention

(1) Where, on an application on oath made by a constable and supported by an information, a magistrates' court is satisfied that there are reasonable grounds for believing that the further detention of the person to whom the application relates is justified, it may issue a warrant of further detention authorising the keeping of that person in police detention.

(2) A court may not hear an application for a warrant of further detention unless the person to whom the application relates—

(a) has been furnished with a copy of the information; and

(b) has been brought before the court for the hearing.

(3) The person to whom the application relates shall be entitled to be legally represented at the hearing and, if he is not so represented but wishes to be so represented—

(a) the court shall adjourn the hearing to enable him to obtain representation; and

(b) he may be kept in police detention during the adjournment.

(4) A person's further detention is only justified for the purposes of this section or section 44 below if—

(a) his detention without charge is necessary to secure or preserve evidence relating to an offence for which he is under arrest or to obtain such evidence by questioning him;

(b) an offence for which he is under arrest is a serious arrestable offence; and

(c) the investigation is being conducted diligently and expeditiously.

(5) Subject to subsection (7) below, an application for a warrant of further detention may be made—

(a) at any time before the expiry of 36 hours after the relevant time; or

(b) in a case where—

(i) it is not practicable for the magistrates' court to which the application will be made to sit at the expiry of 36 hours after the relevant time; but

(ii) the court will sit during the 6 hours following the end of that period,

at any time before the expiry of the said 6 hours.

(6) In a case to which subsection (5)(b) above applies—

(a) the person to whom the application relates may be kept in police detention until the application is heard; and

(b) the custody officer shall make a note in that person's custody record—

(i) of the fact that he was kept in police detention for more than 36 hours after the relevant time; and
(ii) of the reason why he was so kept.

(7) If—
(a) an application for a warrant of further detention is made after the expiry of 36 hours after the relevant time; and
(b) it appears to the magistrates' court that it would have been reasonable for the police to make it before the expiry of that period,

the court shall dismiss the application.

(8) Where on an application such as is mentioned in subsection (1) above a magistrates' court is not satisfied that there are reasonable grounds for believing that the further detention of the person to whom the application relates is justified, it shall be its duty—
(a) to refuse the application; or
(b) to adjourn the hearing of it until a time not later than 36 hours after the relevant time.

(9) The person to whom the application relates may be kept in police detention during the adjournment.

(10) A warrant of further detention shall—
(a) state the time at which it is issued;
(b) authorise the keeping in police detention of the person to whom it relates for the period stated in it.

(11) Subject to subsection (12) below, the period stated in a warrant of further detention shall be such period as the magistrates' court thinks fit, having regard to the evidence before it.

(12) The period shall not be longer than 36 hours.

(13) If it is proposed to transfer a person in police detention to a police area other than that in which he is detained when the application for a warrant of further detention is made, the court hearing the application shall have regard to the distance and the time the journey would take.

(14) Any information submitted in support of an application under this section shall state—
(a) the nature of the offence for which the person to whom the application relates has been arrested;
(b) the general nature of the evidence on which that person was arrested;
(c) what inquiries relating to the offence have been made by the police and what further inquiries are proposed by them;
(d) the reasons for believing the continued detention of that person to be necessary for the purposes of such further inquiries.

(15) Where an application under this section is refused, the person to whom the application relates shall forthwith be charged or, subject to subsection (16) below, released, either on bail or without bail.

(16) A person need not be released under subsection (15) above—
(a) before the expiry of 24 hours after the relevant time; or
(b) before the expiry of any longer period for which his continued detention is or has been authorised under section 42 above.

(17) Where an application under this section is refused, no further application shall be made under this section in respect of the person to whom the refusal relates, unless supported by evidence which has come to light since the refusal.

(18) Where a warrant of further detention is issued, the person to whom it relates shall be released from police detention, either on bail or without bail, upon or before the expiry of the warrant unless he is charged.

(19) A person released under subsection (18) above shall not be re-arrested without a warrant for the offence for which he was previously arrested unless new evidence justifying a further arrest has come to light since his release [; but this subsection does not prevent an arrest under section 46A below][1].

[1] words inserted by Criminal Justice and Public Order Act (1994 c.33), Part II s.29(4) (b).

44 Extension of warrants of further detention

(1) On an application on oath made by a constable and supported by an information a magistrates' court may extend a warrant of further detention issued under section 43 above if it is satisfied that there are reasonable grounds for believing that the further detention of the person to whom the application relates is justified.

(2) Subject to subsection (3) below, the period for which a warrant of further detention may be extended shall be such period as the court thinks fit, having regard to the evidence before it.

(3) The period shall not—

(a) be longer than 36 hours; or

(b) end later than 96 hours after the relevant time.

(4) Where a warrant of further detention has been extended under subsection (1) above, or further extended under this subsection, for a period ending before 96 hours after the relevant time, on an application such as is mentioned in that subsection a magistrates' court may further extend the warrant if it is satisfied as there mentioned; and subsections (2) and (3) above apply to such further extensions as they apply to extensions under subsection (1) above.

(5) A warrant of further detention shall, if extended or further extended under this section, be endorsed with a note of the period of the extension.

(6) Subsections (2), (3) and (14) of section 43 above shall apply to an application made under this section as they apply to an application made under that section.

(7) Where an application under this section is refused, the person to whom the application relates shall forthwith be charged or, subject to subsection (8) below, released, either on bail or without bail.

(8) A person need not be released under subsection (7) above before the expiry of any period for which a warrant of further detention issued in relation to him has been extended or further extended on an earlier application made under this section.

46 Detention after charge

(1) Where a person—

(a) is charged with an offence; and

(b) after being charged—

(i) is kept in police detention; or

(ii) is detained by a local authority in pursuance of arrangements made under section 38(6) above,

he shall be brought before a magistrates' court in accordance with the provisions of this section.

(2) If he is to be brought before a magistrates' court for the petty sessions area in which the police station at which he was charged is situated, he shall be brought before such a court as soon as is practicable and in any event not later than the first sitting after he is charged with the offence.

(3) If no magistrates' court for that area is due to sit either on the day on which he is charged or on the next day, the custody officer for the police station at which he was charged shall inform the justices' chief executive for the area that there is a person in the area to whom subsection (2) above applies.

(4) If the person charged is to be brought before a magistrates' court for a petty sessions area other than that in which the police station at which he was charged is situated, he shall be removed to that area as soon as is practicable and brought before such a court as soon as is practicable after his arrival in the area and in any event not later than the first sitting of a magistrates' court for that area after his arrival in the area.

(5) If no magistrates' court for that area is due to sit either on the day on which he arrives in the area or on the next day—

(a) he shall be taken to a police station in the area; and

(b) the custody officer at that station shall inform the justices' chief executive for the area that there is a person in the area to whom subsection (4) applies.

(6) Subject to subsection (8) below, where the justices' chief executive for a petty sessions area has been informed—

(a) under subsection (3) above that there is a person in the area to whom subsection (2) above applies; or

(b) under subsection (5) above that there is a person in the area to whom subsection (4) above applies,

the justices' chief executive shall arrange for a magistrates' court to sit not later than the day next following the relevant day.

(7) In this section "the relevant day"—

(a) in relation to a person who is to be brought before a magistrates' court for the petty sessions area in which the police station at which he was charged is situated, means the day on which he was charged; and

(b) in relation to a person who is to be brought before a magistrates' court for any other petty sessions area, means the day on which he arrives in the area.

(8) Where the day next following the relevant day is Christmas Day, Good Friday or a Sunday, the duty of the [justices' chief executive][1] under subsection (6) above is a duty to arrange for a magistrates' court to sit not later than the first day after the relevant day which is not one of those days.

(9) Nothing in this section requires a person who is in hospital to be brought before a court if he is not well enough.

[1] words substituted by SI 2001/618 (Access to Justice Act 1999 (Transfer of Justices' Clerks' Functions) Order), Art. 4 (c).

46A Power of arrest for failure to answer to police bail

(1) A constable may arrest without a warrant any person who, having been released on bail under this Part of this Act subject to a duty to attend at a police station, fails to attend at that police station at the time appointed for him to do so.

[(1A) A person who has been released on bail under section 37(7)(a) or 37C(2)(b) above may be arrested without warrant by a constable if the constable has reasonable grounds for suspecting that the person has broken any of the conditions of bail.][1]

(2) A person who is arrested under this section shall be taken to the police station appointed as the place at which he is to surrender to custody as soon as practicable after the arrest.

(3) For the purposes of—

(a) section 30 above (subject to the obligation in subsection (2) above), and

(b) section 31 above,

an arrest under this section shall be treated as an arrest for an offence.

[1] added by Criminal Justice Act (2003 c.44), Schedule 2 paragraph 5.

47 Bail after arrest

(1) Subject to the following provisions of this section, a release on bail of a person under this Part of this Act shall be a release on bail granted in accordance with sections 3, 3A, 5 and 5A of the Bail Act 1976 as they apply to bail granted by a constable.

(1A) The normal powers to impose conditions of bail shall be available to him where a custody officer releases a person on bail under section 37(7)(a) above or section 38(1) above (including that subsection as applied by section 40(10) above) but not in any other cases.

In this subsection, "the normal powers to impose conditions of bail" has the meaning given in section 3(6) of the Bail Act 1976.

[(1B) No application may be made under section 5B of the Bail Act 1976 if a person is released on bail under section 37(7)(a) or 37C(2)(b) above.

(1C) Subsections (1D) to (1F) below apply where a person released on bail under section 37(7)(a) or 37C(2)(b) above is on bail subject to conditions.

(1D) The person shall not be entitled to make an application under section 43B of the Magistrates' Courts Act 1980.

(1E) A magistrates' court may, on an application by or on behalf of the person, vary the conditions of bail; and in this subsection "vary" has the same meaning as in the Bail Act 1976.

(1F) Where a magistrates' court varies the conditions of bail under subsection (1E) above, that bail shall not lapse but shall continue subject to the conditions as so varied.][1]

(2) Nothing in the Bail Act 1976 shall prevent the re-arrest without warrant of a person released on bail subject to a duty to attend at a police station if new evidence justifying a further arrest has come to light since his release.

(3) Subject to subsections (3A) and (4) below, in this Part of this Act references to "bail" are references to bail subject to a duty—

(a) to appear before a magistrates' court at such time and such place; or

(b) to attend at such police station at such time,

as the custody officer may appoint.

(3A) Where a custody officer grants bail to a person subject to a duty to appear before a magistrates' court, he shall appoint for the appearance—

(a) a date which is not later than the first sitting of the court after the person is charged with the offence; or

(b) where he is informed by the justices' chief executive. for the relevant petty sessions area that the appearance cannot be accommodated until a later date, that later date.

(4) Where a custody officer has granted bail to a person subject to a duty to appear at a police station, the custody officer may give notice in writing to that person that his attendance at the police station is not required.

(6) Where a person who has been granted bail under this Part and either has attended at the police station in accordance with the grant of bail or has been arrested under section 46A above is detained at a police station, any time during which he was in police detention prior to being granted bail shall be included as part of any period which falls to be calculated under this Part of this Act.

(7) Where a person who was released on bail under this Part subject to a duty to attend at a police station is re-arrested, the provisions of this Part of this Act shall apply to him as they apply to a person arrested for the first time; but this subsection does not apply to a person who is arrested under section 46A above or has attended a police station in accordance with the grant of bail (and who accordingly is deemed by section 34(7) above to have been arrested for an offence).

(8) In the Magistrates' Courts Act 1980—

(a) the following section shall be substituted for section 43—

43.—"Bail on arrest

(1) Where a person has been granted bail under the Police and Criminal Evidence Act 1984 subject to a duty to appear before a magistrates' court, the court before which he is to appear may appoint a later time as the time at which he is to appear and may enlarge the recognizances of any sureties for him at that time.

(2) The recognizance of any surety for any person granted bail subject to a duty to attend at a police station may be enforced as if it were conditioned for his appearance before a magistrates' court for the petty sessions area in which the police station named in the recognizance is situated."

; and

(b) the following subsection shall be substituted for section 117(3)—

"(3) Where a warrant has been endorsed for bail under subsection (1) above—

- (a) where the person arrested is to be released on bail on his entering into a recognizance without sureties, it shall not be necessary to take him to a police station, but if he is so taken, he shall be released from custody on his entering into the recognizance; and
- (b) where he is to be released on his entering into a recognizance with sureties, he shall be taken to a police station on his arrest, and the custody officer there shall (subject to his approving any surety tendered in compliance with the endorsement) release him from custody as directed in the endorsement.".

[1] added by Criminal Justice Act (2003 c.44), Schedule 2 paragraph 6 (4).

. . . . . .

54 Searches of detained persons

(1) The custody officer at a police station shall ascertain everything which a person has with him when he is—

- (a) brought to the station after being arrested elsewhere or after being committed to custody by an order or sentence of a court; or
- (b) arrested at the station or detained there , as a person falling within section 34(7), under section 37 above.

[(2) The custody officer may record or cause to be recorded all or any of the things which he ascertains under subsection (1).

(2A) In the case of an arrested person, any such record may be made as part of his custody record.][1]

(3) Subject to subsection (4) below, a custody officer may seize and retain any such thing or cause any such thing to be seized and retained.

(4) Clothes and personal effects may only be seized if the custody officer—

(a) believes that the person from whom they are seized may use them—
   (i) to cause physical injury to himself or any other person;
   (ii) to damage property;
   (iii) to interfere with evidence; or
   (iv) to assist him to escape; or

(b) has reasonable grounds for believing that they may be evidence relating to an offence.

(5) Where anything is seized, the person from whom it is seized shall be told the reason for the seizure unless he is—

(a) violent or likely to become violent; or
(b) incapable of understanding what is said to him.

(6) Subject to subsection (7) below, a person may be searched if the custody officer considers it necessary to enable him to carry out his duty under subsection (1) above and to the extent that the custody officer considers necessary for that purpose.

(6A) A person who is in custody at a police station or is in police detention otherwise than at a police station may at any time be searched in order to ascertain whether he has with him anything which he could use for any of the purposes specified in subsection (4)(a) above.

(6B) Subject to subsection (6C) below, a constable may seize and retain, or cause to be seized and retained, anything found on such a search.

(6C) A constable may only seize clothes and personal effects in the circumstances specified in subsection (4) above.

(7) An intimate search may not be conducted under this section.

(8) A search under this section shall be carried out by a constable.

(9) The constable carrying out a search shall be of the same sex as the person searched.[2]

[1] s.54(2)–(2A) substituted for s.54(2) by Criminal Justice Act (2003 c.44), Part 1 section 8(2).

[2] In relation to the investigation of offences conducted by a service policeman under the Army Act 1955, the Air Force Act 1955 or the Naval Discipline Act 1957.

55 Intimate searches

(1) [1]Subject to the following provisions of this section, if an officer of at least the rank of inspector has reasonable grounds for believing—

(a) that a person who has been arrested and is in police detention may have concealed on him anything which—
   (i) he could use to cause physical injury to himself or others; and
   (ii) he might so use while he is in police detention or in the custody of a court; or

(b) that such a person—
   (i) may have a Class A drug concealed on him; and

(ii) was in possession of it with the appropriate criminal intent before his arrest,

he may authorise an intimate search of that person.

(2) An officer may not authorise an intimate search of a person for anything unless he has reasonable grounds for believing that it cannot be found without his being intimately searched.

(3) An officer may give an authorisation under subsection (1) above orally or in writing but, if he gives it orally, he shall confirm it in writing as soon as is practicable.

(4) An intimate search which is only a drug offence search shall be by way of examination by a suitably qualified person.

(5) Except as provided by subsection (4) above, an intimate search shall be by way of examination by a suitably qualified person unless an officer of at least the rank of [inspector] considers that this is not practicable.

(6) An intimate search which is not carried out as mentioned in subsection (5) above shall be carried out by a constable.

(7) A constable may not carry out an intimate search of a person of the opposite sex.

(8) No intimate search may be carried out except—

(a) at a police station;

(b) at a hospital;

(c) at a registered medical practitioner's surgery; or

(d) at some other place used for medical purposes.

(9) An intimate search which is only a drug offence search may not be carried out at a police station.

(10) If an intimate search of a person is carried out, the custody record relating to him shall state—

(a) which parts of his body were searched; and

(b) why they were searched.

(11) The information required to be recorded by subsection (10) above shall be recorded as soon as practicable after the completion of the search.

(12) The custody officer at a police station may seize and retain anything which is found on an intimate search of a person, or cause any such thing to be seized and retained—

(a) if he believes that the person from whom it is seized may use it—

(i) to cause physical injury to himself or any other person;

(ii) to damage property;

(iii) to interfere with evidence; or

(iv) to assist him to escape; or

(b) if he has reasonable grounds for believing that it may be evidence relating to an offence.

(13) Where anything is seized under this section, the person from whom it is seized shall be told the reason for the seizure unless he is—

(a) violent or likely to become violent; or

(b) incapable of understanding what is said to him.

(14) Every annual report—

(a) under section 22 of the Police Act 1996; or

(b) made by the Commissioner of Police of the Metropolis,

shall contain information about searches under this section which have been carried out in the area to which the report relates during the period to which it relates.

(14A) Every annual report under section 57 of the Police Act 1997 (reports by Director General of the National Crime Squad) shall contain information about searches authorised under this section by members of the National Crime Squad during the period to which the report relates.

(15) The information about such searches shall include—

(a) the total number of searches;

(b) the number of searches conducted by way of examination by a suitably qualified person;

(c) the number of searches not so conducted but conducted in the presence of such a person; and

(d) the result of the searches carried out.

(16) The information shall also include, as separate items—

(a) the total number of drug offence searches; and

(b) the result of those searches.

(17) In this section—

"the appropriate criminal intent" means an intent to commit an offence under—

(a) section 5(3) of the Misuse of Drugs Act 1971 (possession of controlled drug with intent to supply to another); or

(b) section 68(2) of the Customs and Excise Management Act 1979 (exportation *etc.* with intent to evade a prohibition or restriction);

"Class A drug" has the meaning assigned to it by section 2(1)(b) of the Misuse of Drugs Act 1971;

"drug offence search" means an intimate search for a Class A drug which an officer has authorised by virtue of subsection (1)(b) above; and

"suitably qualified person" means—

(a) a registered medical practitioner; or

(b) a registered nurse.

[1] In relation to the investigation of offences conducted by a service policeman under the Army Act 1955, the Air Force Act 1955 or the Naval Discipline Act 1957.

. . . . . .

58 Access to legal advice

(1) A person arrested and held in custody in a police station or other premises shall be entitled, if he so requests, to consult a solicitor privately at any time.

(2) Subject to subsection (3) below, a request under subsection (1) above and the time at which it was made shall be recorded in the custody record.

(3) Such a request need not be recorded in the custody record of a person who makes it at a time while he is at a court after being charged with an offence.

(4) If a person makes such a request, he must be permitted to consult a solicitor as soon as is practicable except to the extent that delay is permitted by this section.

(5) In any case he must be permitted to consult a solicitor within 36 hours from the relevant time, as defined in section 41(2) above.

(6) Delay in compliance with a request is only permitted—

(a) in the case of a person who is in police detention for a serious arrestable offence; and

(b) if an officer of at least the rank of superintendent authorises it.

(7) An officer may give an authorisation under subsection (6) above orally or in writing but, if he gives it orally, he shall confirm it in writing as soon as is practicable.

(8) Subject to sub-section (8A) below an officer may only authorise delay where he has reasonable grounds for believing that the exercise of the right conferred by subsection (1) above at the time when the person detained desires to exercise it—

(a) will lead to interference with or harm to evidence connected with a serious arrestable offence or interference with or physical injury to other persons; or

(b) will lead to the alerting of other persons suspected of having committed such an offence but not yet arrested for it; or

(c) will hinder the recovery of any property obtained as a result of such an offence.

[(8A) An officer may also authorise delay where he has reasonable grounds for believing that—

(a) the person detained for the serious arrestable offence has benefited from his criminal conduct, and

(b) the recovery of the value of the property constituting the benefit will be hindered by the exercise of the right conferred by subsection (1) above.

(8B) For the purposes of subsection (8A) above the question whether a person has benefited from his criminal conduct is to be decided in accordance with Part 2 of the Proceeds of Crime Act 2002.][1]

(9) If delay is authorised—

(a) the detained person shall be told the reason for it; and

(b) the reason shall be noted on his custody record.

(10) The duties imposed by subsection (9) above shall be performed as soon as is practicable.

(11) There may be no further delay in permitting the exercise of the right conferred by subsection (1) above once the reason for authorising delay ceases to subsist.

(12) Nothing in this section applies to a person arrested or detained under the terrorism provisions.[2]

[1] s.58(8A)–(8B) substituted for s.58(8A) by Proceeds of Crime Act (2002 c.29), Schedule 11 paragraph 14 (3).

[2] In relation to the investigation of offences conducted by a service policeman under the Army Act 1955, the Air Force Act 1955 or the Naval Discipline Act 1957.

61 Finger-printing

(1) Except as provided by this section no person's fingerprints may be taken without the appropriate consent.

(2) Consent to the taking of a person's fingerprints must be in writing if it is given at a time when he is at a police station.

(3) The fingerprints of a person detained at a police station may be taken without the appropriate consent if—

(a) he is detained in consequence of his arrest for a recordable offence; and

(b) he has not had his fingerprints taken in the course of the investigation of the offence by the police.

(3A) Where a person mentioned in paragraph (a) of subsection (3) or (4) has already had his fingerprints taken in the course of the investigation of the offence by the police, that fact shall be disregarded for the purposes of that subsection if-

(a) the fingerprints taken on the previous occasion do not constitute a complete set of his fingerprints; or

(b) some or all of the fingerprints taken on the previous occasion are not of sufficient quality to allow satisfactory analysis, comparison or matching (whether in the case in question or generally).

(4) The fingerprints of a person detained at a police station may be taken without the appropriate consent if—

(a) he has been charged with a recordable offence or informed that he will be reported for such an offence; and

(b) he has not had his fingerprints taken in the course of the investigation of the offence by the police.

(4A) The fingerprints of a person who has answered to bail at a court or police station may be taken without the appropriate consent at the court or station if-

(a) the court, or

(b) an officer of at least the rank of inspector,

authorises them to be taken.

(4B) A court or officer may only give an authorisation under subsection (4A) if-

(a) the person who has answered to bail has answered to it for a person whose fingerprints were taken on a previous occasion and there are reasonable grounds for believing that he is not the same person; or

(b) the person who has answered to bail claims to be a different person from a person whose fingerprints were taken on a previous occasion.

(5) An officer may give an authorisation under subsection (4A) above orally or in writing but, if he gives it orally, he shall confirm it in writing as soon as is practicable.

(6) Any person's fingerprints may be taken without the appropriate consent if—

(a) he has been convicted of a recordable offence;

(b) he has been given a caution in respect of a recordable offence which, at the time of the caution, he has admitted; or

(c) he has been warned or reprimanded under section 65 of the Crime and Disorder Act 1998 (c. 37) for a recordable offence.

(7) In a case where by virtue of [subsection (3), (4) or (6)][1] above a person's fingerprints are taken without the appropriate consent—

(a) he shall be told the reason before his fingerprints are taken; and

(b) the reason shall be recorded as soon as is practicable after the fingerprints are taken.

(7A) If a person's fingerprints are taken at a police station, whether with or without the appropriate consent—

(a) before the fingerprints are taken, an officer shall inform him that they may be the subject of a speculative search; and

(b) the fact that the person has been informed of this possibility shall be recorded as soon as is practicable after the fingerprints have been taken.

(8) If he is detained at a police station when the fingerprints are taken, the reason for taking them and, in the case falling within subsection (7A) above, the fact referred to in paragraph (b) of that subsection shall be recorded on his custody record.

(8B) The power to take the fingerprints of a person detained at a police station without the appropriate consent shall be exercisable by any constable.

(9) Nothing in this section—

(a) affects any power conferred by paragraph 18(2) of Schedule 2 to the Immigration Act 1971; or

(b) applies to a person arrested or detained under the terrorism provisions.

(10) Nothing in this section applies to a person arrested under an extradition arrest power.

[1] words substituted by Criminal Justice Act (2003 c.44), Part 1 s.9(5).

62 Intimate samples

(1) Subject to section 63B below an intimate sample may be taken from a person in police detention only—

(a) if a police officer of at least the rank of inspector authorises it to be taken; and

(b) if the appropriate consent is given.

(1A) An intimate sample may be taken from a person who is not in police detention but from whom, in the course of the investigation of an offence, two or more non-intimate samples suitable for the same means of analysis have been taken which have proved insufficient—

(a) if a police officer of at least the rank of inspector authorises it to be taken; and

(b) if the appropriate consent is given.

(2) An officer may only give an authorisation under subsection (1) or (1A) above if he has reasonable grounds—

(a) for suspecting the involvement of the person from whom the sample is to be taken in a recordable offence; and

(b) for believing that the sample will tend to confirm or disprove his involvement.

(3) An officer may give an authorisation under subsection (1) or (1A) above orally or in writing but, if he gives it orally, he shall confirm it in writing as soon as is practicable.

(4) The appropriate consent must be given in writing.

(5) Where—

(a) an authorisation has been given; and

(b) it is proposed that an intimate sample shall be taken in pursuance of the authorisation,

an officer shall inform the person from whom the sample is to be taken—

(i) of the giving of the authorisation; and

(ii) of the grounds for giving it.

(6) The duty imposed by subsection (5)(ii) above includes a duty to state the nature of the offence in which it is suspected that the person from whom the sample is to be taken has been involved.

(7) If an intimate sample is taken from a person—

(a) the authorisation by virtue of which it was taken;

(b) the grounds for giving the authorisation; and

(c) the fact that the appropriate consent was given,

shall be recorded as soon as is practicable after the sample is taken.

(7A) If an intimate sample is taken from a person at a police station—

(a) before the sample is taken, an officer shall inform him that it may be the subject of a speculative search; and

(b) the fact that the person has been informed of this possibility shall be recorded as soon as practicable after the sample has been taken.

(8) If an intimate sample is taken from a person detained at a police station, the matters required to be recorded by subsection (7) or (7A) above shall be recorded in his custody record.

[(9) In the case of an intimate sample which is a dental impression, the sample may be taken from a person only by a registered dentist.

(9A) In the case of any other form of intimate sample, except in the case of a sample of urine, the sample may be taken from a person only by—

(a) a registered medical practitioner; or

(b) a registered health care professional.][1]

(10) Where the appropriate consent to the taking of an intimate sample from a person was refused without good cause, in any proceedings against that person for an offence—

(a) the court, in determining—

(i) whether to commit that person for trial; or

(ii) whether there is a case to answer; and

(aa) a judge, in deciding whether to grant an application made by the accused under—

(i) section 6 of the Criminal Justice Act 1987 (application for dismissal of charge of serious fraud in respect of which notice of transfer has been given under section 4 of that Act); or

(ii) paragraph 5 of Schedule 6 to the Criminal Justice Act 1991 (application for dismissal of charge of violent or sexual offence involving child in respect of which notice of transfer has been given under section 53 of that Act; and.

(b) the court or jury, in determining whether that person is guilty of the offence charged,

may draw such inferences from the refusal as appear proper.

(11) Nothing in this section applies to the taking of a specimen for the purposes of any of the provisions of sections 4 to 11 of the Road Traffic Act 1988 or of sections 26 to 38 of the Transport and Works Act 1992.

(12) Nothing in this section applies to a person arrested or detained under the terrorism provisions; and subsection (1A) shall not apply where the non-intimate samples mentioned in that subsection were taken under paragraph 10 of Schedule 8 to the Terrorism Act 2000.[4, 5, 6]

[1] section 62(9)–(9A) substituted for section 62(9) by Police Reform Act (2002 c.30), Part 4 c. 2 section 54 (1).

[2] In relation to the taking of an intimate sample from a person where a person is detained under the Prevention of Terrorism (Temporary Provisions) Act 1989 Schedule 5, any examining officer, constable or prison officer, or any other person authorised by the Secretary of State, may take all such steps as may be reasonably necessary for photographing, measuring or otherwise identifying him.

[3] section 62(9)–(9A) substituted for section 62(9) by Police Reform Act (2002 c.30), Part 4 c. 2 section 54 (1).

[4] In relation to the taking of an intimate sample from a person where a person is detained under the Prevention of Terrorism (Temporary Provisions) Act 1989 section 14, any constable or prison officer, or any other person authorised by the Secretary of State, may take all such steps as may be reasonably necessary for photographing, measuring or otherwise identifying him.

[5] section 62(9)–(9A) substituted for section 62(9) by Police Reform Act (2002 c.30), Part 4 c. 2 section 54 (1).

[6] In relation to the investigation of offences conducted by a service policeman under the Army Act 1955, the Air Force Act 1955 or the Naval Discipline Act 1957.

63 Other samples

(1) Except as provided by this section, a non-intimate sample may not be taken from a person without the appropriate consent.

(2) Consent to the taking of a non-intimate sample must be given in writing.

(2A) A non-intimate sample may be taken from a person without the appropriate consent if two conditions are satisfied.

(2B) The first is that the person is in police detention in consequence of his arrest for a recordable offence.

(2C) The second is that—

(a) he has not had a non-intimate sample of the same type and from the same part of the body taken in the course of the investigation of the offence by the police, or

(b) he has had such a sample taken but it proved insufficient.

(3) A non-intimate sample may be taken from a person without the appropriate consent if—

(a) he is being held in custody by the police on the authority of a court; and

(b) an officer of at least the rank of inspector authorises it to be taken without the appropriate consent.

(3A) A non-intimate sample may be taken from a person (whether or not he is in police detention or held in custody by the police on the authority of a court) without the appropriate consent if—

(a) he has been charged with a recordable offence or informed that he will be reported for such an offence; and

(b) either he has not had a non-intimate sample taken from him in the course of the investigation of the offence by the police or he had a non-intimate sample taken from him but either it was not suitable for the same means of analysis or, though so suitable, the sample proved insufficient.

(3B) A non-intimate sample may be taken from a person without the appropriate consent if he has been convicted of a recordable offence.

(3C) A non-intimate sample may also be taken from a person without the appropriate consent if he is a person to whom section 2 of the Criminal Evidence (Amendment) Act 1997 applies (persons detained following acquittal on grounds of insanity or finding of unfitness to plead).

(4) An officer may only give an authorisation under subsection (3) above if he has reasonable grounds—

(a) for suspecting the involvement of the person from whom the sample is to be taken in a recordable offence; and

(b) for believing that the sample will tend to confirm or disprove his involvement.

(5) An officer may give an authorisation under subsection (3) above orally or in writing but, if he gives it orally, he shall confirm it in writing as soon as is practicable.

(5A) An officer shall not give an authorisation under subsection (3) above for the taking from any person of a non-intimate sample consisting of a skin impression if-

(a) a skin impression of the same part of the body has already been taken from that person in the course of the investigation of the offence; and

(b) the impression previously taken is not one that has proved insufficient.

(6) Where—

(a) an authorisation has been given; and

(b) it is proposed that a non-intimate sample shall be taken in pursuance of the authorisation,

an officer shall inform the person from whom the sample is to be taken—

(i) of the giving of the authorisation; and

(ii) of the grounds for giving it.

(7) The duty imposed by subsection (6)(ii) above includes a duty to state the nature of the offence in which it is suspected that the person from whom the sample is to be taken has been involved.

(8) If a non-intimate sample is taken from a person by virtue of subsection (3) above—

(a) the authorisation by virtue of which it was taken; and

(b) the grounds for giving the authorisation,

shall be recorded as soon as is practicable after the sample is taken.

(8A) In a case where by virtue of [subsection (2A), (3A)][1], (3B) or (3C) above a sample is taken from a person without the appropriate consent—

(a) he shall be told the reason before the sample is taken; and

(b) the reason shall be recorded as soon as practicable after the sample is taken.

(8B) If a non-intimate sample is taken from a person at a police station, whether with or without the appropriate consent—

(a) before the sample is taken, an officer shall inform him that it may be the subject of a speculative search; and

(b) the fact that the person has been informed of this possibility shall be recorded as soon as practicable after the sample has been taken.

(9) If a non-intimate sample is taken from a person detained at a police station, the matters required to be recorded by subsection (8) or (8A) or (8B) above shall be recorded in his custody record.

(9ZA) The power to take a non-intimate sample from a person without the appropriate consent shall be exercisable by any constable.

(9A) Subsection (3B) above shall not apply to any person convicted before 10th April 1995 unless he is a person to whom section 1 of the Criminal Evidence (Amendment) Act 1997 applies (persons imprisoned or detained by virtue of pre-existing conviction for sexual offence etc).

(10) Nothing in this section applies to a person arrested or detained under the terrorism provisions.

(11) Nothing in this section applies to a person arrested under an extradition arrest power.[2, 3, 4]

[1] words substituted by Criminal Justice Act (2003 c.44), Part 1 section 10(5).

[2] In relation to the taking of an intimate sample from a person where a person is detained under the Prevention of Terrorism (Temporary Provisions) Act 1989 Schedule 5, any examining officer, constable or prison officer, or any other person authorised by the Secretary of State, may take all such steps as may be reasonably necessary for photographing, measuring or otherwise identifying him.

[3] In relation to the taking of an intimate sample from a person where a person is detained under the Prevention of Terrorism (Temporary Provisions) Act 1989 section 14, any constable or prison officer, or any other person authorised by the Secretary of State, may take all such steps as may be reasonably necessary for photographing, measuring or otherwise identifying him.

[4] In relation to the investigation of offences conducted by a service policeman under the Army Act 1955, the Air Force Act 1955 or the Naval Discipline Act 1957.

63A Fingerprints and samples: supplementary provisions

(1) Where a person has been arrested on suspicion of being involved in a recordable offence or has been charged with such an offence or has been informed that he will be reported for such an offence, fingerprints or samples or the information derived from samples taken under any power conferred by this Part of this Act from the person may be checked against—

(a) other fingerprints or samples to which the person seeking to check has access and which are held by or on behalf of any one or more relevant law-enforcement authorities or which are held in connection with or as a result of an investigation of an offence;

(b) information derived from other samples if the information is contained in records to which the person seeking to check has access and which are held as mentioned in paragraph (a) above.

[(1A) In subsection (1) above "relevant law-enforcement authority" means-

(a) a police force;
(b) the National Criminal Intelligence Service;
(c) the National Crime Squad;
(d) a public authority (not falling within paragraphs (a) to (c)) with functions in any part of the British Islands which consist of or include the investigation of crimes or the charging of offenders;
(e) any person with functions in any country or territory outside the United Kingdom which-
 (i) correspond to those of a police force; or
 (ii) otherwise consist of or include the investigation of conduct contrary to the law of that country or territory, or the apprehension of persons guilty of such conduct;
(f) any person with functions under any international agreement which consist of or include the investigation of conduct which is-
 (i) unlawful under the law of one or more places,
 (ii) prohibited by such an agreement, or
 (iii) contrary to international law,
 or the apprehension of persons guilty of such conduct.

(1B) The reference in subsection (1A) above to a police force is a reference to any of the following-

(a) any police force maintained under section 2 of the Police Act 1996 (c. 16) (police forces in England and Wales outside London);
(b) the metropolitan police force;
(c) the City of London police force;
(d) any police force maintained under or by virtue of section 1 of the Police (Scotland) Act 1967 (c. 77);
(e) the Police Service of Northern Ireland;
(f) the Police Service of Northern Ireland Reserve;
(g) the Ministry of Defence Police;
(h) the Royal Navy Regulating Branch;
(i) the Royal Military Police;
(j) the Royal Air Force Police;
(k) the Royal Marines Police;
(l) the British Transport Police;
(m) the States of Jersey Police Force;
(n) the salaried police force of the Island of Guernsey;
(o) the Isle of Man Constabulary.

(1C) Where-

(a) fingerprints or samples have been taken from any person in connection with the investigation of an offence but otherwise than in circumstances to which subsection (1) above applies, and

(b) that person has given his consent in writing to the use in a speculative search of the fingerprints or of the samples and of information derived from them,

the fingerprints or, as the case may be, those samples and that information may be checked against any of the fingerprints, samples or information mentioned in paragraph (a) or (b) of that subsection.

(1D) A consent given for the purposes of subsection (1C) above shall not be capable of being withdrawn.][1]

(2) Where a sample of hair other than public hair is to be taken the sample may be taken either by cutting hairs or by plucking hairs with their roots so long as no more are plucked than the person taking the sample reasonably considers to be necessary for a sufficient sample.

(3) Where any power to take a sample is exercisable in relation to a person the sample may be taken in a prison or other institution to which the Prison Act 1952 applies.

(3A) Where—

(a) the power to take a non-intimate sample under section 63(3B) above is exercisable in relation to any person who is detained under Part III of the Mental Health Act 1983 in pursuance of—

(i) a hospital order or interim hospital order made following his conviction for the recordable offence in question, or

(ii) a transfer direction given at a time when he was detained in pursuance of any sentence or order imposed following that conviction, or

(b) the power to take a non-intimate sample under section 63(3C) above is exercisable in relation to any person,

the sample may be taken in the hospital in which he is detained under that Part of that Act.

Expressions used in this subsection and in the Mental Health Act 1983 have the same meaning as in that Act.

(3B) Where the power to take a non-intimate sample under section 63(3B) above is exercisable in relation to a person detained in pursuance of directions of the Secretary of State under section 92 of the Powers of Criminal Courts (Sentencing) Act 2000 the sample may be taken at the place where he is so detained.

(4) Any constable may, within the allowed period, require a person who is neither in police detention nor held in custody by the police on the authority of a court to attend a police station in order to have a sample taken where—

(a) the person has been charged with a recordable offence or informed that he will be reported for such an offence and either he has not had a sample taken from him in the course of the investigation of the offence by the police or he has had a sample so taken from him but either it was not suitable for the same means of analysis or, though so suitable, the sample proved insufficient; or

(b) the person has been convicted of a recordable offence and either he has not had a sample taken from him since the conviction or he has had a sample taken from him (before or after his conviction) but either it was not suitable for the same means of analysis or, though so suitable, the sample proved insufficient.

(5) The period allowed for requiring a person to attend a police station for the purpose specified in subsection (4) above is—

(a) in the case of a person falling within paragraph (a), one month beginning with the date of the charge or of his being informed as mentioned in that paragraph or one month beginning with the date on which the appropriate officer is informed of the fact that the sample is not suitable for the same means of analysis or has proved insufficient, as the case may be;

(b) in the case of a person falling within paragraph (b), one month beginning with the date of the conviction or one month beginning with the date on which the appropriate officer is informed of the fact that the sample is not suitable for the same means of analysis or has proved insufficient, as the case may be.

(6) A requirement under subsection (4) above—

(a) shall give the person at least 7 days within which he must so attend; and

(b) may direct him to attend at a specified time of day or between specified times of day.

(7) Any constable may arrest without a warrant a person who has failed to comply with a requirement under subsection (4) above.

(8) In this section "the appropriate officer" is—

(a) in the case of a person falling within subsection (4)(a), the officer investigating the offence with which that person has been charged or as to which he was informed that he would be reported;

(b) in the case of a person falling within subsection (4)(b), the officer in charge of the police station from which the investigation of the offence of which he was convicted was conducted.[2]

[1] Subsections (1A), (1B), (1C) and (1D) substituted for subsection (1A) by Criminal Justice and Police Act (2001 c.16), Part 3 section 81(2).

[2] In relation to the investigation of offences conducted by a service policeman under the Army Act 1955, the Air Force Act 1955 or the Naval Discipline Act 1957.

64 Destruction of fingerprints and samples

(1A) Where-

(a) fingerprints or samples are taken from a person in connection with the investigation of an offence, and

(b) subsection (3) below does not require them to be destroyed,

the fingerprints or samples may be retained after they have fulfilled the purposes for which they were taken but shall not be used by any person except for purposes related to the prevention or detection of crime, the investigation of an offence or the conduct of a prosecution.

(1B) In subsection (1A) above-

(a) the reference to using a fingerprint includes a reference to allowing any check to be made against it under section 63A(1) or (1C) above and to disclosing it to any person;

(b) the reference to using a sample includes a reference to allowing any check to be made under section 63A(1) or (1C) above against it or against information derived from it and to disclosing it or any such information to any person;

(c) the reference to crime includes a reference to any conduct which-

 (i) constitutes one or more criminal offences (whether under the law of a part of the United Kingdom or of a country or territory outside the United Kingdom); or

 (ii) is, or corresponds to, any conduct which, if it all took place in any one part of the United Kingdom, would constitute one or more criminal offences;

and

(d) the references to an investigation and to a prosecution include references, respectively, to any investigation outside the United Kingdom of any crime or suspected crime and to a prosecution brought in respect of any crime in a country or territory outside the United Kingdom.

(3) If—

(a) fingerprints or samples are taken from a person in connection with the investigation of an offence; and

(b) that person is not suspected of having committed the offence,

they must, except as provided in the following provisions of this section, be destroyed as soon as they have fulfilled the purpose for which they were taken.

(3AA) Samples and fingerprints are not required to be destroyed under subsection (3) above if-

(a) they were taken for the purposes of the investigation of an offence of which a person has been convicted; and

(b) a sample or, as the case may be, fingerprint was also taken from the convicted person for the purposes of that investigation.

(3AB) Subject to subsection (3AC) below, where a person is entitled under subsection (3) above to the destruction of any fingerprint or sample taken from him (or would be but for subsection (3AA) above), neither the fingerprint nor the sample, nor any information derived from the sample, shall be used-

(a) in evidence against the person who is or would be entitled to the destruction of that fingerprint or sample; or

(b) for the purposes of the investigation of any offence;

and subsection (1B) above applies for the purposes of this subsection as it applies for the purposes of subsection (1A) above.

(3AC) Where a person from whom a fingerprint or sample has been taken consents in writing to its retention-

(a) that sample need not be destroyed under subsection (3) above;

(b) subsection (3AB) above shall not restrict the use that may be made of the fingerprint or sample or, in the case of a sample, of any information derived from it; and

(c) that consent shall be treated as comprising a consent for the purposes of section 63A(1C) above;

and a consent given for the purpose of this subsection shall not be capable of being withdrawn.

(3AD) For the purposes of subsection (3AC) above it shall be immaterial whether the consent is given at, before or after the time when the entitlement to the destruction of the fingerprint or sample arises.

[. . .][1]

(5) If fingerprints are destroyed—

(a) any copies of the fingerprints shall also be destroyed; and

(b) any chief officer of police controlling access to computer data relating to the fingerprints shall make access to the data impossible, as soon as it is practicable to do so.

(6) A person who asks to be allowed to witness the destruction of his fingerprints or copies of them shall have a right to witness it.

(6A) If—

(a) subsection (5)(b) above falls to be complied with; and

(b) the person to whose fingerprints the data relate asks for a certificate that it has been complied with,

such a certificate shall be issued to him, not later than the end of the period of three months beginning with the day on which he asks for it, by the responsible chief officer of police or a person authorised by him or on his behalf for the purposes of this section.

(6B) In this section—

"the responsible chief officer of police" means the chief officer of police in whose police area the computer data were put on to the computer.

(7) Nothing in this section—

(a) affects any power conferred by paragraph 18(2) of Schedule 2 to the Immigration Act 1971 or section 20 of the Immigration and Asylum Act 1999 (c. 33) (disclosure of police information to the Secretary of State for use for immigration purposes); or

(b) applies to a person arrested or detained under the terrorism provisions.[2]

[1] repealed by Criminal Justice and Police Act (2001 c.16), Schedule 7(2)(1) paragraph 1.

[2] In relation to the investigation of offences conducted by a service policeman under the Army Act 1955, the Air Force Act 1955 or the Naval Discipline Act 1957.

65 Part V—supplementary

(1) In this Part of this Act—

"analysis", in relation to a skin impression, includes comparison and matching;

"appropriate consent" means—

(a) in relation to a person who has attained the age of 17 years, the consent of that person;
(b) in relation to a person who has not attained that age but has attained the age of 14 years, the consent of that person and his parent or guardian; and
(c) in relation to a person who has not attained the age of 14 years, the consent of his parent or guardian;

["extradition arrest power" means any of the following—

(a) a Part 1 warrant (within the meaning given by the Extradition Act 2003) in respect of which a certificate under section 2 of that Act has been issued;
(b) section 5 of that Act;
(c) a warrant issued under section 71 of that Act;
(d) a provisional warrant (within the meaning given by that Act).][1]

"fingerprints", in relation to any person, means a record (in any form and produced by any method) of the skin pattern and other physical characteristics or features of-

(a) any of that person's fingers; or
(b) either of his palms;

"intimate sample" means—

(a) a sample of blood, semen or any other tissue fluid, urine or pubic hair;
(b) a dental impression;
(c) a swab taken from a person's body orifice other than the mouth;

"intimate search" means a search which consists of the physical examination of a person's body orifices other than the mouth;

"non-intimate sample" means—

(a) a sample of hair other than pubic hair;
(b) a sample taken from a nail on from under a nail;
(c) a swab taken from any part of a person's body including the mouth but not any other body orifice;
(d) saliva;
(e) a skin impression;

"registered dentist" has the same meaning as in the Dentists Act 1984;

"registered health care professional" means a person (other than a medical practitioner) who is—

(a) a registered nurse; or
(b) a registered member of a health care profession which is designated for the purposes of this paragraph by an order made by the Secretary of State;

"skin impression", in relation to any person, means any record (other than a fingerprint) which is a record (in any form and produced by any method) of the skin pattern and other physical characteristics or features of the whole or any part of his foot or of any other part of his body;

"speculative search", in relation to a person's fingerprints or samples, means such a check against other fingerprints or samples or against information derived from other samples as is referred to in section 63A(1) above;

"sufficient" and "insufficient", in relation to a sample, means (subject to subsection (2) below) sufficient or insufficient (in point of quantity or quality) for the purpose of enabling information to be produced by the means of analysis used or to be used in relation to the sample.

"the terrorism provisions" means section 41 of the Terrorism Act 2000, and any provision of Schedule 7 to that Act conferring a power of detention; and

"terrorism" has the meaning given in section 1 of that Act.

(1A) A health care profession is any profession mentioned in section 60(2) of the Health Act 1999 (c. 8) other than the profession of practising medicine and the profession of nursing.

(1B) An order under subsection (1) shall be made by statutory instrument and shall be subject to annulment in pursuance of a resolution of either House of Parliament.

(2) References in this Part of this Act to a sample's proving insufficient include references to where, as a consequence of-

(a) the loss, destruction or contamination of the whole or any part of the sample,
(b) any damage to the whole or a part of the sample, or
(c) the use of the whole or a part of the sample for an analysis which produced no results or which produced results some or all of which must be regarded, in the circumstances, as unreliable,

the sample has become unavailable or insufficient for the purpose of enabling information, or information of a particular description, to be obtained by means of analysis of the sample.[2]

[1] definition inserted by Extradition Act (2003 c.41), Part 4 section 169(6).

[2] In relation to an investigation of offences conducted by a service policeman under the Army Act 1955, the Air Force Act 1955 or the Naval Discipline Act 1957 and to persons held in arrest in connection with such an investigation.

76 Confessions

(1) In any proceedings a confession made by an accused person may be given in evidence against him in so far as it is relevant to any matter in issue in the proceedings and is not excluded by the court in pursuance of this section.

(2) If, in any proceedings where the prosecution proposes to give in evidence a confession made by an accused person, it is represented to the court that the confession was or may have been obtained—

(a) by oppression of the person who made it; or

(b) in consequence of anything said or done which was likely, in the circumstances existing at the time, to render unreliable any confession which might be made by him in consequence thereof.

the court shall not allow the confession to be given in evidence against him except in so far as the prosecution proves to the court beyond reasonable doubt that the confession (notwithstanding that it may be true) was not obtained as aforesaid.

116 Meaning of "serious arrestable offence"

(1) This section has effect for determining whether an offence is a serious arrestable offence for the purposes of this Act.

(2) The following arrestable offences are always serious—

(a) an offence (whether at common law or under any enactment) specified in Part I of Schedule 5 to this Act; and

(b) an offence under an enactment specified in Part II of that Schedule; and

[(c) any offence which is specified in paragraph 1 of Schedule 2 to the Proceeds of Crime Act 2002 (drug trafficking offences),

(d) any offence under section 327, 328 or 329 of that Act (certain money laundering offences).][1]

(3) Subject to subsection (4) below, any other arrestable offence is serious only if its commission—

(a) has led to any of the consequences specified in subsection (6) below; or

(b) is intended or is likely to lead to any of those consequences.

(4) An arrestable offence which consists of making a threat is serious if carrying out the threat would be likely to lead to any of the consequences specified in subsection (6) below.

(6) The consequences mentioned in subsections (3) and (4) above are

(a) serious harm to the security of the State or to public order;

(b) serious interference with the administration of justice or with the investigation of offences or of a particular offence;

(c) the death of any person;

(d) serious injury to any person;

(e) substantial financial gain to any person; and

(f) serious financial loss to any person.

(7) Loss is serious for the purposes of this section if, having regard to all the circumstances, it is serious for the person who suffers it.

(8) In this section "injury" includes any disease and any impairment of a person's physical or mental condition.

[1] Section 116(2)(c)–(d) substituted for section 116(2)(c) by Proceeds of Crime Act (2002 c.29), Schedule 11 paragraph 14(4).

Appendix 3

Relevant sections of the Criminal Justice and Public Order Act 1994

ARRANGEMENT OF SECTIONS

. . . .

Part II Bail

25 No bail for defendants charged with or convicted of homicide or rape after previous conviction of such offences

Part III Course of justice; evidence, procedure, etc.

Inferences from accused's silence

34 Effect of accused's to mention facts when questioned or charged.
35 Effect of accused's silence at trial.
36 Effect of accused's failure or refusal to account for objects, substances or marks.
37 Effect of accused's failure or refusal to account for presence at a particular place.
38 Interpretation and savings for sections 34, 35, 36 and 37.

. . . .

25 No bail for defendants charged with or convicted of homicide or rape after previous conviction of such offences.

(1) A person who in any proceedings has been charged with or convicted of an offence to which this section applies in circumstances to which it applies shall not be granted bail in those proceedings.
(2) This section applies, subject to subsection (3) below, to the following offences, that is to say—
  (a) murder;
  (b) attempted murder;
  (c) manslaughter;
  (d) rape; or
  (e) attempted rape.
(3) This section applies to a person charged with or convicted of any such offence only if he has been previously convicted by or before a court in any part of the United Kingdom of any such offence or of culpable homicide and, in the case of a previous conviction of manslaughter or of culpable homicide, if he was then sentenced to imprisonment or, if he was then a child or young person, to long-term detention under any of the relevant enactments.
(4) This section applies whether or not an appeal is pending against conviction or sentence.

(5) In this section—
"conviction" includes—
(a) a finding that a person is not guilty by reason of insanity;
(b) a finding under section 4A(3) of the [1964 c. 84.] Criminal Procedure (Insanity) Act 1964 (cases of unfitness to plead) that a person did the act or made the omission charged against him; and
(c) a conviction of an offence for which an order is made placing the offender on probation or discharging him absolutely or conditionally;
and "convicted" shall be construed accordingly; and
"the relevant enactments" means—
(a) as respects England and Wales, section 53(2) of the [1933 c. 12.] Children and Young Persons Act 1933;
(b) as respects Scotland, sections 205 and 206 of the [1975 c. 21.] Criminal Procedure (Scotland) Act 1975;
(c) as respects Northern Ireland, section 73(2) of the [1968 c. 34 (N.I.).] Children and Young Persons Act (Northern Ireland) 1968.
(6) This section does not apply in relation to proceedings instituted before its commencement.

. . . .

34 Effect of accused's failure to mention facts when questioned or charged

(1) Where, in any proceedings against a person for an offence, evidence is given that the accused—
(a) at any time before he was charged with the offence, on being questioned under caution by a constable trying to discover whether or by whom the offence had been committed, failed to mention any fact relied on in his defence in those proceedings; or
(b) on being charged with the offence or officially informed that he might be prosecuted for it, failed to mention any such fact,
being a fact which in the circumstances existing at the time the accused could reasonably have been expected to mention when so questioned, charged or informed, as the case may be, subsection (2) below applies.
(2) Where this subsection applies—
(a) a magistrate' court, in deciding whether to grant an application for dismissal made by the accused under section 6 of the [1980 c. 43.] Magistrates' Courts Act 1980 (application for dismissal of charge in course of proceedings with a view to transfer for trial);
(b) a judge, in deciding whether to grant an application made by the accused under—
(i) section 6 of the [1987 c. 38.] Criminal Justice Act 1987 (application for dismissal of charge of serious fraud in respect of which notice of transfer has been given under section 4 of that Act); or
(ii) paragraph 5 of Schedule 6 to the [1991 c. 53.] Criminal Justice Act 1991 (application for dismissal of charge of violent or sexual offence involving child in respect of which notice of transfer has been given under section 53 of that Act);
(c) the court, in determining whether there is a case to answer;
and

(d) the court of jury, in determining whether the accused is guilty of the offence charged,

may draw such inferences from the failure as appear proper.

(3) Subject to any directions by the court, evidence tending to establish the failure may be given before or after evidence tending to establish the fact which the accused is alleged to have failed to mention.

(4) This section applies in relation to questioning by persons (other than constables) charged with the duty of investigating offences or charging offenders as it applies in relation to questioning by constables, and in subsection (1) above "officially informed" means informed by a constable or any such person.

(5) This section does not—

(a) prejudice the admissibility in evidence of the silence or other reaction of the accused in the face of anything said in his presence relating to the conduct in respect of which he is charged, in so far as evidence thereof would be admissible apart from this section; or

(b) preclude the drawing of any inference from any such silence or other reaction of the accused which could properly be drawn apart from this section.

(6) This section does not apply in relation to a failure to mention a fact if the failure occurred before the commencement of this section.

(7) In relation to any time before the commencement of section 44 of this Act, this section shall have effect as if the reference in subsection (2)(a) to the grant of an application for dismissal was a reference to the committal of the accused for trial.

35 Effect of accused's silence at trial

(1) At the trial of any person who has attained the age of fourteen years for an offence, subsections (2) and (3) below apply unless—

(a) the accused's guilt is not in issue; or

(b) it appears to the court that the physical or mental condition of the accused makes it undesirable for him to give evidence;

but subsection (2) below does not apply if, at the conclusion of the evidence for the prosecution, his legal representative informs the court that the accused will give evidence or, where he is unrepresented, the court ascertains from him that he will give evidence.

(2) Where this subsection applies, the court shall, at the conclusion of the evidence for the prosecution, satisfy itself (in the case of proceedings on indictment, in the presence of the jury) that the accused is aware that the stage has been reached at which evidence can be given for the defence and that he can, if he wishes, give evidence and that, if he chooses not to give evidence, or having been sworn, without good cause refuses to answer any question, it will be permissible for the court or jury to draw such inferences as appear proper from his failure to give evidence or his refusal, without good cause, to answer any question.

(3) Where this subsection applies, the court or jury, in determining whether the accused is guilty of the offence charged, may draw such inferences as appear proper from the failure of the accused to give evidence or his refusal, without good cause, to answer any question.

(4) This section does not render the accused compellable to give evidence on his own behalf, and he shall accordingly not be guilty of contempt of court by reason of a failure to do so.

(5) For the purposes of this section a person who, having been sworn, refuses to answer any question shall be taken to do so without good cause unless—
 (a) he is entitled to refuse to answer the question by virtue of any enactment, whenever passed or made, or on the ground of privilege; or
 (b) the court in the exercise of its general discretion excuses him from answering it.

(6) Where the age of any person is material for the purposes of subsection (1) above, his age shall for those purposes be taken to be that which appears to the court to be his age.

(7) This section applies—
 (a) in relation to proceedings on indictment for an offence, only if the person charged with the offence is arraigned on or after the commencement of this section;
 (b) in relation to proceedings in a magistrates' court, only if the time when the court begins to receive evidence in the proceedings falls after the commencement of this section.

36 Effect of accused's failure or refusal to account for objects, substances or marks

(1) Where—
 (a) a person is arrested by a constable, and there is—
  (i) on his person; or
  (ii) in or on his clothing or footwear; or
  (iii) otherwise in his possession; or
  (iv) in any place in which he is at the time of his arrest,
 any object, substance or mark, or there is any mark on any such object; and
 (b) that or another constable investigating the case reasonably believes that the presence of the object, substance or mark may be attributable to the participation of the person arrested in the commission of an offence specified by the constable; and
 (c) the constable informs the person arrested that he so believes, and requests him to account for the presence of the object, substance or mark; and
 (d) the person fails or refuses to do so,

then if, in any proceedings against the person for the offence so specified, evidence of those matters is given, subsection (2) below applies.

(2) Where this subsection applies—
 (a) a magistrates' court, in deciding whether to grant an application for dismissal made by the accused under s.6 of the [1980 c. 43.] Magistrates' Courts Act 190 (application for dismissal of charge in course of proceedings with a view to transfer for trial);
 (b) a judge, in deciding whether to grant an application made by the accused under—
  (i) section 6 of the [1987 c. 38.] Criminal Justice Act 1987 (application for dismissal of charge of serious fraud in respect of which notice of transfer has been given under s.4 of that Act); or

(ii) paragraph 5 of Schedule 6 to the [1991 c. 53.] Criminal Justice Act 1991 (application for dismissal of charge of violent or sexual offence involving child in respect of which notice of transfer has been given under section 53 of that Act);

(c) the court, in determining whether there is a case to answer; and

(d) the court or jury, in determining whether the accused is guilty of the offence charged,

may draw such inferences from the failure or refusal as appear proper.

(3) Subsections (1) and (2) above apply to the condition of clothing or footwear as they apply to a substance or mark thereon.

(4) Subsections (1) and (2) above do not apply unless the accused was told in ordinary language by the constable when making the request mentioned in subsection (1)(c) above what the effect of this section would be if he failed or refused to comply with the request.

(5) This section applies in relation to officers of customs and excise as it applies in relation to constables.

(6) This section does not preclude the drawing of any inference from a failure or refusal of the accused to account for the presence of an object, substance or mark or from the condition of clothing or footwear which could properly be drawn apart from this section.

(7) This section does not apply in relation to a failure or refusal which occurred before the commencement of this section.

(8) In relation to any time before the commencement of section 44 of this Act, this section shall have effect as if the reference in subsection (2)(a) to the grant of an application for dismissal was a reference to the committal of the accused for trial.

37 Effect of accused's failure or refusal to account for presence at a particular place

(1) Where—

(a) a person arrested by a constable was found by him at a place at or about the time the offence for which he was arrested is alleged to have been committed; and

(b) that or another constable investigating the offence reasonably believes that the presence of the person at that place and at that time may be attributable to his participation in the commission of the offence; and

(c) the constable informs the person that he so believes, and requests him to account for that presence; and

(d) the person fails or refuses to do so,

then if, in any proceedings against the person for the offence, evidence of those matters is given, subsection (2) below applies.

(2) Where this subsection applies—

(a) a magistrates' court, in deciding whether to grant an application for dismissal made by the accused under section 6 of the [1980 c. 43.] Magistrates' Courts Act 1980 (application for dismissal of charge in course of proceedings with a view to transfer for trial);

(b) a judge, in deciding whether to grant an application made by the accused under—

(i) section 6 of the [1987 c. 38.] Criminal Justice Act 1987 (application for dismissal of charge of serious fraud in respect of which notice of transfer has been given under section 4 of that Act); or

(ii) paragraph 5 of Schedule 6 to the [1991 c. 53.] Criminal Justice Act 1991 (application for dismissal of charge of violent or sexual offence involving child in respect of which notice of transfer has been given under section 53 of that Act);

(c) the court, in determining whether there is a case to answer; and

(d) the court of jury, in determining whether the accused is guilty of the offence charged,

may draw such inferences from the failure or refusal as appear proper.

(3) Subsections (1) and (2) do not apply unless the accused was told in ordinary language by the constable when making the request mentioned in subsection (1)(c) above what the effect of this section would be if he failed or refused to comply with the request.

(4) This section applies in relation to officers of customs and excise as it applies in relation to constables.

(5) This section does not preclude the drawing of any inference from a failure or refusal of the accused to account for his presence at a place which could properly be drawn apart from this section.

(6) This section does not apply in relation to a failure or refusal which occurred before the commencement of this section.

(7) In relation to any time before the commencement of section 44 of this Act, this section shall have effect as if the reference in subsection (2)(a) to the grant of an application for dismissal was a reference to the committal of the accused for trial.

38 Interpretation and savings for sections 34, 35, 36 and 37

(1) In section 34, 35, 36 and 37 of this Act—

"legal representative" means an authorized advocate or authorised litigator, as defined by section 119(1) of the [1990 c. 41.] Courts and Legal Services Act 1990; and

"place" includes any building or part of a building, any vehicle, vessel, aircraft or hovercraft and any other place whatsoever.

(2) In sections 34(2), 35(3), 36(2) and 37(2), references to an offence charged include references to any other offence of which the accused could lawfully be convicted on that charge.

(3) A person shall not have the proceedings against him transferred to the Crown Court for trial, have a case to answer or be convicted of an offence solely on an inference drawn from such a failure or refusal as is mentioned in section 34(2), 35(3), 36(2) or 37(2).

(4) A judge shall not refuse to grant such an application as is mentioned in section 34(2)(b), 36(2)(b) and 37(2)(b) solely on an inference drawn from such a failure as is mentioned in section 34(2), 36(2) or 37(2).

(5) Nothing in sections 34, 35, 36 or 37 prejudices the operation of a provision of any enactment which provides (in whatever words) that any answer or evidence given by a person in specified circumstances shall not be admissible in evidence against him or some other person in any proceedings or class of proceedings (however described, and whether civil or criminal).

In this subsection, the reference to giving evidence is a reference to giving evidence in any manner, whether by furnishing information, making discovery, producing documents or otherwise.

(6) Nothing in sections 34, 35, 36 or 37 prejudices any power of a court, in any proceedings, to exclude evidence (whether by preventing questions being put or otherwise) at its discretion.

. . . . . .